MANAGEMENT CONTROI SYSTEMS

(Principles & Practice)

Prof. P. Saravanavel

Department of Management Studies
S.R.M. Engineering College,
Kattankulathur-603203.

First Edition : 1994
Reprint : 1997
Reprint : 2000
Reprint : 2003
Reprint : 2007
Reprint : 2022

Published by : Mrs. Meena Pandey for **Himalaya Publishing House Pvt. Ltd.,**
"Ramdoot", Dr. Bhalerao Marg, Girgaon, Mumbai - 400 004.
Phone: 022-23860170, 23863863; **Fax:** 022-23877178
E-mail: himpub@bharatmail.co.in; **Website:** www.himpub.com

Branch Offices :

New Delhi : "Pooja Apartments", 4-B, Murari Lal Street, Ansari Road, Darya Ganj, New Delhi - 110 002. Phone: 011-23270392, 23278631; Fax: 011-23256286

Nagpur : Kundanlal Chandak Industrial Estate, Ghat Road, Nagpur - 440 018. Phone: 0712-2721215, 2721216

Bengaluru : Plot No. 91-33, 2nd Main Road, Seshadripuram, Behind Nataraja Theatre, Bengaluru - 560 020.
Phone: 080-41138821; Mobile: 09379847017, 09379847005

Hyderabad : No. 3-4-184, Lingampally, Besides Raghavendra Swamy Matham, Kachiguda, Hyderabad - 500 027. Phone: 040-27560041, 27550139

Chennai : No. 34/44, Motilal Street, T. Nagar, Chennai - 600 017.
Mobile: 09380460419

Pune : "Laksha" Apartment, First Floor, No. 527, Mehunpura, Shaniwarpeth (Near Prabhat Theatre), Pune - 411 030.
Phone: 020-24496323, 24496333; Mobile: 09370579333

Lucknow : House No. 731, Shekhupura Colony, Near B.D. Convent School, Aliganj, Lucknow - 226 022. Phone: 0522-4012353; Mobile: 09307501549

Ahmedabad : 114, "SHAIL", 1st Floor, Opp. Madhu Sudan House, C.G. Road, Navrang Pura, Ahmedabad - 380 009.
Phone: 079-26560126; Mobile: 09377088847

Cuttack : Plot No 5F-755/4, Sector-9, CDA Market Nagar, Cuttack - 753 014, Odisha. Mobile: 09338746007

Kolkata : 108/4, Beliaghata Main Road, Near ID Hospital, Opp. SBI Bank, Kolkata - 700 010. Phone: 033-32449649; Mobile: 07439040301

Printed at : Infinity Imaging System, New Delhi. On behalf of HPH.

PREFACE

The book is designed mainly for those who have had a course in Commerce / Management and who wish to study management control system

The book continues to focus on the subject of Management Control and Information System. It deals extensively with 'Management' 'Control' and 'System' in a lucid and systematic manner. The text has been divided into five units comprising 33 Chapters. Unit I, with the first six Chapters, gives an introduction / overview of Management explaining the nature and principles of Management Control System. The next six chapters i.e., Chapters 7 to 12 under Unit II explains Information Systems for Management Control System. The Financial Control Techniques viz., Accounting Ratios, Funds flow Statements, Budgeting and Variance Analysis, Break Even Point, etc., are presented in Unit III, comprising nine chapters i.e., Chapters 13 to 21. The significance of Management Control in functional areas like Production including Inventory, Marketing including Distribution and Personnel areas of both Profit and NonProfit (Service) Organisations are examined in Chapters 22 to 29 under Unit IV. Unit V presents Mathematical Models for Management Controls. The various tools of Quantitative Tecniques and Operation Research are explained in such a way that even non-mathematical students can easily grasp the subject. For further readings, a list of useful books are given at the end of the book. Each chapter contains a detailed discussion on the subject, followed by Review Questions.

I am grateful to several authors whose writings have provided me an insight in to the intricacies of the subject. My sincere thanks are due to Shri D.P. Pandey, Himalaya Publishing House, Bombay for his care and continous encouragement in publishing my manuscript.

Suggestions for the improvement of the book would be very much appreciated and acknowledged.

AUTHOR

CONTENTS

UNIT III FINANCIAL CONTROLS

1
Overview of Management

Management : Management is that function of an industrial undertaking which organises, directs and controls various activities of the enterprise directed towards specific ends (objectives). The objectives of the enterprise are accomplished through the use of resources like men, money, material, machines, matters (information) and minutes. The management function of a concern is a major segment of coordination. Management entails the coordination of human effort and material resources toward the achievement of organisational objectives.

Harbison and Myers* observe Management as

(a) An economic source, because the management resources of a firm determine to a large extent its productivity and profitability.

(b) A system of authority, because historically, first of all management developed Authoritarian Philosophy, and

(c) A Class and Status system, because entrance into the class of managers is based upon higher education and brain.

Management embraces all duties and functions that pertain to the initiation of an enterprise, its financing, the establishment of all major policies, the provision of all necessary equipment, the outlining of the general form of organisation under which the enterprise is to operate and the selection of the principal officers.

Principles of Management

'Principles of Management' implies a list of current management practices. -Though F.W. Taylor developed principles of management, credit goes to Henri Fayol, a French management theorist for advocating and publicising certain principles (or laws) for the soundness and good working of the management. - Henri Fayol warned that the principles of management should be, (i) Flexible and not absolute-must be usable regardless of changing conditions, (ii) Used with intelligence and with a sense of proportion, etc. Henri Fayol listed 14 principles, that grew out of his experience; they are briefed as under.

1. Division of Work (or Labour)

- Division of work means dividing the work on the principle that different workers (and different places) are best fitted for different jobs (or things) depending upon influences arising from geography, natural conditions, personal aptitude and skills.

---

* 'Management in Industrial World', Mc Graw Hill Co., N.Y.

- Division of work leads to specialisation.
- Concept of division of labour can be applied to all kinds of work, managerial as well as technical.

Advantages of Division of Labour : Since the same worker does the same work repeatedly, (i) he gains proficiency and skill on the jobs, (ii) rate of production increases, (iii) product quality improves, (iv) he is in a position to suggest changes in product, processing or methods of doing that work.

Disadvantages of Division of Labour : (i) Division of labour gives rise to loss of craftsmanship; workers become machine-minders and no more, (ii) With the passage of time, the same job becomes dull and monotonous, (iii) Workers do not remain all-round and one cannot work in place of another if he is absent.

2. Authority and Responsibility

- Authority and Responsibility should go together, hand-in-hand and must be related.
- An executive can do justice with his responsibility only when he has the proper authority.
- Responsibility without Authority or vice versa is meaningless.

3. Discipline

- Discipline is absolutely necessary for efficient functioning of all enterprises.
- Discipline may be described as-respect for agreements that are directed at achieving obedience, application, and the outward marks of respect.

4. Unity of Command

- Unity of command means, employees should receive orders and instructions from one boss (or supervisor) only. In other words a worker should not be under the control of more than one supervisors.
- Unity of command avoids confusion, mistakes and delays in getting the work done.

5. Unity of Direction

- It is a broader concept than the unity of command.
- Unlike unity of command which concerns itself with the personnel, unity of direction deals with the functioning of the body corporate.
- Unity of direction implies that there should be one plan and one head for each group of activities having the same objective.

In other words, there should be one common plan for an enterprise as a whole.

6. Subordination of Individual to General Interest

- The interests of an individual person should be permitted to supersede or prevail upon the general interests of the enterprise.
- This is necessary to maintain unity and to avoid friction among the employees.

7. Remuneration

- Remuneration is the price paid to the employees for the services rendered by them for the enterprise.
- Remuneration should (i) be fair, and (ii) bring maximum satisfaction to both employees and the employer.

8. Centralisation of Authority

- Centralisation of authority means that the authority is in the hands of centre, i.e., the authority is not dispersed among different sections.
- In a business organisation, authority should be centralised only to that degree or extent which is essential for the best overall performance.
- degree of centralisation is decided by keeping in view the nature, size and complexity of the (business) enterprise.

9. Scalar Chain

- Managers may be regarded as a chain of superiors. There should be an unbroken line of authority and command through all levels from the highest (i.e., general manager) to the lowest ranks (employee).
- The chain of superiors should be short-circuited, when following it strictly will be detrimental to performance.

10. Order

- This promotes the idea that everything (e.g., materials) and everyone (human being) has his place in the organisation.
- Materials and human beings should be arranged such that right material (things)/person is in the right place.

11. Equity of Treatment

- Manager should have equality of treatment for all his subordinates.
- Manager should deal with his subordinates with kindness and justice.
- This will make employees more loyal and devoted towards the management/enterprise.

12. Stability

- Stable and secure work force is an asset to the enterprise, because unnecessary labour turnover is costly.
- An average employee who stays with the concern is much better than outstanding employees who merely come and go.
- Instability is the result of bad management.

13. Initiative

- Initiative is one of the keenest satisfactions for an intelligent employee to experience.
- Managers should sacrifice their personal vanity in order to permit their subordinates to exercise their own initiative.
- A manger should encourage his subordinates to take initiative.

14. Esprit de Corps

- This principle of management emphasises the need for teamwork (harmony, and proper understanding) among the employees and shows the importance of communications in obtaining such team-work.

Functions Of Management

- One way to look at the process of management is to identify the (basic) functions which together make up the process.
- Since some functions are basic to managerial activities at all levels from the foreman to the manager, they are applicable to all business enterprises.
- Though Fayol, Urwick, Davis, Koontz and O'Donnel have specified different number of management functions, the author feels that the following eight functions may be used to describe the job of management.

1. Forecasting.
2. Planning.
3. Organising.
4. Staffing.
5. Directing
   - Leadership
   - Communication
   - Motivation
   - Supervision
6. Coordinating.
7. Controlling.
8. Decision making.

- The above list of the functions of management is a useful analytical device for stressing the basic elements inherent in the job of management.

1. Forecasting

- Forecasting is a necessary preliminary to planning.
- Forecasting estimates the future work or what should be done in future; may be as regards sales or production or any other aspect of business activities.
- Forecasting begins with the sales forecast and is followed by production forecast and forecasts for costs, finance, purchase, profit or loss, etc.

2. Planning

- Planning all aspects of production, selling, etc., are essential in order to minimise intangibles.
- Planning is a process by which a manager anticipates the future and discovers alternative courses of action open to him.
- Planning is a rational, economic, systematic way of making decisions today which will affect the future e.g., what will be done in future, who will do it and where it will be done.
- In fact, every managerial act, whether it be mental or physical, is inexorably intertwined with planning.
- Without proper planning, the activities of an enterprise may become confused, haphazard and ineffective; for example if a refrigerator making concern does not plan in advance-how many refrigerators and of what capacities are to be made before the summer starts and thus it does not procure necessary material, tools, supplies and personnel in time, it cannot reach the production targets and hence may not run profitably.
- Prior planning is very essential for utilising the available facilities (man, material, machines etc.) to the best of advantage.

3. Organising

- Organising is the process by which the structure and allocation of jobs is determined.
- Organising involves determining activities required to achieve the established company objectives, grouping these activities in a logical basis for handling by subordinate (persons) managers, and finally, assigning persons to the job designed. In carrying out the above, the manager will delegate necessary authority to his subordinates (persons) and they, in turn, will take the necessary responsibility.

- Organising means, organising people, materials, jobs, time etc., and establishing a framework in which responsibilities are defined and authorities are laid down.

4. Staffing

- Staffing is the process by which managers select, train, promote and retire their subordinates.
- Staffing involves the developing and placing of qualified people in the various jobs in the organisation.
- Staffing is a continuous process. The aim is to have appropriate persons to move into vacated positions or positions newly created in the enterprise.

5. Directing

- Directing is the process by which actual performance of subordinates is guided towards common goals of the enterprise.
- Directing involves motivating, guiding and supervising subordinates towards company objectives.
- Directing thus includes : (i) Giving instructions to subordinates, (ii) Guiding the subordinates to do the work, (iii) Supervising the subordinates to make certain that the work done by them is as per plans established.
- Directing involves functions such as : (a) Leadership, (b) Communication, (c) Motivation, and (d) Supervision.

(a) Leadership

- Leadership is the quality of the behaviour of the persons (Managers) whereby they inspire confidence and trust in their subordinates, get maximum cooperation from them and guide their activities in organized effort.
- Leadership is more than personal ability and skill.

(b) Communication

- Communication is the process by which ideas are transmitted, received desired results.
- Communication may be verbal or written orders, reports, instructions, etc.
- A manager communicates to his subordinates as what they should do.
- An ineffective communication leads to confusion, misunderstanding, dissatisfaction and sometimes even strikes.

(c) Motivation

- Motivating means inspiring the subordinates to do a work or to achieve company objectives effectively and efficiently.

(d) Supervision

- Supervision is necessary in order to ensure,
  (i) that the work is going on as per the plan established, and
  (ii) that the workers are doing as they were directed to do.

6. Coordinating

- Coordinating means achieving harmony of individual effort towards the accomplishment of company objectives.
- In other words, the dovetailing and harmonising of all the company assets and employees into a coherent whole is known as coordination.
- Ineffective coordination between different functions of a business enterprise (such as production, sales, administration, etc.) can ruin the enterprise.
- Coordination involves making plans that coordinate the activities of subordinates, regulate their activities on the job and regulate their communications.
- Besides other factors, informal relationships within an organisation also tend to facilitate coordination, because workers who like each other outside the factory, prefer to work together on the job also.

7. Controlling

- Controlling is the process that measures current performance and guides it toward some predetermined goal.
- Controlling involves :
  (i) the monitoring of programme activities to make sure that end objectives are being met.
  (ii) the initiation of corrective action as required to overcome problems, if any, hindering the accomplishment of objectives.
- Checks and examinations are required on a periodic basis to ensure that the things are proceeding as per plan established.
- Controlling is necessary to ensure that orders are not misunderstood, rules are not violated and objectives have not been unknowingly shifted. Control means control on persons and other things.
- Controlling is a continuous process which measures the progress of operations (compares) verifies their conformity with the predetermined plan and takes corrective if required.

- Controlling process (i) Sets standards, (ii) Measures job performance, and (iii) Takes corrective action, if required.

8. Decision Making

- Decision making is the process by which a course of action is consciously chosen from available alternatives for the purpose of achieving desired results.
- An outstanding quality of a successful manager is his ability to make sound and logical decisions.
- Management decisions range from establishing consumer operational development needs to the selection of a preferred system design configuration to many other aspects of a business enterprise.

Levels of Management*

Management/Industrial Management has got the following activity levels.

1. Top Management.
2. Upper Middle Management.
3. Middle Management.
4. Lower Management (Foremen etc.).
5. Operating force or Rank and File workman.

1. Top Management : Top Management includes (a) Board of Directors, (b) Managing Directors, (c) Chief Executives, (d) General Managers, (e) Owners, and (f) Shareholders/Financiers.

Top Management Functions are (a) Setting basic goals and objectives, (b) Expanding or contracting activities. (c) Establishing policies, (d) Monitoring performance, (e) Designing/Redesigning organisation and system, and (f) Shouldering financial responsibilities, etc.

2. Upper Middle Management : Upper Middle Management includes (a) Sales executive (Manager), (b) Production executive, (c) Finance executive, (d) Accounts executive, and (e) R & D executive.

Upper Middle Management Functions are (a) Establishment of the organisation, (b) Selection of staff for lower levels of management, (c) Installing different departments, (d) Designing operating policies and routines, and (e) Assigning duties to their subordinates, etc.

3. Middle Management : Middle Management includes (a) Superintendents, (b) Branch Managers, and (c) General Foremen, etc.

---

* Traditionally, it is classified into Top, Middle and Lower management.

Middle Management Functions are (a) To run the details of the organisation, (b) To cooperate to run organisation smoothly, (c) To understand interlocking of departments in major policies, (d) To achieve coordination between different parts of the organisation, (e) To conduct training for employee development and (f) To build an efficient company team spirit.

4. Lower Management : Lower Management includes (a) Foremen, (b) Supervisors or charge-hands, (c) Office superintendent and (d) Inspectors, etc.

Lower Management Functions are (a) Direct supervision of workers and their work, (b) Developing and improving work methods and operations, (c) Inspection function, (d) Imparting instructions to workers, (e) To give finishing touch to the plans and policies of top management, (f) To act as a link between top management and the operating force (i.e., workers) and (g) To communicate the feelings of workers to the top management.

5. Operating Force : Operating Force includes workers, rank and file workman, skilled, semi-skilled and unskilled.

Operating Force Functions are (a) To do work on machines or manually, using tools, etc., (b) To work independently (in case of skilled worker) or under the guidance of supervisor.

Ten Types of Management*

1. Management by Objectives (MBO) : The organisation sets overall objectives, and then all managers set personal objectives. It helps to get everyone thinking in a set time frame but can be slow to respond to new developments.

2. Management by Exception (MBE) : Managers delegate as much responsibility and activity as possible to those below them and stop in only when problems or unusual situations arise. It helps managers focus on critical areas but requires excellent feedback.

3. Management by Decision Models (MBDM) : Decisions are based on projections generated by artificially constructed situations. It helps management see the possible consequences of their actions but tends to be overly simplistic.

4. Management by Styles (MBS) : Managers adjust their approaches to meet situational needs. It is flexible but demands more skill than some managers possess.

---

* Adapted from Henry O. Golightly, Managing with Style and Making It Work for You Hand Book (New York: John Wiley & Sons, 1981)

5. Management by Competitive Edge (MBCE) : Individuals and groups within the organisation compete against one another to see which can achieve the best results. It helps the skillful people rise to the top but can undermine cooperative efforts.

6. Management by Coaching and Development (MBCD) : Managers see themselves primarily as employee trainers. It helps to bring out the best in everyone, but many managers are not good teachers.

7. Management by Information Systems (MBIS) : Managers depend on data generated within the company to help them increase efficiency and inter-relatedness. It helps management to see the organisation as a whole but takes time and money.

8. Management by Matrices (MBM) : Managers study charted variables to discern their interrelatedness, probable cause and effect, and available options. It helps managers to put organisational variables into perspective but can oversimplify those relationships.

9. Management by Work Simplification (MBWS) : Managers constantly seek ways to simplify processes and reduce expenses. It helps management keep red tape to a minimum but may meet employee resistance.

10. Management by Organisational Development (MBOD) : Managers constantly seek to improve employee relations and communication. It helps managers to focus on employees but may net few short term changes.

Ten Management Styles*

In his book 'Managing with Style and Making It Work for You', Henry O. Golightly, founder of Golightly and Company International, a consulting firm, lists the following :

1. Management by Inaction : The manager who does nothing, or at least puts off doing anything. He may be too fearful, uncertain, or bored to take action, but he also assumes that "if you ignore a problem, it will go away, or at least, get better". He functions best in areas where change comes slowly and where he works for people who prefer to make their own decisions rather than to delegate them.

2. Management by Detail : The manager who researches a problem to death instead of solving it. He works best with people who appreciate his information, don't depend on him for quick or dramatic decisions, and will set deadlines for him.

---

* Adapted from Paul Mail : "The Practice of Modern Management", in Management Handbook (New York : John Wiley & Sons , 1981)

3. Management by Invisibility : The manager who makes himself inaccessible for various reasons, thus forcing subordinates to do more of the work and take the heat. He works best with people who don't need to interact with him, but he needs the presence of a few people so he isn't allowed to isolate himself totally.

4. Management by Consensus : The manager who wants decisions to be a group effort. He either wants harmony or is afraid to make decisions by himself. He does not work well with people who won't interact with him or who expect him to generate his own ideas. But he does work well in decentralised companies that stress human relations.

5. Management by Manipulation : The manager who is most concerned with getting people to do what he wants. He values control for control's sake. He works well with people who are not likely to challenge his methods and may even use them for their benefit. He works best in situations with well-defined goals for which he can aim.

6. Management by Rejection : The manager who is overwhelmigly negative. He picks apart all ideas and resists change. He can make a contribution by tempering hastily through-out or ill-advised schemes conceived by more dynamic co-workers.

7. Management by Survival : The manager who looks out primarily for himself. He has a subordinate mentality-a good follower but one unwilling to take risks. He works best "in an organisation large and stable enough to value the consistent performer who is not a 'tiger'".

8. Management by Despotism : The manager who rules with an iron fist and expects complete subjugation. He works best under people who leave him alone to run things and will get cooperation from subordinates by paying them well.

9. Management by Creativity : The manager who manages instinctively. He bases his actions and decisions on hunches, which may or may not be right. He works best with people who will respect his ideas, if not always follow them, who will leave him alone to be creative, or who will organise and implement his good ideas and pass over his bad ones.

10. Management by Leadership : The Manager who listens to his subordinates and then shows them direction. He values both interaction and goals. He adopts techniques from all the other management styles and knows when to use them and how to keep them in balance.

Ten Management Roles*

Henry Mintzberg, professor of management at McGill University, has analysed what managers do all day, and lists the following activities.

Interpersonal Roles

1. **Figurehead.** The ceremonial duties : Greeting VIPs, sending out birthday cards to employees, cutting ribbons, and so on. Twelve percent of all time spent in contact with other people and 17 percent of all the mail coming in are related to status.
2. **Leader.** The most talked-about role : directing sub-ordinates.
3. **Liaison.** Dealing with people "outside (the) vertical chain of command". Forty-four percent of all time spent dealing with others involves outsiders, compared with 48 percent dealing with subordinates and only 7 percent with superiors.

Informational Roles

4. **Monitor.** The gathering of information : reading newspapers and research reports, asking questions of subordinates, picking up bits and pieces from a network of contacts. "A good part of the information a manager collects in his monitor role arrives in verbal form, often as gossip, hearsay, and speculation".
5. **Disseminator.** Passing on to subordinates information that they need.
6. **Spokesman.** Sending information to people outside the unit.

Decisional Roles

7. **Entrepreneur.** Implementing new ideas : starting projects within the unit.
8. **Disturbance Handler.** Reaction to unexpected situations. "Disturbances arise not only because poor managers ignore situations until they reach crisis proportions, but also because good managers cannot possibly anticipate all the consequences of the actions they take".
9. **Resource Allocator.** Deciding "who will get what in (the) organisation unit", including the manager's time.
10. **Negotiator.** "Studies of managerial work at all levels indicate that managers spend considerable time in negotiations...".

Mintzberg notes that sales managers "seem to spend relatively more of their time in the interpersonal roles... production managers give relatively more attention to the decisional roles... staff managers spend the most time in the informational roles...".

---

* Henry Mintzberg, "The Manager's Job : Folklore and Fact", Harvard Business Review, July-August 1975.

REVIEW QUESTIONS

1. Define the term 'management'
2. What are the principles of management?
3. What are the functions of management?
4. Explain the different levels of management?
5. State and explain briefly the ten types of management.
6. Explain briefly the different management styles?
7. Explain the different roles of management?

2
The Control Function

The Control Function : Planning sets forth the objectives a manager intends to pursue. Organising provides the structure, people and responsibility, to attain those objectives. Directing provides the leadership, the motivating environment. Control provides knowledge of deviation from plans and correction for assurance of conformance to plans. Control is the determination or measurement of progress toward objectives in accordance with the established plan. It concerns the attainment of the planning, organising, directing, and staffing objectives.

Control and Supervision : Some people confuse the term 'Control' with 'Supervision'. Control includes supervision to see that employees perform what they are supposed to perform and measurement of deviation from established standards of performance, as well as corrective action. Supervision to an extent, minimises the control function by reducing deviations from the established standards of performance.

Control as a Function

In order to see the managerial function of control in proper perspective, it must be regarded in the light of the other functions of the manager. As seen in the previous chapter, control is one of major functions of the manager at any level of an enterprise- whether president or foreman-and in every organised enterprise- whether business, government, education, church, or other kind. These functions, all of which are necessary to the job of getting things done through people and all of which differ from those of the engineer, accountant, machinist, or personnel expert.

It will be readily seen that all of the functions of the manager are so closely interrelated that it is difficult in practice to ascertain where one function ends and another begins. Indeed, in practice these functions tend to coalesce because the operating manager performs all of them virtually at the same time. Planning and control are particularly closely related since the purpose of control is to make sure that plans are accomplished. Any attempt to control without planning would be meaningless since no one can tell whether his subordinates are doing what he wishes them to do unless he first knows what his wishes are. As Goetz has put it, "Managerial planning seeks consistent, integrated and articulated programs". while "Management control seeks to compel events to conform to plans". Plans thus furnish the criteria for control.

Definition of Control

Controlling is seeing that actual performance is guided towards expected performance. It is an important function of management and is related to all other management functions. All other management functions cannot be completed effectively without performance of the control function. Control is a comparison and verification process and with the help of this process, a balance in the organisation activities directed towards predetermined goals can be achieved and maintained. It helps in taking corrective measure in case of deviation from planned course of action.

According to **Ernest Dale,** "The modern concept of control envisages a system that not only provides a historical record of what has happened to the business as a whole but pinpoints the reasons why it has happened and provides data that enable the chief executive or the departmental head to take corrective steps if he finds he is on the wrong track". **Koontz and O'Donnell** have defined controlling as the measurement and correction of the performance of activities of subordinates in order to make sure that enterprise objectives and the plans devised to attain them are being accomplished. Thus, managerial function of control implies measurement of actual performance, comparing it with the standards set by plans and correction of deviations to assure attainment of objectives according to plans.

According to **Henri Fayol***, the father of modern operational management theory, "control consists in verifying whether everything occurs in conformity with the plans adopted, the instructions issued and principles established. It has for an object to point out weaknesses and errors in order to rectify them and prevent recurrence. It operates on everything, things, people and their actions". Once a plan becomes operational, control is necessary to measure the progress, to uncover deviation from plans and to indicate and implement corrective action. The corrective action may involve even revision of plan, restructuring the organisation, improving staffing and introducing changes in techniques of directing and leading. Thus, the function of control is to compel events to conform to plans**

George R. Terry : "Controlling is determining what is being accomplished, that is, evaluating the performance and, if necessary, applying corrective measures so that the performance takes place according to plans".

The Systems Definition : "That function of a system which provides direction in conformance to the plan" or "The maintenance of variations from system objectives within allowable limits".

---

* Henri Fayol - General and Industrial Management, Page 107 (New York, Pitman Publishing Corporation) 1949 edition.

* Billy E. Goetz - Management Planning and Control, Page 229 (New York, Mc Graw-Hill Book Company) 1949 edition.

Thus, controlling implies determining and stating specifically what is to be accomplished, then checking performance against such standards prescribed with a view to supplying the corrective action required to achieve the planned objectives. The end objective of controlling is, therefore, to ensure that the people's effort in the organisation is continuously directed towards the attainment of the predetermined objectives. Thus, whilst managerial planning seeks to provide consistent, integrated and articulated programmes, management control seeks to compel events to conform to plans. Although the manager cannot affect what has already happened or gone past, he can study the past with a view to learn from it what has happened and where standards were not reached or achieved. He can then formulate the steps required to correct the action so that in the future and expected results are achieved. Thus, control is forward looking and is aimed at ascertaining the deviations from the established goals as quickly as possible with a view to incorporating corrective action.

To sum up, the meaning and purpose of 'Control' is : 1. Knowing exactly what work is to be done as to (a) quantity; (b) quality; and (c) time available. 2. Knowing what resources are available for doing the work as to (a) personnel; (b) materials; and (c) other facilities. 3. Knowing that the work has been done or is being done (a) with the resources available; (b) within the time available; (c) at a reasonable cost; and (d) in accordance with the required standard of quality. 4. Knowing immediately of any delays, hold-ups or variations as to (a) what happened; (b) its cause; and (c) remedy. 5. Knowing what is being done; remove such hindrances as to (a) who is doing it; (b) how it is being done; (c) what it is costing; and (d) when it will be completed. 6. Knowing about the completed work as to (a) time finished, (b) quantity, and (c) final cost. 7. Knowing that resources are guarded against (a) in what way, (b) by whom, (c) at what cost, and (d) with what provision for periodic inspection.

Elements of Control : There are six elements of control, viz., authority, knowledge, guidance, direction, constraint and restraint. To be in a position to exercise control, the Manager must know what the situation is, what it should be, and how to correct it. Besides, he must have the authority to take the appropriate action.

Nature of Control : Managerial control has the following characteristics :

(i) **Control is a function of management :** It is, in fact, a follow-up action to the other functions of management. This function is performed by all the managers in the organisation to control the activities assigned to them.

(ii) **Control is a dynamic process :** It involves continuous review of standards of performance and results in corrective action which may lead to changes in other functions of management.

(iii) **Control is a continuous activity:** It does not stop anywhere. According to Koontz and O'Donnell, "Just as the navigator continually takes reading to ascertain whether he is relative to a planned action, so should be the business manager continually take reading to assure himself that his enterprise or department is on course".

(iv) **Control is forward looking:** It is related to future as past cannot be controlled. It is usually preventive as the presence of control systems leads to minimise wastages, losses, and deviations from standards. It should be noted that control does not curtail the rights of the individuals. It simply keeps a check on the performance of individuals.

(v) **Planning and Controlling are closely related with each other:** Managerial planning seeks consistent, integrated and articulated programme while managerial control seeks to compel events to conform to plans. As a matter of fact, planning is based on control and control is based on planning. The process of control uses certain standards for measuring performance which are laid down by planning. The control process, in turn, may reveal the deficiency of planning and may lead to the revision of planning. It may also lead to setting of new goals, changing the organisational structure, improving staffing and making major changes in the techniques of directing.

'Control' by nature is both restrictive as well as regulative. However, the modern concept of control is concerned more with regulation than with restriction as the latter is a very limited form of control activity. The authority to control vests with the higher level of management because it is the superior who has delegated authority to the subordinate to carry out certain activity. Each higher level of management seeks to ensure that plans are adhered to by those over whom they have authority. Control operates against people, but control is not necessarily restrictive in the sense of one man controlling another. Controls are a method of measuring progress and the present direction of management thinking is towards the desirability of self-discipline in this respect. Peter Drucker* advocates 'Self control' rather than control from higher level. The term 'self control' refers to a system of control wherein each level of management ensures for itself that it follows the planned course and attains the targets assigned to it. The self control thus is more a self regulatory process rather than imposition from the top.

Significance of Control

The significance of control emerges from the need to maximise the use of scarce resources and also to attain an orderly, systematic and purposeful

---

* Drucker, Peter F. - The Practice of Management, Pages 63 and 101 (New York, Harper & Brothers) 1954 edition.

behaviour of an organisation and its members. The need for control arises further from weaknesses which are inherent in the psychological make-up of individuals. In the absence of control, an individual tends to allow results to deviate from plans or orders*. Besides this, employees by nature are generally exposed to various temptations. In the ordinary course of business, many employees have to be entrusted with large amounts of money, valuable materials and trade secrets. In the absence of effective control, employees tend to yield to temptations. Control, therefore, becomes essential to impart strength and to boost morale of an organisation which ultimately affects its output. In a nut-shell, absence of, or laxity in, controls results in total confusion, inefficiency and conflicts.

"Control consists in verifying whether everything occurs in conformity with the plans adopted, the instructions issued and principals established. It has for object to point out weaknesses and errors in order to rectify them and prevent recurrence. It operates on everything, things, people, action".** Control is an important function of management. Without control, a manager cannot "do a complete job of managing". All other functions are the preparatory steps for getting the work done and controlling is concerned with making sure that there is proper execution of these functions. Control is necessary whenever a manager assigns duties and delegates authority to a subordinate. He must exercise control over the actions of his subordinates so that he can ensure that the delegated authority is being used properly.

The road signals at a busy road crossing appropriately illustrate the significance of control. Just as road signals are essential to ensure accident-free and smooth traffic, management control devices are necessary in any organisation for its smooth functioning. By controlling, the manager ensures that resources are obtained and used economically and efficiently for the achievement of organisational objectives. A good control system provides timely information to the manager which is very much useful for taking various operations. Control simplifies supervision by pointing out the significant deviations from the standards of performance. It keeps the subordinates under check and brings discipline among them. It enables the expansion of span of supervision at various levels in the organisation.

Scope of Control

The scope of control is very wide. It virtually covers all the areas of business, namely, policies, procedures, men, money, machines and equipment, public relations, human relations, research and development and so on. Generally,

---

* Dalton E. Mc Farland : Management Principles and Practices, Pages 390-393 (New York : McMillan Publishing Co. Inc.) 1974 edition.

** Henri Fayol : General and Industrial Management

control is exercised by concentration on key areas of business on which the success of the business depends. It is known as 'Key-point Control'. The key-points vary from enterprise to enterprise.

Control may (i) physical, and (ii) financial. Physical control may be either quantitative or qualitative. They are exercised by personal supervision and checking. Either the entire lot or the sample is compared with the standards. Financial control is exercised through budgetary control and cost accounting control.

Standards of Performance

A standard is a criterion against which performance and results of the individuals is measured or judged. Standard should be based on scientific analysis and should not be subjective in nature. It should possess the following characteristics :

1. Standard should be capable of achievement with reasonable amount of effort and time.
2. Standards should concentrate at results and not the procedures.
3. Standards should not be rigid. They should be capable of being changed whenever the need arises.
4. As far as possible standard should be expressed in quantitative terms and should be based on the result of work measurement carried with the help of time and motion studies.
5. Standards should be consistent with the overall organisation objectives.

Standards may be expressed in physical terms or monetary terms. Physical standards are generally, applied at the operative levels where the quantity and quality of production is to be controlled. Monetary standards are expressed in terms of costs and revenues.

Thus, there are many types of standards which can be fixed for measuring performance, which include the following important ones, namely : 1. Physical standards, 2. Cost standards, 3. Revenue standards, 4. Capital standards, and 5. Intangible standards.

1. Physical Standards ; These physical standards, like quantitative in units and man-hours, deal with non-monetary measurements and are used more often at the operating level where materials are utilised, labour employed and goods manufactured. These can be quantitative or qualitative in nature. **Quantitative** standards may, for example, define the number of units to be produced per hour, or the man-hours per unit of output or the tonne-miles of weight traffic carried or units of production per machine-hour and so on. Physical standards can also measure **quality** such as closeness of tolerances, fastness of a colour, the durability of a product and so on. These physical standards are "the building blocks of managerial planning", and simultaneously they constitute the physical standards for control.

2. Cost Standards : These monetary measurements are also common at the operating level and give some monetary value to the cost of the operations involved, e.g., direct or indirect cost per unit produced, material cost per unit and selling cost per rupee or unit of sales. Thus, these cost standards state the expense involved in monetary terms for attaining the various goals.

3. Revenue Standards : These standards attach a monetary value to the sales, e.g., per capita in defined market area. Again, the annual sales for a department store can be stated in rupees by multiplying the forecasted number of units by the selling price per unit and can become the expected revenue volume of the enterprise for a defined period.

4. Capital Standards : These standards are in terms of the capital invested by the organisation and are thus related to the balance sheet, e.g., rate of return on capital invested and several ratios such as the ratio of current assets to current liabilities.

5. Intangible Standards : These standards are expressed in neither physical nor monetary measurements and yet they exist in an organisation. They relate to the measurement of intangibles such as the competence of managers and employees or the success of a public relations programme or the benefits of a training programme. Psychological tests and attitude surveys are being continuously developed by psychologists and behavioural scientists as an aid measuring such intangibles. However, it is difficult to set quantitative standards to these highly qualitative factors.

The standards may be tangible or intangible. It is relatively easy to measure performance against tangible standards as compared with intangible standards. The tangible standards are mostly physical, cost, revenue or capital standards. It is impractical if not impossible for a manager to attempt to check the performance of the various activities under his supervision against all these numerous goals. The manager, therefore, must select certain points in the operation which will be the strategic points to reflect the goals of his department and to show him whether or not these goals are being met. Through this technique a manager will be in a position to concentrate his energies on controlling operations.

Further, the strategic points should be such as will (i) facilitates timely control, (ii) permit economic observation and (iii) provide comprehensive coverage and promote balanced control.*

* William H. Newman : Administrative action, Pages 409-415 (Englewood Cliffs, N.J. : Prentice Hall, Inc.) 1951 edition.

STEPS IN THE CONTROL PROCESS

In order to perform his control functions, a manager follows three basic steps. First of all, he establishes the standards of performance to ensure that performance is in accordance with the plan. After this, the manager will appraise the performance and compare it with predetermined standards. This step will lead the manager to know whether the performance has come up to the expected standard or if there is any deviation. If the standards are not being met, the manager will take corrective actions which is the final step in controlling as shown in Fig. 2.1 The detailed discussion of these steps is given below :

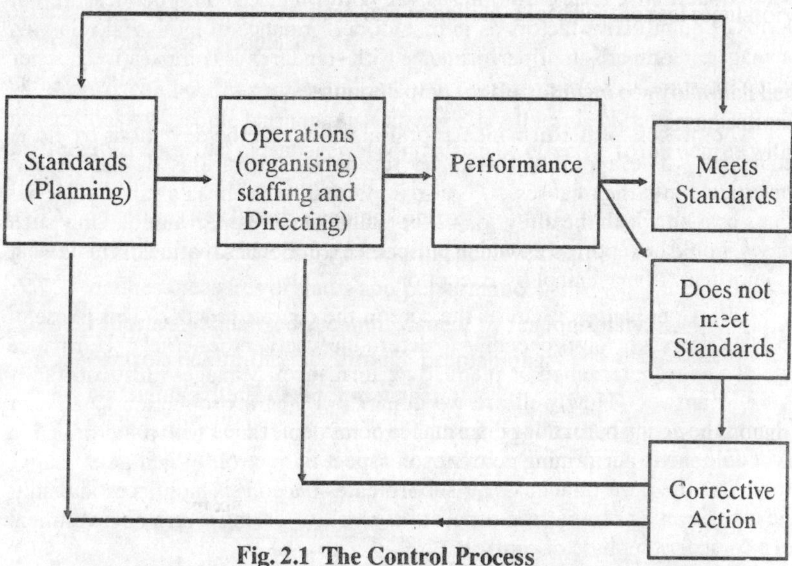

Fig. 2.1 The Control Process

(i) Establishing standards : A standard acts as a reference line or basic of comparison of actual performance. Standards should be set precisely and preferably in quantitative terms. It should be noted that setting standards is also closely linked with and is an integral part of the planning process. Different standards of performance are set up for various operations at the planning stage which serve as the basis of any control system. Establishment of standards in terms of quantity, quality or time is necessary for effective control because it is essential to determine how the performance is going to be appraised. Standards should be accurate, precise, acceptable and workable. Standards should be flexible, i.e., capable of being changed when the circumstances require so.

As seen in the previous pages, different types of standards are used for measuring the performance of different operations. Many standards are of a physical nature, such as number of units, man-hours, etc., and there are other standards which are expressed in monetary terms relating to sales, revenues, expenses, costs and so forth. In addition to these standards, there are also standards of an intangible nature like reputation of the firm. Whenever standards are intangible, it is essential to lay down quantitative factors which will determine whether the standards are being met or not.

(ii) Appraising performance : This step involves measuring of actual performance of various individuals, groups or units and then comparing it with the standards which have already been set up at the planning stage. The quantitative measurement should be done in cases where standards have been set in quantitative terms. In other cases, performance should be measured in terms of quantitative factors as in case of performance of industrial relations manager. Comparison of performance with standards is comparatively easier when the standards are expressed in quantitative terms.

The process of performance appraisal will reveal the deviations from the standards. The appraisal should try to analyse the various deviations and investigate into their causes. It is also important to establish a range of deviations beyond which the attention of top management is warranted. Only such cases should be reported up which pin-point exceptional situations. This is what is known as 'Management by Exception'.

(iii) Comparison : This is the core of the control process. This phase of control process involves checking to determine whether the actual performance meets the predetermined or planned performance. Manager must constantly seek to answer, "How well are we doing?". When a production supervisor checks the actual output or performance of his department with the production schedule, he is performing comparison aspect of control. When an executive evaluates the performance of his subordinates once in six months or annually, he is performing comparison aspect of control. Checking return on investment is a comparison phase of control.

(iv) Taking corrective action : The final step in the control process is taking corrective actions so that deviations may not occur again and the objectives of the organisation are achieved. This will involve taking certain decision by the management like replanning or redrawing of goals or standards, reassignment or clarification of duties. It may also necessitate reforming the process of selection the training of workers. Thus, control function may require change in all other managerial functions. If the standards are found to be defective, they will be modified in the light of the observations.

Some innovative people and organisations have already built-in corrective actions in their control process, if the deviations are due to controllable factors. Some even go to the extent of identifying the uncontrollable factors and developing alternative courses of action for deviations. When deviations occur and the procedures regarding corrective actions are given in advance to the performers of job, actions can be taken without delay. The following are important phases of corrective action :

1. **The Operative Phase :**
   (a) Prompt investigation of the causes of the deviation.
   (b) Decision concerning the required corrective action.
   (c) Prompt direction for correcting the situation in accordance with the decision.
   (d) Close supervision of the corrective action to ensure that it is taking place according to the instructions and is effective.
2. **The Administrative Phase :**
   (a) Further investigation of recurring difficulties to determine the basic factors, either human or physical, that are responsible.
   (b) Disciplinary action, either positive or negative, as the situation requires.
   (c) Creative planning to prevent a recurrence of the situation.
   (d) Recognition of the situation and the introduction of the planned measures.

Follow-Through : Recommending corrective actions also is not sufficient and the manager shouldn't assume that his responsibility is over with this action. Often control process is ineffective or fails because the corrective action recommended is not followed through. Specific procedures must be established and the responsibility must be clearly assigned to carry out the corrective action. Say, for instance, the performance evaluation of a subordinate indicates weaknesses in supervisory practices, the superior of this individual recommends a corrective action by which the individual is to undergo some training in supervisory practices. The responsibility for that corrective action is not over just by making this recommendation. The superior must follow through his recommendation to see whether the individual participates and makes progress in the training programme and to what extent he relates to his actual work situation whatever he has learned in the training programme.

Feedback in Control : We have noted in the control process that performance is measured and reported back to the manager. Performance information thus measured and channeled back to management is known as **Feedback.** It tells what kind of job is being done, what variations have occurred, and what kind of temporary measures taken to make adjustments, modifications and so on. This feedback information may include quality, quantity, market share, customer service and financial information. The information gained through feedback is useful for future planning and decision-making processes.

There are two types of feedback controls. One is **self-correcting** and the other is **non-correcting.** The self-correcting or servo- mechanism is one which regulates itself without outside intervention for corrective action to be taken. In steel mills, thermostat systems are used to make sure that heat remains uniform in various production process.

The non-correcting system requires outside intervention before corrective action can take place. Statistical quality control is an example of this type. Through statistical sampling, deviations are identified. Quality control charts are used for this purpose.

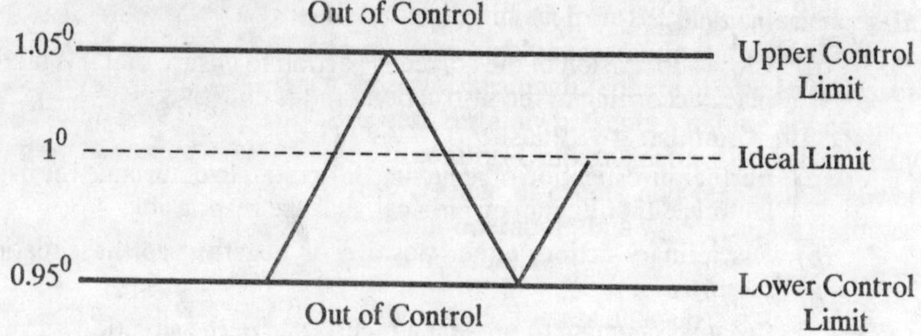

Fig 2.2 Quality Control Chart

In the above chart, let us say the predetermined standards set for the diameter of pipes as 1 inch. Due to the condition of machines and other factors the acceptable deviations were set at 1.05" (upper limit) and .95" (lower limit). When the diameter of the pipe goes beyond these limits, it is said to be **out of control.** At this point the process is halted and necessary adjustments are made with outside intervention and the system is brought back **into control.**

THE TEN COMMANDMENTS OF EFFECTIVE CONTROL SYSTEM

The following are the ten essential or basic requirements of an effective control system :

1. Suitable : The control system must be suitable for the kind of activity it is intended to serve. Apart from differences in the systems of control in different business, they also vary from department to department and from one level of the organisation to the other. A system of control useful at a higher level of management will be different in scope and nature from that in use at the operative level. Several techniques are available for control purposes such as budgets, break-even points, financial ratios and so on. The manager must be sure that he is using the technique appropriate for control of the specific activity involved. The tools appropriate are not necessarily the same as between different departments or between two different organisations. For example, the sales department and production department may use different tools of control. Again, a small business will not have as elaborate a control system as a large organisation.

2. Understandable : The system must be understandable, i.e., the control information supplied should be capable of being understood by those who use it. A control system that a manager cannot understand is bound to remain ineffective. The control information supplied should be such as will be used by the managers concerned. What may be considered valuable and understandable to one manager may not be so to another. It is, therefore, the duty of the manager concerned to make sure that the control information supplied to him is of a nature that will serve his purpose. As an illustration, it is quite possible that top managers may understand a complicated system of control based on statistical break-even charts and mathematical formulae whilst to the lower level manager such information would be of very doubtful utility, being beyond their powers of comprehension. In this sense, the data supplied as information must be understandable and helpful.

3. Economical : The system must be economical in operation, i.e., the cost of a control system should not exceed the possible savings from its use. The extent of control necessary should be decided by the standard of accuracy or quality required. A very high degree or standard of accuracy or quality may not really be necessary. Undue complexity of the control system should be avoided to keep a check on the costs of control. It, therefore, becomes necessary to concentrate the control system on factors which are strategic to keep the costs down and the system economical.

4. Flexible : The system of control must be flexible, i.e., workable even if the plans have to be changed. In case the control systems can work only on the basis of one specific plan, it becomes useless if the plan breaks down and another has to be substituted. However thoroughly the plans may have been formed or the planning premises established, unforeseen circumstances can upset the best-laid plans. A good control system would be sufficiently flexible to permit the changes so necessitated. For example, Goetz pointed out that it was possible that some particulars within the managerial plan might fail. "The control system should report such failures and should contain sufficient elements of flexibility to maintain managerial control of operations in spite of such failures".

5. Expeditious : Nothing can be done to correct deviations which have already occurred. It is, therefore, important that the control system should report deviations from plans expeditiously. No useful purpose can be served by a deviation detected months after its occurrence. The objective of the control system should be to correct deviations in the immediate future. This requires that the time-lag between the occurrence of a deviation and its reporting be kept at the minimum possible.

6. Forward Looking : The control system must, therefore, be forward-looking as the manager cannot control the past. In fact, the control system can at times be so devised as to anticipate possible deviations or problems. Thus, deviations can be torecast so that corrections can be incorporated even before the problem occurs. Cash forecasts and cash control is an example in point where a financial manager can forecast the future cash requirements and provide for them in advance.

7. Organisational Conformity : Since activities are carried on by people, and events must be controlled through people, it is necessary that the control data and system must conform to the organisational pattern. The control data must be so prepared that it is possible to fix responsibility for the deviations within the areas of accountability. For example, where factory costs are accumulated in a manner other than on the basis of areas of responsibility, they may lost much of their values as an instrument of control. In this case, the actual costs in a department may be out of line with the standards set without the department knowing whether the deviation has been caused by something within its control. In this sense, organisation and control are difficult to separate, being dependent on one another for effective management.

8. Indicative of Exceptions at Critical Points : The management principle of exception should be used to show up not only deviations but the critical areas must also be fixed for most effective control.

9. Objectivity : As far as possible, the measurements used must have objectivity. Unfortunately, particularly whilst appraising a subordinate's performance, the subjective element cannot be entirely removed. Here the personality of both the manager as well as his subordinate would be reflected in the final judgement and can bias the appraisal. The use of indefinite terms can frustrate the subordinate like being told that he is not doing a good job. He is likely to react more favourably to objective standards.

10. Suggestive of Corrective Action : Finally, an adequate control system should not only detect failures, but must also disclose where they are occurring, who is responsible for them, and what should be done to correct them. Overall summary information can cover up certain fault areas. For instance, it is insufficient to show merely a decline in the profits. The reason for such decline must also be indicated, such as a drop in the sales volume or an increase in the costs. Even this is insufficient. The information should also disclose in which market areas the sales declined or which specific costs had increased. Where a system merely detects deviations but does not indicate corrective action, the control system becomes an exercise in futility.

Benefits of Control

Following are the advantages of an effective system of control :

1. **Control provides the basis for future action.** It will reduce the chances of mistakes being repeated in future by suggesting preventive steps.

2. **Control facilitates decision making.** The process of control is complete only when corrective measures are taken. This requires taking a right decision as to what type of follow up action is to be taken.

3. An effective system of **control facilitates decentralisation of authority** because the top executives get the feedback information constantly which helps them to ensure that the decisions taken at the lower levels are consistent with the policies of the enterprise and are in the interest of the enterprise.

4. **Control and planning go hand in hand.** Control is the only means to ensure that the plans are being implemented in real sense. Control points out the short comings of not only planning but also other functions of management such as organising, staffing and directing.

5. The existence of a control system has a **positive impact on the behaviour of the employees.** They are cautious while performing their duties as they know that they are being observed by their superiors.

6. **Control helps in co-ordination** of the activities of the various departments of the enterprise by providing them unity of direction.

Limitations of Control

A control system may be faced with the following limitations :

1. An enterprise cannot control the external factors such as government policy, technological changes, fashion changes, etc.

2. Control is an expensive process because sufficient attention has to be paid to observe the performance of the subordinates. This requires an expenditure of a lot of time and effort.

3. Control system loses its effectiveness when standards of performance cannot be defined in quantitative terms. For instance, it is very difficult to measure human behaviour and employee morale.

4. The effectiveness of control mainly depends on the acceptance of subordinates. They may resist control because they may feel that it will reduce or curtail their freedom. Control also loses its significance when it is not possible to fix the accountability of the subordinates.

REVIEW QUESTIONS

1. Define the concept of managerial control. Discuss the nature of control.
2. Explain the importance of control to a business enterprise.
3. Why is control a must in business management? What are the requirements of an effective control system?

4. Examine important features of controlling. What are basic steps in the process of controlling?
5. "Planning is an empty exercise without contolling". Comment.
6. Examine the benefits and limitation of Managerial Control.
7. What is Controlling? Discuss its need. What do you think are the characteristics of a good control system?
8. Critically examine the following statement : "Planning is meaningless without control and control is aimless without planning".
9. Explain the different steps involved in the control process
10. Explain the following :
    (a) Forward looking control.
    (b) Principle of Exception

3

The Nature of Management Control

Management control is the process of assuring that resources are obtained and used effectively and efficiently in the accomplishment of the organisation's objectives. Management control is a process carried on within the framework established by strategic planning. Objectives, facilities, organisation, and financial factors are more or less accepted as "givens". Decisions about next year's budget, for example, are limited by policies and guidelines prescribed by top management. The management control process is intended to make possible the achievement of planned objectives as effectively and efficiently as possible within these "givens". The purpose of a management control system is to encourage managers to take actions which are in the best interests of the company. For example, if the system is structured so that a certain course of action increases the reported profits of a division, and at the same time lessens the profits of the company as a whole, there is something wrong. Technically, this purpose can be described as goal congruence.

Defining Management Control

Management control can be defined as a systematic effort by business management to compare performance to predetermined standards, plans, or objectives in order to determine whether performance is in line with these standards and presumably in order to take any remedial action required to see that human and other corporate resources are being used in the most effective and efficient way possible in achieving corporate objectives.

All control starts with an enterprise's plans and expectations for the future because the objectives and standards against which performance is measured are based on those plans and expectations. In an operational control situation, a means of obtaining accurate and up-to-date information about current performance must be developed next. The actual is then compared with the expected. Depending upon the evaluation of the meaning of any variation from standard, some sort of action is then taken. In those situations that involve developing controls for planning decisions - an aspect of management control frequently overlooked - a realistic means of quantifying possible future events must be developed, so that all alternatives can be stated in comparable terms. These projections of performance can then be compared with the predetermined performance requirements set for the company or operation involved, and a choice can be made among alternative courses of action.

Some Distinguishing Characteristics

While management control has characteristics common to all forms of control, it also has a number of distinguishing characteristics. First, management control refers specifically to the control functions within a business enterprise. Second, it concerns the business manager's control functions. Third, it is control designed to help a business enterprise reach its over-all objectives, and it is always viewed as an extension of a company's long-range plan. In other words, management control is another means managers have to achieve corporate objectives more effectively, whether it be at the staff, management, or operational level, whether the controls are used to protect assets or to stimulate creative use of those assets, or whether the controls are used to maintain production efficiency or to make decisions to purchase equipment.

Management Control and Planning

Because management control is designed to help a corporation reach its long-term objective, management control begins with corporate planning. Corporate planning is an intellectual process which requires analysis of future circumstances, both external (environmental) and internal (company), and the development of an objective, policies, and programmes within the context of that future. The type of business planning defined here is always done within the framework of the entire corporation's long-term future, whether the plan itself is for one or ten years, and may be either for the corporation as a whole or for only one of its major operations. In most instances the corporate planning process includes the creation of an intermediate or long-range plan for a business enterprise.

Management control is an extension of the corporate planning process, for a good plan should have controls built into it. And a management control system cannot be developed, nor can management control be exercised effectively, unless the company has a specific objective and over-all plan for reaching that objective. For example, in building a control system, one must know not only what kind of business the company is in now, but also the kind of business it plans to be in three, five, or even ten years from now. Nor can one establish standards for measuring performance without knowing the company's expectations for the future.

By definition, therefore, management control is always exercised within the perspective of the over-all corporate plan, although the two functions are distinct : the management planning process leads to the creation of a corporate plan; the management control process controls performance within the framework of that corporate plan.

In order to understand just how performance is controlled and control decisions are made, it is necessary to examine in detail the two major management control processes. The first is the process followed in solving control problems and in setting up effective controls or a system for effective control. The second is the process of controlling the operation and making decisions once the controls or control system have been developed.

The Process Followed in Solving Control Problems and Setting Up Controls

The approach to solving management control problems closely parallels the fundamental approach to problem solving/decision making. The steps in the problem-solving/decision making process, as outlined by Peter Drucker, are as follows :

1. Diagnose the situation and review all of the facts in order to find and define the problem.
2. Examine the problem and review the facts in order to find the key factors affecting the problem and its solution. This step is sometimes referred to as premising.
3. Develop alternative solutions to the problem.
4. Test and evaluate the alternatives to determine the best solution.
5. Construct a clear statement of the solution selected, and convert the decision into a plan of action.

The following is an outline of how this process can be applied to management control problems :

1. Diagnose the situation in order to find and define the control problem. The investigation should result in definitions (i.e., simple statement) of :

* The control problem which must be solved.

* The scope of the problem, its management implications, and tangential areas related to the control problem.

* The extent of the solutions needed and the method to be used in solving the problem.

2. Examine the control problem and review the facts in order to find the key factors affecting the problem and its solution. The principal areas of investigations would be :

* Corporate planning factors, such as the nature of the company's business, the company's objective and major policies, the timing of major steps in the plan, and other factors related to the corporate long-range plan.

* The nature of the control problem being solved or of the operation for which the controls or control system is being created. For example, the problem could be an information system, capital equipment acquisition, production, inventory or other operational control, or any of wide range of control situations.

* The purpose for which the controls or control system is being developed.

* The standards or criteria against which performance will be measured or compared.

3. Develop alternative solutions. The areas covered would be :

* Mechanics. The specific tools of analysis or the actual control system to be used. These would include the reporting forms needed and the precise information wanted on these forms, a design for the information system proposed and the organisation needed, the mathematical and analytical models which will be used, and the assumptions to be used for quantifying risk and uncertainty.

* Implementation. The way to put the new solution (if one is proposed) into operation.

* The exercise of control. Where the controls or control system are automatic, this step in solving the control problem would be included as part of the mechanics. If executive judgement and action are required, principles of action and attitude and procedures must be spelled out. How control is exercised and how decisions are made on the basis of the control information developed are discussed in the next page.

4. Test and evaluate these alternatives to determine the best control tools, techniques, or system, how they can best be put into operation, and how they can be used most effectively by managers to achieve over-all corporate objectives.

5. Prepare a written statement of the solutions selected in all major areas and proceed to carry it out. As the analysis of the situation proceeds, he develops tentative alternative solutions to assist in testing and checking the feasibility of certain courses of action. For example, he may first examine the various alternative computerised information systems. After investigating each of these alternatives, he may come to the conclusion that a computerised information or control system is too costly, and that a combined manual and punched card processing system will be best for his operation. At this point he will develop additional alternatives.

As the analysis progresses further, therefore, revised solutions are usually developed. This is the phase during which the executive has the opportunity to correct, adjust, or confirm the earlier solutions in the light of subsequent analysis and evaluation.

Lastly, he develops final solutions. This is the stage during which the solutions are stated in the formal written plan presented to management.

This same process is at work in Step 2 of the management control process when the executive is seeking, defining, and quantifying the over-all key factors affecting his solution. For example, while it is important to know that standards must be established, the executive's real job is to develop the specific standards and the format in which they will be presented. Such questions as how those using the standards will respond to them and use them and whether the standards are a true reflection of the corporation's long-term goals and crucial to the success or failure of the control system. Constant probing, testing, and hypothesising are necessary before a clear definition of the most relevant key factors can be formulated.

The process is repeated again when developing plans for putting the new system into operation, when, for example, developing ways to get operating managers to accept a new control system. And nothing can be done to by-pass or simplify this continual process of investigation and evaluation so necessary for successful management control. The existence of these difficulties and complexities does not mean that management control is not a science, for underlying the back-and-forth intellectual searching described above are the familiar steps of problem definition, premising, and developing, testing, and implementing the solution.

What the complexities do mean is that knowing management control theory is only a small beginning. Adapting that theory to solving the problem at hand is the art of management control, which complements the science. It is an art which is critical to the successful application of the science of management control in a business situation. It is an art which requires considerable experience and judgement, and so is learned principally by doing.

Exercising Control

Once a control problem has been resolved and a new control tool or system developed, then the question of how to use the system or tool most efficiently for controlling and making control decisions must be explored. In many instances control is exercised automatically - performance is checked and adjustments are made by automated equipment. A home-heating system is an example of this type of automated control, as are many modern chemical plant operations. The type of control being discussed here is not, however, automatic control, but the type of control that involves executive judgement and executive action in using the control tools or system to achieve broad corporate objectives.

Above all, management control requires that a balance be maintained between compliance and stimulation in exercising control. For example, when variances from budget occur, what balance can be struck between criticising operating personnel for noncompliance and taking constructive steps for educating them in corporate goals? Or how much use can be made of the discussions of the variances to better coordinate functional operations, such as production and marketing, without at the same time destroying the system's value in maintaining compliance ?

In exercising control, the executive can limit himself merely to insisting upon compliance - protecting assets, policing, checking accuracy, gathering more information, reprimanding, and the like. However, this is too restrictive a viewpoint. Management control dictates that the executive strive to attain more positive goals in exercising control. The primary aim of management control is to stimulate better use of assets, create new ways to do business, better coordinate the efforts of individual operating departments, educate operating personnel so that their efforts are more closely geared to accomplishing specific corporate objectives-in short, to create an enabling atmosphere, whose vistas are broadened, not narrowed, by the controls.

A study of the introduction of a new control system at H.J. Heinz, Inc., in the Mid-1950s illustrates this point. At Heinz the development of the new control system started with long-range planning. The six development steps were :

1. Establishing the goals of the business.
2. Forecasting conditions.
3. Developing plans.
4. Preparing and scheduling estimates.
5. Controlling commitments and expenditures.
6. Reporting and appraising results.

The organisation for control was then established and the responsibility for introducing new controls was fixed.

Factors Affecting Managerial Philosophy

Application of the concept of management control requires as a minimum the following :

1. identifying key factors in the business operation which need to be controlled in order to achieve a given over-all result;
2. specifying the basis for establishing standards of performance for each control factor, such as forecasts, budgets, standard costs, turnover ratios, and lead times;
3. defining the information-accounting and operating data and statistics-that must be accumulated to measure status and performance;
4. establishing a reporting structure that identifies performance in each control area, relates causes and effects, signals trends, and identifies results by responsibility under the plan of organisations.

The development of such a management control system requires careful study of the total enterprise and its separation into controllable components. A close scrutiny must also be made of each component in terms of its operational characteristics.

What has been so far stated represents "received doctrine". recognising that, although some firms incorporate such measurements and information into their control systems, most of them do not. But we must go beyond the minimum steps outlined for developing a philosophy of control. As Peter F. Drucker explains, "We are recently acquiring a great capacity to design 'controls' in businesses, based upon a great improvement in techniques, especially in the application of logical and mathematical tools to business data, and in the ability to process and analyse large masses of data very fast".*

Drucker then raises the question : "What do these improved techniques mean for control?" ... Might we simultaneously be enlarging the means to control (that is, the measurement and information systems) without achieving the end results of control which we seek? This may well be the case, because in too many instances the measurements and information pertain to historical data; yet the most effective controls are known to deal with the future, about which we know far too little. Frederic G. Donner, chairman of the board of General Motors, for example, points out that he spends far more time contemplating forecasts of future conditions than reviewing financial data of past operations. Management has at its disposal three positive actions by which control can be exercised : 1. planning ahead; 2. day-to-day scheduling, direction and supervision; 3. after-the-fact response to data systems feedback.

Any present or prospective controller considering his own philosophy of control would do well to bear in mind one distinction : we may find ourselves with too many controls and too little control. The individual in a firm who is most directly charged with producing the means to control (information and measurement systems) is the "controller". Most knowledgeable executives, controllers included, quickly agree that it would be a gross mistake for controllers to use the controls to exercise personal control in the business. As staff executives, controllers must recognise that line executives at the various levels in administration determine whether the firm can truly be said to be "in control". A further distinction has been made by the Financial Executives Institute : the functions of controllership include establishing, coordination, and maintaining an integrated plan for the control of operations, through authorised management. According to James L. Peirce, vice president-finance of A.B. Dick Company, these last three words need emphasis if such a plan is to become operational.*

Because we deal with human beings in the conduct of business enterprises, effective control cannot be achieved unless measurement and information

* Peter Drucker, "Controls, Control and Management", in Management Controls : New Directions in Basic Research (New York:Mc Graw-Hill Book Company, 1964), p. 286.

* James L. Peirce, "The Planning and Control Concept", The Controller, XXII, (1954), pp. 403-6, 422-25.

systems allow latitude for personal accomplishment and contribution. Therefore, a valid philosophy of managerial control utilises the premise that even the most complete system of quantitative control must be consonant with the qualitative control provided by the human organisation.

Four additional factors stated by Drucker which operate to affect the managerial philosophy are :

1. Measuring business data interferes with the data measured.
2. Measures of business data must be appropriate.
3. There are diminishing returns on internal management controls.
4. Business is a unique control situation.

These factors warrant consideration at this point.

1. Measuring business data interferes with the data measured : In the physical sciences, measurement is an objective process : it changes neither the object measured nor the individual making the measurement. In business, however, as in many other areas of the social sciences, quite often the act of measuring interferes with the event being measured. The mere fact that an item (such as return on investment, inventory, turnover, or sales revenues) has been selected for measurement attaches an undesirable bias and lack of objectivity to the item. We are aware that the item has been selected for measurement and control-therefore it must be important !

Actions may be taken which are irrational in over-all company terms in order to "window dress" the item being measured. Executives who have operated under budgetary control may over- emphasize the need to stay within the budget, often losing sight of what should be their goal : economical and profitable operations. Changed circumstances may well justify deviation from the original budget, but even then, only an experienced executive willingly abandons the carefully prepared budget target.

What, then, should we measure in our control system?

We should measure those events and results which managers at various levels believe are of over-all importance as well as critical in their own areas of supervision. Unless executives in a company satisfactorily determine what should be measured, the measurement and information systems they design will make the business even more difficult to control. The manager will all too soon be buried in controls which do not effectively provide control.

2. Measures of business data must be appropriate : Drucker cites as an example a report of an industrial relations department which showed grievances from the working force were running one-half of one percent (.005) for "five grievances per thousand employees per month". On the surface this appeared minimal, because most managers in business implicitly apply a normalisation concept which interprets this to mean that one department with 200 employees had one grievance on the average. The fact was that one department with 20 employees had all five of the experienced grievances !

Similar non-normalised statistics reflect that "10 percent of the inventory items account for 75 percent of the rupee value of inventories held", or "90 percent of the rupee volume of business is usually represented by less than 5 percent of the number of products a company handles". There are certainly implications here for what the manager needs to control, as well as for the nature of the measurement and information systems and how they should reflect such data for him. These are isolated illustrations of the kind of measurements on which many managers must rely. The traditional measurement systems, accounting included, too often conceal rather than highlight most of the truly significant data needed by managers.

A critical need in management is to increase the ability to perceive the essential items in a given situation and to direct attention to them, for proper identification of the problem and its essential elements often provides the solution to the problem. An information and measurement system which would focus attention only on crucial events and results would give any manager much more aid and would result in much better performance than we have any right to expect under typical reporting systems.

3. Diminishing returns on internal management controls : The last two decades have witnessed concentration on internal operating efficiencies. In many industrial firms today further substantial internal operating economies may no longer be reasonably expected. Although it is perfectly logical to continue to monitor through internal control devices a firm's processes and operations to assure their continuation in a "state of control", nevertheless the highest "payoffs" from additional control efforts lie outside the firm. Using an example from industry, it may be argued that the 50 percent of the consumer's dollar which is typically expended in the distribution process (after the product is physically completed) offers far greater opportunities for added control benefits. But, at present, little of the total control effort is being expended outside of the producing firm.

Admittedly the information and measurements in our control systems are more readily adaptable to internal rather than external monitoring; but the greatest opportunity lies outside the firm. One aspect of this control system should be evaluation of outside earnings possibilities. Diversification and merger studies have made substantial advances in recent years, yet the external facets of control have been barely explored by most companies. The whole field of entrepreneurship offers an opportunity for control system applications. Drucker pointed as an example to the field of electronic data processing, which he believes offers proof that, because the basic idea of electronic data processing was sound, IBM's internal efficiency was irrelevant for over a decade. They were efficient internally, but the opportunities external to the firm in this field were so massive that they overshadowed the internal aspects. As the EDP industry matures, this imbalance may disappear, but the point remains that the great opportunity for profits at the time was external.

4. Business is a unique control situation : We have seen many control applications transferred to business almost intact from the physical sciences. In many cases such applications have been highly successful. But should not the business field be regarded as a separate, meaningful sphere or human endeavor which is subject to control? Business certainly presents a unique appearance to those interested in controls and in control. Unlike all natural or mechanically operated systems, it exhibits a wide range of events and results that are of profound importance to its successful operation, but which cannot easily be quantified within existing systems of measurement.

Business may well be the only system possessing such a wealth of both quantifiable and non-quantifiable results and events of primary importance to successful control. This offers a unique opportunity for controls if we are but cognizant of the non- quantifiable as well as the quantifiable results and events. Management scientists in particular, having a background in physics or engineering, have had difficulty in realising that practically every definition underlying measurement of accounting data (accounting entities, accrual accounting, conservatism, consistency, cost, going concern, disclosure, matching cost against revenue, materiality, objectivity, realisation, stable measuring unit, and uniform accounting period) is based on assumptions and practices which were not always easily rationalised and cannot presently be physically verified. We have defined the concepts-and then measured. Only within very rigid limitation are accountants permitted to change the definitional ground rules as they operate in areas where they have been bold enough to attempt measurements of business data. Certainly these conventions and practices have facilitated measurement of many business data, but we need to extend the areas where measurement can be achieved. As an accountant, it worries me that far too many of the measurements in accounting are the recorded facts about past events. Unfortunately, accountants seem to be too little concerned about the "facts" of the future. And, as we have pointed out, too great a preponderance of the measured facts of the past concern internal, rather than external, events and results.

For these two reasons, important developments on the outside- especially as they pertain to the future-are not measurable until it is too late to exercise control. It follows that we are whipsawed by day-to-day events and results outside our control. A balance between the measurable and non-measurable-between the past and the future, and between the internal and the external- will remain for some time as a crucial problem facing those concerned with management control.

Where does this leave us in our search for a philosophy of control? Accountants, more than most professional men, recognise that a business is a separate entity and at the same time realise that this is a legal "fiction", in more ways than one. A business is presumed to possess its own resources and objectives; on the other hand, a business is comprised of persons, each with his own purposes, ambitions, ideals, and needs. Successful businesses satisfy the ambitions and needs of their members, as individuals, and do so through systems of incentives, rewards, deterrences, and penalties. Here lies the real regulatory control of business : people at work.

Approached with a proper appreciation for the ultimate control which lies in decisions by "people harmoniously at work" at all levels of the organisation, the "received doctrine" of managerial control can be effective to the degree with which it :

1. identifies key factors needing control;
2. establishes standards for measuring achievement;
3. defines measures of status and performance;
4. reports and analysed accomplishment by responsibility;
5. controls before-the-fact through preplanning;
6. highlights critical data for managers;
7. increasingly seeks to monitor events external to the firm, even though in the past they may have been regarded as non- quantifiable.

REVIEW QUESTIONS

1. Define the term 'management control'.
2. What are the distinguishing characteristics of management control?
3. Management control begins with corporate planning. Do you agree? State your views.
4. Explain the different steps involved in problem solving/decision making process.

4

Principles of Management Control

Classification of Principles : One of the major purposes of a theory is to explain the nature of a subject by presenting a clear and systematic view of it With this in mind, it appears that managerial control can be analysed by placing the basic principles of control into the categories of 1. those dealing with the nature and purpose of control, 2. those having to do with the structure of control, and 3. those explaining the process of control. (The same classification of principles could, no doubt, be used for the managerial functions of organising and planning, and perhaps also for staffing and direction.

Nature and Purpose of Control

The nature and purpose of managerial control seem to be reflected in five principles, which may be summarised as follows :

1. **Principle of Assurance of Objective :** Controls must contribute to the accomplishment of group objectives by detecting deviations from plans in time and in a manner to make corrective action possible.

It is obvious that the purpose of all organised enterprise is the accomplishment of group objectives, ends which cannot be accomplished by individuals acting along. This essential fact has been recognised in many analyses of management.

For example, a company's objective in instituting a new product programme may be to maximise return on investment; but if, as the programme proceeds, a forecast of revenues and expenses indicates that the programme (perhaps because of a competitor's action) will yield a negative of a negligible return, control should make it possible to reconsider the original decision and modify or replace the programme before it is too late. If a control were designed to show only the state of progress in the development of the product itself, the company might find itself with a fully developed, but relatively unprofitable new product which had already absorbed its resources.

Therefore, controls must have as their essential reason the attainment of objectives or goals, just as the other functions of the manager must have as their **raison d'etre** the accomplishment of objective. In the case of control, this purpose can only be accomplished if the techniques used make it possible to detect failures in plans. This is a simple truth, but one which often is overlooked by the practicing manager.

2. **Principle of Efficiency of Control :** Controls are efficient if they effectively detect deviations from plans and make possible corrective action with the minimum of unsought consequences.

Chester Barnard has very clearly pointed out the applicability of the scientific concepts of effectiveness and efficiency to systems of human coopera-tion.* A control may be effective in the sense that it does assure the attainment of objectives, but it is inefficient if it does so at unnecessarily high cost in rupees, hours, lost morale, or individual dissatisfaction.

Techniques of control have a way of becoming costly, complex, and burdensome. It is entirely possible for a manager to spend considerably more than it is worth to detect deviations from plans. And such costs go beyond rupees. For example, a control technique so vigorous and thorough that it negates authority delegations or seriously impairs the morale of those who must execute plans can easily result in costs beyond any possible value it might have. Among the countless instances of costly control found in practice are complex engineering procedures and controls which hamstring creativeness and human efficiency, detailed budget control which place a strait jacket on the manager, and purchasing controls which not only delay deliveries but involve costs beyond the value of the items purchased.

3. **Principle of Control Responsibility :** Control can be exercised only by the manager responsible for the execution of plans.

The principle follows logically from the two preceding it. If the organisation structure, through its delegation of authority and assignment of tasks, gives a manager responsibility for the accomplishment of certain plans or portions of plans, this responsibility cannot be waived without changing the organisation. It is logically and practically inconsistent to expect a manager to make and accomplish plans and not to expect him to exercise control to make and sure that these plans are being accomplished. Yet this principle is sometimes misunderstood in practice. Some managers expect control to be exerted only from some top point in an enterprise, or they wait to be told from above what controls to exercise and when.

The principle of control responsibility also appears to clarify the often misinterpreted role of controllers and centralised control units. Although these agencies may, in a staff or service capacity, assist the manager by furnishing him information needed to control his department, they cannot assume the part of actually exercising these controls without destroying the unity and meaning of the manager's job.

4. **Principle of Future Controls :** Effective control should be aimed at preventing present and future deviations from plans.

---

* Barnard, Chester I., *The Functions of Executive,* Harvard University.

It has sometimes been said that planning is looking ahead and control is looking back. This seems to be a distorted view of control. Just as planning must be forward looking, so must control. Since the manager cannot possibly control the past, and too seldom can move fast enough to detect and correct current deviations from plans, his controls should be aimed at the future.

The tendency to regard control as looking back has arisen largely because managerial control has been so dependent upon accounting and statistical data instead of forecasts and predictions. In the absence of any means to look forward, reference to history, on the assumption that what is past is prologue, is admittedly better than not looking at all. But this principle does point to the need for more control information based on forecasts.

One can hardly deny that the alert manager would prefer a forecast of what will happen in the execution of a given plan, even though this projection has a margin of error in it, to a decimately accurate report of the past, about which he can do nothing. Of course, what a manager would probably like best of all is a system of control that would operate with instantaneous feedback, like the servo-system of an automated machine tool, so that deviations might be corrected before they occur by means of correcting tendencies to stray from desired performance.

That managers are increasingly looking ahead for purposes of control is apparent from the great attention being given to expense and revenue projections and the forecasting of cash. Well managed companies always forecast cash requirements carefully for periods varying from four to twenty-four months in advance. By seeing their cash needs well ahead of time, they are usually able through careful planning to provide for them before cash stringencies occur. On the other hand, many companies have found themselves in desperate circumstances by suddenly awakening to the fact that they do not have the cash to meet commitments. And it is almost tradition that cash is difficult to get in emergencies, but easy to obtain if arranged for well ahead of needs.

5. **Principle of Direct Control :** The most effective technique of control in an enterprise is to assure the quality of subordinate managers.

Most controls used by managers are actually indirect controls because they are based on the need to keep subordinates, particularly managerial subordinates, from making mistakes. Unquestionably, the best and most direct kind of control is to assure the best possible quality of managers. Able and well trained managers plan well and thoroughly, delegate authority, assign tasks, and do the most effective job of selecting, training, and directing subordinates. They make fewer mistakes and require fewer indirect controls.

The Structure of Control

A second group of three principles are significant for the structure of control techniques, particularly in their relation to plans, organisation, and the managerial incumbent.

6. **Principle of Reflection of Plans :** Controls must be designed so as to reflect the character and structure of plans.

This principle underlines the fact that controls must be tailored to individual plans. Thus, if the control of costs is the aim, the control techniques used must be based on planned costs of a definite and specific type. If one would control inventory, clearly the controls must take into account and follow those plans which influence inventory; and true inventory control must be based upon the entire programme of production planning and scheduling, purchasing, shipping, warehousing, sales, and finance. Too often, in these and similar cases, the manager deceives himself by thinking he is controlling an aspect of operation when is control technique is not designed to reflect the pertinent plans involved.

7. **Principle of Organisational Suitability :** Controls must be designed to reflect organisation structure.

Since managers and their subordinates are the means through which the events of planning must be accomplished, it follows that effective controls must be applicable to a manager's authority area and must therefore reflect the organisation structure. Consequently, any device of control must be tailored to the manager and his position in the organisation, and information to appraise performance against plans must be suitable to the manager who is to use it. Urwick has expressed this as the principle of uniformity and has emphasised that "all figures and reports used for purpose of control must be in terms of the organisation structure".

As can be readily seen, this principle is similar to the principle of control responsibility outlined above. The principle of control responsibility, however, emphasises that control of events can be exercised only through people, with the manager the focal point of control. But control techniques must be structured so that a certain manager can be held responsible. This can only be done by making the controls consistent with organisation structure. It does no good to hold a manager responsible for costs, for example, if the cost reports do not pinpoint which manager in an organisation position is responsible. In other words, one principle has to do with the personal responsibility for control, the other with the orientation of control information to the organisation structure.

8. **Principle of Individuality of Controls :** Controls must be designed to meet to personal needs of the individual manager.

An important factor in any system of control is the fact that people do vary in terms of personal biases, training, and ability to comprehend information. No matter how much a statistician, mathematician, or accountant might like to mould a manager into his own image, it is a fact of life that what a manager control understand or will not understand cannot be useful to him for control. What might be a delight to the figure-minded treasurer might be abhorrent to the plant superintendent. What might be meaning ful to the chief engineer might be incomprehensible to the sales managers. Some managers may like reports, others tables, some charts, and still others mathematical formulae or curves. Control devices and information are important enough that they should be tailored to these needs.

The Process of Control

In the operation of controls, there appear to be six principles which point to the most effective possible techniques of control. To be sure, control, being so much a technique, rests heavily on the art of management, on "know-how" in a given instance. But experience in control yields certain benchmarks which no manager should overlook in practice.

9. **Principle of Standards :** Effective and efficient control requires objective, accurate, and suitable standards.

Standards are authoritative criteria by which performance can be measured. The principle of standards implies that every plan must have measures of effectiveness which are as specific and simple as possible and which accurately measure whether a planned programme is being accomplished.

Not only are such standards highly desirable from the standpoint of giving the manager a precise measurement of operations in relation to plans, but they are desirably because events are controlled through people. Actual performance is sometimes camouflaged from the manager by a subordinate's sparkling or dull personality or by his ability to "sell" a deficient performance. Thus measurements of performance that are not objective can often be wrong. Moreover, good standards objectively applied as a measure of a subordinate's performance are most likely to be accepted by the subordinate as fair and reasonable.

10. **Principle of Strategic Point Control :** Effective and efficient control requires that attention be given to those factors which are strategic to the appraisal of performance.

It is ordinarily wasteful and unnecessary for a manager to follow every detail of the execution of plans. What he must know is that plans are being executed in such a manner that their goals can be accomplished. He should, therefore, concentrate his attention on selected parts of performance which will indicate whether significant deviations in the total plan are occurring or will occur.

There are no easy guidelines which might be applied by a practicing manager to determine the strategic points he should watch, since the selection of these is predominantly a matter of the managerial art. Perhaps the manager can reach his own solution to the problem by asking himself what things in his operations will show him best whether the plans for which he is responsible are being accomplished.

11. The Exception Principle : Efficiency in control requires that attention of the manager be given primarily to significant exceptions.

This principle, which was pointed out many years ago by Frederick Taylor,* is sometimes confused with the principle of strategic point control. But they are essentially different concepts even though both have to do with the utilisation of standards. Strategic point control refers to the selection of certain key factors which determine whether performance conforms with plans, while the exception principle has to do with watching for (and taking action with respect) significant deviations at these points.

The difference between the exception principle and the principle of strategic point control can be illustrated by the techniques a sales manager might employ to control field sales. He might select as critical points to watch such items as sales per salesman, sales by products and by territories, or gross profits from sales by product. However, in watching these critical points, he would see no need for action unless he detected deviations beyond limits he regarded as normal, that is, deviations which constitute noteworthy exceptions.

The exception principle is often quoted as an essential requirement of managerial control efficiency. However, the manager who first chooses the fewest practicable strategic points to watch, and then concentrates on exceptions increases his efficiency markedly. The necessary number of strategic points to be watched will depend upon the importance of the plan and the extent to which strategic points showing progress under the plan can be found or devised. This difference might be illustrated by practices in quality control. It may be important to test carefully every part of a missile guidance and control system and hold each part to close performance tolerances; but in the missile fuselage shell there might be only few points to be checked, and the allowable tolerance might be relatively broad.

12. The Principle of Flexibility of Controls : Controls should incorporate sufficient flexibility to remain effective despite the failure of plans.

Stated negatively, this principle, first given clear form by Goetz,** means that controls should not be so inextricably bound into a particular plan that, should unforeseen events or shifts in goals make the plan unworkable, all control is lost. This principle is best illustrated by the considerations which led to the flexible, or variable, budget. Such budgeting, which provides for budgets to be changed quickly and virtually automatically if the business outlook changes,

---

* **Shop Management (New York : Harper & Brothers, 1919), pp. 126-127.**

** **Billy E. Goetz, Management Planning and Control (New York : Mc Graw Hill Boom company, 1949), p 229.**

arose from fears that under fixed budgets control might be lost through continuation of managerial authority to spend at a level determined by previous sales forecasts but not justified by actual sales volume.

While this principle is difficult to implement in practice, the manager should be aware of the desirability of such flexibility. Otherwise, the manager may go long blithely thinking that he has proper control of the execution of a plan, only to find that the situation for which the plan was tailored has been changed. Many managers tend to lose control over such ventures cause to mount- while the elusive rabbit of completion seems to be around one more corner.

13. **Principle of Review :** The control system should be reviewed periodically.

Because of the dynamics of enterprise and the environment in which it operates, not only should controls be kept flexible but the system and techniques of controls should periodically be reviewed. Controls, like plans, are never final. Just as the manager should continually re-evaluate his plans and take navigational readings to see if he is on course, so should he periodically and systematically review his controls to make certain that the standards used, the strategic points selected, and the tolerances permitted are consistent with his plans and goals.

14. **Principle of Action :** Control is only justified if measures are undertaken to correct indicated or experienced deviations from plans through appropriate planning, organising, staffing, and directing.

Control is meaningless and wasteful and the application of the principles above a fruitless exercise unless action is taken to correct deficiencies detected. These corrections may be in the form of revised or new plans, new or different delegations of authority and assignments of tasks, better training or selection of subordinates, or a better order of counselling and guidance by the manager.

This principle not only underscores the action aspect of control but also the fact the control tends to coalesce with the other functions of the manager. It emphasises the basic unity of management and the essential fact that control functions cannot be delegated, cannot be centralised in a staff or department which does not have the authority to execute a plan, and cannot be taken away from the manager without destroying managership itself.

REVIEW QUESTIONS

1. **What are the principles of management control? Explain them briefly.**
2. **Explain the principles of managerial control dealing with the nature and purpose of control.**
3. **State the principles of managerial control significant for the structure of control techniques.**
4. **What are the six principles of managerial control explaining the process of control?**

5

Strategic Planning Management Control And Operational Control

Management planning and control begins with the establishment of the fundamental objectives of the organisation, and continues as the process by which necessary resources are provided and employed effectively and efficiently toward achievement of the goals. A management planning and control system provides the comprehensive framework within which this process is carried out. Such a system encompasses all aspects of an organisation's operations, and thus is seen as a "total" system.

Three Levels of Management : An organisation can be looked at in terms of three distinct levels of management, namely, corporate management, divisional management and operating management. The corporate management level consists of executives who are responsible for the performance of the organisation as a whole. The chairman or managing director and executives in charge of specific functions such as finance, manufacturing, marketing or personnel constitute the corporate management. Jointly, they are responsible for the overall performance of the organisation. The divisional management consists of executives responsible for total performance of particular regions or product divisions. For example, in the case of a multi-product company, the divisional managers in charge of production and marketing of products under its division, constitute the divisional management. In the case of a large banking company, the total geographical area is divided into regions, each comprising several branches in that geographical area. Regions may be in the charge of regional managers who also constitute divisional management. The operating management consists of executives charged with the management of unit operations/or responsible for the accomplishment of specific operational tasks. A branch manager in charge of a specific branch or a production manager in charge of a specific production unit in a product division constitute the operating management.

Three Levels of Decision-making : The following are the three levels of decision-making :

1. The institutional level for strategic thinking and planning, i.e., those concerned with general company objectives and general problems of the position of the organisation in its environment;

2. The managerial level which focuses on gathering, coordinating and allocating resources for the organisation, e.g., planning budgets, deciding on capital expenditures, formulating personnel practices;
3. The technical level, involving the acquisition and utilisation of technical knowledge for operational controls, e.g., inventory controls and production scheduling.

Framework for Planning and Control : Anthony and Dearden's Framework*

Consistent with the three levels of management and three levels of decision-making, the total planning and control system could be subdivided into three categories as shown in Fig. 5.1

(i) Strategic planning (ii) Management control (iii) Operational control

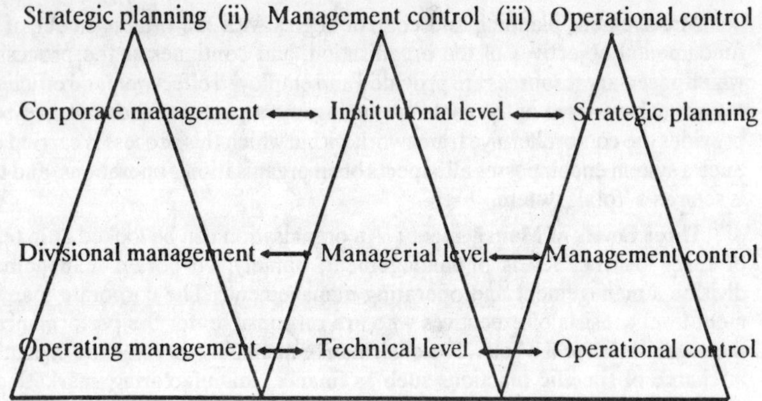

Fig.5.1 Three levels of management, three levels of decision-making and the corresponding three activities of planning and control

Although three distinct levels of decision-making have been identified, they do not operate in watertight compartments. In fact, the interrelationships are so strong they complement each other. The same is true of the three categories of planning and control. The important aspects of the three categories are briefly outlined.

Strategic Planning

Strategic planning is the process of deciding on the goals of the organisation, on changes in these goals, on the resources used to attain these goals, and

* Robert N. Anthony and John Dearden, Management Control Systems. Richard D. Irwin, Homewood, Illinois, 1981 and Robert N. Anthony, Planning and Control Systems : A Framework for Analysis, harvard university Press, Cambridge, mass., 1965

on the policies that are to govern the acquisition, use and disposition of these resources.

The word strategy is used here in its usual sense of deciding on how to combine and employ resources. Thus, strategic planning is a process having to do with the formulation of long-range, strategic, policy-type plans that change the character or direction of the organisation. In an industrial company, this includes planning that affects the goals of the company; policies of all types (including policies as to management control and other processes); the acquisition and disposition of major facilities, divisions, or subsidiaries; the markets to be served and distribution channels for serving them; the organisation structure (as distinguished from individual personnel actions); research and development of new product lines (as distinguished from modifications in existing products and product changes within existing product lines); sources of new permanent capital, dividend policy, and so on. Strategic planning decisions affect the physical, financial, and organisational framework within which operations are carried on.

Strategic planning is long term planning and is carried on at the top level of management. It is concerned with deciding the goals of the organisation. Management, after analysing its own strengths and weaknesses and on the basis of the threats it faces and the opportunities available to it, directions of the enterprise. Strategic planning has become a crucial exercise for the top management of enterprises because of the greater turbulence in environments in which such enterprises operate. Decisions to expand or diversify quite often emerge from the exercise of strategic thinking. Companies with large turnover and operating in diverse fields usually have a corporate planning department which is involved in the process of evaluating the changes in environment and its implication for the enterprise. It is also involved in the evaluation of new opportunities. Since organisation continuously interact with their environment, and since only the top management can take decisions which have far-reaching, long-term implications on the organisation, the top management continuously scans the environment for possible opportunities. Thus only few individuals are involved in this process. At times, strategic decisions require secrecy and are not communicated till the decisions are actually taken. Most of the data for planning is derived from the external environment, e.g., industry demand, estimates of investments in new facilities and new plants. There is also a high degree of uncertainty associated with the projections made over a long period of time and therefore strategic planning has to recognise this fact.

Management Control

Management control is the process of evaluating, monitoring and controlling the various sub-units of the organisation so that there is effective and efficient allocation and utilisation of resources in achieving the predetermined goals. Thus, the focus of management control is on the managers of organisational sub-units and hence its focus is on line managers responsible for the performance of their departments. Management control, therefore, is the control exercised by the management over the managers. Who controls the managers and what is the process involved in controlling them? Management control is exercised by evaluating the performance of each 'responsibility centre' against planned performance. Planned performance is decided in consultation with the managers of responsibility centres, taking into consideration the activities being managed by them and the resources available to them in terms, of men, materials money etc. Planned performance is usually translated into monetary terms, although physical achievements are also planned for. Managers are not only responsible for the achievement of physical targets, but also for the corresponding monetary values. Thus, management control is generally built around a financial structure. Actual and planned performance are compared at regular intervals so as to identify resource gaps and, if need be, provide managers with more resources or transfer resources from one organisational unit to another. The end-of-the-year review may be too late to take corrective action. The whole purpose of management control is to decide on corrective action if there are substantial deviations from the planned performance. The management control system also provides mechanisms for proper coordination and integration of various organisational sub-units by interrelating the tasks being performed and deciding on the resource allocation. In the process of management control conflicts are inherent between managers for resource mobilsation, allocation and snatching. Thus, there is intense interaction among managers.

Distinctions between Management Control and Strategic Planning : Briefly, here are some ways in which the strategic planning process differs from the management control process.

A strategic plan usually relates to some part of the organisation, rather than to the totality; the concept of a master planner who constantly keeps all part of the organisation at some coordinated optimum is a nice concept, but an unrealistic one. Life is too complicated for any human, or computer, to do this.

Strategic planning is essentially **irregular.** Problems, opportunities, and bright ideas do not arise according to some set timetable; rather, they are dealt with whenever they happen to be perceived. The appropriate analytical techniques depend on the nature of the problem being analysed, and no over all approach (such as a mathematical model) has been developed that is of much help in analysing all types of strategic problems. Indeed, an overemphasis on a systematic approach is quite likely to stifle the essential element of creativity. In strategic planning, management works now on one problem, then on another, according to the needs and opportunities of the moment.

The estimates used in strategic planning are intended to show the expected results of the plan. They are neutral and impersonal. By contrast, the management control process and the data used in it are intended to influence managers to take actions that will lead to desired results. Thus, in connection with management control it is appropriate to discuss how tight an operating budget should be. Should the goals be set so high that only an outstanding manager can achieve them, or should they be set so that they are attainable by the average manager? At what level does frustration inhibit a manager's best efforts? Does an easily attainable budget lead to complacency? And so on. In strategic planning, the question to be asked about the figures is simple: Is this the most reasonable estimate that can be made?

Strategic planning relies heavily on external information-that is, on data collected from outside the company, such as market analysis, estimates of costs and other factors involved in building a plant in a new locality, technological developments, and so on. When data from the normal information system are used, they usually must be recast to fit the needs of the specified problem being analysed. For example, current operating costs that are collected for measuring performance and for making pricing and other operating decisions usually must be restructured before they are useful in deciding whether to close down the plant. Another characteristic of the relevant information is that much of it is imprecise. The strategic planner estimates what will probably happen, often over a rather long time period. These estimates are likely to have a high degree of uncertainty, and they must be treated accordingly.

In the management control process, the communication of objectives, policies, guidelines, decisions, and results throughout the organisation is extremely important. In the strategic planning process, communication is much simpler and involves relatively few persons; indeed, the need for secrecy often requires that steps be taken to inhibit communication. Wide communication of the decisions that result from strategic planning is obviously important; this is part of the management control process.

Both management control and strategic planning involve top management, but middle managers (i.e., operating management) typically have a much more important role in management control than in strategic planning. Middle managers usually are not major participants in the strategic planning process and sometimes are not even aware that a plan is being considered. Many operating executives are by temperament not very good at strategic planning. Also, the pressures of current activities usually do not allow them to devote the necessary time to such work. Currently, there is a tendency in companies to set up separate staffs to gather the facts and make the analysis that provide the background material for strategic decisions.

Distinctions Between Strategic Planning and Management Control

Characteristics	Strategic Planning	Management Control
Focus of plans	On one aspect at a time	On whole organisation
Complexities	Many variables	Less complex
Degree of structure	Unstructured and irregular; each problem different	Rhythmic; prescribed procedures
Nature of information	Tailor-made for the problem; more external and predictive; less accurate	Integrated; more internal and historical; more accurate
Communication of information	Relatively simple	Relatively difficult
Purpose of estimates	Show expected results	Lead to desired results
Persons primarily involved	Staff and top management	Line and top management
Number of persons involved	Small	Large
Mental activity	Creative; analytical	Administrative; persuasive
Source discipline	Economics	Social psychology
Planning and control	Planning dominant, but some control	Emphasis on both planning and control
Time horizon	Tends to be long	Tends to be short
End result	Policies and precedents	Action within policies and precedents
Appraisal of the job done	Extermely difficult	Much less difficult

Strategic planning and management control activities tend to conflict with one another in some respects. The time that management spends in thinking about the future is taken from time that could otherwise be used in controlling current operations, so in this indirect way strategic planning can hurt current performance. And, of course, the reverse also is true.

More directly, many actions that are taken for long-run, strategic reasons make current profits smaller than they otherwise would be. Research and some advertising expenditures are obvious examples. The porblem of striking the right balance between strategic and operating considerations is one of the central problems in the whole management process.

Operational Control or Technical Control

Operational control is the process of assuring that specific tasks are carried out effectively and efficiently. As the definition suggests, the focus of operational control is on individual tasks or transactions : scheduling and controlling individual jobs through a shop, as contrasted with measuring the performance of the shop as a whole; procuring specific items for inventory, as contrasted with the management of inventory as a whole; specific personnel actions, as contrasted with personnel management; and so on. The definition does not suggest another characteristic that applies to most activities that are subject to operational control, namely, that these activities are capable of being programmed.

Distinction Between Management Control and Operational Control : As an example of an activity to which operational control is applicable, consider the inventory area. If the demand for an item, the cost of storing it, its production cost and production time, and the loss involved in not filling an order are known, then the optimum inventory level and the optimum production or procurement schedule can be calculated. Even if these factors cannot be known with certainty (as, of course, is the case with all future events), sound estimates nevertheless can be made, inventory levels and production or procurement schedules based on these estimates can be calculated, and reasonable men will agree with the results of these calculations. An inventory control system using rules derived from such calculations is an example of operational control.

By contrast, consider the legal department of a company. No device can measure the quality, or even the quantity, of the legal service that constitutes the output of this department. No formula can show the amount of service the department should render or the optimum amount of costs that should be incurred. Impressions as to the "right" amount of service, the "right" amount of cost, and the "right" relationship between the service actually rendered and the cost actually incurred are strictly subjective. They are judgments made by management. If persons disagree of these judgments, there is no objective way of resolving the disagreement. Yet the legal department, as a part of the whole organisation, must be controlled; the chief counsel must operate within the framework of policies prescribed by top management. The type of control necessary in this situation is management control.

Examples of activities that are susceptible to operational control are automated plants, such as cement plants, oil refineries, and power generating stations; the direct production operations of most manufacturing plants; production scheduling; inventory control; the order-taking type of selling activity; and order processing, premium billing, payroll accounting, cheque handling, and similar paperwork activities.

Examples of activities for which management control is necessary are the total operation of most manufacturing plants, which includes such judgement inputs as indirect labour, employees' benefit and welfare programmes, safety activities, training, and supervision; most advertising, sales promotion, pricing, selling (as distinguished from order-taking), and similar marketing activities; most aspects of finance; most aspects of research, development, and design; the work of staff units of all types; and, of course, the activities of top management.

The type of control appropriate for the whole of any unit that carries on both programmed and nonprogrammed types of activities is management control. Thus, the control of one division of a company is management control, even though operational control is appropriate for certain aspects of the work such as posting and cheque writing.

Some people believe that the distinction between the two classes of activities described above is merely one of degree rather than of kind; they say that all we are doing is distinguishing between situations in which control is easy and those in which control is difficult. We think the distinction is more fundamental, and hope this will be apparent from the following brief list of characteristics that distinguish management control from operational control.

Management control covers the whole of an organisation. Each operational control procedure is restricted to a subunit, often a narrowly circumscribed activity. Just a management control occurs within a set of policies derived from strategic planning, so operational control occurs within a set of well-defined procedures and rules derived from management control.

Control is more difficult in management control than in operational control because of the absence of a valid, objective standard with which actual performance can be compared. A good operational control system can provide a much higher degree of assurance that actions are proceeding as desired than can a good management control system.

An operational control system is a rational system; that is, the action to be taken is decided by a set of logical rules. These rules may or may not cover all aspects of a given problem. Situations not covered by the rules are designated as exceptions and are resolved by human judgement. Other than these exceptions, application of the rule is automatic. The rules in principle can be programmed into a computer, and the choice between using a computer and using a human being depends primarily on the relative cost of each resource.

In management control, psychological considerations are dominant. The management control system at most assists those who take action; it does not directly or by itself result in action without human intervention. By contrast, the end product of an inventory control system can be an order, such as a decision to replenish a certain inventory item, and this order may be based entirely on calculations from formulas incorporated in the system. (The formulas were devised by human beings, but this is a management control process, not an operational control process).

In a consideration of operational control, analogies with mechanical, electrical, and hydraulic systems are reasonable and useful, and such terms as feedback, network balancing, optimisation, and so on are relevant. It is perfectly appropriate, for example, to view an operational control system as analogous to a thermostat which turns the furnace on and off according to its perception of changes in temperature. These analogies do not work well as models for management control systems, however, because the success of these systems is highly dependent on their impact on people, and people are not like thermostats or furnaces; one can't light a fire under a human being simply by turning up a thermostat.

The management control system is ordinarily built around a financial structure, whereas operational control data are often nonmonetary. They may be expressed in terms of man-hours, number of items, pounds of waste, and so on. Since each operational control procedure is designed for a limited area of application, it is feasible to use the basis of measurement that is most appropriate for that area.

As new techniques are developed, there is a tendency for more and more activities to become susceptible to operational control. In the factory, the production schedule that was formerly set according to the foreman's intuition is now derived by linear programming. And although not very long ago it was believed that operational control was appropriate only for factory operations, we now see models and formulas being used for certain marketing decisions, such as planning salesman's calls and planning direct- mail advertising. This shift probably will continue; it is a large part of what people have in mind when they say, "management is becoming increasingly scientific".

The managers of responsibility centres are concerned with effectively and efficiently managing the tasks allocated to the centres. They exercise operational control, to perform these tasks and activities. Thus, it is concerned with individual tasks or transactions, such as procurement of raw material according to prescribed quantity and quality, scheduling of jobs, selling of products to specific customers, and so on. Most activities that fall in the realm of operational control are subject to being programmed and are repetitive in nature. It is easier to develop quantitative models that would lead to optimal decision-making. Consequently, optimum relationship can be determined between inputs and outputs of specific tasks. In the case of operational controls, it is also easy to find relationships between the level of activity and the cost incurred. Engineered costs play an important role in operational control.

Thus, operational control is essentially concerned with the control of activities within the department, e.g., the materials manager exercise operational control on the specific activities of his department and is concerned with day-to-day control and follow-up on activities. The data for operational control is concerned with individual events and activities and is reported as the events occur, e.g., data is reported on daily output in the production department. Exactness in data is another essential characteristic number. Further, the data generated is often non-monetary and control is exercised on the basis of physical achievements, e.g., number of units produced by each worker in a shop, so many units sold areawise per week/month and so on. It is in the area of operational control that techniques of operations research find wide applications, because the activities are programmable. Mathematical models can be developed and these can prescribed decision rules and hence solutions are obtained from models rather than from the subjective judgement of managers.

The differences between management control and operational control are summarised below.

Distinctions Between Management Control and Operational Control

Characteristics	Management Control	Operational Control
Focus of activity	Whole operation	Single task or transaction
Judgment	Relatively much; subjective decisions	Relatively little; reliance on rules
Nature of structure	Psychological	Rational
Nature of information	Integrated; financial data throughout; approximations acceptable; future and historical	Tailor-made to the operation; often non-financial; precise; often in real time
Persons primarily involved	Managament	Supervisors (or none)
Mental activity	Administrative persuasive	Follow directions (or none)
Source discipline	Social Psychology	Economics; physical sciences
Time horizon	Weeks, months and years	Day-to-day
Type of costs	Discretionary	Engineered

Interrelationship Among Strategic Planning, Management Control and Operational Control

Although total management planning and control activities have been classified into three distinct categories, namely strategic planning, management control and operational control, all three are interdependent and interrelated.

Strategic planning is concerned with deciding the goals of an organisation, changes in goals, resources needed for attaining goals and policies related to the acquisition, use and disposition of resources. Thus, strategic planning lays the foundation for management control, because, once goals are determined, the management has to translate them into specific tasks aimed at achieving the goals. The process involved is that of management control. Management control, exercised by the top management focuses on the overall performance of each responsibility centre. It results in the control of managers by higher level managers and sets guidelines for operational control. Managers of responsibility centres in turn exercise control over the specific tasks and activities of their respective departments. If operational control is not properly exercised, the department will not be able to achieve its planned targets. This may, in turn, create imbalances in other departments, e.g., if the marketing department is not able to meet the planned sales targets, the inventories will pile up and production may have to be cut down.

Distinctions between Strategic Planning, Management Control and Operational Control

The strategic planning process is carried on at the top and the involvement of the middle management is small, as against management control in which both the top management and middle management are closely involved. While strategic planning relies heavily on external information, management control largely uses data generated within the organisation. Operational control uses data generated on specific tasks or activities. The reliability of data generated during the process of strategic planning is subject to a high level of doubt, because of the uncertainties involved. Data generated in management control and operational control is more accurate and reliable because it relates to events taking place or likely to occur in the near future or having taken place in the past.

In the management control process, performance is evaluated against standards determined by managers. How tight or loose standards are will depend upon how the standards are set. Thus, while the management control process involves data that is personalised, the estimates in strategic planning are impersonal and neutral.

The focus of activity in operational control is on specific tasks, while in management control it is on the whole operation of the organisation. In the case of operational control, decision rules can be developed to decide about optimum decisions, while in the case of management control, a lot of managerial judgement is required and the scope of quantitative models is limited. While the focus of operational control is on efficiency, management control essentially focuses on organisational effectiveness. In the case of management control, difficulties arise in developing valid, objective standards with which performance can be compared. Control is more difficult because it is difficult to develop approximate measures of performance for a department which performs various types of tasks. Human considerations are dominant in the management control process. The success or failure of the management control process also depends on the personalities of the managers involved. The system can either act as a motivational device or kill initiative. This will depend upon how the system has been designed and how it is being used. The basic purpose of this system is to facilitate constructive actions and control, not to restrict such actions. In the case of the operational control system, the system is more important than the human element, because it is system that makes/indicates the decision rather than the managers. The management control system is usually built around a financial structure. Thus, it emphasises the measurement of performance both in physical as well as in financial terms. The operational control system, on the other hand, closely monitors physical achievements such as labour hours, machine hours, units produced, units sold, units defective, quantity procured, loss percentage and yield.

Perhaps it will be helpful in clarifying certain distinctions between strategic planning, management control, and operational control if all three are examined in terms of certain fundamental characteristics. To summarise :

Characteristics	Strategic planning	Management control	Operational control
Level	Top management	All level-top to front line supervision	Supervisory
Scope	Total	Overall, consisting of related subsystem	Operating unit
Time frame	Long range	Short to intermediate (1 to 5 years)	Short periods - daytoday, weekly, monthly
Environment	External, toward developing internal	Internal, adjusting to external factors	Internal only
Goals and Objectives	Basic objectives	Tangible goals, with in framework of over all objectives	Short-term, tangible to operating unit

Structuring	Relatively unstructured	Fairly highly structured but flexible	Quite rigid pre estabilshed
Activity patterns	Irregular	Rhythmic, regular	Highly repetitive
Character of activity	Creative	Administrative, persuasive	Following directions little initiative
Focal point	Entire organisation	All operations, line management	Operating unit

TYPES OF CONTROL

The control influences have been classified in three categories namely organisational controls (administrative control), informal group controls, and individual level controls (self-control). These are interdependent and mutually reinforce each other. The **organisational controls** usually consist of formal rules and standard operating procedures plus the informal procedures that are also communicated throughout the organisation. The **informal group controls** are based on the principal of mutual controls, which envisage checks and balances on each other's activities as a result of the mutual commitments of the members of the group to each other. The **individual level control or self-control** is the result of control exercised by the individual on himself or herself with a view to achieving personal goals and aspirations.

We may add an additional type of control, namely **political control**. Since an organisation operates in a given socio- economic environment, it has to work within the policies formulated by the political system of a country. Thus, all organisations are subject to political control exercised through government ministries and parliament. In Table. 1 shown in page 61 shows the goals, performance criteria, rewards and punishments, and feedback elements under each category of control, are outlined.

Internal Controls : Developing an appropriate system of internal controls is another important technique of instituting controls within an organisation. Internal controls are based on two basic principles, namely that accounting responsibilities are divided among employees in such a way that no single person is given complete control of a transaction and one person's work is checked by another without unnecessary duplication of effort. Thus, this system is based on internal check and mutual control. Internal control is primarily concerned with checking the reliability of accounting data, monitoring operational efficiency and checking adherence to managerial policies with which the accountant is concerned. In a broader sense, internal control encompasses every type of accounting technique and can be extended beyond in internal audit to encompass management audit. It is procedure-oriented to ensure that employees act in accordance with instructions, rules and regulations as specified in various manuals. It could also be used as an instrument for promoting operational efficiency. The management should recognise that an internal control system's purpose is as much a positive one (promoting efficiency) as a negative one (preventing errors and frauds).

Insidious Controls : Besides formal control in organisations there exist a variety of insidious controls. Since the former are static in nature they fail to capture the dynamics of insidious and unobtrusive controls. "The insidious controls are more dangerous and powerful because they are so deceptive. Their deceptivencess is shown in their not causing participants to feel their presence- there is no feeling of being oppressed by a despot. Instead there is perhaps just the experience of conforming to the logic of a situation.

The various kinds of insidious controls include control through indicating intentions, pleasures and displeasures, control through dominant coalition, control through employees' loyalty, control by keeping insiders at key strategic positions, control by constantly reminding employees of their dependence on the organisation and by not allowing individuals to become bigger than the organisation, control through rewarding loyal employees, control through punishing vocal employees, control through informal dinner and business meetings, control through distorting facts and information, control through spouse's tales and so on. Details about the successful use of insidious controls in the context of management of a state can be found in the work of Kautilya and Machiavelli, namely **Arthasastra** and The **Prince** and is best illustrated in the stories of the **Panchtantra.** Situations illustrated in the **panchtantra** can be found in the management-jungle within an organisation. Insidious controls though not visible like formal controls sometimes exert more pressure. They gain importance because of the failure of formal control systems to measure what they intend to measure. Since the measurement process becomes subjective in respect of several tasks and activities, insidious controls gain dominance.

Of various insidious controls, control through dominant coalition and by keeping loyal employees in key positions is most prevalent. Dominant coalition exercises power and control through instantaneous transmission of information through its network. We often hear the expression 'the boss knows everything that is happening here'. Such controls are exercised through a group of informers who act as spies. Dependence on this method could vitiate the working environment within the organisation because of distortions in information and generation of misinformation. In the other case the finance man for example, even in professional Marwari organisations, is always a man from the family/caste/village, even though he may not be a professionally qualified accountant. Experience shows that managements place a lot of reliance on indirect control.

TABLE 1 Types of interdependent controls

Particulars	*Political Control*	*Organisational Control*	*Informal Group Control*	*Self-Control*
1. Goals	Conformity to national goals and objectives	Profits, market share, quality of service	Mutual commitment, group ideal	Personal goals, aspirations
2. Performance criteria	Organisation's contribution to society and meeting other obligations such as pollution control	Budgets, standard costs, past performance	Group norms	Self-expectations, interim targets
3. Feedback	Feedback through investigative journalism indicating defaults by the organisation, safety hazard like Bhopal gas tragedy	Quantitative variances	Deviant behaviour	Perceived impending failure, reaching or missing targets, fear of failure
4. Rewards (positive reinforcement/ carrot	National/industry level awards for excellence in management and meeting social obligations	Commendation, promotion, salary increases	Appreciation, by peer, membership, leadership	Self-satisfaction, elation
5. Punishments (stick)	Government ordering the closure of the plant and criminal proceedings, imprisonment of top executives	Condemnation, dismissal, stoppage of regular increment in salary	Kidding, ostracism, hostility	Sense of disappointment and frustration, feeling of failure, self-hatred

Source: G.W Dalton and P.R Lawrence, Adapted from *Motivation and Control in Organisations*, Richard D. Irwin, Homewood, Illinois, 1971, 15, and Charles T Horngren, *Cost Accounting: A managerial emphasis*, Prentice Hall, Englewood Cliffs, 1983, 319. The dimension related to political control has been added by the author.

The Feedback Control

The systems can, in general, be classified as **open-loop systems and closed-loop systems.** In an open-loop system, the output of the system is not coupled to the input and for each reference input there is a corresponding fixed operating condition. The illustrations of open-loop systems include home appliances such as the toaster and washing machine, and city traffic systems. In a close-loop system, output is measured against a goal and the difference is used as a means of control. Thus, a course of action is taken on the basis of feedback information. Feedback is the transmission of a signal from a later to an earlier stage. Several open-loop systems can be made closed- loop by relating output to a standard, i.e., by providing for measurements against goals.

An important feature of the closed-loop system is the concept of feedback. Feedback is of two types, namely **positive feedback and negative feedback.** Positive feedback refers to utilisation of the part of output as input to the system, and thus achieve deviation-amplification. The saying 'nothing succeeds like success' is an illustration of positive feedback. All growth processes involve positive feedback as a part of output gets amplified. Negative feedback utilises the deviation between standard and actual performance as input to the system. Therefore negative feedback systems are deviation-counteracting. While positive feedback leads to growth-promotion, negative feedback results in control-maintenance.

Feed Forward Controls

In control system engineering, feed forward control refers to advance control of input variables in anticipation of the changes in output. Thus, feed forward control is anticipatory in nature. This control is similar to what William Newman* calls steering controls, in which the results are predicted and corrective action is taken before completion of the task. A hunter always aims ahead of a pigeon's flight to make correction for the time between the shot and the pigeon's position. In several managerial situations, a similar future-directed control is needed, because there is generally a time-lag in getting feed- back, e.g., in budgetary controls, the data on actual performance say for the month of March, will be available in April/May, and the analysis may reveal that the variance was due to certain decisions taken in January/February. Such time-lags are generally observed in organisations, unless they have some kind of instantaneous information system. Managers are more interested in taking action today in anticipation of problems tomorrow, i.e., they need a system that will indicate to them the need for immediate corrective action. In practice, managers are always engaged in future-directed controls, e.g., they make

---

* William Newman, 'Constructive Control : Design and Use of Control Systems,' Prentice Hall Inc, Englewood Cliffs, N.J. p. 25.

forecasts for sales, and then plan future actions to achieve the anticipated level of sales. Project Evaluation and Review Technique is another illustration of future-directed controls.

In designing feed forward systems, we may develop a model, indicating the input-output variables, and the interrelationships among them. We then monitor inputs to ascertain whether inputs are as planned. If not, the inputs or the process are changed to ensure the desired result. Thus, the focus of feed forward controls is on the input side of the system so that a corrective action is taken before the output of the system is affected. An important problem in feed forward controls is the effect of what control system engineers call disturbances. Since the occurrence of disturbance or random shock may upset the output, it is necessary to watch it. Therefore, besides monitoring the regular inputs, unusual and unexpected disturbances should also be watched for and monitored.

Variations in Controls

In the ideal world, all these controls would be working in the same direction, but in the real world this ideal is never fully achieved. The general nature of control that is appropriate in a given situation varies according to the nature both of the work involved and of the individual manager. Three dimensions of the work are important :

1. The amount of management discretion.
2. The amount of interdependence, and
3. The time span of performance.

Management Discretion : The work done by an organisation unit can be located along a scale with routinized production or clerical operations at one end, and creative, unspecifiable activities, such as research at the other. For activities at or near the routine end, specific performance standards can be established, and rewards (for example in the form of bonuses) can be related to how actual performance compares to these standards. For activities at the other end of the scale, specific standards are not feasible; indeed, an attempt to impose them is likely to have dysfunctional consequences.

Interdependence : Organisation units can also be located along a scale according to their degree of independence from, or interdependence with, other units. To the extent that the work of the whole organisation requires that individual units cooperate closely with one another, controls that focus on the performance of an individual unit can be dysfunctional.

Time Span : Finally, organisation units can be arrayed according to the time span between the initiation of action and results. A selling organisation whose job is to visit customers and take orders is at one extreme (with a short time span), and an organisation responsible for all the efforts involved in introducing a new product is at the other extreme (with a long time span). When the time span is short, performance measurement can be, and should be, frequent, and actual performance can be compared with short-run standards. When the time span is long, any measurement of interim performance should be regarded as being highly tentative.

Personal Differences : In addition to these differences in the nature of the work, the control system should also take account of differences in the motivation and other personality characteristics of individual managers to the extent that this is feasible. Generally, these differences affect the way one manager deals with another in using the system, rather than differences in the way the formal system is constructed.

MANAGEMENT CONTROL PROCESS

Management control has two aspects, namely system and process. These are intimately interrelated. The system outlines authority relationships, autonomy delegation, relationship among various organisational sub-units, parameters for performance evaluation, reward and punishments for achievement and non-achievement of targets, and information flow among various responsibility centres of the organisation. The processes are managerial processes involved in establishing goals and objectives, performance appraisal of responsibility centres, ensuring achievement of targets and budgets by various organisational sub-units, follow-up of remedial action plans, implementation of decisions taken in performance review meetings. The control system provides the necessary feedback and other relevant information and thus affects the quality of the decisions. The effectiveness of the control process is dependent on the quality of feedback received and the way it is used by the senior management for performance appraisal.

In hierarchical organisations with appropriate decentralisation of authority the control process begins with a review of the past performance of strategic business units and responsibility centres, and negotiation of specific objectives and targets for the next year. This is followed by a periodic recording of actual results and reporting of actual results against the targets. The senior management reviews the performance of responsibility centres on the basis of this reported information. During this process, areas where improvement is necessary, are identified and reasons for shortfall are analysed. Then, remedial actions are decided upon. In the next review meeting, results of past corrective action together with the current performance are analysed. This process is carried through in each review meeting.

In the process of reviewing the performance, specific targets may also get altered as a result of negotiation with the senior management. Thus, the management control process is primarily managerial in nature, secondarily accounting-oriented and involves behavioral issues related to superior-subordinate relationship. While the management must identify the objectives of various sub-units and contributions expected from managers, accountants should help in methods of measuring and reporting results as they are achieved. Fig. 5.2 indicates various components of the management control process.

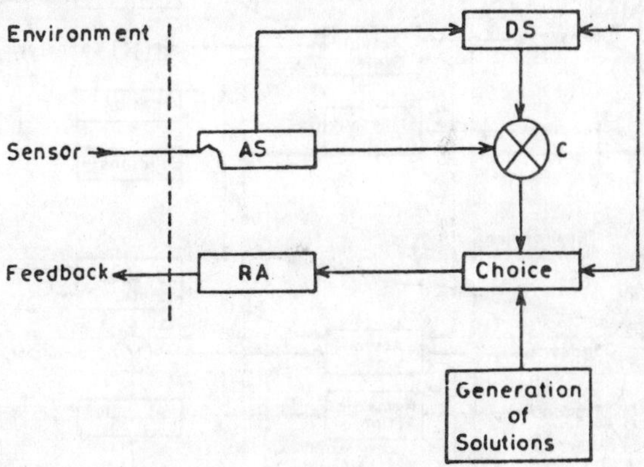

Fig. 5.2 Components of Control Process

AS—measurement of actual state

DS—desired state as indicated in goals or standards

C—comparator, i.e. comparison of actual with standard

RA—initiation of remedial action

Multi-level Controls

Hierarchical organisations have multiple layers of responsibility centres. The organisation as a whole can be treated as an overall responsibility centre. Its major sub-parts are first- level responsibility centres which can be further sub-divided into second-level responsibility centres, this process can be continued further to subsequent levels, depending upon the size and complexity of tasks performed by the responsibility centres. Thus regional offices of a bank are the first-level responsibility centres, divisional offices the second level responsibility centres and branches, the third-level responsibility centres. It is possible to identify further responsibility centres within each branch. Corresponding to organisational hierarchy, there exists control hierarchy. The overall goals are divided by the top management and these are communicated to the first-level responsibility centres for deciding specific objectives for this level. This centre communicates with the next level and the process continues. Each level of responsibility centre also influences the upper level responsibility centres. During the review meetings, each level reviews the performance of the level below it. Fig. 5.3 represent the control hierarchy interlinking the control process at each level.

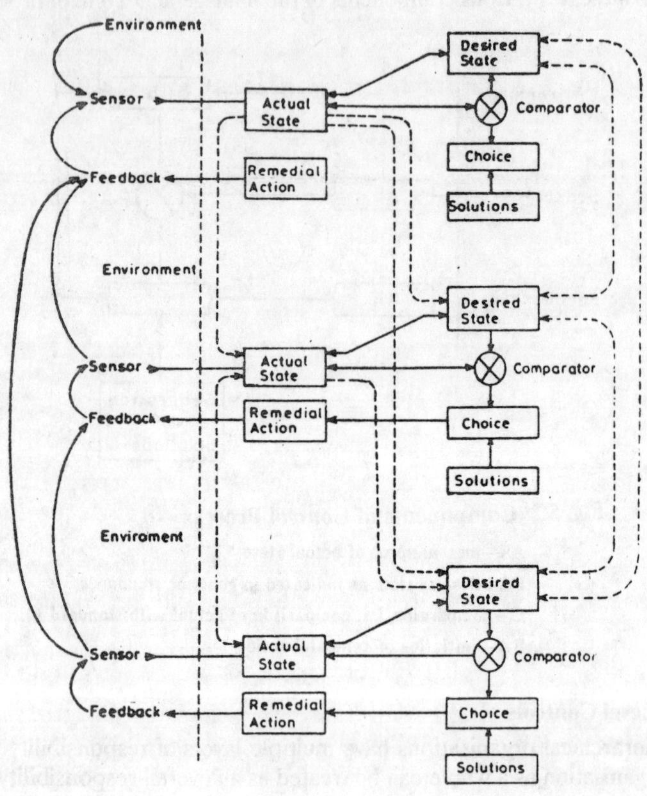

Fig. 5.3 Control hierarchy interlinking the control process at multiple levels

In a multidivision, multiproduct situation, the process of management control involves performance evaluation of strategic business units and responsibility centres both for the short-term as well as long-term achievements. Since it also involves the resource allocation by corporate headquarters, intense competition among various Strategic business units can be witnessed for resource snatching. This process can be compared to centre-state relations in a country. While the states want to get as much share of the national resources as possible, the centre has the difficult tasks of satisfying the demands of the states, given the limited resources. States express their aspirations through the formation of regional parties representing regional interests, while the centre has the key role of developing a national perspective. The same is true of management control. An over emphasis on the evaluation aspect of a responsibility centre, without giving adequate resource support, is likely to result in resentment among the managers and foster an individualistic viewpoint rather than a corporate viewpoint. This, it is likely to lead to regionalism. A senior executive from a large corporate organisation having several different manufacturing plants once pointed out how difficult it was for plant managers to overcome the plant perspective and develop the corporate perspective. Although it is difficult to generalise, organisations do face the pressure of centrifugal tendencies on the part of divisional managers and the role of corporate management is to provide the necessary centripetal force to keep the system in balance.

System's Thinking and Control System Design

Stafford Beer* the well known writer and practitioner of cybernetics has classified systems according to the characteristics of complexity, probabilism and self-regulation. A system with a large number of components and interrelationship is complex, and a system that can not be described in a precise fashion is exceedingly complex. Probabilism refers to the probabilistic nature of the system. In a deterministic system, the parts interact in a perfectly predictable way. In the case of probabilistic systems, this is not so. However, what may occur can be described in probabilistic terms. Self-regulation refers to control from within, utilising the margin of error as a means of control. Self-regulation is essential if the system has to maintain its structure. Depending upon the characteristics of the system, specific tools of analysis have been developed. For analysing the extreme complexity, the black-box technique is used, for probabilism, the information theory is used and for self- regulation, the feedback principle. The classification of systems according to complexity and probabilism, is useful in identifying the type of control required. The concept of cybernetic control is applicable in exceedingly complex and probabilistic systems such as a firm, a human being, and an economic system.

The Law of Requisite Variety : As interrelationships among the parts of a system increase, the system's variety also increases. Therefore, the larger is a system, the larger is its variety. Thus, when an organisation grows from a simple one with few employees and few interdependencies to a larger one, its variety increases. As the reduction in variety makes the system more predictable, the control mechanisms are designed to reduce the variety. The reduction in variety is achieved through information. Ashby has proposed the law of requisite variety for the design of control mechanisms. By this we mean that the control mechanism (controller) should have at least as many alternatives as the system

---

* Stafford Beer, Cybernetics and Management, John Wiley and Sons, New York, 1964, P. 18

can exhibit. Thus, in the case of a machine, the control mechanism is said to have requisite variety, if all the causes of stoppage are known and corrective action can be taken for all such causes.

The law of requisite variety demands the same amount of variety in the control mechanism as there is in the system being controlled. If the control mechanism does not possess the requisite variety, it may not be possible to control the system as many things may go wrong and the control mechanism does not possess as many alternatives as the system can exhibit. One way of achieving better control is by reducing the variety in the system, so that the requisite variety of the control mechanism will be smaller. Thus, various organisational policies aim at reducing the variety, by serving as a guideline for taking action.

The Black Box Technique

The major determinants of the complexity of a system include*

(i) the number of elements comprising the system, (ii) the attributes of the specified elements of the system, (iii) the interactions among the elements of the system and (iv) the degree of organisation inherent in the system, i.e., the existence or absence of predetermined rules and regulations which guide the interactions of the elements or specify the attributes of system's elements.

The black box technique involves manipulation of the input and classification for the output by observing the response of the system , and thereby deducing something about the mechanisms within the system, in terms of regularities or repetitiveness. It may be observed that the experimenter may himself be affecting the system that he is studying and thus, his behaviour may be affecting he system under study, i.e., the box, and he may himself be getting affected by the system's behaviour. Thus the experimenter may be coupled to the box and form together a feedback system. This is particularly true of business systems. The more the regularities or repetitiveness identified on the basis of classification of the output, the more knowledge is said to have been obtained about the box, and more the reduction in complexity of the system. Once the output is classified distinctively on the basis of degree of similarity, these similarities are then converted into many-to-one transformations, with a view to reducing the system's variety. As mentioned earlier, it is essential to reduce variety to ensure proper controls in the system.

Consider the case of business systems. If the manager or analyst makes an attempt to understand all possible combinations of the elementary units of the system, he is likely to be overawed by the details. Considering the system as

* Peter Schoderbek, et. al. Management Systems : Conceptual Considerations, Business Publications Inc., Dallas, USA, 1975, p. 76.

undefinable in detail, the technique of black box can be used in arriving at 'many to one transformations' for instance various policies to direct the organisation. Thus, the black box technique involves (i) input manipulation, (ii) output classification, and (iii) many-to-one transformation.

An important lesson to be learnt from this technique is the formulation of principles of self-regulation without knowing the exact nature of all causal relationships between inputs and outputs. As organisations can be considered black boxes because of their complexity, in order to achieve control it should be sufficient to know about the inputs that lead to desirable outputs. Though our aim is usually to improve knowledge of causal relationships, it is not necessary to acquire complete knowledge if the objective is to achieve control.

GOALS AND STRATEGIES

The management control process takes place within the context of goals, and of strategies for achieving these goals, that have been decided upon in the strategic planning process. The management control process is concerned with the attainment of goals and the implementation of strategies, not with their formulation. A management control system is situational, that is, it is tailored to the particular goals and the particular strategies of the organisations. In order to carry out the management control process managers must know what the company's goals and strategies are, and in particular, must understand how they influence the process. Moreover, the systems designer should insure that the control system is consistent with the organisation's goals, whatever they are. It is appropriate, therefore, that we discuss the identification of goals and strategies and how they are communicated to those involved in management control. In implementing strategies, an important concept is that of the key variable. Key variables are those relatively few variables that must be watched with particular care if the company is to achieve its goals.

Goals

Goals Distinguished form Objectives : We use the term goals to mean broad, fairly timeless statements of what the organisation wants to achieve and the term objectives for more specific statements of ends, the achievement of which is contemplated within a specified time period. Others use these terms as synonyms, and still others reverse the meanings given above. Our use is consistent with the etymology of these terms (although abridged dictionaries typically do not distinguish clearly between them), but more importantly, our meaning of "objectives" is consistent with its meaning in "management of objectives", which is a phrase used with increasing frequency in both business and government control systems. Goals are developed in the strategic planning process, and objectives are used in the management control process. There is the possibility of confusion if a clear distinction between them is not made. They differ with respect to the time period and the degree of specificity.

1. Time Period : Goals are usually stated without reference to a time period, whereas objectives are intended to be accomplished by a specified date, sometimes in one year, sometimes in five years or longer. For example, a goal of government is to improve health; establishes objectives for medical education, research, insurance programmes, construction of health care facilities and the like, each of which is to be attained by a certain time, and each of which presumably contributes toward the broad goal.

2. Specificity : Goals are stated in broad, general terms. Objectives are stated in more specific terms, preferably in such a way that there is some measurable basis for determining the extent to which the objective has been achieved. For example, an objective of Spencer group is to open a certain number of additional fast food outlets next year; indeed, its objective may be stated even more specifically in terms of the number of outlets that are to be opened in each geographical area. A company may set as an objective, the attainment of Rs. 20 million sales volume five years from now. To the extent that objectives are stated in this ways, the management control system can measure the degree of their attainment, but if they are vague or ill defined, no system can measure them.

Profitability as a Goal : It is safe to say that an important goal of most businesses is to earn a profit. A business is owned by its shareholders. They have invested money in the business, and they expect a return on this investment. Profit is a measure of this return. Presumably, the higher the profit, the better off are the shareholders. It follows that, in a general way, a goal of the business should be to earn as high a profit for the shareholders as is feasible.

Statement of Goals

A statement about profitability, along the lines discussed above, and a statement about growth, express the economic goals of the organisation. In addition although often unstated, an organisation has the fundamental goal of survival, and therefore will not knowingly adopt strategies that are so risky that they threaten its very existence. The organisation also has social goals which, although difficult to formulate in meaningful words, are appropriately part of its goals.

The list of goals is desirably short. The more numerous they are, the greater the possibility that one criterion will conflict with another when a proposed strategy is being discussed, and this conflict will hamper, rather than assist in, the resolution of the issue. To take an obvious example, if a company states its economic goals to be a 18 percent return on shareholders investment, a 15 percent return on capital employed, a 12 percent annual increase in earnings per share, and a 10 percent increase in sales volume, a proposed strategy may be consistent with some of these goals, but not with others. Less obviously, some companies state a long list of goals, some of which are little more than platitudes, and a serious attempt to analyse proposed strategies in terms of these criteria can be frustrating. Actually, when the list is long and vague, the tendency is to disregard many of the stated goals when proposed strategies are being analysed, and such a list therefore serves no useful purpose.

Strategies

Although most companies have the goal of a satisfactory return on investment, each company selects its own paths that it hopes will lead to the achievement of this goal. These paths are its strategies. Although strategies can be classified in various ways, for our purposes, it is sufficient to call them either (i) charters or (ii) policies*

Charters : Although most companies legal charters are written in such broad terms that the company is permitted to engage in any type of lawful economic activity, in practice a company's management draws boundaries around the territory in which it will operate. In a conglomerate these boundaries may be very wide; at the extreme, a company may be willing to enter any industry in which it believes there are promising profit opportunities. One company states, for example, "Our policy is planned profitable growth in any market we can serve well". Few companies, including most conglomerates, have such wide boundaries, however. Most companies state. "We are in the steel business", "We are in the air transport business", or "We are in the food business". Such statements are a beginning for the delineation of the company's charter, but it is desirable that they be made more specific.

Within an industry, each company presumably tries to find the best niche for itself. (The current marketing term for this is "positioning"). Its decision in this regard is much affected by the personality of its chief executive officer, and is influenced by his background, his drive, and his attitude toward expansion and toward risk taking. The possible permutations are too large to enumerate, but to give an indication. The company can aim at the quality end of a market, at the low-price end, or at the whole spectrum; it can manufacture what it sells, or buy what it sells from vendors, or assemble components that it buys from vendors; it can seek a dominant market share, or accept a steady market share, and so on.

Divisional Charters : Within the general boundaries set for the company as a whole, charters are established for each division or other principal operating unit. These divisional charters are an important factor in the management control process, for they set limits to divisional planning. In some companies, divisions are permitted to grow and to extend their activities without regard to a specific charter. When this happens, programmes of two or more divisions

* Some authors include the determination of goals as one component of strategy. See Alfred D. Chandler, Jr., Strategy and Structure (Cambridge, Mass. : M.I.T. Press, 1962), p. 13.

may overlap in an undesirable way. Two divisions may compete against one another in the same market. Or, one division may be counting on orders from another division to fill its production capacity, without knowing that the other division has made plans to obtain its products from another source. Or, an important market segment may be overlooked by all the divisions. Under certain circumstances competition among the divisions is sound practice. For example, the various car divisions of T.V.S. compete vigorously with one another. The point is not that such competition be eliminated but rather that it be carried on knowingly, and as a part of the overall strategy of the corporation.

Although divisional charters are set by top management, divisional managers usually participate actively in the process. For various reasons, Division A may wish to invade the territory assigned to Division B, and the Division A manager will argue vigorously the case for doing so. Because the manager of Division B usually does not want his own boundaries to be constricted, he opposes such a move, and top management must then decide.

Polices : In addition to the corporate charter and divisional charters, the strategies also comprise the broad policies that are to govern corporate activities. These policies are essentially constraints within which subordinate managers are expected to operate. They include promotion, transfer, compensation, retirement, and other personnel policies; dividend, debt structure, short-term borrowing and other financial policies; capital investment criteria; quality levels and other product policies; and policies regarding discrimination, pollution, and other social issues. The formulation of policies that are specific enough so that they are more than platitudes, yet broad enough so that they do not unduly restrict the operating manager is a difficult task.

Formulation of Strategies

Strategies are intended to remain in force for a reasonably long time. They must, however, be dynamic, for a company's environment changes, and its strategies must be adapted to the current environment. Thinking about strategy is an important top management activity, although not a time consuming activity. Andrews says that the strategist considers four questions simultaneously : What might we do? What can we do? What do we want to do? and What should we do?* These questions are addressed in the context of the company's environment as it is currently perceived and taking account of the resources which are, or may be, available to the company. Strategy is a match between environmental opportunities and organisational resources, both as perceived by management.

A few companies have developed systematic approaches to the formulation of strategy. Bharat Heavy Electricals Limited (BHEL), for example, has

---

* Kenneth R. Andrews, The Concept of Corporate Strategy (Homewood, Ill. : Dow Jones-Irwin, Inc., 1971), Page 41.

developed a model that incorporates the principal factors that, according to its studies, govern return on investment and use this model both to search out strategic opportunities at the corporate level and also to analyse strategies proposed by division managers.* Aguilar describes companies that systematically re-examine their environment as a basis for making changes in strategy.* Most companies do not make systematic strategic studies. Instead when an opportunity or a threat is identified, it studies and the study may lead to a change in strategy. Some of the possibilities originate at corporate head quarters; others originate when a division perceived an opportunity that is outside of its existing charter.

In evaluating present and proposed strategies, the following questions are suggested.*

1. Is the strategy identifiable and has it been made clear.either in words or practice? (The unstated strategy cannot be tested or contested and is likely therefore to be weak. If it is implicit in the intuition of a strong leader, his organisation is likely to be weak and the demands his strategy makes upon it are likely to remain unmet).

2. Does the strategy exploit fully domestic and international environmental opportunity? (Unless growth is incompatible with the resources of an organisation or the aspirations of its management, it is likely that a strategy that does not purport to make full use of market opportunity will be weak also in other respects. Vulnerability to competition is increased by lack of interest in market share).

3. Is the strategy consistent with corporate competence and resources, both present and projected? (Although additional resources, both financial and managerial, are available to companies with genuine opportunity, the availability of each must be finally determined and programmed along a practicable time scale).

4. Are the major provisions of the strategy and the program of major policies of which it is comprised internally consistent? (One advantage of making as specific a statement of strategy as is practicable is the resultant

---

* Sidney Schoeffler, Robert D. Buzzell, and Donald F. Heany, "Impact of Strategic Planning on Proft Performance", Harvard Business Review, March-April 1974, pp. 137-45.

* Francis J. Aguilar, Scanning the Business Environment (New York : The Macmillan Company, 1967).

* C. Roland Christensen et. al., Business Polciy : Text and Cases (Homewood, Ill : Richard D. Irwin, Inc., 1973), pp. 114-17.

availability of a careful check on coherence, compatibility, and synergy-the state in which the whole can be viewed as greater than the sum of its parts).

5. Is the chosen level of risk feasible in economic and personal terms? (Strategies vary in the degree of risk willingly undertaken by their designers, but the choice should be made knowingly).

6. Is the strategy appropriate to the personal values and aspirations of the key managers? (Conflict between the personal preferences, aspirations, and goals of the key members of an organisation and the plan for its future is a sign of danger and a harbinger of mediocre performance or failure).

7. Is the strategy appropriate to the desired level of contribution to society? (Although it can be argued that filling any economic need contributes to the social good, it is clear that a manufacturer of cigarettes might well consider diversification on grounds other than his fear of future legislation).

8. Does the strategy constitute a clear stimulus to organisational effort and commitment? (Some undertakings are inherently more likely to gain the commitment of able men of goodwill than others. Generally speaking, the bolder the choice of goals and the wider the range of human needs they reflect, the more successfully they will appeal to the capable membership of a healthy and energetic organisation).

9. Are there early indications of the responsiveness of markets and market segments to the strategy? (A strategy may pass with flying colour all the tests so far proposed, but if within a time period made reasonable by the company's resources and original plan the strategy does not work, then it must be weak in some way that has escaped attention).

Key Variables

In addition to measuring profitability, the system highlights certain variables that have a significant effect on profitability. These are called key variables. (Also "strategic factors", "key success factors", "key result areas", and "pulse points"). In most situations, there are relatively few such variables, six being the number most commonly cited. There will be key variables for the organisation as a whole and other, perhaps different, key variables for the divisions or other organisation units.

Nature of Key variables : The identification of key variables requires a thorough understanding of the economics of the business. In some cases they can be found by constructing a model of the business and using it to discover the sensitivity of profits to various factors. Usually, however, the variables are uncovered by discussions with persons who have acquired a deep understanding of the business through long experience with it. These persons know intuitively the important things to keep an eye on, and these are the key variables. More specifically, a key variable has the following characteristics :

1. It is *important* in explaining the success or failure of the organisation.
2. It is *volatile,* that is, it can change quickly, often for reasons that are not controllable by the manager.
3. *Prompt action* is required when a significant change occurs.
4. The change is *not easy to predict.*
5. The variable can be *measured*, either directly or via a surrogate. For example, *customer satisfaction* cannot be measured directly, but its surrogate, *number of returns* can be a key variable.

One way to attempt to isolate the key variables is to look at the raison d'etre of the industry itself, and of the particular firm within that industry. A useful question is, "Why, in a free- enterprise economy, should this company be able to operate at a satisfactory profit?". A hardheaded rethinking of this fundamental question should lead to a careful spelling out of just what functions the company is performing that its customers are willing to pay for. Further thought should then be devoted to the question of why this company, rather than its competitors, is able to attract profitable volume. Then, finally, it may be possible to pinpoint those activities that need to be done particularly well if the company is to enjoy even greater success.

Another approach that may be useful for an analyst who is trying to improve his understanding of the interplay of economic forces on a company is to examine the way in which decisions are made. What decisions does management regard as major ones? What are the factors that management is concerned about in making these decisions? And specifically, for many types of intangible, discretionary expenditures, what will be the source of revenue from which the company will recover this cost and earn a profit? Questions such as these should also eventually lead to the identification of those elements which are critical to the success of a company in a competitive environment.

Marketing Variables : Some aspect of marketing effort is key variable in most businesses, not only because of the need to take prompt action in the marketing area if results are unsatisfactory, but also because of the need to make prompt adjustments in production and other plans if a significant change in the volume of business seems to be on the horizon. Among the specific measures used are the following :

1. **Sales :** This item is especially important in retailing and in other businesses in which the customer's action is immediately reflected in sales revenue.

2. Bookings : In companies that manufacture for future delivery, the nature and volume of sales orders booked is more important than current sales volume, both as an indicator of marketing success and as a warning that other plans may require adjustment.

3. Market Share : Unless market share is watched closely, a deterioration in the company's competitive position can be obscured by a reported increase in sales volume that results from generally favourable business conditions. Automobile dealers report their sales to automobile manufacturers every ten days, and detailed information on market share is published a few day later. In some industries, however, market share is difficult to determine, or can be determined only several months after the fact.

4. Gross Margin Percentage : A change in the average gross margin percentage of a product line may signal a change in the sales mix of products, or in the proportion of sales that cannot be made at regular prices. Either situation can be cause for concern. An increase in off-price sales may be indication of trouble in the production operation (resulting, e.g., from poor quality or from over production of certain styles) as well as in the marketing function itself.

5. Key Account Orders : In companies that sell to retailers, the order received from certain important accounts-large department stores, discount chains, super markets, mail order houses-may provide an early indication of the success of the entire marketing effort. If the company does not get its "fair share" of the business from these accounts, this is a signal of grave trouble with its, styling, its pricing, its promotional efforts, or other aspects of its marketing programmes.

6. Lost Orders : A variation on the above in the number of customers who should be expected to place orders but who do not.

7. Promotional Indicators : The renewal rate on magazine subscriptions, the direct mail response rate for companies that rely on direct mail as a marketing tool, the coupon returns for companies that use advertisements with coupons, are all indicators of the success of marketing efforts. Because of the difficulty of predicting success and because of the importance of these efforts on profitability, in certain companies variables such as these are watched closely. Some of them, such as the subscription renewal rate for a magazine, may signal a basic weakness in the product rather than in the promotional effort per se.

8. New Customers : In organisations such as banks, newspapers, and service establishments that thrive by attracting new customers who, once acquired, tend to provide revenue for along period of time, the number of such customers is a key variable. In automobile companies, the owner body, which is the number of people who now own the company's car, is a similar variable because there is a high probability that these owners will buy the same make of car again.

Production and Logistics Variables

In the ideal world, products would flow through a factory as smoothly and uneventfully as a river normally flows between its banks.But just as floods cause havoc in a watershed, so unexpected events can causes havoc in the factory, or in the distribution network that leads from factory to consumer. Some variables that may warrant special management attention and prompt action if an unsatisfactory situation develops are as follows :

1. Cost Control : In many companies, management can safely assume that actual costs will be in line with standard costs, and it need not pay attention to cost control unless a "red flag" is raised in accordance with the exception principle. In some companies, however, costs must be monitored all the time. This is particularly the case when the profit margin as a percentage of sales in small, as in the case of super markets; a small change in costs can have a major impact on profits. Output per manhour or overtime are indicators of cost control that are key variables in some companies.

2. Capacity Utilisation : Unit costs, and hence profits, are strongly influenced by production volume, because of the impact of fixed costs. In part, volume fluctuations are the responsibility of the marketing organisation, and are identified by variables listed above, but in part they reflect the ability of production people to schedule properly and to adjust capacity to current requirements. In a professional organisation, sold time, which measures the percentage of the total available professional hours that is billed to clients, is a key measure of resource utilisation. In a hotel, occupancy rate, the percentage of rooms occupied each day, is a similar measure. In these and certain other organisations, products cannot be produced for inventory; if available resources are not sold today, they are lost forever. Thus, a measure of capacity utilisation is almost always a key variable in such organisations.

3. Backlog : This can be an important indication of the need to change production plans, either in total or for particular items.

4. Quality : In many companies, acceptable quality can be taken for granted. In some, such as aircraft or drug manufacture and the operation of transportation systems of all types, a departure from the highest quality standards can be catastrophic, and some measurement of quality is a key variable. In other companies, such as the manufacture of integrated circuits, the level of quality has a significant effect on unit costs. (If 10 percent of each batch of "chips" is of acceptable quality, unit costs are considerably higher than if the percentage is 90). Customer return is another measure of quality.

5. Yield : In many process industries, they yield, which is the amount of salable product that is obtained from a given input of raw material, has an important effect on profitability, and prompt action needs to be taken when unexpected changes are reported.

6. Raw material Costs : If the company's raw materials tend to fluctuate widely in cost, their price movements need to be watched closely, so that appropriate management action can be taken to change inventory levels, change product prices, or adopt alternative product formulations. In such companies, raw material prices are a key variable all the time, and under unusual economic conditions (such as unforeseen inflation) they may temporarily become a key variable in most companies. By contrast, labour costs are rarely a key variable; changes in labour rates occur only annually or semi-annually; these changes can be foreseen, and their consequences can be taken account of without a special signalling system.

7. On Time Delivery : In companies in which fulfillment of delivery promises is important and in which delivery on time is difficult, the percentage of shipments that are late is a variable that may warrant special management attention.

REVIEW QUESTIONS

1. How will you link the three levels of management with the three levels of decision making ?
2. What is strategic planning? Distinguish it from management control.
3. What is operational control? How does it differ from management control?
4. Explain, in detail, the inter-relationship among strategic planning, operational control and management control.
5. What are the different types of controls used in management control systems?
6. Explain the nature of and reason for variations in controls?
7. Explain the different aspects of management control process.
8. Write short notes on (a) The Law of Requisite Variety (b) The Black Box Technique.
9. Explain the meaning of the term 'Goals'. How do they differ from objectives?
10. What do you understand by 'Strategies'. Are Policies and Charters of a business be called Strategies?
11. How will you formulate and evaluate the strategy of a car manufacturing firm?
12. Explain the nature of key variables. List out some of the important key variables in production and marketing of electronic goods.

6
Management Control System

Meaning and Design : The control process comprises setting targets (which will lead to achievement of the company's objectives) to be achieved in a given period (through a given amount of resources), reviewing performance vis-a-vis targets set and taking corrective action when and wherever necessary to ensure that the targets are achieved. In this process there are actually two major activities involved, viz., (i) The role of the controlling authority in planning (target fixing) and in taking control action and (ii) the system or routine framework or arrangements, which provide relevant information to facilitate the control action with a view to ensuring the efficient and effective use of resources in the accomplishment of targets.

The management control system refers to a framework or set-up by which the manager can ensure control over the actions of his subordinates as well as control over the whole operations in an organisation. It is the whole net-work by which a manager ensures that the targets will be achieved. The main purpose of the control system is to assist in target fixing, collecting information on actual performance, comparing actuals with targets, reporting the variations and initiating suitable action to ensure that the targets are achieved efficiently and effectively. According to Anthony*, "It is a total system in the sense that it embraces all aspects of the firm's operations because an important management function is to assure that all parts of the operation are in balance with one another and in order to examine balance, management needs information about each of the parts".

Characteristics : Following is the list of the principal characteristics of a management control system.

1. A management control system focuses on programmes and responsibility centres. A programme is a product, product line, research and development project, or similar activity that the organisation undertakes in order to achieve its goals. A responsibility centre is an organisation unit headed by a responsible manager.

2. The information in a management control system is of two general types : (i) planned data, that is, programmes, budgets, and standards; and (ii) actual

---

* Anthony, R.N. : Management Accounting Principles, page 308 (Homewood, Illinois : Richard D. Iriwin, Inc.) 1970 revised edition.

data, that is, information on what is actually happening, both inside the organisation and in the external environment.

3. Ordinarily, a management control system is a total system in the sense that it embraces all aspects of a company's operation. It needs to be a total system because an important management function is to assure that all parts of the operations are in balances with one another; and in order to co-ordinate these activities, management needs information about each of them.

4. The management control system is usually built around a financial structure; that is, resources and revenues are expressed in monetary units. Money is the only common denominator which can be used to combine and compare the heterogeneous elements of resources (e.g., hours of labour, type of labour, quantity and quality of material, amount and kind of products produced). Although the financial structure is usually the central focus, non-monetary measures such as minutes per operation, number of employees, and reject and spoilage rates are also important parts of the system.

5. The management control process tends to be rhythmic; it follows a definite pattern and timetable, month after month and year after year. In budget preparation, which is an important activity in the management control process, certain steps are taken in predescribed sequence and at certain dates each year : dissemination of guidelines, preparation of original estimates, transmission of these estimates up through the several echelons in the organisation, review of these estimates, final approval by top management, and dissemination back through the organisation. The procedure to be followed at each step in this process, the dates when the steps are to be completed, and even the forms to be used can be, and often are,set forth in a policies and procedures manual.

6. A management control system is, or should be, a coordinated, integrated system; that is, although data collected for one purpose may differ from those collected for another purpose, these data should be reconcilable with one another. In particular, it is essential that data on actual performance be structured in the same way- that is, have the same definitions and the same account content-as data on planned performance. If this is not done, valid comparisons of actual and planned performance cannot be made. In a sense, the management control system is a single system, but for some purposes it is useful to think of it as a set of interlocking subsystems, one for programming, another for budgeting, another for accounting, and another for reporting and analysis.

Overview of Management Control Systems

Much of the management control process involves informal communication and interactions. Informal communication occurs by means of memoranda, meetings, conversations, and even by such signals as facial expressi

Although these informal activities are of great importance, they are not amenable to a systematic description. In addition to these informal activities, most companies also have a formal management control system. It consists of some or all of the following phases :

1. Programming.
2. Budgeting.
3. Operating and Accounting.
4. Reporting and Analysis.

As indicated in Diagram 6.1, each of these activities leads to the next. They recur in a regular cycle, and together they constitute a "closed loop". These four phases are described briefly below, and are discussed in depth in later chapters.

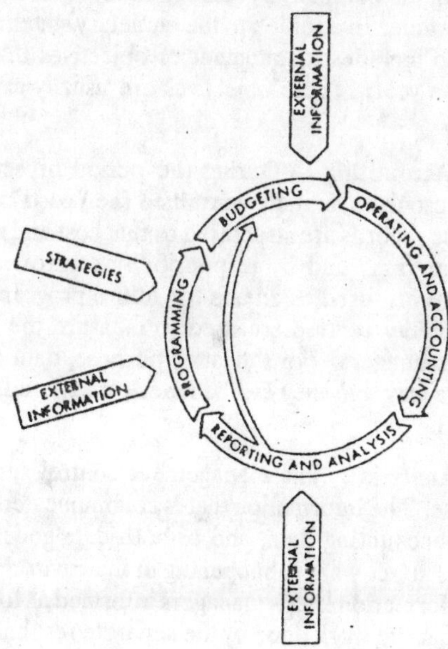

Fig. 6.1 Phases of Management Control

Programming : Programming is the process of deciding on the programmes that the company will undertake and the approximate amount of resources that are to be allocated to each program. Programs are the principal activities that the organisation has decided to undertake in order to implement the strategies that it has decided upon. In a profit-oriented company, each principal product or product line is a program. If several product lines are manufactured in the same plant, the plant itself and additions or modifications to it may be identified as a programme. There are also various research and development programmes, some aimed at improving existing products or processes, others searching for marketable new products.

Budgeting : A budget is a plan expressed in quantitative, usually, monetary terms that covers a specified period of time, usually one year. In the budgeting process each programme is translated into terms that correspond to the sphere of responsibility of each manager who is charged with executing the programme or some part of it. Thus, although the plans are originally made in terms of individual programmes, in the budgeting process the plans are translated into terms of responsibility centres. The process of developing a budget is essentially one of negotiation between the manager of responsibility centre and his superior. The end product of these negotiations is an approved statement of the revenues that are expected during the budget year, and the resources that are to be used in achieving the company's goals for each responsibility centre and for the company as a whole. In addition to the monetary statement of plans, the plan for the year also includes a statement of objectives that are to be accomplished during the year. These objectives are usually expressed in non-monetary terms.

Operating and Accounting : During the period of actual operations, records are kept of resources actually consumed (i.e., costs) and of revenues actually earned. These records are structured so that cost and revenue data are classified both by programs and by responsibility centres. Data classified according to programs are used as a basis for future programming, and data classified by responsibility centres are used to measure the performance of responsibility centre managers. For the latter purpose, data on actual results are reported in such a way that they can be readily compared with the plan as set forth in the budget.

Reporting and Analysis : The management control system serves as a communication device. The information that is communicated consists of both accounting and non-accounting data, and of both data generated within the organisation and data about what is happening in the environment outside the organisation. This information keeps managers informed as to what is going on and helps to insure that the work done by the separate responsibility centres is co-ordinated.

Reports are also used as a basis for control. Essentially, such reports are derived from an analysis that compares actual performance with planned performance and attempts to explain the difference. Based on these formal reports, and also on information received through informal communication channels, managers decide what, if any, action should be taken. They may, for example, decide to change the plan as set forth in the budget, and this leads to a new planning process. It is for this reason that the phases shown in diagram 6.1 are depicted as a closed loop with one phase leading to the next.

Management control was defined as "the process by which managers assure that resources are obtained and used effectively and efficiently in the accomplishment of the organisation's goals". Depending on the situation in a given organisation, this process may relate to either or both of two structures : (i) the organisation structure and/or (ii) projects. A key concept in this discussion is that of the responsibility centre. A responsibility centre is an organisation unit headed by a manager who is responsible for its activities. All responsibility centres produce outputs (that is, they do something), and all have inputs (that is, they use resources). They can be classified on the basis of the measurement of inputs and outputs into one of four types : revenue centres, expense centres, profit centres and investment centres.

The Management Control System is designed by incorporating the following five basic steps :

(a) The classification of organisation into Responsibility Centres.
(b) Fixing up responsibility in accordance with the firm's objectives and deciding critical variables/key factors for each Responsibility Centre.
(c) Developing information system which facilitates real time information* regarding operations which deviate from the desired results, specifically critical variables and relate results to individual accountability.
(d) Performance reporting to management for remedial measures.
(e) Real time control** action by Management.

In a revenue centre, outputs are measured in monetary terms, but does not measure inputs in monetary terms. In a profit centre, the management control system measures both inputs and outputs in monetary terms; that is, inputs are measured in terms of cost and outputs in terms of revenue. Profit is the difference between cost and revenues. Many profit centres transfer products (either goods or services) to other profit centres within the company. The price used in measuring the amount of products transferred is called a transfer price. Because of its importance in the management control system of profit centres, a whole chapter, chapter 2 is devoted to a discussion of transfer pricing. In an investment centre, the control system measures not only the inputs and outputs in monetary terms, but it also measures the investment that is employed in the responsibility centre.

---

* The real time information refers to information on what is happening as events are occurrring. The use of computer and other electronic data processing devices has made possible the collection of Real time information

** The real time control means correction of deviations as soon as they are reported.

Responsibility Centres and Their Identification

According to Shillinglaw, "Responsibility centre is an organisation unit headed by a single person (sometimes by a committee) answerable to higher authority and obliged to perform certain tasks",* It refers to departmental or sectional classification of a business in such a manner that the responsibility is fixed on the departmental or sectional head for the target fixed in respect of that department or section. Responsibility Centres can be classified as (a) Revenue Centres, (b) Profit Centres, (c) Cost Centres and (d) Investment Centres. In a Profit Centre, targets may be fixed in terms of Profit. This is possible only if the department's output can be measured in terms of 'Revenue'. If a department's output is neither feasible nor necessary to be measured in terms of revenue (for example, Accounting Department, Research and Development Department, Law Department etc.), it can be referred to as a Cost Centre. For such centres a system of accounting is designed to measure only the expenses incurred by each centre. An Investment Centre is a responsibility centre in which the manager is held responsible for the use of assets as well as for revenues and expenses. His performance is evaluated in the light of target fixed for the rate of return on investment.

The targets for the various Responsibility Centres may be evolved keeping in view the nature of the Responsibility Centre as well as overall objectives of the business. In identifying responsibility centres in an organisation, five broad consideration may be kept in view.

1. A manager should be responsible for attaining results in relation to operations within the responsibility centre.

2. It should be possible to measure clearly the inputs required by the responsibility centre. The inputs may be the cost of raw materials, supplies, power and fuel, machinery, men etc.

3. If the responsibility centre is a profit centre, the value of its output e.g., the finished products, assemblies, intermediate products or services produced by it, should be measurable as far as possible in terms of revenue.

4. The method of operation in the responsibility centre through which the inputs are converted into desired outputs, should be distinct for the responsibility centre. We may call it the conversion process or technology employed by the responsibility centre.

5. The units within the organisation or external markets served by the responsibility centre should be clear and distinct so that the management can easily measure the value of goods and services provided by the responsibility centre in the form of output, and its value to the receiving unit or the market.

* Gordan Shillinglaw : Cost Accounting Analysis and Control, Page 24 (Homewook, Illinois : Richard D. Irwin Inc.); 1968, Indian reprint.

Control can be effective only if a manager has authority over his department and each manager in this way is accountable to some authority or the other. The manager's authority and responsibility in respect of a responsibility centre should be clearly defined, otherwise no control can be exercised over him. Also he cannot exercise control over others. Duality of authority and responsibility is virtually responsibility to none, which will weaken a control system. Further, each responsibility centre should be coded as this will facilitate the collection and arrangement of information generated from various sources.

Management Control Structure

The financial responsibilities are delegated to the departmental or divisional managers. It is also necessary, then to evelve a control structure so that the divisons entrusted with financial reponsibility are constrained to diacharge their duties towards fulfilment of the over all objectives. The tree below depicts the types into which a financial control system can be divided.

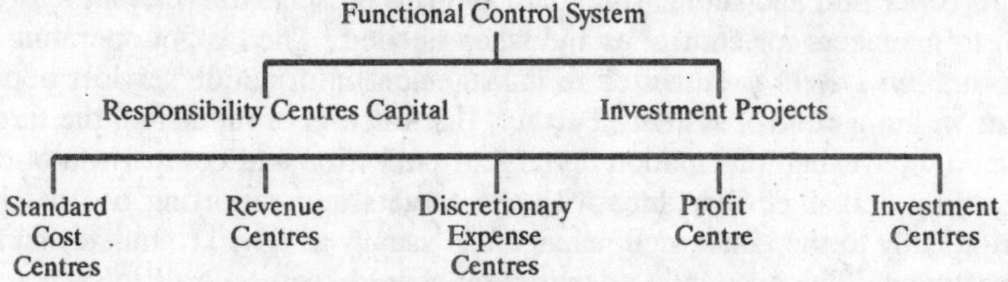

All these reponsibility cantres would have certain inputs and certain outputs. There exists some relationship between inputs and outputs. The divisional manager-in-charge of a responsibility cantre can manipulate some of these inputs atleast, to achieve greater or optimal output. It is to be noted that the projects has discrete beginning and discrete end over time basis, whereas, all the responsibility centres have usually indefinite time.

Critical Variables : A critical variable is that aspect of the operation at the responsibility centre, which if carried out ineffectively, the realisation of the goals of the organisation will be adversely affected irrespective of the fact that other operations in the organisation are being performed effectively and efficiently. For example, in a textile mill the 'Waste' ratio in spinning process, and 'damage' in weaving and finishing of cloth are considered as critical vairables.* The point selected for control should be critical in the sense either of being limiting factors in the operation or of showing better than other factors whether plans are working out. With such critical points a manager can handle a larger group of subordinates and activities and thereby increase his span of management, effect cost savings and improve communication.

Developing System for Information Collection and its Analysis

Information is a pre-requisite for control. The word 'Information' means data relevant for a particular purpose. Any data relevant to a manager for the purpose of control would constitute information for him. Information about

---

* S.K. Bhattacharya : Managerial Planning & Control System (New Delhi : I E Learning System Pvt. Ltd.) 1977 edition.

critical variable is a must for managerial control purposes. A piece of information if conveyed properly and understood correctly would add to the knowledge of the recipient. When a person gains knowledge he is prompted to act. In the case of a manager he is prompted to take control action. Such information could be obtained either through a formal system or through grape-vine. However, as companies grow, managers become more dependent on formal rather than on informal systems.* Further, the formal systems provide a crutch for the orderly succession of management. As such the emphasis is on the development of formal information systems.

The formal information system should be so structured that it (i) provides regular collection of data regarding each and every responsibility centre, (ii) yields processed and summarised data and (iii) presents the relevant information to managers for control as and when needed. The task of operating the information system is entrusted to management information services department within a control system. Further, the function of tabulating the targets framed, conveying information on targets, collection and comparison of data regarding actual performance with the targets and reporting of variations periodically to the concerned managers is usually assigned to the accounting department. The accounting department should keep records in such a way that cost and revenue data are collected, summarised and presented alongwith variations both by product, department and by responsibility. The product-wise data are used for determining product-wise profitability and for exercising activity control whereas the responsibility-wise data are used to measure the performance of the heads of responsibility centres. The information collected and reported responsibility centre-wise, produces below stated intangible effects some of which are intentional and some unintentional** :

(i) They may prepare employees to investigate the causes and take suitable corrective action.

(ii) They may instil attitudes of loyalty and pride of accomplishment.

(iii) They may prompt the superior to locate those activities and people in the organisation in need of help so that assistance can be rendered and the scarce resources of the firm can be most effectively utilised.

(iv) They may effect the image of the whole organisation that is perceived by the outside world.

Management Reporting System

Management reporting system, in general, may be divided into three segments, namely, statutory reports, routine control & accounting reports and

---

* Charles T. Horngren : Cost Accounting - A managerial emphasis (New Delhi : Prentice-Hall of India Pvt. Ltd.) 1976 edition.

** A.W. Willsmore : Accounting for Management Control, Chapter 1. (London : Sir Isaac Pitman and Sons Ltd.) 1971 edition.

management control reports. Statutory reports include maintenance of statutory records and submission of reports and returns to various authorities as directed by law.

Routine control and accounting reports include routine stock records, sales records, ledgers, bank and cash position statements, expenses statements, etc., which are needed for general control and for accounting and auditing purpose.

Management Control Reports : Management plans and budgets the operations of each division, department or unit. Time-bound targets are set and the management would like to ensure that the company's operations run as per the predetermined plan and targets set are met. The reports and the reporting system evolved to review that the company's operations are proceeding as per plans is known as management control reporting system. Hence for evolving appropriate management reporting system, it is necessary (i) to identify operations that need be reviewed, (ii) the path or the course of action planned and (iii) the time bound targets or budgets fixed.

Action Orientation : Since these reports are meant to review that the pre-set objectives are persued and predetermined targets are achieved, these reports must incorporate (i) the action being taken to improve the performance and to overcome impediments if any and (ii) assistance required from corporate management. The reports must not be alibis for non-achievement.

Management by Exception : Management controls must be exercised where operations go or are likely to go haywire. It is therefore not essential to review everything but to review only those areas where performance is not as per plan. This principle is called "management by exception". Thus the system based on "management by exception" (i) deletes unnecessary information about operations that are running as per schedule and (ii) clearly points out operations of areas where action is needed.

Periodicity : The control reports must be submitted at interval where effective action can be taken. Too frequent reporting loses interest and enthusiasm of the recipients. Similarly, too infrequent reporting, when action cannot be taken, will be of academic interest only.

Timeliness : It is essential that the reports are submitted at a specified date. Delays will make the reports ineffective and stale.

Accuracy : It must be understood that management control reports are not accounting documents and hence about 95 percent accuracy is good enough. Expense figures, for example, may be given in thousands or lakhs of rupees. For getting exact figures, precious time will be lost. Moreover, unnecessary lengthy figures will divert the attention from the subject.

Evolving Management Reporting System : Having reviewed the basic tenents of the management reporting system, let us see as to how to evolve and to establish the management reporting system.

Organisational Structure : It is absolutely essential to know the organisational structure of a unit for which the MIS (management information system) is being evolved. The designations of the persons or positions, the responsibilities at each level and the reporting structure must be clearly understood. The management control information need at each level varies and hence the need to study the structure. At the highest management level overall review of divisional departmental operations will be sufficient, whereas at lower levels detailed information of each expense account, each product on customer may be required.

Studying Information Needs : Two methods are adopted for studying the information needs at each level of management.

Upside Down : Study critically the information needs at each level of management commensurate with the responsibilities. Find out and record all areas for which an executive will be accountable. The information system must cover all these areas and report to him the happenings and the progress in each area at regular intervals.

Down to Up : Each organisation evolves knowingly or unknowingly some reporting system to review its operation. Over a period, some reports are evolved. Record all these reports. Find out their frequency, information contents, source of information, usefulness of each piece of information, action taken after studying report, etc. many of the reports will be found totally useless. Discard these. You may change the frequency of submission or change their contents, etc. Such critical analysis will indicate and trim the reports to bear necessity.

Integrated Reporting System : It takes considerable efforts and time to prepare and submit reports and recipient has also to study each report. Hence it is advisable to reduce the number of reports to the bear necessity.

As we saw above, statutory reports and routine control and accounting reports are required to be made in addition to management control reports. Hence it is advisable to evolve an integrated reporting system, which can serve all the three objectives. Such a system will considerably reduce the number of reports, the efforts gone in, to collect and to compile data to make reports and studying the reports by the recipients.

An Essential Control Tool : Good management control reporting system - M.I.S. - is extremely useful for controlling operations of any organisation. Executives are flooded with papers on day- to-day activities and unless a good reporting system to control the company's operations is evolved, a lot of paper work and unwanted operations pile up resulting in tensions, bickerings, late hours and inefficiency.

Nature and Contents of Management Control Reports

The reports are the vehicles of communication. The purpose of a control report is to communicate series of data related to the performance of specific responsibility centres and their organisational heads. Fundamentally, they report actual results with desired performance and pinpoint both efficient and inefficient performance.

The following aspects of reporting for managerial control are of crucial importance for an effective and efficient management control system :

1. Frequency of reporting.
2. Format of control reports.
3. Contents and periodic review of management reports.

Frequency of Reporting : The frequency of submission of management report in terms of time would vary depending upon the importance and cruciality of the information communicated*. For instance, daily or weekly information will usually be required on sales and production performance and weekly or monthly information on assets, liabilities, sales, profits and broad categories of expenses and cost. Certain financial information like overhead expenses which are very susceptible to change or control once their broad levels have been determined, may even be reported every quarter. External environment data which are of great use and relevance to corporate management might be reported half yearly, since reporting at shorter intervals might not bring out the trend characteristics of such information.

If there is a special problem of financial liquidity, top management may also want daily figures of cash balances, as well as frequent reports on the source and application of funds, with projection of future cash requirements. In other circumstances, special reports on new researches, or some other aspect may be needed on a regular periodic basis or on special occasions when a change is contemplated. At all levels, promptness may be regarded as more important than complete accuracy. Often speed or greater frequency can be achieved by sacrificing a little bit of accuracy. Approximations may well be good enough to serve as signals that will enable the important things to be spotted. The purpose of the control report is not to provide exact information but to draw attention to the matters that demand correction, and to the need for further examination and analysis.**

* Hingorani, Ramanathan and Grewal : Management Accounting, Page 315 (New Delhi : Sultan Chand and Sons) 1981 edition.

** Deardon, J. : "How to Organise Information Systems". Page 68, Harvard Business Review, Vol. 43 No. 2, 1965 edition.

Format of Control Reports : Format of a management report should be so designed that it highlights the actual achievement or performance in relation to original plan or budgets for respective items like output, sales, revenue, costs, researches, receivables and other operational aspects of performance like yield, wastage, utilisation, quality level achieved etc.

It is also very useful that the reader of the report must be able to see the shortfall from the plan or the target and identify relatively easily and quickly the major or the primary factors contributing to such shortfalls. One additional requirement also needs to be covered. Once having ascertained the reasons for the shortfall if the manager concerned wishes to analyse in detail the particular activity or operation leading to the shortfall, he should know precisely the type of the detailed reports to be called for, even though he might not be receiving them as a routine at his management level.

The designer of the format of control reports should ensure that reports do not get too cramped and crowded with data. Good reports are those which are of use and interest to the reader indicating to him readily the results of performance and the factors which are causing significant variations. This will attract his attention towards the area for control action in time. Further, the format for report should be designed in such a way that it suits the requirement of the level aimed at.

Contents of Management Report : "A good reporting system lays emphasis on tailoring the contents of the reports according to the needs of the executives who use them".* This tailoring should be carried down to the individual report rendered to each supervisor. The Supervisor of each department determines within the general framework, the extent of the detailed information he requires to control operations for which he is held accountable. Too much information in the management report for control purposes creates a problem of information indigestion** and this ultimately delays control action. To combat information indigestion, there arises the need to design information suited for special use at all levels of management. All managers must choose points of information which would assist them in exercising control over the department and employees therein, under their supervision. The nature of the information that needs to be supplied differs from one operating level to another. At the top level in all businesses the most important report is a condensation or summary of the essential operating and financial information to serve as a means of overall appraisal.

---

* Reginald, L. et. al. : Budgeting-Key to Planning and Control. Page 20 (New York : The American Management Association Inc.) 1966 edition.

** Deardon, J. : "How to Organise Information Systems". Page 68, Harvard Business Review, Vol. 43 No. 2, 1965 edition.

The requirements of operating management are rather different. The operating managers are more concerned with volume, quality and technical performance. They usually find such data useful which provides them information about the targets achieved. However, they also need information relating to costs incurred by them and the revenues generated by their operations. It is important to ensure that only those costs which are controllable by the manager receiving the report and revenues generated by his operations are included in the report.

From the above discussion the essentials of a good control report can be laid down as below :

1. It is tailored to the organisational structure and controllability by responsibility centre.
2. It is designed to draw attention of concerned manager towards deviations related to responsibility for judging performance and for adopting measures for correction and improvement.
3. It is repetitive and related to short time period.
4. It suits the requirements of its principal user.
5. It should be simple, understandable and further it should include only essential information.
6. The information contained in it should be lucidly presented either in written or graphic form or both.
7. To minimise gap between the decision point and performance reporting, it should be prepared and presented promptly.
8. It should not report only faults but embody constructive actions for improving the situation.

Pre-requisites of a Successful Management Control System

The successful operation of a management control system depends upon the presence of the following preconditions* :

(i) Control requires plans.
(ii) A clear cut organisation structure.
(iii) Top management involvement.
(iv) Motivation of employees.
(v) Full communication.
(vi) Accounting system which supports control

Controls Require Plans : Control pre-supposes feed forward, that is, the objectives, plans, policies and standards have been developed and communi-

* Glenn A. Walsh : Budgeting, Profit Planning and Control (New Delhi : Prentice hall of India Private Limited) 1976 Indian reprint.

cated to those managers who have performance responsibility for their accomplishment. Consequently, effective control necessarily must rest upon a firm foundation of management planning. In the absence of it there is no way that managers can determine whether their organisational units are accomplishing what is desired and expected unless they first know what is expected.

Top Management Involvement : The effective and efficient implementation and administration of management control system depends to a great extent on top management attitude and involvement in the system.* Top management involvement entails managerial support, confidence, participation and timely action by top management in the implementation and administration of the management control system. The whole control system will be a failure if it receives just a light hearted treatment at the hands of top management. Any slackness of top management towards the system will have its reflection in the indifferent attitude and half- hearted commitment of executives towards the administration of the control system. Hence to solicit full commitment and co-operation of executives towards the system, it is very essential that the top management takes such action which rewards good performance and removes the causes of poor performance. Further, the management should impress on their subordinates that they have been fair in their actions.

Motivation of Employees : The term 'motivation' here refers to mental disposition of employees towards the control system. Dalton and others** have stated that the controls are usually disliked. So it is considered that no control system can be effective if concerned managers are not motivated to the system. The following is a list of measures the managers have found helpful in eliciting a positive response to controls :

1. Maintaining dispassionate view of control.

2. Encouraging subordinate's participation in setting standards. This will minimise the usual negative reaction of employees towards a control system.

3. Maintaining internal consistency between the standards desir management and the standard as perceived by the subordinates under diffe separate control systems.

4. Using "Fact Control" (i.e., the emphasis should be on the facts in situation, rather than on the pressure of a supervising executive that should call for the necessary corrective action).

---

* Braj Raj Mohanty : "Implementation and Administration of a Management Control System" (An unpublished Doctoral Dissertation submitted under Fellowship Porgramme of Indian Institute of management, Ahmedabad) 1976 edition.

** Dalton, C.W. and P.E.Lawrance: Motivation and Control (Homewood, Ill : Richard D. Irwin Inc.) 1970 edition.

5 Being sensitive to personal needs and social pressure in the administration of controls.

6. Devising incentive system which takes into account the individual difference in their needs and reactions to various forms of incentives.

7. The control system should encourage goal congruence, that is, it should be so structured that the goals of the people in the organisation are as far as feasible consistent with the goals of the organisation as a whole.

8. The employees should be impressed that the idea behind the management control is not to dominate subordinates but to guide and direct their efforts to achieve the pre-determined goals and objectives.

9. A control system should be designed in a way that it minimises the usual negative reaction to controls and provides constructive help to individuals in meeting their accepted goals. To achieve this goal the management must set not only acceptable standards but evolve right criteria of performance measurement, measures of output correctly and provide prompt and direct feedback. All these will help the management in inspiring employees to co-operate with the system voluntarily.

Proper Communication System : Communication is a process of imparting ideas and getting one self understood by others. To be assured of good control, a system of regular formal reporting should be in existence. Every manager should give attention to whether the report system in his department and company provides the right kind of information, to the right people and at the right time to enable him to control the work effectively.

Accounting System for Control : A good accounting system is the backbone of a management control system as it is a major source of data generation for control purposes. The accounting system should be so devised that it assists in the formation and implementation of management objectives.

Diagram 6.2 clearly demonstrates the design of the accounting system for planning and control. The right hand side of the diagram shows that accounting formalises plans for expressing them in the language of figures as budgets. Accounting formalises control (i.e., action and evaluation) as performance reports compare results with plans and spotlight deviations from plans. The system should generate such information that encourages managers to act in harmony with the overall objectives of organisation.* The principal task of accounting for management control is to draw attention towards shortcomings

---

* Charles T. Horgren : Accounting for Management Control - An Introduction, Page 6 (New Delhi : Prentice - Hall of India Private Limited) 1976 edition.

from planned performances, to provide clues and to fix the responsibility for the same with the object of bringing business activities on right lines.

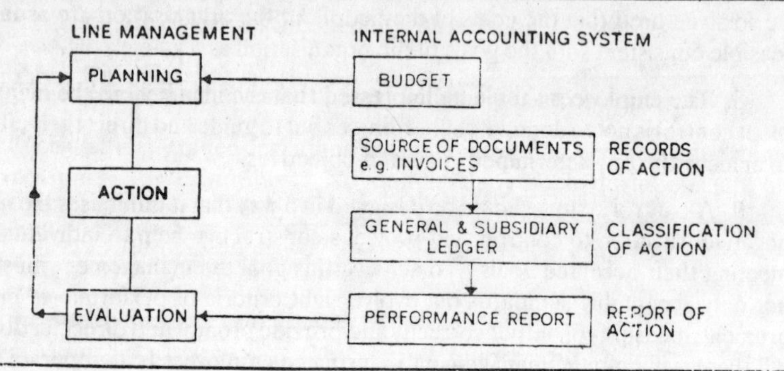

Fig. 6.2 Accounting Framework for Planning and Control

This is done through designing the accounting system in such a way as to keep the records of resources actually consumed and output actually achieved both products of programme and responsibility centre-wise and report the accurate and relevant data for measuring, analysing the performance and assessing effectiveness and the efficiency of the head of each responsibility centre in attainment of his organisation goals.

According to William L. Farrare*, a good accounting system for control is based on concept of responsibility accounting under which the cost and revenues, assets and liabilities (where pertinent) figures are traced to the individual managers (sometimes a committee) who are responsible for making decisions about the cost in question. The essence of responsibility accounting system is the accumulation of cost and revenues according to areas of responsibility in order that deviation from standard costs and budgets can be identified with the person or group responsible. It is done through by showing controllable and non-controllable cost separately in statement of cost related to a cost centre effectively and efficiently. This helps in (1) measuring the performance and identifying shortfalls of individual managers in attaining their departmental

* William L. Farrare : Responsibility Accounting - A Basic Control Concept, Pages 152-163 (An article included in William E. Thomas, Readings in Cost Accounting, Budgeting and Control Published by South-Western Publishing Company, U.S.A.) 1970 Indian Reprint.

goals, (2) identifying the managers who need assistance for corrective action and (3) effectively utilising scarce resources.

For control purpose, the accounting system be further developed on standard cost concept, particularly in a manufacturing organisation. Under this concept the cost recorded in an account is a scientifically pre-determined cost i.e., cost which should have been as opposed to what it is. The variance account. thus on the very day of transaction recorded the comparison between actual cost and standard cost is done and loss is pointed out. Besides the above, accounting system for effective control purposes should also underlie the concept of vairable costing.

Controller and his Role in Management Control System

The control process involves two major functions, namely, the planning and control action on the one hand and the routine set- up which provides informative assistance for planning and control on the other hand. This routine set-up for supplying control information is operated by a responsible person known either as controller, chief management accounting executive or financial controller. Sachar Committee in Chapter 8 para 8.13 recommended that each company whose paid up capital is Rs. 25 lakhs or above should be statutorily required to appoint an accountant or a financial controller in addition to a cost accountant and Internal Auditor, director for planning and control or a budget officer or a budget director. The controller's responsibility usually encompasses all phases of accounting including Income-taxes and routine reporting to outside parties. But accounting techniques for planning and control are his main tools for helping managers to get things done. The controller is a staff authority with responsibility for providing the managers and also other staff managers with specialised services.* The point is that the controller does not do any controlling in terms of line authority, except over his own departmental staff whether working in the central set-up or in different wings of the organisation. In other words he is not entrusted with any authority to control in a sense a production or a sales executive is vested with. The role of controller is to assist the management in completing the events in conformity with the plans.

The functions of controller in a management control system include the following :

(i) to ensure that the data are collected from all the input centres in time.

(ii) to see that data are processed speedily and expeditiously for developing performance reports.

(iii) to review reports at successive levels to identify remedial actions.

* There are three types of authority : Line, staff and functional. Line authority is exerted downward over subordinates. Staff authority is the authority to advise but not command others. It is exercised laterally or upward. Functional authority is the right to command action laterally and downward with regard to specific function or speciality.

(iv) to analyse the reports with a view to identifying trends and highlighting the areas requiring follow up action.

(v) to assist in formulating corrective actions.

Besides above accounting routines, which of course provide the figures for the control system, a controller has to co-ordinate different functions in the process of operating the control system. He is also entrusted with various types of work relating to accounting, control and finance. The Financial Executive Institute of United States of America lists the functions of controller as follows.*

(i) Planning for control.

(ii) Reporting and Interpreting.

(iii) Evaluating and consulting.

(iv) Tax administration.

(v) Government reporting.

(vi) Protection of assets through internal control, internal audit.

(vii) Insurance coverage.

(viii) Economic appraisal.

Planning for Control : It means to establish, co-ordinate and administer as an integral part of management, an adequate plan for the control of operations. Such a plan would provide to the extent required in the business profit planning programmes for capital investing and for financing sales forecasts, expense budgets and cost standards, together with the necessary procedures to implement the plans.

Reporting and Interpreting : It seeks to compare performance with operating plans and standards and to report and interpret the results of operations to all levels of management and to the owners of the business. This function includes the formulation of accounting policy, the co-ordination of systems and procedures, the preparation of operating data and special reports as required.

Evaluating and Consulting : It refers to consulting with all segments of management responsible for policy or action concerning any phase of the operation of the business as it relates to the attainment of objectives and the effectiveness of policies, organisational structure and procedures.

Tax Administration : It aims to establish and administer the policies and procedures for taxes.

---

* William E. Thomas : Readings in Cost Accounting, Budgeting and Control, Page 344 (Bombay : D.B. Tarporeval Sons & Co. Private Ltd.) 1970 Indian Reprint.

Government Reporting : It means to supervise or co-ordinate the preparation of reports to Government agencies.

Protection of Assets : It aims to assure the protection of the assets of the business through internal control, internal auditing, and proper insurance coverage.

Economic Appraisal : It appraises continuously economic and social forces and government policies and interprets their effect upon the business.

Diagram 6.3 as given below shows how a controller's department may be organised to carry out the functions entrusted to the controller.

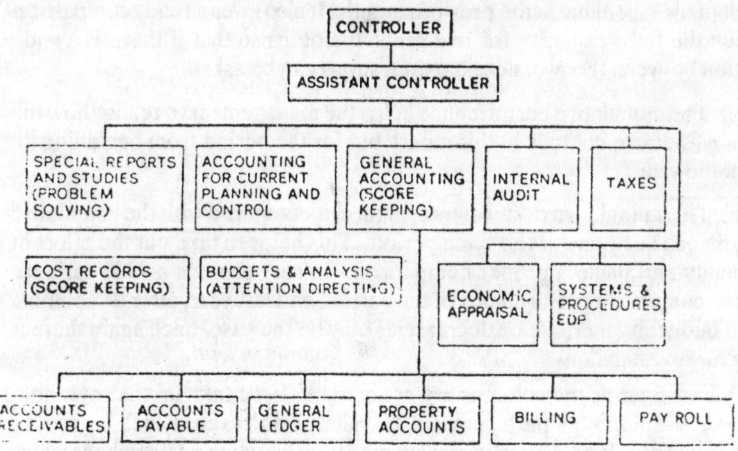

Fig. 6.3 Organisation chart of a controller's Department

Operating Performance Reporting to Top Management

Several surveys have been carried out which reveal that top management spends considerable time in (a) meetings, and (b) in reading reports. This is understandable, for the chief objective of top management is not execution of tasks but laying down of policy guidelines and monitoring of performance. For this purpose they need a constant flow of information on current operations which will influence decisions for the future.

What is the relevant information that the top executives of a company must receive which will assist in discharging this responsibility? The discussion that follows is limited to information relating to operating performance.

* **Charles T. Horgren : Accounting for Management Control - An Introduction, Page 6 (New Delhi : Prentice - Hall of India Private Limited) 1976 edition.**

1. Performance statement : The performance statement indicates the working result for a designated period, usually a month. An example of such a statement is indicated in Table I Some of the important features of this statement are :

(a) It lists both budgeted and actual performance, and the variance thereof indicating, thereby, how much the company has deviated from the plan.

(b) Simultaneously, it also records alongside the previous month's performance as well as the cumulative performance till date.

(c) The previous month's performance serves to determine whether any shortfall in the last month has been made up or any shortfall in this month is as a result of over-booking in the previous month. It also gives a ready comparison between the fixed expenses for two running months so that if there is a wide deviation between the two, necessary questions can be asked.

(d) The cumulative performance helps the management to realise how the company is doing, not only in this month but for the period from beginning till date of the year.

(e) This cumulative performance, in turn, is compared with the cumulative performance last year for the same period. This helps to take out the effect of seasonality and make a proper comparison. In case there is a wide variance between cumulative performance of the current and last year, after discounting for the budgetary increase or decrease as may be the case, once again there is a case for investigation.

This is so far as the columns are concerned. If we take up the rows now, the report is spilt into 4 parts, namely, (i) sales performance which is given by the sales revenue, both domestic and export, (ii) production performance which is indicated by contribution and factory indirect and direct costs, (iii) administrative performance indicated by administration and selling expenses, and (iv) financial performance indicated by the interest costs.

The idea of separating these is that it helps in quickly and exactly pinpointing which operational area is responsible for deviation from the budget and to what extent. This, in turn, will facilitate taking of corrective action.

NOTE : The format will, of course, be duly modified for an individual organisation depending on what particular item of revenue or expense is important to merit an individual mention instead of being grouped under a category head.

2. Cash flow statement : Next to the performance statement, the most important information is the cash flow statement - Table II. This is a very important document, though it is rarely that people look at it or are even informed about it. The month's cash flow statement updated every week should be flashed to the senior executives which will tell them how operations stand. merely getting profits on books without realising it in terms of cash is of little use.

In the cash flow statement, the cash inflow part is based on the expected collections for the month as well as any other sources of income, while the cash outflow is based on fixed expenses/outgoings, as well as payment due to suppliers. This statement would indicate on a week-to-week basis whether the cash flow position is under control or whether the company is going to face a liquidity crunch.

Whenever there are any pointers to the latter kind of situation developing it is necessary that immediate attention of the concerned department heads be focussed on the problem so that necessary action can be taken to forestall such an eventuality. In drawing up this statement, in the first instance, a draft statement should be made that lists all normally expected revenues plus all payments normally due and expenses that are planned for or need to be incurred.

If, on the basis of this statement, it is found that there is a cash short fall (i.e., a negative cash flow) then either credit may be taken for additional funds to be brought in (by borrowing, sale of some disposable asset etc.) or planned but non-mandatory expenses pruned down or (as is usually done) withholding certain payments that are due. A final cash flow statement for the month may be drawn up where the "expected" revenue and expense columns lists the additional revenue expected or the curtailed expense payment planned to be incurred made.

It might be pertinent here to mention that a good cash flow position does not imply excess of cash; in fact too much of cash lying idle is also undesirable. If or any reason there appears to be such a possibility developing, the senior management must consider immediately what short-term investment avenues are open to them to earn the maximum out of this excess temporary cash.

3. Capital equipment commitments and procurement : Another statement that must be seen by the senior management is the capital equipment commitments and procurement monitor. At the beginning of each financial year of the company, a capital equipment budget is made. Interalia, this budget lists three important figures, namely, (a) the total carry forward amount of sanctioned commitment and cash flow from the previous year, (b) the fresh additional commitment and cash flow for the current year, and (c) the total commitment and cash flow for the current year. Therefore, what must be watched by the senior management in the capital equipment report is to see whether (a) the sanctioned equipment has been ordered in time or not; (b) if ordered, whether it has been delivered in time or not; (c) if delivered, whether it has been installed, and (d) if installed, whether it is working satisfactorily (see Tables IIIA and IIIB).

It is most important to monitor this, equipment by equipment at the senior most levels. Of course, some line may be drawn in terms of value, but basically, capital equipment represents the heart of any investment that a company makes and it is important and necessary for the senior management to be concerned in its entirety with its timely installation, proper and efficient use, and regular maintenance.

Very often it has been seen in large organisation, that machine tools, plant and equipment get ordered without much careful scrutiny, chiefly because of the value limits that are sanctioned for their approvals. Thus, a large number of relatively low value equipment gets ordered because it is not necessary to obtain approval for their procurement from the seniormost of corporate level of management. Operating managers often tend to misuse, or casually exercise the discretionary value-limits below which they are not required to seek approval in ordering any kind of equipment which takes their fancy. This is why, even though for reasons of operating autonomy some discretion must be given, equally, for ensuring proper deployment of funds, this discretion must be monitored at the highest level.

Secondly, there are often, instances when machinery is procured but is not being used due to a variety of reasons, ranging from faulty equipment; poor servicing, change in production plan, dropping of project that calls for this equipment, insufficient power, and so on and so forth.

It is obvious, therefore, that it is not sufficient for top management to monitor the ordering of the equipment or even its timely installation. What the top management must ensure is, whether the newly ordered equipment is being used or not and if not, why not; and if the answer is that it cannot be used in the foreseeable future, for any reason whatsoever then immediate disposal action must be contemplated. This is because otherwise the equipment represents an idle lock-up of funds. The recent report about jobless machines in various hospital of Bombay is a case in point.

4. Sales and Production - Quantitative Report : As will be seen from Table IV, this report lists the production of various items for the period and compares it with the budgeted, the previous month and the previous year's cumulative production for the same period. This enables one to pinpoint - productwise - the cause for variance and make investigations for necessary corrective action.

The second half of the report similarly deals with the sales of each product, further analysing it regionwise. This enables one to identify the products and the regions or branches that are responsible for the deviation from the budget. Necessary action can then follow.

There is an important reason why the sales and production reports are proposed to be presented together. It enables the reader to assess at a glance whether there is over-production of a low- selling product, or under-production of a hot-selling item. It is not uncommon to find in many companies, especially large, multi-product units, that the factory produces what they can "easily manufacture" while the marketing pushes what can "easily sell".

Further, the "easy to manufacture" products and the "easy to sell" product are not always coincident leading to accumulation of unwanted finished goods. Stock, on the one hand, and starving of the market for required goods, on the other.

Whether such a situation is arising will be immediately reflected by this statement and corrective action can immediately be initiated.

These four reports form the key to reporting to the top management. It is essential that all these four reports be sent to each and every member of the top management team. In this connection, it is to be emphasised that it is equally important that the functional heads of personnel, administration and technical activities receive these reports also.

It is all too common a practice to believe that the performance report need be seen only by the chief executive and the finance chief or at best by the marketing chief also. Similarly, the cash flow is usually seen only by the finance chief and if necessary by the chief executive. This is a practice that must be forthwith stopped. Each and every department makes a contribution to performance - some in a quantitative manner, some in an intangible manner. Some by earning revenue, all by incurring costs. But the knowledge of how a company is doing in terms of its measurable parameters will effect the input given by the supporting department, even if the latter is of an intangible nature. For example, if it is found that cash flow position is very stringent, personnel, administration and technical could all contribute by (a) stopping or delaying procurement of equipment that is not urgently required; (b) cutting back on overtime; and (c) curtailing expenses that are not of an immediate and unavoidable nature. If the sales performance is lagging in a particular area and it is due to lack of proper staff, personnel department could make a special effort for that particular area to recruit somebody, or to scan the list of existing staff to see if somebody could be transferred. If product quality has deteriorated, which is affecting sales and this is due to poor airconditioning, perhaps the administration and technical could get together. But all these things will happen

TABLE I PERFORMANCE STATEMENT FOR THE MONTH OF ——

All values in Rs. Lakhs (of thousands)

Previous month Budget	Previous month Actual		Budget	For the month Actual	For the month Variance	Budget	Cumulative Actual	Variance	Cum. same period last year	Incr/Decr over cum. acti. same period last year
		1. Sales								
		1.1 Domestic								
		1.2 Export								
		1.3 Sub-total								
		1.4 Add Closing Stock								
		1.5 Sub-total								
		1.6 Less Opening Stock								
		1.8 Less Commission								
		1.9 NET REVENUE								
		2. DIRECT COST								
		2.1 Direct Materials								
		2.2 Power & Fuel								
		2.3 Sub-total								
		3. CONTRIBUTION (1.9 - 2.3)								
Budget	Actual	4. MFG. COSTS								
		4.1 Direct Exp. at Factory								
		4.2 Indirect Exp. at Factory								
		4.3 Depreciation								
		4.4 Sub-total								
		5. GROSS MARGIN (3-4.4)								
		6. GENL. ADMN. & SELLING EXP.								
		6.1 Genl. Admn. Exp.								
		6.2 Sub-total								
		7. NET MARGIN (5-6.3)								
		8. FINANACIAL EXPENSES								
		9. PROFIT BEFORE TAX (7-8)								

(FOR TABLES II, IIIA, IIIB, IVA, IVB SEE APPENDIX AT THE END OF THE BOOK) only if these service departments are also fed by (a) the profit performance, and (b) the reason for it being what it is.

It must not be forgotten that profits are earned as a result of revenue received minus expenses incurred in earning that revenue. And while only a few departments bring in revenue, all departments incur expenses which influence the earning, viz., profits. Thus it is necessary that each and every functional head must be kept fully informed of the profit performance and how the department has contributed to it.

To summarise, top management need four essential reports for monitoring operating performance, namely, (i) performance statement, (ii) monthly cash flow statement, (iii) capital equipment procurement monitor and (iv) sales and production quantitative report.

These reports must be seen by all members of the top management team and the deviations from budget performance discussed every month, jointly, for taking timely corrective action to steer the performance back to the annual plan.

REVIEW QUESTIONS

1. What do you know about 'Management control systems'?
2. Explain the nature and contents of management control reports?
3. What are the pre-requisites of a successful and effective management control system?
4. What are the functions of a controller? Examine his role in management control system

7
Systems Theory and Management

The systems concept can be a useful way of thinking about the job of managing. It provides a framework for visualising internal and external environmental factors as an integrated whole. It allows recognition of the proper place and function of subsystems. The systems within which businessmen must operate are necessarily complex. However, management via systems concepts fosters a way of thinking which, on the the one hand, helps to dissolve some of the complexity and, on the other hand, helps the manager recognise the nature of the complex problems and thereby operate within the perceived environment. It is important to recognise the integrated nature of specific systems, including the fact that each system has both inputs and outputs and can be viewed as a self-contained unit. But it is also important to recognise that business systems are a part of larger systems - possibly industry-wide, or including several, may be many, companies and/or industries, or even society as a whole. Further, business systems are in a constant state of change - they are created, operated, revised, and often eliminated.

System

The term 'system' is in common use. One speaks of an educational system, computer system and many others. A system is composed of integrating parts that operate together to achieve some objective or purpose. In other words, a system is not a randomly assembled set of elements, but consists of elements which can be identified as belonging together because of a common purpose, goal, or objective. Systems can be abstract and physical deterministic and probabilistic and closed and open. An abstract system is an orderly arrangement of interdependent ideas or constructs. A physical system is a set of elements which operate together to accomplish an objective. A deterministic system operates in a perfectly predicable manner. The inter action among the parts is known with certainty. The probabilistic system can be described in terms of probable behaviour, but a certain degree of error is always attached to the prediction of what the system will do e.g., an inventory system. A closed system does not exchange material, information, or energy with its environment but an open system exchange information, material, or energy with the environment e.g., biological systems such as man.

Definition of Systems

A system is "an organised or complex whole; an assemblage or combination of things or parts forming a complex or unitary whole". The term system covers an extremely broad spectrum of concepts. For example, we have mountain systems, river systems, and the solar system as part of our physical surroundings. The body itself is a complex organism including the skeletal system, the circulatory system, and the nervous system. We come into daily contact with such phenomena as transportation systems, communication systems (telephone, telegraph, etc.), and economic systems.

The antonym of systematic is chaotic. A chaotic situation might be described as one where "everything depends on everything else". Since two major goals of science and research in any subject area are explanation and prediction, such a condition cannot be tolerated. Therefore there is considerable incentive to develop bodies of knowledge that can be organised into a complex whole, within which subparts or subsystems can be interrelated. Before proceeding to a discussion of systems theory for business, it will be beneficial to explore recent attempts to establish a general systems theory covering all disciplines of scientific areas.

Elements of the System : Five basic elements are worthy of examination :

1. The total system's **objectives**, and the related performance measures. A common fallacy in stating objectives is to emphasize the obvious, since it is no easier to determine a system's real objectives than it is to determine those of an individual. As a result, the controller must move from a vague statement of objectives to a more precise and specific set of measures of performance for the overall system.

2. The **environment** must be studied once objectives and performance measures have been determined, since this sets fixed constraints. The environment determines to a large extent how the system will perform, but, by definition, its characteristics are beyond the system's immediate control.

3. The system's **resources** (or inputs) enable it to perform its role. The system has control over these, and information systems can therefore be constructed to record all the relevant data for decision-making purposes-including lost opportunities, since these indicate lessons from utilising resources for one purpose rather than another. Balance sheets and profit and loss accounts exclude certain resources (e.g., personnel factors) and foregone alternatives, thereby rendering them inadequate as complete statements of system resources.

4. The **sub-systems**, or **components**, of the total system must be delineated, and measures of performance, activities, and goals determined. Traditional thinking has been limited to departments or divisions as sub-systems, but the 'Production Department' is not necessarily the same thing as the 'Production Sub-system'. It is more logical to think in terms of missions (i.e., the rational breakdown of tasks that the sub-systems must perform). Only in this way can

a sub-system's contribution be measured, and the controller will be involved in clearly specifying cost centres that are congruent with the systems approach. The aim should not be the simple accumulation of costs, as this is another measure of inputs, but should be a measure of how the output contributes to the goals of the system.

5. All the previous factors, along with the **generation of system plans,** are aspects of the management of the system. Not only must the firm's management devise the plans, it must also be ensured that the system is carrying them out. It is the definition of objectives, the allocation of resources, and the degree of adjustment necessary to co-ordinate the multiple purposes of the numerous systems and sub-systems in a firm that make the task of management so difficult and exacting.

General Systems Theory

General systems theory is concerned with developing a systematic, theoretical framework for describing general relationships of the empirical world. A broad spectrum of potential achievements for such a framework is evident. Existing similarities in the theoretical construction of various disciplines can be pointed out. Models can be developed which have applicability to many fields of study. An ultimate but distant goal will be a framework (or system of systems) which could tie all disciplines together in a meaningful relationship.

There has been some development of interdisciplinary studies. Areas such as social psychology, biochemistry, astrophysics, social anthropology, economic psychology, and economic sociology have been developed in order to emphasise the inter-relationships of previously isolated disciplines. More recently, areas of study and research have been developed which call on numerous subfields. For example, cybernetics, the science of communication and control, calls on electrical engineering, neurophysiology, physics, biology, and other fields. Operations research is often pointed to as a multidisciplinary approach to problem solving. Information theory is another discipline which calls on numerous subfields. Organisation theory embraces economics, sociology, engineering, psychology, physiology, and anthropology. Problem solving and decision making are becoming focal points for study and research, drawing on numerous disciplines.

With these examples of interdisciplinary approaches, it is easy to recognise a surge of interest in larger-scale, systematic bodies of knowledge. However, this trend calls for the development of an over-all framework within which the various subparts can be integrated. In order that the **interdisciplinary** movement does not degenerate into **undisciplined** approaches, it is important that some structure be developed to integrate the various separate disciplines while retaining the type of discipline which distinguishes them. One approach to providing an over-all framework (general systems theory) would be to pick out phenomena common to many different disciplines and to develop general models which would include such phenomena. A second approach would include the structuring of a hierarchy of levels of complexity for the basic units of behaviour in the various empirical fields. It would also involve development of a level of abstraction to represent each stage.

We shall explore the second approach, a hierarchy of levels, in more detail since it can lead toward a system of systems which has application in most business and other organisations. The reader can undoubtedly call to mind examples of familiar systems at each level of Boulding's classification model.

1. The first level is that of static structure. It might be called the level of **frameworks**; for example, the anatomy of the universe.

2. The next level is that of the simple dynamic system with predetermined, necessary motions. This might be called the level of **clockworks**.

3. The control mechanism or cybernetic system, which might be nicknamed the level of the **thermostat**. The system is self regulating in maintaining equilibrium.

4. The fourth level is that of the "open system", or self- maintaining structure. This is the level at which life begins to differentiate from not-life; it might be called the level of the **cell.**

5. The next level might be called the genetic-societal level; it is typified by the **plant**, and it dominates the empirical world of the botanist.

6. The animal system level is characterised by increased mobility, teleological behaviour, and self-awareness.

7. The next level is the "human" level, that is, of the individual human being considered as a system with self-awareness and the ability to utilise language and symbolism.

8. The social system or systems of human organisation constitute the next level, with the consideration of the content and meaning of messages, the nature and dimensions of value systems, the transcription of images into historical record, the subtle symbolisations of art, music and poetry, and the complex gamut of human emotion.

9. Transcendental systems complete the classification of levels. These are the ultimates and absolutes and the inescapables and unknowables, and they also exhibit systematic structure and relationship.

With the general theory and its objectives as background, let us, direct our attention to a more specific theory for business, a systems theory which can serve as a guide for management scientists and ultimately provide the framework for integrated decision making on the part of practicing managers.

Systems Theory for Business

The biologist Ludwig von Bertalanffy has emphasised the part of general systems theory which he calls open system. The basis of his concept is that a living organism is not a conglomeration of separate elements but a definite system, possessing organisation and wholeness. An organism is an open system which maintains a constant state while matter and energy which enter it keep changing (so-called dynamic equilibrium). The organism is influenced by, and influences, its environment and reaches a state of dynamic equilibrium in this environment. Such a description of a system adequately fits the typical business organisation. The business organisation is a man-made system which has a dynamic interplay with its environment - customers, competitors, labour organisations, suppliers, government, and many other agencies. Furthermore, the business organisation is a system of interrelated parts working in conjunction with each other in order to accomplish a number of goals, both those of the organisation and those of individual participants.

A common analogy is the comparison of the organisation to the human body, with the skeletal and muscle systems representing the operating line elements and the circulatory system as a necessary staff function. The nervous system is the communication system. The brain symbolises top-level management, or the executive committee. In this sense an organisation is represented as a self-maintaining structure, one which can reproduce. Such an analysis hints at the type of framework which would be useful as a systems theory for business - one which is developed as a system and that can focus attention at the proper points in the organisation for rational decision making, both from the standpoint of the individual and the organisation.

The scientific-management movement utilised the concept of a man-machine system but concentrated primarily at the shop level. The so called "efficiency experts" attempted to establish procedures covering the work situation and providing an opportunity for all those involved to benefit - employees, managers, and owners. The human relationists, the movement stemming from the Hawthorne-Western Electric studies, shifted some of the focus away from the man-machine system per se to interrelationships among individuals in the organisations. Recognition of the effect of interpersonal relationships, human behaviour, and small groups resulted in a relatively widespread reevaluation of managerial approaches and techniques.

The concept of the business enterprise as a social system also has received considerable attention in recent years. The social- system school looks upon management as a system of cultural interrelationships. The concept of a social system draws heavily on sociology and involves recognition of such elements as formal and informal organisation within a total integrated system. Moreover, the organisation or enterprise is recognised as subject to external pressure from the cultural environment. In effect, the enterprise system is recognised as a part of a larger environmental system.

Since World War II, operations research techniques have been applied to large, complex systems of variables. They have been helpful in shop scheduling, in freightyard operations, cargo handling, airline scheduling, and other similar problems. Queuing models have been developed for a wide variety of traffic- and service-type situations where it is necessary to programme the optimum number of "servers" for the expected "customer" flow. Management-science techniques have undertaken the solution of many complex problems involving a large number of variables. However, by their very nature, these techniques must structure the system for analysis by quantifying system elements. This process of abstraction often simplifies the problem and takes it out of the real world. Hence the solution of the problem may not be applicable in the actual situation.

Simple models of maximising behaviour no longer suffice in analysing business organisations. The relatively mechanical models apparent in the "scientific management"era gave way to theories represented by the "human relations" movement. Current emphasis is developing around "decision making" as a primary focus of attention, relating communication systems, organisation structure, questions of growth (entropy and/or homeostasis),and questions of uncertainty. This approach recognises the more complex models of administrative behaviour and should lead to more encompassing systems that provide the framework within which to fit the results of specialised investigations of management scientists.

The aim of systems theory for business is to develop an objective, understandable environment for decision making; that is, if the system within which managers make the decisions can be provided as an explicit framework, then such decision making should be easier to handle. But what are the elements of this systems theory which can be used as a framework for integrated decision making? Will it require wholesale change on the part of organisation structure and administrative behaviour? or can it be woven into existing situations. Organisations will remain recognisable. Simon* makes this point when he says :

1. Organisations will still be constructed in three layers; an underlying system of physical production and distribution processes, a layer of programmed (and probably largely automated) decision processes for governing the routine day-to-day operation of the physical system, and a layer of nonprogrammed decision process (carried on in a man-machine system) for monitoring the first-level processes, redesigning them, and changing parameter values.

2. Organisation will still be hierarchical in form. The organisation will be divided into major subparts, each of these into parts, and so on, in familiar forms of departmentalisation. The exact basis for drawing departmental lines may change somewhat. Product divisions may become even more important than they are today, while the sharp lines of demarcation among purchasing, manufacturing, engineering, and sales are likely to fade.

We agree essentially with this picture of the future. However, we want to emphasise the notion of systems as set forth in several layers. Thus the systems that are likely to be emphasised in the future will develop from projects or programmes, and authority will be vested in managers whose influence will cut across traditional departmental lines.

There are certain key subsystems and/or functions essential in every business organisation which make up the total information- decision systems, and which operate in a dynamic environmental system subject to rapid change. The subsystems include :

1. A **sensor subsystem** designed to measure changes within the system and with the environment.
2. An **information** processing subsystem such as an accounting, or data processing system.
3. A **decision-making** subsystem which receives information inputs and outputs planning messages.
4. A **processing subsystem** which utilises information, energy, and materials to accomplish certain tasks.
5. A **control component** which ensures that processing is in accordance with planning. Typically this provides feedback control.
6. A **memory or information storage subsystem** which may take the form of records, manuals, procedures, computer programmes, etc.

A goal setting unit will establish the long range objectives of the organisation, and the performance will be measured in terms of sales, profits, employment, etc., relative to the total environmental system. This is general model of the systems concept in a business firm. In the following pages a more specific model illustrating the application of the systems concept is established.

An Illustrative Model of the Systems Concept

Traditionally, business firms have not been structured to utilise the systems concept. In adjusting the typical business structure of fit within the framework of management by system, certain organisational changes may be required. It is quite obvious that no one organisation structure can meet operational requirements for every company. Each organisation must be designed as a unique system. However, the illustrative model set forth would be generally operable for medium to large-size companies which have a number of major products and a variety of management functions. The primary purpose of this model is to illustrate the application of systems concepts to business organisations and the possible impact upon the various management functions of planning, organising, communication and control. The relationships which would exist among the top management positions are shown in Figure 7.1

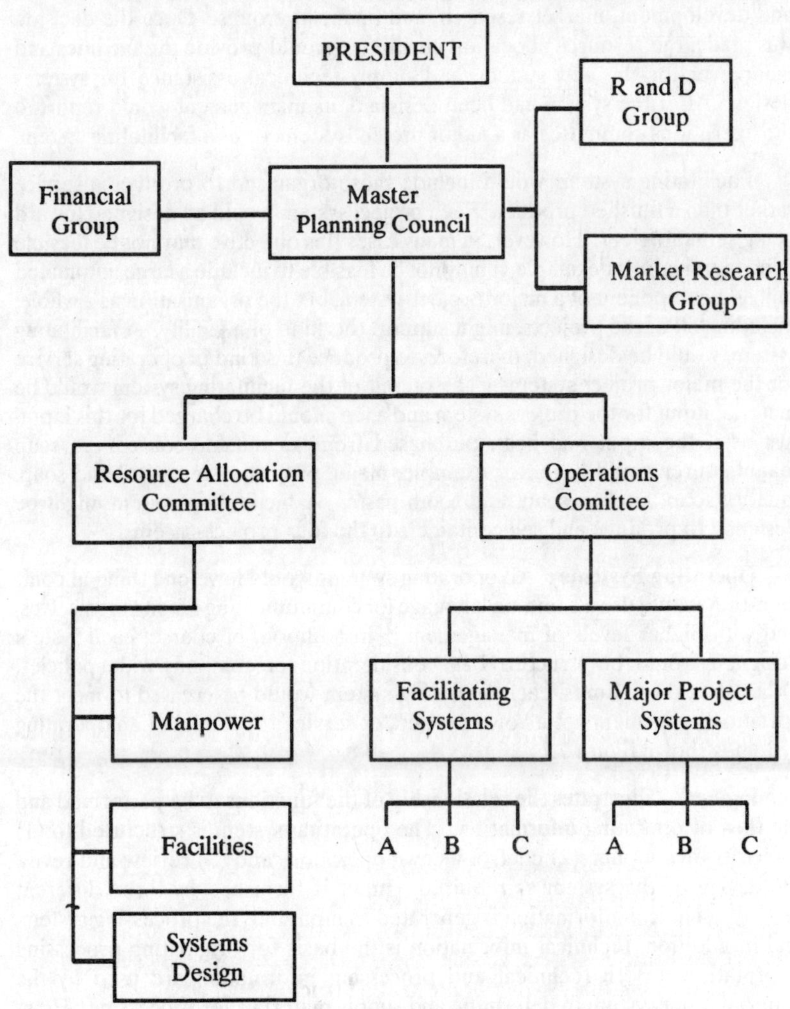

Fig. 7.1 The Systems Model : Top Management

The master planning council would relate the business to its environmental system, and it would make decisions relative to the products or services the company produced. Further, this council would establish the limits of an operating programme, decide on general policy matters relative to the design of operating systems, and select the director for each new project. New project decisions would be made with the assistance and advice of the project research and development, market research, and financial groups. Once the decision was made, the resource allocation committee would provide the facilities and manpower for the new system, and supply technical assistance for systems design. After the system had been designed, its management would report to the operations committee as a major project system, or as a facilitating system.

Facilitating systems would include those organised to produce a service rather than a finished product. Each project system would be designed toward being self-sufficient. However, in many cases this objective may not be feasible or economical. For example, it may not be feasible to include a large automated mill as a component of a major project system, but the organisation as a whole, including all of the projects, might support this kind of a facility. A facilitating system, would be designed, therefore, to produce this kind of operating service for the major project systems. The output of the facilitating system would be material input for the project system and a fee should be charged for this input, just as if the input had been purchased from an outside source. A soap manufacturer could have, for example, major project systems in hand soap, laundry soap, kitchen soap, and tooth paste. A facilitating system might be designed to produce and sell containers to the four project systems.

Operating Systems : All operating systems would have one thing in common-they would use a common language for communicating among themselves, and with higher levels of management. In addition, of course, each system designed would be structured in consideration of company-wide policies. Other than these limits, each operating system would be created to meet the specific requirements of its own product or service. A model of an operating system is shown figure 7.2

Figure 7.2 illustrates the relationship of the functions to be performed and the flow of operating information. The operating system is structured to (1) direct its own inputs, (2) control its own operation, and (3) review and revise the design of the system as required. Input is furnished by three different groups: technical information is generated as input into the processing system, and in addition, technical information is the basis for originating processing information. Both technical and processing information are used by the material input system to determine and supply materials for processing. However, corrective action, when necessary, would be activated by input allocation.

This model can be related to most business situations. For example, if this represented a system to produce television sets, the technical information would refer to the design of the product, processing information would include the plan of manufacture and schedule, and the material input would pertain to the raw materials and purchased parts used in the processing. These inputs of information and material would be process and become output. Process control would measure the output in comparison to the standard (Information Storage) obtained from input allocation, and issue corrective information whenever the system failed to function according to plan. The design of the system would be reviewed continually and the components rearranged or replaced when these changes would improve operating efficiency.

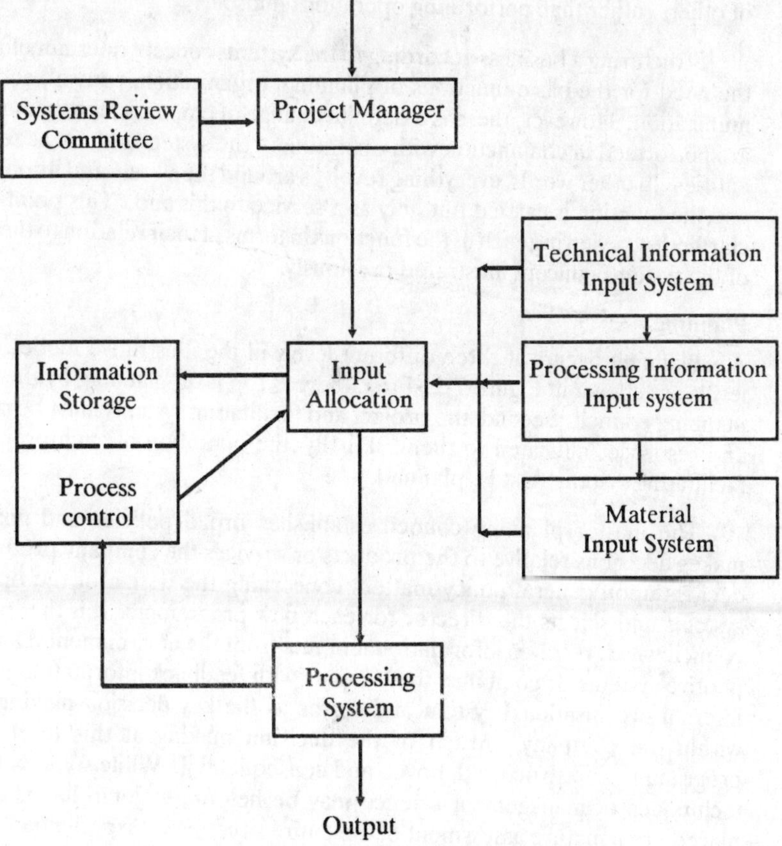

Fig. 7.2 An Operating System Model

Basically, the operating systems would be self sustaining with a high degree of autonomy. Therefore, they could be integrated into the over-all organisational structure (Figure 7.1) with a minimum of difficulty.

Systems Concepts And Management

Managers are needed to convert the disorganised resources of men, machines, and money into a useful and effective enterprise. Essentially, management is the process whereby these unrelated resources are integrated into a total **system for objective accomplishment**. A manager gets things done by working with people and physical resources in order to accomplish the objectives of the system. He co-ordinates and integrates the activities and work of others rather than performing operations himself.

Structuring a business according to the systems concept does not eliminate the need for the basic functions of planning, organisation, control, and communication. However, there is a definite change of emphasis, for the functions are performed in conjunction with operation of the system and not as separate entities. In other words, everything revolves around the system and its objective, and the function is carried out only as a service to this end. This point can be clarified by reviewing each of the functions in terms of their relation to the model of the systems concept illustrated previously.

Planning

Planning occurs at three different levels in the illustrative model. These levels are shown in Figure 7-1. First, there is top level planning by the master planning council. Second, the project and facilitating systems must be planned and resources allocated to them. Finally, the operation of each project and facilitating system must be planned.

The master planning council establishes broad policies and goals and makes decisions relative to the products or services the company produces. It decides upon general policy matters concerning the design of the operating systems and selects the director for each new programme. It is the planning council which receives informational inputs from the environmental and competitive systems. It combines these inputs with feedback information from the internal organisational system and serves as the key decision-making centre within the company. Much of the decision making at this level is non-programmed, unstructured, novel, and consequential. While some of the new techniques of management science may be helpful, major reliance must be placed upon mature assessment of the entire situation by experienced, innovative top executives.

Once these broad decisions have been made, the planning function is transferred to the resource allocation and operating committees. They plan and allocate facilities and manpower for each new system and supply technica assistance for individual systems design. At this planning level it is possible to utilise programmed decision making - operations research and computer techniques.

The third level, planning the operations of each project or facilitation system, is concerned primarily with the optimum allocation of resources to meet the requirements established by the planning council. This planning can most easily be programmed to automatic decision systems. However, the project director would still have to feed important non-quantifiable inputs into the system.

Under the systems concept of planning there is a direct relationship between the planning performed at each of the three levels. The first planning level receives informational inputs from the environment and competitive system and feedback information from within the organisation. It translates this into inputs for the next planning level which in turn moves to a more detailed level of planning and provides inputs for the third or project level. One of the major advantages of this systems model is to provide a clear-cut delineation of the responsibility for various types of planning. This concept facilitates integrated planning on a systems basis at the project level within the organisation. Given the inputs (premises, goals, and limitations) from the higher levels the project managers are delegated the function of integrated planning for their project.

Organisation

Traditional organisation theory emphasised parts and segments of the structure and is concerned with the separation of activities into tasks or operational units. It does not give sufficient emphasis to the interrelationships and integration of activities. Adapting the business organisation to the systems concept places emphasis upon the integration of all activities toward the accomplishment of over-all objectives but also recognises the importance of efficient subsystem performance.

The systems basis of organisation differs significantly from traditional organisation structures such as line and staff or line, staff, and functional relationships. As shown in Figure 7.1, there are three major organisational levels, each with clearly delineated functions. The master planning council has broad planning, control, and integrative functions; the resource allocation committee has the primary function of allocating manpower and facilities, and aids in systems design for the facilitating or project systems. One of the major purposes of this type organisation is to provide an integration of activities at the most important level - that is the individual project or programme.

Staff specilisation of skills is provided for the master planning council through such groups as financial, research and development, and market research. Their activities, however, are integrated and co-ordinated by the planning council. There are specialists at the operating level who are completely integrated into each project system. Thus, the activities of these specialists are geared to the effective and efficient performance of the individual project system. This type organisation minimises a major problem associated with staff and functional personnel - their tendency to associate their activities with specialised areas rather than with the optimum performance of the over-all operation. Yet, under the model the importance of initiative and innovation are recognised. In fact, the major function of the master planning council is planning and innovation. Specific provision for receiving information inputs from product and market research are provided in the model.

One of the great advantages of the systems concept for organising pertains to the decentralisation of decision making and the more effective utilisation of the allocated resources to the individual project system. This has the merit of achieving accountability for performance through the measurability of individual systems of operation.

Control

The systems concept features control as a means of gaining greater flexibility in operation, and, in addition, as a way of avoiding planning operations when variables are unknown. It is designed to serve the operating system as a subsystem of the larger operation. Its efficiency will be measured by how accurately it can identify variations in systems operation from standard or plan, and how quickly it can report the need for correction to the activating group.

We must conclude that error is inevitable in a system which is subject to variations in input. When the lag in time between input and output is great, more instability is introduced. Feedback can reduce the time lag; however, corrective action which is out of phase will magnify rather than overcome the error. Every system should be designed to make its own corrections when necessary. That is, a means should be provided to reallocate resources as conditions change. In our model the Systems Review Committee (see Figure 7.2) should be aware of any change in operating conditions which might throw the system "out of control". Replanning or redesign may be required.

In controlling a system it is important to measure inputs of information, energy, and materials; and outputs of products and/or services. This will determine operating efficiency. In addition it may be important to establish points of measurement during critical or significant stages of processing. Such measurements would be used principally to help management to analyse and evaluate the operation and design of individual components. The best approach is to spotlight exceptions and significant changes. Management can focus their attention on these areas. One important thing to remember is that the control group is not a part of the processing system - it is a subsystem, serving the operating system. Cost control can be used as an example to illustrate this point. The cost accountant must understand that his primary objective is to furnish managers with information to control costs. His task is to inform, appraise, and support; never to limit, censure, or veto. The same principle applies to every control group serving the operating system.

Communication

Communication plays a vital role in the implementation of the systems concept. It is the connecting and integrating link among the systems network. The flow of information, energy and material - the elements of any processing system - are co-ordinated via communication systems. As shown in the model (Figure 7-2) the operating system requires information transmission to ensure control. Communication systems should be established to feedback information on the various flows - information, energy, and material. Information on the effectiveness of the planning and scheduling activities (as an example of information flow) would be helpful in adjusting the nature of this activity for the future. Similarly, reports on absenteeism are examples of communication concerning the energy flow (the people in the system) to the processing activity. Information on acceptance inspections an example of information stemming from the material flow aspect of an operating system. All to these feedback communication systems provide for information flow to a sensor and a control group. Comparison between the information received and the information stored (the master plan for this particular operating system) would result in decisions concerning the transmission of corrective information to the appropriate points.

Relationships within and among various project systems and between the levels of the system as a whole are maintained by means of information flow which also can be visualised as a control device. Moreover, any operating system maintains contact with its environment through some sensory element. Referring to Figure 7-1, the sensory elements in this case are the groups reporting to the master planning council. The master planning council makes decisions, concerning the product or service the organisation will produce, based on information gained from market research, research and development, and financial activities. In a sense, these activities function as the antenna of the organisation, maintaining communication with the external environment. The master planning council melds the information received through these activities with other premises covering the internal aspects in order to make decisions about future courses of action. Here again, communication or information flow can be visualised as a necessary element in controlling the course of action for the enterprise as a whole. Based on the feedback of information concerning the environment in general, the nature of competition, and the performance of the enterprise itself, the master planning council can continue its current courses of activity or adjust in light of developing circumstances.

Thus, communication or information flow facilitates the accomplishment of the primary managerial functions of planning, organising and controlling.

Communication by definition is a system involving a sender and a receiver, with implications of feedback control. This concept is embodied in the lowest level projects or subsystems, in all larger systems, and in the system as a whole. Information-decision systems, regardless of formal charts or manuals, often flow across departmental boundaries and are often geared to specific projects or programmes. The systems concept focuses on this approach and makes explicity the information-decision system which might be implicit in many of today's organisations.

Pervasiveness of System Concepts

Many of the most recent developments in the environment of businessmen and managers have involved systems concepts. For example, the trend toward automation involves implementation of these ideas. Automation suggests a self-contained system with inputs, outputs and a mechanism of control. Yet the concept also recognises the need to consider the environment within which the automatic system must perform. Thus the automated system is recognised as a subpart of a larger system.

The kinds of automation prevalent today range in a spectrum from sophisticated mechanisation to completely automatic, large-scale production process. Individual machines also can be programmed to perform a series of operations, with automatic materials-handling devices providing connecting links among components of the system. In such a system, each individual operation could be described as a system and could be related to a larger system covering an entire processing operation. That particular processing operating could also be part of the total enterprise system, which in turn can be visualised as a part of an environmental system. Completely automated processing systems such as oil refineries are also common place today. In such cases the entire process from input of raw material to output of finished products is automated with pre-programmed controls used to adjust the process as necessary, according to information feedback from the operation itself.

Physical distribution systems have received increasing attention on the part of manufacturers and shippers. The concepts of logistics, or materials management, have been used to emphasise the flow of materials through distribution channels. The term **rhochrematics** has been coined to connote the flow process from raw-materials sources to final consumer. In essence, these ideas embrace systems concepts because emphasis is placed on the total system of material flow rather than on functions, departments, or institutions which may be involved in the processing.

In recent years increasing attention has been focused upon massive en, gineering projects. in particular, military and spare programmes are becoming increasingly complex, thus indicating the need for integrating various elements of the total system. Manufacturing the product itself (a vehicle or other hardware) is quite complex, often involving problems of producibility with requirements of extremely high reliability. This is difficult to ensure for individual components or subsystems. In addition, each subsystem also must be reliable in its interrelationship with all other subsystems. Successful integration of sub components, and hence successful performance of a particular product, must also be integrated with other elements of the total system.

REVIEW QUESTIONS

1. Explain the term 'system' and bring out its characteristics.
2. Explain the salient features of general systems theory.
3. Explain in detail the concept of system theory as applied to business.
4. How will you apply systems concepts to functional management areas?

8

Information Theory

Meaning of Information : Information is a fact, datum, observation, perception or any other thing that adds to knowledge. The number 1,000 taken by itself is not information; it doesn't add to anyone's knowledge. The statement that 1,000 students are enrolled in a certain college is information. Information is obtained either by direct observation or by communication. Most of a manager's information is obtained by communication. Even in the simplest responsibility centre, the manager could not observe with his own senses everything that is going on, nor would he want to devote his time to doing so, even if it were possible. Instead, the manager relies on information that is communicated to him in various ways, ranging from informal conversations to formal reports.

Definition of Information : Information, as commonly understood, refer to raw data, organised data, the capacity of a communication channel, etc. In the owrds of Gordon B. Davis "Information is data that has been processed into a form that is meaningful to the receipient and is of real or perceived value in current or prospective decisions".*

The information processing system processes data in unusable form into usable data that is information to the intended receipient. In a world of uncertainty, information reduces uncertainty. It changes the porbabilities attached to expected outcomes in a decision situation and therefore has value in the decision process. Information may have several **attributes** :

(i) **True or false :** It may coincide with reality or not. If the receiver of false information believes it to be true, the effect is the same as if it were true.

(ii) **New :** It may be completely new and fresh to the receipient

(iii) **Incremental :** it may update or new increments to information already available.

(iv) **Corrective :** It may be a correction of past false information.

(v) **Confirmatory :** It may confirm existing information.

This is still valuable because it increases the receipients perception of the correctness of the information.

---

* Gordon B. Davis : Management Information System, PHI, 1990, p.22

It was John Diefold who coined the term "Information Resource Management" (RIM). The concept is that information has a value and cost. It must be preserved, protected, controlled, planned and utilised like any other valuable asset in a corporation such as money, material, equipment or people. Though this may not sound revolutionary, instances are not wanting where companies are not treating information with this understanding.

The Diefold Research Programme report on the administration of information resources states, "The ultimate goal of IRM is to put in place mechanisms to enable the company to acquire or produce the data or information it needs, of sufficient accuracy and quality, in time and with avoidable cost. This is accomplished by creating conditions whereby all levels of the organisation come to look upon information not as free goods but as a costly and valuable asset that must be treated with the same management discipline as is currently afforded to financial assets, human resources, materials assets and other resources the company utilises to achieve its aims".

The similarities between information as a source and other corporate assets are many. It possesses fundamental value like money, raw-materials or labour. It has measurable characteristics such as method, difficulty and cost of acquisition. It comes in various forms and degrees of reliability. It is to be refined and processed before it can be made use of. It is transported through many hands. Synthetic substitutes are also available. It is an expenditure which can be standardised and its cost and benefits could be analysed.

In a modern corporation, the IRM concept and function is considered important enough to warrant a separate IRM officer. He is responsibile for establishing policies and procedures for information resources. Control over information with policies as to who should have access to what information and how to avoid pilfering is also necessary. It is also possible that the management information services (MIS) incharge can have the responsibility over IRM as it is integral to the operation of MIS. The concept of IRM broadens the conventional dimensions of MIS. In fact MIS normally covers only a portion of the overall information reservoir in a corporation. As such management of information as an entity should go beyond the MIS. High efficiencies can be achieved by optimising the total inflow of information. Information can be about money, people, facilities or materials. It operates along side all of them. It is one of the inputs for the business system. Feedback from the system is also necessary for reforming or modulating the IRM.

Valuable Asset : Pervading the entire organisation must be the concept that information is a valuable resource, particularly in the management control and strategic planning areas and that it must be properly managed. This is a subtle but important change in thinking. If fact, in many ways, IRM and MIS are more than a support for the business. It is inextricably bound up with the business itself. One of the manifestations of IRM is the MIS which will have a higher reporting relationship in the organisation and will become more a part of its executive committee.

The Seventies ushered in the term information as opposed to data. Data is defined as raw numbers and files. Tó be useful to management, data must be processed into meaningful information. The term Information Systems more closely characterised the function performed by the computer or EDP manager. To this term the word "management" was then appended. It indicated the need for management involvement in the information systems. The Eighties brought about a further shift. The word system was replaced by resource, thereby shifting the emphasis not merely on managing the information but on managing the source of information itself.

Information is to be distinguished form reality (or "the state of nature" in the language of information theory). Suppose that a petroleum company is considering the purchase of drilling rights on a certain piece of property. There is in reality a certain quantity of crude oil on that property. No one knows what that quantity is, however. The petroleum company does have some information that helps it to estimate the amount of oil that probably exists-information derived from knowledge of geological formations, drilling on nearby properties, seismic explorations, and so on. This information is useful in helping the company decide whether to buy the drilling rights, but it is not, and cannot be, a perfect description of reality, which is the actual amount of crude oil that exists on the property.

Value of Information

Suppose the oil company can buy drilling rights to the property for Rs. 10 million, and it is convinced that the Rs. 10 million investment would be worth while if the property contained at least 10 million barrels of crude oil. It is uncertain as to how much oil the property does contain. It can reduce this uncertainty by obtaining additional information, for example by conducting additional seismic shots or by asking the opinion of a petroleum geologist. In order to obtain this information, it must incur additional costs. Information theory describes a technique for deciding how much the company can afford to pay for this additional information. Since the technique is usually described in the context of problems involving sampling, the amount that the company can afford to pay is called the **expected value of sample information.**

More generally, the approach can be used to describe the nature of an optimum information system in a company. In an optimum system, the difference between the expected value of sample information furnished by the system and the cost of obtaining this information is at a maximum.

There are several catches to the use of information theory in the real world, however. Catch 22 is that the expected value of information depends on the decision maker's judgment. If the petroleum company, on the basis of information now available, is already pretty well convinced that the property does contain at least 10 million barrels of crude oil, additional information is much less valuable to it than would be the case if it were more uncertain about the true state of nature, that is, the quantity of crude oil. Information theory provides a technique for probing the decision maker's own judgment as to how valuable additional information would be, but the technique requires the identification of the decision maker's **subjective probabilities** (i.e., his current belief as to the likelihood that various quantities of crude oil exist on the property) and his utiles (i.e., how strongly he feels about the necessity for making the right decision). In order to identify these amounts, a lengthy dialogue between the decision maker and the analyst is required, and its outcome is tentative at best. Thus, although the approach has the appearance of being objective, the values used in the technique actually are highly subjective.

Furthermore, the theory requires that there be a clear specification of the problem under consideration and of the nature and cost of the additional information that might be purchased as an aid in making the decision. Most business problems are not that clear cut. In the usual case, the problem is not sharply defined and there are several alternative solutions. Moreover, information is an information system is used for several purposes, and it is usually not feasible to associate a specific piece of information with a specific problem and hence compare its value with its cost.

Finally, many decision makers draw on the information that flows through an information system. The problem of quantifying the judgments of each of them as to the expected value of additional information can be insuperable.

Thus, the practical application of information theory is limited to problems like the oil well drilling rights situation described above; that is, problems in which the decision is both important enough to warrant the expenditure of much management time in quantifying the value of additional information and also specific enough so that the nature of additional information that might be obtained, the extent to which it will reduce the decision maker's uncertainty, and its cost can all be stated.*

For our purposes, this aspect of information theory provides only some useful general notions (which could perhaps be derived equally well by common sense) : The purpose of information is to reduce a decision maker's uncertainty about the "state of nature". that is, about what is the actual situation in the real world; and the value of additional information should exceed its cost.

---

* For a thorough explanation of the technique and how to apply it to such problems, see Howard Raiffa, Decision Analysis : Introductory Lectures on Choices under Uncertainty (Reading, Mass. : Addison Wesely, 1968).

Characteristics of Information

1. Purpose : Information must have purpose at the time it is transmitted, otherwise it is simply data. Information communicated may have many purposes because of the variety of activities of people employed in an organisation. The basic purposes of information are to inform, evaluate or pursuade and information is needed for identifying problems, solving problems, decision making, planning and controlling. The purpose of supplying information to machines is to give instructions to get upon.

2. Frequency : The frequency with which information is supplied affects its value. Financial statements prepared weekly may not be very useful as they show very little change, whereas annual financial statements may be very useful to the recipients as they show changes big enough to indicate hundreds. Information communication too frequently tends to act as interference and the receiver does not take it seriously. Further, the frequency with which information is transmitted depends upon the operational needs of the receiver of the information. At operating levels such as accountant, accounting information may be transmitted immediately the financial transaction takes place. At the top management level, this may not be the case as they require information on important matters which need their attention.

3. Cost : Cost is a limiting factor in obtaining information. Value of the information should be evaluated against its cost. It may be difficult to know the value of the information but even then efforts should be made to know the value before designing any information system,.

4. Reliability : Reliability is the degree of confidence the decision-maker places in the information. It is more expensive to obtain more reliable information. Reliability should be evaluated with value and best of the information and information system should be designed accordingly.

5. Continuous or Discrete : The information transmitted may be continuous or discrete in form. The accounting information to the accountant is of continuous nature whereas information given to the managers in the form of reports on sales, production, cost or financial position at different periods of time is discrete nature.

Noise : Suppose that the chief executive officer reads in a report that the actual profit of one of the divisions in the company in the preceding month was 10 percent below the budgeted profit. This message could convey to him the signal that the performance of this division was unsatisfactory; the division was not contributing as much to the company's profit goal as the budget indicated that it should. This signal might be correct, but, on the other hand, for any of a number of reasons it might not be correct; the performance of the division might in fact be perfectly satisfactory. An information system that conveys ambiguous messages of this sort is said to be noisy. Information theory provides approaches to measuring the amount of noise in an information system. These techniques have turned out to be valuable in studying ways to improve electrical systems, such as the telephone system, but they have no practical application to management systems, beyond suggesting the common sense ideas that noise is present in all such systems, that it never can be eliminated, but that measures to improve the clarity of the messages in the system as worthwhile.

Relevance : A person receives through his senses vast quantities of information, more than he possibly needs or can use, but his brain acts to filter most of it, and he is consciously aware of, and acts on, only a tiny fraction. For example, the ears of an automobile driver pick up innumerable sounds which are disregarded, but if the sound of an engine knock appears, the brain brings this message to his consciousness for appropriate action. Similarly, a business information system is constructed with the objective of filtering out unneeded information and conveying only relevant information to the decision maker. Designers of management information systems cannot know exactly what information about the organisation will be relevant. They nevertheless attempt to extract from reality that information that they believe to be relevant, to filter out irrelevant information, and to communicate various types of information to users of the system according to their perception of the needs of each user. The idea of relevance has great practical importance, particularly since the advent of the computer. It is easy to design a system that spews forth mountains of information; it is much more difficult to decide what small fraction of that information is likely to be useful.

Precision : There are two types of quantitative information : **counts and measurements.** Counts can be precise; if one counts twelve persons in a room, the number is exact, in the sense that there are not twelve and a fraction. A measurement is never precise. Measurements are always approximations. With modern radar, the distance from a point on the earth to a point on the moon can be measured within an accuracy of a few feet, but there is that margin of error of a few feet. All measurements are estimates that are accurate only within a range. Most messages in a management information system are measurements, rather than counts. All accounting information (with the trivial exception of the amount of cash in a small business) is derived from measurement. Inventory quantities may be obtained by counts, but the monetary amount of inventory is a measurement. Measurements of such items as the expenses of an accounting period are likely to be fairly rough approximations. In a management information system, there is usually a tradeoff between precision and timeliness. An estimate of sales revenue for a month that is made available on the first day of the following month is usually more useful to the manager than an estimate that reaches him two weeks later, even though the latter is more accurate because it has been double checked, reports from outlying offices have been included, and so on.

Types of Information

Information can be either **systematic or nonsystematic.** Our discussion is generally limited to information that flows through a formal system, but it is important to keep in mind the fact that a great deal of information reaches the manager from sources outside the formal system. Newspaper and other news media, conversations, and even a manager's perception of a colleague's facial expressions are important sources of information. Many managers give more attention to such sources than to the formal reports.

Information can be **external or internal.** Much information that is relevant to the manager flows into the organisation form the outside environment. This information can be systematic-regular reports from trade associations, government agencies, and so forth-or it can be unsystematic. Information from and about the environment that surrounds the organisation is important, but we do not discuss it extensively in this book because of its wide variety. Our description is primarily concerned with information that is generated inside the organisation.

Accounting Information : Information can be accounting or nonaccounting. Although both types of information are important, we tend to give more attention to accounting (i.e., financial) information. The reason is that the management control system is built around an accounting core. The outputs of a responsibility centre are the goods and services that it provides to other responsibility centre or to customers; accounting provides a way of aggregating these often heterogeneous products into a single amount revenue. The inputs of a responsibility centre are the hours of labour services, kilos of materials, and units of various services that it uses; accounting provides a way of aggregating these heterogenoeus inputs into a single amount, expense. Profit, which is the difference between revenue and expense, is an overall measure of the performance of the responsibility centre, encompassing within it the results of actions that create revenue and the expenses associated with those actions.

Not only does accounting provide a way of aggregating physically unlike elements, an accounting system is also a disciplined way of doing this. The fundamental rule that debits must always equal credits, and the safeguards built into the system of recording and summarising transactions provide assurance that there is appropriate support for the validity of the numbers that flow through the system and that part of a given transaction has not slipped through a crack and disappeared. Errors, and even fraud, can sometimes occur, but these are relatively uncommon, and users, in most circumstances, can trust accounting numbers more than they can trust numbers that come from a system that is not governed by the debit-and-credit mechanism.

Obviously, accounting information is not perfect. The reported profitability of a responsibility centre is never a complete or accurate measure of its performance. Furthermore, in many responsibility centres it is not feasible to measure output in monetary terms and therefore it is not feasible to measure profitability. Also, in certain responsibility centres, accounting measurements are relatively unimportant. In certain staff units, for examples, the control of the unit's expenses is a trivial matter; the quality of the work that it does is the most important criterion of performance, even though quality cannot be measured in accounting terms.

Another inadequacy of accounting informations is that considerable time elapses between the occurrence of an event and the issuance of an accounting report on that event. If an automated machine starts to turn out parts that exceed prescribed tolerance limits, someone needs to get information on that event immediately; they cannot wait for an accounting report on spoilage costs.

Because of these inadequacies, accounting information is supplemented by various types of nonaccounting information : reports of labour efficiency and personnel turnover as well as labour costs; reports of materials usage and spoilage, as well as material costs, and so on. This information is important, and in some cases it is more important than the accounting information. For example, a report of orders booked, which strictly speaking is not an accounting number, is usually a more important indicator of the performance of a marketing organisation than the accounting number called revenue. Nevertheless, bookings do not tell the whole story; profitability depends on how much of the revenues generated by these bookings ultimately flows down to the bottom line.

When we refer in this book to a **financial control system,** we mean that part of the management control system that collects, reports, and uses accounting numbers. In emphasising the financial control system, we do not intend to minimise the importance of other information. Our reason for focusing on accounting information is that it provides a coherent framework for the management control system in the organisation as a whole. Most nonaccounting information can be related to appropriate parts of this framework. Thus, information about increased spoilage from a machine is originally presented in nonaccounting terms, but the effect of this situation ultimately shows up in an accounting report of the increased costs in the responsibility centre and a corresponding decrease in the profitability of the company.

Operating Information : By far the largest quantity of information that flows through a business is **operating information,** that is , information that is generated in the course of day-to-day operations. There is great variety in this information, but in general terms it can be classified into a relatively few main streams, some of the most important of which are :

A production stream, consisting of records showing the detail on orders received from customers, instructions for producing the products to meet these orders, and records of work in process and finished goods inventories. The nature of the production stream varies widely in different industries, but it tends to be similar for companies within a given industry. In some industries, such as banks and insurance companies, the majority of employees process "paper" in essentially the same way that employees in a factory process material.

A purchasing and materials stream, consisting of records having to do with materials and services ordered, with their receipt, with keeping track of materials while they are in inventory, and with their issue to the production departments.

A payroll stream, consisting of records which show how much each employee has earned, the nature of the work that employees did, and how much they have been paid. Because payroll records must conform to requirements set forth in social security regulations, there is a great deal of similarity in the payroll records of most companies.

A plant and equipment stream, consisting of records showing the cost, location, and condition of each significant noncurrent asset, together with the related depreciation data.

A sales and accounts receivable stream, consisting of detailed data on each order booked, each sales transaction, the credit to accounts receivable that is generated by the transaction, amount that customers pay, and amounts that customers currently owe.

A finance stream, consisting of records of cash movements and cash balances, investments, borrowings and payments made to lenders, and dividends and other transactions with shareholders.

A cost stream, consisting of records of costs incurred in manufacturing goods or rendering services.

A responsibility accounting stream, consisting of the revenues, expenses and investment of responsibility centres.

With the exception of the responsibility accounting stream, these streams of information are required for purposes other than management control. Much information used in the management control process is derived by summarising data that was originally generated for other purposes. The additional cost of using these data for management control purposes is relatively small. Indeed, there is such a tremendous difference in the cost of summarising information that exists in these operating streams and the cost of collecting data *de nove*, that systems designers often specify that management control information be obtained from operating information, even though the available data are not quite what is desired.

Management Control Information

In the management control process, information is used for planning, for co-ordinating, and for control. It is appropriate here to make some general comments, particularly on the nature of information that is used for the control process *per se*.

Information Reports Vs. Control Reports : To the extent that the manager's needs for information can be predicted, reports can be designed that will meet these needs; one such report is the **control report,** which essentially reports actual performance compared with planned performance. However, in planning and co- ordinating the work of the organisation, management needs information beyond that contained in control reports. Management therefore also receives information reports, that is, reports intended to tell management what is going on, but not specifically designed to facilitate the control process. These reports may or may not lead to action. Each reader studies them to detect whether or not something has happened that is worth looking into. If nothing of significance is noted, which is often the case, the report is put aside without action. If something does strike the reader's attention, an inquiry or action is initiated. The information on these reports comes both from the accounting system and also from a wide variety of other sources. Included are reports of orders received, the status of accounts receivable, the status of inventories, general news summaries, stock market prices, actions of competitors, and government regulations.

The important point is that a management control systems cannot be viewed as consisting entirely of a set of reports, each designed to show information that is relevant in the control process. It also consists of a wide variety of reports which may, but also may not, contain relevant information.

Control Information : Diagram 8.1 is the essentials of the management control process that provides a basis for making comments about the type of information that is useful in that process. The process starts with the preparation of plans. These plans are made within the context of goals and strategies which have been decided on in the strategic planning process, and they take account of other relevant information that bears on the problem of how the organisation can operate most effectively and efficiently to reach its goals. The plans are expressed as programmes, budgets, objectives, and in other terms.

Each responsibility centre uses the plans as a guide to operations. They are, however, not a complete guide because operations are also influenced by other information, particularly current information from both external and internal sources. This information may suggest that operations should not proceed in exact conformance with the plan. If the production budget was based on a sales estimate of Rs. 1,000,00 and a current estimate is that sales will be Rs. 1,500,000, the actual production schedule should take account of this new information.

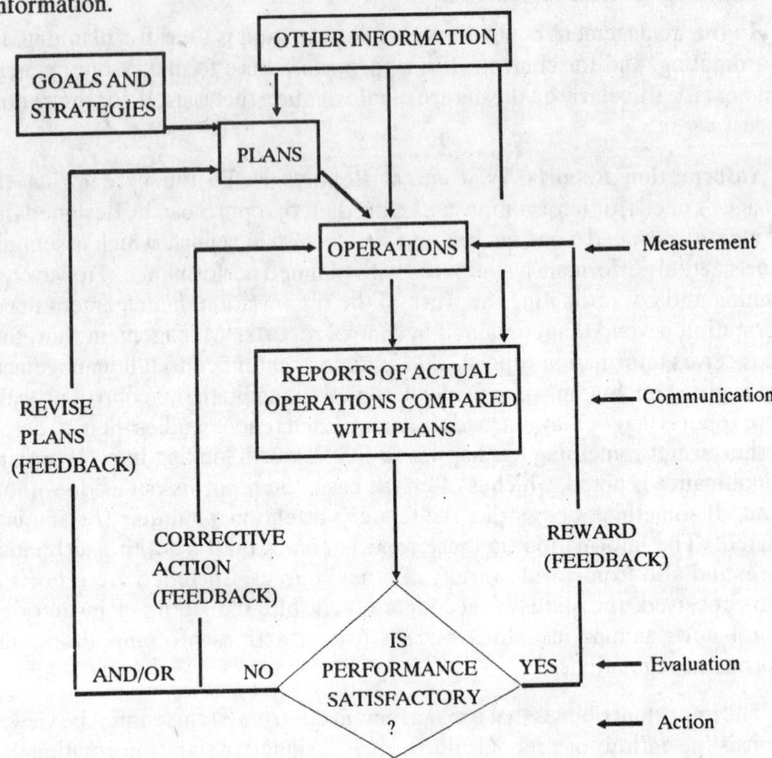

Fig. 8.1 The Control Process

During the conduct of operations, actual performance is **measured.** Periodically, the results of these measurements are **communicated** to the manager who supervises the manager of the responsibility centre, and this information is **evaluated.** The evaluation process starts with a comparison of reported actual performance with planned performance. Based on this comparison, and on other information which may help to explain why actual performance differed from planned performance, the manager makes a judgment on whether or not the performance was satisfactory.

The judgment gives rise to various types of **feedback.** If the performance was judged to be satisfactory, this is communicated to the responsibility centre manager with appropriate commendation, and this signals to the responsibility centre manager that he is judged to be performing in a way that is consistent with over-all goals. If the performance is judged to be unsatisfactory, either or both of two types of feedback signals are communicated : (1) the manager of the responsibility centre may be motivated to take corrective action, and/or (2) the plans may be revised.

Motivational Reports and Economic Reports : Control reports are of two general types. One is intended to report on personal performance, and the other to report on economic performance. Since the first type is intended to motivate managers, it is often called a motivational report. Essentially, such a report compares actual performance for a responsibility centre with what performance should have been under the prevailing circumstances. Presumably, the budget states the responsibility manager's commitment to a certain level of performance, and reports show how well he has carried out this commitment. Behavioural considerations are important in using such reports.

An economic report is designed to show how well the responsibility centre has performed as an economic entity. The content of such a report may be quite different from that of a motivational report. For example, an economic report would ordinarily include all the costs of the responsibility centre, including allocated costs, whereas a motivational report may show only those elements of cost that the responsibility manager can influence. Economic reports are prepared much less frequently than motivational reports.

The motivational report may show that the responsibility manager is doing an excellent job, considering the circumstances, but if the economic analysis shows that the responsibility centre is not earning an adequate profit, or otherwise is not making an adequate contribution to company goals, action may nevertheless be necessary. The manager of a down town department store may be doing the best job possible, but if the economic report indicates that the store is operating at a loss (because, say, of the movement of business out of the downtown area and into suburban shopping centres), the store may be closed. This action does not reflect unfavorably on the manager's performance.

Critics of a management control system sometimes overlook the fact that the system contains these two types of reports. Depending on their bias, they criticise reports because, for example, they report full costs including allocated costs, or alternatively because they do not report full costs. It must be appreciated that each type of cost construction has its place in a management control system.

Appropriate Standards : Standards used in control reports are of three types : (1) predetermined standards or budgets, (2) historical standards, or (3) external standards.*

* Refer to the Chapter 13 - 'Ratio Analysis'

Information for Managerial Decision

The increasing complexities of modern management demand new tools and skills. The most profound and promising of these new tools is advanced and accurate information. The systems of information are changing the process of management in many ways.

The basic management functions-planning, organisation and control-depend increasingly on up-to-date information while management decision making which is becoming more and more structured relies, for its accuracy and effectiveness, on the availability of information at every decision centre. Management organisation itself is being changed to provide for information systems. Even technical functions of management like marketing, finance and manufacturing are dependent on up-to-date and accurate information for decision making and invariably provide for their own information systems.

Management theory and practice continue to change at a rapid rate. It is no longer sufficient for a manager to be skilled in one functional specialty, such as engineering or accountancy. To be effective, he should be proficient in planning, organising and controlling. He must be familiar with systems approach to management and utilisation of information for decision making.

These functions of management are not performed one after the other. They interface and often they are performed simultaneously. Planning involves studying objectives for the area of activity, identifying opportunities and designing a programme for achieving the objectives. Organising involves providing leadership and supervision of the action plan through the organisation. Controlling involves measurement of performance and applying correctives through feedbacks. The place of information in all these three basic functions is important. Recognition of a problem or an opportunity is prompted by information-internal or external. Defining the problem, evaluating alternative courses of action and preparing the final plan also need information. Once a decision is made or a plan developed, to implement it through the organisation, information has to be given to the various sub-areas.

The managers plan for allocation of resources and the work of the other people is based on information regarding past performance and future needs. It starts with a strategic plan as the framework. The strategic plan fixes a long track and the ultimate goals, keeping in view current environmental conditions. From this, intermediate and short term goals are derived. For short term goals an operations plan or short term plan is evolved. It is evident that these concepts in the planning process need critical information. Without gathering necessary planning terms and without evaluating alternatives no goals can be fixed nor plans evolved. The planning information can be classified under environmental competition and internal.All are important and basic for the planning process.

Environmental information should cover government, society, economy, technology and factors of production. competitive information will have to cover own firm, total industry and the competitors. Internal information for planning should cover sales, availability of finance, supply factors and organisation's policies. The information system should conform to the organisation structure and the decision centres within the enterprise. Only then, the information supplied will be relevant. This means information flow and organisation design should be done together.

Control systems can best be regarded as information systems, because the rapidity and appropriateness of corrective action, the end result of all control processes, depends on the kind of information received. Standards of performance are always a part of any good plan. Performance against standards cannot be measured unless some type of communication, report or information on actual performance is supplied to the controlling individual. Information required for performance control is different in both type and characteristic, from that needed for planning. It has to be faster and timely. This constitutes the feedback. Apart from this feedback, the modern management control systems need feed-forward also. This means anticipating lags in output by monitoring the inputs and correcting their effects. By so doing action can be taken to change the input and thereby bring the system output into equilibrium with desired results before the measurement of the output discloses a deviation from the targets. This involves real time information regarding inputs, careful analysis of input variables and their relationship to the results desired and predicting the results. The feed-forward again depends on accurate and faster information systems.

The major management functions-planning, Organising and controlling-cannot be separated. They are linked functionally by a common system of information. For example, planning affects the standards for control and the feedback affect future planning. Moreover, the information flow has to include information regarding various resources like money, manpower, materials and machines to provide a system of planning and control. Suitable sensors and standards must be developed to cover attributes of the input and output and give information.

Goals are achieved by solving problems, taking decisions and performing operations. Decisions for operations must be based on information regarding all the problem solutions. These decisions have to be communicated to many other decision makers or operators for its achievement. They in turn receive and give information as part of the network. All these elements constitute the Management Information Systems (MIS). In the design of the system the following have to be kept in view :

- Decision centres.
- Action points.
- Channels of communication.
- Information needs.

The decision centres are also control points and sources of feedback information. Problem solving and decision making have to be distinguished. Problem solving seeks answers to a question. Decision making is taking follow up decisions after a solution has been given for its implementation. It is the commencement of action. As such, decisions are made at a number of points in the process like decisions as to goals, decisions as to inputs and decisions as to feedback and control. Problem solving is complete with the decision for implementation. Not every problem can be solved. This may be due to limitation of resources or cost of the solution itself. Consequently, managers have to set priorities and select the problems to be solved. They have to organise human efforts into synergistic systems which conduct further problem solving at the operational levels. To every level information is required for decision making. This is provided by the MIS. For setting priorities in problem solving, the MIS should provide information to identify the critical problems. This is also part of the information system. The institutionalisation of problem solving is becoming more formal with the development of management systems and decision processes. In this, computer systems are playing an increasing role. They can be applied for structured problems readily. For ill-structured problems human effort is still required.

User-oriented MIS

The detailed decision process is a function of information and behavioural and environmental factors that shape the process. The quality, quantity, flow and timing of information supplied by the MIS to the decision makers are critical. The value of information is closely linked with its timeliness. Moreover, the degree of processing of the information depends on the ultimate user, namely, the Board, the chief executive, the manager, the operators, or the chief accountant. What is highlighted and how it is presented will have to vary depending on the user.

The decision maker must find ways of selecting important elements and evaluating them before reaching a decision. In olden days it was the rule of thumb and past experience. In modern days guidelines are evolved for this purpose. Similarly, the requirements will vary for short range decisions and long range decisions.

The modern management assignment or decision making process consists of the following steps :

- **Search for the problem;**
- **Stating a problem;**
- **Collection of data;**
- **Development and testing a model representing the problem solution;**
- **Manipulation of the model to determine outcomes of various input conditions;**
- **Selection of the best course of action;**
- **Implementation of the course;**
- **Feedback and correctives.**

The formulation of the model and its manipulation distinguishes the modern decision making process from the earlier ones.

For a dynamic business system, it is necessary to review, either periodically or continuously, the nature of output in order to attune the systems for the changes in its own operations or changes in the environment. In addition, in a business system, one has to observe whether the output is profitable or acceptable. By means of models and assessed quantitative methods, the various solutions can be quantified, analysed, compared and in all these processes, information plays a very important role.

An illustrative list of information for strategic planning and management control is presented below :

Information for Strategic Planning and Management Control

Strategic Planning :

Economic trends and forecasts :

- Economic developments and forecasts for next five years;
- Growth of specific process and other industries the company serves;
- Trends in population, price levels, labour forces;
- Demand forecasts for major products and equipment;
- Major projects in different industries to be implemented in next five years;
- Demand/capacity ratios in various industries;
- International developments of interest to the company.

Political trends and developments :

- Analysis of political developments leading to investment opportunities;
- Implications of new regulatory legislation;
- Political shifts of particular significance to the company.

Social trends and forecasts :

- Major social trends and their impact on the company;
- Trends in education, health, living habits and leisure-time activities.

Competitive information :

- Past performance, present activities and future plans of the major competitors;
- Planned development and launching of new products and facilities;
- Planned mergers/acquisitions, plant re-locations, R & D activities.

Technological trends and forecasts :

- Major breakthroughs in process plant technology;
- Equipment design trends;
- Predicted obsolescence of products and services.

Market data :

- Analysis of current and projected market shares;
- Sales forecasts for major products and equipment;
- Innovations in marketing, advertising and sales promotion;
- Analysis of customer buying habits and preferences.

Internal data for planning :

- Analysis of past performance and product profitability;
- Plant productivity and manpower; and facilities utilisation.

Management Control

Overall company performance :

- Financial performance, monthly profit and loss, and balance sheet;
- Company budget performance and utilisation;
- Progress of capital expenditure projects;
- Company performance statistics.

Sales and marketing performance :

- Sales invoiced, (actual Vs. forecast), disvisionwise, regionwise, etc.).
- Orders booked and order backlog;
- Profit margins, actual Vs. forecast;
- Sales expensed (actual Vs. budget, disvisionwise).

Production performance :

- Actual shop output Vs. planned output, plantwise;
- Manufacturing statistics, plant utilisation, scrap, rework, overtime, etc.

Material and inventory status :

- Actual level of stocks Vs. planned stocks, storewise and categorywise;
- Work-in-progress, plantwise;
- Major purchase orders placed and outstanding;
- Performance measures.

Personnel status and performance :

- Company personnel status report, plantwise and category/skillwise;
- New recruits Vs. requisitions;
- Personnel statistics, staff turnover, absenteeism, promotions etc.

Financial and cost performance :

- Profitability and overhead recovery, plantwise and divisionwise;
- Cost-over, under-runs, and variance analysis;
- Facilities control report.

REVIEW QUESTIONS

1. What do you know about 'information'? State its important characteristics.
2. Explain the value of information in business planning and control decisions.
3. "The value of information is inversely proportional to the degree of uncertainty: thus, the value of information is maximum for the least probable even". Elucidate.
4. What are the different types of information? List out the various information generated in the course of day to day operations of a business.
5. Explain in brief the nature of management control information.
6. Givan an illustrative list of information required to a multinational corporation for strategic planning and management control.

9

Installation of Management Information and Control System

The decision to establish a formal management information and control system (MICS) becomes almost inevitable in today's business climate. The accelerating needs for uniform, concise and timely information by all levels of management dictate the establishment of such a system. The results can be better control of and greater profitability from the enterprise. Essentially, the functioning of a MICS involves transmission of all pertinent data necessary to the conduct of a business to one or more management information centres, where it is maintained and then disseminated in discrete form to all levels of management. This description provides no reference to computers or any other specific type of data processing equipment. This is to emphasize that possession of data processing equipment is not a pre-requisite for a MICS. Computers, punched card equipment, data collection and transmission equipment, etc., are excellent tools that can, if costs and volume warrant, be extremely useful in a MICS programme.

Reluctance of many managements to undertake a MICS programme can be traced to the confusion and lack of understanding surrounding the subject of information systems, and how they can be effectively installed. Management is continuously faced with the frustrations of receiving inadequate, incorrect or untimely information. As a result the validity of management decisions and actions based on this type of information is at times questionable. Timely, adequate and correct information - the means through which management can effectively monitor, control, and plan - is becoming increasingly elusive as businesses grow in size and complexity.

Progressive companies recognising this situation are at various stages of development and installation of MICS. In many cases the management of these companies, although disillusioned at times with the progress, costs and results achieved, still continues on the path toward MICS. The reasons for this continued determination on the part of management to pursue MICS can be found in its desire to achieve a state in information storage, use and handling that will achieve.

Uniformity of Information : With a single source generating the required information.

Reliability of Information : resulting from adequate controls established and constantly monitored on all input and output of the system.

On Time Response : communication of established information needs as often and as quickly as desired.

As these items are achieved the benefits resulting from an MICS become evident : the potential for achievement of substantial reductions in operating costs, information that management can refer to quickly and simply to assist in its decision process, and a smoother more efficient organisation that can supply the information when needed. With these benefits available, management can realise such basic contributions to cost reduction and higher profits as improved sales forecasting and production control, increased inventory turnover rate, increased productivity of all facilities, etc. The realisation and extent of any savings is completely dependent upon management's ability to understand and effectively utilise the information generated by the system.

An additional cost savings aspect of installing MICS is achieved through the elimination, modification and/or combination of systems and procedures previously used by the organisation. These more immediate savings can be impressive, but not nearly as much as the potential long range savings that can be achieved once the system is installed. Management should also realise that both short and long range savings can start being attained without waiting for the installation of the entire system.

Following is a representative listing of the type of information that can be made available to management from a well designed and installed MICS. The ability of the system to produce this type of information on time and in a usable form depends on the means employed to design and install the system.

- Sales status by product, territory, salesman, etc., with variances.
- Cash position.
- Inventory position in units and/or dollars - comparison to budgeted.
- Inventory items not meeting minimum turnover rate for an established period.
- Profit position - by profit centres for an established period.
- Production status - by product, plant, etc., including orders not on time and reasons for variances.
- Projection of inventory and sales position using a simulation model.
- Budget variances of expenses, capital expenditures, projects, etc., by budget centres.
- Personnel skills inventory of all company employees.

Prerequisites to Undertaking MICS

Once management has agreed to consider MICS, but prior to the commitment of any company facilities, it is necessary to review certain aspects of the organisation to make sure that MICS will be built on a firm base. This base is composed of the prerequisites described below. These pre-requisites are all related to people-the key factor is the design, installation and continued growth and success of MICS. Until management feels that these items are in place, or can reac y be achieved, it would be best to delay the start of company involvement in ICS.

1. Auequate corporate discipline so that common inter-functional procedures can be implemented.

2. Documentation of potential savings anticipated from installation of MICS. This documentation must include reasonable supporting data to substantiate the savings, and to justify the investment of company facilities for such an undertaking.

3. A relatively stable management, especially at the policy- making level. A company undergoing continual reorgansiation at this level does not have an environment conducive to effective systems design and installation of this nature. Paradoxically, an MICS, if properly designed, will help stabilise an organisation as a result of the well defined responsibilities and controls required for such a system.

4. Management that is willing to commit its time and interest to understand the various plans, techniques and equipment associated with the proposed system. This understanding should be in sufficient detail to enable intelligent monitoring of the costs and progress of the system.

5. The willingness of management to start acquiring and training a core of experienced systems personnel. This core can range in size from one man in a small company to a full staff of 20 or more in a major corporation.

6. The presence within the organisation of operational personnel who are knowledgeable in depth concerning the information requirements, methods, procedures and techniques within the functions they are associated with. These personnel will play a major role in the design and implementation of such a system. Management must be willing to relinquish considerable time from the regular duties of these personnel since they will become members of the design and installation committee discussed later.

Key Steps Required

Companies with success in undertaking the installation of MICS have found the following key steps vital to their installation plans. These steps are listed in the required sequence, but in many cases it is not necessary to await the total completion of one before starting on the next. This overlapping can best be illustrated by use of the flow chart shown in next page. This chart is a modification of PERT chart and can be, with the necessary elaboration, used as an effective tool for the planning and control of this programme.

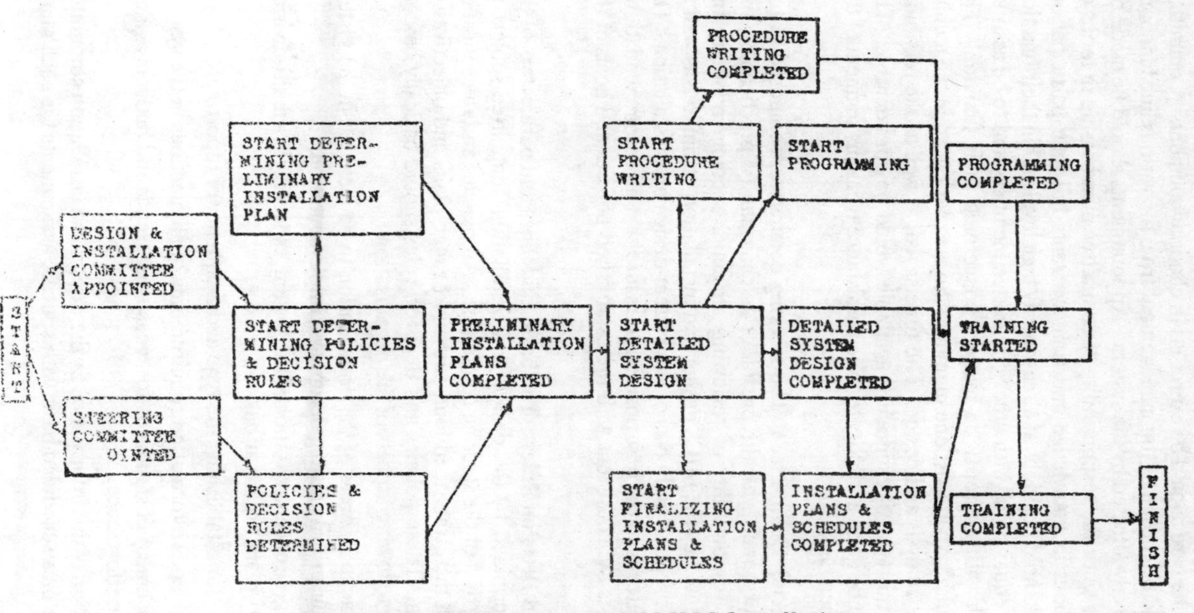

Steps required for a Successful MICS Installation

This modified PERT chart can, with the necessary elaboration, be used as an effective tool for the planning and control of steps vital to installing an MICS.

Design and Installation Committee : Members appointed to this committee will be responsible for the complete design and installation of the system; therefore extreme care should be exercised in choosing members. Committee members should be chosen by top management from the various line functions that will be directly affected by the system. Appointments should be made on a full time basis since the responsibility of committee membership in terms of what contributions in knowledge and time warrants full-time participation. Members should hold positions at a reasonably high level within their function to ensure their equal status with other committee members and to be assured that they speak with authority on matters concerning their function. The committee should have at least one member who is experienced in the techniques of systems analysis and design. The time saved, as well as the reliability achieved, with this type of experience available would be considerable. The committee must be given authority to solicit assistance from any segment of the organisation when needed.

MICS Steering Committee : The steering committee, composed of top management personnel, with the president as chairman (if practicable), will have the basic responsibility of reviewing all major recommendations and proposals presented by the MICS design and installation committee as well as monitoring the progress and costs of the system design and installation. The steering committee is in the best position to insure that all recommendations, designs and costs are consistent with the established policies and goals of the company.

Policies and Decision Rules : The basic guidelines and parameters of the system are determined by the design and installation committee subject to review and approval of the steering committee. All policies and rules must be compatible with the established long and short range plans and objectives of the organisation. These policies and decision rules should basically be concerned with the following aspects of the organisation :

1. The functional areas of the organisation to be included in the system and their priority during design and implementation.
2. The degree of centralisation of the system, especially in a multi-division or multi-plant organisation.
3. Criteria for establishing the type and frequency of reporting.
4. The universal information requirements of all functions in the system.
5. Establishment of standards for measuring trends and budgets against actual performance.

Determination of this information by the design and installation committee should be made on a scheduled basis with specific assignments for each member.

The Preliminary Installation Plan : With the knowledge gained by members of the design and installation committee from the previous step, development of a preliminary installation plan should be developed at this point by the committee. The plan should include : (i) A listing of all steps needed for installation of the system in each functional area of the organisation, the estimated time to accomplish each step and the person responsible for its successful completion. (ii) Manpower requirements for achieving full installation. (iii) Any equipment requirements and estimated funds needed for their acquisition.

This data should be thoroughly documented and submitted to the MICS steering committee for approval. Once approved, this data will from the basis for monitoring the programme. Because of the tentative nature of any schedules and requirements developed at this stage, it becomes extremely important to establish effective communications between the two committees. Progress review meetings and appropriate progress reports must be established on a scheduled basis.

Detailed Systems Design Specifications : This step produces the complete details required by the design and installation committee for completing the installation plan and schedule. In addition to detailed specification produced at this point will be used by programmers, procedure writers and training personnel for preparing their output.

Any system specification for which use of data processing equipment appears feasible should be submitted to selected equipment manufacturers for purposes of soliciting proposals. The submitted proposals should be reviewed with each manufacturer by members of the design and installation committee. The procurement or rental of data processing equipment should be approved by the steering committee.

The detailed systems specifications, written and documented, should include :

(a) **Input Specifications** - including form content, form design, means of preparation and transmission, current and anticipated volumes, etc.

(b) **Output Specifications** - including content and format, distribution, frequency, current and anticipated volumes, etc.

(c) **Processing Requirements** - defining in detail what is required to be done with the input to achieve the required output.

(d) **File Descriptions** - the detailed contents and volumes (present and anticipated) of all files needed for the system.

(e) **Control Requirements** - all controls necessary to ensure accuracy of input and output.

Documentation of these specifications should be under the direction of a senior systems designer who is thoroughly trained and experienced in this type of effort. Line personnel members of the design and installation committee will play a major role by contributing the necessary detailed operating information and systems design suggestions in this step.

The Final Installation Plans and Schedules : At this point the design and installation committee should establish the final installation plan as a result of the detailed data generated from the systems design specifications. Before starting installation of any part of the system, the following must be considered.

Preparation of a detailed installation plan and schedule for each segment of the system should be accomplished through the joint effort of the design and installation committee and operating personnel of the functions involved. The plan should include the means of phasing in the new procedures and phasing out the old (if any exist). For each installation step, assignment of responsibilities to a specific individual must be made, and detailed instructions for accomplishing each installation step must be written. This will lessen the possibility of error or misunderstanding. Training for those involved in any special tasks required for installation should be instituted when necessary.

Programming : If data processing equipment will be used by the system, the design specifications described previously are furnished to trained programmers who are responsible for the documenting of instructions (programmes) that will enable the equipment to efficiently process the input and produce the required output. In addition, the testing of the programme to insure reliability and accuracy in meeting the systems design specifications is included as part of the task required to complete this step.

Procedure Writing There are two types of procedures required at this stage in system installation. Both types should be written and maintained on a permanent basis.

1. Standard Operating Procedures (S.O.P.) cover in detail the specific duties and responsibilities of each person assigned to perform a job within the system. This type or procedure should include the detailed actions to be taken under varying conditions, relationships with other functions, etc. These procedures will form the basic curriculum for the training programmes to follow.

2. Policies and procedures are applicable to interfunctional information flow. Included should be specified control requirements and control points, assignment of responsibilities, etc.

Training : The training programme is intended for all personnel whose positions expose them to the new system, even indirectly, and is composed of two segments : (i) A description of the total system to indicate in general terms the relationships and responsibilities of each function to the whole system. (ii) A detailed description of a segment of the system to be performed by specific operating personnel, e.g., order processing. In this segment training should cover the step-by- step duties and responsibilities of each person. The use of S.O.P. and policies and procedures as training tools is a necessity. Members of the design and installation committee should assist the training staff in all phases of the training programme.

General Comments : In addition to the steps discussed above, the following comments related to a MICS installation are presented because of their importance.

1. During and following installation of any portion of the system, the need for changes in the design will become evident. Causes for changes can range from some overlooked piece of information required by a function to a major reorganisation of a department. The design and installation committee must, therefore, have the ability to react rapidly to such causes in order to determine the system changes required and to modify installation plans to reflect these changes.

2. The need for adequate planning and control of all installation steps has been mentioned before. PERT or CPM techniques have been used with great success in this area, and the author strongly recommends the use of similar techniques for the planning and control of any MICS installation.

3. The impact on personnel of a company undertaking such a programme as MICS can be significant, either positively or negatively, depending role in the system. There is no doubt that the key to success of an undertaking such as MICS rests to a considerable extent on the amount of understanding and support of the system engendered in a company personnel by management. To achieve positive reactions, management must be willing to undertake an educational programme that is comprehensive enough to overcome the ever present (but usually unjustified) fear created by a pending change in the manner of doing things. This is especially true when the employment of computers and other data processing equipment is anticipated by the company.

4. The committees described should not be considered luxuries that can be afforded only by the larger company. These committees can be informal and small, e.g., in some small companies two or three men could perform the duties of the design and installation committee. The larger and more complex the company, the greater the representation should be.

5. The need for a detailed written description of all information that is produced during the design and installation of the system is absolutely necessary. This is especially true of all completed procedures, policies, programmes,

specifications and operating instructions. Many information systems have been documented assuming that any detailed information can be obtained from the system designers, machine operators, programmers, etc., when needed. This approach is an invitation to potential disaster, since there never is a guarantee that these personnel will be available when needed.

REVIEW QUESTIONS

1. Explain the reasons for installation of management information and control system.
2. What are te pre requisites for the installation of management information and control system.
3. Explain the sequential steps involved to instal a management information and control system.

10

Structured and Unstructured Decision : Implications for Control

Nature of Decision Making : According to Simon* the manager's job consists of recognising circumstances that require decisions, identifying appropriate actions and finally choosing the most effective action. Simon** has categorised decisions as structured (programmed) and unstructured (unprogrammed) decisions. **Programmed decision** is a process which is in the form of a formula to be adopted by anyone. This demands the least amount of creativity, problem-solving ability and model building need. For example, the reorder point level in inventory management is a programmed decision. When the inventory level falls below the reorder point, the pre-determined or order quantity is used for purchase. For a given level of operation, bank teller deciding to process the cheque presented across the counter is going through the programmed decision.

In the case of **non-programmed decision**, information availability is low, the need for environmental information is fairly high, is not repetitive and calls for creative intervention by the executive. For example, product mix or production plan is a non-programmed decision. In some organisations promotion may be a programmed decision and in some it may be non-programmed. These two are extreme cases and the most frequently occurring situation is the mixed case of semi-programmed decision. A semi-programmed decision is a situation needing when it is not falling into the expected human intervention pattern.

For example, if there is a condition in the reorder point formula that if the price of the commodity does not exceed a given value, the order quantity is as given. Otherwise, the order quantity will have to be obtained with due consideration to many other factors. Most of the management techniques are developed for the purpose of converting a major part of executive decisions into the programmed category. Thus, most operational decisions fall in the category of programmed decisions and therefore decision-making is highly structured and circumscribed. In these situations, a set of instructions or programme unambiguously defines the action to be taken in all conceivable circumstances. As against this, at the strategic planning level, decisions are unstructured. The

---

* Jay W. Forrester, Industrial Dynamics, MIT press, Cambridge, Mass. 1961.

** Herbert Simon, The New Science of Management Decisions, Harper and Row, New York, 1960.

task of control is easier in cases of programmed decisions, as appropriate operations research models can be formulated for them. As has been indicated earlier, operational controls involve a larger component of programmed decisions.

The Simon framework and the Anthony-Dearden framework are closely interlinked. Strategic planning involves a greater degree of the unstructured component of decision-making, while operational controls involve a high degree of the structured component of decision-making. It may be difficult to put an exact numerical figure that would indicate the extent of structured decision-making involved in strategic planning, management control and operational control. However, an understanding of the Simon framework of programmed and unprogrammed decisions would help in identifying areas in the management control process for which definite procedures can be worked out. Table 10.1 indicates the increasing extent of structured decisions as we move from strategic planning to operational controls.

Table 10.1 Interlinkage Between the Nature of Task and Control Activities

Activity / Nature of task	Strategic Planning	Management Control	Operation Control
Structured	Structured	Structured	Structured
Unstructured	Unstructured	Unstructured	Unstructured
Decision aids	i Environmental Information System ii Management Information System iii SWOT analysis	i Management Information System ii Decision Support Systems iii Management Science Models	i Follow up Charts ii Executive Diary iii Management Science Models

The Simon framework coupled with the recent advances in computer technology, forms the basis for designing the decision support systems (DSS). The DSS are systems in relation to key decisions and tasks with a view to improving the effectiveness of the manager's problem-solving process. The concept of DSS has basically evolved from two major streams of research and thought. The first stream is the Simon framework of **programmable** (structured) and **non-programmable** (unstructured) tasks and the second stream is the technical advances in interactive computer systems. Integrated research in the two streams has lead to decision support as a distinctive concept and methodology for developing computer-based decision aids. The DSS aims at utilising analytical power and the data processing capabilities of the computer for managerial decisions. It implies the use of computers to:*

1. assist managers in their decision processes in semi-structured tasks;
2. support, rather than replace, managerial judgement;
3. improve the effectiveness of decision-making rather than its efficiency.

Therefore, the DSS is essentially computer-based support for taking managerial decisions in semi-structured decision situations.

Organisation Structure to Control Systems Design

A major factor differentiates the automatic control system from the management control system, is the exercise of control by human beings in the latter case. In automatic control systems, the human element is missing. It is for this reason that an understanding of organisation behaviour is important for the proper perception of management control systems and processes. Further, as the major focus of the control system is on the performance evaluation of the organisational sub-units, the control system designer should also have an understanding of the organisation structure. Structure refers to the way the enterprise is organised so as to enable the total task of the organisation to be performed in an efficient and effective way. The organisational structure is essentially the arrangement of its sub-systems with authority and responsibility relations. Thus, it refers to whether the organisation is centralised or decentralised or whether it emphasises line or staff or how the 'boxes' are arranged.

In the past, designers of organisation structure recommended the following broad guidelines: (i) clear lines of authority running from top to bottom of the organisation. It should be possible to trace a chain of command from chief executive to every employee; (ii) there must be unity of command. No one in the organisation should report to more than one boss; (iii) the accountability and authority of each responsible person should be clearly defined o avoid overlapping of tasks and authorities; (iv) the responsibility should always be coupled with corresponding authority and the responsibility of the higher authority for the acts of his subordinate is absolute, i.e., a manager may delegate

---

* Peter G.W. Keen and M.S. Scott Morton, Decision Support System: An Organisational Perspective, Addison-Wesley Publishing Co., Reading, Mass. 1980, p.1

authority. However, he cannot dissassociate himself from the acts of his subordinate; (v) the work of every person in the organisation should be confined as far as possible to the performance of a single leading functions, thereby permitting specialisation in tasks, (vi) line functions should be separated from staff functions. Line functions are essentially those that accomplish the main goal or objectives of the organisation such as manufacturing, selling, etc. These are also referred to as operating departments. Staff functions aid in or are auxiliary to line functions. These are generally advisory in nature; (vii) there are limits to the number of persons that can be co-ordinated by a single manager. This limit is known as 'span of control'.

These traditional principles of organisational design could not meet the test of the new organisational forms that had to be designed to meet the complexities of the organisations, which were not necessarily bureaucratic in nature. A contingency theory was evolved to explain some of the complexities. Contingency means it depends. Therefore, the contingency theory aims at analysing each situation and designing structure taking into consideration task performance and individual group satisfaction, rather than using universal models and fitting them to any situation. There are multifarious relationships between design variables and therefore it is necessary to draw up a task- analysis matrix, indicating tasks and their relationship with design variables, such as objective of the organisation, technology, size, people, managerial styles, and so on. If task profiles are similar or interdependent, such tasks can be combined in a department or section. Theses tasks should therefore be integrated into an efficient and satisfying whole. One of the most important integrative mechanism is hierarchy, which is also the most important characteristic of structure. Other techniques for integrating are the drawing up of rules and procedures for the expected behaviour, devising of mechanism for handling information, delegating and referring fewer decisions upwards for approval and making planning a culture in the organisation.

In using a contingency approach to design an organisation structure rather than transplanting perhaps an outmoded model from a similar institution, the following variables need to be analysed : (i) objectives, (ii) time orientation,(iii) task differentiation, (iv) people involved, including experience, motives, numbers, (v) market (or external) pressure, (vi) technical system, (vii) managerial style, (viii) ethos and culture of the organisation.

Major Forms of Organisation Structure

On the basis of analysis of various design variables, organisational structure can be broadly categorised into four major forms : (i) a functional organisation, in which the tasks are differentiated on the basis of each major function such as marketing, production, etc., with each manager responsible for the specified function; (ii) a divisional organisation in which differentiation is on the basis of a product line or group of product lines with the manager responsible for all the functions related to such a product line or group of product lines, (iii) a matrix organisation, in which there is two way differentiation, namely according to functions and according to projects, with both superimposed on each other; (iv) a network structure aimed at closer inter-institutional co-ordination among a network of agencies involved in implementing a programme or a project.

Functional Structure : In a functional structure, the tasks are differentiated on the basis of each major function and each manager is responsible for one of these. Thus, there is functional specialisation such as marketing, production, finance, personnel, R & D, etc. In such a structure, those with authority can tell others what to do in that function. Such structures have a high degree of centralised decision-making.

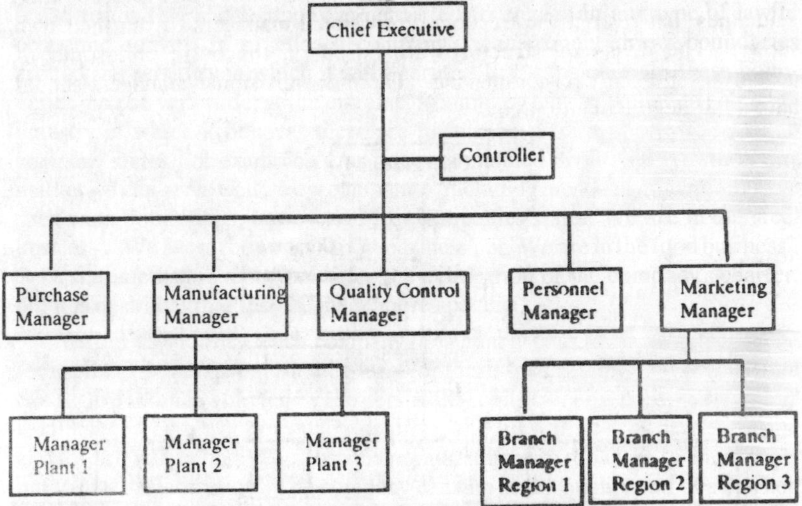

Fig. 10.1 Functional Organisation Structure

Organisations with functional structure can benefit from the economies of scale and also improve the quality of output because the activities of a given function are centralised. One of the major questions in such organisations is whether one functional manager has staff or a functional authority in relation to other functions, e.g., can the head of marketing tell the head of production what to produce (functional) or can he play only an advisory role (staff)? In such organisations, therefore, the top management must plan and co-ordinate the activities of the various functions and resolve conflicts between various functions. In such organisations, since profits are the result of joint efforts, it is difficult to identify the responsibility for profits to individual managers. Further, except for the chief executive, others do not have an overall perspective of the enterprise, and managers tend to have a functional bias. Figure 10.1 depicts an illustrative functional organisation structure.

Divisional Structure : In case of divisional structure, the divisional manager is responsible for all or almost all the functions related to a product line or group of product lines. Thus, the responsibility for earning profits can be assigned without ambiguity to the divisional manager. The divisions can operate almost as independent entities. They can formulate their own product/market strategies and even compete with other divisions. All the important decisions affecting the product line are taken by divisional managers and thus, there is a high level of decentralisation in a truly divisionalised company. In case of such structures, there is always a high level of inter-divisional competition, particularly over allocation of funds which may lead to major conflicts in the company. There would also be situations of conflict between head office and divisions, particularly if there are a whole range of head office guidelines that restrict the freedom of divisional managers to run their own shows. The divisional structures are based on the basic philosophy of decentralisation in decision-making. Therefore divisional managers should have a fair degree of autonomy.

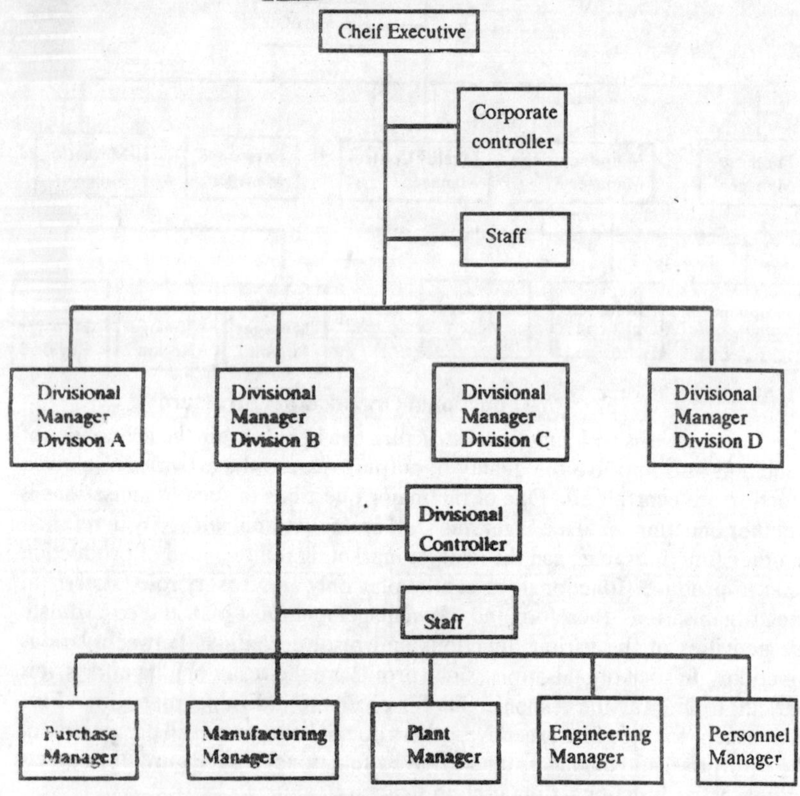

Fig. 10.2 Divisional Organisation Structure

Matrix Structure : In matrix structure, task forces are created to solve a problem. There is a basic permanent organisation structure; superimposed on it is another structure in which the focus is on projects. Therefore, in such structures there is shared responsibility on people who must please tow bosses, the functional manager and the project manager. Thus, a person reports administratively to one manager and functionally to another. A project manager is like a contractor who hires his personnel from various departments. Hence, he relies heavily on the resources from other departments. The illustration of a matrix organisation is construction of a thermal power station on turnkey basis. The time duration for the project would be around three years. For executing the project, the project manager will have to get people, material and services from other departments and therefore his task involves close co-ordination with other departments-managing people and getting work from them, even though they are not under his control administratively. A large number of other enterprises such as research and development institutions, training institutions, consultancy organisations and construction companies usually operate with matrix structure. Matrix organisations pose more difficult problems of managing delicate human relations as against hierarchial organisation, because the manager (a better word would be co-ordinator) often has to deal with a large number of professional staff who may be organisationally equal or even senior to the person in charge of the project. An illustration of this would be a research project in a research organisation. The team leader of such a project may be comparatively a junior person, who has special skills, while members of the team may be hierarchically senior. Figure 10.3 depicts a matrix-type organisation structure.

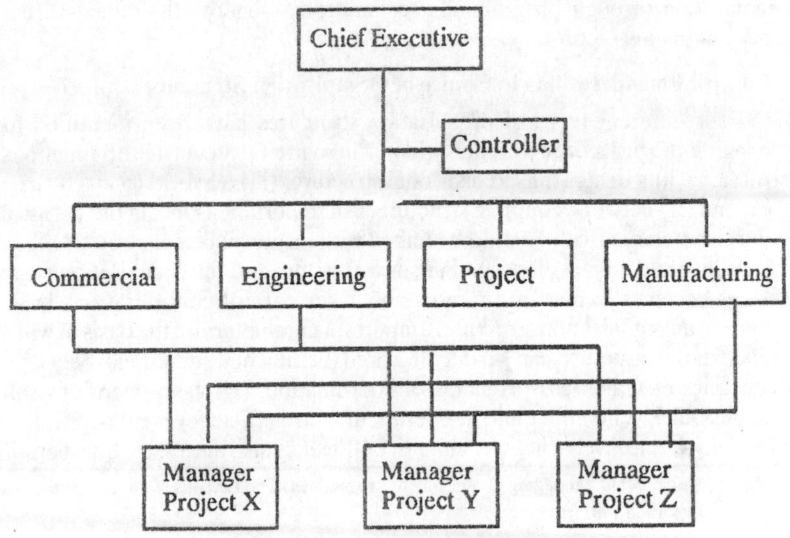

Fig. 10.3 Matrix Structure

Network/Coupling Structure : The network of the organisation is used to implement large national development programmes. In such cases,

> A national programme agency works in co-ordination with a network of organisations or institutions which jointly provide the components of the programme service. The network concept permits a high degree of decentralisation which in turn is a response to the existence of extreme environmental complexity.*

In the case of network structures, an important aspect of control is how to achieve effective inter-agency and inter-institutional co-ordination. This can be achieved by developing appropriate mechanisms for reciprocal interdependence and seeking lateral influences. In case of network organisations the role of authority, as the primary source of power decreases, while sources of lateral influence such as the use of funds, joint planning, political support, mobilisation of demand among beneficiaries, and participation of beneficiaries in programme operations, assume greater significance.*

The coupling structures are structures with inter-locking autonomous but mutually dependent institutions. The three-tier structure in co-operative organisations consisting of an autonomous village co-operative society, an autonomous district- level union and an autonomous state-level federation is an example of such structures. Since mutual interdependence is of a very high order, the viability of each subsystem is dependent upon the performance of the next level. Further, assignment of profit responsibility assumes greater significance in such organisations. Coordination among various units is achieved through involvement of the chief executives in the management of next level organisation through programming committees. Figure 10.4 depicts a network/coupling structure.

Control Considerations in Choice of Organisation Structure

Four different types of organisation structures have been identified for managing the tasks of the organisation. These are (i) a centralised functional structure, (ii) a decentralised divisional structure, (iii) a hybrid (matrix) structure, and (iv) network/coupling structure. An important aspect in the design of control systems is that it should be linked with responsibility centres. Because of this intimate linkage between the control system and the organisation structure, it becomes important to know about key control considerations in the choice of an organisation structure. Important parameters on the basis of which choice of the structure can be decided are (i) efficiency and effectiveness, (ii) economics of scale, (iii) problems of coordination, (iv) assignment of profit responsibility, (v) conflict and cooperation. Since efficiency is related to level of activity, as the level of activity increases efficiency also increases. Size permits

* Sameul Paul, Managing Development Progammes : The Lessons of Success, Westview, Colorado 1982, p.118

the division of labour and specialisation within each discipline, which in turn results in increased productivity as a result of better learning of the tasks to be performed. Therefore, functional structures offer better potential for increa ing efficiency. However, the benefits of efficiency are available only up to optimum size, i.e., the size at which it operates at the minimum cost per of output.

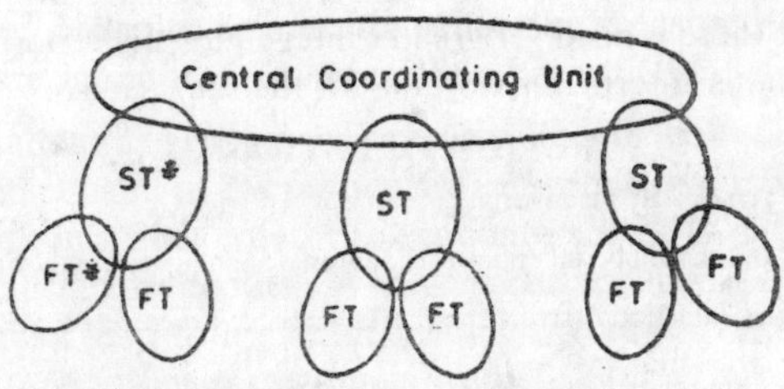

*FT stands for first tier organisations
+ST stands for second tier organisations

Fig. 10.4 Network/Coupling Structures

Though functional structures offer the advantage of economies of scales, once optimum size is surpassed, a subdivision will be called for to take the advantage of economies of scale. In practice, it is usually difficult to determine the optimum size for the organisation. The assignment of profit responsibility, is another important consideration for organisation structure design. While the assignment of profit responsibility is difficult in the case of functional organisations, the divisional structure offers the advantage of assignment of profit responsibility to the divisional manager. From the control systems point of view, this is an important factor in favour of divisional structure. It may, however, be pointed out that within a division, the departments are organised on functional basis and therefore the control problem within the division is similar to the control problem confronted in functional structures.

The issues related to conflict and cooperation assume importance if there is greater interdependence and if it is difficult to assign specific responsibilities for non-achievement of targets. In functional structure, inter- functional conflict is likely to be more intense compared to divisional structures, because by design, divisional structures are more autonomous except in cases where there are significant inter-divisional transfers. The matrix structure provides the advantage of improved coordination, because it vests total responsibility for the project/programme with the manager whose exclusive task is to plan, coordinate and integrate the activities that cut across several functions. In such structures, functional managers have technical responsibility and are expected to provide all the necessary support to the project/programme managers. As this structure suffers from the weakness of diffused responsibility, it becomes difficult to fix accountability in case of failures to achieve targets. The network/coupling type of structure is more suited when there is need to create autonomous but mutually interlocked organisations such as the three-tier structure of coopera-tive organisations, in which each tier is an autonomous organisation but is interlocked with the next level. These structures are also better suited in those situations where there is need for greater inter-enterprise coordination among various autonomous enterprises working for the same cause.

REVIEW QUESTIONS

1. How will you classify managerial decisions?
2. What factors should be taken into account in designing an organisational structure?
3. Expalin (a) Functional structure (b) Divisional structure (c) Matrix structure (d) Coupling structure.
4. Explain the need for control considerations in choosing of organisation structure.

11
Managerial Behaviour and Control Process

Organisation Structure : Certain characteristics of organisations and of the behaviour of people who work in organisations influence the design and use of management control systems.

Although organisations come in all sizes and shapes, for the purpose of analysing the appropriate management control structure, we can refer generally to three main types : (i) a functional organisation, in which each manager is responsible for a specified function, such as production; (ii) a divisional organisation, in which each divisional manager is responsible for all, or almost all, of the functions that are involved in a product line or group of product lines, and (iii) a matrix organisation, in which there are two organisational structures, one arranged by functions and the other by objects. Abbreviated organisation charts for each type are shown in next page.

Functional Organisations

In a functional organisation, each manager is responsible for one of the several functions that collectively are involved in generating profits or doing whatever the goals of the organisation may be. Functional organisations have the potential of great efficiency. For a great many activities, efficiency increases as the size of the activity increases, up to some point where there are no further "economics of scale" to be realised. The reason that efficiency increases is that large-scale operations permit the utilisation of increasingly specialised inputs. A general purpose machine tool operated by a skilled machinist may be able to produce 100 parts per hour, whereas a specially designed piece of equipment may produce 1,000 parts per hour and require only a part time operator. Specialisation of human resources can also yield economies of scale; the learning curve of a production worker is perhaps the most common example.

Further, the quality of manufacturing supervision and technical services, such as engineering and quality control, is likely to be better when those activities are centralised under one manufacturing manager. Scattering those resources across product divisions would both lower the quality of the personnel that might be used and reduce the efficient utilisation of their services. Similar arguments might be made about the efficiency of the marketing organisation as a large functional activity.

Fig. 11.1 Types of Organisation

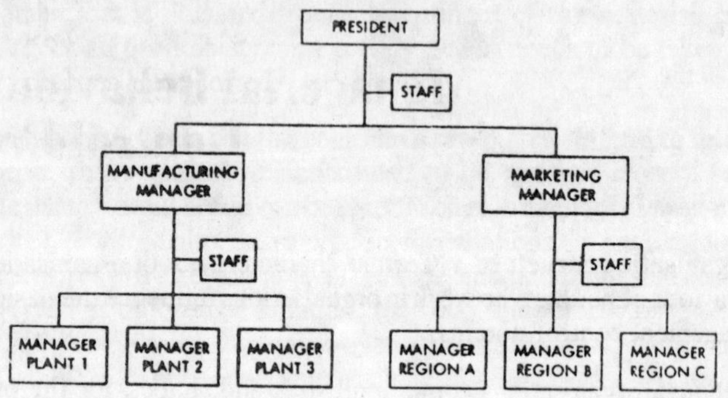

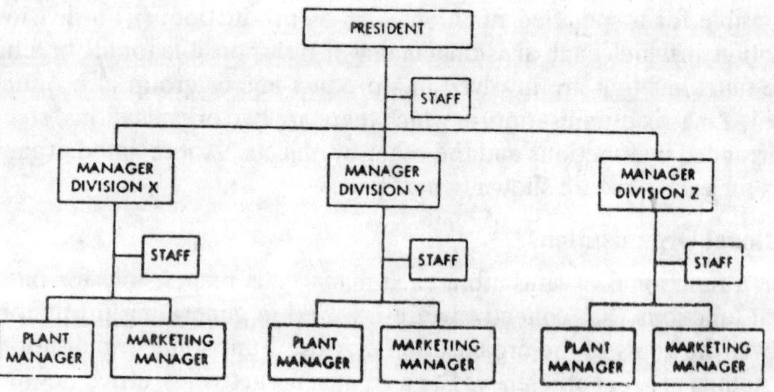

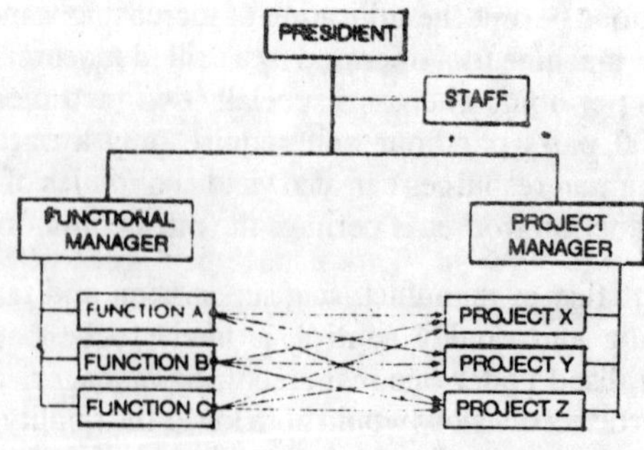

A disadvantage of a functional organisation is that responsibility for earning profits cannot be assigned unambiguously to individual managers. If one manager is responsible for manufacturing a product and another manager is responsible for marketing that product, then the profits on that product result from the joint efforts of each. It may be quite difficult or impossible, to identify how much of the total profit is attributable to each manager. Further, in a functional organisation, top management must plan and coordinate the activities of the functional units and resolve disputes between their managers. These factors make control more difficult in a functional organisation.

Effective decision making in a functionally organised business is hampered by the fact that no subordinate has the same broad perspective of the business that the president or general manager has. Many decisions, and almost all of the important ones, will affect more than one function in the business. Delegating the authority for such decisions to one functional manager may result in a different decision (because of his functional bias) than if the decision were made by another functional manager or by the general manager.

Divisional Organisations

For control purposes, a division in a divisional organisation can be treated almost as if it were an independent entity. The division manager can develop a strategy for his particular business, finding a competitive niche for it that may be different from the strategy being pursued by other division managers with different product lines. Tactically, a product division manager has the authority to change the production schedule in response to the request of an important customer; in a functional organisation, such a request must go "through channels", which may be ponderous and time-consuming. Moreover, divisions may be an excellent training ground for young managers, fostering entrepreneurship and increasing the number of centres of initiative in a corporation.

Since division managers are responsible for both the manufacturing and the marketing activities for the products in the division, they control the main elements that affect the division's profitability, and they therefore can be held accountable for their division's results. They cannot be held quite as accountable as if the division manager were the chief executive of an independent company because the division is a part of the larger organisation and decisions made by higher management and interactions with other divisions do impinge on the division manager's responsibility; nevertheless, the division manager can be held accountable for profits to a greater degree than the manager of a unit in a functional organisation. The management control process is therefore inherently more straight-forward in a divisional organisation than in a functional organisation.

Of course, responsibility centres within a division are functional units, and the control problem is the same for these units as for a whole company that is functionally organised except that it is on a smaller scale.

Matrix Organisations

In a matrix organisation, there is one basic organisation structure in which responsibility centres are arranged by functions, and alongside this structure-or superimposed on it - there is another structure in which the focus of responsibility is by projects. As used in this context, a project is any task or group of tasks involved in reaching a specified end objective. Preparing an advertising campaign, developing a new project, or building a new plant are examples of such objectives. Each project is set up for a specific purpose. The project manager used personnel, material, and/or services from the various functional units in accomplishing that objective, and when the objective is achieved the project is terminated.

A shipyard is an example of a matrix organisation. The basic organisation structure is by function shops-plumbing shop, electrical shop, machine shop, and so on. Each ship overhaul is a project. The project manager calls on the functional shops for the resources required for the job. If these resources are personnel, they work under the supervision of the project manager while assigned to the project. If the shop furnishes material or services, the responsibility for the cost, quality, and timely delivery of these items is partly that of the shop manager and partly that of the project manager.

Consulting firms, research/development organisations, construction companies, manufacturers of aircraft and other complicated equipment, and many other companies have a matrix organisation. In most companies, teams are created for various special purposes, and these teams are equivalent to projects.

The management control problems in a matrix organisation are obviously more difficult than those in the other two types. Planning must mesh the requirements of the projects with the resources that are available in the functional units. Coordination involves scheduling the activities of the several units so that projects are completed on time but personnel are not idle. Control is difficult because profitability is the joint responsibility of several managers.

Implication for Systems Design

If case of control were the only criterion, companies would be organised into divisions whenever it was feasible to do so because in a divisional organisation each divisional manager is held responsible for the profitability of the division's product line and presumably plans, coordinates, and controls the elements that affect its profitability. Control is not the only criterion, however. A functional organisation may be more efficient because the larger functional units give the economies of scale. A divisional organisation requires a somewhat broader type of manager than the specialist who manages a function. A matrix organisation permits personnel with similar skills to have a home base in a functional unit whose manager is responsible for developing these skills.

Because of the apparently clearcut nature of the assignment of profit responsibility in a divisional organisation, designers of a management control system sometimes recommend such an organisation without giving appropriate weight to the other considerations involved in organisation design. In the final analysis, the systems designer must fit the system to the organisation, not the other way around. In other words, although the control implications of various organisation structures should be discussed with top management, once management has decided that a given structure is best, all things considered, then the system designer must take that structure as a given and design the best system he can for it. Enthusiasts for some control technique may overlook this essential point.

This point is also important in other contexts. For example, many advertising agencies follow the practice of shifting account supervisors from one account to another at fairly frequent intervals, so as to bring a fresh point of view to the various advertising programmes. This practice increases the difficulty of measuring the performance of an account supervisor because the fruits of an advertising campaign may require a long time to ripen. Nevertheless, the systems designer should not insist that the rotation policy should be abandoned simply because to do so would make performance measurement easier.

KEY BEHAVIOURAL CONCEPTS

The control system aim at evaluating the performance of responsibility centres. The manager heading a responsibility centre is rewarded on the basis of performance evaluation of his department. This reward could be monetary or an enhancement of status or appreciation of work. He may also be punished if he fails to achieve the target. This could be in the form of stoppage of normal increments, delayed promotion, or general rebuke. Thus, control systems operate as double-edged swords. This is particularly true in situations where the linkages among various responsibility centres are high and one responsibility centre may get the reward at the cost of another. No doubt a large number of managers dread the formal control system and resist the introduction of such systems. Since the control process is primarily behavioural in nature, designer of the control system should have an understanding of how managers would react to formal systems. Since there is an intimate link between organisation behaviour and the control systems, it is essential to know what motivates managers to achieve the results and what organisational processes lead to better goal congruence between the individual and the organisation. The field of behavioural science deals with such questions in detail. Here, we will restrict ourselves to key behavioural concepts that have relevance for control systems. These are (i) perception, (ii) attitudes and beliefs, (iii) motivation, (iv) goal congruence, (v) inter unit conflict and cooperation, (vi) managerial styles, (vii) resistance to change (viii) force field analysis, (ix) entrapment, (x) compromising and sacrificing and (xi) socio- cultural influences.

Perception

The control process involves interactions among various levels of management. In such interactions, the perception of what the other party wants in an important factor in determining the achievements. This is because it may not be possible to specify the actions in advance with absolute clarity. Further, managers, in informal discussions, may get a different impression about the seriousness of senior management for achievement/non achievement of results. They may also perceive the control system as being unjust and unfair, particularly, if some colleagues get rewards on the basis of manipulation of performance or through credit snatching. Thus, the success of the control system will depend upon the perception of managers in terms of what is expected of them. Since the organisations have two dimensions namely formal and informal, distortion in communication can take place at various levels. The existence of informal organisations, which is reality, may lead to not so desirable perceptions.

Attitudes and Beliefs

Attitudes and beliefs are important determinants of managerial behaviour. The attitudes and beliefs are the results of manager's learning and experiences in his social, religious, cultural and organisational settings. In the context of management control, attitudes acquire importance because the achievement of targets to some extent depends upon a positive attitude towards work. As attitudes serve as a frame of reference, they provide a bench mark against which facts and events are viewed. If, in a review meeting, person in charge of a particular responsibility centre gets snubbed without reason, and if this has happened in an earlier meeting, his actions in future meetings may be influenced by these experiences and by a belief that his superior wants to settle scores with him.

Motivation

The managerial behaviour can be influenced by providing appropriate stimuli. Since human beings behave as they do because of certain needs and motives, it is necessary to know about the various types of motives that propel managers to act in a certain way. In order to direct managerial behaviour towards attainment of overall goals of organisations, the top management has to provide the necessary motivating stimuli. Maslow's model of needs hierarchy indicates the various needs such as physiological, safety, love, ego and self-actualisation. In order to motivate managers positively these needs have to be taken care of. Herzberg proposed the two-factor model. According to him, there are two sets of factors, namely factors that may prevent dissatisfaction (hygiene factors) and factors that may provide satisfaction (motivators). Hygiene factors include salary, working conditions, company policy, supervision and work group, and motivators include advancement, development, responsibility, recognition, achievement, and the work itself. This framework is useful in understanding what motivates managers in achieving the targets. Mc Clelland identified the need for achievement as a significant need. The other needs include need for power and need for extension. Achievement motivation is characterised by calculated risk taking, personal responsibility for success and failure, use of feedback for improving performance. Power motivation is characterised by an urge to make an impact, to influence and to control other person, situations and events. Extension motivation is characterised by concern for others, to be of service to the community and society at large. The management control process should provide the necessary opportunities to managers to get these needs satisfied.

Incentives : Individuals are influenced both by positive incentives and negative incentives. A positive incentive, also called a reward or a reinforcement, is the satisfaction of a need, or the expectation that a need will be satisfied. A negative incentive, also called a punishment, is the deprivation of satisfaction of a need, or the fear of such deprivation. Most of the research studies on human incentives use students as subjects, and those few studies conducted in a business environment tend to focus on sales persons, production workers, clerical employees, and other nonmanagers. There are obvious difficulties in conducting controlled experiments with managers as subjects. Despite the paucity of research evidence, there seems to be support for the following generalisations :

Individuals are more motivated by positive incentives than by negative incentives.

Monetary compensation is an important incentive, but beyond the subsistence level the amount of compensation is not necessarily as important as non-monetary rewards. Nevertheless, the amount of person's earnings is often important indirectly as an indication of how his achievement and ability are regarded. (a person earning Rs. 50,000 a year may be disgruntled if a colleague whom he perceives to have only equal ability earns Rs. 51,000 a year).

The effectiveness of incentives diminishes rapidly as time elapses between an action and the reward or punishment administered for it. This is why it is important that reports on performance be made available and acted on quickly. Management control cannot wait for the annual financial statements that appear three months or so after the year has ended.

Needs may be unconscious, or they may be expressed as aspirations or objectives. Motivation is weakest when the person perceives an objective as being either unattainable or too easily attainable. Motivation is str when the objective can be attained with some effort and when the individual regards its attainment as important in relation to his needs.

The incentive provided by a budget or other statement of objective is strongest when the manager participates actively in the process of arriving at the budgeted amounts.

A person who perceives his work as being worthwhile or important is more highly motivated than one who does not.

A person needs to know, on some fairly regular basis, whether the results of his efforts are regarded by his superior as being satisfactory.

Objectives are likely to provide strong incentives only if the manager perceives these objectives to be fair.

Objectives are likely to provide strong incentives only if managers feel committed to attaining them. The commitment is strongest when it is a matter of public record, that is, when the manager has explicitly agree to the objective.

Managers tend to accept reports of performance more willingly and to use them more constructively when the reports are presented to them in a manner that they regard as objective; that is, without personal bias.

Persons are receptive to learning better ways of doing things only when they personally recognise the inadequacies of their present behaviour.

Beyond a certain point, pressure for improved performance accomplishes nothing. This optimum point is far below the maximum amount of pressure that conceivably could be exerted.

Individuals differ in their needs and in their reactions to incentives of various types. An important functions of the manager at each level is to adapt his application of the management control system to the personalities and attitudes of the individuals whom he supervises. Thus an impersonal system can never be substitute for interpersonal actions; rather, the system is a framework that should be adapted by the manager to fit individual situations.

Compensation : In many companies managers are compensated in part by a salary and in part by a bonus that is based on performance. This bonus can be a powerful incentive. The bonus and the method of arriving at it can take any of several forms, and the direction and strength of motivation is greatly affected by the particular forms that are selected.

The basis for the bonus can be entirely objective, entirely subjective, or anywhere in between. An objective bonus is one that is based strictly on a formula, such as the calculated profitability of a division. The measure of profitability can be for the individual division, for the company as a whole, or for the combination of the two. The time span for the bonus calculation can be single year, or a period of two, three, or four years.

A bonus system which is primarily objective, which focuses on a division's profitability, and which has a short time span is appropriate when the division manager has a considerable degree of autonomy, when cooperation with other divisions is relatively unimportant, and when the division manager is unlikely to take short-run actions that hurt long-run profitability. By contrast, a bonus system which is based primarily on top management's subjective appraisal, which focuses on the profitability of the company as a whole, and which may cover a period of several years, is appropriate when top management exerts a direct influence on decisions that affect the divisions, when divisions must cooperate with one another, when the short-run profitability of a division cannot be measured with reasonable accuracy, and when a long-run view is encouraged. Many permutations of these sets of characteristics are obviously possible and lead to a wide variety of bonus plans.

Alternatives also exist for the form of bonus payment. It may be paid in cash or in stock options, and in either case the payment may be made immediately, or it may be deferred for a number of years. These payment options also affect the motivation that the bonus provides. Clearly, the power of the bonus and the existence of such a variety of alternatives suggest that it is worthwhile to devote much study and thought to devising a bonus plan which will provide the optimum motivation.

Goal congruence

Each individual has his personal goals. He joins an organisation to achieve these goals. The personal goal may just be to get a job that assures safety and monetary rewards. The organisation, through its top management, sets for itself goals that is desired to achieve. At times there is a conflict between individual goals and organisational goals. Such conflict is more clearly evident in non-profit organisations such as research and development institutions, and educational institutions. Top management wants these organisational goals to be attained, but other participants have their own personal goals that they want to achieve. These personal goals are the satisfaction of their needs. In other words, participants act in their own self- interest. Here individuals may grow bigger than the organisation and this may lead to goal conflict. The control system should be designed so as to integrate the personal goals with organisational goals, and thereby achieve goal congruence. As managers tend to take action according to their perceived self-interest, the control system should ensure that these actions are also in the interest of the organisation. Thus, the system should discourage individuals acting against the interests of the organisation, e.g., a cost reduction should not be achieved at the cost of quality if the organisation has concern for quality products.

In the language of social psychology, the management control system should encourage goal congruence; that is, it should be structured so that the goals of participants, so far as is feasible, are consistent with the goals of the organisation as a whole. If this situation exists, a decision that a manager regards as being good from his own viewpoint will also be good decision for the organisation as a whole. As Mc Gregor states :

The essential task of management is to arrange organisational conditions and methods of operations so that people can achieve their own goals best by directing their own efforts towards organisational objectives.*

Perfect congruence between individual goals and organisational goals does not exist. One obvious reason is that individual participants want as much salary as they can get, whereas from the view point of the organisation, there is an upper limit to salaries, beyond which profits will be adversely affected. As a minimum, however, the system should not encourage the individual to act against the best interests of the company. For example, if the management control system signals that the emphasis should be only on reducing costs, and if a manager responds by reducing costs at the expense of adequate quality or if he responds by reducing costs in his own responsibility centre by measures that cause a more than offsetting increase in costs in some other responsibility centre, he has been motivated, but in the wrong direction. It is therefore important to ask two separate questions about any practice used in a management control system :

1. What action does it motivate people to take in their own perceived self interest, and
2. Is this action in the best interests of the company?

There is a close link between motivation and goal congruence. As motivation involves desire for a selected goal and the drive or pursuit towards the goal, it has two aspects, namely congruence and effort. The achievement of goal congruence may also be affected by the degree of freedom to make decisions, i.e., autonomy given to the managers. Therefore, while designing a control system, the three important aspects related to goal congruence, managerial effort and autonomy should be given due consideration, with a view to motivating managers to achieve organisational goals.

Inter-unit Conflict and Cooperation

The conflict and cooperation are fundamental to all living systems. We observe the predator prey relationships and other similar situations in life. This

---

* David Mc Gregor, The Human Side of Enterprise (New York : Mc Graw-Hill, 1960).

phenomenon is also observed in the context of organisations. Conflicts are inherent among various responsibility centres because of their conflicting goals, e.g., the marketing department may like to keep as much inventory as is possible while the finance manager may insist on reduction of inventory. The conflict between two mutually interdependent divisions is generally evident, because each is trying to optimise its profits. This conflict is resolved by the top management through appropriate transfer price mechanism. An important task of senior management is to resolve inter-unit conflicts. The control system can provide necessary inputs for resolving such conflicts. While a certain amount of conflict is desirable for keeping the organisation healthy, it should not be allowed to reach unmanageable proportions, as it may lead to dysfunctional consequences. As conflict arises partly because of competition, the management may like to keep healthy competition within limits. Since collaborative efforts are also required to achieve overall goals, the control system should foster the cooperation among various responsibility centres. This can be achieved through appropriate coordinative mechanisms, such as creation of coordination committees consisting of those in charge of strategic business units. Khandwala has summed up the various aspects related to conflict and cooperation as follows.

> The greater the interdependence between organisation units, the more specialised their functions and the greater the differences between their personnel in terms of goals, the means for achieving goals and the procedures for resolving agreements, the greater is likely to be conflict between them. The more restrictive, diverse or technologically complex the environment, the more professionally oriented the top management style (including an emphasis on participation and optimisation) and the higher the aspirations of the top management with respect to organisational goals, the greater is the variety of coordinative mechanisms employed in the organisation.*

Organisation Climate : As noted above, perceptions about an organisation's goals and about decisions that a manager should take to achieve these goals come not only from the formal control system but also through the informal organisation. Both the formal and informal structure combine to create what is called the organisational climate. As defined by Andrews :

The term 'climate' is used to designate the quality of the internal environment which conditions in turn the quality of cooperation, the development of individuals, the extent of members dedication or commitment to organisational purpose, and the efficiency with which that purpose becomes translated into results. Climate is the atmosphere in which individuals help, judge, reward,

---

* Pradip Khandwala, The Design of Organisation, Harcourt Brace Jovanovich, New York, 1977, p. 551,

constrain and find out about each other. It influences morale-the attitude of the individual toward his work and his environment.*

Organisational Climate has important influences on motivation. Since to a certain extent an organisation is "the lengthened shadow of an individual", the attitude of the chief executive officer toward control is an important ingredient of the climate. The nature of the management control process in a given organisation is much affected by the "style" of the top management in that organisation. Some chief executive officers rely heavily on reports and other formal documents; others prefer conversations and informal contacts. The formal system must be consistent with top management's preferences. It follows that if a new top management, with a different style, takes over, the system should change correspondingly.

By its very nature, "climate" cannot be described concretely. Some alternative characteristics are as follows :

Focus on results versus focus on following the rules.

Individual accomplishment versus being a member of the team.

Initiative and risk taking versus "not rocking the boat".

Individual gains versus enhancement of organisational objectives.

Tough mindedness in dealing with people versus avoidance of unpleasant actions.

The purpose of the management control system is to insure compliance with polices versus the purpose is to obtain results.

The management control system is an aid to managers versus the system should be circumvented or disregarded.

The relative importance of participatory management versus authoritarian management.**

Managerial Styles

The management control process involves determination of targets and setting up the standards. This can be done by two diametrically opposite styles viz., the authoritarian (autocratic) and the democratic styles. The authoritarian leader sets the standards without consulting the persons who are expected to achieve them, while a democratic leader ensures that policies, strategies and standards are determined by group. An autocratic leader unilaterally decides

* Kenneth R. Andrews, The Concept of Corporate Strategy (Homewood, Ill. : Dow Jones-Irwin, Inc., 1971), page 232.

** This list is adapted from an unpublished paper by Professor Robert H. Caplan.

what is to be done and assigns the specific tasks to each individual. Quite often he does not indicate the overall purpose of the activity and just tells the people as to what is to be done. He gives general feedback which is often punitive and fires at failures. A democratic leader decides along with the group what is to be done and lets the group decide who is to do what and makes sure that a decision is made. He ensures that everybody understands the overall goals, objectives and plans. He gives specific feedback and uses mistakes as an opportunity for coaching and guidance, and tolerates failures. Although the autocratic and democratic styles in theory represent two ends of spectrum, however, in reality, the leaders use a mix of both styles. They are autocratically democratic or democratically autocratic, i.e., they are tough as nails for certain values, ideals and ideas, and adopt an open door policy on other issues or vice versa, if the clarity on goals and values is not of high order. Thus, managers usually use a mix of theory X and theory Y, and rarely theory X or theory Y.

Force Field Analysis

Kurt Lewin developed the field-force analysis using the field concepts of physics. His field theory is concerned with the dynamics of human motivation. Lewin defines the concepts of 'lifespace' consisting of the person and the psychological environment, and, life space being the union of these two. According to him, there are two dimensions for every situation facing a person, namely what is possible and what is not possible in that situation. Accordingly, there are certain facilitating factors and certain inhibiting factors related to the situation faced by the individual. These may facilitate or retard progress towards particular events such as achievement of targets, effective performance of the tasks assigned to the individuals. The managerial behaviour is determined by the relationship between the person and environment as revealed by facilitating (driving forces) and inhibiting factors (restraining forces) that lead to possible rather than impossible events. The driving forces are those that push the existing situation towards the desired goal while restraining forces are those that hinder the movement towards the goals. The equilibrium is attained as a result of these two forces, just as in Newtonian mechanics.

Lewin's framework of force-field analysis is closely interlinked with management control process. During the review meetings for performance appraisal of the responsibility centres, the focus is on identifying the facilitating and inhibiting factors in the achievement or non-achievement of targets. These are then divided into factors that were within the control of the manager of the responsibility centre and factors beyond his control. The reasons are analysed for non-achievement and remedial action plan is drawn up. This process is very close to the force-field approach advocated by Lewin.

Resistance to Change

It has been a common experience that organisations tend to follow the law of inertia. As the introduction of control systems tends to move the organisation from one level of equilibrium to a higher level of equilibrium, there is an inbuilt tendency on the part of the organisation to resist. A proper understanding of resistance to change is important for the designer of the control systems.

The inertial resistance which indicates the resistance to change, depends upon the size and age of the organisation, technology, age of managers, etc. We quite often hear about removing the dead wood from the organisation in order to infuse new thinking and reduce the resistance to change, so as to make the organisation an adaptive organisation. An important objective of introducing a formal control system is to reduce inertial resistance and make the organisation more effective.

Entrapment

At times, managers are hesitant to backtrack or make changes that can be construed as an admission of error. They get entrapped because of their own previous decisions and will spend more time and energy justifying their earlier decisions rather than taking any policy shift. This entrapment can be observed in several organisational conflicts. When negative results occur, managers intensify their efforts by putting more resources than are justifiable in a given situation. The U.S. intervention in vietnam is an illustration of entrapment. In the context of the organisation, it must decide on how much R & D expenditure is needed to build a new or improved product. It should decide on how much advertising is needed. A voluntary agency must decide about its representative's withdrawal from the host agency. These represent situations in which managers get entrapped. Entrapment has been more specifically defined as follows.

> The term escalation refers to an increase in the perceived or actual size of a conflict. Entrapment is formally defined as a special form of escalation in which parties involved expend more of their time, energy, money or other resources in a conflict than seems appropriate or justifiable according to some external standards.*

Compromising and Sacrificing

Herbert Simon's research related to administrative behaviour, indicated that managers depict a 'satisficing' behaviour. According to Simon,

> In actual organisational practice, no one attempts to find an optimal solution for the whole problem. Instead, various particular decision or

* Percy H. Hill, et.al., Making Decision : A Multidisciplinary Introduction, Addison - Wesley Publishing Co., Reading, Massachusetts P. 69

groups of decisions within the whole complex are made by specialised members or units of the organisation. In making these particular decisions, the specialist units do not solve the problem but find a "satisfactory" solution.*

Thus, in real life the managers tend to seek satisficing solutions rather than optimal solutions.

Several times managers tend to seek compromising solution rather than satisficing or optimal solution. While the logic of a situation may demand a particular decision, however, because of pressures and counter pressures, the actual decision taken may be compromising solution. As an illustration of compromising solution we can cite the allocation of portfolios to ministers or allocation of responsibilities in an organisation. The ministerial position may not necessarily be given to the most able person but to a person representing a particular pressure group. Compromising is particularly applicable in those dynamic situations where constant readjustments are required to be made because of changes in underlying forces. it may be pointed out that compromising should not be construed in the negative sense.

Another important aspect is 'sacrificing'. The person in charge of one responsibility centre may adopt a sacrificing behaviour towards other responsibility centres. Such managerial behaviour may be observed particularly in those cultures which inculcate a feeling of sacrificing such as in Japan and India. The sacrificing behaviour can be observed in transfer price decisions.

Socio Cultural Influences

A Chief Executive who was assigned the task of turning around a government owned public sector unit, indicated that he derived his inspiration from Rabindranath Tagore and immediately narrated a verse whose translation is as follows : "Who will take the charge of my work, says the setting sun. Hearing this, the world keeps mum, like a picture dumb. One earthern lamp was there, it said : My lord, I shall strive to do the best I can". Another chief executive, in a briefing session to managers, spoke out several verses from poet Thiruvalluvar's work, Thirukkural, which was written a few centuries before Christ. The author happened to be present in the briefing session, and found the verses inspiring and containing lessons of motivation and leadership. The author was told that a lot of South Indian managers derive inspiration from this scripture. Just to illustrate, here is the English translation of two selected verses. "He (the leader) has capacity to tolerate those who speak harsh words and greet them with a smile (Verse 389). "Get information from independent sources and if they are consistent, accept the information as right" (Verse 586). A

---

* Herbert A. Simon, Administrative Behaviour, (3rd ed), Free Press, New York, 1976,). 272.

businessman highlighted the importance of inaugural ceremony for the newly acquired business premises and indicated that such occasions help in creating an extended family, which is very essential for long-term business growth. One chief executive experimented with Gandhiji's concept of Trusteeship and said that his actions are guided by the principle of sum total good and not the individual good. Another chief executive derived inspiration from the teachings of Lord Buddha and said he attempted to follow the path of Buddha, according to which 'the only real victory is one in which no one is vanquished and everyone is victor'. At least some of the Indian managers and businessmen are deeply influenced by the profound teaching of various scriptures of different religions, which have now become part of the Indian cultural heritage. The organisational culture to some extent gets influenced by cultural and religious stimuli to which every person in the society gets exposed, explicitly or implicitly. The culture and religion affect our managerial actions through their impact on collective subconscious.

Since the control process involves motivating subordinates to achieve the targets, the meaningful learnings from our scriptures could assist managers in performing their tasks more effectively. As the scriptures shape attitudes and beliefs, their impact on management control process is revealed implicitly or explicitly, in the way managers handle certain situations. If our attitude is shaped by the path of Buddha, in which no one is vanquished and everyone is victor, then our managerial actions will be determined accordingly. On the other hand if we are trained through the methodology of 'win as much as you can', our managerial actions will follow this rule.

REVIEW QUESTIONS

1. Explain in brief the key behavioural concepts that have relevance to control systems?
2. "Control systems operate as double edged swords". Elucidate.
3. Do you think that managerial behaviour can be influenced by providing the necessary motivational stimuli?
4. How does the managerial style affect the management control process?
5. 'A proper understanding of resistance to change is important for the designer of the control systems'. Why?
6. Explain the key behavioural concepts that have relevance to control systtems .
7. Explain briefly the following : (a) Perception, (b) Goal Congruence, (c) Entrapment and (d) Socio-Cultural Influences.

12
Management By Objectives

Definition & Concept : Many approaches have been utilised to integrate individual and group goals with overall goals of the organisation of an enterprise. Management By Objectives is basically a process whereby the superior and subordinate managers of an enterprise jointly (i) identify its common goals, (ii) define each individual's major areas of responsibility in terms of results expected of him, and (iii) use these measures as guides for operating the unit (or enterprise) and assessing the contribution of each of its members. The goals are jointly established by the manager and his subordinates and agreed upon in advance. These goals emphasize either output variables or intervening variables, or some combination of both. At the end of the predecided time period, the subordinate's performance is reviewed in relation to preset goals. Both superior and the subordinate participate in this review/evaluation. If, after evaluation, it is found that there is some discrepancy between the work planned (to be done) and the work accomplished, steps are suggested to overcome the problems or to make necessary adjustments in the original plan. This sets the stage for the determination of objectives for the next time period. To conclude, MBO implies managing by properly identifying the objectives of an organisation.

Objectives : An objective is an intended goal which prescribes definite scope and suggests direction to efforts of a Manager.

Need for Objectives : Management is the art of getting things done through people. In a competitive economy, things will not get done well unless everyone concerned in an enterprise knows what the objectives and targets are and accepts them as being worth attaining.

Requirements of Objectives : Objectives, whether those of individuals or those of the organisation must (i) work in the same direction towards achieving company goals; (ii) be clearly defined and communicated to all; (iii) be such that they can be reasonably attained; (iv) be reviewed after definite time period for adjustments if necessary.

Nature of Objectives : Objectives may be (i) Short term, e.g., expediting the works lagging behind the schedule; (ii) Long term, e.g., planning for diversification; (iii) Specific, e.g., decision of pricing policies; (iv) General, e.g., profit objective, objective of increasing productivity.

Types of Objectives : There are three basic types of objectives : 1. Broad objectives 2. Major objectives 3. Minor or Lesser objectives.

1. Broad or Corporate Objective is a wordy statement of the standing the company wishes to achieve. e.g., (i) To supply to public with the best of modern utility services at reasonable rates; (ii) To manufacture high quality products and to strive to make them better at lower costs, etc.

2. Major objectives are distilled from Broad objectives and set the tactical areas into which the company wishes to move. Major objectives include market shares, product plans and plans to expand the customer population.

3. Minor or Lesser objectives are targets, budgets, and departmental objectives, including those governing the performance standards of managers and the other members of the staff.

Steps in Setting up MBO

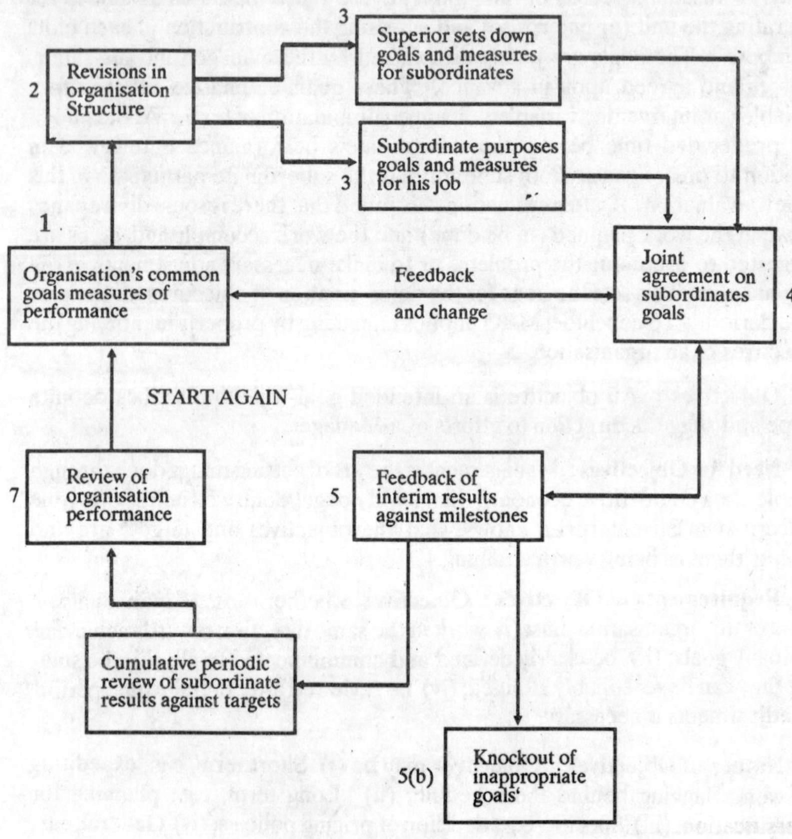

Fig. 12.1 Steps of the Cycle of MBO

1. The first step is to clarify and set the common goals of the entire organisation.

2. To achieve the goals of the organisation, any appropriate changes in the organisation. structure may be made : changes in titles, duties, relationships, authority, responsibility, span of control, and so forth.

3. Superior sets down goals for his subordinates; subordinates also propose goals for their jobs and select the areas in which they must be effective during the period of compauy plan. Usually there are five or six vital areas where the subordinates concerned must think to obtain the desired results. These results may be straight drive to (a) Some targets of growth, (b) Achievement of greater efficiency, productivity or profitability, (c) Elimination of certain problems etc.

4. Superior and subordinates sit together, discuss the objectives and reach on joint agreement on a subordinates' goals to be achieved by him during a stated time period. In other words, the goals are jointly established and agreed upon in advance.

5. Throughout the time period what is to be accomplished should be compared with what is being accomplished; necessary adjustments should be made and inappropriate goals or unattainable goals should be discarded so that resources are not unnecessarily wasted.

6. The performance of all subordinates against their MBO plan (or targets) must be formally reviewed at predetermined times during the plan. Usually a major review is made annually but it is advisable for lesser quarterly reviews to be undertaken. In the latter, attention is given to the areas where progress has been slow or where some unforeseen bottlenecks have occurred. These may be due to poor performance of some other subordinates' MBO achievements.

7. Ultimately the performance of the entire organisation should be reviewed with respect to the objective set at the start. If there is a discrepancy between the objectives decided and those achieved, efforts should be initiated to determine the steps to be taken to overcome the problems responsible for the discrepancy. This sets the stage for the determination of objectives for the next time period and the entire cycle of MBO is started again from step 1.

Till a couple of decades ago, 'Management by Objective' was a little known concept. Its phenomenal circulation, all over the world, and in all kinds of undertakings happened in the last forty years or so. The first among management writers to introduce the concept was Peter Drucker writing in the 1950's. Other high priests of the concept were George S. Odiorne and Jhon Humble. Odiorne stated the concept as :

> "a process whereby the superior and the subordinate managers of an enterprise jointly identify its common goals, define each individual's

major areas of responsibility in terms of the results expected of him, and use these measures as guides for operating the unit and assessing the contribution of each of its members".

Launching the M.B.O. - The Logic and the Steps

Setting objectives is the first task of all management. Reaching the objective (goal) is the very logic of the management process through organising, directing and control. In this context to talk elaborately or to introduce the theme of M.B.O., as an innovation might appear naive and labouring a truism. Yet, most organisations which have seriously introduced M.B.O. have reaped distinct improvement in their management. It is, therefore, to outline the system - step by step - logically as it must be introduced in an enterprise.

Step 1 : The first step is to **set down, formally, the goals of the enterprise.** This is essential; for it is often that an enterprise of them this question in a television interview. The chances are nine to one that after half an hour of rambling eloquence, the Chief of the organisation will leave the audience no wiser or himself no clearer about it than when he began his televised dissertation.

Step 2 : Objectivise the goals so set out and define measures of performance. Perhaps the most important mandate of M.B.O. is that the objectives (at all levels) must be set out in concrete terms; they must be measurable to serve as yardsticks of accomplishment.

Step 3 : The goals (sub-goals) at all management levels must then be set out. The process is both deductive and inductive. The sub-goals at the top and lower management and supervisory levels are deduced from the enterprise goal; they are also worked upward (induced) from the bottom of the management pyramid. When these two stream meet-and found to diverge-starts the process of sifting and adjustment. The result is an agreed set (system) of goal network harmonising with the enterprise goal. The horizontal levels of goal-centres are simultaneously brought into the net. They support one another, collaterally (at parallel levels) and fit into the goal network up and down the management pyramid.

Step 4 : The compulsion of the first three steps is likely **to demand adjustment in the organisation structure-which must be put through.** The goal network when it is built between step 1, through step 3, has a logic of its own. The organisation frame needs to sustain this logic as a close fit.

Step 5 : The goals to be set at all levels must be joint and agreed ones. As previously suggested, goal-setting is not a matter of **direction** from the top; not even a process of deduction from the top management objective. Contrarily, it is also not a derivative of bottom-level management thinking synthesised into enterprise goal. It is a two-way process, in fact, a participative all-level wisdom put together in cordial discussions out of which emerge the (a) enterprise goal (b) objective and task of top management and (c) the several tasks and targets at all levels of management.

(a) The senior (up in the management ladder) advises goals for the junior levels; the latter suggest their own goals (as they see it) and the overall goal for the enterprise. The several merits accrue from the process : (a) The goals set at the top levels reflect more keenly the interface of the enterprise with the outside environment. It provides the much-needed link between the organisation sub-system and the social system. The goals set by juniors and employees reflect, more closely the hard reality and constraints within the enterprise. The goals set at the top (for all levels) set the dimensions and the challenge; the goals set at the bottom (for all levels), the drags and warnings. From out the marriage of the two is born the **optimum goal** which the enterprise can reach within its constraints after they are stretched and broken with the skill and urge of the management team.

(b) The searchlight of attention flashed through the details of the enterprise status-illumining in the process, its visible future as it can be carved out of the present; and the whole of the management team is witness to the great act of searching analysis. This leaves the **communication line** flushed and clear.

(c) The whole team gets **involved** as a participative network; and the best in them comes out in the process. Their individual goals and several motives are set to compass-point that directs to the common enterprise goal. Goal-erosion, wasted and militating efforts, and cantankerous self-service tend to meet away-fused in the cooperative team work.

(d) **Management by objective,** undergoes a mutation toward **management by self-appraisal** (the utopia of the behavioural theorists) **and management by results.** Management is no longer a mere series of actions; no longer (as it is, so often) a string of excuses for failures, missed opportunities, fatal unpreparedness. Ideally and managed imaginatively, M.B.O. can indeed unleash the fissionable energies and closeted wisdom of the human beings-all harnessed in the common task.

(e) The **leadership** is released from the routine of administration. His time (so circumscribed) and energies (of which the fund is sorely strained) are set free for the task of piloting the enterprise through the shoals and turbulence of the frightening dynamics of the modern economic and socio-economic spectrum.

Step 6 : There is a continuous feed back from appraisal (review) of internal (and several) goals and the enterprise goal as it is set. The result is two-way interaction by which the internal goals are set to a higher pitch and the enterprise goal is fettled (continuously) to an updated form.

Step 7 : Appraisal of results proceed continuously against the goals at all levels-and the closed-system is set a new in its self-correcting cycle. Since all levels are committed to their distinct and local results, the correction process is self- starting without waiting for advice or mandates from the top.

Step 8 : Review of sub-results (at lower levels) throws light on organisation results. This helps control and correction and, secondly, monitor and adjust the organisational goal.

The following diagram is visualisation of the closed sub-system of the functioning of M.B.O.

Fig. 12.2 The Eight-step of M.B.O. Cycle

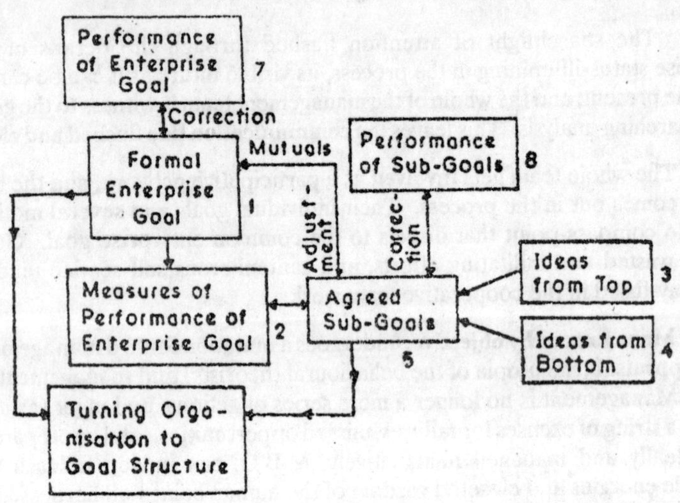

Advantages of M.B.O.

(a) Management by objectives may become a powerful tool in gaining mutual commitment and high productivity for an organisation.

(b) M.B.O keeps company objectives\targets constantly in view.

It gives meaning and direction to people in an organisation

(c) It coordinates the efforts of various departments of an organisation

(d) It provides motivation to people because they work on objectives decided with their consent.

(e) It prevents flittering away of efforts and money.

(f) It allows greater consistency in decision making.

(g) It forces management to think ahead in respect of its short-term and long-term goals.

(h) It helps an enterprise to focus on the areas where it is vital that management should be effective and isolate the problems preventing progress towards company objectives.

(i) It assists managers in their own self-development and leads to an analysis of training requirements if subordinates are to improve their performance in future years.

(j) MBO leads to a better understanding between superiors and the subordinates.

What's Wrong with M.B.O. - Its Limitations

Many organisations, in this country and elsewhere in the world, have reaped large benefits from a serious application of M.B.O. At the same time, many more prominent organisation (in the private but more so in the public sector) have not adopted this relatively simple and logical system. The process of catching up seems too slow for the process to become a force in business management. The question must be asked, and answered (however tentatively), why this is so. Observations in many empirical situations suggest certain reasons :

(a) In a scheme of M.B.O. the leadership quality and contribution does not find a central place. The leader, of course, (with his team) suggests the goal-at the top and at lower levels-but that is open for a debate and discussion. An over- reliance is placed on rational attitudes and intelligent consensus. Too often, the reality situation does not support these premises.

(b) Somewhat allied to the first point is the consensus on the **leadership style** on which the top and the lower levels must sit down together and agree. a particular leadership style goes well (and another does not) with a certain (available) combination of **men and goals** that they must accomplish. Of the **four** broad leadership styles, each one would suit a typical (actual) situation that controls managers and their goals. These are-(a) hight task-high relation (supervision); (b) high task low relation; (c) low task-high relation; and (d) low task-low relation. These are only different combinations of the **level** (difficulty and challenge) of the task set and the **level** (quality, experience, etc.) of the managers available to accomplish them. M.B.O., to be more rewarding, has to reach not only agreed goals down the line but a combination of **goal-leadership-style** nexus appropriate to the situation. This does not convey that agreement on this **combination** is either rigid or irreversible. In fact, this agreement ought to be an understanding, open for continuous review and discussion (and therefore adjustment) between the levels of management concerned.

(c) The scheme does not assign sufficient weightage to goal conflicts. It does lean heavily on continuous adjustment of goals-at all levels in the light of actual performance and evolving environment but the basic (almost total) assumption is that the whole system moves objectively and rationally. This is not realised inpractice.

(d) Society being what it is (and there are no signs of the symptoms abating), **three levels** (at least) of motives work toward setting managers' and employees' goal. Not necessarily all of them are on the surface. These are : (i) Rational and objective motives, (ii) Irrational and idiosyncratic motives-which will include personal equations, and (iii) Motives that spring from the mischief-element in management. This is the misty area of all reality management which breeds factions, groups, concerted self-service-worsening (in the extreme situation) into intrigues, conspiracies, corruption. M.B.O. is at once a victim and a corrective to these forces. So long as the two latter motives are not effectively bottled up the bed is too inhospitable for the seeds of M.B.O. to flower. With all these comments, let it be recorded that energetic pursuit of the theme of M.B.O. can do no harm. It is a healing process; and by the very act of attacking cobwebs and dank musty areas of management it holds back the germs of plague that ever threaten to engulf the unwary management.

(1) One of the pre-requisites for effective implementation of MBO is a **clear thinking at the corporate level translated into long-term plans.** Many organisations have over the years, implemented MBO and improved their operations and performance. (2) Effective implementation of MBO **requires a good reporting system.** This is necessary for taking timely remedial action in case deficiency is noticed in any area. As organisation grows in size, this reporting system becomes complex and time consuming. It may not be possible for top management to directly supervise each and every activity at lower interested in critical activities rather than every activity. Thus, as a **by-product of MBO,** large organisations introduced what is called **Management By Exception**(MBE).

In this management technique, higher levels of management will concentrate only on exceptional situations, i.e., critical areas.

Both MBO and MBE are scientific forms of management. However, they can be successful only and only if corporate level executives are capable of thinking ahead and have a real interest in promoting the organisations rather than selves.

Combination of these two qualities are not frequently found and when MBO is introduced in an organisation where these are lacking, different distorted versions of MBO will appear on the scene. **Four such distorted versions** in the reverse order of their scientific efficiency which can be occasionally seen in and around us are given below.

1. Management By Crisis (MBC) : In this type of management, decisions are taken only when a crisis develops. This happens when the organisation as a whole is incapable of thinking systematically and scientifically about its future. Because of this, ad hoc decisions are the order of the day. When crisis develops executives are forced to take decisions at least to put out fire. But such decisions most often - though they temporarily put out fire - create future crisis and the organisation moves from one crisis to another, demoralising the entire system in the process. Even with all the drawbacks of this style of management one has to agree that a certain amount of courage is required by the management to take decisions when crisis develops. Unfortunately there are managements which do not act even in situations of crisis. Such type of management is called "Management by Inertia (MBI)".

2. Management By Inertia (MBI) : In this type of management the manager believes that, left to itself, a problem will get solved automatically and any action by him is likely to jeopardise his present and future position in the organisation. Thus, no actions or decisions are taken on very many important issues. A classic example of this type of management is found in organisations where representations from especially individual employees are not listened to for years together. Having waited for so long a period, the employee may feel that the management may not consider his request at all. Having, no other avenue to redress his grievance, he reconcilies to his situation and later turns out to be a frustrated employee for the rest of his life.

3. Management By Telegrams (MBT) : This is a fall-out of Management by crisis. When decisions are taken at the last moment, normal communication channels break down mostly due to lack of time. In this type of management telegrams are the order of the day. In addition to the heavy expenditure which eats the profitability of the organisations, MBT creates other problems also related with non and wrong delivery of telegrams and distorted message communication. Telegrams, a communication media, which normally should have been used only in case of unforeseen exigencies, today are the major source of communication for many inefficient organisations. In fact, the level of efficiency of an office is directly inverse to the number of telegrams issued and received by that office.

4. Management By Judges (MBJ) : In all the above types of management, even though some of them are highly unscientific, a ray of hope remains in the sense that management is still in the hands of persons working in the organisation. However, when on majority of the occasions decisions are not taken or decisions are taken on the basis of personal equations rather than merits of the case; persons affected by the issues, be they employees or creditors or customers, feel that justice and fairplay cannot be expected at the hands of the management and the only course left to them will be to approach courts obtaining justice. In such cases decisions are taken by courts rather than by managements. While efficiency and equity of this method can never be disputed it tells upon the quality of internal management. While every organisation may have to adopt all these types of management styles at one time or the other, the overall quality of the management is decided by the ratio of each type of management style adopted to the total management style

Relevance to Indian Conditions

The critical question is how realistic are the assumptions under Indian conditions. How many are creative and imaginative? How many can be trained or led (as distinct from directed) to a commitment to organisational goals? How many employees in India feel a pressing need for self-actualisation when their bellies are bullied by hunger? It is absurd to have the lever which controls a machine requiring 200 lb of pull to move it if workers are strong enough to accept only 18 lb to pull. Similarly, it will be foolish to install a system of sharing information, participation and self-control, if it is found that the employees have little or no capacity for initiative, individual action and leadership because of the factors that condition them from infancy to live in a well- defined, almost all-inclusive structure.

Lack of infrastructure

Let us consider the lack of infrastructure to introduce MBO in most of our industries. How can an employee like his job when his main criterion in selecting or applying for a job is monetary benefit rather than aptitude? Any number of instances where post-graduates and graduates apply for lowly paid jobs because of economic reasons can be cited. Whatever care one may take in job recruitment and selection, one cannot altogether avoid the possibility of job dissatisfaction in them. When one has no job satisfaction one naturally tries to evade the work which in turn results in the need for supervision.

Class conflict : Another problem that makes the introduction of MBO rather difficult is the element of class conflict which has been pushed to the foreground in recent years by various political parties. Also, opposition to the profit concept must be removed from the employee's mind if MBO is to be effective.

Public sector industries are in no better position. The frequent changes in government policies make introduction of MBO rather difficult. Most public sector undertakings are headed by administrators sent on deputation who carry with them bureaucratic practices and hoard authority, a *sine qua non* of MBO.

Managers often overlook the fact that MBO requires a new way of life or new style of management. It may require a high degree of concentration on one's own leadership style for giving up some of the old authoritarian ways and establishing new and more participative ways. Are we prepared to shed out old authoritarian ways which we have cherished so long? Even if we assume that there is no opposition to the profit motive it raises many issues because it is based on a reward- punishment psychology. The managers must also realise that the objective plea will not serve the purpose because every organisation is a social system, a network of interpersonnel relationship. A man may do an excellent job of objective measurement, but may fail miserably as a partner, as a subordinate, or as a colleague. It is common knowledge that people fail to be promoted more for personal reasons than for performance inadequacy.

Furthermore, since every subordinate is a component of his superior's efforts to achieve his own goals, he will inevitably be apprised on how well he works with his superior and helps the latter to meet his needs. A heavy subjective element in performance appraisal creeps in. The undue complexity in explaining the philosophy of MBO to the Indian illiterate or semi-literate employee should also be taken into account by managers. To alien character of the literature on MBO written against a western socio-economic background and organisational process has complicated the process of its introduction in India. But this by itself should not deter us in our efforts. It is necessary to modify our current management practices and orient out organisational climate to relate MBO to our needs. To conclude MBO is not a panacea for all management problems. But it enables a working arrangement for integrating all that is relevant to achieving organisational effectiveness.

REVIEW QUESTIONS

1. Explain the term 'objective'. State the need for and requirement of objectives.
2. What do you understand by management by objectives?
3. Explain the various steps involved in setting up M.B.O.
4. Explain, in detail, the step-by-step logic in launching M.B.O. in an 'enterprise'.
5. Outline the advantages and limitations of M.B.O. as an aid to control process.

13
Financial Ratio Analysis

The term 'Financial Control' here refers to control over financial resources as to ensure their effective and efficient utilisation in the attainment of financial management goals of profitability and liquidity which ultimately lead to firm's objective of maximisation of profits and value or wealth with respect to owner's interests. The financial control is exercised through financial accounting and reporting vis-a-vis analysis and interpretation of financial statements.

Accounting Control System

Although the firm consists of the sub-systems of production, marketing, R&D, personnel, administration, etc., the controller, by the very nature of his duties, is above to see the total spectrum of corporate activities in an integrated manner. In the final analysis, money becomes the only common yardstick for planning and gauging performance; this is the controller's domain by emphasising his service (as opposed to stewardship) function, and by having a complete grasp of his information and control systems. In fact, he can only adequately discharge his responsibility if he appreciates the types of decisions made and the nature of the activities to be controlled. Complete control can never be achieved purely on the strength of quantitative information. However, management accounting does provide a suitable quantitative base, to which the manager can add both qualitative data and other quantitative factors to balance control action.

Accounting is useful control process in three major ways: (a) as a means of communicating information on what management wants done; (b) as a means of motivating the organisation to act in ways most likely to attain the objectives of the business; and (c) as a means of appraising performance and reporting on performance to those concerned. In addition, control information can be used as a basis for future planning, but it must be emphasised that the aim of control is not to correct past mistakes, it is rather to guide current and future a activities to achieve corporate objectives. The internal control systems of business activities have been custodial and efficiency control in this present contex.

Accounting and Controllership

Accounting, being neither restricted to one particular area of business nor to a specific industry, was one of the first general management methodologies. As a quantitative method, its underlying problems are those of observation, measurement, systems analysis, model construction, and decision theory. To this extent, it paroles the problematic aspects of operations research. The economic objectives of a business in any given period of time, may be diverse and perhaps unique to that firm. But in so far as any such objectives are relevant to accounting, they can be listed as follows:

(a) to achieve the target revenues and costs- the income problem;

(b) to achieve the target figure of available money at all times during the period-the financial or liquidity problem; and

(c) to achieve the target pattern of resources, other than money, at all times during the period-the asset structure problem.

To facilitate the accounting control function-with its many dimensions- there is not one single accounting system, but rather several acceptable and complementary systems, each capable of contributing significantly to our understanding of economic events as they affect business firms.

The orthodox approach to accounting simply divides its functions into two basic categories: (a) the stewardship function, involving the maintenance of records for asset control, with particular reference to the function of responsibility to the absent owners; and (b) the service function, which treats accounting as a tool of managerial decision-making via planning and control systems. This latter function has greatly increased in importance in recent years, while the record-keeping function has been relegated to the background. Financial accounting is essentially of a stewardship nature, reporting to outsiders on management, rather than to management. The traditionally aggregated figures must meet the criterion of objectivity, but this often conflicts with the more important control criterion of usefulness. While financial accounting reports focus on the whole business, they must be complied in accordance with rigid statutory and professional standards. Being historical in perspective, it will be evident that financial accounting is of little value in exercising control.

In contrast, cost accounting is concerned with specific segments of the business-relating costs and revenues (hence profits) to products, processes, and divisions. Operational control is made effective via variances from standard, but cost accountings is essentially concerned with planning and controlling costs in great detail-too great for top management. The development of management accounting has been based on the criterion of usefulness-the main consideration being 'Why' rather than 'How' in designing reporting systems. The objectivity criterion of financial accounting differs is largely irrelevant, and the approach of management accounting differs from that of cost accounting in being problem oriented and geared to management control. Financial analysis is permitted by the derivation and comparison of ratios, as well as by the preparation of funds-flow statements from balance sheets and income statements (or profit and loss accounts).

Internal control is the process and means of safeguarding assets, checking the reliability of accounting data, promoting operational efficiency, and encouraging adherence to managerial policies. However, in its broadest sense, internal audit to the rigorous management audit. In essence, since every system of control requires human application, internal control exists to ensure that the human factor acts in accordance with instructions, plans, and policies. Control accounting, as a refinement of management accounting, and exists to indicate how successful the firm is in its goal- striving behaviour. It permits the inclusion of goals other than profit, and pays special attention (via the planning phase) to accruing goal-sub goal consistency. Inevitably, these four broad types of accounting overlap considerably, but the demands of a variety of primary and secondary goals within the firm requires that control accounting be central in the management process, supplemented by the other forms as appropriate.

The Requirements of an Accounting Control System

A good accounting system is far more than just an accounting system. It is a true managment control system. You should expect the following minimums :

(1) You should get both present and future probable performances instead of just past performances. This includes the present month, next month, the next quarter, the next half year, and the next year. These projected (proforma) predictions are actually more important to you than your past performances because they allow you to intelligently establish your priorities, correct problems that will occur, and allow you to "close the door before the horse escapes."

(2) You should get a readable warning-flag report (exceptions forecast) which will predict the impact of problems unless corrective actions are taken.

(3) You should get a built-in security system which will allow information to flow to even the lowest of employee levels on an as-needed basis without concerning yourself with confidential information getting to your competitors. Once this security system is reliable, your profit centre control system is an effective tool to disseminate meaningful information to

all levels of management. The savings in meetings and conferences is sisgnificant.

(4) You should establish a relatively tamper-proof system. The checks and balances are there to discourage dishonesties, paddings, disguisings, and buck passing.

(5) Your accounting system should be the foundation of your incentives (both rewards and punishments) systems. It keeps the scores and disburses the earned incentives.

(6) Your control system should "float" with conditions as they exist and will exist. If sales are going to increase, the budgets for each group will likewise increase when the timing (a management decision) is correct. The floating budgets and reserves can be made so that they neither lead nor lag conditions.

(7) Your system should give you frequent (about twice weekly) scan reports on who and what is generating your profits and your losses.

(8) You should receive reports on your past performances that are accurate and on time.

(9) Periodically financial analysis should be carried out from accounting data and financial statements to determine the operating and financial characteristics of your firm.

Financial Statement Analysis

Meaning of Financial Statement: The term 'Financial Statement' or 'Published Accounts,' as used in business usage, refers to a package of financial statements such as Balance Sheet, Profit and Loss Account, etc. In the case of a limited company, financial statements also include Profit and Loss Appropriation Account, Statement of Retained Earnings, Statement of Sources and Uses of Funds, Directors' Report, Auditors Report and a copy of the Chairman's speech delivered at the Annual General Meeting. Some times the term also includes in its fold the 'schedules' and explanatory 'footnote' connected with buildings, investments, depreciation, description of contingent liabilities and disclosure of events after the statement date. They are intended to supplement the data contained in financial statements and increase the value of such statements to the reader.

Purpose : Financial Statements are prepared for the purpose of presenting a periodical review of report on the progress by the management and deal with the status of investments in the business , and the results achieved during the period under review. They reveal the financial health in terms of progress, position and prospects of a business on a certain date.

Nature of Financial Statement : As to nature of the financial statement the American Institute of Accountant remarked that such statements reflect a combination of recorded facts, accounting conventions and personal judgments and the judgments and conventions applied affect them materially. Recorded facts convey data brought in statements that have been written in accounting records such as figures relating to cash in hand, cash at bank, sales, purchases, debtors, creditors, etc. The financial statements do not disclose such facts which are not and can not be recorded in the accounting books, whether or not such facts are material. For instance, the market value or replacement cost of a fixed asset is not stated in the balance sheet because as per the accounting records the cost price, not the replacement cost of the fixed asset is a recorded fact. Accounting principles, concepts, and conventions, also influence the construction of financial statements, e.g., the principle matching cost and revenues, allocation of expenditure between capital and revenue in different accounting periods, conservative basis of valuation of assets, etc. But the application of these concepts and conventions depends upon the personal judgment of accountant. For instance, the selection of depreciation method either 'straight line method' or 'written down method' and 'pricing methods of issuing materials' viz., First In First Out (FIFO) or Last In First Out (LIFO) mostly depend upon the personal judgment or opinion of the accountant.

Analysis and Interpretation of Financial Statement

The financial statements prepared in an absolute manner are not more than a group of accounting figures and convey nothing to a layman. Of late, corporate managers are becoming increasingly interested in the information presented to them by accountants and are beginning to question the need for and the use of such statements prepared by finance and accounts divisions. But it is a challenge to those who are being presented with such information. It, therefore, becomes necessary to regroup, analyse and present the financial figures in a more meaningful manner for the use of all non-financial executives at all levels.

Analysis Leads to Interpretation : The first step in the interpretation of financial statements is analysis. Analysis means splitting or regrouping of the total figures contained in the statements into their component parts, It is largely a study of relationship among the various financial factors in a business.

Interpretation Through Comparison : The second step in the interpretation of financial statements is comparison. Mere examination of the components of a statement cannot be expected to lead to a definite conclusion in regard to the financial status of a business. In order to interpret the position or progress of an enterprise it is necessary not only a separate the totals given in its financial statements into their components but also to make comparisons of the various components and to examine their content. Thus interpretation requires analysis and comparison.

Objects of Financial Statement Interpretation : The primary objectives of interpreting financial statements are-

(i) to estimate the profitability or earning capacity of the enterprise;

(ii) to gauge the financial (both liquidity and solvency) position and financial performance of the concern;

(iii) to determine the measure of efficiency of operations;

(iv) to decide about the future prospects to the firm. As a matter of fact, the objectives of analysis and interpretation of these statements, depend to a large extent on the view-point of analyst.

Procedure for Interpretation : Whenever, a Management Accountant is called upon to interpret the financial statement of such companies, he should take the following steps;

(a) Ascertain the purpose and the extent of the analysis and interpretation;

(b) Study all available data contained in the financial statements to gain an insight into the meaning and significance of the financial figures;

(c) Obtain such additional information as is considered necessary for the work;

(d) Tabulate the data in a logical manner.

(c) Analyse the data by preparation of comparative statements, ratio analysis, trend analysis, etc.

(f) Interpret the facts revealed by the analysis;

(g) Present the findings in the form of a report, supplemented by charts, diagrams, etc., where necessary.

Techniques of Analysis and Interpretation: For analysing the financial data and interpreting them in a systematic manner, a number of techniques or tools are available. Chief among them are-

(i) Comparative Statements, (ii) Common-size statements

(iii) Trend Analysis (iv) Average Analysis
(v) Ratio Accounting (vi) Funds Flow Statement
(vii) Cash Flow Statement (viii) Working Capital Forecast.

Types of Financial Analysis: According to the *Modus operandi* of analysis, a financial analysis may be vertical or horizontal. When financial statements for a certain period only are analysed the analysis is called *vertical* analysis. Where a series of statements relating to a number of years are reviewed and analysed, there is said to be an *horizontal* analysis. The first is a *static* analysis, measuring the position at a point of time or for a period; the second is a *dynamic* analysis, measuring change of position or trend of the business over a number of years.

According to materials used, an analysis may be internal or external. Internal Analysis is conducted within the business itself, the analyst being associated with the business itself. For such an analysis, the analyst has full access to the books of account, and complete information about the business is at his disposal. In external analysis he is not connected with the enterprise, and the only data available to him are the published statement and such information as the business is willing to partwith. Analysis for purpose of investment and granting credit is of external type, whereas analysis for managerial purposes is of the internal type.

Limitations of Financial Statement Analysis: Any person using the techniques and analysis of financial statement should keep in mind the very limitations of financial statement themselves. The basic nature of financial statement is historic and essentially they are interim reports. The figures drawn from one year statements have limited utility of such analysis. An analyst should also be cautious from window-dressing in the accounts. Many items are influenced by personal judgment. The soundness of the judgment necessarily depends on the competence and integrity of those who make them.

Comparative Financial Statement : Comparative financial statements are statements of the financial position of a business so designed as to provide time perspective to the consideration of various elements of financial position embodied in such statements. In any Comparative statement, columns for more than one year's position or working can be drawn and figures may be provided. The annual data can be compared with similar data for previous years. Comparative statements may be made to show: (i) absolute data (in rupee); (ii) increase or decrease in rupee values; (iii) increase or decrease in absolute data in terms of percentages and (iv) common-size statements. The more important of such statements are (a) Comparative Balance Sheet; (b) Comparative Income statement; (c)

Comparative Statement of Working Capital and (d) Comparative Statement of Manufacturing costs.

Common-Size Statements : Comparative statements that give only the vertical percentages or ratios for financial data without giving rupee values are known as common-size statements. They are also known as 100 per cent statements. Total assets, liabilities and total net sales are stated as 100 per cent. The ratio of each statement item to the statement total is found by dividing individual rupee amounts by total amount in the statement.

Trend Analysis : Trend analysis or Tend percentage also plays a significant role in the interpretation of horizontal financial statements. An analysis of the trend of certain business facts is extremely helpful in budgeting, forecasting, etc. Under this technique, a statement of one period is taken as a base with reference to which all other statements are to be studied. Every item is to be stated as 100 in the statement, that is taken as the base. If the amount of an item in another statement, is less than that in the base statement, the trend percentage will be below 100 and, if the amount is more than the base amount, trend percentage would be above 100 per cent. Thus, the ratios or percentages of different items for various periods are calculated and then a comparison is made.

An analysis of the ratios over the past few years suggests the trend or direction in which the enterprise is moving-upward or downward. It is like an Index Number showing relative changes in the financial data resulting with the passage of time. There are many companies in India and abroad which present the trends of certain vital figures like trend of sales, cost of sales, profits and wages, etc., over a number of years through the media of statistics, tabular form, charts, graphs, etc., in their published annual reports.

It may be noted that the trend analysis and interpretation cannot always reveal an accurate picture of the state of the business when compared with the base year. The base year itself may not be a representative year for the comparison of the items of Profit & Loss Account and of the Balance Sheet items. Trend analysis also does not distinguish between significant items as it bases all the items of financial statements at par in relation to the base year.

Average Analysis : Averages are another important tool of interpretation and this technique is an improvement over trend analysis method. When trend ratios have been determined for the firm, these figures are compared with industry averages. Some of the important averages which the management can use are the average stocks, average monthly sales, average gross profit, etc. In using averages for the purpose of interpretation, the Management Accountant will have to enter the realm of the mathematician or the statistician.

Other tools and techniques of analysis and interpretation of financial statements, viz., Ratio Accounting and Funds flow including Cash flow statements are explained in depth, in subsequent pagess.

FINANCIAL RATIO ANALYSIS

Meaning : The relationship between the two figures expressed mathematically is called a 'Ratio'. It is a numerical relationship between two numbers. It is calculated by dividing one into another. Ratio Accounting or Ratio Analysis is the process of determining and interpreting numerical relationships based on financial statements. It is the technique of interpretation of financial statements with the help of Accounting Ratios derived from the Balance Sheet and Profit and Loss Account. It involves the comparison of existing ratios against standards established. The standards may be set by management as goals expressed in the budgets (i.e. budgetary standard) ; or may be historical figures showing performance of the same concern in the past (i.e., historical standard), or may be figures reflecting the performance of other companies (i.e. industrial or market standard).

Mode of Expression: Accounting Ratios can be expressed in various ways, such as (i) a pure ratio, say current ratio is 2:1; or (ii) a rate, say, current assets are 2 times of current liabilities; or (iii) a percentage, say, current assets are 200% of current liabilities. Each method of expression has a distinct advantage over the other. The analyst will select that mode which will best suit his convenience. There are certain accounting ratios which can be best expressed if stated as a pure ratio only, e.g. current assets : current liabilities. Some other ratios can best be expressed if stated as a rate only, e.g., Turnover of Debtors ratio, while some others can most advantageously be expressed as a percentage only, e.g., Gross profit Margin or Return on Capital. Ratios are expressed in such a way that the first appears in numerator and the second as denominator.

Classification of Ratios

Accounting Ratios may be classified in a variety of ways. Some of the possible methods are presented below:

(a) Classification according to Statement (Source)

(i) *Balance sheet (Position) Ratios* :- Where both numerator and denominator figures are taken from the balance sheet, such as Current ratio, Quick ratio, Proprietory ratio, etc.

(ii) *Profit and Loss (Revenue) Ratios*: - Ratios calculated out of the figures found in the profit and loss account. At times also called operating ratios. Examples are Gross profit ratio, Operating profit ratio, Expense ratios, etc.

(iii) *Position cum Revenue Ratios:* - Where ratios are calculated by taking one figure from Balance Sheet and another from Profit and Loss account. These ratios are also known as Consolidated or Combined or Complex Ratios. Examples of such ratios include Return on total resources. Return on capital employed, Return on Proprietor's fund, Turnover of debtors and creditors, Earnings ratios, etc.

B. Classification according to Time

(i) *Structural ratios* i.e. ratios computed from data referring to the same point of time. e.g. ratios of a particular month or year.

(ii) *Trend ratios*, i.e. ratios computed between the items referred to different periods of time.

C. Classification according to Nature

(i) *Primary ratio* e.g. Operating Profit to Capital Employed.

(ii) *Secondary or Supporting ratio* e.g. Stock velocity, Debtors Velocity, Expense ratios, etc.

D. Classification according to Functions

(i) *Financial Ratios* include liquidity and solvency ratios: Ratios indicating the liquidity position of the firm are current ratio, quick ratio, absolute liquidity ratio, turnover of stock ratio, turnover of debtors and creditors, etc. Solvency ratios include proprietary ratio, debt equity ratio, capital gearing ratio, ratio of security, interest coverage ratio, cash flow debt service ratio etc.

(ii) *Profitability Ratios* e.g. Gross Profit ratio, Net profit ratio, Operating ratio, Return on capital employed, Expense ratio, etc.

(iii) *Turnover or Activity Ratios* e.g. Turnover of stock, Turnover of debtors, Turnover of creditors, etc.

(iv) *Market Test Ratios* e.g. Dividend yield ratio, Fixed dividend cover, Equity dividend cover, Earnings per share, Price earnings ratio, Net cash inflow, Book value per share, etc.

BALANCE SHEET RATIOS

1. Current Ratio

Meaning: Current ratio is the relationship between the total current assets and current liabilities. This is a barometer of general measure of liquidity and state of trading. It is also known as Working Capital Ratio or Net Working Capital Ratio.

Formulation : Current ratio = Current Assets - Current Liabilities.
Alternatively, Current Assets : Current Liabilities.

Components : Items which are usually included in current assets are cash in hand, cash at bank,readily realisable investments, bills receivable, trade debtors, stock in trade, prepaid expenses, etc. The components of current liabilities are bills payable, sundry creditors, bank overdrafts, outstanding expenses, short-term borrowings, provision for taxes, dividend, bonus, etc., and other sundry liabilities. Normally those assets expected to be converted into cash within a year and those liabilities including such long term liabilities to be paid off within same period out of current assets or by creating current liabilities are included under current items.

This ratio is is expressed in the form of pure ratio. A current ratio of 2:1 is considered ideal as a rule of thumb. That is, the current assets must not only be equal to current liabilities but should leave a comfortable margin of working capital after paying off the current debts. But in actual practice 1:1 ratio is found acceptable than 2:1. A high ratio i.e., more than 2:1 say 3:1 indicates under-trading and the same also indicates one of the signs of over-capitalisation. Conversely, a low ratio indicates over-trading and under-capitalisation of business.

Precaution: While calculating this ratio, the analyst should observe the following guidelines.

(i) Current assets and current liabilities should be properly valued; Loose Tools though called current assets are not included.

(ii) Reserves and other accounts relating to the valuation of current assets are deducted from the total current assets;

(iii) Contingent liabilities need not be given proper consideration.

(iv) As regards investments, note the purpose behind them; if they are made from long-range point of view and not for immediate cash realisation, exclude them from current assets.

(v) Consider the type of business and nature of business transactions e.g., speculative or seasonal. In case of seasonal business, peak sales and slack sales like tides and ebbs, which in turn influence the stock in trade.

(vi) Give due attention to the composition or quality of current assets.

(vii) Note the current ratio is susceptible to 'Window dressing' and manipulations. An equal increase in both current assets and current liabilities would decrease current ratio and similarly equal decrease in current assets and current liabilities would increase current ratio.

Significance: It includes: (a) Liquidity in a rough fashion, (b) Adequacy of working capital - gross and net, (c) State of trading - over or under or fair. (d) Capitalisation - over or under or optimum, (e) Margin of safety for short term creditors.

Limitations: Current ratio suffers from the following limitations:

(i) Current ratio differs among various industries and also between manufacturers and retailers in the same line of business;

(ii) All such current assets are treated alike but they are not equally and readily realisable in cash to meet the demand of the total current liabilities.

(iii) The credit given to the debtors and available from the creditors in a particular business can affect the position of this ratio. If these periods are different the desirable ratio would also differ.

It is, therefore, dangerous to use current ratio alone as a sole index of liquidity.

2. Quick Ratio

Quick ratio (Acid Test Ratio) is concerned with the relationship between liquid assets and liquid liabilities. It is a refinement of the current ratio and its other names are Liquid Ratio and Acid Test Ratio.

$$\text{Quick Ratio: } \frac{\textit{Quick or liquid assets}}{\textit{Quick or liquid liabilities}}$$

$$= \frac{\textit{Cash + Debtors + Bills receivables + Temporary Investments}}{\textit{Creditors + Bills payables}}$$

Stock-in-trade is excluded from current assets because it is usually liquid current asset and considered to be the graveyard of a business. Prepaid Expenses are also excluded from the list of quick asset because they

are not expected to be converted into cash. Debtors are included in. current assets after providing for bad and doubtful debts. Similarly, out of current liabilities bank overdraft is also exculded to arrive at quick liabilities, because in most cases bank overdraft is more or less a permant arrangement and renewed periodically. Some analysts prefer to include'overdraft' under quick liabilities in consonance with the concept of conservation. The former view is debtor's concept and the latter one is creditor's concept.

A quick ratio of 1:1 is usually considered to be good and satisfactory. Thus it is a better test of financial liquidity because it places more emphasis on immediate conversion of assets into cash than does the current ratio.

3. Cash Position Ratio

Cash Position Ratio relates the sum of cash and marketable securities to the total quick liabilities.

$$\text{Cash Position Ratio} = \frac{\textit{Cash + Marketable securities}}{\textit{Quick liabilities}}$$

This ratio is obtained by subtracting both the debtors and bills receivables from the quick assets dividing the same by quick liabilities. A ratio of 75 : 1 is considered to be safe. It is a more rigorous test of liquidity than the previous two ratios. This ratio is also known as Absolute Liquidity Ratio or Super Current Ratio.

4. Proprietary Ratio (Asset Backing)

This ratio establishes the relationship between the proprietors' funds (equity + preference + capital reserves + free reserves + undistributed profits) and total assets. In other words, it brings the relationship between equity of the proprietors and the creditors. This ratio is also called Net worth to total assets ratio or simply Equity ratio.

$$\text{Proprietary Ratio} = \frac{\textit{Proprietor's Funds}}{\textit{Total Assets}} \textit{ or } \frac{\textit{Capital Employed}}{\textit{Total Liabilities}}.$$

It is a sound principle that proprietors should subscribe sufficient capital to cover fixed, intangible assets, investments in other companies and a reasonable figure for working capital. Some analyst deduct intangible assets from the proprietors' funds; but whether this practice should be followed or not will largely depend upon the realisable value of intangibles and the purpose of analysis ; Losses should also be deducted and funds payble to others should not be added.

A ratio 0.75 : I (or 75%) is deemed to be a desirable one. Higher the ratio, better it is for all concerned e.g. A higher ratio say 100% means that there are no outside liabilities and all the funds are employed are those of shareholders. In such a case the return to Shareholders would be a lower rate of dividend and this is also a sign of 'over-capitalisation'.

5. Assets-Proprietorship Ratio

This ratio is subdivided into- (a) Ratio of Current Assets to Proprietor's Funds

$$= \frac{\textit{Current Assets}}{\textit{Proprietors' Funds}}$$

(b) Ratio of Fixed Assets to Proprietor's Funds $= \dfrac{\textit{Fixed Assets}}{\textit{Proprietors' Funds}}$

6. Capital Gearing Ratio

The term "capital gearing" is used to describe the capital mix *i.e* the relationship between the equity share capital (including all reserves and undistributed profits) and fixed interest bearing secruities of a company. Fixed interest dividend bearing securities are preference shares, debentures, public deposits, etc.

$$\text{Capital Gearing Ratio} = \frac{\textit{Equity Capital}}{\textit{Fixed interest/dividend bearing securities}}$$

Gearing is said to be high if capital carrying fixed rate of interest/dividend is more than the equity capital. Similarly, gearing is low if capital carrying fixed rate of interest/dividend is less than the equity capital. When both the capital are equal it is said to be evenly geared. Thus, the gearing is in inverse ratio to the equity share capital. *i.e.*

Higher gear = low equity share capital
Low gear = high equity share capital

The capital gearing also reveals the suitability, or otherwise of the company's capitalisation. i.e.
Equity capital > Loan capital = Overcapitalisation = Low gearing
Equity capital < Loan capital = Undercapitalisatyion = High Gear
Equlty Capital = Loan = Optimum capitalisation = Even Gear

Whether or not high gear ratio is good for the enterprise will depend upon its profitability trend. Thus if the company can foresee a trend of continuous increase relatively more and more profit will be available to equity shareholders as compared to preference shareholders and debenture holders, in such a case high gearing would be better.

Capital gearing may be 'planned' or may be 'historical', the latter describing a state of affairs where the capital structure has evolved over a period of time, but not necessarily in the most advantageous way. Capital gearing ratio is not only important to prospective investors but also to the company because it affects distribution policies, the building of reserve as well as a stable dividend policy. Hence, it must be properly planned.

Leverage Ratio: This is an American term which has approximately the same meaning as 'gearing'. It indicates the relationship of bonds to equity. Leverage may be either operational or financial. Operating leverage may be defined as the employment of an asset with a fixed cost in the hope that sufficient revenue will be generated to cover fixed / variable costs. Financial leverage is defined as the use of funds with a fixed cost in order to increase earnings per share. Favourable or positive leverage is said to occur when the enterprise earns more on the assets purchased with the funds than the fixed cost of their use. Unfavourable or negative leverage occurs when the firm does not earn as much as the funds cost. The favourability of financial leverage is sometimes termed as 'trading on equity'.

The incidence of corporate tax has had its influence in recent times on the capital gearing of companies, since it has encouraged them to raise loan capital in larger proportions than would normally be justified as loan interest paid is allowable for taxation purposes.

7. Debt-Equity Ratio

It establishes the relationship between shareholder' funds and the outsider's funds.

$$\text{Equity Ratio} = \frac{Equity}{Total\ Assets} \qquad \text{Debt Ratio} = \frac{Debt}{Total\ Assets}$$

$$\text{Debt to Equity Ratio} = \frac{Debt\ \%\ Total\ Assets}{Equity\ \%\ Total\ Assets}$$

$$i.e.\ \frac{External\ Equities\ (Long\ term + Short\ term)}{Internal\ equities\ (Equity + Pref. + Reserves\ \&\ Surplus)}$$

Debt-Equity ratio of 1:1 is ideal. For industrial concerns, a ratio of 2:1 is considered appropriate, though it may be higher in public utility concerns. In some financial circle, this ratio is computed with (redeemable) preference shares classed as creditors rather than as ownership claims. But it all depends upon the nature of preference share and the purpose of financial analysis.

PROFIT AND LOSS ACCOUNT RATIOS

12. Gross Profit Ratio

This ratio is a measure of general profitability of the business. It is an important tool to ascertain the trend on increase or decrease in the gross profit ratio. This ratio is calculated by dividing the gross profit by net sales and is usually expressed a percentage.

$$\text{Gross Profit Ratio} = \frac{\text{Gross Profit}}{\text{Net Sales}} x100$$

There is no rigid standard to this ratio. Generally the gross profit should however be adequate to cover the operating expenses and to provide for fixed charges, dividends, building up of reserves, etc. Normally, 30% to 40% margin is anticipated.

An increase in gross profit ratio may be on account of following factors:

1. The sale price of the goods may increase without an increase in the cost of the goods sold.
2. A reduction in cost while the sale price remains the same.
3. A reduction in costs accompanied by comparatively lower reduction in the sale price e.g. costs may be reduced by 5 per cent while the sales price may go down by 2 per cent.
4. The absence of expenses on purchases since the same might have been written off completely in the previous year.
5. Sales might be inflated in other ways too e.g. goods sent on consignment included in sales as well as stock-on-hand.
6. The change in the method of valuation of the closing stock so that it is valued at prices which were too high.

On the other hand, a decrease in the ratio, compared, of course, with the previous year, may be due to following factors:

(i) A decrease in the sale price of the goods sold without corresponding decrease in their costs.

(ii) An increase in the costs without corresponding increase in the sale price.

(iii) The expenses on purchases incurred last year but recorded this year.

(iv) Stock at the end valued at very low figure.

(v) Misappropriation of stock at the end.

(vi) The rise in wages and other direct costs of production.

(vii) The understatement of closing stock due to change in the method of valuation.

(viii) The goods purchased for the personal use of owner(s) included in the purchases of the business.

13. Operating (Expenses) Ratios

This ratio matches operating expenses (*i.e.* cost of goods sold plus factory expenses, office and administrative expensise, selling and distribution expenses with net sales. The purpose of this ratio is to ascertain the operational efficiency of the management in their business operations.

$$\text{Operating Ratio} = \frac{\textit{Cost of good sold plus Operating expenses}}{\textit{Net sales}} x100$$

In general, for manufacturing concerns, operating ratio is expected to touch a percentage of 60% to 70%. Lower the ratio, the more favourable it is because it would leave higher margin of operating profit and vice versa. Operating ratio should be analysed further to throw light on the levels of efficiency prevailing in different elements of total cost. The ratios that help us in analysing the operating ratio are the following:

(a) Materials Consumed Ratio $= \frac{\textit{Materials Consumed}}{\textit{Net Sales}} x100$

(b) Conversion Cost Ratio

$$= \frac{\textit{Labour + Manufacturing (factory) expenses}}{\textit{Net Sales}} x100$$

(c) Office & Admn. Expenses Ratio

$$= \frac{\textit{Office \& Admn. Expenses}}{\textit{Net Sales}} x100$$

(d) Selling & Distribution Expenses Ratio

$$= \frac{\textit{Selling \& Dist. Exp.}}{\textit{Net Sales}} x100$$

The totals of these four ratios will be equal to the operating ratio.

(*e*) Financial Expense Ratio $= \frac{\textit{Financial Expenses}}{\textit{Net Sales}} x100$

(*f*) Non-Operating Expenditure Ratio

$$= \frac{\textit{Non Operating expenses}}{\textit{Net Sales}} x100$$

14. Operating Profit Ratio

This ratio establishes the realationship between operating profit and sales and is calculated as follows:

$$\text{Operating Profit Ratio} = \frac{\textit{Operating Profit}}{\textit{Net Sales}} x100$$

OR = 100 *minus* Operating Ratio.

This ratio indicates the portion remaining out of every rupee worth of sales after all operating costs and expenses have been met. For the calculation of this ratio, non-operating expenses and non-operating incomes are ignored.

15. Net Profit Ratio

It expresses the relationship between net profit or net operating profit and net sales. This ratio is calculated as follows:

$$\text{Net Profit Ratio} = \frac{\textit{Net Profit}}{\textit{Net Sales}} x100$$

Net profit ratio differs from the ratio of operating profit to net sales in the sense the former is calculated after adding non-operating income *e.g.* interest or dividend on investments, rent received, profit on sale of fixed assets, etc. to such profit and deducting non-operating expenses *e.g.* loss on sale of old fixed assets, provision for legal damages, etc. from such profit. Higher the ratio, the better it is because it gives an idea of improved efficiency of the firm.

16. Inventory (Turnover of Stock) Ratio

It is the relationship between the cost of goods sold during a given period and the average stock holding during the period *e.g.* it tells us as to how many times stock has turned (sold) over the period. It indicates the operational and marketing efficiency of the business. It is also known as stock velocity ratio.

$$\text{Inventory Ratio} = \frac{\textit{Cost of sale}}{\textit{Average inventory at Cost}}$$

This ratio is expressed in number of times; Average inventory is calculated by dividing the opening stock plus closing stock by two. Some analysts take net sales or cost of goods sold instead of cost of sale and average inventory at selling price instead of cost price.

17. Net Sales to Inventory Ratio $= \frac{\textit{Closing Stock}}{\textit{Net Sales}}$

18. Raw materials Turnover (Material Velocity) Ratio

$$= \frac{\textit{Stock of raw materials}}{\textit{Average monthly consumption of raw material.}}$$

COMPOTITE RATIOS

19. Return of Total Resources

This ratio acts as an yardstick to assess the efficiency of the operations of the business. In otherwords, this ratio of net profits to total assets indicates the extent to which assets employed in the business are utilised to result in net profits.

Return on Total Resources =

$$\frac{\textit{Net profit before taxes} + \textit{Interest on L. T. loans}}{\textit{Capital Employed}} x100$$

20. Return on Capital Employed (ROCE)

It is the most appropriate indicator of the earning power of the capital employed in the business.

Return on Capital Employed =

$$\frac{\textit{Net profit before taxes} + \textit{Interest on L. T. loans}}{\textit{Capital employed}} x100$$

Capital Employed = (Properitor's capital + Undistributed Profits + Reserves and Surplus – Fictitious assets) + Long term liabilities.

= Net worth + Long Term Liabilities

This ratio acts as a pointer to the management showing the progress or deterioration in the earning capacity and efficiency of the business.

21. Return of Proprietor's Fund

In this ratio net profit is compared with the investment of the proprietor's funds.

Return on Proprietor's fund

$$= \frac{\textit{Net Profit (after tax and interst)}}{\textit{Proprietor's Fund}} x100$$

This ratio is invariably calculated by the prospective investor in the business to find out whether the investment would be worth making in terms of return as compared to the risk involved in the business. This ratio is also used in making inter-firm comparison.

22. Return on Equity Shareholder's Fund

$$= \frac{\textit{Net Profit after tax} - \textit{Pref. Dividend}}{\textit{Equity shareholder's Fund}} x100$$

23. Return on Equity Capital

$$= \frac{Net\ Profit\ after\ tax - Pref.\ Dividend}{Equity\ capital} x100$$

24. Dividend Yield $= \frac{Dividend\ (in\ Rs)\ paid\ per\ share}{Market\ price\ per\ Equity\ share}$

If refers to the percentage or ratio of dividend paid per share to the market price per share. This ratio indicates the effective rate of return on investment which potential investors may hope to earn.

25. Preference Dividend Cover

$$= \frac{Net\ Profit\ \ (after\ tax)}{Annul\ preference\ Dividend}$$

It indicates how many times the preference (fixed) dividend is covered by profit after tax. This ratio measures the margin of safety for preference shareholders. Such investors normally expect their dividend to be covered about three times by profits available for dividend purposes.

26. Equity Dividend Cover

$$= \frac{Net\ profit\ (after\ tax) - pref.\ Dividend}{Dividend\ paid\ on\ Equity\ Capital}$$

$$\text{or } \frac{Earnings\ per\ equity\ share\ (Rs)}{Dividend\ per\ equity\ share\ (Rs)}$$

Equity Dividend cover is the number of times the dividend is covered by the amount of profit available for equity shareholders *i.e.* net profit after tax less preference dividend. Higher the dividend cover, the higher is the extent of retained earnings and higher is the degree of certainty that dividend will be repeated in future years also. A typical standard cover is 2 *i.e.* out of every Rs. 100 profits available for dividend, Rs. 50 is distributed, and Rs. 50 is retained and ploughed back in the business.

27. Earnings Per Share (EPS)

$$= \frac{Net\ profit - -Pref.\ Dividend}{No.\ of\ (outstanding)\ Equity\ shares}$$

The earnings per share are of great importance to determine the value of a share and hence its market price. The product of estimated earnings per share and the estimated price-earnings ratio gives a fair idea about the potential market price of a share. The market price of share can be obtained by dividing estimated earnings per share by capitalisation rate.

28. Price Earnings Ratio (PER)

$$= \frac{Average\ Market\ price\ per\ share}{Earnings\ per\ share}$$

Price Earnings Ratio shows how many times the annual earnings the present shareholders are wiling to pay to get a share. This ratio helps investors to know the effects of earnings per share on the market price of the share. This ratio when calculated for several years can be used in trend analysis for predicting future price earnings ratios and, therefore, future stock prices.

29. Capitalisation (Earnings Price) Ratio

$$= \frac{\textit{Earnings per share}}{\textit{Average Market price per share}}$$

This ratio indicates the rate at which the stock exchange investors are capitalising the value of current earnings.

30. Pay-Out Ratio $= \dfrac{\textit{Dividend paid per share (Rs)}}{\textit{Earnings per Share (Rs)}}$

This ratio indicates the proportion of earnings available which equity shareholders actually receive in the form of dividend. An investor primarily interested should invest in equity shares of a company with high pay-out ratio. A company having low pay-out ratio need not necessarily be a bad company. A company having income may like to finance the expansion out of the income earned and thus may have low pay-out ratio. An investor interested in stock price appreciation may well invest in such a company even though the pay-out ratio is low. The reverse of the payout ratio is the ratio of Retained Earnings: –

$$= \frac{\textit{Profit retained}}{\textit{Profit earned}} x100$$

31. Book Value Per Share

$$\frac{\textit{Shareholders' Funds} - \textit{Preference Share Capital}}{\textit{Number of Equity Shares}}$$

The computed figure may be compared with the actual Stock Exchange quotation, if the company is a listed one. But this can only be a very general guide, as stock market prices are influenced by many factors not directly related to the performance of companies.

32. Interest Coverage Ratio (I.C.R.) or Fixed Charges Cover

This ratio is calculated by dividing fixed interest charges into net profit.

$$\text{ICR} = \frac{\textit{Net profit before interest \& income tax}}{\textit{Fixed Interest charges}}$$

This ratio indicates the financial position of the enterprise to meet interest payments out of current earnings. Fixed interest charges should be covered by six to seven times.

33. Cash Flow to Debt Coverage Ratio

$$\frac{C.F.}{1+\frac{SFD}{I-T}}$$

CF – Annual cash flow before interest and taxes.

I – Interest payments

T – Income-tax Rate

SFD – Sinking Fund Appropriation on Debt.

This ratio gives an idea of firm's long term liquidity position by which it meets its interest charges out of operational cash flow of the period.

34. Turnover of Debts (Debtors' Velocity) Ratio

This ratio explains the relationship of net credit sales of a firm to its books debts indicating the rate at which cash is generated by turnover of receivables or debtors. The purpose of this ratio is to measure the liquidity of the receivables or to find out the period over which receivables remain uncollected *i.e.* ageing of receivables.

Turnover of Debtors Ratio (Number of times in a year)

$$= \frac{\textit{Net (Credit) sales}}{\textit{Average or year end Debtors}}$$

If the annual turnover rate is say 6, this means that, on an average receivables are collected in 2 months, *i.e.* average collection period is 2 months time. Alternatively, average collection period is calculated thus: –

Average collection period (Number of days in a year) $= \frac{\textit{Accounts receivable}}{\textit{Annual Credit sales}} x365$

Trade debtors include bills receivables along with book debts, Bills arising not from regular sales *i.e.*, a bill receivable from the buyer of fixed assets, should be excluded. Bad and doubtful debts and their provisions are not deducted from the total debtors in order to avoid the impression that a larger amount of receivables have been collected. If the break up of sales into cash and credit sales are not available, the analyst has to use the total sales for computation of the ratio. As to the calculation of daily sales, the number of working days of the firm during the year is customarily taken as 360 days rather than 365 days exactly; some others use 300 days owing to the fact that remainder of days being holidays. Average collection period is analysed with reference to the (billing) terms of sale and then, overdues are counted after the expiry of credit period allowed.

Ageing of Accounts Receivables

Ageing of accounts is yet another method of analysing the liquidity of receivables. This involves classifyig the amounts due in each accounts according to the period that it is outstanding or categoristing the receivables at a point of time according to the proportions billed in previous months. For instance, such a classification as on 31 December of any year may reveal that 60% of the amounts outstanding are not more than a month old, 20% may be more than a month but less than 2 months old, 12% may be outstanding for more than 60 days (2 months) but less than 90 days (3 months) and 8% of the amount may be more than 3 months old. If the terms of sale require payment within 30 days, the information as regards again of accounts shows that 40% of the amount of receivables are overdue, 20% are upto one month over due, 12% upto 2 months overdue and 8% are more than 2 months overdue, Evidently, the accounts with outstanding dues which are long overdue need to be investigated and written off, if they are uncollectable. With the information on aging of accounts, the analyst can get an accurate picture of the investment in receivables and changes in the basic composition of the investment over time.

Ageing Schedule

Outstanding Period (days)	Outstanding Debtors (Rs.)	Percentage of total Debtors
1--30	2,40,000	60%
31-60	80,000	20%
61--90	48,000	12%
Over 91	32,000	8%
	4,00,000	100

The Ageing Schedule breaks down debtors according to length of time for which they have been outstanding and gives a detailed idea of the quality of debtors. The average collection period measures the quality of debtors in an aggregative way while ageing schedule very clearly spots out the slow paying debtors.

35. Creditors' Ratio (Creditors' Velocity)

This ratio shows the velocity of the credit discharged by matching annual credit purchases to the outstanding payables (both trade creditors plus bills payable) at the accounting date.

$$\text{Creditors or Payables Ratio (Number of times in a year)} = \frac{\textit{Net (Credit) Purchase}}{\textit{Average or year end payables}}$$

Smaller the payables ratio, greater the credit period enjoyed and consequently larger the benefit reaped from credit suppliers.

$$\text{Average Payment Period (Number of days in a year)} = \frac{\textit{Payables}}{\textit{Net credit purchases}} x365$$

Other turnover ratios are Turnover of total assets, Turnover of fixed assets, Turnover of investment, Turnover of cash, Turnover of working capital, Turnover of capital, etc.

The Du Pont Chart

Any discussion on ratio analysis will not be complete without a reference to the Du Pont Chart. This chart, a schematic description of which is given below, has been developed by the giant Du Pont group in United States of America, to monitor performance of individual units in the group. Du Pont Analysis is a system of analysis showing the relationship between return on investment, asset turnover and the profit margin. In the Du Pont analysis, asset turnover is multiplied by profit margin to obtain Return On Investment (ROI).

Every company should aim at maximising return per unit of investment. Hence, the executive of the company should constantly monitor earnings in relation to investment. Here earnings refer to profit before tax, interest and depreciation. While the rate of taxation is based on government policy, depreciation and interest are dependent upon the cost, life-span of plant, the level of borrowings, etc. By excluding these items, the top management of the company can find out the efficiency or otherwise of the operatives at the plant level. Consequently, the original value of fixed assets is recknoned for computing total investment.

To maximise the return, one should either increase the numerator or depress the denominator. This can be achieved by (i)increasing sales, (ii) decreasing investment which, in short period, is possible only in respect of current assets for a given sale of operations; and (iii) increasing net profit by reducing cost of sales. This ratio has been split into two components, *i.e.*,

Sales/Investment and Net Profit/Sales would gnerally be available in many companies as routine control data.

This is generally useful for constant monitoring of the performance of a company. Hence, a creditor (Banker) need resort to this chart only in exceptional circumstances like nursing a sick unit or financing the entire cost of a small scale unit, where the banker becomes the full financier of the venture.

Inter-Firm Comparison Through Ratio Analysis

Appraisal of firms refers to performance appraisal of an unit or enterprise. It is a systematic and periodic evaluation of an unit's performance (both physical and financial) with a view to finding out how well it does its present job and assessing its potential ability to do other work.

Methods of Comparison: There are several standards to compare and contrast the performance of a company. First of all, current performance of a company may be compared with its own past performance. Since the general economic and the state of technology constantly undergo changes, comparisons with the past performance have but limited value. The second alternative is to compare the current performance with the budgets prepared earlier with estimates and guesses. But a budget is a plan or document prepared yesterday based on the facts of the day before yesterday and hence it is not fully dependable for ever. The third and most informative standard is Inter-firm Comparison (IFC).

Meaning of IFC

Inter-firm Comparison is a management technique by which information concerning performances, efficiencies, costs, and profits of firms in an industry (firms in the same line of business) are voluntarily exchanged and studied and a relative comparison is made. That is, it involves a process of bringing together a number of identical firms and collecting their business figures and statistics through a neutral organisation in which participant firms repose their full confidence. The figures under comparison may relate to (i) Financial results, (ii) Cost structure of products, and (iii) Physical and operation performance. It is a tool for control - control by comparing own performances with those of other competitors in the field, for improving efficiency and indicating the weakness, and thereby maximising profits. The appraisal is more 'macro' oriented.

Inter-firm Comparison: When the performance, financial results, etc., of one department or branch of a firm are compared with the other departments or branches, of the same firm, it is known as intra-firm comparison. This techniquc will be highly helpful to large companies managing a number of similar works.

Purpose: The main purpose of Inter-firm comparison is (as indicated above) to improve efficiency by showing management the present achievement *i.e.,* operating performance and financial results and indicating the possible weakness.

Selection of Ratios

Before any ratios can be selected for an organisation, the objective or objectives of that organistion must be defined. Only if it is known where an organisation is trying to go can one measure how far it has gone. If an organisation has a number of objectives, they must be ranked in some order or relative importance. Then, if there is a conflict between two objectives, it is known which must yield to the other. However, it must be appreciated that this ranking is not immutable. The relative order of importance of objectives is likely to change over the course of time. As on objective is achieved, another becomes more importance. Priorities will also change in response to changes in outside pressures.

It must be known, too, how the achievement of these objectives has been divided up within the organisation and what are the sub-objectives of different parts of the organisation. Each part should have a reasonably clearly defined objective to aim for and the definition should be such that the sub-objective can be achieved without prejudicing the main objective of the organisation. This leads to the **ten basic principles of ratio selection :**

1. If possible, a manager must be provided with a single key ratio that indicates unequivocally the degree of his success, together with subsidiary ratios explaining how this success can be imporved. In choosing the subsidiary ratios, it is useful to bear in mind the next six principles.

2. Ratios should be logically interrelated. A test of this is that they are mathematically related (the converse is not, however, true.)

3. Pseudo ratios must be avoided. *Pseudo* ratios-the results of dividing items that are not logically related - may be mathematically related to real ratios but do not measure any underlying business reality. The following examples of pseudo ratios may help to clarify the point :

(a) Interest paid/sales (per cent). Interest paid, particularly if it is on a fixed loan such as a debenture, is not affected by the level of sales, so it should not be shown as a ratio of sales but of the amount borrowed.

(b) Sales per production employee (Rs.). Many firms sell, in additon to goods of their own manufacturer, goods made or largely made by other firms (factored goods). This is done to offer a wide range of products to a firms' customers. The value of the sales of these factored goods is in no way the result of the efforts of production employees and should therefore not be included in a ratio relating to them.

4. A manager must be given ratios which cannot lead to action by him (either as an individual. or, if necesary, jointly with colleagues).

5. A ratio must measure a material factor of the business, not a trivial one.

6. The ratio of the cost of obtaining the information to the likely benefit to management of having it must always be borne in mind.

7. The number of ratios provided to any one manager must be kept to the minimum.

There is no such thing as an ideal set of ratios suitable for all firms, all industries, all managers, at all times. Hence the next three basic principles :

8. Different ratios are required for different industries and even for different firms within an industry if they are operating in different ways.

9. Within a firm, different levels of management require different ratios and so do managers with different functional responsibilities but at the same level in the hierarchy.

10. A manager's need for specific ratios changes as his problems change.

This means that selecting ratios is an exercise which must be done for each firm and manager individually. There will however be considerable similarities between the results. It also means that from time to time (say once a year) each manager should review the ratios he receives and ruthlessly weed out those which are no longer providing information that he needs for action. There is an insidious tendency for the amount of information provided is vastly imporved if, as with roses, the growth is vigorously pruned.

It is important that the key ratio, or the way in which it is used and interpreted, is such that neither: (a) the desire to achieve a 'good' figure for it does not inhibit the undertaking of activities which would be of benefit to the organisation; nor (b) a 'good' figure for it may be achieved by undertaking activities which are not of benefit to the organisation. The risk of (a) may occur, when, for example, cost are incurred in one period and the benefits do not show through untill a latter period. The risk of (b) may occur, particularly at the subsidiary ratio level, where an action may benefit a part of the organisation but cause greater damage to the whole, and also, for example, when expenditure (or, for example, maintenance) is deferred to a later period.

DEVELOPMENTS IN RATIO ANALYSIS

Altman's Bankruptcy Prediction Model

Historical ratio analysis as described so far in this chapter appears to be a useful management technique, particularly when used on a comparative, interfirm basis but it is not without limitations. Consequently a number of attempts have been made to refine ratio analysis in order to make it more effective and forward looking. A particular example of this is the work of Professor Altman is known as *bankruptcy prediction model* (1968).

Altman and other workers have developed a technique based on identifying a small, selected group of 5 ratios which are combined using calculated weightings to produce a single value, known as Z or Zeta score. The procedure, which is a form of multiple discriminant analysis, is designed to replace the conventional norms which are used in traditiional ratio analysis, by empirically tested weights and groups that provide a clear datum level above which the firm is likely to be healthy and profitable and below which there are likely to be financial crisis.

The original equation developed by Altman was,

$$Z = .012x_1 + .014x_2 + .033x_3 + .006x_4 + .999x_5$$

where, x_1 = Working Capital to Total Assets Ratio
x_2 = Retained Earnings to Total Assets Ratio
x_3 = EBIT to Total Assets Ratio
x_4 = Market Value of Equity to Book Value of Total Debt Ratio
x_5 = Sales to Total Assets Ratio
Z = Discriminant score (overall index).

It may be stated that by selecting the above five ratios Altman attempted to consider financial problems (viz., ratios 1, 2 & 4) and operating problems (viz. ratios 3 & 5).

A score of 2.675 was established as a cut-off point by Altman. His zone of ignorance was from Z = 1.81 to Z = 2.99. This indicated that while a company was likely to go bankrupt (if below 2.675) or likely to remain a going concern (above 2.675), there was the possibility that an error in classification could exist for a score within this zone.

Example

Using Altman's function calculate Z score in case of AB Ltd. whose five accounting ratios are as follows :

x_1 = 25% x_3 = 15%
x_2 = 30% x_4 = 150% x_5 = 2.0 times

and interpret the result.

$$Z = .012x_1 + .014x_2 + .033x_3 + .006x_4 + .999x_5$$
$$= .012 \times 25 + .014 \times 30 + .033 \times 15 + .006 \times 150 + .999 \times 2$$
$$= 0.3 + .42 + .495 + .9 + 1.998 = 4.113.$$

Since AB Ltd.'s Z score of 4.113 is well above the 2.99 upper limit of Altman's zone of ignorance, the data indicate that there is virtually no chance that AB Ltd. will go bankrupt within the next two years. (Altman's model could predict bankruptcy reasonably well for about two years into the future.)

Using his discriminant function Altman found that he could predict bankruptcy with 95 per cent accuracy in the first year before failure and 72 per cent accuracy in the second year.

Value Added (or Added Value)

Value added is the difference between sales income and bought in goods and services. Value added statements can help to assess the relative efficiency of the firm without the analysis being obscured by extenal input cost which may be largely uncontrollable. Value added is the wealth that a firm creates by its own efforts. The value added performance of a company is a good measure of the overall productivity of the firm and it is out of the total amount of the value added that the firm rewards all interested partie including sharesholders, staff, Revenue authorities and others.

The Corporate Report advocated that a statement of Added Value should be prepared as this was considered to be the simplest and most effective way of putting profit into proper perspective in relation to the amount of value added paid out to employees, shareholders, the Government, and suppliers of loan capital.

A typical format of a Value Added Statement is given next page.

Statement of Added Value for year to . . . . .

			Rs.
less	**Sales**		6,500,000
	Bought in goods and services		4,250,000
	Added Value		2,250,000
	Applied As Follows		Rs.
	To employees (Wages, pensions, and other benefits)		1,750,000
	To suppliers of capital	Rs.	
	Dividends to shareholders	1,40,000	
	Interest on loans	75,000	2,15,000
	To pay Government Taxation		50,000
	To provide for maintenance and expansion of assets		
	Depreciation		100,000
	Retained profits		135,000
	Added Value		2,250,000

Value Added Ratios : In addition to the production of a summary value added statement such as that shown above the concept of value added can be included in ratio analysis.

Value added is a prime measure of productivity and ratios using value added could easily be included in the pyramid of ratios. Typical ratios involving value added include:

Value added/Fixed Assets
Value added/Current Assets
Value added/Per Employee
Value added/per Rs. of direct wages

and others of a similar nature.

Value Added and Motivation : It can be argued that value added is a better measure of performance than profit and if this viewpoint is accepted then there is likely to be more favourable motivational effects if performance is judged on value added rather than profit. To change the whole range of management accounting reports and statements from conventional profits and contributions to statements of value added would be a formidable task but on a selective basis the concept might be worthwhile.

Advantages of Ratio Analysis

1. Accounting ratios are most commonly used for management control purpose, by comparing own performance with the performance of other similar types of business.
2. Accounting and financial ratio can play a significant and important role in cost accounting, financial accounting, budgetary control and auditing.
3. It is one of the media to 'link between the past and the future.'
4. Besides, it aids to management; it helps the general public to understand the financial health of the business. From ratio analysis it is possible, without any difficulties, to have a general impression of the past performance of the business and to have a forecast about the uncertain future.
5. Identification of financial responsibility is possible from thorough and critical ratio analysis.
6. It is one of the factors which accelerates the development of the art of institution in the field of financial management.

All these are some of the important advantages. However, it should be noted in this context that whether accounting and financial ratios will render valuable services to all concerned, it all depend on the persons who handle it.

Limitations of Ratio Analysis

1. The ratio so drawn are based on the historical figures appearing in the balance sheet. So the performance of one enterprise based on the historical data gives a wrong direction to the approach.

2. In preparing different ratios, assets and liabilities are not grouped under money-value items. This could have given a realistic approach to the concept.

3. Financial and Accounting ratio will tend to interpret wrong direction if based on unauthentic data.

4. One particular ratio is not sufficient to review the whole operation of the business. It should be considered along with other ratios.

5. In practice, ratio analysis is useful only to understand the trend of the particular business, not particular type of business as a whole. This can be done by comparing the past result with that of the present. Management and financial policies differ from concern to concern. For this practice, it is difficult to compare the performance of one company with another. However, this study will give us some guidelines. Because a ratio which is

satisfactory for one particular enterprise, may be the reverse in the case of another.

Illustration 1. The following are the summarised Profit and Loss Account of Hindusthan Products Limited for the year ending 31st December, 1993 and the Balance Sheet as on that date.

PROFIT AND LOSS ACCOUNT

		Rs.			Rs.
To Opening Stock		99,500	By Sales (including Credit sales Rs. 6,80,000)		8,50,000
" Purchases		5,45,250			
" Incidental Expenses.		14,250			
" Gross Profit		3,40,000	" Closing Stock		1,49,000
		9,99,000			**9,99,000**
To Operating Expenses:			By Gross Profit		3,40,000
" Selling and Distribution	30,000		" Non-Operating income		
Administration	1,50,000		" Interest	3,000	
Finance	15,000	1,95,000	" Profit on Sale of Shares	6,000	
					9,000
" Non-Operating Expenses:					
" Loss on Sale of Assets		4,000			
" Net Profit.		1,50,000			
		3,49,000			**3,49,000**

BALANCE SHEET

	Rs.		Rs.
Issued Capital :		Land and Buildings	1,50,000
2000 Equity Shares of		Plant and Machinery	80,000
Rs. 100 each.	2,00,000	Stock in Trade	1,49,000
Reserves	90,000	Sundry Debtors.	41,000
Other Current liabilities	90,000	Cash and Bank Balance	30,000

Profit and Loss Account.	60,000	Bills Receivable	30,000
Bills Payable.	40,000		
	4,80,000		**4,80,000**

From the above statements, you are required to calcululate the following ratios:

(i) Stock Turnover Ratio (ii) Receivable Turnover Ratio (iii) Creditors Turnover Ratio (iv) Sales to Working Capital (v) Sales to Fixed Assets (vi) Sales to Capital Employed (vii) Current Ratio (viii) Operating Ratio (ix) Return on Total Resources (x) Turnover of Fixed Assets (xi) Turnover of Total Assets.

Additional information: (i) Average Debtors Rs. 34,000 (ii) Average Credit Purchases Rs. 80,000.

Solution

i. Turnover of Stock Ratio $= \frac{\textit{Cost of goods sold}}{\textit{Average Inventory}}$

$$= \frac{(Sales - GrossProfit)}{\frac{Opening\ stock + Closing\ Stock}{2}} \qquad \frac{8{,}50{,}000 - 3{,}40{,}000}{\frac{99{,}500 + 1{,}49{,}000}{2}}$$

$$= \frac{5{,}10{,}000}{1{,}24{,}250} = 4.1:1$$

ii. Turnover of Receivable Ratio $= \frac{\textit{Net Credit Sales}}{\textit{Average Debtors}} = \frac{6{,}80{,}000}{34{,}000} = 20\ \textit{Times}$

iii. Turnover of Creditors Ratio $= \frac{\textit{Account Payable}}{\textit{Average Credit Purchases}}$

$$= \frac{40{,}000}{80{,}000} = \frac{1}{2} \text{ or .5 times.}$$

iv. Sales to Working Capital $= \frac{\textit{Sales}}{\textit{Working Capital}} = \frac{8{,}50{,}000}{1{,}20{,}000} = 7.08:1$

v. Sales to Fixed Assets $= \frac{\textit{Sales}}{\textit{Fixed Assets}} = \frac{8{,}50{,}000}{2{,}30{,}000} = 2.36:1$

vi. Sales to Capital Employed $= \frac{\textit{Sales}}{\textit{Capital Employed}} = \frac{8{,}50{,}000}{3{,}50{,}000}$ 2.43:1

vii. Current Ratio $= \frac{\textit{Current Assets}}{\textit{Current Liabilities}}$

$= \frac{\textit{Stock + Sundry Debtors + Cash} \text{ and } \textit{Bank Balances}}{\textit{Current Liabilities}}$

$= \frac{Rs.\ 1{,}49{,}000 + Rs.\ 71.000 + Rs.30{,}000}{Rs.\ 1{,}30{,}000}$

$= \frac{Rs.2{,}50{,}000}{Rs.\ 1{,}30{,}000} = 1.923:1$

The ratio is very near the standard ratio of 2:1

viii. Operating Ratio $= \frac{\textit{Cost of Goods Sold + Operating Expenses}}{\textit{Net Sales}} \text{ X } 100$

$= \frac{Rs.5{,}10{,}000 + Rs.1{,}95{,}000}{Rs.8{,}50{,}000} \text{ X } 100$

$= \frac{Rs.7{,}05{,}000}{Rs.8{,}50{,}000} \text{ X } 100 = 83\%$

Cost of goods sold = Opening Stock + Purchases + Incidental expenses - Closing stock or Sales - Gross profit

ix. Return on Total Resources $= \frac{\textit{Net Profit}}{\textit{Total Assets}} \text{ X } 100$

$= \frac{Rs.1{,}50{,}000}{Rs.4{,}80{,}000} \text{ X } 100 = 31\%$

The business has given a return of 31% on total resources during the year 1993 i.e., for every Rs. 100 of total resources Rs. 31 are earned.

x. Turnover of Fixed Assets $= \frac{\textit{Net Sales}}{\textit{Fixed Assets}}$

$= \frac{Rs.8{,}50{,}000}{Rs.2{,}30{,}000} = 3.7:1$

Fixed assets here are land and buildings and plant and machinery.

xi. Turnover of Total Assets $= \frac{\textit{Net Sales}}{\textit{Total Assets}}$

$= \frac{Rs{,}8{,}50{,}000}{Rs.4{,}80{,}000} = 1.77:1$

The ratio is less than the desirable ratio of 2:1 i.e., the value of sales is not as much as it should be.

Illustration 2. From the following figures relating to the accounts of Alpha Ltd., comment upon the present state and trend in respect of rofitability, solvency and capialisation of the company.

Consider only two significant ratios under each head:

	1992-93 Rs.	1993-94 Rs.
Sales	12,00,000	15,00,000
Net Block	5,00,000	8,00,000
Receivables	2,00,000	2,95,000
Payables	1,00,000	2,00,000
Cash and Bank	50,000	20,000
Closing stock	2,00,000	4,00,000
Bank O/D	1,00,000	2,50,000
Purchases	9,00,000	12,00,000
Expenses	1,00,000	1,50,000
Depreciation	75,000	1,20,000
Interest on O/d	15,000	40,000
Loan	...	2,00,000
Interest on Loan	...	35,000
Share Capital	4,00,000	4,00,000
Reserve & Surplus	1,90,000	2,07,500
Provision for Income Tax	1,20,000	1,97,500
Proposed Dividend	40,000	60,000
Stock on 1.4.93		Rs. 1,80,000

Solution

i. Working notes :		**1992-93 Rs.**		**1993-94 Rs.**
Sale		**12,00,000**		**15,00,000**
Less:				
Cost of Goods sold :				
Opening stock	1,80,000		2,00,000	
Add Purchases	9,00,000		12,00,000	
	10,80,000			

Less : Closing stock	**2,00,000**			
			14,00,000	10,00,000
Expenses (Execluding Interest Depreciation				**5,00,000**
			4,00,000	
	1,00,000	8,80,000		
	75,000	**3,20,000**		**2,70,000**
Less : Interest on overdraft				2,30,000
			1,50,000	
		1,75,000	**1,20,000**	**40,000**
Less : Interest on Loan		1,45,000		1,90,000
				35,000
Provision for taxation		**15,000**		1,55,000
Balance		1,30,000		77,500*
Proposed Dividend		.....		77,500
Transfer to Reserve		**1,30,000**		60,000
				17,500

ii. Balance sheet as on.		**1992-93 Rs.**		**1993-94 Rs.**
Net Block		5,00,000		8,00,000
Net Current Assets :				
(a) - (b)				
Receivables	2,00,000		2,95,000	
Cash at Bank	50,000		20,000	
Quick Assets	2,50,000		3,15,000	
Stock	2,00,000		4,00,000	
(a)	**4,50,000**		**7,15,000**	
Liabilities other than overdrafts :				
Payables 1,00,000		2,00,000		
Provision for taxation 2,00,000		1,97,500		
Proposed Div 40,000	2,60,000	**60,000**	4,57,500	
Bank overdraft	1,00,000		2,50,000	
(b)	**3,60,000**	90,000	**7,07,500**	7,500
		5,90,000		**8,07,500**
		4,00,000		4,00,000
Share Capital	1,90,000		2,07,500	
Reserve & Surplus	5,90,000		6,07,500	
Loan	.....		2,00,000	
Capital Employed	**5,90,000**		**8,07,500**	

At the end of the year 1992-93 the provision for taxation appears to be disproportionate to the amount of the profit before tax of Rs. 1,30,000. It is possible that the figure of tax of previous years contain excess provision.

I Profitability **1992-93** **1993-94**

1. Gross Profit Ratio = $\frac{\textit{Gross Profit}}{\textit{sales}}$ X 100 $\frac{3,20,000}{12,00,000}$ X 100 $\frac{5,00,000}{15,00,000}$ X 100

2. Return on Capital = $\frac{\textit{Profit before Interest * \& Tax}}{\textit{Capital Employed}}$ $\frac{1,30,000}{5,90,000}$ X 100 $\frac{1,90,000}{8,07,500}$ X 100
   = 22.03% = 23.53%

II. Solvency

1. Current Ratio = $\frac{\textit{Current Assets}}{\textit{Current Liabilities}}$ = $\frac{4,50,000}{3,60,000}$ = $\frac{7,15,000}{7,07,500}$
   = 1.25 = 1.01

2. Liquid Ratio = $\frac{\textit{Liquid Assets}}{\textit{C. Liabilities}}$ = $\frac{2,50,000}{3,60,000}$ = $\frac{3,15,000}{7,07,500}$
   = 0.78 = 0.45

3. Fixed Assets Ratio = $\frac{\textit{Fixed Assets}}{\textit{longterm funds}}$ $\frac{5,00,000}{5,90,000}$ $\frac{8,00,000}{8,07,500}$
   (Security Ratio)
   = 0.85 = 99.1

*** Interest on long term borrowing has been taken in to account**

III. Capitalisation

1. Debt Equity Ratio
   (ignoring bank overdraft as debts)
   = $\frac{\textit{Long terms Loans}}{\textit{Share holders fund}}$ = $\frac{0}{5,90,000}$ $\frac{2,00,000}{6,07,500}$
   = Nil = 0.33

2. Capital Gearing Ratio:
   $\frac{\textit{Preference share + Debentures+Loan}}{\textit{Equity share}}$ = $\frac{\textit{Nil}}{5,90,000}$ $\frac{2,00,000}{6,07,500}$
   = Nil = 0.33 : 1

3.Fxed Assets Ratio = $\frac{\textit{Fixed Assets}}{\textit{Long term Funds}}$ = $\frac{5,00,000}{5,90,000}$ $\frac{8,00,000}{8,07,500}$
   = .85 = .99

Comments

Profitability: Gross profit ratio has increased from 26.7% in 1992-93 to 33.3% in 1993-94 reflecting better production and sales management. However return on long-term funds (capital employed) has increased marginally from 22.03% to 23.53%. This is so because sales have increased by 25% whereas expenses and depreciation charges have gone up by 50% and 60% respectively. As also the amount of net block has gone up by 60% but corresponding increase in sales in 1993-94 over 1992-93 has not been achieved. As a result fixed assets turnover ratio which was 2.4 times in 1992-93 has come down to 1.88 times in 1993-94. On the whole, it may be said bout the trend of profitability that till the company achieves higher sales 'thout further increase in fixed expenses, the net profitability ratio. cannot be considered satisfactory.

Solvency: Current ratio has gone down from 1.25 times in 1992-93 to 1.01 times in 1993-94 against the universally accepted standard of 2:1 Sundry Debtors which were 16.7% of sales in 1992-93 have increased to 19.7% of sales and investment in stock in trade has increased by 100% in 1993-94. This has been partly financed by postponing payment to creditors which have increased by 100%. Higher provision for taxation and proposed dividend also accounted for deterioration in this ratio.

Quick ratio or acid test ratio further confirms decline in solvency of the firm. It has come down to .45 : 1 in 1993-94 compared with .78:1 in 1992-93. This is mainly because of proportionately higher increase in current liabilities compared to increase in quick assets. Some long term sources may therefore be tapped to augment core working capital requirements. Steps should be taken to arrest declining trends in both the solvency ratios.

Capitalisation : In the year 1992-93 the company did not have any debt component in its capital structure. However in 1993-94 company did raise some funds by means or long term loans to finance the expansion in assets. But debt equity ratio of .33:1 is still much on the lower side. Generally the accepted norm for debt equity ratio is 2 : 1. It shows that there is ample scope for the company to raise further loan capital.

The fixed assets ratio also shows that in 1993-94 the company has raised long-term funds only to partly finance fixed assets. The sound financial management would require that core current assets should also be financed from long term sources. In conclusion it may be said that company should make efforts to increase sales volume and introduce more long-term funds preferably from loans to improve, profitability and capitalisation.

Illustration 3. On the basis of the following figures derived from the accounts of a company, prepare a Report on the level of efficiency of financial and operational.

Years	Capital Turnover Ratio	Net Profit % on Sales	ROI Percentage	Current Ratio
	Ratio			
1	1.0	8%	8%	6.0
2	2.0	10%	20%	4.0
3	3.0	11.5%	34.5%	2.0
4	5.0	13%	65%	0.5

Solution

The Managing Director,
Alert Company.

New Del
November 19,1993.

Dear Sir,

Re: Level of efficiency of financial and operational management.

As desired by you we have studied the figures submitted to us from the accounts of your company. Our observations on the level of efficiency of financial and operational management of this company yearwise are as follow:-

Year 1 In this year capital turnover ratio is very low i.e. 1 only. It indicates that the company has not been able to use its assets profitably resulting in poor capacity utilisation. Very high current ratio i.e. at 6 also reaffirms that company had too much unutilised funds in this year. The whole situation represents under trading or the case of over capitalisation. The low net profit to sales ratio and low ROI precentage in comparison to future years are also the result of low capital turnover ratio and high current ratio.

Year 2 From financial and operational management point of view, the situation is more or less the same as in Year 1. But, trend is quite satisfactory as capital turnover ratio has doubled and current ratio has come down to 4.

Year 3 In this year it appears that the company has reached an optimum level of effeciency of financial and operational management in the company. It is evident by the faact that company's capital turnover ratio has gone upto 3 and current ratio has come down to 2. These ratios represent a satisfactory situation. In this year ROI percentage is also quite good i.e.

34.5%. Company should have made efforts to maintain this level of efficiency in future years also.

Year 4 In this year ROI level percentage is very high which may generally be considered a welcome feature. However, current ratio has gone down tremendously. It indicates that the company is not ploughing back profits for working capital requirements. Very low current ratio poses a situation technical insolvency inspite of the fact that company has high profitability as is evident by 13% net profit to sales ratio. Such a situation gives signs of over trading or represents a case of under capitalisation.

Conclusion : In conclusion we would like to say that the company should try to maintain level of effeciency of financial and operational management as in Year 3. From a long term point of view, under trading or over capitalisation and over trading and under-capitalisation are not good. In view of the developments in Year 4 it is suggested that immediate remedial measures should be taken to set the things right. This may be possible by infusing more capital in the company.

We shall be glad to be of assistance in case any further analysis or elucidation is required in the matter.

Yours faithfully,

X Y Z Co.

Chartered Accountants.

REVIEW QUESTIONS

1. For what purpose financial statements are prepared? Also explain the inherent nature of financial statements?
2. What do you understand by 'analysis' and 'interpretation' of financial statements?
3. Explain the procedure of financial statement interpretation.
4. What is the significance of accounting ratios in the analysis of financial statements?
5. As a financier what safeguards would you ensure in assessing the credit-worthiness of a company from published accounts?
6. Why do bankers require financial statements of several years when examining a proposal for an advance?
7. Are there any limitations on the interpretation of financial statements?
8. Describe how would you study (i) the liquidity (ii) the solvency and (iii) the profitability of a business enterprise from an analysis of its published accounts.
9. What are the reasons for percentage of gross profit being normally calculated on turnover than on cost? Do you think that equally effective information would be made available if the percentages were calculated on cost?

10. The current ratio of a Company is 2:1. Which of the following suggestion would improve the ratio, which would not change it.
(a) To pay a current liability.
(b) To sell a motor car for cash at a slight loss.
(c) To borrow money on an interest-bering Promissory Note.
(d) To purchase stocks for cash, and
(e) To give an interest-bearing Promissory Note to a creditor to whom money was owed on current account.

[Ans: (a) improve (b) improve (c) reduce (d) no change e) no change]

14

Cash Funds Flow Statement

Traditional financial statements of a business tell very little about its flow of funds. Particularly, the nature of the balance sheet is criticised as merely a statement of the assets and liabilities as on a particular day. The balance sheet may depict the effect of various transactions in a particular period and show the resources position after all transactions in a period but does not show the movement of funds (*i.e.*, working capital). The income statement also summarises the results of its periodic operating activities without indicating the manner of financing them. It is to be noted that all the time the ultimate success or failure will depend on availability and better utilisation of fund, given a particular situation. Hence, the need for another statement to account for the periodic increase or decrease of working capital of an enterprise. The statement, called funds flow statement, portrays the sources and applications of working capital, and highlights the basic changes in the resources and financial structure of a concern between its two balance sheet dates. These dates conform to beginning and ending financial statement dates whatever period of examination is relevant - a quarter or a year. Thus, it is clear that the funds flow statement is intended to supplement, and not to supplant, the balance sheet and profit and loss account in whole or part.

Concept of 'Fund' : In a flow analysis the main ingredient is the 'fund'. The word 'fund' can be defined in different ways as follows:

(i) Cash Fund, (ii) Working Capital Fund, (iii) Capital Fund and (iv) Total Resources Fund.

The cash fund means and includes only the inflow and outflow of fund involving actual cash transactions. The working capital fund means and includes the cash fund claims against cash and near- cash items which are payable or recoverable within a period of twelve months. A somewhat broader approach to the concept of fund lies in interpreting fund in the sense of total or all financial resources.

Meaning of Cash Flow : Cash flow signifies the actual movement of cash in and out of an enterprise. When the cash flows in, it is called positive cash- flow while the cash flowing out is known as negative cash flow. The difference between them is net cash flow.

The primary sources of cash inflow are capital from owners, borrowings, cash sales, collection on accounts receivable, sale of assets, etc. Cash outflows take place intermittently on account of payments made to outsiders for interest, dividend, income tax, repayment of loans, acquiring fixed assets etc. Regular outflows of cash generally take place for purchase of inventories of rawmaterials and supplies, payment of wages and various manufacturing, selling, and administrative expenses. To sum up, inflows (sources) imply decreases in other current or non-current assets and increases in current or non-current liabilities; Conversely, outflows (uses or applications) entail increases in current or non-current assets and decreases in current or non-current liabilities. Cash trading/operating profit as a result of operations during the year gives a very important internal source of cash flow.

Object of Cash Flow Analysis: The chief object of cash flow analysis is to show the causes of changes in cash balances, between two balance sheet dates. The analysis relates to the movement of cash rather than to the inflow and outflow of working capital. It depicts a penetrating review of cash movements over an operating cycle. The next object of cash-flow analysis is to throw light on the factors contributing to the reduction of cash balance in spite of increase in profits or vice versa. It helps the management in short range financial decisions relating to liquidity and ways and means position. This statement helps to answer such questions as:

1. Where did the profits go?
2. Why were the dividends not larger?
3. How was the expansion of fixed assets financed?
4. What happened to the proceeds from selling off plant?
5. How was the repayment of debts achieved?
6. What became of the proceeds of debenture issues?
7. How was it possible to distribute dividends in excess of current earnings?
8. Why must money be borrowed to finance purchase of a new plant and equipment when the necessary amount is exceeded by ;the 'cash flow' i.e., net income plus depreciation?
9. How is it that the net current assets are up even though there was a net loss for the period?
10. How was the increase in working capital financed?
11. Why were the net current assets down although the net income is up?

12. What became the assets derived from an increase in outstanding capital stock?

Techniques for Construction of Cash Flow Statement: The cash flow statement is prepared with the help of balance sheet, income statement, and some additional information. There is no set of format for a cash flow statement. Like funds flow statement it can also be prepared in two ways either in a report form on in an account form. Generally, it is of reconciliation type where cash at the beginning is reconciled with cash at the end.

A proforma "Cash Flow Statement" is given below:

CASH FLOW STATEMENT FOR THE PERIOD.....

Sources	Rs.	Uses	Rs
Cash balance (opening)	...		
Add: (i) Cash from Operation	...	Cash lost in operation	...
(ii) Sale of Shares/Bonds	...	Redemption of Shares/ Bonds	...
(iii) Sale of Non current assets	...	Purchase of Non current assets	...
(iv) Raising new loans		Repayment of loans	
(v) Income from outside investments	...	Payment of Interest/ Taxes/Dividends	...
(vi) Other sources eg., damages from law suits, subsidies, gifts, prizes, etc., ...	...	Meeting of unsual Expenses like damages in legal action, loss by embezzlement, etc.,	
		Cash balance (closing)	...
	...		...

The preparation of cash flow statement involves the calculation of cash flows related to operations and the calculation of cash flows on account of other transactions.

There are two methods of determining cash flow from trading operations: (i) Cash Sales method and (ii) Net Profit method. Under the first method, cash from operation is determined by deducting cash purchases and cash operating expenses from cash sales. Thus, to determine the cash sales, credit sales must be deducted from total sales of the year; Credit sales can be determined from total debtors a/c. In the absence of any other information, all the items appearing in income statement are assumed to be cash items.

Statement of computing Cash from Trading Operations (Cash sales Method).

			Rs.
Sales			...
Less :	Increase in Accounts Receivable		...
	Cash Sales		...
Less :	Purchases		
	Increase in Accounts Payable	...	
	Cash Paid to creditors		
	Cash Operating Expenses	...	...
(after adjusting accruals and payments)			
	Cash From Trading Operations		...

Under the second method, cash from trading operations can be determined with the help of net profits also. In this method, depreciation, loss on sale of fixed assets, amortisation of fictitious assets, credit purchases, outstanding expenses, provisions and reserves made during the year are added back to the amount of net profit. The reason for this is very simple that they do not result in outflow of cash and, therefore, should not be treated as payments. On the other side all non-business incomes, increase in account receivables, stock in trade, prepaid expenses, reduction from deferred credits and decrease in bills payable should be reduced from the net profit. Decrease in accrued income, increase in income received in advance, etc. are added to and increase in accrued income, decrease in income received in advance, etc., are deducted from the net profit. The increase or decrease in current assets and currents liabilities influences the flow of cash from operations. Therefore, these increases and decreases shall be adjusted in net profit. To summarise –

Operating Net Profit + Decrease in Current Assets
+ Increase in Current Liabilities,
Or
– Increase in Current Assets.
—Decrease in Current Liabilities.

It would be better if increase or decrease in each item of current assets/liabilities is considered separately for calculating cash from trading operations.

Statement of Calculating Cash from Operation (Net Profit Method)

		Rs.
Reported Net Profit for the period		...
Add : *Non-Cash Expenditures (Adjustments)*	Rs.	
(i) Goodwill, Trade Mark, etc., written off	...	
(ii) Preliminary Expenses	...	
(iii) Depreciation charged for the year	...	
(iv) Discount on issue of Shares/Debentures	...	
(v) Appropriation of Reserves and provisions	...	
(vi) Dividend paid/provided for the period	...	
Add: *Non-Operating Losses :*		
(vii) Loss on Sales of Fixed Assets charged to current year's P & L a/c	...	...
Less: *Operating gains:*		
(i) Gain on Sale of fixed assets credited to current year's P & L a/c		
(ii) Dividend/Interest Received from outside Investment	...	...
Profit After Adjustments/Operating Cash Profit		
Add : (1) Decrease in Current Assets	...	
(2) Increase in Current Liabilities	...	...
Less: (1) Increase in Current Assets	...	...
(2) Decrease in Current Liabilities	...	...
Cash From Trading Operation		...

Illustration 1

PSG. Rayon Corporation made the profit of Rs. 3,70250 after considering the following:

(i) Depreciation of fixed assets Rs. 7,500

(ii) Amortisation of development cost Rs. 5,000;

(iii) Loss on sale of a machine Rs. 600

(iv) Provision for doubtful debts Rs. 1,2000, Provision for taxation Rs. 50,000,

(v) Transfer to general reserve Rs. 20,000

(vi) Gain on sale of fixed assets Rs. 2,500;

The following additional information is given to you:

	December 31			December 31	
	1993	1994		1993	1994
	Rs.	Rs.		Rs.	Rs.
Creditors	20,000	25,000	Debtors	36,000	39,000
Bills payable	15,000	13,000	Bills receivable	12,000	10,000
Outstanding expenses	7,000	6,000	Prepaid expenses	1,600	1,700

You are required to determine the Cash From Operation.

Solution

		Rs.	Rs.
(i)	Adjustment of Profit :		
	Profit made during the year :		3,70,250
Add:	**Non-cash items:**		
	Depreciation on fixed assets	7,500	
	Amortisation of development cost	5,000	
	Loss on sale of machine	600	
	Provision for doubtful debts	1,200	
	Provision for tax	50,000	
	Transfer to general reserve	20,000	84,300
			4,54,550
Less :	Gain on sale of fixed assets		2,500
	Cash Profit from operation		4,52,050
(ii)	Calculation of cash from operation :		
	Profit as per (i) above		4,52,050
Add :	Decrease in Current Assets :		
	Bills receivable	1,500	
Add :	Increase in Current liabilities :		
	Creditors	5,000	6,500
			4,58,550

Less : Decrease in Current liabilities :			
Bills Payable	2,000		
Outstanding expenses	1,000	3,000	
Less : increase in current assets :			
Debtors	3,000		
Prepaid expenses	100	3,100	6,100
Cash from Operation			4,52,450

Illustration 2

Vijaya Nagar Textiles Ltd., finds on 1st January, 1994 that it is short of funds with which to implement its programme of expansion.On 1st January, 1993, it had a credit balance of Rs. 1,80,000. From the following information, prepare a statement for the Board of Directors to show the overdraft of Rs. 68,750 as at 31st December, 1993 has arisen.

Figures as per Balance Sheet as at 31st December

	1993 Rs.	1994 Rs.
Fixed Assets	750000	1120000
Stock and stores	190000	330000
Debtors	380000	335000
Bills Receivable	87500	95000
Bank Balance	180000	68750 (o/d)
		350000
Trade Creditors	270000	
Share Capital (in		300000
shares of Rs.10 each	250000	

The profit for the year ended 31-12-1993 before depreciation and taxation amounted to Rs. 2,40,000. 5000 shares were issued on 1st January, 1993 at a premium of Rs. 5 per share. Rs. 1,37,500 were paid in March 1993 by way of income tax. Dividend was paid as follows:

1992 (final) on the capital 31-12-1992 at 10% less tax at 25%

1993 (interim) 5% free of tax.

Cash Flow Statement of Vijayanagar Textiles Ltd. for 1994

Inflows	Rs.	Outflows	Rs.
Bank balance on 1-1-93	180000	Purchase of fixed assets	370000
Issue of shares	50000	Income tax paid (2)	137500
Share Premium	25000	Final dividend for 1992	18750
Cash from Operation (1)	217500	Interim dividend for 1993	15000
Bank overdraft as on 31-12-1993	68750		
	541250		541250

Workings

(1) Cash from Trading Operation;

	Rs.	Rs.
Operating Profit as given		240000
Less Increase in stock	140000	
Increase in bills receivable	7500	147500
		92500
Add Increase in creditors	80000	
Decrease in debtors	45000	125000
		217500

(2) It is assumed that the figures of incometax paid, i.e., Rs. 1,37,500 includes income-tax deducted at source from final dividend of 1992.

Illustration 3

The financial position of M/s Tall and Short on 1st January, 1994, and December 31, 1994 was as follows:

Liabilities	1-1-94	31-12-94	Assets	1-1-94	31-12-94
	Rs.	Rs.		Rs.	Rs.
Current Liabilities	36000	41000	Cash	4000	3600
Mrs. Tall's Loan	---	20000	Debtors	35000	38400
Loan from Bank	30000	25000	Stock	25000	22000
Capital	148000	149000	Land	20000	30000
			Building	50000	55000
			Machinery	80000	86000
	214000	235000		214000	235000

During the year the partners withdrew Rs. 26,000 for domestic expenses. The provision for depreciation against machinery as on 1-1-1994 was Rs. 27,000 and on 31-12-1994 Rs. 36,000.

Prepare the Cash Flow Statement for the year ended 31st December, 1994.

Solution

Cash Flow Statement of M/s Tall & Short for the year ended 31-12-1994

Inflow	Rs.	Outflow	Rs.
Cash balance		Bank loan repayment	5000
on 1-1-1994	4000	Partner's Drawings	26000
Mrs. Tall's Loan	20000	Purchase of land	10000
Cash from operation	40600	Building (additions)	5000
		Machinery Purchase	15000
			61000
		Cash balance as on 31-12-1994	3600
	64600		64600

Workings

Cash from operation		Profit earned during the year	
Profit earned during 1994	27000	Capital at the end	149000
Depreciation	9000	*Add*: Drawings	26000
			175000
Add: Decrease in Stock	3000	Less: Capital in the beginning	148000
Increase in current Liabilities	5000	Profit earned during 1994	27000
	44000		
Less: Increase in Drs.	3400		
	40600		

Uses of the Cash Flow Statement

1. One of the most important functions of the management is to manage company's money in such a way that adequate cash is available to meet its liabilities. To determine the availability of cash payments, management needs cash flow statement.
2. It helps the manager or financial controller in explaining how despite the profits, the company is short of cash.
3. The projected cash flow statements help financial manager in exploring the possibility of repayment of long-term debts which depends upon the availability of cash.
4. From the projected cash flow statements, management can determine the likely inflow or outflow of cash from operations; and the amount of cash required to be raised from other sources to meet the future needs of the business.
5. It supplements the analysis provided by Fund Flow Statement as cash is a part of the working capital
6. Comparison of actual and budgeted cash flow statement will disclose the failure or success of the management in managing cash resources. Deviations will indicate the need for corrective actions.
7. For payment of liabilities which are likely to mature immediately cash is more important than the working capital. Cash flow statement is certainly a better tool of analysis than fund statement as far as short-term analysis is concerned.

Limitations of Cash Flow Statement

Cash flow Statement is usually criticised on the following grounds:

1. Inter-industry comparison of cash flow statement can be misleading. It does not measure the economic efficiency of one company in relation to another. Usually a company with heavy capital investment will have more cash inflow.
2. Comparison over a period of time can also be misleading. A company is not better off in the current year than the past year because its cashflow has increased.
3. Again, inter-firm comparison of cash inflow and outflow can also be misleading. The terms of purchase and sale may differ from company to company. After all, cash flow does not always mean profit.

4. Compared with the previous years, cash flow statement may be vitiated due to changes in purchases or/and sales and other policies.
5. The cash can be easily influenced by the managerial decisions, by making certain payment in advance or by postponing payments.

REVIEW QUESTIONS

1. What is a Cash Flow Statement and state the objects of preparing such a statement?
2. How will you determine cash flow from
3. Discuss the usefulness of cash flow statement for cash management. Would such a statement be helpful to outsiders also?
4. State and explain the main sources and applications of 'cash Fund'
5. Differentiate a cash flow statement from (a) Cash Budget, (b) Fund Flow Statement.
6. State whether the following transactions would be a source or an application of cash:
   (i) Sale of fixed assets on cash terms.
   (ii) Issue of shares as purchase consideration.
   (iii) Purchase of fixed assets on cash terms.
   (iv) Redemption of debenture against cash.
   (v) Redemption of debentures converting them into shares.
   (vi) Payment of dividend declared earlier.
   (vii) Payment of long-term loans.
   (viii) Sale of investment.
   (ix) Issue of bonus shares.
   (x) Recording the provision for taxation.

   [Ans: (i) Source (ii) no effect (iii) application (iv) application (v) no effect (vi) application (vii) application (viii) source (ix) no effect (x) no effect]

15
Working Capital Funds Flow Statement

Meaning of Funds Flow Statement: A Statement of Sources and Application of Funds is a technical device designed to analyse the changes in the financial condition of a business enterprise between two dates. Thus a funds flow statement is a report on movement of funds explaining wherefrom working capital originates and where into the same goes during an accounting period. In nut-shell, funds flow statement is a technical device designed to highlight the changes in the financial condition of a business enterprise between opening and closing balance sheet dates. Here, the term 'funds' denotes the working capital. The difference between the current assets and liabilities is working capital and the net movement in the working capital may only be entered.

Main Objects of the Funds Flow Analysis: The important objectives of the funds flow statement are: (i) to indicate the results of current financial management, (ii) to lay emphasis on the most significant changes that have taken place, during specific period, (iii) to show how general expansion in a business has been financed, or to describe the sources from which additional funds were derived, (iv) to illustrate the relatationship between profits from operation, distribution of dividend and raising of new capital or contracting the loans and, (v) to give recognition to the fact that a business exists on flow of funds and is not a static organisations.

Preparation of Funds Flow Statement

Generally speaking, the funds flow statement consists of two parts – viz, (1) Schedule of Changes in Working Capital and (ii) Statement of Sources and Uses of Funds.

Schedule or Statement analysing changes in working capital is prepared with the help of current assets and current liabilities of the two (periods) balance sheets (one being the previous year *i.e.,* opening balance sheet and other being current year *i.e.,* closing balance sheet). An increase in the amount of any current asset in the current year in comparison to that in the previous year results in an increase in the working capital. A decrease in the amount of any current asset in the current year in comparison to that in the previous year results a decrease in working capital. Similarly current liabilities are also compared. That is, an increase in any current liability in the current year in comparison to the previous year results in a decrease in the working capital and vice versa. Finally, the total increase and total decrease is compared and the difference shows the decrease or increase in the working capital. An increase of working capital is the application of funds and decrease of working capital is the source of funds. In other words, increase in working capital over a period implies generation of more working capital than the use thereof for various purposes over that period; conversely occurs on a decrease in working capital.

List of Current Assets and Liabilities

	Current Liabilities		**Current Assets**
(i)	Trade Creditors	(i)	Cash in Hand
(ii)	Bills Payables	(ii)	Cash at Bank
(iii)	Band Overdraft	(iii)	Temporary Investments
(iv)	Outstanding Expenses	(iv)	Trade Debtors
(v)	Provision Against Current Assets	(v)	Bills Receivables
		(vi)	Inventories
(vi)	Provision for Taxation	(vii)	Prepayments
(vii)	Proposed Dividend		

List of Non-Current Assets and Liabilities

	Non-current Liabilities		**Non-current Assets**
(i)	Equity Share Capital	(i)	Land and Building
(ii)	Preference Share Capital	(ii)	Plant and Machinery
(iii)	Long Term Loans	(iii)	Furnitures and Fixtures
(iv)	Debentures	(iv)	Long Term Investments
(v)	Share Premium Account	(v)	Discount on Issue of Shares and Debentures
(vi)	Forfeited Shares	(vi)	Good will, Patent, Trade Marks
(vii)	Capital Reserve, capital Redemption Reserve, etc.	(vii)	Preliminary Expenses
(viii)	General Reserves, Insurance Fund, Dividend Equalisation Fund, Debenture Sinking Fund. Investment Fluctuation Reserve, etc.	(viii)	Other Deferred Expenditures like Advertisement cost
(ix)	P & L A/c. (Credit Balance)	(ix)	P & L A/c. (Debit Balance)
(x)	Provision for Depreciation on Fixed Assets		

It should noted that the above two lists are not exhaustive.

The terms used above are explained below:

1. *Non-Current (Fixed) Liabilities:* These liabilities are not payable within a year out of current assets. These liabilities are generally payable either in the long period or at the close of the business.

2. *Current Liabilities:* These liabilities are payable within a year out of current assets. The values of these liabilities generally change within one

year. Long Term liabilities, if matured, and are to be paid in the current period, will become current liabilities.

3. *Non-Current (Fixed) Assets:* Those assets which are obtained in the business for use over a long period of time for earning purpose are called non-current assets. These assets are not purchased for the purpose of selling.

4. *Current Assets:* Those assets which are reasonably expected to be realised in cash or sold or consumed within one year or during the normal operating cycle of the business are called current assets.

After learning the meaning of these terms we have to see as to when there is flow in funds. Whenever there is change in the funds it is presumed that flow in funds has taken place. Transactions that bring working capital into the enterprise are sources of funds. On the contrary, if the working capital decreases, it is an application of funds. Out of all transactions now we have to see which transactions bring flow in funds and other transactions which do not affect the flow of funds.

Transactions which bring the change in the working capital.

i. *Current Assets and Non-current (Fixed) Assets:* Whenever in any transaction one aspect affects the current assets and the other non-current assets, there is flow in the working capital. For example, when building is purchased for cash, non-current assets will increase and current assets will reduce without any corresponding change in current liabilities. So working capital will decrease. Similarly, if any fixed asset is sold, there is increase in current assets (without corresponding change in current liabilities) and reduction in fixed assets; it will increase the working capital.

ii. *Current Assets and Non-current (Fixèd) Liabilities*: If in any transaction, one aspect affects the current assets and the other non-current liabilities there will be flow in the working capital. For example, if equity shares are issued for cash, it will increase the (current assets) without any corresponding increase in current liabilities and also increase the equity share capital (Non-current liabilities) there is increase in the working capital. On the other hand, if long term liabilities *i.e.,* debentures are paid in cash it will decrease the current assets and decrease the non-current liabilities without any change in current liabilities, so it will reduce the working capital.

iii. *Current Liabilities and Non-current Liabilities*: If in any transaction, one aspect affects the current liabilities and the other non-current liabilities, there will be flow in the working capital. For example, if debentures are issued to the creditors, it will increase the non-current liabilities and decrease the current liabilities without any change in current assets, so there will be increase in the working capital.

iv. *Current Liabilities and Non-Current Assets*: In in any transaction, one aspect affects the current liabilities and the other non-current assets, there is flow the working capital. For example if building is purchased on credit, it will increase the non-current assets and also current liabilities (without any change in current assets), so there will be decrease in the working capital.

Transactions not affecting the flow of funds

The following transactions will not bring any change in the working capital and thus, there will be no flow in funds.

a. *Current Assets and Current Liabilities:* When in any transaction one aspect affects the current assets and the other current liabilities, there is no flow in funds. For example, if goods are sold on credit, it will increase the debtors (current assets) and will reduce the stock of goods. So there will be no change in the working capital. Similarly, if cash is paid to creditors it will decrease the current assets and decrease the liabilities; there will be no change in the working capital.

b. *Non-Current Assets and Non-Current Liabilities:* In in any transaction, one aspect affects the non-current assets and the other non-current liabilities, there will be not be any change in the working capital. For example, if building is purchased by the issue of Equity Shares it will increase the non- current assets and non-current liabilities, but there will not be any change in working capital. Similarly, if debentures are redeemed out of the non-current assets and non-current liabilities, but there will be no change in working capital.

c. *Non-Current Assets and Non-Current Liabilities:* If there is any transaction both aspects of which affect non-current liabilities or non-current assets, it will not affect the working capital. For example, if debentures are converted into share capital it will on one hand increase the non-current liabilities and on the other hand decrease the non-current liabilities.

Statement of Changes in Working Capital

This statement is prepared from current assets and current liabilities in order to calculate increase or decrease in working capital and is prepared in the following proforma:

STATEMENT OF CHANGES IN WORKING CAPITAL

	Previous year figures Rs.	Current year figures Rs.	Changes in Current Assets and Liabilities	
			(Increase) Dr.	(Decrease) Cr.
Current Assets :				
Cash	--	--	--	
Bill Receivable	--	--		--
Debtors	--	--	--	
Stocks	--	--		
Advance Payment	--	--	--	
Accured Income	--	--	--	
Investment (short term)	--	--	--	
Total Current Assets	--	--		
Current Liabilities :				
Creditors	--	--	--	
Bills Payable				
Bank	--	--		--
Overdraft	--	--	--	
Outstanding Expenses	--	--		--
# Provision for Taxation	--	--	--	
# Proposed Dividend	--	--		--
Short term Loan	--	--	--	
Total Current Liabilities	--	--		
Working Capital	--	--		
		-		
Decrease in Working Capital			--	
Total		-	-	-

Note: Current liabilities marked with arterisk # can be alternatively dealt with as non-current liabilities. If these are treated as non-current liabilities then no treatment is to be given in statement of changes in working capital and accounts relating to these items should be prepared separately to find out hidden transactions of taxes or dividends paid or provided during the year. It is better to prepare accounts of these items separately because payments of taxes and dividends are important applications of funds.

The following rules may be remembered for current assets and current liabilities:

(i) An increase in current assets increases working capital;

(ii) A decrease in current assets decreases working capital;

(iii) An increase in current liabilities decreases working capital; and

(iv) A decrease in current liabilities increases working capital.

While preparing funds flow statement, the following rules must be remembered:

1. An increase in a fixed asset indicates an application of funds.
2. A decrease in a fixed asset indicates a source of funds.
3. An increase in a fixed liability indicates a source of funds.
4. An decrease in a fixed liability indicates an application of funds.
5. An increase in shareholders' funds indicates a source of funds-
6. A decrease in shareholders' funds indicates an application of funds.

The following will illustrate these rules:

Source of Funds	**Application of Funds**
- Fixed Assets	+ Fixed Assets
+ Fixed Liabilities	- Fixed Liabilities
+ Shareholders' Fund	- Shareholders Funds

Note: Prepare fixed assets and liabilities accounts to find out the hidden transactions which have taken place between the opening and closing balance sheet dates. Such transactions can be purchase or sale of fixed assets, depreciation on fixed assets, amount written off from discount on shares, goodwill, patents, trade marks, etc., amount transferred to reserves, taxes or dividend paid or provided during the year, first issue of shares or debentures during the year, redemption of preference shares of debentures etc. Working of some accounts is given below:-

Machinery Account

	Rs.		Rs.
To Opening Balance	--	By Depreciation (Bal. fig.)	--
To Purchase of Machinery (Bal. fig.)	--	By Sale of Machine (Bal. fig.)	--
		By Loss on sale (Bal. fig.)	--
		By Closing Balance	--
	--		--

Note: One item can be balancing figure, others will be given and balancing figure is taken as hidden transaction.

Discount on Shares Account

	Rs.		Rs.
To Opening Balance b/d	--	By Profit & Loss A/c. Amount written off during the year (Bal. fig)	--
		By Closing Balance c/d	--
	--		--

Provision for Taxation Account

	Rs.		Rs.
To Cash (Tax paid)	--	By Opening Balance b/d	--
To Closing Balance c/d	--	By Profit & Loss A/c. provision made (Bal. fig.)	--
	--		--

Proposed Dividend Account

	Rs.		Rs.
To Cash [Payment of dividend of last year]	--	By Opening Balance b/d	--
To Closing Balance c/d	--	By Profit & Loss A/c. [Provision made for the Current year - Bal. fig.]	--
	--		--

Equity Share Capital Account

	Rs.		Rs.
		By Opening Balance b/d	
To Closing Balance c/d.	--	By Cash [Fresh issue]	--
	--		--

Illustration 1

From the following two Balance Sheets as on 31st December 1992 and 1993 you are required to prepare a Schedule of Changes in Working Capital.

Capital & Liabilities	1992 [Dec. 31] Rs.	1993 [Dec. 31] Rs.	Assets	1992 [Dec. 31] Rs.	1993 [Dec. 31] Rs.
Share Capital	2,00,000	2,50,000	Cash	30,000	47,000
Trade Creditors	70,000	45,000	Debtors	1,20,000	1,15,000
Retained Earnings	10,000	23,000	Stock in trade	80,000	90,000
			Land	50,000	66,000
	2,80,000	3,18,000		2,80,000	3,18,000

Solution

Schedule of Changes in Working Capital

Particulars	1992 Rs.	1993 Rs.	Changes in Working Capital Increase (Rs.)	Changes in Working Capital Decrease (Rs.)
Current Assets				
Cash	30,000	47,000	17,000	
Debtors	1,20,000	1,15,000		5,000
Stock in trade	80,000	90,000	10,000	
Total Current Assets	2,30,000	2,52,000		
Current Liabilities				
Trade Creditors	70,000	45,000	25,000	
Working Capital	1,60,000	2,07,000		
Increase in Working Capital	47,000			47,000
	2,07,000	2,07,000	52,000	52,000

From the above, it is to be noted that the statement of working capital is prepared with two additional columns for the changes in working capital i.e., increase or decrease in current assets and current liabilities. The balancing figure of these columns is always equal to the balancing figure of the columns meant for current assets and current liabilities.

After preparing the statement or schedule of working capital, statement of sources and applications of funds is prepared with the help of remaining items in the Balance Sheets of the two periods, i.e., all non-current assets and liabilities and other information given in the problem. Any transaction increasing the amount of working capital is a source (inflow) of funds, and decreasing this amount is an application (outflow) of funds. Increase or decrease in working capital occurs only when a transaction causes a change in both the current and non-current items. Changes confined to either of these items do not alter the funds as detailed in the previous pages.

(i) Conversion of a current asset into another, e.g., substitution of trade debtors by bills receivables, prepayment of expenses, collection of receivables, etc.

(ii) Increase or decrease in current assets accompanied by increase or decrease in current liability in the same amount offset each other and therefore, cause no changes in working capital; yet working capital ratio changes e.g., discharge of trade creditors, credit purchases of inventories, etc.

(iii) Replacement of current liability with another, e.g., substitution of trade creditors by bills payable.

(iv) Exchange of non-current asset with another such as acquisition of machinery for long-term investment.

(v) Substitution of non-current liability with another e.g., conversion of debentures into shares, and

(vi) Exchange of non-current assets with non-current liabilities, for instance, purchase of land by issuing shares or redemption of mortgage loan by forgoing building offset each other and therefore cause no effect in working capital.

In other words, it may be said that working capital varies only when variation in current items is accompanied by a corresponding variation in any non-current items. Therefore, increase in working capital (source of funds) is indicated by increase in equities (share capital and borrowing e.g., receipt of cash from the issue of shares, debentures) and decrease in non-current assets e.g., sale of land, building, etc. Similarly, decrease in working capital (uses of funds) is indicated by increase in non-current assets e.g., purchase of land, plant etc., and decrease in equities and long-term debts e.g., redemption of preference shares and debentures. To sum up, working capital analysis deals with flow of funds between current and non-current items.

The Principal Sources and Applications of Funds are listed below:

	Sources of Funds	Uses of Funds
1.	Funds from operation (operating profit)	Funds lost in operation (operating loss)
2.	Issue of share capital	Redemption of preference Shares
3.	Borrowing long term loans such as debentures, mortgages, deposits, etc.	Repayment of long-term loans
4.	Sale of non-current [fixed] assets e.g., land, building, plant, long term investment, intangibles, etc.	Purchase of non-current [fixed] assets Drawings in case of proprietary, partnership business.
5.	Non-trading receipts such as dividend and interest earnings, gifts received, damages recovered in legal action etc.	Non-trading payments e. g., loss arising from legal action, loss of cash by exbezzlement, etc. and payment of taxes & dividends.
6.	Exccess of Uses over the Sources of funds i.e., Decrease in working capital [as per schedule]	Exccess of Sources over the Uses of funds i.e., Increase in working capital [as per schedule]

Calculation of Funds from Operation

The profit of a period is an important source of funds. Funds from operations which are internal in character are arrival after making adjustments in the net profit. These adjustments are necessary because the net profit has been determined after deducting noncash expenses such as depreciation, writing of Goodwill, etc., which do not result in the flow of funds. That is, transactions like depreciation, goodwill written off, etc., are shown as expenses, in fact, are book adjustments, and do not involve use of resources, so that the actual funds generated from operations are larger by the amount of such non-cash expenses. Funds from operations may be arrived at by adding back all non- cash debits [expenses] to the net profit, and deducting all non- cash credits [incomes] therefrom. If there has been a net loss, non-cash expenses have to be deducted therefrom and non-cash income added thereto. It can be calculated as under :

CALCULATION OF FUNDS FROM OPERATION

		Rs.	Rs.
Net profit as shown in P & L A/c.			...
Add.	(a) Depreciation and Depletion charges	...	
	(b) Amortisation of fictitious and intangible assets like amount written off by way of preliminary expenses, goodwill, patents, discount on shares, or debentures, premium on redemption of debentures or preference shares, deferred charges etc.	...	
	(c) Provision for taxation	...	
	(d) Loss on sale of fixed assets if debited to P&L A/c	...	
	(e) Dividend (paid out of current year's profit)	...	
	(f) Appropriation of retained earnings	...	...
Less:	(a) Dividend received from outside	...	
	(b) Retransfer of excess provisions	...	
	(d) Profit on sale of fixed assets (if already credited to P & L A/c.)	...	
	(d) Appreciation in the value of fixed assets	...	...
	Funds From Operations		...

Note 1: Provisions for tax may be treated either as a current or non-current liability. As a current, (i.e., as a charge on profit) provision for taxation is considered while preparing statement of working capital and not used for adjusting the profit made during the year for calculating the funds from operation and also tax paid during the year is not treated as an application of fund. As a non-current liability, the provision for tax is treated as internal appropriation of profit made during the year and also tax paid during the year is treated as a application of fund.

Note 2: Proposed dividend is also treated like tax provision either as current or as non- current liability. But after the dividend is declared in general meeting, the amount becomes as current liability.

Note 3: Trade Investments should be treated as long term investments and they should not be included in statement of changes in working capital.

However, if investments represent surplus fund temporarily invested in marketable securities, they are to be treated as current asset, and as such, are to be considered in determining working capital.

Note 4: When investments or fixed assets have been sold or purchased and provision for taxation have been increased and taxes have been paid, various ledger accounts should be prepared - Asset A/c; Accumulated Depreciation A/c., Investment A/c., Provision for Taxation A/c., etc.

A Proforma "Funds flow Statement" is given below :

Statement of Sources and Uses of funds

		Rs.
A.	**Inflow (Sources) :**	
	(a) Share capital	...
	(b) Debentures	...
	(c) Loans	...
	(d) Sale of investment and fixed assets	...
	(e) Trading / Operating Profit	...
	(f) Non-trading / Non-Operating Income	...
	Total	...
B.	**Outflow (Uses) :**	
	(a) Redemption of shares (redeemable)	...
	(b) Repayment of loans	...
	(c) Redemption of debentures and fixed assets	...
	(e) Payment of dividend (last year or interim)	...
	(g) Non-trading expenses	...
	(h) Trading, operating loss	...
	Total	...
	Increase or decrease in working capital (as per statement of changes in working capital)	

OR

Sources And Applications Statement

	Sources (inflow)	Rs.	Applications (outflow)	Rs.
1.	Share capital	...	Redemption of redeemable shares	...
2.	Debentures	...	Redemption of debentures	...
3.	Loans	...	Repayment of loans	

4.	Sale of Investments and fixed assets,.	...	Purchase of investments and fixed assets	
5.	Trading / Operating profit	...	Trading/Operating loss	
6.	Non-trading income	...	Non-trading expenses Payment of dividends (last year or interim) Payment of Income tax	...
7.	Decrease in working capital (as per statement of changes in working capital)		Increase in working capital (as per statement of changes in working capital)	
	Total	...	**Total**	...

Illustration 2

Calculate Funds from operation from the following Profit and Loss Account :

PROFIT AND LOSS ACCOUNT

	Rs.		Rs.
To Expenses paid and outstanding	3,00,000	By Gross profit	4,50,000
Depreciation	70,000	" Gain on sale of land	60,000
Loss on sale of machine	4,000		
Discount	200		
Goodwill	20,000		
Net profit	1,15,800		
	5,10,000		5,10,000

Solution

Net profit as per profit and loss account		Rs.	1,15,800
Add. Depreciation	Rs. 70,000		
Loss on sale of machinery	4,000		
Discount	200		
Goodwill	20,000	Rs.	94,200
			2,10,000
Less : Gain on sale of land			60,000
Funds from Operation			1,50,000

Uses and Significance of Funds Flow Statement

(i) **Analysis of Financial Operation :** A funds flow statement shows how the resources have been obtained and the uses to which they are put.

The funds statement determines the financial consequences of business operations. It is also useful in judging whether the firm has expanded at too fast a rate and whether financing is strained. It also points out to the effectiveness with which the management has handled working capital during the period under review.

(ii) **Evaluation of the firm's financing :** This statement can assist the financial manager in planning intermediate and long-term finance for obtaining resources in the further and determining how they are to be used. That is, analysis of the major sources of funds in the past reveals what position of the firm's growth was financed internally and what position externally.

(iii) **Comparison with the Budget:** The statement defines the past flow of funds and gives insight into the evolution of the present situation. it provides certain useful information about the firms' financial policies to the outside world like bankers, Government, etc.

Funds flow statement is becoming popular with the management because it helps to explain why inspite of earning sizable amount of profits, the company is experiencing difficulty in making payments to creditors, the rate of dividend on equity shares can not be increased and the bank balance is getting thinner.

Limitations of Funds Statement

(a) **Disclosure of overall variation only :** The funds flow statement shows overall change in working capital and not the variations in individual items, including on most significant item cash, constituting the working capital.

(b) **Manipulation by Management :** Since non-monetary assets such as inventories are included in working capital, the management may manipulate the net change in working capital and the resources of funds from operation by applying any of the widely varying methods of inventory valuation most suited to it.

(c) **Grouping of Heterogeneous items :** The concept of 'working capital' bundles monetary and non-monetary current assets, together. Consequently it includes widely divergent items such as cash, receivables, inventories prepayments, etc., and hence lacks homogeneity. Particularly, a stock of standard product ready for sale, may resonabable by treated as a liquid source, but often a large part of the inventory represents work in progress throughout the various stages of production. Thus, it is not proper to refer to inventories or prepayments as 'funds'.

(d) The Funds statement, however cannot also disclose (i) a true and fair or current view of liquidity and (ii) factors responsible for liquidity to change.

Distinction Between Funds Flow Statement and Cash Flow Statement

(1) 'Fund Flow Statement' is based upon working capital concept while 'Cash flow Statement' is based on cash concept of the term fund.

(2) 'Cash Flow Statement' can be described as a supplement to 'Funds Flow Statement' as it is based on just one important element of working capital.

(3) A separate Schedule of changes in working capital is not required in Cash flow Statement as changes in working capital items are also explained in the statement itself.

(4) Funds Flow Statement is prepared in consonance with the 'Accrual concept' while in Cash Flow Statement 'accrual data' is converted into 'cash data'.

(5) Fund Flow Statement matches the source of funds with their uses while Cash Flow Statement begins with the opening balance of cash and after recording uses and sources of cash, reaches the closing balance of cash.

(6) Funds Flow Statement is more useful in long term planning. It is not important to know what will be the cash position after 10 years but it is certainly desirable to estimate what will be the funds at that time.

(7) Classification of accounts and transactions into current and non-current is relevant only for the purpose of Fund Flow Statement. If notional concept of cash is taken, no such classification is required in the case of Cash Flow Statement.

Distinction Between Funds Flow Statement and Balance Sheet

(1) Balance sheet is a statement showing the financial position of the concern on a particular date. The asset side portrays the deployment of resources in various types of properties and liabilities side indicate the manner in which the resources are obtained. It shows all assets and liabilities whether current or fixed, tangible or intangible, etc., while Funds Flow Statement shows the changes in current assets and current liabilities during a particular period of time.

(2) Balance sheet shows the total financial position on a particular date and in this way, it is of a historical nature and therefore, its utility is very limited for the management. On the other hand, Funds Flow Statement is a comparative statement of assets and liabilities and depicts the changes in working capital during the period of two Balance Sheets.

(3) Funds Flow Statement is an analysis and control device for the management. Management can ensure the long term and the short term solvency of the firm by studying the internal funds flow cycles. It is modern technique of knowing the inflows and outflows of funds during a particular period. Balance sheet represents the balance of various assets and liabilities and does not present analysis of any kind.

(4) There are two views of financial position of the firm long term and short term. Short term financial position means the technical solvency of the firm in the near future while on the other hand, long-term financial position means future financial structure of the firm. Both are inter-related but there is a difference in their analysis. The short-term view of the financial position of the firm cannot be had from the Balance Sheet.

Funds Flow Statement and Income Statement / Profit & Loss Account

(i) A funds Flow Statement deals with the financial resources required for running the business activities. It explains how the funds were obtained and how were they used. Whereas as Income Statement discloses the results of the business activities. i.e., how much has been earned and how it has been spent.

(ii) A Funds Flow Statement matches the "funds raised" and "funds applied" during a particular period. The sources and application of funds may be of capital as well as of revenue nature. An Income Statement matches the income of a period with the expenditure of that period which are both of a revenue nature. For example, where shares are issued for cash, it becomes a source of funds while preparing a funds flow statement but it is not an item of income for an Income Statement.

(iii) Sources of funds are many besides operations such as issue of share capital and debentures, sale of fixed assets, etc. Income Statement which discloses the results of operations cannot even accurately tell about the funds from operations of non-fund items such as depreciation, writing off of fictitious assets, etc., being included therein.

Thus, both Income Statement and Flow Statement have different functions to perform. Modern management needs both. One cannot be a substitute for the other rather they are complementary to each other.

Illustration - 3

The Balance Sheets of Senthil Industries Ltd., as on 31st December 1993 and 31st December 1994 are as follows:

Liabilities	1993	1994	Assets	1993	1994
	Rs.	Rs.		Rs.	Rs.
Share capital	150000	200000	Land & Building	20000	40000
General Reserve	63250	68250	Machinery	150000	240000
Despreciation Fund	50000	55000	Prepaid Insurance	3000	3500
Sundry creditors	122750	114850	Stock	108000	60000
Accrued expenses	9000	18000	Sundry Debtors	75000	80000
Tax payable	5000	5400	Cash	29000	28000
			Preliminary expenses	15000	10000
	400000	461500		400000	461500

Sales for the year 1994 were Rs. 10,50,000. In arriving at the net profit items deducted from sale include among others: cost of goods sold Rs. 8,25,000, depreciation on machinery Rs. 25,000, wages and salaries Rs. 1,00,000 and a profit of Rs. 5,000 on the sale of a machinery. The machinery had cost Rs. 30,000; depreciation of Rs. 20,000 had been accumulated for it and it was sold for Rs. 15,000. The Company declared and paid Rs. 30,000 as dividends during the year 1994.

Prepare a schedule of changes in working capital and a statement showing the Sources and Applications of funds for the year ending 31st December 1994.

Solution

Schedule of Changes in Working Capital

	1993	1994	Changes in Working Capital	
			Increase	Decrease
	Rs.	Rs.	Rs.	Rs.
Current Assets:				
Prepaid insurance	3000	3500	500	
Stock	108000	60000		48000

Sundry debtors	75000	80000	5000	
Cash	29000	28000		1000
Total current Assets	215000	171000		
Current Liabilities:				
Sundry Creditors	122750	114850	7900	
Accrued expenses	9000	18000		9000
Income tax payable	5000	5400		400
Total Current Liabilities	1367500	138250		
Working Capital	78250	33250		
Decrease in Working Capital		45000	45000	
	78250	78250	58400	58400

Statement of Sources and Applications of Funds

Inflow	Rs.	Outflow	Rs.
Funds from operations (1)	60000	Purchase of land & building	20000
Issue of shares	50000	Purchase of Machinery	
Sale of Machinery	15000	(2)	120000
		Payment of dividend	30000
Decrease in working capital	45000		
	170000		170000

General Reserve Account (1)

	Rs.		Rs.
To Depreciation	25000	By Balance b/d	63250
To Preliminary expenses (written off 15000-10000)	5000	By Machinery (Profit on sale)	5000
		By Funds from operations (balancing figure)	60000
To Dividend	30000		
To Balance c/d	68250		
	128250		128250

Machinery Account (2)

	Rs.		Rs.
To Balance b/d (at cost)	150000	By Cash (Sale)	15000
To General Reserve (Profit on sale)	5000	By Depreciation Fund	20000
To Cash (Purchase of machinery)	120000	By Balance c/d	240000
	275000		275000

Depreciation Fund

	Rs.		Rs.
To Machinery a/c (accumulated depreciation)	20000	By Balance a/c	50000
		By Depreciation for the year	25000
To Balance c/d	55000		
	75000		75000

REVIEW QUESTIONS

1. Why is it necessary to prepare Funds Flow Statement in addition to financial statement?
2. What is meant by 'flow' of fund?
   Is depreciation a "source of fund"?
3. What is Funds Flow Statement?
4. What is a non-fund item? Give examples.
5. List four examples of the uses of working capital.
6. In what way does a Statement of Sources and Uses differ from a statement of Receipts and Disbursements?
7. "Expenses reduce working capital, whereas charge of depreciation does not." Do you agree? Give reason to support your answer.
8. Outline the main sources and applications of funds.
9. What are the principal ways in which working capital may be (a) increased; (b) decreased.
10. Distinguish between Funds-flow analysis and cash-flow analysis.
11. Discuss in detail the procedure of making a funds flow statement.
12. Why is management posed, sometimes, with the paradox of huge profits and yet impossible to pay dividends or even taxes?
13. State the effect of each of the following transitions considered individually, on working capital fund:
    (a) Purchase of merchandise for cash
    (b) Purchase of merchandise on account
    (c) Purchase of building against long term Note payable

(d) Borrowed Rs. 10,000 issuing a short term Pro-note
(e) Sold for Rs. 10,000 cash merchandise that has cost Rs.7,000
(f) Bonus paid in the form of fully paid shares
(g) Redemption of debentures by payment in cash
(h) Redemption of debentures by converting them into equity.
(i) Issues shares for cash Rs.50,000
(j) Received from a customer Rs. 3,000 in payment of his account
(k) Machinery with cost of Rs 20,000 and accumulated depreciation Rs. 18,500 was sold for Rs. 2,000 cash
(l) Bad debts amounting to Rs. 1,000 written off against a provision for bad and doubtful debts
(m) Prepayment of expenses
(n) Acceptance of bill of exchange
(o) Endorsement of B/R to creditor

14. State the individual effect of the following transactions on the funds flow and also cash flow:

1. Proprietor transfers his Rs. 4,00,000 private building to the business.
2. Owner purchases from his private estate Rs. 15,00,000 merchandise for the business.
3. Subscription of Rs. 10,000 shares in the Binny Co. Ltd.
4. Acquisition of inventory for cash Rs. 25,000.
5. Purchase of equipment in exchange of Rs. 10,000 shares of Binny Co. Ltd.
6. Sale of merchandise costing Rs. 5,000 for Cash Rs. 7,000
7. Issue of Rs. 20,000 shares to acquire merchandise of Rs. 15,000 and furniture Rs. 5,000.
8. Issue of shares worth Rs. 5,000 in redemption of debentures.
9. Conversion of Rs. 3,000 debentures into Rs. 3,000 equity shares.
10. Borrowing of Rs. 1,200 by accepting a 6 months bill.
11. Purchase of building for Rs. 6,00,000 in exchange of a 10 year bond.
12. Collection of Rs. 3,00,000 from a customer and payment of Rs. 70,000 to a supplier.
13. Fully depreciated equipment originally costing Rs. 40,000 fetches nothing as salvage when declared.
14. 1,000 debentures of Rs. 1,000 each issued at Rs. 900 to public are duly subscribed and paid.
15. Equipment originally costing Rs. 75,000 is sold for Rs. 20,000 when its accumulated depreciation amounts to Rs. 60,000.
16. Redemption of Rs. 8,000 Redeemable Preference shares at a premium 10%

[**Ans:** Cash flow: (S) 10, 12, 14, 15 (A) 3, 4, 12, 16 Funds flow: (S) 2, 5, 7 (Rs. 1, 5000), 12, 14, 10; (A) 12, 16 No Effect: 1, 5 7 (Rs 5000), 8, 9, 11, 13]

16

Break Even Analysis

Break even analysis indicates at which level costs and revenues are in equilibrium. To speak broadly, break even analysis means an analytical technique that can be used to determine the probable profit at any level of production or sales. It is basically an extension of marginal costing. Break even analysis may be performed both graphically as well as algebraically; it establishes and explains the relationship among costs (fixed and variable cost) of production, volume of production, profit and sales value. Hence, this analysis is also designated as 'Cost-Volume-Profit' (CVP) analysis.

Break Even Chart: When the break-even analysis is performed graphically it is known as a break even chart (BEC). It is a graphical representation of marginal costing. It has been defined as a chart which shows the profitability or otherwise of an undertaking at various levels of activity and indicates the point at which neither profit nor loss is made.

Break Even Point: A break even point may be described as specified level of activity or volume of sales which breaks the revenue and costs evenly *i.e.,* income just balances with expenses. This point is also known as no loss, no profit point, balancing point, neutral point, equilibrium point, loss ending point.Sales in excess of this point show profit.

Construction of Break Even Chart

Production volume is plotted on the X (horizontal) axis, costs and sales revenue are shown on the Y (vertical) axis. The fixed cost line on the vertical axis is drawn parallel to horizontal axis. The variable costs at different levels of (budgeted) activity are plotted over the fixed cost line. Note that the variable cost line is joined to fixed cost line at zero volume of production. This gives the total cost line. Total sales line is marked on the right side of vertical axis. The sales line cuts the total cost line at a point where the total costs are equal to total revenues and this point of intersection of two lines is known as break even point – the point of no profit no loss. Draw a perpendicular to the X axis from the point of inter- section and horizontal distance from the zero point to the point where the perpendicular is drawn represents the break even output. Draw a perpendicular to the Y axis from the point of intersection and the vertical distance from the zero point to the point at which the perpendicular is drawn represents the break-even sales. The angle formed by the inter-section of the sales line and total cost line is known as the angle of incidence. The area to the left of the break even point is the loss area while to the right of it, there is the profit area. The variable cost is represented by the gap between the total cost and the fixed cost. The distance between any selected level of output/sales from the break even output/sales represents the margin of safety.

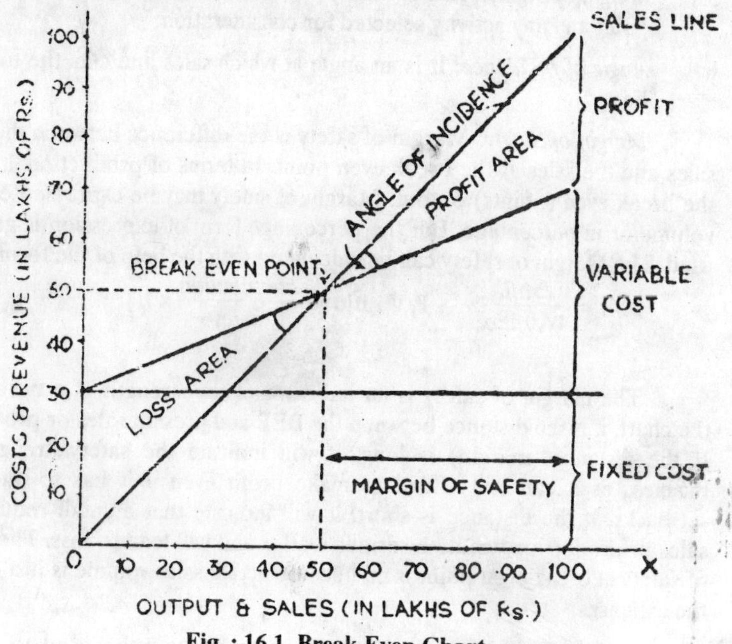

Fig. : 16.1 Break-Even Chart

Total Production/Sales Rs. 100 lakhs; Fixed cost Rs. 30 lakhs; Variable costs Rs. 40 lakhs; Total costs Rs. 70 lakhs; Break even point Rs. 50 lakhs

Break even chart can be drawn alternatively with variable cost either at base or at top. A break even chart may also be drawn in a from which is suitable to show the components of the variable cost or profit appropriations.

Features of Break Even Chart: The following are the chief features of a break even chart:

1. *Cost line :* The total cost, fixed cost and variable cost can be directly read for any chosen level of activity.

2. *Sales Revenue:* Like, costs, sales revenue can also be directly noted for any level of activity.

3. *Profit or Loss:* The gap between the total cost line and the income line at any level of activity measures the profit or loss at that level.

4. *Break Even Point:* When the income line crosses the total cost line income and total costs are equal then neither a profit nor a loss is made, the firm breaks evenly. This point is called the break-even point, and is usually measured in terms of activity.

5. *Margin of Safety:* This is simply the difference between the break-even point and any activity selected for consideration.

6. *Angle of Incidence:* It is an angle at which sales line cuts the total cost line.

Margin of Safety: Margin of safety is the difference between the actual sales and the sales at the break even point. In terms of production it is over the break even (points) output. Margin of safety may be expressed either in volume or in percentage. But the percentage form of expression is generally used. The Margin of safety can be calculated with the help of the formula:

$$M/S = \frac{Profit}{P/V\ ratio} \quad (\text{P/V ratio} = \frac{contribution}{sales} \times 100$$

The margin of safety is an indicator of the strength of a business. In the chart, it is the distance between the BEP and present sales or production. If the distance (margin) is long, it will indicate the safety/strength of a business as it can still afford to make profit even if it has to face some set-backs. If the distance is short, it will indicate that a small reduction in sales or production will be a serious matter and will lead to loss. The margin of safety at break even point is nil because actual sales volume is just equal to the expenses.

In interfirm comparison, margin of safety may be used to indicate relative position of firms. If the margin of safety is unsatisfactory the possible steps to rectify the position are : (a) Increase the selling price (b) Increasing the volume of output (c) Reduce the fixed costs (d) Reduce variable costs, and (e) Substitution of the existing product or products by more profitable lines i.e., improving sales mix.

Angle of Incidence: This is the angle formed at the break-even point at which the sales line cuts the total cost line. This angle is an indicator of profit-earning capacity over the break even point. If the angle is large, it indicates that the profits are being made very satisfactorily at a high rate. If the angle is small it indicates that the profits are being earned at a relatively low rate of return revealing that variable costs form a large part of costs of sales. However, if margin of safety and angle of incidence are considered together, they will be more informative. For instance, a large angle of incidence with a high margin of safety will indicate the most favorable conditions of a business or even the existence of monopoly position.

It is clear that if the contribution margin is higher, the angle of incidence will also be higher. The angle of incidence can be improved: (i) by raising the selling price and/or (ii) by reducing the variable cost. It should however be noted that angle of incidence is not affected by fixed costs, even though the break even point is affected by the fixed costs.

Position of Break Even Point: Firstly, if the break even point appears in the centre of the chart, it is an optimum favorable position. Secondly, if the Break Even Point sets on the right wide of the chart, it means that the position of profit earning is not favorable. The margin of safety is low and the causes may be either (i) the amount of fixed overhead is too great for the amount of sales being achieved or (ii) the variable costs are high and consequently, the contribution is low. In either case, close scrutiny would have to be made of the costs and the possibility explored of substituting another product for one now being made in order to provide a greater contribution. Lastly, if the break even point is one to the left of the chart and is coupled with a large angle of incidence and good margin of safety it would indicate a high favorable situation for greater production an greater profits by larger sales.

Variables Affecting Break Even Point: The following are the three variables that affect break even point:

(i) *Marginal cost* - An increase in marginal cost (i.e. Variable cost per unit) raises the break even point whereas a decrease in the marginal cost lowers the break even point.

(ii) *Fixed cost* - An increase in fixed cost raises the break even point whereas a decrease in fixed cost lowers the break even point.

(iii) *Marginal revenue* - An increase in marginal revenue (i.e., sale price per unit) lowers the break point whereas a decrease in the marginal revenue raises the break even point.

Assumption of Break Even Analysis

The following assumptions usually underlie break even analysis.

(1) The behaviour of costs and revenues has been reliably determined and is linear over the relevant range.

(2) Cost may be resolved into fixed and variable elements.

(3) Fixed cost remains constant over the volume range on the break even chart.

(4) Variable costs fluctuate proportionately with volume.

(5) Selling prices remain unchanged.

(6) Prices of cost factors i.e. raw materials, wages, rent etc., remain unchanged.

(7) Operating efficiency of men and machines, production techniques and productivity are to remain unchanged.

(8) There is only one product or in the case of many products, Product mix will remain constant. Product mix and Sales mix will be constant in case of multiproduct analysis.

(9) Revenue and costs are to be compared with a common activity base.

(10) The volume is the only relevant factor affecting costs.

(11) The number of units produced and sold will remain the same i.e., there will not be any opening stock or closing stock.

(12) There is no improvement or deterioration in cost control.

(13) Inventory is maintained at an uniform level.

Profit / Voume Ratio : Here profit means the contribution and volume means the sales value. The profit/volume ratio, popularly known as the P/V ratio expresses the relation between contribution and sales and makes the change in the percentage of contribution in relation to changes in the volume of sales. It is one of the most important ratios for studying the profitability of operation of a business, and it is another method to determine the cost volume profit relationship. This ratio is also known as the Marginal Income Ratio or Contribution Ratio or Profit volume Ratio. The formula for calculating P/V ratio is expressed in symbols-

$$\text{P/V Ratio} = \frac{Contribution\ x\ 100}{Sales} i.e., \frac{C}{S} x100$$

$$\text{or} = \frac{Fixed\ Expenses + Profit}{Sales} x100 i.e., \frac{F+P}{S} x100$$

$$\text{or} = \frac{Sales - Variable\ Costs}{Sales} x100 i.e., \frac{S-V}{S} x100$$

$$\text{P/V Ratio} = \frac{Change\ in\ Contribution}{Change\ in\ Sales} = \frac{Change\ in\ Profit\ (or\ loss)}{Change\ in\ Sales}$$

The real significance of P/V ratio lies in its use for appraising profitability of different operations, product lines, sales area, method of sales, classes of customers, etc. A higher ratio reflects greater profitability and lower ratio indicates lesser profitability. The P/V ratio is useful for determination of the break even point, level of output or sales, to earn a desired amount of profit, calculation of variable cost, and profit for any volume of sales.

(i) Break Even Point $= \dfrac{\textit{Fixed Costs}}{\textit{P/V Ratio}}$

(ii) Sales required to earn a desired amount of profit:

$$\frac{\textit{Fixed Cost+Profit}}{\textit{P/V Ratio}} = \frac{F + P}{\textit{P/V Ratio}} = \frac{\textit{Contribution Margin}}{\textit{P/V Ratio}}$$

(iii) Variable cost = Sales (1-P/V Ratio)

(iv) Profit = P/V Ratio x Margin of safety

(v) Fixed cost = Sales at B.E.P. x P/V Ratio

(vi) Contribution = Sales x P/V Ratio

The P/V Ratio is normally expressed in percentage by multiplying it by 100. A high ratio indicates that a slight increase in the volume without an increase in the fixed costs would give higher profit. A product with low P/V ratio means low profitability of that product. A steady P/V ratio of a business during the past several years means that the business is going along steadily.

The P/V Ratio is improved if contribution is increased and this can be done by any of the following ways:

(a) By increasing the selling price.

(b) By altering the sales mixture i.e., products having low P/V ratio will be substituted by a product with a higher ratio.

(c) By increasing the production of such products whose P/V ratios are favourable.

(d) By reducing the variable costs.

It should, however, be noted that P/V ratio is not affected by any decrease in fixed costs, although this decrease would increase the total profit.

General Conclusions of Break even Chart

(a) The location of the break-even point is determined by the magnitude of fixed costs.

(b) The location of the break even point measures the margin of safety of the business.

(c) The magnitude of the angle of incidence is determined by the magnitude of the variable costs and hence the need to control the variable costs. This will help to maintain the rate at which profit grows.

(d) To assess the efficiency and stability of the business, both the location of the break even point and angle of incidence have to be studied.

(e) Fixed costs play a dominant role in the profit structure and hence business with low fixed costs can weather a slump more successfully than those with large fixed costs. Uses of Break Even Analysis

Uses : Break even analysis helps management in a number of ways. Some of the noteworthy uses of this analysis are listed below:

(i) **Product planning** i.e., adding a new product line to the existing product line or dropping an existing product from a product line in the light of its estimated revenue and cost.

(ii) **Activity planning** i.e., expansion or reduction of capacity.

(iii) **Profit planning** i.e., deciding quantum of profits to be earned based on the projections regarding the level of activity.

(iv) **Make or Buy decisions** / Expand or Buy decisions.

(v) **Lease decisions** i.e., whether to lease or purchase capital assets, (like ownership or lease / sale or leaseback / lease or hire, etc.,)

(vi) **Capital Projects decision** (i.e., studying the effects of installing an equipment initially or replacing it with a new one in case it has become obsolete, on costs, revenues and profits, and arriving at such equipment selection and replacement decisions.

(vii) **Choosing Promotion** Mix, i.e., determining the best promotion mix which consists of personal selling advertising and sales promotion.

(viii) **Distribution channels decision i.e.,** a manufacturer to make a choice between exclusive distribution (having one retailer in a city) and selective distribution (having several retailers in a city).

(ix) **Price decisions** : If the demand schedule and the cost pattern are known, it is helpful for determining the best price so as to yield maximum profit.

(x) Decision regarding **profitability of products or departments:** The decision whether a department should continue or a particular product should be eliminated rests on the contribution made or the loss incurred by the product or department. It is also useful to decide about the suspension of operative activity or permanent closing down of a business.

Limitations of Break even Analysis

1. When break even analysis *based on accounting data*, as it usually happens, it may suffer from various limitations of such data *e.g.*, neglect of imputed cost, arbitrary depreciation estimates and inappropriate allocation of overhead costs.
2. Break even analysis is *static* in character. Costs and prices are subject to constant change from unit to unit as also from period to period.
3. Costs in a particular period need not be caused entirely by output in that period.
4. Selling costs are specially difficult to handle in break even analysis.
5. The straight line total revenue curve presumes that any quantity might be sold at that one price. In real world, perfect competition is rare.
6. A basic assumption in break even analysis is that the cost revenue volume relationship is *linear.* This is realistic only over narrow ranges of output.
7. Break even analysis is not an effective tool for long range use and its use should be restricted to the *short run* only.
8. The area include in the Break even Analysis should be limited. If too many products, too many departments or too many plants are lumped together and graphed on a single break even chart, both good and bad performances can easily be buried in the total picture of the group.
9. Break even analysis assumes that profits are a function of output ignoring the patent fact that they are also caused by other factors such as technological changes, improved management, changes in the scale of fixed factors of production, and so on.

Conclusion : In spite of these limitations, break even analysis is an effective medium for dramatising the impact of volume in cost and profit.

Calculation of Break Even Point

A. Break Even Point in terms of Physical Units: The selling price of a unit covers not only its variable cost but also leaves a margin (contribution margin) to contribute towards fixed cost. The break-even point is reached when sufficient number of units sold is equal to the fixed costs.

$$\text{B E.P.} = \frac{\textit{Total Fixed costs}}{\textit{Marginal contribution (per unit)}} \text{ OR}$$

$$= \frac{\textit{Fixed overheads}}{\textit{Price Per Unit} - \textit{Variable Cost per unit}}$$

Illustration 1

Determine the Break-Even Point (in units) from the following data: Variable cost per unit Rs. 20. Selling price per unit Rs. 30. Fixed overheads Rs. 1,00,000 per year.

Solution

$$\text{B.E.P.} = \frac{1{,}00{,}000}{30-20} = \frac{1{,}00{,}000}{10} = 10{,}000 \textit{units}$$

B. Break Even Point in terms of Sales Value or Revenue: If total sales volume, total variable costs and total fixed costs are given (sale price and variable cost per unit are known) it is convenient to determine the Break Even Point in terms of total rupee sales.

$$\text{B.E.P.} = \frac{\textit{Total Fixed Costs}}{\textit{Contribution Ratio}} = \frac{\textit{Total Fixed Costs}}{\text{P/v } x \text{ } 100}$$

Illustration 2

Sales Rs. 2,00,000. Variable costs Rs. 1,20,000. Fixed costs Rs. 40,000 Calculate Break Even Point (in sales value).

Solution

$$\text{B.E.P.} = \frac{40{,}000}{40\ \%}$$

= Rs. 1,00,000

C. Break Even Point in terms of Percentage Capacity: If total units of production/sales, details regarding the variable costs and fixed costs are given, it is possible to calculate the Breaks Even Point in terms of production/sales capacity (in percentage). With the calculated break-even capacity it is convenient to determine full/under/over utilisation of plant capacity.

Illustration 3

Transactional Tractors Ltd. have an installed capacity of 5,000 tractors per annum. For the coming year they have budgeted as follows:

Production/Sales		4,000 Units
	Costs:	Rs. in crores
(i)	Direct Material	18.00
(ii)	Direct Wages	0.60
(iii)	Factory Expenses	0.80
(iv)	Administrative Expenses	0.20
(v)	Selling Expenses	0.20
	Profit	1.00

Factory Expenses as well as selling expenses are variable to the extent of 20%. Calculate the Break Even capacity utilisation in Percentage.

Solution

Calculation of Variable Cost			**Calculation of Fixed Cost**		Rs.
Direct Material		8,00,00,000	Administrative Expenses		20,00,000
Direct wages		60,00,000			
Factory Expenses (20%)	To the extent vari- able	16,00,000	Factory Expenses (80%)	To the extent fixed	64,00,000
Selling Expenses (20%)		4,00,000	Selling Expenses (80%)		16,00,000
Total Variable cost		8,80,00,000	Total Fixed Cost		1,00,00,000

$$\text{Variable Cost per Unit} = \frac{Rs.\,8{,}80{,}00{,}000}{4{,}000\ units}$$

$$= \text{Rs. } 22{,}000$$

Sale = Fixed Cost + Variable Cost + Profit

$$= 1{,}00{,}00{,}000 + 8{,}80{,}00{,}000 + 1{,}00{,}00{,}000 = \text{Rs.}10{,}80{,}00{,}000$$

$$\text{Sale per Unit} = \frac{10{,}80{,}00{,}000}{4{,}000} = Rs.27{,}000$$

Contribution = Selling Price per unit - Variable Costs per unit = Rs. 27,000 - 22,000

= 5,000

$$\text{Break Even Point} = \frac{Fixed\ Cost}{Contribution} = \frac{1{,}00{,}00{,}000}{5{,}000} = 2{,}000\,Units$$

Break even capacity utilisation percentage

$$= \frac{Break\ even\ production}{Total\ capacity} x100$$

$$= \frac{2{,}000\ units}{5{,}000\ units} x100 = 40\% \quad \text{OR} \quad \frac{Total\ Fixed\ Costs}{Total\ Contribution} x100$$

$$= \frac{Rs.\ 1{,}00{,}00{,}000}{Rs.\ 5{,}000\ x\ 5{,}000} x100 = 40\%$$

D. Calculation of Break Even Point for Multi-Products: Multiproduct firms are not able to measure Break Even Point in terms of common unit of product. Hence the firms usually resort to the analysis of total contribution margins of all the products to overall fixed costs of the firm, which implies calculating overall Break Even Point for the firm.

For the purpose of calculating overall Break Even Point an overall weighted contribution ratio is calculated from various contribution ratios of the individual products, weights being given in the proportion of sales of individual products to the firm's total sales of all the products. Once this overall contribution ratio is calculated, the overall Break Even Point can easily be calculated in the same way as it is calculated for a single product. The sales mix is an important factor in calculating the overall Break Even Point; if the composition of the sales mix changes, the overall Break Even Point also changes.

Illustration 4

A firm produces and sells three products X, Y and Z. From the following data calculate the overall Break Even Point for the firm.

Product	No. of Units sold	Sale Price per Unit (Rs)	Variable cost per unit (Rs)	Contribution ratio
X	10,000	10	6	40%
Y	5,000	12	9	25%
Z	8,000	5	2.5	50%

Fixed costs are Rs. 60,000 per year.

Solution

Statement Computing The Overall Contribution Ratio

Product	Sales Proceeds No. of units x selling price (Rs)	Proportionate Sales Proceeds of total sales	Contribution ratio	Overall contribution ratio (%sales proceeds x contribution)
X	1,00,000	50%	40%	20.0%
Y	60,000	30%	25%	7.5%
Z	40,000	20%	50%	10.0%
	2,00,000	100%		37.5%

Hence oerall contribution ratio is 37.5%

$$\text{Break Even Point is} = \frac{\textit{Fixed Costs}}{\textit{Overall contribution ratio}}$$

$$= \frac{60,000}{37.5\%}$$

$$= \text{Rs. } 1,60,000$$

The break-down of the total sales of Rs. 1,60,000 is as under--

Product	Propritionate % of sales	Sale Proceeds	Number of units
X	50%	80,000	8,000
Y	30%	48,000	4,000
Z	20%	32,000	6,400
		1,60,000	

Illustration : 5

The XYZ Co. has the following budget for the year 1993-94:

	Rs.
Sales (1,00,000 units @ Rs. 20)	20,00,000
Variable cost	10,00,000
Contribution	10,00,000
Fixed Cost	4,00,000
Net Profit	6,00,000

From the above information find out

(a) The adjusted profits for 1993-94 if the following two sets of changes are introduced and also suggest which plan should be implemented.

Plan A		Plan B	
Increase in price	20%	Decrease in price	20%
Decrease in volume	25%	Increase in volume	25%
Increase in variable cost	10%	Decrease in variable cost	10%
Increase in fixed cost	5%	Decrease in fixed cost	5%

(b) The P/V ratio and break even points under the two plans referred above.

Solution

XYZ Co. Budget - 1993-94.

Units : 1,00,000

	Rs. (Per unit)	Rs. (Total)
Sales	20	20,00,000
Variable Cost	10	10,00,000
Contribution	10	10,00,000
Fixed Cost	4	4,00,000
Profit	6	**6,00,000**

(a)	Plan 'A'	Plan 'B'
Units: (1,00,000 - (1,00,000X25%) (1,00,000 + (1,00,000X25%)	75,000	1,25,000
	Rs.	Rs.
Selling price per unit	24	16
Variable cost per unit	11	9
Contribution per unit	13	7
Total Constribution	9,75,000	8,75,000
Fixed Cost (4,00,000 + (4,00,000X5%)	4,20,000	3,80,000
Profit	**5,55,000**	**4,95,000**

It can be clearly seen from the above workings that estimated profit for 1993-94 is the higherst in case of the original budget. and therefore neither 'A' nor 'B' should be implemented and the original budget should be followed.

(b)	Budget	Plant 'A'	Plant 'B'
Contribution (Rs.)	10,00,000	9,75,000	8,75,000
Sales (Rs)	20,00,000	18,00,000	20,00,000
Fixed Cost (Rs.)	4,00,000	4,20,000	3,80,000
P/V Ratio C/S	50%	54.17%	43.75%
B.E. Point (sales) F.C ÷ P/V Ratio (Rs.)	8,00,000	7,74,385	8,68,571
or,			
B.E. Point (unit) (F.C. % Contribution per unit.	40,000	32,308	54,286

Illustration : 6

A company has a capacity of producing 1,00,000 units of a certain product in a month. The sales department reports that the following schedule of sales price is possible :

Volume of Production	Selling price per unit Re.
60%	0.90
70%	0.80
80%	0.75
90%	0.67
100%	0.61

The variable cost of manufacture between these levels Re. 0.15 per unit. Fixed Costs Rs. 40,000.

You are required to prepaare a statement showing incrementai revenue and differential cost at each stage. At which volume of production will the profit be maximum ?

If there is a bulk offer at Re. 0.40 per unit for the balance capacity over the maximum profit volume for export and the price quoted will not affect the internal sale, will you advise accepting this bid and why?

Solution

Statement of Incremental Revenue and Differential Cost

Volume of Pro duction	Sales Value	Cost of Production			Differ ential cost 10,000 units	Incre mental of revenue for 10,0 00 units
		Variable	Fixed	Total		
Rs.	Rs.	Rs.	Rs.	Rs.	Rs.	Rs.
60,000	54,000	9.000	40,000	49,000	-	-
70,000	56,000	10,500	40,000	50,500	1,500	2,000
80,000	60,000	12,000	40,000	52,000	1,500	4,000
90,000	60,300	13,500	40,000	53,500	1,500	300
1,00,000	61,000	15,000	40,000	55,000	1,500	700

It will be observed that maximum profit will be earned at 80% capacity (80,000 units), as upto this level, incremental revenue is greater than differential cost. Profit will be maximum when incremental revenue will be equal to differential cost. Above 80% capacity, incremental revenue will be less than the differential costs and hence the practical capacity should be fixed at 80% for earning a maximum profit of Rs. 8,000.

However, the bulk offer for export will increase the profit by Rs. 5,000 as shown below:

	Internal Sales (80,000 units) Rs.	Export Sale (20,000 units)	Total (1,00,000 units) Rs.
Sales	60,000	8,000	68,000
Less : Costs	52,000	3,000	55,000
Profit	8,000	5,000	13,000

Hence, the bulk offer for export may be accepted.

REVIEW QUESTIONS

1. What is Breakeven analysis?
2. Define Breakeven point and give the formula for calculating it.
3. What is a Breakeven chart?
4. What are the main considerations to be taken into account in formulating profit objectives?
5. What conclusions can be drawn from the position of the break even point and the angle of incidence in a break even point?
6. What is profit-volume ratio? What purpose does it serve?
7. Compared with Company A, Company B has a high P/V ratio and high non-variable costs. Which of two companies has the greater profit potential? Why?
8. Discuss the possible steps to rectify the position when the margin of safety is unsatisfactory.
9. What is the effect of the following on the break even point, margin of safety and the profit-volume ratio.
   (a) Increase in total fixed costs
   (b) Increase in physical sales
   (c) Decrease in variable cost per unit
   (d) Discount on selling price
   (e) Increase in selling price per unit
   (f) Increase in raw material cost
   (g) Increase in plant capacity
   (h) Retrenching labour, surplus to requirements
10. Enumerate the assumptions underlying the break even analysis?
11. State the limitations of break even (analysis) chart.
12. What general conclusions can be drawn from a break even chart?
13. "Profit usurpers are constantly challenged and checkmated by good Break Even Control". Discuss and illustrate how Break Even Analysis aids planning and control.

17

Budgetary Control and Variance Analysis

Budgetary control refers to the principles, procedures, and practices of achieving given objectives through budgets and budget reports. It has been defined as "the establishment of departmental budgets relating to the responsibilities of executives to the requirements of a policy and the continuous comparison of actual with budgeted results, either to secure by individual action to the objective of their policy or to provide a basis for its revision."

Classification of Budgets

Budgets can be classified on the basis of (a) Time (b) Nature (c) Activity and (d) Functions.

I. Classification of Budgets according to Time : (a) Long-term budget - extending five to ten years: (b) Short-term budget - ranging for a period of one or two years. (c) Current budget upto one year; (d) Interim budget in between two budget periods.

II. Classification of budget according to Nature : (a) Operating budgets relating to the operations of the enterprise. (b) Financial Budgets concerning with the financial implications of the operating budgets i.e. relating to the capital structure and liquidity of the enterprise; e.g., Cash budget, Capital budget etc.

III. Classification according to Activity Level or Capacity: Budgets, according to activity, may be of two types (i) Fixed Budget and (ii) Flexible (variable) Budget. Fixed budget is one which remains unchanged inspite of changes in volume of output or level of activity. This budget is prepared for a specific planned activity and it is not adjusted according to activity level attained. On the other hand, a flexible or variable budget is one which is prepared for changing level of activity. It is also known as 'Sliding Scale Budget'. The principle of flexible budget lies in making a series of fixed budgets for different levels of activity. A flexible budget considers the difference in the behaviour of fixed and variable costs.

IV. Classification according to Functions Involved: (a) **Sales Budget:** This is probably the most important budget and is prepared to show what finished products can be sold in what quantities and at what prices. It may be prepared (a) product-wise (b) territory-wise (c) customer-wise (d) period-wise and (e) according to salesman. In preparing a sales trend, the following factors should be considered analysis of past sales trend, estimates of salesman, available plant capacity, orders on hand, seasonal fluctuations in demand competition and market conditions.

(b) Production Budget: This budget is based on sales budget as it has to provide for the output needed to meet the requirement of the sales budget. The following points are kept in view while preparing this budget: Production cycle, availability of plant capacity, make or buy decisions, desired inventory levels and sales requirements.

(c) Raw Materials (Purchase) Budget: It is based upon production budget, as this budget provides for the materials needed for production. Materials may be direct or indirect. The materials budget generally deals only with the direct materials. Indirect materials are generally included in the works overhead budget. Quantities of raw materials to be used, cost of such materials, desired inventory levels, storage space, economic size of order, price, order already placed, etc., are the main factors influencing this budget.

(d) Direct Labour Budget: Direct Labour or Personnel budget covers the estimates of direct labour requirements - trained and untrained, essential for carrying out the budgeted output. This budget is generally prepared on the basis of the different grades and trades of workers needed for each job/process/production.

(e) Plant Utilisation Budget: This budget is also based on production budget. The plant utilisation budget determines the machine load in each department during the budget period.

(f) Overheads Budgets: Overheads budgets may be (a) Factory Overheads Budget (b) Administrative Overheads Budget (c) Selling and Distribution Overheads Budget. Manufacturing or Factory overheads budget will provide an estimate of cost of indirect labour, indirect material and indirect expenses to be incurred in the budget period. Administrative Overhead budget covers the expenses of all the central offices, and management salaries. Selling and distribution overhead budget includes all expenses relating to selling, advertising, delivery of goods to customers, etc.

(g) Research and Development Budget: This budget tells the estimated expenditure for development and research during the budget period. It is drawn up taking into account the research projects in hand and the new projects to be taken up.

(h) Cash/ Finance Budget: It is one of the most important component of the financial budget. The cash budget usually consists of two parts giving detailed estimates of (i) cash receipts and (ii) Cash payments. Estimates of cash receipts are prepared on a monthly basis and depend upon estimated cash sales, collection from debtors, and anticipated receipts from other sources e.g., sale of assets, borrowings, etc. Estimates of cash payments are based on estimated purchases of assets etc.

(i) Capital Expenditure Budget: This budget plans for expenditure on fixed assets. It involves heavy amount : its impact is very much felt on the productction capacity or profitability of the unit. Usually the plan period of this budget stretches beyond the budged period.

(j) Master Budget: It is the summary budget, incorporating its component functional budget, which is finally approved, adopted and employed. The budget may take the form of a Profit and Loss Account and a Balance Sheet at the end of the Budget Period.

These functional budgets can also be regrouped into (i) physical budgets, (ii) cost budgets, (iii) profit budgets and (iv) financial budgets.

Administration of Budgetary Control

The process of budgetary control can be reasonably divided into two stages (1) preparation of budgets and (2) implementation of the budget performance. The preparation of a budget can be viewed as an accounting process and its implementation as a management process. Its effectiveness to a large extent depends upon the organisation efficiency. In a large-sized organisation, an effective budgetary control system can be organised on the following lines:

(i) Determining Objectives: A budget being a plan for the achievement of certain operational objectives, it is desirable that same are defined very precisely. The objectives should be written out and the areas of control should be clearly demarcated in order to give a clear understanding of the plan and its scope to all those who must cooperate to make it a success.

(ii) Establishment of Budget Centres : A budget centre is a section of the organisation of an undertaking defined for the purpose of budgetary control. A budget is prepared for each budget centre and, therefore, the budget centres should be properly selected. A budget which refers to a budget centre is a departmental budget. A budget centre may again consist of a number of cost centres representing different groups of machines.

(iii) Introduction of Adequate Accounting Records and Their Codification: The budget department depends on the accounts department for reliable historical data which form the basis of many estimates.

(iv) Preparation of Budget Organisation Chart: Organisation chart defines the functions and responsibilities of each member of management and ensures that each one knows his position on the organisation and his relationship to other members. It should also be supplemented by written directives concerning the function of the staff members. The organisation chart depends upon the nature and size of the enterprise; however, a simple chart is given below.

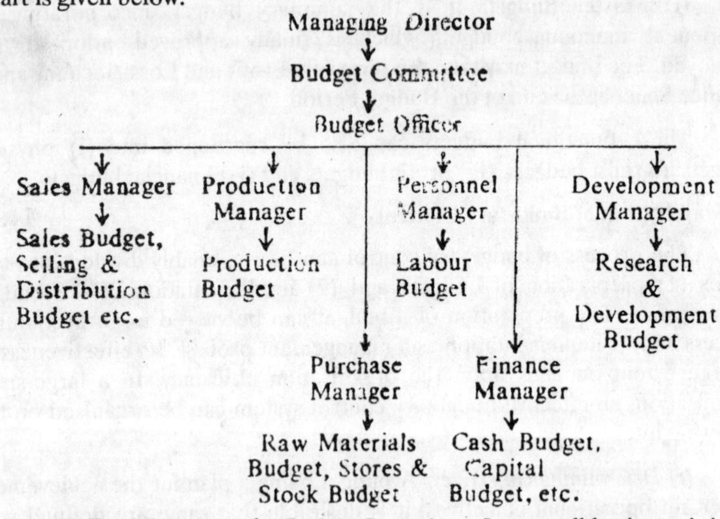

(v) Establishment of a Budget Committee: In a small business, it is the (Cost) Accountant who prepares the budget, but in big undertaking, a Budget Committee is appointed for this purpose. The Budget committee consists of Chief Executive or Managing Director, Budget officer or Director or Controller and the heads of main departments. The Chief Executive acts as the chairman, and cost accountant as its secretary. The Managers of different departments prepare their budget and submit to this Committee. This Committee makes necessary adjustments, coordinates all the budgets and prepares a Master Budget. The functions of a budget committee are:

(a) ensuring that everyone appreciates the budget efforts;

(b) reconciling divergent views;

(c) offering technical advice;

(d) co-ordinating budgeting activities;

(e) reviewing individual budgets;

(f) suggesting revisions, or approving budget proposals without further revision; and

(g) scrutinising control reports in the latter stages of the budgetary process.

(vi) Preparation of Budget Manual: It is document or schedule or rule book which sets out the responsibilities of the persons engaged in the routine of and the forms and records required for budgetary control. This manual lays down the budget programmes, and the specific and general duties of the executives, departmental managers and the Budget Committee. The budget manual usually contains the following:

(a) responsibilities of the persons engaged in budgetary control;

(b) length of budget periods and control periods;

(c) the budget calendar showing the dates of completion for each part of the budget and submission of reports; dates of review, revision and instructions issued;

(d) forms and records required for budgetary control;

(e) the accounts code and classification used by the Company; method of accounting to be adopted; procedure for preparation of financial statements and reporting the same;

(f) budget proforma, etc;

(g) the follow-up Procedures.

Budget Time Table: The budget manual should give a schedule as to who is responsible for what in an organisation. Each responsible person should know by what date he should finish his work.

The following list describes the activities for which different persons are generally responsible for:

Manager	Responsible for
Sales	Sales in terms of quantity, selling prices, discounts, rebates, etc; sales forecast, selling costs including those of sales managements; representation, advertising, etc; forecast of selling and distribution costs; capital requirements.
Distribution	Distribution costs including those of transports storage etc., quantity of finished goods stock.

Production	Production in terms of quantity; production costs; forecast of production costs - material, labour and overhead; raw material stocks and work-in-progress; capital requirements.
Research and Development	Research costs; forecast research and development costs, capital requirements.
Managing Director	Profit planning; capital expenditure; depreciation; current assets and liabilities e.g. level of trade debtors and the cash position.
Company Secretary	Administration costs - legal expenses, audit fees, etc; forecast administration costs; capital requirements.
Budget Committee	Review of sales forecast, current operating results; review and approval of master budget; long-term budget; approval of department budget, monthly cash forecast.

Performance Report Time Table: A budget manual should specify as to when performance reports will be ready and given to managers. For example, performance reports may be made available after 15 days of the end of the accounting period. The accounts departments should ensure that this timetable is being adhered to. Likewise, the budget committee will review the performance results. Reports from managers of budget centres should be submitted to the budget committee before they are discussed in the meeting.

(vii) Level of Activity: It is essential to establish a normal level of activity since it forms the basis of the budget. Level of activity can be attained by efficient working under the existing condition.

(viii) Selection of the Budget Period: The period covered by a budget is known as budget period. The length of the budget period normally depends upon the nature of the plan, circumstances of the business, the control aspect, production period and timings of availability of finance. Most manufacturing industries use one year as the budget period. For control purposes, the annual totals are divided by 12 to obtain monthly budgets; but if seasonal fluctuations are important, separate budget estimates can be made for each month or season. A budget prepared for a very long time cannot be very accurate as it is very difficult to forecast events for a longer period.

(ix) Locating the Principal Budget Factor: Budgets should be evolved around the Principal budget factors (or limiting, scarce or key factors) in business. Every business has its own key factors, which limits the level of

activities. These key factors should be correctly identified and diagnosed. In most of the enterprises, sales (demand) is normally the key factor. The success of the budgetary control rests on the accuracy of the sales forecast. If the sales figure proves to be inaccurate, most of the budgets will be affected. Similarly, materials, labour, cash, space, equipment, management etc., may also be the key factors. The following is a detailed list of key factors.

(a)Sales : (i)marketing potentialities and consumer demand,
(ii)Shortage of pushing salesmen,
(iii)Inadequate advertising.

(b)Materials : (i)Availability of supply,
(ii)Restrictions imposed by licences, quota etc.

(c)Labour : (i)General shortage of workers,
(ii)Shortage in certain grades e.g., operation of modern complex mechinery.

(d)Plant : (i)Insufficient capacity due to shortage in supply,
(ii)Insufficiennt capacity due to lack of capital,
(iii)Bottlenecks in certain key processes, operations or departments.

(e)Management : (i)Shortage of efficient executives,
(ii)Lack of capital,
(iii)Insufficient research into product, design and methods.

Sometimes there may be two or more limiting factors at the same time and the budget committee has to take greater care so as to assess the relative influence of the key-factors. This problem is generally solved with the help of graphs, linear programming, operational research, etc. It may be mentioned that the key factor is not a permanent factor and in the long run managemnt may get suitable opportunities to overcome the key factor limitations by working overtime of shifts, introducing new methods, changing materials mix, hiring new machinery or buying new equipment on hire purchase, providing incentive schemes and producing and selling more profitable products, selecting the optimum level of production, etc.

(x) Determination of Budget Cost Allowance: It is the cost which a budget centre is expected to incur during a given period of time in relation to the level of activity attained by the budget centre.

(xi) Implementation of the Budget and Recording of Actual Performance: A copy of the section of the master budget appropriate to each department sphere of activity is issued to their respective heads for execution.

(xii) Budget Variance Analysis & Reporting: A variance is the divergence between any planned result and the actual result measured in monetary terms. A budget variance is the difference between a budgeted figure and an actual figure. The overall variance between a planned cost and an actual cost is usually due to a number of factors. Ascertaining the contribution of each factor to the over all variance is known as variance analysis. Any budget variance can be either (i) a favourable variance which on its own would result in the ultimate profit being better than that planned or (ii) an adverse variance which on its own would result in the ultimate profit being worse than that planned. A budget variance may be either controllable or uncontrollable. A controllable cost variance is one which be identified as the primary responsibility of a specified person. It should be borne in mind that when computing budget variance it is always the budget allowance (allowed figures) that is compared with the actual figure and the original figure has no relevance.

Elements of a Successful Budgetary Control System

The success of the budgeting process in an organisation depends on the following essential elements:

1. Objectives: All planning presupposes that objectives have been established, since the plan is merely a means to an end, not an end in itself. Objectives are the end.

2. Knowledge of Cost Behaviour: It is essential that there be an awareness of the firm's particular cost patterns, and the influences thereon. Cost-volume-profit analysis is a useful adjunct to the budgeting exercise, as it aids considerable in understanding cost behaviour.

3. Accurate Forecasting of Business Activities: Forecasting is a prerequisite in a budgeting process. It is not only the starting point, but is also critical to the development of an accurate budget. Forecasting can be done regarding activities which are internal and external to an organisation. Internal activities are easier to forecast than external activities such as production forecast. But external factors like state of and nature of market conditions, inflation or deflation and its effect on company products are difficult to predict. Business firms require competent market researchers to forecast accurately such external factors.

4. Coordinating Business Activities: Budgeting needs to coordinate all the individual budgets into an integrated plan as each budget has certain implications for the other budgets. There must be coordination between sales, production, purchasing, personnel budgets. Budgets are useful tools in communicating budgetary expectations and goals and in bringing necessary adjustments among organisational activities.

5. Education: All levels of management must be convinced of the usefulness of budgets, and know the part that each must play in planning and control through budgets. This requires a continuous programme of training in budgeting methods and their value.

6. Communicating the Budgets: The success of a comprehensive budgeting programme depends on communication of individual budgets to the different units in the organisation. The basic point is that the preparation of the budget is of no value unless it is known to the person for whom it is meant. Managers are not responsible for budget unless the budget is communicated clearly, concisely and in an authoritative manner to them.

7. Acceptance and Cooperation: Successful budgeting also requires that budgets should be accepted by the people who must execute them. Budgeting should have the active cooperation of the entire organisation from the top to the bottom. Cooperation for the budget can be achieved in number of ways.

8. Reasonable Flexibility: The budgeting programme should contain reasonable flexibility if the situation so demands. However, it should be noted that too much flexibility and too much tightness are both undesirable. Too much flexibility will weaken the cost control and the budget will become inoperative. Similarly, too much regidity not permitting reasonable deviations will create problems and restrictions in the implementation of the budget. If conditions have changed making the estimates and budgets inaccurate, the budgets should be revised. A budget is simply a tool of to serve managements needs and not an irrevocable contract.

9. Adequate Systems Support: This will come mainly from the accounting sphere, where it must be ensured that records and procedures are sufficient for the task in hand. Thus, the budget should be linked to the accounting system in such a way that the same definitions, etc., relate to common elements. (For example, if inventories in the budget system are valued at standard cost, so should the inventories in the accounting system.)

10. Providing a Framework for Evaluation: Budgeting provides a basis to evaluate the performance of different departments. A comprehensive budget, properly developed, will contain initially organisational goals and expectation and subsequently can be used as an effective evaluation technique.

Budget and Forecasts

A forecast is an assessment of probable future events, while the budget relates to planned events. The budget is based on the implications of a forecast and thus forecasting precedes the preparation of a budget. The major differences in forecasts and budget are summarised as follows:

	Forecast	**Budget**
1. Nature of data	physical or financial.	Financial backed up by physical.
2. Ti	May be valid for any period of time.	Predefined budget period usually one year
3	Forecaster not responsible for forecasting result.	Managers accept responsibility for results
. by top ement.	May be necessary	Always approved by top management
ision	Revised on the availability of new information.	Revised only under completely changed conditions.
6. Use as control instrument.	Exclusively a planning tool	Both a planning and control tool.
7. Analysis of variance	Not analysed formally or periodically.	Formal periodic analysis.
8. Objective of variance analysis.	To improve ability to forecast	To use for performance appraisal.

Financial forecasting, which is one of the segments of the total forecasting process, involves systematic projection of the expected results in the form of proforma financial statements and cash inflow-outflow forecasts. Cash forecasts help in cash planning and proforma financial statements serve as analytical documents for funds from banks and financial institutions. Although financial forecasting is a useful tool for financial planning, the managers cannot be held responsible if the actual results do not conform to the forecast. Further, there is no need to get these forecasts approved by the top management and they can be changed on the basis of new information or changes in the environmental forces related to marketing, raw material prices etc. Again, no approval is needed for such changes, which can be made even weekly or daily. Thus, forecasting is used as a planning tool by managers for proper planning of activities within their boundaries.

The essential difference between budgeting and forecasting is in the use of budgeting as a tool for the performance appraisal of the various responsibility centres in respect of achievement of predetermined performance levels. A budget not used as a control instrument may turn out to be a mere forecast. At times, budgets prepared by the accountant without the active participation of the managers responsible for achievement of budgeted results, may turn out to be unrealistic and impractical. Budgets, in this sense, are the forecasts in the accountant's diary. This is a situation which the management should strive to a void if it wants to enjoy the real benefits of a budgeting system.

SALES BUDGET

The sales budget, generally, forms the fundamental basis on which all the other budgets are built up. The budget is essentially a forecast of sales to be achieved in a budget period. The Sales Manager should be made directly responsible for the preparation and execution of this budget. He should take into consideration the following factors while preparing the Sales Budget :

(a) Past sales figures and trend,

(b) Salesman's estimates,

(c) Plant capacity.

(d) *General Trade Prospects :* The general trade prospects considerably affect the sales. Valuable information can be gathered in the connection from trade papers and managers.

(e) Orders on hand.

(f) *Proposed Expansion and Discontinuance of Products :* It affect sales and, therefore, it should also be considered.

(g) *Seasonal Fluctuations :* Past experience will be the best guide in this respect. However, efforts should be made to minimise the effects of seasonal fluctuations by giving special concessions or off-season discounts thus increasing the sales volume.

(h) *Potential Market :* Market research should be carried out for ascertaining the potential market for the company's products. Such an estimate is made on the basis of expected, population, growth, purchasing power of consumers and their buying habit.

(i) *Availability of Material and Supply :* Adequate supply of raw materials and other supplies must be ensured before drafting the sales programme.

(j) *Financial Aspects* : Expansion of sales usually require increase in capital outlay also;.Therefore, sales budget must be kept within the bounds of financial capacity.

(k) *Other Factors :* (i) The nature and degree of competition within the industry, (ii) Cost of distribution of goods, (iii) Government controls, rules and regulations related to the industry, and (iv) Political situation - national and international - as it may have an influence upon the market.

The Sales Manager, after taking into consideration all these factors, will prepare the Sale Budget, in terms of quantities and money, distinguishing between products, periods and areas of sale.

Methods of Sales Forecasting

Production requirements, inventory levels, and cost incurrence generally are geared to the rate of sales-the usual measure of activity, so the sales forecast represents the cornerstone of the short-term plan. As such, the sales forecast is the sales objective, which is equivalent to the co-ordinated contribution (i.e., output) of all functions within the company.

The method of forecasting sales must consistent with the peculiarities of the situation, and constantly revised and improved to keep up with the growth and needs of the company.

The selection and adoption of a particular method will depend upon:

(a) the characteristics of the concern-such as its size, nature of business, etc.,

(b) the firm's environment-competitive, technological, traditional, volatile, etc.,

(c) te costs involved-field surveys cost more than projections of past sales data;

(d) availability of qualified personnel; and

(e) the time period to be covered.

Some of the more frequently means of forecasting sales are outlined below:

1. Factor Listing : This is an unsophisticated means of projecting historical results in the light of expected changes in the conditions affecting the firm's operations. For example, the analyst may believe that anticipated economic factors will weaken the company's position (e.g., credit restrictions may be expected,inflation may be continuing but the firm is unable to pass increased costs on to its customers, etc.). On this basis, he may conclude that these factors will cause sales to fall off. The other relevant factors, such as competition, will be assessed in similar qualitative manner, and a projection made.

2. Salesman's Estimates : This is as weak as factor listing, since salesmen are, by nature, optimistic, and usually unable to appreciate all the relevant aspects that must be taken into account in arriving at a realistic forecast.

3. Statistical Methods : Trend analysis, correlation studies between sales and economic indicators, and cyclic models are typical of the staistical methods in use. They are more objective than (1) and (2) above, but are based, as a rule, on the assumption that past conditions will prevail into the future. Allowance should be made for expected future conditions, and the risk of chance variations arising that result in a new trend path.

4. Group Judgement Method : The combined experience and judgement of senior employees (such as chief executive, sales director, and finance direcor) may be thought sufficient to produce an accurate forecast. Such group opinion is, however, hardly likely to be of much value. It ignores the need for a scientific and rigorous approach.

5. Economic Analysis Method : This is based on the use of various indices-such as the rate of capital investment in the engineering and related industries, or the ratio of durable to non-durable manufacturing output, and the relationship between sales levels and these indicators. These 'pressure' indicators are thought to predict general trends, but are rarely specific enough to result in the production of accurate sales forecasts.

6. Opinion Survey Methods : This is a form of marketing research survey, the outcome of which is an average of expectations based on the views of persons directly involved with the firm's products-especially its actual and potential consumers. If carefully conducted, with suitable samples, this means of forecasting sales can be very accurate, but it is also very expensive.

7. Econometric Method : Econometrics aim to predict changes in economic activity by specifying and manipulating the relationships that exist amoungst selected economic variables. It is a rigorous, quantitative science, but requires the availability of highly skilled econometric model-builders, and an econometric model is only as accurate in its predictions as the parameters and relationships within it allow it to be.

All forecasting methods have certain features in common, as they are all concerned in greater or lesser detail with future conditions and past performance. But this is not to suggest that they are all equally accurate. The best methods are quantitative, objective, and concerned with both expected future conditions as well as expected future sales.

The translation of expected sales quantities into expected revenue gives rise to the sales budget. The development of this particular budget (which is the revenue side of the master profit plan) must be carried out in detail with rspect to products, time, and responsibility. Thus it should indicate, in adition to expected total annual sales and revenues:

(a) sales by division (or territory);
(b) sales by month and quarter; and
(c) sales by individual product line.

While the principle of full participation of the part of sales management in setting budget levels should not be ignored, it is an area that must of necessity depend largely on the services of professional marketing researchers and, perhaps, economists.

An inability to overcome the obstacles to acurate sales forecasting by no means nullifies the value of the budget as a major management tool. It simply means that in most cases the budget must not be a rigidly predetermined plan, but should be sufficiently flexible to allow it to be adapted to meet changing conditions.

Illustration (Sales Budget): 1

A B C Distributors Ltd., has three sales divisions at Bombay, Delhi and Calcutta. It sells two products - Product A and product B. The budgeted sales for the year ending 31st December 1993 at each place are given below:

Bombay	: Product A	100, 000 units ar Rs.	8 each
	Product B	70, 000 units at Rs.	5 each
Delhi	: Product B	1,10, 000 units at Rs.	5 each
Calcutta	: Product A	1, 50, 000 units at Rs.	8 each

The actual sales during the same period were as follows -

Bombay	: Product A	1, 25, 000 units at Rs.	8 each
	Product B	75, 000 units at Rs.	5 each.
Delhi	: Product B	1, 25, 000 units at Rs.	5 each
Calcutta	: Product A	1, 55, 000 units at Rs.	8 each

From the reports of the sales personnel it was considered that the sales budget for the ending 31st December 1994 would be higher than 1993 budget in the following aspects -

Bombay : Product A 8, 000 units.
: Product B 5, 000 units
Delhi : Product B 13, 000 units.
Calcutta : Product A 10, 000 units.

Intensive sales compaign in Delhi and Calcutta is expected to result in additional sales of 25,000 units of Product A in Delhi and 18,000 units of Product B in Calcutta. You are required to prepare a Sales budget for the period ending December 1994.

Solution

ABC Distributors Ltd.
SALES BUDGET

Divisions.	Pay ment	Budged for the year 1994		Budget for the year 1993			Actual sales for the year 1993		
	Qty.	Price Rs.	Amt. Rs.	Qty.	Price Rs.	Amt. Rs.	Qty.	Price Rs.	Amt. Rs.
Bombay :									
A	1,08,000	8	8,64,000	1,00,000	8	8,00,000	1,25,000	8	10,00,000
B	75,000	5	3,75,000	70,000	5	3,50,000	75,000	5	3,75,000
	1, 83, 000		12,39,000	1,70, 000		11,50,000	2, 00 000		13,75,000
Delhi :									
A	25,000	8	2,00,000						
B	1,23,000	5	6,15,000	1,10,000	5	5,50,000	1,25,000	5	6,25,000
	1,48,000		8,15,000	1,10,000		5,50,000	1,25,000		6,25,000
Calcutta :									
A	1,60,000	8	12,80,000	1,50,000	8	12,00,000	1,55,000	8	12,40,000
B	18,000	5	90,000						
	1,78,000		13,70,000	1,50,000		12,00,000	1,55,000		12,40,000
Total									
A	2,93,000	8	23,44,000	2,50,000	8	20,00,000	2,80,000	8	22,40,000
B	2,16,000	5	10,80,000	1,80,000	5	9,00,000	2,00,000	5	10,00,000
	5,09,000		34,24,000	4,30,000		29,00,000	4,80,000		32,40,000

Illustration (Procuction Budget): 2

From the following data, prepare a production Budget for the Sunlight Co. Ltd:

Product	as on 1st Jan. 1994 (Units)	as on 30th June, 1994 (Units)
A	80,000	1,00,000
B	90,000	80,000
C	1,20,000	1,40,000

Requirements to fulfil sales programme :

A 6,00,000 units; B 5,00,000 units; C 8,00,000 units

Normal loss in production:

A 4%; B 2%; C 6%

Solution

Production Budget of Sunlight Co. Ltd. During 1st Jan-30th June 1994

	Products			
	A	B	C	Total
Sales during the period	6,00,000	5,00,000	8,00,000	19,00,000
Add: Estimated stock as on 30th June	1,00,000	80,000	1,40,000	3,20,000
	7,00,000	5,80,000	9,40,000	22,20,000
Less : Desired stock as on 1st January:	80,000	90,000	1,20,000	2,90,000
Required Units	6,20,000	4,90,000	8,20,000	19,30,000
Add: Loss in Production	26,000	10,000	52,000	88,000
Production Budget	6,46,000	5,00,000	8,72,000	20,18,000

Preparation of Cash Budget

The preparation of the cash budget is based upon such information as:

(i) The amount of budget monthly cash sales and credit sales,

(ii) The number of months within which bills in respect of credit sales are realised, i.e., credit period allowed.

(iii) The selling and distribution expenses to be incurred during the month,

(iv) The amount of budgeted monthly cash purchases and credit purchases,

(v) The number of months allowed for meeting the bills in respect of purchases, i.e., credit period availed.

(vi) The amount of salaries and wages to be paid,

(vii) The overhead expenses to be incurred,

(viii) The details of capital expenditure to be incurred, and

(ix) The details of administrative expenses, payment of dividend, debenture interest and miscellaneous income.

The cash budget usually extends over the same period as the master budget. However, for control purposes, it should be analysed to show monthly or weekly requirements of cash.

Advantages of Cash Budget

(a) To ensure that sufficient cash is available for meeting the business requirements.

(b) To reveal the expected shortage of cash so that arrangement may be made for a bank overdraft or loan.

(c) To reveal the any expected surplus of cash so that the same may be invested outside.

(d) To reveal the availability of cash so that an advantage may be taken of cash discounts.

(e) To show whether capital expenditure projects can be financed internally.

The main objectives of preparing the cash budget are as follows:

(a) To ensure that sufficient cash is available for both revenue and capital expenditure.

(b) To indicate any expected shortage of cash, so that arrangement may be made by borrowing in advance.

(c) To show any expected surplus fund which may be invested profitably outside the business.

The main source for the receipts of cash are cash sales, and collection of account receivables. A forecast of the collection from the account receivable is to be made on the basis of company's past sales trend, proceeds from the sale of assets, bank loans, etc. Likewise the requirement of cash for purchase of raw-materials, wages, salaries, repayments of loans, dividend, taxes, purchase of plant or equipments, etc., is determined.

Illustration (Cash Budget): 3

National Products Limited wants to approach its bankers for temporary overdraft facility for the period from 1st October 1994 to 31st December 1994. During the period of these three months the company will be manufacturing mostly for stock. You are required to prepare cash budget for the above period from the following data indicating the overdraft facility required by the company at the end of each month.

	Sales Rs.	Purchase Rs.	Wages Rs.
August 1994	3,60,000	2,49,600	24,000
September 1994	3,84,000	2,88,000	28,000
October 1994	2,16,000	4,86,000	22,000
November 1994	3,48,000	4,92,000	20,000
December 1994	2,52,000	5,36,000	30,000

(a) 50 percent of credit sales are realised in the month following sales and the remaining 50 per cent in the second month following.

(b) Creditors are paid in the month following the month of purchase.

(c) Estimated cash at bank as on 1st October 1994 Rs. 50,000

Solution

Cash Budget for the Period from 1st October to December 1994

Receipts	October	November	December
Opening balance of cash	50,000	1,12,000	- 94,000
Cash Sales	--	--	---
Cash realised from debtors	3,72,000	3,00,000	2,82,000
Total Receipts	4,22,000	4,12,000	1,88,000
Payments :			
Purchase	2,88,000	4,86,000	4,92,000
Wages	22,000	20,000	30,000
Total payments	3,10,000	5,06,000	5,22,000
Closing balance c/d	1,12,000	- 94,000	- 3,34,000

Working Notes : **Cash realised from debtors**

October $\frac{3,60,000}{2} = 1,80,000 + \frac{3,84,000}{2} = 1,92,000$ = Rs. 3,72,000

Novemebr $1,92,000 + \frac{2,16,000}{2} = 1,08,000$ = Rs. 3,00,000

December $= 1,08,000 + \frac{3,48,000}{2} = 1,74,000$ = Rs. 2,82, 000

MASTER BUDGET

The Master Budget is "the summary budget incorporating its commponent functional budgets which is finally approved, adopted and employed." It sets out the plan of operations for all departments in considerable detail for the budget period. The budget may take the form of Profit and Loss Account and a Balance Sheet as at the end of the budget period.

The Master Budget requires the approval of the Budget Committee before it is put into operation. It may happen sometimes, that a number of master budgets have to be prepared before the final one is agreed upon. The budget generally contains detailss regarding sales (net), production costs, cash position and key account balances (Debtors, Stock, Fixed Assets, B/R A/c etc.). It also shows the gross and the net profits and the important accounting ratios.

MASTER BUDGET

	Period..............................	Period 1 Rs.	Period 2 Rs.	Budgeted Period 3 Rs.	Capital.... Total Rs.
	Sales				
	Cost of Sales :				
	Direct Materials				
	Direct Labour				
	Factory overhead (Variable)				
	Overhead (Fixed)				
Add :	Opening Stock				
Less :	Closing Stock				
	Gross Profit Rs.				
Less :	Administration Cost				
	Selling and Distribution Cost				
	Net Profit				

Assets : Fixed / Current

Profit/Capital Employed	----------
Ratios :	==========
Sales/Capital Employed	
Profit/Turnover	
Current Ratio	
Acid Test Ratio	----------
	==========
Appropriation from Profit ;	
Dividends	
Reserves	
Taxes	

Balance of Profit & Loss	
	==========

Thus a master budget represents the overall plan of the enterprise.

Preparation of Flexible Budget

A flexible Budget is known as a Variable or Sliding Scale Budget or Control Type Budget. It is constructed in such a manner that a ready made budget is available in advance in relation to the actual volume of sale and production under varying conditions. A fixed budget which is subject to revision should not be confused with a flexible budget. A flexible budget automatically adjusts itself to the actual level of activity whereas fixed budget, after revision, is again fixed in character and may not conform to the actual volume of output. By providing a budget which is based on the same level of activity as actually attained, a flexible budget provides a much more useful aid in controlling operations than a fixed budget.

The need for a flexible budget can be simply illustrated as follows. The owner of a lorry knows that the more he uses his lorry per year the more it costs him to operate it; he also knows that the more he uses his lorry the less it costs per klm. The reason for this lies in the nature of the expenses, some of which are fixed while others are variable or semi-variable. Insurance, taxes, registration, and garaging are fixed costs; they remain the same whether the lorry is operated 1,000 or 20,000 klms. The costs of tires, gas, oil, and repairs are variable costs and depend largely upon the klms driven. Obsolescene and depreciation result in a combined type of cost that, although fluctuating to some degree with the usage of the lorry, is semi-variable, for it does not vary directly with the usage. The cost of operating the lorry per klm. depends on the number of klm. the lorry is used. Kilometre constitutes the basis for judging the activity of the lorry. If the owner prepares an estimate of total costs and compares his actual expenses with the budget at the end of the year, he cannot tell how successful he has been in keeping his expenses within the allowed limits unless he takes the kilometrege factor into account.

The underlying principle of a flexible budget is that for any given volume of business there should be some norm of expenditures and that norm should be known before hand to provide a guide to actual expenditures. To recognise this principle is to accept the fact that every business is dynamic, ever-changing, and never static. It is erroneous, if not futile, to expect a business to conform to a fixed, pre-conceived pattern.

Originally, the flexible budget idea was applied principally to the control of departmental factory overhead. In recent years, however, the idea has been applied to the entire budget so that production budgets as well as selling and administrative budgets are prepared on a flexible basis.

The construction of a flexible budget is identical with that of a fixed budget except that a budget is calculated for each volume ranging from a possible 60 per cent to 100 per cent of capacity. When actual figures are available, estimates previously determined for the level attained are compared with actual results, and differences are noted. This end-of-period comparison is used to measure the performance of each department head. It is this ready-made comparison that makes the flexible budget a valuable instrument for cost control. The flexible budget assists in evaluating the effects of varying volumes of activity on profits and on the cash position.

Flexible budget has the following **advantages:-**

(1) Ascertainment of Costs: Costs can be ascertained with greater degree of accuracy. Under or over-recovery of overhead can be kept at a minimum level.

(2) Control over Costs: Flexible budget enables management to control cost as it predetermines what the costs should have been at various levels of activity.

(3) Management by Exception: As flexible budget shows the expenses at various levels of activity, management can compare actuals with the figures as shown by the flexible budget. Any deviation from flexible budget should be brought to the notice of top management for taking remedial measures.

(4) Determination of Maximum Return Level: A carefully prepared flexible budget enables management to keep a watch on the production, sales and inventory levels and to make periodic adjustments to attain a level of activity which should give management the best result.

It may be mentioned that flexible budget has its limitations. Fixed costs do not remain fixed in the long run and patten of variable and semi-variable costs changes with change of managerial policy and circumstances prevailing in the market conditions.

Difficulties in Developing Flexible Budgets

(i) It is difficult to segregate costs into fixed and variable categories;

(ii) Determination of costs relating varying volumes of output is difficult to determine with reasonable accuracy in advance of production because costs may not behave in the same manner as anticipated;

Fixed Budget is suitable for Sales Deptt., Cash Dept., capital additions. Flexible budgets are suitable for manufacturing costs, selling costs, distribution costs, and administrative costs.

Illustration (Flexible Budget);4

Draw up a flexible budget for overhead expenses on the basis of the following data and determine overhead rates at 70%, 80% and 90% plant capacity.

	At 70% capacity Rs.	At 80% capacity Rs.	At 90% capacity Rs.
Variable Overheads:			
Indirect labour		12, 000	
Stores including spares		4, 000	
Semivariable Overheads :			
Power (30% fixed, 70% variable)		20, 000	
Repairs & Maintenance (60% fixed, 40% variable)		2, 000	
Fixed Overheads :			
Depreciation		11, 000	
Insurance		3, 000	
Salaries		10, 000	
Total Overheads		62, 000	
Estimated direct labour hours		1, 24, 000	

Solution

Flexible Budget for the Period

	At 70% capacity Rs.	At 80% capacity Rs.	At 90% capacity Rs.
Variabe Overheads :			
Indirect labour	10,500	12,000	13,500
Stores including spares	3,500	4,000	4,500
Semivariable Oveheads:			
Power : Fixed	6,000	6,000	6,000
Variable	12,250	14,000	15,750
Repairs & Maintenance : Fixed	1,200	1,200	1,200
Variable	700	800	900
Fixed Overheads :			
Depreciation	11,000	11,000	11,000
Insurance	3,000	3,000	3,000
Salaries	10,000	10,000	10,000
Total Overheads	58,150	62,000	65,850
Estimated direct labour hours	1,08,500	1,24,000	1,39,500
Direct labour rate	Re. 0.536	Re. 0.500	Re. 0.472

Workings :

Calculation of direct labour hour rates :

$$\text{At 70\% capacity} = \text{Rs. } \frac{58{,}150}{1{,}08{,}500} = \text{Re. } 0.536$$

$$\text{At 80\% capacity} = \text{Rs. } \frac{62{,}000}{1{,}24{,}000} = \text{Re. } 0.500$$

$$\text{At 90\% capacity} = \text{Rs. } \frac{65{,}850}{1{,}39{,}500} = \text{Re. } 0.472$$

Budgeting and Motivation

In order to implement strategy the organisation needs to have a reasonable commitment to the achievement of the goals by those charged with ensuring that the enterprise succeeds. So motivation on the part of those managers is a most important part of the budgeting system.

Motivation may be accomplished by the reward-punishment system, part of which may be linked to the planning and control system. A motivation system may use positive (bonuses, promotion, etc) or negative (demotion, etc) incentives. The establishment of a motivation system that blends the attainment of personal aspirations with goals of the organisation is a problematic task.

Once the budget is recognised to be an element that helps to motivate people in the organisation attention must be paid to individual and group needs and values. When these elements are incorporated in the overall planning and control process then the resulting budget is likely to fulfil its function as an aid to employees' motivation. If the process of developing plans and budgets, and their associated control system, is properly conceived and utilised, involving real participation by all levels of management, then it becomes an indispensable element.

For example, actual sales revenue for a period might be less than budgeted revenue for any or all of the following reasons:

1. Sales volume in units was below the budgeted level;

2. Due to deliberate or inadvertent (i.e., offering a volume discount which most customers took advantage of) action on management's part, average selling price was below the budgeted selling price;

3. The sales mix differed from the planned mix; for example, sales were projected at a 65/35 ratio for two products, but actual sales were at a 55/45 mix.

Each of these sources of variance could lead management to a different interpretation of the underlying cause, and suggst different strategies for subsequent periods.

The Influence of Budgets on Behaviour

Accounting systems do not always have a passive or neutral effect on those who participate in them and this is particularly so in relation to budgeting systems. Since the relationship of a manager's performance to the budget is usually an important part of his overall performance appraisal, managers often regard it with some distance or even hostility. It has been argued that the methods of preparation and operation of budgets and budgetary control systems can have a very significant effect on the attitudes and hence behaviour of managers who have a responsibility for the fulfillment of sections of the overall budget. Recall that the budget is often used by top management to satisfy two purposes: to motivate managers to achieve the corporate objectives embodied in the budget, and to provide a benchmark against which managers' performance can be evaluated.

Goal Congruence : Managerial behaviour may also be influenced by the rewards that are perceived to be available for regular achievement of budget results. If such desirable outcomes for the managers as enhanced salary awards or increased promotional prospects are seen to exist, both the personal goals of the managers and the goals and objectives of the organisation will be realized by the attainment of the budget. Thus the action of the managers will be in harmony with the objectives of the organisation. This situation is described as goal congruence. The budgetary control system should be designed so that, as far as is possible, the goals of the individual managers are consistent with the goals of the organisation as a whole. Incentive systems based on short-term results, combined with emphasis on long-term planning, will lead to incompatible goals for the individual and the firm, and incompatible goals result in dissonance. Individual managers, seeking salary and promotional rewards, might favour courses of action which show short-term favourable results, even if the longest-term implications for the organisation are less favourable. Or if generous cost budgets are set, based largely on the level of the previous year's actual expenditures, and no significant rewards are perceived by managers for achieving savings, managers may deliberately spend up to their budgeted allowance simply to prevent tighter budgets being imposed in the future.

Discretionary Costs : In order to be effective for control and performance evaluation purposes, the working of the system must be seen to be fair and unbiased to the participant managers. Managers should only be held responsible for those costs that they actually control. This is particularly important in the allocation of overhead costs to individual departments. Certain allocation schemes, while perfectly acceptable for product costing purposes, may impose a "tax" on particular divisions which is beyond the control of the manager. Thus attention should be paid to the controllability of the costs for which managers are being held responsible.

DEVELOPMENTS IN BUDGETING

Having discussed some of the traditional views of budgeting let us turn to some more recent developments in budgetary control. We will emphasis the provision of additional information to the managers of an organisation. In doing so particular attention will be paid to ways in which the traditional budgetary control system can be improved. In general, none of the developments require a major upheaval in an organisation's management information system, or in particular in its budgetary control system. The effect of any change is dependent upon (i) the depth to which any of the techniques are applied; (ii) the additional costs involved in their implementation; and (iii) any additional benefits that they would provide.

Probabilistic Profit Budgeting

One relatively recent development in budgeting which has its roots in statistics, concerns the use of probability. What are termed probabilistic profit budgets (PPB) can be drawn up to help provide better budgeting information for decision making purposes, especially under conditions of uncertainty. However, before discussing probabilistic profit budgeting it is used to briefly remind oneself about flexible budgeting. This is because it is possible to confuse flexible and probabilistic profit budgets. Although flexible budgets will be drawn up on an *ex ante* basis their use tends to be exposes in that they help to analyse the actual performance against that section of the budget drawn up for the level of activity achieved; the probabilistic profit budget is both up and use on an exante basis as an aid to decision making.

The major assumption upon which the concept of PPB is based concerns the use of probability to provide an indication of the potential variability of each time within the budget. Flexible budgeting, although moving away from the traditional approach of the single point, most expected budget, does not consider the potential variability of individual items within the budget. It merely extrapolates the expected budget to various levels of possible activity on either side of the single point most expected estimate. the probabilistic approach to budgeting also provides a range of budgets, but draws these up under quite different assumptions. The technique also associates subjective probabilities with the various levels of activity that could occur, to provide probable or expected values for each major budget classification or item. This provides management with an aid to decision-making under conditions of uncertainty. Management is then provided with a range of probabilistic budget information to examine which enables them to carry our a deeper analysis of potential situations before they decide upon their profit plans.

At its simplest the probabilistic profit budget may be based upon three-level estimates. These will show the most likely, the optimistic, and the pessimistic figures that could be either associated with global budgets or various, probably major, items within a budget. This immediately introduces a high degree of sophistication in the budgeting process. Simulation can also be used in conjunction with this approach to further enhance the quality of the decision-making information provided. (Although the discussion in this section revolves around probabilistic profit budgets based upon three level estimates, the range of estimates made in such a budget will depend upon the situation and circumstances involved.)

Example

Probabilistic Profit Budget based on three-level estimates.

	Attitude towards expected activity					
	Pessimistic		Most Likely		Optimistic	
Sales (units)		70		80		100
		Rs.	Rs.	Rs.	Rs.	Rs
Revenue	(90p)	63	(50 p)	80	1.2)	120
Variable costs	(60p)	42		40	(45p)	45
Contribution		21		40		75
Fixed costs		35		30		25
Budgeted profit (loss)		(14)		10		50
Probabilty		0.2		0.7		0.1
Expected monetary value		Rs.2.8)		7		5
Expected monetary value (overall)		Rs. 9.2				

It can be seen that the most likely column, (which would be the 100 percent budget under a flexible budgeting system), is based upon the expected outcome of future performance. This is the first column to be established. The next stage is for management to discuss their view of the possible outcome of the budget if they take a pessimistic approach. Sales and other items would be less favourable under this approach. In fact, both unit scales and the price that could be charged for the items would be lower if things turn out badly. The overall effect is to make the budgeted profit position very much worse than it would have been if a linear relationship had been considered for all the items involved.

A repeat of this exercise is then carried out, but this time taking an optimistic view of the future.

Although an examination of the columns of a probabilistic budget, just as they stand, will provide useful management information, an additional stage would be to assign subjective probabilities to each of the columns. Such probabilities are referred to as subjective because they are established based on the 'subjective views' of those who assign them. Armed with subjective probabilities the expected values associated with each column can then be computed. The columns can then be summed to provide an expected value of the overall outcome of the situation. The ultimate extension of this would be the production of a probabilistic profit budget showing the likely outcome of operations in situations of uncertainty using a broader range of operations and wider range of assumptions than those associated with three-level estimates. For example, a pessimistic view of the prices that would be obtained for each unit sold. Or a pattern of pessimistic costs could be matched with one of optimistic revenues. In fact there are numerous possible combinations that could be used in the analysis of even three-level probabilistic profit budget information.

Using a computer enables an organisation to deal with the numerous possible relationship and interrelationships. The various elements of many more than three-point estimates could be combined to produce dozens of different relationship profiles by use of a suitable program. Simulation can also be used to show the effects of any changes, or the interrelationships of changes, in the budget's components.

Measures of Variability

A number of approaches can be taken to measure the variability of an item, or items, within a probabilistic profit budget. Measures that can be used for this purpose include those associated with the following parameters.

* **Probability intervals.** Probability intervals enable an analysis to be made of the percentage of items which are seen to fall within given ranges of distribution.

* **Confidence intervals.** Where the parameters concerning the probability are not known any reliability these will have to be estimated. Confidence intervals are all about the level of confidence associated with the estimates of parameters.

* **Co-efficients of variation.** To enable the variability of discrete probability distributions to be described co-efficients of variation can be used. These concern the percentage relationship between the standard deviation and the mean of the distribution. They enable the prediction of the potential variability of the items within a budget. This variability will be large when the co-efficient of variation is high.

PPB can be used to provide a range of data and information to decision makers on the possible outcomes of budgets and the probability of the occurrence of these outcomes. They assist decision makers who examine them by enabling them to evaluate the information presented and which of the profiles presented they would prefer to work towards. This enables management to ensure that effort is focused in the right direction.

Rolling Budget

A rolling budget is "the continuous updating as a short term budget by adding, say a further month or quarter and deducting the earliest month or quarter so that budget can reflect current conditions." Thus a rolling budget is a device which attempts to help an organisation overcome the problems resulting from frequent unexpected or unforseeable changes in activities and/or further costs. Every quarter (or month if that period is chosen) all normal budgeting activities are repeated in respect of the next quarter, for which a budget has not yet been prepared: eg on 31st March, 1994, the budget for the quarter ending 31st March, 1995 is prepared. The comparison is then made between the quarter just completed and the new quarter just budgeted. The master budget for the year and for the intervening quarters, ending 30th June, 30th September and 31st December, 1994 are then adjusted to reflect the difference disclosed by the comparison. Actual results for subsequent quarters can be then compared with the updated budgets.

Advantages

1. Management is able to concentrate on a suitable time-span which it can visualise and for which it can more fairly be held accountable.
2. Management is forced to think in the light of the implications of practical changes/developments rather than in theoretical or generally optimistic terms. The budgets may thus have more motivational impact.
3. This approach minimises the historical elements in budgeting (i.e.what people planned for up to 11 months ago). It eliminates the artificial separation of one financial year from another-as regards operational activities-and allows a more evolutionary type of development.
4. This approach is entirely different from conventional budgets (fixed and flexible). Both fixed and flexible budgets artificially separates on financial year from another.

Performance Budgeting

The conventional budgeting emphasises upon the financial aspects and does not generally take into account the physical aspects of performance. As a result, control of the performance in terms of physical units and the related costs cannot be achieved. Performance budgeting, which was evolved in the United States during 1920's, seeks to overcome this limitation. Performance budgeting provides a meaningful relationship between estimated inputs and expected outputs as an integral part of the budgeting system. 'A performance budget is one which presents the purpose and objectives for which funds are required, the cost of the programmes proposed for achieving those objectives, and quantitative data measuring the accomplishments and work performed under each programme. Thus, performance budgeting is a technique of presenting budgets for costs and revenues in terms of functions, programmes and activities and correlating the physical and financial aspects of the individual items comprising the budget, The necessary steps in performance budgeting are as follows:

1. Establishment of goals, objectives and policies.
2. Formulation of programmes for the achievement of goals, and objectives.
3. Execution of the budget in terms of responsibility and achievement of targets as far as possible within the given time and cost elements.
4. A systematic process of evaluation and appraisal for control as well as updating the budget.

An essential adjunct to the performance budgeting is an adequate 'information system' for performance reporting.

Effectiveness : Performance budgeting is extremely useful in planning and controlling limited resources. Accordingly, it has been put to use by the private and public sector firms as well as by many Government departments. It has been established that performance budgeting is equally helpful both in profit and non-profit-making organisations. It's effectiveness can be summarised as follows:

1. It ensures progress towards long-term objectives.
2. It correlates the physical financial aspects of programmes and activities.
3. It facilitates budget review and decision-making at all levels of management.
4. It facilitates more effective performance audit.
5. It helps to measure progress in time bound objectives so that timely remedial action may be taken.

Zero-Base Budgeting

The 'zero-base' refers to a 'nil-budget' as the starting point; it starts with the premise that the budget for the next period is 'zero' so long the demand for a function, process, project or activity is not justified for each rupee. The assumption is that without such justification no spending will be allowed. The onus lies with each manager to justify why the money should be spent at all and to indicate what would happen if the proposed activity is not carried out and no money is spent. In effect, each manager or functional head is required to carry out cost-benefit analysis of each of the activities etc., under his control and for which he is responsible.

Why ZBB : In the conventional budgeting current year's budgets are generally arrived at based on past figures, say, adding some percentage to the last year's figures. Complaints are often heard that there is no relationship between the expenditures made and the results obtained and there is no control over the inputs to the system and the outputs obtained. Thus, there may be lack of objectivity in the process of formulation of budgets under the conventional budgeting technique. ZBB overcomes these limitations by starting with zero and then objectively determining the budget figures.

Is ZBB a new technique? The idea of ZBB is not absolutely a new one because every firm might have experienced this approach once in its life time. This could happen, for example, when a firm is formulating its first budget or when a re-organisation of the firm calls a budget revision. However, this implies that the application of this organisation and most of the firms of the world still formulate their budgets on the conventional incremental budgeting technique. Thus, ZBB is nothing more than an extension of the logical approach to spending decision.

The historical background : ZBB is originated from the United States of America. In 1964, the United States Department of Agriculture used ZBB approach to prepare their budget. It was, however, an additional exercise on the top of normal process. Later, Peter A. Pyhrr, a Staff Control Manager at Texas Instruments Corporation, developed the technique and implemented it for the first time during 1969-70 in Taxes in the private sector. Pyhrr wrote an article on 'Zero-Base Budgeting' in Harvard Business Review (November-December, 1970) and later wrote a book on it in 1973.

Jimmy Carter, the then Governor of Grorgia, read about ZBB in Harvard Business Review and invited Pyhrr as a temporary consultant to help him apply the approach to the State of Georgia. In 1972 Governor Carter introduced the new Zero-Base Budgeting system in the State of Georgia. Later, after winning the election of presidential post, Carter strongly supported the uses of ZBB in state budgetary control machinery. The technique appeared so fascinating to the former president that during his first year in office, he mandated the use of ZBB throughout the Federal Government in the Fiscal Year 1979.

Application of ZBBB : ZBB is nothing but a budgeting process and hence can be used as a tool in the hands of management. Thus, for application of ZBB, there two basic requirements: (a) there must have a budgeting system within the organisation; (b) it requires managers to develop quantitative measures for use in performance evaluation. The ZBB process consists of identifying decision packages and then ranking them in order of importance through a cost-benefit analysis. Therefore, ZBB can be used on any activities, functions, or operations where a cost-benefit relationship can be identified even if this evaluation is highly subjective.

(a) **Industry :** ZBB is applicable to the following areas: Administrative, Technical e.g. Research & Development, Engineering, Laboratories, Quality control, Maintenance, Production Planning, commercial e.g. Market research, Technical support, Transportation and distribution, etc.,

Thus, ZBB is more applicable to discretionary cost areas.[1] Direct manufacturing costs, such as direct material, direct labour and variable manufacturing overhead, are controlled better through standard costing technique as in these cases relationship between the inputs and outputs can be determined, standards and deviations of the actual from those standards can be measured. Where standards are determinable, those costs associated with the inputs should be controlled through the use of standad costing. On the other hand, if the output as a function of the input cannot be specified, then other means of cost control must be used. ZBB is a planning, resource allocation and control tool. According to ZBB system, justification of the expenditures may be required of the basis of expected output. So, while ZBB may be applicable to only a portion of the total budgeting effort in an enterprise, those areas to which it is directly applicable are the hardest to plan and control.

(b) **Government :** ZBB can be readily adapted to all government activities and agencies since government is a service organisation that

---

[1]Horngren divides fixed cost into two groups viz. (i) committed fixed costs, and (ii) discretionary or managed or programmed fixed costs. Committed fixed costs consist largely of those items arise from the possession of plant, of equipment, and of a basic organisation. Example: rent, rates, taxes, depreciation, insurance, salaries etc. These costs are affected by long-run capacity needs. Discretionary fixed costs arise from period (usually yearly) appropriation decisions that directly reflect top management policies. these costs may have no particular relation to volume or activity. Examples are Research and Development, advertising, sales promotion, donations, management consulting fees, and employee training programmes. Conceivably, these costs could be reduced almost entirely for a given year in dire times, whereas the committed cost would be much more difficult to reduce. An increase in such costs may be due to management's authorisation to spend "because we can afford it" rather than because there is an obvious cause-and-effect relationship between such costs and volume [Charles. T. Horngren, Cost Accounting: A Managerial Emphasis, PHI, 1988 pp. 241-244].

supposedly provides some benefit for the tax payers. It may be stated that in the U.S.A. when ZBB was first used in the State of Georgia it was applied to all 65 budgeted agencies (e.g. health, highway, education, agriculture, public safety, game and fish, family and children's services, etc).

Steps in ZBB *There are three basic steps in Zero-Base Budgeting. These are:*

(a) identify 'decision'and develop 'decision packages' ;

(b) evaluate and rank all 'decision packages' in order of importance through cost/benefit analysis or subjective evaluation,and

(c) allocate resources accordingly.

A *'decision unit'* is a tangible activity or group of activities for which a single manager has the responsibility for successful performance. The decision unit may be identified in different ways in different areas and under different managers. For example, a decision unit may be a traditional cost centre, it may be identified as research and development, capital expenditure, may be a decision unit, service provided or received, such as computer service, legal counsel etc. may be the focus of a decision unit. In short, a decision unit should be related directly to one or more of the 'functions' in the existing accounting system or be relatable to the organisation chart. After identifying the decision unit, *'decision packages'* are to be formulated. A decision package is a document or form which details :

(a) a description of the function or activity

(b) the goal(s)or objective(s) of the function or activity

(c) specific measures of performance

(d) benefits to be derived from financing the activity

(e) the consequences of its non-funding

(f) the projected costs of the package

(g) alternative ways of performing the same activity.

Decision packages may be formulated in either of two ways as follows:

(a) *Mutually exclusive packages:* This represents identifying alternative means of performing the same function. The alternatives are ranked and the best one is chosen. The other packages are discarded.

(b) *Incremental packages :* This represents identifying sequential levels of effort and funding that may be expended on a specific function.

For each function there generally will exist several approaches to accomplishing it-these are mutually exclusive. But within each of the several choices, incremental levels of activities in achieving the ultimate objective of the function can be identified. In other words, the mutually exclusive alternative packages generally must be further defined into incremental levels of effort in excess of the basis effort. Therefore, frequently the initial effort is to define the activity, analyse it in terms of feasible ways to accomplish the objectives (i.e., alternative packages), then analyse the different levels of effort for performing the activity (i.e. incremental packages).

After formulating the decision packages, they are to be ranked and resources to be allocated accordingly. The decision packages are reviewed and ranked in the order of decreasing benefit to the firm. The focus upon benefit-achieving the organisation's goals allows an allocation of limited resources on the basis of projected results. After the available resources are forecasted, it is a simple process to match the ranked decision packages on a cumulative amount basis. The total available resources will determine the acceptable expenditures. If any change in funding occurs during the budget year, the ranking of decision packages should be reexamined and resources allocated accordingly.

Should ZBB be done every year? This question is a common topic of discussion for there is no simple yes or no answer. There are some arguments against yearly repetition. Some managers are concerned about not repeating the process every year. There are some alternative suggestions also, namely :

- Repeat the process every 2 to 3 years.
- Rotate the activities or organisation that use ZBB each year, so that some organisations are doing the process every year.
- Repeat the process only for those prorammes with major changes and problems so that management can concentrate on these areas.
- Repeat the process with changes of management of government administrations so that these new managers can completely review all activities, programmes and priorities.
- Use some combinations of the above.

It is clearly acceptable to repeat the process every 2 to 3 years if an organisation makes its major funding allocations for such a time frame. However, if annual budgets are used, the following two criteria should be met before ZBB should be discontinued as a standard practice every year:

1. Management must be satisfied that the operations are effective and efficient.

2. The work environment must be reasonably stable, without major changes in work loads, problems, needs, and so on.

If the above two conditions are met, ZBB need not be continued every year. It may be mentioned that at Texas Instruments (U.S.A.), the possibility of not repeating ZBB every year was not contemplated primarily because changes was the rule rather than the exception.

Effectiveness of ZBB

1. It improves the planning and control activities in the organisation by relating costs with benefits.

2. It ensures active participation from all concerned. It therefore facilities co-ordination both in planning and control.

3. It helps to pinpoint responsibilities and thus makes possible responsibility accounting more effective. In other words, it facilitates better control and maintaining operating efficiency in the organisation.

4. Allocation of resources are made according to needs and the benefits derived.

5. It develops skills and interpersonal relationship for mangers at all levels.

The Parata System

Parata is the pre-determined budget of the net cash inflows operations, before tax and dividend. The amount of parata is agreed upon between the chairman and the unit incharge. While arriving at the agreed parta, due consideration is given to market position, targeted sales volume, pricing strategy, manufacturing efficiency and standard cost of raw materials. Once parta is agreed, it becomes an instrument of control. The actual parta performance is compared with budgeted parta on a daily basis. The parta system emphasises cash generation, which is quite often an over-riding objective. According, to G.P.Birla, the parta system was started because of the financial problems of the depression years. "Money was tight, credit was not easily available and you had to worry about money more than anything else." If the firm had adequate cash, it could get much more mileage im many areas of strategic importance, e.g. acquisition of new companies at a lower purchase price, and ensuring long- term supplies of critical raw material.

The total parta system is essentially a system of daily budgeting and reporting. Every day, a report of the previous day's production, sales, inventories, cash flow position and profit or loss is sent to the chairman. This is compared with norms. The deviations are identified for consumption of material, other important expenses and for profit.

Proforma of Parta Reporting.

S.No.	Particulars	Today	To date Total	To date Average
A	Production			
1.	Liquid quantity (kls) utilisation Eff %			
2.	Power Quantity (Kg) utilisation Eff %			
3.	Production value Rs (000)			
B				
1.	Raw materials consumed Rs (000)			
2.	Variable conversion cost Rs. (000)			
3.	Total Variable cost Rs(000)			
C	Contribution (A3-B3) Rs.(000)			
D	Fixed cost Rs. (000)			
E	Surplus Rs. (000)			

Remarks :

BUDGETARY CONTROL AND VARIANCE REPORTING

Preparation of the budgets is the first step in the budgetary control system. Implementation of budgets is the second phase which needs continuous reporting of budget performance at short intervals. Preparation of budgets alone will not achieve much unless a comparison is made regularly between the actual performance and the budgeted performance. Thus proper reporting is an essential element in budgetary control. The daily/weekly/monthly reports depending on the nature of operations involved on the results of various functions are regularly submitted to the management and follow up action has to be taken immediately. In this respect, budget reports showing the following information will prove useful:

(a) Budgeted level of activity and budgeted cost of the same.

(b) Budgeted cost of actual level of activities.

(c) Actual cost of actual activity.

(d) Variance between budgeted figures and actual figures.

(e) **Reasons of Variance.**

The importance of reporting lies in the fact that it brings into light the areas which need management attention. It will help in taking timely action for taking corrective measures. Thus, reporting will disclose the persons who are responsible for the variance may not be due to employees but may be due to external factors (i.e. change in wage rates, prices of materials, slack market etc.) which are uncontrollable for which no operative or executive can be held responsible. Budget reports to top management should explain the difference between the profit involved in quantitative and financial terms, show the flow of funds and projections in this regard and provide feedback about the achievements of goals and objectives of the firm.

Various budget reports such as sales budget report, production budget report, purchases budget report, labour budget report etc., are used in budgetary control system.

BUDGETARY CONTROL REPORT

Selling and Distribution Cost Statement

Month Year

Particulars	Total	Territory A	Territory B
Selling Cost:			
Market Research			
Advertisement			
Bad Debts			
Distribution Cost:			
Warehouse Rent			
Warehouse Staff			
Salaries			
Insurance			
Packing			
Transport			
Total Selling & Distribution cost.			
Sales			

Total cost
as % to Sales
Variance Analysis
for the month:
Expenditure
Volume
Cumulative:
Expenditure
Volume

Prepared by....
Submitted by 1......................... 2.............................. 3...........................
Expenses budget report, cash budget report, capital expenditure budget report, research and development budget report etc. can be prepared to highlight the activities of various functional budgets.

Variance Analysis Reports

The primary purpose of variance analysis as discussed here, is to facilitate management control. Therefore, reports should be made available just after the completion of actual performance otherwise their purpose will be lost. Further, a routine may be established whereby the monthly performance reports reach the individual who has to exercise control. Managers should be provided with variance reports relevant to their own area of control. Reports to the top management should be comprehensible and concise. "Brevity is the soul of wit' applies to such reports as it is unrealistic to expect that the management would be interested in uninteresting and perhaps boring technical details of a large number of variances. The top management may be provided with flash reports/first information reports, focusing on specific problems.

The interpretation of the reports should be done with caution. There may be interdependencies between various variances. One variable may effect several variables and it may be difficult to isolate the effects. One may pass on the inefficiency to others without being particularly noticed. In some situations, the inefficiencises in one department are caused due to inefficiencies in earlier departments. Suppose the material purchased is of a poor quality, it may result in increased usage variance and perhaps an unfavourable labour efficiency variance. In such circumstances, it would be wrong to hold the production supervisor responsible. However, if variance analysis is followed blindly, the production supervisor may get a firing from the production manager, while the purchase manager can sit back an relax.

Therefore, the basic lesson to be learned in the use of variance analysis is that one should not jump to conclusions and value judgements immediately. A significant variance is only an indicator of further analysis. Variance, if used as pressure tactics, are likely to motivate managers to find ways and means to beat the system, which be a self-defeating exercise.

When the budget is to be used as an instrument of control, it is necessary to compare actual results with the budget, which can be done by preparing a periodic performance report indicating the deviations. Such deviations, if significant, should be reported to the management using the concept of 'Management by Exception', the purpose being to make the reports concise, selective and action-oriented. The variances are then investigated to determine the underlying causes and once this has been done, the management can decide on the appropriate corrective actions. The variances could be caused because of three major reaosns. Firstly, the reason may be that specific managerial decisions were taken to respond to some new developments not initially planned for e.g. special advertising campaign not planned earlier. Variances on account of such specific managerial decisions need no further investigation. Secondly, it may be caused because of some uncontrollable factors due to exogeneous variables e.g. changes in government policy for import of raw material; such variances should be identified. Thirdly, it may be due to controllable factors which need to be carefully investigated because it is in this area that corrective action is most needed.

The technique of variance analysis involves the arithmetical manipulation of the budget and actual data. Since such arithmetical tricks can be performed in more ways than one, one may find different treatment in different text books. However, this should not compound the confusion because what is important is the logic of variance analysis rather than the mechanics. Some of the important variances are discussed as below.

Sales Budget Variances

Actual sales will differ from the budget and therefore, it is necessary to understand what factors have caused this diviation. The principal reason for the deviations are; first, the actual price realised is different from the price envisaged at the time of budget formulation. It may have become subsequently necessary to revise the price due to competitive forces or other similar reasons. Second, the quantity (volume) of product sold is different from the quantity planned to be sold and some reasons for this may have been within the control of management while some others may not. Third, in case of a multiproduct situation, the actual sales-mix may be different from the budgeted sales- mix, a possible reason for this being that salesmen may have concentrated on their favourite products and therefore, sold larger quantities of such products than as envisaged in the budget. Thus, the sales budget variance can be categorised as a price variance and a volume variance. In case of a multiproduct situation the volume variance can be further analysed in terms of a sales mix variance and a quantity variance. It may be pointed out that the same approach can be used to analyse a territory-wise sales performance report. If in a particular sales district, there is a very high variance, it needs to be analysed further to understand the cause underlying the symptoms reflected by high variance.

Illustration 5 (Sales Budget Variances)

Budget and Actual Sale during the Month of January

Product	Budget			Actual		
	Units	Price/Unit	Value	Units	Price/Unit	Value
A	750	4.00	3000	1100	3.80	4180
B	750	5.50	4125	1000	5.70	5700
C	750	6.00	4500	900	6.50	5850
		Total	11625		Total	15730

Solutions

a) Price Variance

Product	Actual Sale (Units)	Budget Price	Actual Price	Budget Minus Actual	Price Variance
A	1100	4.00	3.80	(0.20)	(220)
B	1000	5.50	5.70	0.20	200
C	900	6.00	6.50	0.50	450
				Total	430

b) Volume Variance

(1) Product	(2) Actual Quantity	(3) Budgeted Quantity	(4) Actual sale - Budgeted	(5) Budget Price	4 x 5 Variance
A	1100	750	350	4.00	1400
B	1000	750	250	5.50	1375
C	900	750	150	6.00	900
			Total		3675

c) Mix Variance

(1) Product	(2) Budgeted	(3) Actual sale Mix	(4) Actual at Sale	(5) Difference (3)-(4)	(6) Budgeted Price	Mix Variance (5) x (6)
A	1/3	1000	1100	100	4.00	400
B	1/3	1000	1000	-	5.50	--
C	1/3	1000	900	(100)	6.00	(600)
					Total	(200)

d) Quantity Variance

(1) Product	(2) Actual volume at Budgeted Mix	(3) Budgeted Volume	(4) Difference (2) - (3)	(5) Budgeted Price	Quantity Variance (4) x (5)
A	1000	750	250	4.00	1000
B	1000	750	250	5.50	1375
C	1000	750	250	6.00	1500
			Total		38 75

Material Budget Variances

The deviations in the case of the material budget could be either because the price at which the material is procured is different from that envisaged in the budget and/or because the quantities purchased and subsequently consumed are different from the budget. The purchase manager is responsible for both purchase price as well as timing and quantity of purchases. Thus, the performance report of the purchasing department will show variances on account of quantity and price.

Once the material has been purchased according to the technical and quality specifications, it is used by the production department for producing the planned output. The manager of the using department has no control on the prices, but he has complete control on the usage of the material. In case of multiple raw materials such as for the cattlefeed factory, the production manager may consume raw materials in a mix different from what was envisaged in the budget besides which, the actual yield may differ from the budgeted yield. Therefore, the usage variance can be further analysed in terms of a mix variance and a yield variance. It may be pointed out that for computation of usage variance, we make use of the actual number of units used by the using department as the manager of this department is responsible for variance on the actual units consumed.

Illustration 6 (Material Budget Variance)

	Budget			**Actual**		
Materials	Quantity (Kg)	Price Rs.	Amount Rs.	Quantity	Price Rs.	Amount Rs.
A	500	20.00	10000	800	25.00	20000
B	1000	30.50	30500	1300	30.00	39000
Less Normal loss(10%)	150			200		
Total	1350		40500	1900		59000

Solution

a) price Variance

(1) Material	(2) Actual Quantity	(3) Budget Price	(4) Actual Price	(5) Difference (3) - (4)	(6) Price Variance (2) x (5)
A	800	20.00	25.00	(5.00)	(4000)
B	1300	30.50	30.00	0.50	650
				Total	3350

b) Mix Variance

(1) Material	(2) Actual Quantity at Budget Proportion.	(3) Actual Qantity.	(4) Difference (2) - (3)	(5) Budget Price Rs.	(6) Mix Variance (4) x (5) Rs.
A	700	800	100	20.00	2000
B	1400	1300	(100)	30.50	(3050)
				Total	(1050)

c) Yield Variances

Budgeted normal loss (10%) = 2100 x 0.10 = 210

Actual loss = 200

Budgeted loss less Actual loss = 210-200 = 10

Budgeted material cost per unit of output $= \frac{40500}{1350} =$ Rs. 30

Yield variance = (Budgeted loss - Actual loss x Budgeted material cost per unit of output) = 10 x 30 = Rs. 300

Labour Budget Variance

The variances in the labour budget arise because of two major factors namely, due to differences in the actual wage rate and the budgeted wage rate and due to differences between actual labour hours and the budgeted labour hours for the achieved level of activity. Therefore, the labour budget variance can be broken into two components namely, wage rates variance and labour efficiency (usage) variance. The labour usage is controllable at the supervisor's level while the wage rates are often determined in union management negotiations. However, a wage rate variation may also take place if the supervisor uses the workers with a higher wage rate than the rate called for in the manufacturing operations. Such a wage rate variation is controllable as the supervisor has used a high proportion of lower paid employees with the result that wage rate variation is low, however, these employees, being less skilled may take more hours to complete the task. Thus,there may be interdependencies in wage rate and labour efficiency.

Illustration 7 (Labour cost variances)

Budget			**Actual**		
Hours	Rate/Hour Rs.	Amount Rs.	Hours	Rate/Hour Rs.	Amount Rs.
6000	5.00	30000	6400	5.20	33280

Hours for production 6200 excluding Idle time 200

Solution

Variances		Rs.
Rate Variance	= 6400 (5.20 - 5.00)	= 1280
Efficiency Variance	= (6200-6000)x5.00	= 1000
Idle Time Variance	= 200 x 5.00	= 1000
	Total Labour Cost Variance	3280

Manufacturing Overhead Variances

This is the grey area where arithmetical tricks have been performed by different authors in different ways. The confusion has been confounded because of lack of standardised terminology.

The analysis of manufacturing overhead variances is somewhat complex that for sales, raw materials, and direct labour, and it has been a primary concern of cost accountants for many years. As a result, practically every book discussing cost accounting and management accounting describes this analysis. Although the mathematical analysis of manufacturing overhead variances is fairly simple, the analysis itself is imprecise because of the numerous opportunities for theoretical and practical distinctions by a lack of standardisation in terminology; almost every writer on the subject has his own"pet" terms. The student pursuing this subject may be understandably confused by the maze of terminology, theoretical distinctions, practical differences, and the resulting alternative procedures. Another factor adds to the complexity, that is, the type of budget data available. If variable budget data (where overhead expenses are identified by their fixed and variable components) are available, a realistic analysis of overhead variances generally can be computed. Alternatively, when only static budget data are used (that is, where the fixed and variable components of overhead expenses are not differentiated), attempts to develop a useful analysis are difficult at best. Some analysis, however, actually try to support an illogical result.

The main thing in variance analysis is to understand the significance of the reported variances and to know what action can be initiated to correct the adverse trends. Our purpose is use the variances for management control, rather than to open variances accounts for ultimately disposing them off in the books of accounts. The approach should be basically to investigate the underlying causes.

In case of materials and labour, the variances were analysed in terms of price (rate) and usage (efficiency). In case of overheads also, the prices of certain items such as rent, rates,electricity and, insurance may change and this will give rise to an overhead price variance. A change in prices may take place, immaterial of whether overheads are fixed or variable. The variable overhead services such as power, consumable materials, tools, etc., may be either used efficiently or wastefully. Therefore, there is need to evolve a control indicator that will indicate the efficiency with which the variable overheads are being used. Such an indicator could be a variable overhead efficiency variance. The following illustrates the computational aspects of variance reporting under flexible budgeting.

Illustration 8

Variance reporting under Flexible Budget

	Budget at 100% Capacity	Budget Adjusted for 80% Capacity.	Actual Cost	Variance		
				Price	Efficiency	Total
Indirect labour	1500	1200	1300	20	80	100
Fuel and oil	3000	2700	2900	160	40	200
Electricity	400	360	430	20	50	70
Consumable stores	300	270	250	10F	10F	20F
Tools	200	150	180	--	30	30
Overtime allowance	100	25	-50	--	25	25
Insurance	100	100	100	--	--	--
Total	5600	4805	5210	190	215	405

Fixed overheads such as rent, insurance and, depreciation have to be incurred, immaterial of what is the output of the department. The department supervisor or manager can do hardly anything to control them. Therefore, the major concern of the departmental manager is to ensure that the output level is high enough to absorb the fixed overheads at a reasonable rate. Of course, it is the major responsibility of the marketing department to ensure that the plant is operating at as near full capacity as is possible.

At the time of budgeting for overheads, we may have calculated the overhead rate using the following formula:

$$\text{The budgeted overhead rate} = \frac{\textit{Total budgeted overhead for the period}}{\textit{Estimated volume of output}}$$

As has been pointed out, the total overhead is a sum of two components viz., the fixed portion and the variable portion. Hence, a variation in overheads can be due to a change in either or both. Further, in the case of the variable portion, there will be a variation in proportion to activity and there can also be a variation in the amount of expenditure per unit. Similarly, the actual level of output will differ from the budgeted level of output. Therefore, any analysis of overhead variances has to recognise a variance in the overhead cost incurred and a variance due to the volume of activity. The former is referred to as 'expenditure variance' and the latter as 'volume variance'.

We can now proceed to discuss a framework for the analysis of manufacturing overhead variances on the assumption that the variable budget data is available. In case of variable budget data, we have fixed and variable costs identified by each department. One approach would be to use only variable cost is components for the purpose of variances analysis. Since the fixed cost is fixed at the department level within the 'relevant range', there is no need to use it for variance analysis. However, if the actual output is beyond the relevant range., the fixed costs may jump from one level to another. If the equation $Y = a + bx$, (where 'a' represents the fixed overhead and 'b' is the rate of variable overhead) has been used to formulate the budget for a particular manufacturing department, then the variance analysis should be based on this equation.

It has been pointed out that the actual overhead may differ from the budgeted overhead because firstly, the actual level of activity (output) is different from the planned level of activity and secondly, the overheads actually incurred may differ from the planned overheads at the actual output. Thus, the total overhead variance can be attributed to the above mentioned two factors namely, volume and expenditure and accordingly, there are tow components of overhead variance known as volume variance and expenditure variance. If we analyse the cause of low level of activity it may either be because of (i) a lesser number of working days in a month then was envisaged at the time of the formulation of the budget, (ii) the capacity usage being lower or higher than budgeted, (iii) the actual machine hours or any other base of activity in the department being different from the budget hours for the actual output. Therefore, the volume variance can be analysed in terms of calendar variance, capacity usage variance and volume efficiency variance. Since the volume arises due to actual level of activity being different from the budgeted, this also indicates the idle capacity in comparison to that budgeted. Therefore, the variance arising due to this factor is also known as idle capacity variance.

It may be pointed out that as far as the production department is concerned, volume variance is uncontrollable because it is the major responsibility of the marketing department to make sure that the plant is working as near full capacity as is possible.

The expenditure variance also referred to as spending or budget variance can be further analysed in terms of price variance, efficiency variance and usage variance.

Illustration 9

Overhead Variances

	Budget	Actual
Number of working days	20	21
Manhours	40000	43000
Output per manhour (units)	3.2	3.0
Total output (units)	128000	129000
Overheads: Fixed	32000	31500
Variable	102400	114400

(a) Variable Overhead Variance

= (Budgeted variable overhead rate per unit of output) x Actual output - Actual variable overhead.

$$= \frac{102400}{128000} \times 129000 - 114400$$

$$= 0.8 \times 129000 - 114400 = 11200$$

(b) Fixed Overhead Variance

1. Expenditure Variance = Budget - Actual = 32000-31500 = 500 (Fav.)

2. Volume Variance.

$$\text{Budgeted overhead rate per unit} = \frac{32000}{128000} = 0.25$$

Volume Variance = (Budgeted output-Actual output) x overhead rate.

$$= (128000 - 129000) \times 0.25 = 250 \text{ (Fav.)}$$

$$\text{Calender Variance} = \frac{32000}{20} \text{ (21-20)} = 1600 \text{ (Fav.)}$$

Efficiency Variance

Output per manhour Budget 3.2 units
Actual 3.0 units

---

loss pei hour 0.2 units

Loss in 43000 hrs. = 8600 units.

Monetary loss
(Efficiency Variance) = (Loss in units) x (overhead rate/unit)

= 8600 x 0.25 = 2150

Capacity Variance

Manhours for 21 days	= 42000
Actual manhours	= 43000
Excess manhours	= 1000

Capacity variance per hour = (Excess/Deficit manhours) x overhad rate

$$= 1000 \text{ x } \frac{32000}{40000} = 800$$

COST CONTROL RATIOS

Apart from expressing the budget variances in absolute figures, certain ratios are also commonly used in measuring deviations from budget and are incorporated in budget reports. The important ratios are :-

1. Standard Capacity Usage Ratio : This is the relationship between the budgeted number of working hours and the maximum possible number of working hours in a fixed period. This ratio is generally expressed in percentage and indicates the production of available facilities which is intended to be used during the budget period.

$$\frac{\textit{Budgeted number of working hours}}{\textit{Maximum hours in a budget period}} x100$$

2. Actual Usage of Budgeted Capacity Ratio : This is the relationship between the actual number of working hours and the budgeted number of working hours. This ratio indicates the extent to which facilities were actually utilised during the period.

$$\frac{\textit{Actual number of working hours}}{\textit{Budgeted number of working hours}} x100$$

3. Actual Capacity Usage Ratio : This is the relationship between the actual number of working hours and the maximum possible number of working hours in a period. Thsi is expressed as-

$$\frac{\textit{Actual number of working hours}}{\textit{Maximum possible hours is a period}} x100$$

4. Activity Ratio : This is the number of standard hours equivalent to the work produced, expressed as percentage of the budgeted standard hours.

This ratio measures the level of activity at which the firm is operating. The ratio is expressed in this manner-

$$\frac{\textit{Actual production in terms of standard hours}}{\textit{Budgeted production in terms of standard hours}} x100$$

5. Efficiency Ratio : This is the standard hours equivalent to the work produced, expressed as a percentage of actual hours spent in producting that work. This ratio measures the efficiency with which the firm is operating and is expressed thus-

$$\frac{\textit{Actual production in terms of standard hours}}{\textit{Actual hours worked}} x100$$

6. Calendar Ratio : This is the relationship between the actual number of working days in a period and the number of working days in the relative budget peiord. This ratio indicates whether all the working days in a budget period have been available in actual practice and is expressed as-

$$\frac{\textit{No. of actual working days in a period}}{\textit{No. of working days in the budget period}} x100$$

Illustration 10

(i) From the following information calculate the important ratios used for control purpose and comment on the results :

(a)Maximum possible working hours in a budget period	5,000 hrs.
(b)Budgeted number of working hours	4,000 hrs.
(c)Actual number of working hours	3,600 hrs.
(d)Budgeted production in standard hours	6,000 hrs.
(e)Actual production in standard hours	5,400 hrs.

(ii) If the number of actual working days during the month be 24 corresponding to 25 days in the budget, find out the Calendar Ratio.

Solution

Standard capacity usage ratio

$$= \frac{4,000}{5,000} x100 = 80\% \text{ (Adverse)}$$

Actual usage of budgeted capacity

$$= \frac{3,600}{4,000} x100 = 90\% \text{ (Adverse)}$$

Actual capacity usage ratio

$$= \frac{3,600}{5,000} x100 = 72\% \text{ (Adverse)}$$

Efficiency Ratio (attained)

$$= \frac{\textit{Actual production hrs.}}{\textit{Actual No. of working hrs.}} x100 = \frac{5,400}{3,600} x100 \ 150\% \text{ (Favourable)}$$

Activity Ratio

$$= \frac{\textit{Standard houurs} \text{ for } \textit{actual production}}{\textit{Budgeted hours}} x100$$

$$= \frac{5,400}{6,000} x100 = 90\% \text{ (Adverse)}$$

Efficiency anticipated, expeccted or budgeted efficiency

$$= \frac{\textit{Budgeted production standard hours}}{\textit{Budgeted number working hours}} x100$$

$$= \frac{6,000}{4,000} x100 = 150\% \text{ (Favourable)}$$

$$\text{Calendar Ratio} = \frac{24}{25} \text{ x } 100 = 96\% \text{ (Adverse)}$$

Comments : The budget was prepared on the basis of 4,000 working hours, which was only 80% of the available capacity ; during the period only 3,600 hours were worked i.e., 90% of the capacity budgeted for or 72% of the available capacity.

Only 5,400 standard hours were produced during the priod, this represented 90% activity ratio. The efficiency attained was 150%, budgeted efficiency was also 150%, which is thus equivalent to 100% of actual efficiency.

Advantages of Budgetary Control

(a) Forecasting and Planing : Budgetary control system guides the management in planning formulation of policies in advances. It secures planned allocation of productive facilities and resources, viz, men, money, material, machinery, market, method, matter and minuts for their optimum utilisation.

(b) Communication : Being a means of communication, it enables the lower level of management to understand the basic objectives and policies of the concern. The budget communicates managements' expectations. They serve as communication links between different levels of management and between management and workers.

(c) Coordination: It coordinates effectively the activities of different departments viz, production, purchase, marketing, financial, administrative, etc., It also develops a sound communication system through budget committee meetings and discussions. The coordination of the main divisions of a concern makes for smoother opeation and less internal friction which results in the achievement of the budget goal.

(d) Decentralisation of Responsibilitty : Budgeting facilitates delegation of authority. It also enables the management to decentralise responsibility, without loosing control of the business. It pinpoints operational inefficiency and establishes divisional and departmental responsibility which prevents 'buck passing' when the budget figures are not achieved.

(e) Imperfect Control : It exercises an efficient control over all aspects of production operations of the commodity to be manufactured. The budget is an impersonal policeman that maintains ordered effort and brings about efficiency in results. Any expenditure in excess of what is provided for in the budget cannot be incurred without prior sanction at higher levels. It thus acts as an instrument of control.

(f) Appraisal of Performance : Budget serves as a tool for measuring the managerial performance. The budgeted targets are compared with the actual ones, variations are spotted out and responsibility fixed. It also assists in measuring the efficiency of departments and individuals in achieving the budget targets.

(g) Cost-Concious : It makes all the executives cost conscious and thus paves the way for an efficient utilisation of the available resources. The whole course of action being planned in advance, wastage and losses of all types are avoided.

(h) Avoiding Financial imbalance : The budget of cash expenditures and cash receipts makes it possible for the financial management to forecast their need for credit and arrange for it in advance. It also aids in obtainng bank credit.

(i) Basis for Incentives : It provides a basis for the introduction of incentive systems of remuneration by results.

(j) Adoption of Standard Costing : Budgets are the forerunners of standard costs; they create necessary conditions for introduction of a system of Standard Costing.

Limitations of Budgetary Control

The following are some of the major limitations of budgeting :

(a) Budgets are essent lly *based on estimates* and forecasts, whose accuracy depends up correctness of facts and good judgement.

The subjective elemention in interpretation of facts often creates several doubts as to their reliability.

(b) There is a *danger in overbudgeting,* through spelling out major expenses in detail and depriving managers of freedom of action managing their departments.

(c) Under fast *changing business conditions and government policies* budgeting involves a tight-rope-walking, between yesterday, today and tomorrow. Due to the inflationary pressure and changing taxation policies of the government, it is difficult to prepare the budget in such a way as to give a realistic position of the firm's affairs as it will stand in future.

(d) The technical persons always resent any paper work. It should, therefore, be seen as little paper work is involved in the operation of the budget as possible.

Despite these limitations, budgets provide guidelines to managerial action in more definite terms. However, budgets should be used only as a tool of planning and control, and the various limitations should also be kept in mind while administering budgetary control system.

REVIEW QUESTIONS

1. (a) What are the essentials of a budget and budgetary control?
(b) What is the difference between a forecast and a budget?
(c) What are the main steps in budgetary control?
(d) What is flexible budget? State its significance.
(e) What is 'Principal budget factor'?
(f) What do you understand by 'Budget Manual'?
(g) How does the budget serve as an instrument of control?
(h) What do you understand by Master Budget?
(i) What are the uses of a cash budget?
(j) What does Labour Budget represent? To which other budgets is it linked?
(k) What are control ratios in budgetary analysis?
(l) What is budget allowance and why it is important?
(m) What is a budget centre?
(n) Is it deirable to prepare a budget for each budget centre?
(o) What is a budget report? State the importance of a good budget report.
(p) Distinguish between fixed budgets and flexible budgets.
(q) What factors generally determine a budget period?
(r) What is the difference between an operating budget and financial budget?
(s) On what does the success of budgetary control depend?
(t) What is a zero base budget?
(u) Explain the basic steps involved in zero base budgeting?

2. (i) Explain the different variances in budgetary control system.

(ii) What are the limitations of budgetary control?

(iii) Briefly explain the role of budgetary control as an instrument of financial planning and control?

(iv) Explain the nature of a system of budgetary control, and list the advantages to management of such a system.

(v) Explain the advantages expected from the introduction of s system of budgetary control in a small factory producing a variety of products.

(vi) What is 'Sales forecast'? State briefly the procedures adopted in making forecasts.

(vii) What are the essential features of efficient system of budgetary control?

(viii) What are the basic principles that are common to both Standard Costing and Budgetary Control?

(ix) Distinguish between Budgetary Control and Standard Costing.

3. Explain briefly the following :

(a) Probabilistic Profit Budgeting

(b) Performance Budgeting

(c) Roling Budget

18

Standard Costing and Variance Analysis

Standard Cost is a predetermined cost which is calculated from management's standard of efficient operation and the relevant necessary expenditure. Standard Costing is the preparation of standard costs, and their comparison with actual costs and the analysis of variances to their causes and points of incidence.

Applicability of Standard Costing: Standard Costing technique can be applied to any class of production or service but it is appropriate in those case where production or service is of a repetitive character. This implies that this technique is of maximum value when it is used with a process costing system in process industries like bricks, cement, fertiliser, paper, sugar, biscuits, etc.

Establishment of a Standard Costing system

The installation of standard costing system in a manufacturing concern involves the following steps:

(*a*) *Standardisation of functions i.e.,* all activities should be standardised and the technical processes of operations should also be susceptible to planning.

(*b*) *Establishment of (Standard) Cost Centres.*

(*c*) *Classification of Accounts i.e.,* the different accounts can be codified and different symbols may be used to facilitate speedy collection, analysis and reporting.

(d) *Fixation of Activity or Capacity Levels :* The level of production estimated would be the standard production linked with any of the following activity levels, also known as the 'capacity levels. *The Maximum Theoretical capacity* in relation to a plant is that which can be achieved without interruptions of any kind such as breakdowns, waiting time, absenteeism of employees, shortage of materials, etc. But this capacity is very rarely achieved as much as interruptions are normal occurrences which affect every business. Hence, the use of maximum capacity as a basis for calculating overhead costs is not recommended. *The Practical Capacity* is the maximum capacity minus the unutilised capacity due to normal interruptions. It is also known as the practical operating capacity or normal capacity to manufacture. The physical plant capacity to produce, as indicated by the manufactures, is known as the rated capacity. This is usually taken as the 100% capacity. The difference between the practical capacity and the actual capacity based on expected sales is known as the idle capacity. This is represented by the unutilised capacity due to a lack of the sales demand

(*e*) *Setting up of Standards:* Standards may be basic (long period) and current (short period). From the point of view of efficiency level they will fall into three broad categories: (*a*) strict or ideal; (*b*) attainable or expected/actual and (*c*) loose. The standard should be realistic and attainable. Unrealistic standard provoke resentment and depress performance. Loose standard leads the management to indulge in self-congratulation. Normally, a period of one year is more realistic, as it coincides with the budget period and the normal accounting period.

(f) *Setting of Standard Costs:* Standard Costs should be determined for each element of cost separately and accurately. Like a budget committee in big industries, there should be a Standards Committee or Standards Division which will be vested with the work of setting standard costs. The Standards Committee generally consists of all functional heads like production manager, personal manager, etc. In determining the output regard must be had to the limiting factors affecting sales, production, etc. Setting up of standard cost involves the determination of cost standards. A cost standard is a usage, price or other standard upon which a standard cost is based.

For any given unit of product the following standards must be determined. (*i*) Standard material costs/ (*ii*) Standard labour costs, (*iii*) Standard direct costs, (*iv*) Standard variable overhead costs, (*v*) Standard fixed overhead costs, and (*vi*) Standard selling price and profit.

The Standard Direct Material Cost is found by multiplying the quantity of materials to be purchased with the rate or price at which they are available. Thus determination of standard material costs involves deciding upon (i) standard material specifications, (ii) standard material utilisation or usage and (iii) standard material price. The standard material cost includes not only net purchase but also freight, carriage inwards, receiving and inspection, octroi, insurance and storage charges. Spoilage allowances including shrinkage, waste and scrap of materials in the course of production should be provided for amounts regarded as normal or unavoidable. The normal wastage should be carefully standardised, as a high allowance would conceal inefficiency, and a low allowance would give undue adverse variance.

Determination of *Standard Direct labour Cost* involves fixation of (a)standard labour grades (b) standard labour times *i.e.*, standard hours through Time, Motion and Fatigue Study with the help of work study engineers (c) standard wages rates based on time rate, piece rate and premium plans. Due regard should be given to incentive payments and other fringe benefits; standard rates of pay should be established for every category of labour. Labour rates are subject to fluctuating demand and supply and fixed by contracts, law, wage boards, wage tribunals, and awards. Personnel Department will help the cost accountant in determining standard rates of pay.

Standard Direct (expense) cost is any expenditure (other than direct material and direct labour) which is directly to be incurred on a specific cost unit. Such special expense is charged directly to the particular cost standard (account) concerned. Direct expenses are also known as chargeable expenses and also form part of the prime cost of a product. Example of direct expenses include (a) hire charges of a special purpose machinery or tool hired for a particular process, (b) maintenance cost of such equipment, (c) cost of special designs, drawing or moulds made for a specific product or process, (d) royalty, (e) excise duty, (f) experimental expenses or pilot projects, etc.

Standard overhead Costs are classified as manufacturing, administration, selling and distribution overheads. They are also categorised into fixed, variable and semi-fixed or semi-variable, so that correct estimates in respect of each class may be prepared for the budget period. Standard overhead rate is determined on the basis of past records and future trend of prices. Fixation of overhead standard involves (*a*) the estimation of the overhead (rates or costs) components such as indirect labour, power, depreciation, taxes, rent, etc., (*b*) determination of estimates of production. It should be remembered that the following expenses are to be excluded from the computation of (standard) total costs: (i) all excluded expenditure such as purchase of plant, buildings, etc. (ii) capital losses like loss on sale of fixed assets, (iii) profit based allocations like bonus to directors and employees, (iv) items of pure financial nature such as interest on capital, charity, donations, cash discounts, etc.

The *Standard selling and Distribution costs* are found by making a careful study of the costs involved in selling and distributing a cost of unit. Packing material, packing time, freight, commission and a share of advertising and sales administration costs are the various components of the cost.

Setting Standards for Sales Price and Margin : A profit improvement plan of an organisation includes not only cost plans aiming for cost reduction to result in to increase the profit but also standards for sales. Other things remaining constant, profits may be increased by increasing the volume of sales, even by reducing the the selting price, or by increasing the selling price, provided the market condition permit such a course being taken. The management may, therefore, also like to set standards for sales they expect to make in the coming period by setting (a) Quantity Standards and (b) Price Standards. Quantity standards regarding sales will have to be fixed up for each of the products in which the business deals while determining quantity standards certains factors like post sales figures, presence of competitors, production capacity etc.,

The Standard Selling Price at which it is planned to sell the cost unit, may be determined by the Sales Manager in consultation with the managing Director. The Standard Sales Margin is the difference between the total standard cost of a product and its standard selling price,

(g) *Preparing Standard Cost Card or Cost Sheet*: After standards have been computed for material, labour and overhead, they are recorded in standard cost cards or standard cost sheets. The standard cost cards give the standard unit cost of a product. A card may be prepared for each product to show the quantity and prices of each class of material required, the time and rate of each grade of labour, the overhead rate and the total of each element of cost for each operation or product. This card is very similar to a job card.

(*h*) *Standard Cost of Production:* When the standard quantity which shall be manufactured during a particular period has been decided upon, the standard cost of standard production can be computed by a simple multiplication of the Standard Units to be produced by the standard per Unit Cost of Production.

(i) *Standard of Sales:* Standards are to be laid down both for the probable quantity of sales and the selling price, so as to know the standard value of sales. The budgeted estimate of the expected volume of sales and the selling price can be made by the management. The deviations of actual volume of sales and the price at which the goods are actually sold are also important for effecting managerial control over costs.

(j) *Recording of Actual Costs i.e.,* ascertainment of actual results.

(k) *Comparison of Actual with Standard, to find the differences between the two (known as variance).*

(l) *Reporting the variances to management*, identifying causes and persons responsible for such variances, so that appropriate action can be taken as may be necessary.

(m) *Monitoring and Feedback.*

(n) *Taking Corrective Measures / Revision of Standards.* Standards established are not permanent in nature and they have to be revised from time to time taking into consideration the change in the circumstances. The chief object of revising a standard is to facilitate better control over costs and improve the over all working and probitability of the organisation. There should not be frequent changes in the standards, otherwise, the very purpose of the fixation of the standards will be defeated. Generally, standards should be revised only on account of those causes which are beyond only on account of those causes which are beyond the control of the management. Current standards are reviewed every year as new current standards are reviewed every year as new budgets are prepared and the entire standard cost structure is revised owing to any of the following changes.

(a) the prices of materials and labour change,

(b) the manufacturing methods change;

(c) the product designs or specifications change;

(d) there are errors in setting the standards, and

(e) there are other relevant circumstances such as, technological advancements.

The basic standards are revised in the course of the year itself under the following circumstances :

(a) When there are permanent changes in the methods of manufacture,

(b) When the plant capacity changes, and

(c) When the disparity between the standards and the expected performance becomes so great that the standard loses its significance.

Essentials of Effective System of Standard Costing

The sucessful implementation of cost control plan under Standard Costing depends upon certain essential or pre-requisotes which are as follows:

(a) *Planable Technical Process :* Technical process of operation must be ssusceptible to planning.

(b) *Settingy Cost of Process/Operation :* Standards must be designed to give cost of operation or process rather than products, so that variances may be traced to their origin/source without laboious investication.

(c) *Support of Top Management :* Standard Clsting technique should have the full support and co-operation of every member of the management team. In other words management must take an interest in controlling costs and be aware of the advantages affered by standard costs and use of variance report.

(d) *Reasonably attainable Standards :* Standards must be properly set so as to have confidence in the fairness of standards both by management and operating personnel.

(e) *Adequate Accounting System :* Since historical data form the basis for future of standard costs, the accounting system in the business should be adequate such as to hold each port of the organisation to its responsibilites.

(f) *Periodic Reporting :* Reports must be prepared constantly keeping management at all levels informed of progress relative to standards. a periodical compearison of the actual costs with the standard costs may reveal variances. these variances should be reported by those responsible for execution to their superiors and, in turn get instructions for correction of the diviations communicated to then.

Budgetory Control and Standard Costing

(1) *Nature of Cost*: The budgets are 'should be' cost while the standards are 'ought to be' costs.

(2) *Indices*: Budgets are indices, adherence to which keeps a business out of difficulties. Standards are pointers to further possible improvements.

(3) *Basis*: Budgets are based on estimated cost and past actuals and adjusted to the future needs. They have roots in the past experience and eyes on the future. Standard costs, on the other hand, are scientifically planned on technical assessment under a set of working conditions.

(4) *Cost Plan*: Budgets are plans of action for a definite period. Standard costs are criteria for operative efficiency.

(5) *Projection*: Budgets are projection of financial accounts whereas standard costs are projection of cost accounts.

(6) *Scope*: Budgets are complete in as much as they are framed for all the activities and functions of a concern such as production, purchase, selling and distribution, research and development, capital expenditure, etc., Standard costing relates only to the function of production and the related manufacturing costs. Moreover, budgets include both income and expenditure whereas standards are usually for expenditure only. Thus budgetary control is extensive whereas standard costing is intensive.

(7) *Applicability*: Budgeting can be adopted in any industry or business. But standard costing cannot fully be adopted in job-order industries and contracts.

Despite the above dissimilarities, both standard costing and budgetary control have certain common basic principles. They are: (1) The establishment of predetermined targets of performance, (2) the measurement of actual performance, (3) the comparison of actual performance with the predetermined targets. (4) the analysis of variances between the actual and the standard performance, (5) the taking of corrective measures, where necessary. Both are the techniques of importance in their respective fields and complementary to each other. Usually the two system are used in conjunction with each other to obtain most fruitful results. They are inter-related but not interdependent.

Advantages of Standard Costing

(*i*) Standard costs help the management in *fixation of prices* and in laying down *production policies.*

(*ii*) They provide constant and uniform bases for management on the *operational efficiency* of workers and other members of the Staff.

(*iii*) Through study of variances management need to concentrate only on areas and problems which call for its attention *i.e.,* the system of *management by exception* can be practised.

(*iv* Standard costs help in readily showing up and, then, *elimination of avoidable wastages and losses.*

(*v*) *Performance of employees* at all levels can be judged objectively; this enables the concern to promote and reward the right person.

(*vi*) *Delegation of authority* becomes effective since the men concerned know what they have to achieve and by what standard they will be judged.

(*vii*) The whole concern in imbued with a dynamic forward looking mentality.

VARIANCE ANALYSIS

Variance analysis is the process of analysing variances by sub-dividing the total variance in such a way that management can assign responsibility for off-standard performance. If the effect of the variance is to increase the profit, the variance is said to be favourable, shown as (F). Favourable variance would result when the actual costs are lower than the standard costs; it is also known as *positive* or *credit variance* and viewed only as savings. In the reverse case, it is adverse or unfavourable, shown as (A). That is when actual costs exceed the standard, unfavourable or adverse variance would result. It is also known as *negative* or *debit variance* viewed as additional cos or loss.

The profit variance can be divided into (*a*) total cost variance and (*b*) total sales margin variance. Total cost variance can be further sub-divided into (*i*) direct material cost variance, (*ii*) direct wage variance and (*iii*) overhead variance. In another way, they can also classified into price variance and volume variance, controllable variance and uncontrollable variance, revision variance and methods variance.

The price variance is concerned with price factor and relates to prices of materials, rates of labour, expenditure on overheads or selling price of products; the volume variance refers to quantity of units in terms of raw materials consumed, number of hours worked, utilisation of plant or number of unit sold.

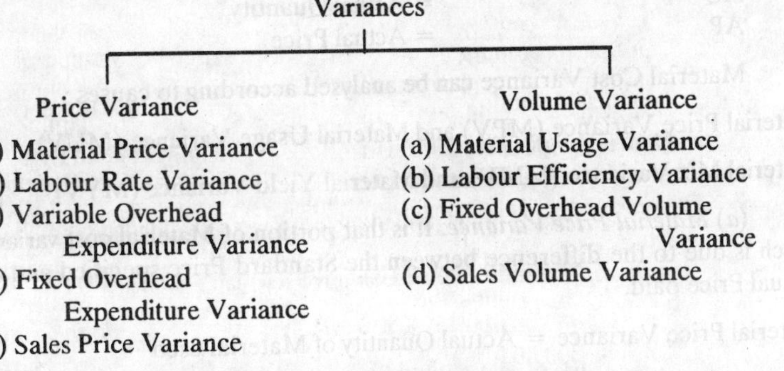

In variance analysis responsibilities are allocated to different managerial persons and that is why it is also known as Responsibility Costing. If a variance can be identified as the primary responsibility of a specified person it is said to be a controllable variance; if the variance is due to the factors beyond the control of an individual, then the variance is said to be uncontrollable.

When the circumstances have changed after the standards have been set up, but a permanent change of budget or standard is not desired, either due to shortage of time or due to temporary nature of the change, the budget and standards are temporarily revised; and the amount by which the budget requires revision for such a temporary change is called Revision Variance. *i.e.,* the variance between between the basic standard cost and the revised standard cost.

Standards are set having regard for a certain method of production to be adopted. If for some reason a different method is adopted the a variance may result which is termed as Method Variance. It is the portion of total cost variance which is due to the use of methods other than those specified.

I Direct Material Cost Variance (MVC)

Material cost variance is the difference between the standard cost of direct materials specified for the output achieved and the actual cost of direct materials used.

Material cost variance = Total Sandard Material Cost-Total Actual Material Cost

MCV	= (SQxSP)-(AQxAP)
SQ	= Standard Quantity (for actual production)
SP	= Standard Price
AQ	= Actual Quantity
AP	= Actual Price

Material Cost Variance can be analysed according to causes :

Material Price Variance (MPV) and Material Usage Variance (MUV)

Material Mix Variance (MMV) and Material Yield Variance (MYV)

(a) *Material Price Variance*: It is that portion of Material cost variance which is due to the difference between the Standard Price specified and the Actual Price paid.

Material Price Variance = Actual Quantity of Material used

(Standard Unit Price-Actual Unit Price)

MPV = AQ (SP-AP)

(b) *Material usage or Quantity Variance* (*MUV*): It is the difference between the standard quantity specified and the actual quantity used.

Material Usage Variance = Standard Unit Price

(Standard Quantity--Actual Quantity)

MUV = SP (SQ-AQ)

Illustration 1

Calculate Material Cost Variances from the following

	Standard	Actual
Quantity	200 Kgs.	230 Kgs
Price	Rs. 2 per Kg.	Rs. 1.50 per Kg.

Solution

(a) Material Cost Variance (MCV) = Standard Cost--Actual Cost
= Rs. 400--Rs. 345 = Rs. 55 (F)

(b) Material Price Variance (MPV)
= Actual Quantity (Standard Price--Actual Price)
= 230 (Rs. 2-1.50) = Rs. 115(F)

(c) Material Usage Variance (MUV)
= Standard Price (Standard Quantity--Actual quantity)
= Rs. 2 (200-230) = Rs. 60 (A)

Verification : MCV = MPV + MUV
Rs. 55 (F) = Rs. 115 (F) + Rs. 60 (A)

Material Usage Variance can be sub-divided into two.

(*i*) Material Mix Variance and (*ii*) Material Yield or Scrap Variance.

(*i*) *Material Mix Variance*: It is that portion of the direct material usage variance which is due to the difference between the standard and the actual composition of a mixture. When the ratio of mix is different but the total quantities of standard mix,

Material Mix Variance = Standard Price (Standard Quantity of Mix--
(Actual Quantity of Mix)

When the total actual quantity and total standard quantity and the ratio of mix are different, then the standard quantity of the each material will be revised –

Material Mix Variance

$$= \frac{\textit{Total weight of Actual Mix}}{\textit{Total weight of Standard Mix}} \times \textit{Standard cost of Standard Mix}$$

-- Standard cost of Actual Mix.

or MMV = (RQ – AQ) X SP.

Revised Standard Quantity

$$= \frac{\textit{Total weight of Actual Mix}}{\textit{Total weight of Standard Mix}} \times \textit{Standard Quantity.}$$

(*ii*) *Material Yield or Scrap Variance*: It is that portion of the direct material usage variance which is to the difference between standard yield specified and actual yield obtained. Thus,

Material Yield Variance = Standard Price x Abnormal Loss/Gain

or

= Standard output Rate (Standard Yield

of Actual input--Actual Yield)

MYV = SR (SY--AY)

The difference between standard yield and actual yield is called abnormal loss or gain. In case standard yield is less than the actual yield the difference is called abnormal gain and vice versa for abnormal loss.

To sum up, the Material Cost Variance is the aggregate of Material Price Variance + Material Mix Variance + Material Yield Variance.

Material Cost Variances : Causes & Controllability

Variance	Possible Causes	Person Responsible
A. Material Price Variance	1. Market Price Fluctuations	Uncontrollable
	2. Emergency Purchases	Manager for Stores/ Sales/Production
	3. Insufficient Purchasing (Uneconomical, Bad buying)	Purchase Manager
	4. Scarcity of Material	Uncontrollable
	5. Off season purchasing especially for seasonal products like jute, cotton etc.	Purchase Manager
	6. Failure to get discount (Cash/Trade)	Accounts Officer
	7. Change in delivery cost	Uncontrollable
B. Material Quantity/ Usage Variance	1. Difference in quality of material	Purchase Manager
	2. Use of defective materials causing spoilage, scrap, inefficiency of workers	Foreman
	3. Wrong specification or design	Planning Engineer
	4. Incorrect booking of material usage	Stores Department
	5. Wrong mix (Other than std. mix)	Production Manager

6.	Defects in Plant & machinery	Foreman/Maintenance Engineer
7.	Faulty material processing	--Do
8.	Pilferage of materials	Security/Stores Dept
9.	Rejection of completed work necessitating additional material withdrawal from store	Foreman

II. Labour Cost Variances (LCV)

Labour Cost Variance is the difference between standard direct wages specified for the activity achieved and the actual direct wages paid.

Labour Cost Variance = Standard Labour Cost-Actual Labour Cost.

LCV = SLC -- ALC

SLC = Standard Time for Actual Production X Standard Rate.

ALC = Actual Time x Actual Rate

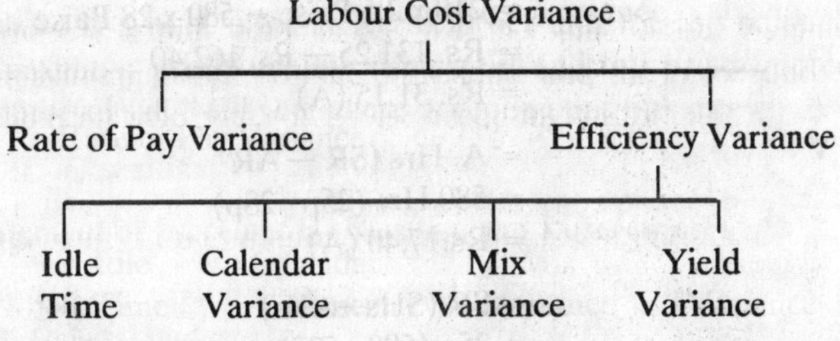

Labour cost variances can be analysed into (i) Labour Rate of pay Variance. (ii) Labour Efficiency (or Time) Variance, (iii) Labour Idle Time Variance. (iv) Calendar Variance (v) Labour Mix or Gang Composition Variance and (vi) Labour Yield Variance.

(i) Labour Rate of Pay (or Wage Rate) Variance (LRV): It is that portion of Labour Cost Variance which is due to the difference between the standard rate of pay specified and the actual rate paid.

LRV = Actual Time (Standard Rate – Actual Rate)

(ii) Labour Efficiency Variance (LEV): It is that portion of labour cost variance which is due to the difference between the standard labour hours specified for the output achieved and the actual labour hours expended. This is also known as Labour Time Variance, Labour Quantity Variance, Labour Usage Variance and Labour Spending Variance.

LEV = Standard Rate (Standard Time -- Actual Rate)

Note: Actual time should be taken after excluding abnormal idle time if any.

Illustration 2

The information as per Standard cost card is given below:

Labour rate	25 Paise per hour
Hours set per unit for production	2.5

The actual production date is given below :

Units produced	210
Labour rate	28 Paise per hour
Hours worked	580

Calculate (a) the labour cost variance (b) labour rate variance and (c) labour efficiency variance.

Solution

(a) L C V = S L C − A L C
= SHsxSR—AHsXAR
= 210 x 2.5 Paise — 580 x 28 Paise
= Rs. 131.25 — Rs. 162.40
= Rs. 31.15 (A)

(b) L R P V = A. Hrs (SR — AR
= 580 Hrs (25p—28p)
= Rs.17.40 (A)

(c) L E V = SR (SHs—AHs)
= 25p (580—525)
= Rs. 13.75 (A)

Proof : L C V = LRPV + LEV
Rs. 31.15 (A) = Rs. 17.40(A) + Rs. 13.75 (A)

(iii) Labour Idle Time Variance: It is that portion of labour cost variance which is due to the (abnormal) idle time of workers on account of failure of power supply, machine break- down, shortage of materials, etc.
Labour Idle time Variance = Idle Hours x Standard Rate per Hour
Note : This Variance is always adverse.

(iv) Labour Calendar Variance (LCV): This variance arises only when workers are paid for the days for which they have not worked and for which no provision was made while determining Standards. This happens only when

some special public holidays are declared.
Labour Calendar Variance = Standard rate X Unbudgeted Holidays.

(*v*) *Labour Mix Variance (LMV)* It is the variance due to the difference in standard composition of labour and the actual composition of labour. It is calculated as follows:

(*a*) If there is no change in the standard composition of labour force and total time expended is equal to the total standard time.

LMV = Standard Cost of Sandard Mix-Standard Cost of Actual Mix

(*b*) If the standard composition of labour force is revised due to shortage of a particular type of labour and the total labour time expended is equal to the standard time

LMV = Standard Cost of Revised Standard Mix -- Standard Cost of Actual Mix

(*c*) If the total actual time of labour differs from the total standard time of labour.

$$\text{LMV} = \left(\frac{\text{Total Time of Actual Labour Mix}}{\text{Total Time of Standard Labour Mix}} x \text{ Standard Cost of Standard Mix}\right) - \text{Standard Cost of Actual Mix.}$$

(*d*) If the standard is revised and the actual time of labour differs from the total standard time of labour.

$$\text{LMV} = \left(\frac{\text{Total Time of Actual Labour Mix}}{\text{Total Time of (Revised Std. Labour Mix}} x \text{ Standard Cost of Revised Standard Mix}\right) - \text{Standard Cost of Actual Mix}$$

(*vi*) *Labour Yield Variance (LYV)*: Like material yield variance, it is due to the difference in the standard output specified and actual output obtained.

LYV = Standard Labour Cost per unit (Actual Output-Standard Output). If the actual production is more than standard production, it is a favourable variance and vice versa.

Labour Cost Variance: Causes and Responsibility

Variance	Possible Causes	Person Responsible
A. Labour Rate Variance	1. Use of non-standard grade employees, high grade workers, employing workers of different wage rates.	Foreman
	2. Overtime or shift work wages	Production or Sales Manager
	3. Changes in the basic work wages	Uncontrollable
	4. Use of a different method of wage payment e.g., payment of piece rate instead of time rate.	--Do
B. Labour Efficiency	1. Improper Supervision	Foreman
	2. Bad working conditions e.g., frequent break downs	Production/Personnel Manager
	3. Insufficient Training	Foreman
	4. Incorrect instructions and delay in briefing	--Do--
	5. Poor quality material	Purchase Manager
	6. Faulty Planning and Scheduling	Production Manager
	7. Change in the method of operation	Planning Engineer
	8. Incorrect booking of labour time	Personnel Manager
C. Idle Time	1. Machinery Breakdown	Maintenance Engineer
	2. Power failure	Electrical Engineer
	3. Shortage of materials	Purchase Manager

III. Overhead Cost Variance

Overhead Cost Variance can be classified into (a) Variable Overhead Cost Variance (b) Fixed Overhead Cost Variance.

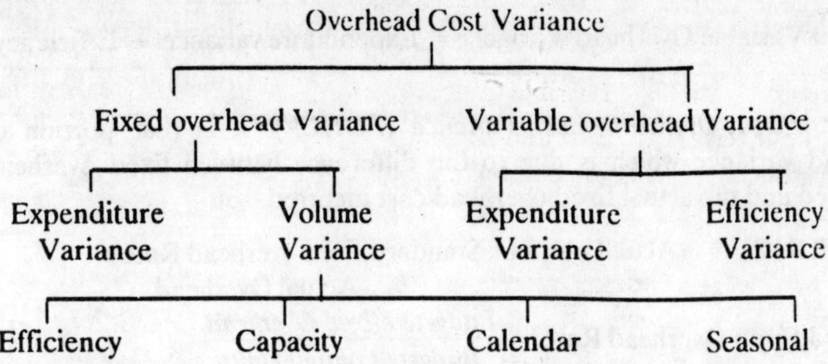

1. *Variable Overhead Variances*: They are caused by difference between the actual variable overhead expenditure incurred and the standard allowed.

VOHV = SOHC – AOHC

Variable Overhead Cost Variance = Standard variable overhead cost on actual output—Actual variable overhead cost

= (Actual Output x Standard Overhead Rate – Actual overhead

Standard Overhead Rate = $\frac{\textit{Budgeted Variable Overhead}}{\textit{Budgeted output in units}}$

Alternatively, the following variable overhead variances may be computed to make the position more clear:

(i) *Variable Overhead Expenditure Variance* (*VOHExV*) Cost This is the difference between the standard overhead allowed and the actual overhead incurred, for the actual time worked.

VOHExV = (Actual time worked) Standard Variable Overhead Rate – Actual Variable Overhead rate for the period

or Budgeted cost – Actual cost

(ii) *Variable Overhead Efficiency Variance* (*VOHEff. V*): This is the difference between standard variable overhead allowance of actual output, and the standard variable overhead of actual time.

VOHEfficiency Variance = Standard Overhead Rate (Actual time – Standard time for actual production)

Total Variable Overhead Variance = Expenditure variance + Efficiency variance

2. *Fixed Overhead Cost Variance (FOHCV)*: It is that portion of overhead variance which is due to the difference between fixed overhead recovered and the actual fixed overhead cost incurred.

FOHCV = (Actual output x Standard fixed overhead Rate)— Actual Overhead

$$\text{Standard Fixed Overhead Rate} = \frac{\textit{Budgeted fixed Overhead}}{\textit{Budgeted output Units}}$$

This variance is divided into (1) Fixed Overhead Expenditure Variance and (ii) Fixed Overhead Volume Variance.

(i) Fixed Overhead Expenditure Variance (FOHExCV): It is the difference between actual overhead expenditure and the budgeted expenditure.

FOHExV : = Budgeted Fixed Overhead - Actual Fixed Overhead
= (Standard Recovery Rate x Budgeted Production) — Actual Fixed Overheads

If the actual output is more than the budgeted output, it leads to over-recovery of overhead costs and a favourable variance results and vice versa. This variance is also known as Budget Variance or Cost Variance or Spending Variance.

(ii) Fixed Overhead Volume Variance (FOHVOV): It is the difference between the standard cost of overhead absorbed in actual output and the standard allowance allowed for that output. This variance is caused due to the difference between the budgeted output and the actual output.

FOHVV = Standard Fixed Overhead Rate (Actual Quantity — Budged Quantity)

or = Actual output x Standard Rate — Budged Fixed Overhead

If the actual output is more than the budgeted output, it leads to over-recovery of overhead costs and a favourable variance results and vice versa.

The Fixed Overhead Volume variance can further be analysed as under:

(a) Fixed Overhead Efficiency Variance (FOHEff. V): It is that portion of volume variance which is due to the difference between the budgeted

efficiency (in standard unit) and the actual efficiency achieved. This variance is like labour efficiency variance.

FOHEff. V = Standard Overhead Rate per unit (Actual Quantity — Standard Quantity)

When the actual output is more than the standard quantity of output, there would be excess recovery of fixed overheads and a favourable variance arises and vice versa.

(b) Fixed Overhead Capacity Variance (FOHCapV): It is that portion of volume variance which arises due to working higher or lower capacity usage than standard.

Capacity variance (in terms of output) = Standard Overhead Rate per unit x (Standard Quantity — Budgeted Quantity)

or = Fixed Overhead Standard Rate per Hour (Standard hours for the period — Actual Hours for the Period)

If standard overheads are more than the budgeted overheads, the variance is favourable and vice versa.

(c) *Calendar Variance:* It is the difference between the number of working days anticipated in the budgeted period and the actual working days in the budgeted period.

Calendar Variance (in Hours) = Standard Rate per Hour (Actual Hours-Budgeted Hours)

Calendar Variance (in Days) = Standard Cost of Fixed Overheads per Day (Actual Days - Budgeted Days)

If the actual days exceed the standard or the budgeted days, the variance is favourable and vice versa. It should however be noted that the sum of the calendar variances in the whole year would be zero.

(d) *Seasonal Variance:* A seasonal variance is that portion of the volume variance which is due to the difference between the seasonality of budgeted output and the average output on which standards have been calculated. If a complete year were taken as cycle, the sum of the variances over a complete year would be zero.

Overhead Cost Variances: Causes & Controllability

A.	Overhead Expenditure Variance	1.	Rate in Wages	Uncontrollable
		2.	Lack of control over Expenditure	Dept. Manager
		3.	Change in Production Method	Production Manager
		4.	Change in nature of service e.g., using gas in lieu of electricity	do
B.	Volume Variance	1.	Declining sales (Lack of orders) or customer demands	Sales Manager
		2.	Lack of proper supervision	Foreman
		3.	Defect in Machinery (breakdown)	Maintenance Engineer
		4.	Low efficiency of worker	Foreman/Personnel Manager
		5.	Poor quality material	Purchase Manager
		6.	Abnormal idle time (if not booked as part of time spent on jobs)	Foreman/ Uncontrollable
		7.	More or less working days/Calendar Variations (if using a standard month)	Uncontrollable
		8.	Strikes, absenteeism including lateness	Personnel Manager

Illustration 3

The Standard cost per unit for Product 'A' is as under --

Standard Cost	Rs.	The cost of operations to produce 1000 units during January 1994 is as under	Rs.
Materials per unit at Rs. 10	10	Material 950 units at Rs. 11	10,450
Labour 5 hours at Rs. 2	10	Labour 4,500 hours at Rs. 2.20	9,900
Overheads :		Overheads:	
Variable 5 hours at Rs. 2	10	Variable	11,000
Fixed 5 hours at Re.1	5	Fixed	6,500
Total cost per unit	35	Total cost of 1000 units of Product A	37,850

The flexible budget for this department for normal monthly activity was called for 6,000 direct labour hours of operation. At this level the fixed indirect cost was budgeted at Rs.6,000.

You are required to compute the various variances from the above information.

Solution

(i) Material cost variance = Standard cost for Actual output-- Actual cost of Actual Material used
= Rs. 10,000—Rs. 10,450 = Rs.450(A)

(ii) Material price variance = AQ (SP -- AP)
= 950 (10—11) = Rs. 950 (A)

(iii) Material usage variance = Standard Unit Price (SQ—AQ)
= Rs. 10(1,000—950) = Rs. 500 (F)

Varification :
Material cost variance = Material Price variance + Material usage variance
Rs. 450 (A) = Rs. 950 (A) + Rs. 500 (F)

(iv) Labour Cost Variance = SLC—ALC
= 5,000X Rs. 2—4,500 X Rs. 2.20
= Rs. 10,000—Rs. 9,900
= Rs. 100 (F)

(v) Labour Rate of Pay Variance = Actual Time (Standard Rate —Actual Rate)
= 4500 (2 — 2.20) = Rs. 900 (A)

(vi) Labour Efficiency Variance = Standard Rate (Standard Time — Actual Time)
= Rs. 2 (5,000—4,500)
= Rs. 1,000 (F)

Check : LCV = LRV + LEffV
Rs. 100 (F) = Rs. 900 (A) + Rs. 1,000 (F)

(vii) Total Overhead Cost Variance = (Actual Output x Standard Overhead Rate)—Overhead incurred
= (1,000 x 15) — 17,500
= Rs. 2,500 (A)

(viii) Variable Overhead Variance = (Actual Output x Standard Rate of Variable overhead) — Actual Variable overhead incurred
(1,000 x 10) — 11,000
= Rs. 1,000 (A)

(ix) Fixed Overhead Variance = (Actual Output x Standard Rate of fixed overheads) — Actual fixed overheads incurred
= (1,000 x 5) — 6,500
= Rs. 1,500 (A)

Proof:

Overhead Cost Variance = Variable overhead variance + Fixed overhead Variance

Rs. 2,500 (A) = Rs. 1,000 (A) + Rs. 1,500 (A)

IV. Sales Variance

The cost variance so far explained ultimately affects profit favourably or adversely. Budgeted profit may be affected due to increase or decrease (i) in the selling price and (ii) the quantum of sales. There are two distinct methods of computing and presenting sales variances: (i) Sales Value or Turnover Method and (ii) Sales Margin (Profit) Method. The first method shows the effect of variances in terms of turnover and the second shows the effect in terms of profits.

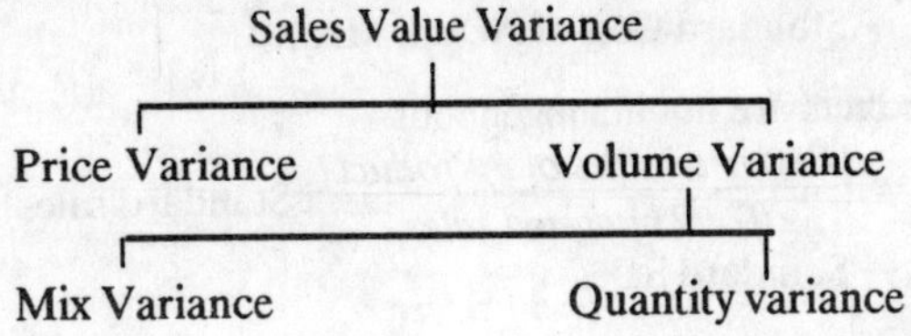

Sales Value Method

(i) **Sales Value Variance:** It is the difference between standard or budgeted sales and the actual sales.

Sales Value Variance = Standard Sales - Actual sales

Note : Standard Sales = Standard Price x Actual Quantities of sales.

If actual sales are more than the budgeted or standard sales, a favourable variance would result and vice versa.

(ii) **Sales Price Variance:** It is that portion of the sales value variance which is due to the difference between standard price specified and the actual price charged.

Sales Price Variance = Actual Quantity Sold (Standard Price — Actual Price)

(iii) **Sales Volume Variance** : This is the difference between the budgeted sales and the standard value of the actual mix of sales.

Sales Valume Variance = Actual Quantity Sold (Standard Quantity - Standard Quantity)

or = Budgeted Sales - Standard Sales

Note: Budgeted sales = Standard Selling Price x Budgeted or Standard Quantity of Sales.

If actual sales at standard price exceed the budgeted sales, there is a favourable variance and vice versa.

Thus, Sales Value variance = Price Variance + Volume Variance.

The Sales Volume variance can further be analysed into (a) Mix Variance and (b) Quantity Variance.

(a) **Sales Mix Variance**: It is that portion of the sales value variance which is due to the difference between the standard and the actual interrelationship of the quantities of each product or product group of which sales are composed, where products are homogeneous

Mix Variance ($\frac{\textit{Total Quantity of Actual Mix}}{\textit{Total Quantity of Standard Mix}}$ x Standard Cost of Standard Mix

— Standard Cost of Actual Mix.

Where the products are not homogeneous--

Mix Variance = ($\frac{\textit{Budgeted sales of a Product}}{\textit{Total budgeted sales}}$ x Standard sales)

— Standard Sales

Where the nature of product is not known--

Mix Variance = Standard Value of Actual Quantity at Standard Mix

-- Standard Value of Actual Mix.

(b) **Sales Quantity or Sub-Volume Variance:** This is the difference between the sales volume variance and the sales mix variance, arising purely due to difference in the quantity sold.

Quantity Variance = (Total Standard Quantity — Total Actual Quantity) X Total Standard Price Rate

Illustration 4

Standard sales 60,000 units @ Rs. 10 per unit = Rs. 6,00,000
Actual sales 1,00,000 units @ Rs. 9 per unit = Rs. 9,00,000
Calculate sales variances.

(i) Sales Value Variance = Actual sales value — Standard sales value

= Rs. 9,00,000 — Rs. 6,00,000

= Rs. 3,00,000 (F)

(ii) Sales Price Variance -- Actual Volume (Actual Price — Standard Price)

= 1,00,000 (Rs. 9 — Rs. 10)

= Rs. 1,00,000 (A)

(iii) Sales Volume Variance = Standard Price (Actual Sales — Standard Sales Volume)

= 10 (1,00,000 — 60,000)

= Rs. 4,00,000 (F)

Varification :

Sales Value Variance = Sales Volume Variance + Sales Price Variance

Rs. 3,00,000 (F) = Rs. 4,00,000 (F) — Rs. 1,00,000 (A)

Sales Margin or Profit Method

Total Sales Margin (Value) Variance: This is the difference between the actual margin from sales and budgeted margin.

Margin (Value) Variance = Budgeted Profit - Actual Profit

Sales Margin Price Variance: It is that portion of total margin variance which is due to the difference between the standard price of the quantity of the sales effected and the actual price of those sales.

Margin Price Variance = Actual Quantity of Sales x Standard price - Actual Quantity of Sales x Actual Price

or Standard Profit - Actual Profit.

Sales Margin Volume Variance: It is that portion of total margin Variance which is due to the difference between the budgeted quantity and the actual quantity of sales.

Margin Volume Variance = Standard Margin per Unit (Budgeted Units - Actual Units sold)

Sales Margin Mix Variance: This is that portion of the sales margin variance which is due to the difference between the budgeted and actual quantities of each product of which the sale mixture is composed, valuing sales at the standard net selling price and cost of sales at standard.

Margin Mix Variance = Standard Margin (Standard proportion of Mix - Actual Mix)

Sales Margin Quantity Variance: This is the difference between sales sales margin volume variance and sales margin mix variance.

Margin Quantity Variance = Standard Margin Rate (Standard Quantity - Actual Quantity)

Sales Margin Variance Due to Sales Allowance: It is that portion of total margin variance which is due to the difference between the budgeted rebates, discounts, etc., allowed on those sales.

Profit (or Loss) Variance: It is the difference between the budgeted profit (or loss) and the actual profit (or loss).

Sales Variances : Causes & Controllability

A. Sales Price Variance	1.	Unexpected Competition	Uncontrollable
	2.	Rise in general price level	-Do-
	3.	Poor quality of material	-Do-
B. Sales Volume Variance	1.	Unexpected competition	Uncontrollable
	2.	Ineffective Sales Promotion	Publicity Manager
	3.	Ineffective supervision and control of salesman	Sales Manager

Control of Variances

After the variances have been analysed, the management shall be reported as to the extent of favourable and unfavourable variances due to various causes. Cost reports presented to management would clearly indicate where the scope for action lies. The causes of variance should be disclosed in the reports to the management. Management would take corrective action so as to control the adverse variances. Responsibility should be assigned to persons concerned in case of adverse variances resulting because of factors which were within the control of the business. The factors like changes in the market conditions, demand and supply position etc., are beyond the reach of management and hence responsibility cannot be placed for such uncontrollable factors. The management would try to bring down the actual costs to the level of standard cost and will apply a system of strict inspection and supervision for effecting cost control. In case of controllable factors, the responsibility can be assigned to the different departments for different reasons of variances.

Variances	The department to be held responsible
Materials	
Price	Purchasing Department
Usage	Stores, Purchase/Process as the case may be
Wastage, scrap, spoilage	Production Deptt.
Wages	
Rate	Personnel Deptt.
Time-lack of proper supervision	Production Deptt.

Overheads	
Volume	Sales Deptt.
Efficiency	Production Deptt.
Expenses	
Higher rate of indirect workers	Personnel Deptt.
Higher prices of indirect material	Purchasing Deptt.
Higher consumption of indirect material	Production Deptt.
Excessive expenditure in factory	Production Deptt.
Excessive expenditure for selling & distribution	Selling Deptt.
Sales	
Price & Volume	Selling Deptt.

In order to keep the variances at the minimum it is necessary to fix the standards carefully and after scrutinising all aspects of the problem throughly. Standards should be reliable. Should make due allowance for incidental expenses, change in market situation, possible losses, wastages, scrap or spoilage in materials, labour waste, administration waste, changes in managerial policy etc. As far as possible corrective action should be taken promptly and immediately, whenever, during the period any variation is located. The trend in prices and changes in production should be duly accounted for. Moreover, standards might have to be revised from time to time in view of the changed circumstances.

Variance analysis, in itself, would not help in achieving the objective of minimising cost unless managerial action is prompt and in the right direction. The direction, of course, shall be indicated by the analysis of variances but it is the executive side which would be responsible for taking immediate action, exercising proper control, having a close watch over operations etc., so that economies may be effected, inefficiencies minimised and performance improved. A continuous and rigorous effort in the direction of cost control would help the management to have th goal of standard costing achieved.

The direction along with their causes should be reported to the management regularly and at the opportune time so that corrective action can be taken immediately. The person or department may be held responsible for any adverse variations after duly accounting to it. The information as to the profit earned by the business is presented through a simple Profit and Loss Account where a system of historical costing is prevalent. But when a system of standard costing is in operation, the information about the standards, the actual and the variances, along with their causes should be depicted through a statement, so that the management may be able to take quick action in respect of any inefficiencies revealed. After the statement in the report to be submitted to the management, certain notes may be appended to explain the causes for the variances. Particularly, since the rule of management by exception, is followed, greater attention is drawn in the report towards the adverse variations i.e., the reason for the failures or unsuccesses are highlighted in particular along with the comments on overall performance in general.

Disposal of Variances

There is difference of opinion among accountants as regards disposal of cost variance. However, the following methods are usually used to close the standard cost variances: (i) Transfer to Profit and Loss Account; (ii) Allocation to Finished Stock, Work in Progress, and cost of sales; (iii) Transfer to Reserves Account i.e., to carry forward to the next financial year and to be set off in the subsequent year or years.

The standard costs are also incorporated in the accounting system so as to increase its statistical utility. The following are the methods used for accounting based on standard costing: (i) Partial Plan Method, (ii) Single Plan Method, and (iii) Dual Plan Method.

REVIEW QUESTIONS

1. (a) Define Standard cost, standard costing and cost standard.
   (b) In which type of industries standard costing is employed?
   (c) Consider the three broad categories of the word 'Standard' as applied to standard costing.
   (d) What are the techniques of standard costing?
   (e) How is a standard fixed?
   (f) What is a standard cost card? State the uses of such a card?
   (g) Explain the terms 'variance' and 'variance analysis'
   (h) Draw up a variance analysis chart.
   (i) What purpose do the variance reports serve?
   (j) What are the causes for material cost variance?
   (k) State the causes for labour cost variance.
   (l) Summarise the causes giving rise to labour efficiency.
2. (i) State the advantages of standard costing.
   (ii) What are the major limitations of standard costing system?
   (iii) State the main differences between standard costs and budgetary control.
   (iv) What are the various circumstances in which material price and usage variances are likely to arise?

19

Responsibility Centres and Divisional Control

Responsibility Accounting: The cornerstone of every management control system is the concpt of responsibility acccounting. Each manager of a company has responsibility for part of the total activity. Thus organisation can be viewed as a collection of different responsibility centres, each headed by a manager who is responsible for the achievement of the goal assigned to him, which in turn will help for the achievement of the overall goal of the organisation. The planning identifies the desired performance of each responsibility centre, shows the inter- relationships among units and controls/ aids in the successful implementation of the plan for each centre. Hence the accounting system sholud be designed in such a way that a manager is responsible for and thus helps in the process of appraisal of each responsibility centre.

In spite of several drawbacks, both objectives and results of actions of each responsibility centre are measured in financial terms. Responsibility accounting tries to develop suitable methods to measure the performance of each responsibility centre taking into account the authority and responsibility enjoyed by each of them. Thus one single method cannot be used simultaneously to measure them while their decision making authority varies.

Concept of Responsibility Accounting ; Responsibility accounting is a system of control by delegating and locating the responsibility for costs. It is similar to any other system of cost such as standard costing or budgetary control but with greater emphasis towards fixing of the responsibility of the person entrusted with the execution of specific job. It is not probably understood to be a separate accounting like financial or costing system. It is neither a substitute for the traditional cost accounting nor it involves a drastic change in accounting theory and practice. It is only a system of control by delegation and location of responsibility for costs; its essence is to provide the right information to the right people at the right time.

Responsibility accounting measures both inputs of the responsibility centres in monetary terms wherever possible. The input is termed as the "cost" while the output is termed as "revenue" of the resposibility centre. However, where montary measurement of output is not possible (e.g., services rendered by the accounting department to the organisation), it may be measured in terms of total cost of goods and srevice transferred or number of units of output.

Steps for Control through Responsibility Accounting

Follwoing steps are necessary to effect control through the Responsibility Accounting:

(a) Plan the whole activity of the responsibility area;

(b) Set up budgets, standards, and estimates for the execution of the plan (with the realistic targets),

(c) Divide the plan into self-contained units and allocate them to the responsibility centres, with the detailed instruction necessary for correct execution;

(d) Evaluate the actual performance of each responsibility centre and compare the actual results with the budgeted estimates or the standards set, and to work out the variances;

(e) Analyse the variances, fix up responsibility for the variances upon the responsibility centres, and take corrective measures.

The personal factor in responsibility accounting is most important. The management may prepare the best plan or the budget and put before its staff, but its success depends upon the initiative and the will of the workers to execute it. In order to implement this system of accounting/reporting, it is necessary that

(i) the palns should be prepared in consultation with the persons responsible for it;

(ii) the targets fixed should be precise, clear and realistic;

(iii) the plans and their method of execution should be made clear to staff;

(vi) the staff should be trained properly in the work required of them; and

(v) due incentives and encoragements should be provided to the persons working well. In other words, there should be a system of reward or executive compensation to provide incentives for the executives to attain higher levels of performance.

Responsibility Centres

Responsibility accounting focuses attention on responsibility centres. Responsibility Centre (also known as Responsibility Unit or Control Centre) refers to any organisational unit that is headed by a responsible person. It is the segment of business with reference to which information will be communicated to pinpoint responsibilities. Taking the heirarchy as the basis of defining the responsibility unit there can be six levels of responsibilities, viz., 'the worker,' 'a group of workers,' 'the department' and 'the plant' (or the factory as the case may be), 'the division', and 'the Company or Corporation'. Targets for the various responsibility centres may be evolved keeping in view the overall objectives of the business. The process of evolution of targets involves participation of the responsible executives in the process.

The Principal Types of Financial Responsibility: Responsibility Centres may be divided into for categories: (i) Expense Centres, (ii) Revenue Centres, (iii) Profit Centres and (iv) Investment Centres or Asset Centres. In responsibility centres the targets may be in terms of cost, cost and revenue or even assets; in certain responsibility centres, the output may be in physical terms instead of values. All the more, they are also responsibility centres.

The Management Control Structure

Responsibility Accounting for Divisional Performance

Responsibility Centres

Expense Centre Revenue Centre Profit Centre Investment Centre

Expense Centres: Expense Centres also known discretionary expense centres can be formed by dividirg the whole organisation in to a number of divisions for whom a standard amount of expense to be incurred is predetermind and the performance of each is appraised by comparing the actual amount with the standard amount. Each division is recognised as an expense centre. It is also sometimes termed as the cost centre. Certain activities such as legal department, personnel department (i.e., Service functions) can only be cost centres because it is neither possible nor necessary to measure the output in terms of monetary units. This approach emphasises that the performance of certain division should be measured against specific cost standards.

The term 'cost centre' is also used in responsibility accouting approach. In cost accounting parlance, a 'cost centre' is a location, person or item of equipment (or group of these) for which costs may be ascertained and used for purposes of cost control. A responsibility centre is essentially a personalised concept, whereas cost centres are frequently impersonal. For example, the machine shop of an engineering company is composed of several cost centres, milling machines, turret lathes, auto- meter, etc but it is the whole shop that is under the authority of the foreman. This is the responsibility centre. Thus cost centre is used as a means of assembling items of cost, so that they can be assigned to goods and services. Thus, emphasis in case of cost centre is more on the jobs, products or processes whose cost are to be ascertained rather than on persons who may be managing them. On the other hand, responsibility centres are formed on the basis of responsibility delegated to responsible members of the organisation with a view to identify cost which can be controlled by each one of them for facilitating working of management control process. Of course, sometimes, cost centres are also used as responsibility centres but they are merely a means to an end.

Revenue Centre: A revenue centre is primarily responsible for marketing or selling products or services eg, a given sales territory or geographical division. The primary responsibility of the centre's manager would be to raise revenue through sales. Administrative selling could also be involved. However, such cost would be secondary, and would normally be expected to occur in proportion to revenue.

Profit Centre: The entire organisation is divided into a number of divisions and each division is treated as a profit centre. It is responsible for generating a specified quantum of profits from its activities. The performance of each division being judged in terms of both the income that is earned and costs that are incurred. It is an important system of control in large undertakings where each divisional manager is given a profit objective and the performance is measured accordingly. It is also sometimes termed as the 'Contribution Centre' or 'Financial Performance Centre.' In non-profit organisation, the term 'revenue centre' is used in the place of profit centre. Thus the profit centre approach emphasises that the performance of certain divisions should be measured against specified profit target.

A profit centre is an entity for accounting and control purposes that is responsible for a particular group of products and all revenue and most or all expenses associated with these products. Profit Centres may be a division of a large firm that are separately incorporated, and have their own 'book' and financial statement. Profit centres are essentially established for one of three reasons:

1. Cost-benefit decisions and trade-offs are delegated to manager close to the sources of necessary information. These managers can often make better decisions than their superiors, who are more remote from necessary information sources.

2. It is believed that manager will do a better job (be more highly motivated) if they can identify their own personal business, and that there

will be a greater goal congruence with the profit objectives of top management.

3. A profit centre will provide good experience and act as a training ground for future top management.

The output of a responsibility centre may either be meant for internal consumption or for outside customers. In the latter case the revenue is realised when the sales are made. However, in case of internal transfers, responsibility centre is a profit centre only when the management decides to measures its output in monetary terms. For example, in case of a process industry the output of one process/division may be transferred as raw material (input) for another process/division at a price called 'transfer price'. Transfer Pricing is the notional price at which the output of one department in a factory is transferred to another. This facilitates the preparation of separate departmental profit and loss account. It should be clearly understood that such internal transfers do not increase the company's assets but definitely help sometimes in the management control process*.

Prerequisites for the Successful Implementation of the Profit Centre System

(i) **Sound System of Transfer-Prices**: When one division takes the goods or services of another division, the goods or services of the latter division must be transferred to the former at a price. Transfer prices should be fair to both divisions. That is, a price must be determined to use as a basis of assigning a cost to the division acquiring the goods or services. Likewise, a price must be used as the basis for reporting the revenue of the division selling the goods or service.

(ii) **Independence to the Divisional Manager:** If the manager of a profit centre has little authority to decide on the quality and quantity of its output or on the relation of output to costs then a profit centre is usually of little use as a control device. This does not imply that the manger of a profit centre must have complete control over output and inputs, for few, if any managers have such complete authority. Some authorities insist that the divisional manager should have the liberty to buy it from another division of the company or from the open market.

(iii) **Existence of Market:** There must exist a market for the goods/services rendered by one division to another. If identifcal products are not available, at least, substitutes must be available. The market must be fairly stable and reliable.

* For more details read Chapter 20

(iv) **Negotiation by Divisional Managers:** Divisional Managers must be allowed to freely negotiate and bargain among themselves. Usually, the purchasing division is interested in maximising the transfer prices.

(v) **Uniform System of Accounting:** There should be fool proof and uniform system of accounting to measure the profits. Realistic standards of profits and profitability should be evolved to compare against actuals.

(vi) **Arbitration to Settle Disputes:** There must be some institutional arrangement to settle disputes relating to transfer prices. An official arbitrator may be appointed.

(vii) **Free Service must be furnished, if required:** When top management requires the responsibility centre to use a certain service furnished by another responsibility centre within the company, the service probably should be furnished at no charge, and the service unit, therefore, should not be a profit centre. For example, if the top management requires the internal audits be made, the responsibility centres probably should not be asked to pay for the cost of the internal auditing, and the internal auditing unit should therefore not a profit centre.

(viii) **Adequate Understanding of the Management Job:** To the extent that a profit centre puts a manager business for the himself, it promotes a spirit of competition In many situations competition provides a powerful incentive for good management. In other situations, however, organisation units should cooperate closely with one another. In these situations the profit centre device may generate excessive friction between profit centre to the detriment of the whole company's welfare. Also it may generate too much interest in short run profits deterimental to the long-run results. These difficulties are likely to arise when managers have an inadequate understanding of the management job, and the problems often can be overcome by education. If however they can not be overcome, the profit centre technique should not be used.

(ix) **Organisational Requirements:** The Organisation requirements are : (a) A well-knit organisation chart delineating clearly the levels of authority and responsibility; (b) A sound and prompt system of information and reporting i.e., an effective Management Information System to take care of both collection of data ad presentation of analysis. (c) Preferably a low rate 'employee turnover' and not too frequent transfers of staff, at least at responsibility levels.

(x) **Implementation in Phases:** Though the profit-centre concept has got a very wide purview, still its implementation should be taken up in phases, initially with one functional area, preferably marketing. The

Budgeting and Budget revision mechanism should be geared towards the profit-centrewise requirements This would obviate the need for subsequent arbitary break-up of all relevant Budget figures.

The important advantages attached to the concept are : (i) profitability is the simplest way of analysing the effectiveness of a segment of a complex business and (ii) Managers understand pretty well what profit is and aggressive managers always welcome the opportunity of having their performance measured by real entrepreneurial yardstick.

Mechanics of setting up Profit Centre Controls

A Profit Centre is defined as any service, any product, or any family of products and services which generates profits. The steps involved in setting up your profit centre controls are:

1. Assign one person as each profit centre manager. This individual has both the responsibility and the authority to maximise the profits of his centre. This manager should be a "bulck stops here" type of guy.

2. Segment your company into its cash producing components (profit centres) and treat each centre as a separate division or company. Each centre must have its own set of books to which its manager must answer.

3. Utilise simple accounting for each centre by divorcing all ledgers over which the profit centre manager has no controls. In this step you are breaking out all overhead, G & A, facilities, support staffs, service staff, taxes, and that capital equipment shared by more than one single profit centre. This action forces all overhead people to be evaluated alone.

4. Divide each profit centre's materials and production stages into their smallest increments. Give each increment full ledger status. In other words, if your profit centre has four production stations, one QA station, and is made up of six parts, then this profit centre has 11 ledgers for these 11 items.

5. Introduce a ledger linkage system which will allow your accountants to combine ledgers of identical items used by the various profit centres. This linkage will allow your purchasing department to combine identical items for quantity discounts, it will allow your administration to optimise manpower loading, it will allow your production people to more efficiently schedule work stations and inventory, and it will allow your sales people to priority key customers' deliveries.

6. Establish a security system which willl allow information to disseminate to all levels on a need-to-know basis. The usual security sytem is to classify each ledger on a 1-to1- basis.

7. Develop a reliable system in which all "input" informatin flows from the groups to accounting and all "output" information flows from accounting back to the groups. There are probably a dozen different ways that you can accomplish this, however you'll be wise to make it accounting's responsibility to make whatever way you select work.

8. Decide what kind of information you want from accounting. Feel free to dictate the formats and leave ample space for reader notes. You'll observe that your accounting reports will gather all kinds of scribbled notes and be sent back and forth in place of typed memos.

9. Determine the frequencies for each report. Some marketing, inventory, production, purchasing, and administration reports may be generated on almost a daily basis, whereas some financial reports may be needed only on a monthly or quarterly basis.

10. Establish your management-by-exceptions flags and make certain that they are reliably tripped, your exceptions reports will then become the backbone of your operation's management.

11. Implement your reward/punishment incentives into this accounting system so that it will reliably disburse both rewards and punishments.

12. Since all past information is developed from actual expenses and payments, your ledgers already handle this aspect. However, since your proforma (projected) management information comes from both back orders and sales forecasts and the floating budgets to satisfy these predicted sales, both your marketing and accounting groups must work well together. Your short-range sales forecasts should be within + 10% your mid-range forecasts should be within + 20% and your long-range forecasts should be within + 30%. Implement the forecasting systems which will give you these reliabilities.

13. Establish a floating budget for each group. The budget varies both upwards and downwards with sales. Establish your lead/lag time periods with this floating concept.

14. Determine what percentage of profits of each profit centre will flow into the company treasury. Deduct this percentage plus the cost of sales percentages from the selling price and that is the value at which each profit centre must sell the product or service to your company. This value minus the

costs of producing the product is the profit the centre realises. This can be divided amongst the company and the centre's team.

15. Establish a series of mini-reserves and allow the proper level manager authority to release funds from these reserves. If "front money" is necessary to test a production cost savings idea, then the profit centre managers and the production manager can withdraw funds from their respective reserves to determine the viability of the idea.

16. Agree to perform both periodic and random audits of this system. Though profit centre controls have dozens of built-in checks and balances that make the systems hard to beat, it should be policed by audits. Your accounting group can perform the periodic audits, however consider bringing in an outside Chartered Accountant for the random audits so that everyone is kept honest.

17. You have now developed a flexible system that restricts no one from performing company business. Therefore, there is no reason for anyone to try to disguise, pad, end run, shoot, or buck pass the system. Make it a well published company policy of how you'll deal with those who do attempt to violate your system.

Investment Centre

Profit centres, by definition, are really not quite like independent firms. Profit centres do not incorporate allocation of invested capital and appropriate cost of such capital. Where the profit-centre concept for control purposes is extended to include such items, the result is known as an investment centre. Investment centres may be thought of as profit centres with the addition of an asset base. Investment centre is the ultimate extension of the responsibility idea. It is a centre in which the head of the centre is held responsible for the use of the assets as well as revenues and expenses. In other words, he is expected to earn a satisfactory return on the assets employed in his responsibility centre. However, the selection of the appropriate asset base can present difficulties.

Three fundamental question must be resolved in arriving at an asset base appropriate for a particular investment centre:

(a) Which assets should be included?
(directly identifiable non-monetary assets or productive assets)

(b) How should the assets selected be measured? (book value or replacement cost or original cost)

(c) Should the base be assets or net assets?
(owner's investments/assets employed) (assets-liabilities)

Essentially, the issue of which assets should be included involves the choice between all assets directly and indirectly involved in the investment centre's activities and only those productive assets that are currently in use. Firms that establish investment centres for control purposes rarely decentralise the management of cash, receivables and marketable securities Also, certain fixed capacity assets may be commonly or jointly used with other investment centres, and therefore, not really be controllable.

Responsibility Accounting for Service Centres

It is apparent from the above discussion that a responsibility unit can be planned and controlled as a cost, revenue profit, investment centre, depending on the scope of decision making authority delegated to the unit. This range of authority is the most important factor in the choice of a monetary performance measurement. Cost, revenue profit and investment centres usually coincide with the allocation of authority for decisions over cost, revenues and investment respectively. The purpose is to explore the possibility of treating service departments as profit centres and hence to measure the performance of these units on the basis of profit, which are otherwise generally being treated as cost centres and evaluated on the basis of how well it succeeds in keeping down the cost.

Service activities difffer from regular activities in that they provide services to other segments rather than sell their services or products on the market. As the products or services of the service departments are not generally sold in the market - rather they are being consumed by other segments of the organisation - the scope of adjusting cost and revenue to determine profit and to treat it as a profit centre is limited. On the other hand, different regular products which are generally being traded in the market are considered as separate unit having profit responsibility. It is suggested that this difference is to be ignored, and the service departments are to be considered as profit centres whenever possible, like any productive segment.

It may well be argued the utility of measuring the perfromance of a service department on the basis of profit. The answer is obvious. Firstly, profit is the most objective basis for measuring theperformance of any manager and profit responsibility is a powerful motivator of man. Managers understand what profit is all about, and aggressive managers welcome the opportunity to have their abilities measured by the only real entrepreneurial yardstick. Secondly, income is the prime motivating factor of running a business and it is assumed that the income is generated by the continuous operation of the total firm. Hence every attempt is to be made to assess the contribution of each segment to the overall profit objective of the firm and to determine the centre where from income generates. Economicaly and practically speaking, refraining from spending effect, the firms income just as does additional rvenue. Thus, saving Rs. 1,00,000 (net of cost) in producing in plant electricity is equivalent to a gain of Rs. 1,00,000 (revenue minus cost) from an increase in sales volume of some other product. This will increase profit consciousness of the service department manager.

Thirdly, it is not a very impractical suggerstion. As a matter of fact, it is easy to find many independent business concerns which sell only services as, for example, electricity, transportation, legal asistance, cleaning or research. Applying the same logic, an organisation can treat us service department as a profit centre, which are "selling" their services to other productive department of an organisation. In this circumstances, a steel mill producing electricity instead of purchasing it can be considered as an integrated firm incorporating two kinds of businesss - steel and electricity; a dairy firm can be considered as integrating milk and butter production and transportation services and so on.

Lastly, the reports thus produced can be analysed to discover the locations where income is generated. Consider, for example, a profitable mining concern which uses trucks to a large extent for hauling ore. Trucks may be considered as a profit centre instead of a service centre. Suppose the report indicates that the mining activity has a loss and the truck activity has profits. This is important information as to whether there is a readily available opportunity to render trucking services outside the firm or not. This information should initiate an analysis of the reasons for the inefficient mining operations and a search for a market for the efficient trucking operations - for either, substituting for the ore hauling for expanding the trucking operations.

Thus, it is suggested that the service departments whenever possible are to be considered as profit centres instead of cost centres. Under the present accounting practices, it is assumed that the service department "sells" its services at a predetermined standard price. This procedure implies that if costs are kept down, "profit" will emerge. Under conventional standard cost accounting, the "profits" are termed as favourable variance. When the standard price is based on market price or even on a pseudo market price, there is no material difference between two centres.

When there is market for the service, there is no problem in assigning transfer prices and considering the service activity as a profit centre. When a regular market does not exist, management can search for a market and market price. For example, a firm may be quite successful in arriving at market prices for its service centres by soliciting bids. To make the bids real rather than fictitious, management may accept some of them to substitute for those jobs which the firm might conduct ineffciently. When there is no market for the service, a pseudo market price might be used. One of the important uses of pseudo market price is to price non-marketable services.

Though the suggestion prescribed above may sound well, problems associated with it cannot be undermined, specially, arriving at market price for some of the services as very difficult because of its peculiar nature, such as research and development. Though there are difficulties. it is strongly believed that these difficulties are technically feasible to solve. Extensive research of this type is currently taking place among economists, accountants, management scientists and other disciplines such that the resulting capability in this area is growing at a rapid rate. A meaningful transfer pricing system can be developed for some of the service departments because of its peculiar nature but for the time being, these areas can be treated as cost centres.

Advantages of Responsibility Accounting

(a) Responsibility accounting is an effective tool of cost control and cost reduction applied with budgetary control and standard costing.

(b) Accounting information provided by the system of responsibility accounting is used by the top management as an aid in planning and controlling the activities of responsibility centres and in motivating the persons responsible for carrying out these activities.

(c) It facilitates the fixing of divisional responsibilities.

(d) It assists in the evaluation of performance job wise and total monthly and annual performance. It permits an objective evaluation of the performance of individual managers / divisions.

REVIEW QUESTIONS

1. Define 'Responsibility Accounting'
2. Define the term 'Responsibility Unit'.
3. Distinguish between Cost Centre and Expense Centre.
4. What do you understand by 'Investment Centre?
5. What is a Profit Centre? State the prerequisites for the successful implementation of the profit centre system.
6. Explain the mechanics of setting up Profit Centre Control.
7. What are the advantages of Responsibility Accounting?

20
Transfer Pricing and Management Control

As pointed out in the previous chapter one of the principal problems in operating a profit centre system is to devise a satisfactory method of accounting for the transfer of goods and services from one profit centre to another. Since in most companies there are significant amounts of intracompany transactions, this problem is a common one. In this chapter we discuss various approaches to arriving at transfer prices for transactions between profit centres and the system of negotiation and arbitration that is essential when transfer prices are used.

Objectives of Transfer Prices : A sound transfer price system should accomplish the following objectives :

1. **Divisional Autonomy :** It should motivate the division manager to make sound decisions, and it should communicate information that provides a reliable basis for such decisions. This will happen when actions that the division manager takes to improve the reported profit of his division also improves the profit of the company as a whole.
2. **Divisional Performance Appraisal :** It should result in a report of divisional profits that is a reasonable measure of the economic performance of the division.
3. **Goal Congruence :** The prices should be set so that the divisional management's desire to maximise divisional earnings is consistent with the objectives of the company as a whole. The transfer prices should not encourage sub-optimal decision-making.

These objectives cannot be achieved perfectly. In striving to increase the profits of his division, the division manager may make decisions that hurt the profits of other divisions and thus hurt the company as a whole; the transfer price system can minimise, but it probably cannot eliminate, this tendency. Up to a point, the system should motivate division managers to act as if they were the heads of independent companies; but division managers must, beyond this point, act for the good of the corporation as a whole, even at the expense of the reported profitability of their own divisions.

Issues in Transfer Pricing

Establishing a theoretical frame-work for equitable transfer prices is not an impossible task. However, at the operational level, the subject matter has varied ramifications and for want of clear guidance and timely decisions on behalf of the management, transfer prices become a source of seemingly interminable conflicts among divisional managers at the cost of corporate interests.

Transfer prices measure exchange of products and services between responsibility centres within a company. They could cover pricing of (i) service rendered by service departments to user departments, (ii) transactions between divisions entrusted with profit responsibility, (iii) transactions between legally independent organisations but under the same management, and (iv) under bilateral monopolistic conditions.

When profits are used as a measure of divisional performance, the concept of transfer pricing is conducive to the promotion of goal congruence. If the corporate management can establish profit centre concept by assignment of responsibility for cost and revenue, and a transfer price can be established which, given a volume of sales, would cause a divisional manager to make the same decision that would be made by the top management, it can delegate unlimited authority to divisional managers whether they purchase or sell, within or outside the organisation.

Usefulness of Transfer Pricing : The concept of transfer pricing could be used to : (i) identify unit contribution to the total profit, (ii) encourage profit consciousness, (iii) measure management performance, (iv) maximise operating unit profitability, (v) locate profits to minimise tax, (vi) facilitate decentralised decision making, (vii) motivate divisional managers, towards goal congruence, and (viii) serve as a tool for control.

It has disadvantages too, namely. (i) unit managers tend to prefer divisional profits over corporate, (ii) lengthy disagreements on prices, (iii) extra administrative costs, (iv) need for conventions, if no market prices are available, (v) arguments over disposition of variances, (vi) prices to minimise tax liabiliies, and (vii) task of eliminating book profits arising from interdivisional profits.

Organisational framework : There is no one method of arriving at transfer prices which could be considered as ideal in all circumstances. As a matter of fact a form of transfer pricing suitable under one situation may cause difficulties under another. A study of the nature of industry, organisation structure, its culture, degree of centralisation etc., would be helpful before an attempt is made to arrive at a suitable basis for determining transfer prices. When evolving procedure for determining transfer prices, factors which could be considered are (i) the role of the corporate office and if the prices will be centrally administered, (ii) the extent of **internal negotiations**, (iii) accountants' role and (iv) whether the prices will be related to costs or derived from selling prices.

The company's organisational structure would be quite relevant. When considering the same, the following will have to be considered : (a) nature of industry and size of operations, (b) extent of vertical and leteral integration, (c) extent of decentralisation, and (d) objectives before the management.

Other significant aspects that need to be considered are :

1. Sourcing decisions : Both the divisions, viz., buying and selling, can take sourcing decisions independently on their own; they cannot take such decisions, and only some of the divisions can take such decisions.

2. Manufacturing processes : (a) Mass, batch or unit, (b) for stock or against specific orders, and (c) whether raw material, intermediate or and products.

3. Market situation : (a) Buyer's Vs. seller's market, (b) if market price is readily available, and (c) extent and nature of competition.

4. Control exercised by the centre would cover areas such as : (a) sourcing, (b) pricing, (c) profitability, (d) return on investment, (e) cost performance, (f) approval of unit budget, (g) cash flow, (h) approval of capital expenditure,(i) turnover and, (j) market share.

Types of Transfer Prices

1. Market Based Transfer Price : In a competitive situation, transfer prices are more likely to be related to selling prices. But complications set in because a perfectly competitive situation is largely a theoretical assumption of economists which is rarely found in existence in reality. The problem areas arising from the use of market prices for determining transfer prices are : fluctuating prices, different markets, product differentiation, varying level of quality and service and extra features.

The **advantages** of using selling prices for determining transfer prices are : i) divisional managers are assured of independence in respect of sourcing decisions, ii) market prices represent true opportunity costs, and iii) they provide incentive for efficient production because excessive cost cannot be passed on to the buyers.

The **disadvantages are :** (i) it can be applied only to fairly standard products under stable market conditions, (ii) it breaks down when there is excess capacity, (iii) low initial prices are often quoted to get a foothold in the market and (iv) there are problems of quality differentials between outsider's products and the company's own standards.

2. Cost Based Transfer Price : The concept of cost is subject to varied interpretations. In the process, the basic assumptions and sometimes, even the arithmetic of it get challenged. Various alternatives are, namely, variable cost;

direct cost; full cost; full cost plus profit; two part consisting of standard variable cost to manufacture plus lump sum share of fixed manufacturing cost; three part which consists of two parts as above plus a charge to cover return on capital employed.

Problem areas when using costs as a basis for transfer pricing could be broadly covered under materials and labour and overheads :

Materials : (a) Purchase costs could vary from consignment to consignment. (b) One could dispute the percentage to be added on account of manufacturing losses. (c) One has to decide if abnormal losses have to be provided. (d) Control prices Vs. market prices. (e) FIFO, LIFO, average or derived from specific consignment .

Labour and Overheads : The following are areas which could lead to disputes : (a) Level of activity to be adopted. (b) Efficiency variables. (c) Abnormal items. (d) Basis of overhead allocations. (e). Expenditure incurred to derive long term benefits. (f) Varying capacity utilisation each year and impact thereof on overhead allocation. (g) Share of R & D and corporate office expenses.

3. **Negotiated Transfer Prices :** In theory, a transfer price based on negotiations between buying and selling divisions would be more acceptable. This presupposes that the divisional managers and those who are involved in determining transfer prices have adequate information and market situation and product costs. This will enable them to arrive at transfer prices which are fair to both the parties. In practice, negotiations do not always result in harmonious relations as they should because of varying positions of strengths, unresolved conflicts and cases going by default for either lack of information or bad presentation of one's case.

Transfer pricing problems in the Public Sector

Of late, public sector industries are also charged with the task of earning adequate return on capital. There is renewed emphasis on decentralisation setting targets and management by objectives. Transfer pricing will, therefore, be not unique to industries in the private sector. However, there are some problems peculiar to the public sector such as (i). social objectives vs. profit objectives. (ii) divisional managers do not have full control over his resources and (iii) large turnover of divisional managers.

International trade : With liberal cash incentives available on exports and complicated tax laws, transfer pricing has special relevance in the export trade. Some of the areas that need to be looked into are : utilisation of spare capacity, tax implications, and taking full advantage of various government concessions.

Behavioural aspects : The problems associated with transfer prices have outgrown the field of accountants. Management specialists and behavioural scientists are now equally interested in the subject. Problem situation arise from weak leadership, lack of relevant information and cost data and lack of confidence. There could be no formal or informal agency to resolve conflict situations and where it is in existence their interventation could be irregular and extent of their effectiveness doubtful. There could also be no regular review of existing transfer prices and systematic revision. For this, issues such as how often, to what extent and timings have to be decided.

Transfer prices is a management tool besides being an instrument of accountants. Its effectiveness depends upon how well it is structural and used. It calls for clear divisional objectives, an operational manual which is revised regularly, institutionalised mechanism to resolve conflict situations, and regular review of transfer prices.

Illustration 1

Your Co. fixes the inter-divisional transfer prices for its products on the basis of cost plus a return on investment in the division. The budget for division A for 1994-95 appears as under :

Investment in Division 'A' :

	Rs.
Fixed Assets	5,00,000
Current Assets	3,00,000
Debtors	2,00,000
Annual Fixed cost of the Division	8,00,000
Variable cost per Unit of Product	10

Budgeted volume - 4,00,000 units per year

Desired ROI - 28%

Determine the transfer price for Division 'A'.

Solution

Investment in Division :

	Rs.
Fixed Assets, Current Assets & Debtors	10,00,000
Desired return on investment (ROI) 28% on 10,00,000 =	2,80,000
Variable cost 4,00,000 x 10 =	40,00,000
Annual fixed cost of the Divn. A	8,00,000
Total cost :	48,00,000
Add return on investment	2,80,000
	50,80,000

$$\text{Inter-Divisional transfer price} = \frac{50{,}0{,}80{,}000}{40{,}00{,}000} = \text{Rs. 12.70 per unit.}$$

llustration 2

Transferor Ltd. have two process - preparing and finishing. The normal output per week is 7500 units (completed) at a capacity of 75%

Transferee Ltd. had production problems in preparing and require 2000 units per week of prepared material for their finishing process.

The existing cost structure of one prepared unit of Transferor Ltd. at existing capacity :

Material Rs. 2.00 (variable 100%)
Labour Rs. 2.00 (variable 50%)
Overhead Rs. 4.00 (variable 25%)

The sales price of a completed units of Transferor Ltd. is Rs. 16 with a profit of Rs. 4 per unit.

Contrast the effect on the profits of Transferor Ltd. for six months (25 weeks) of supplying units of Transferee Ltd., with the following alternative transfer prices per unit : (i) Marginal cost; (ii) Marginal cost + 25%; (iii) Marginal cost + 15% Return on capital (assume capital employed Rs. 20 lakh); (iv) Existing cost; (v) Existing cost + a portion of profit on the basis of

$$\frac{\text{Preparing cost}}{\text{Total cost}} \text{ x Unit profit.}$$

(vi) At an agreed market price of Rs. 8.50

Assume no increase in fixed cost.

Solution

Existing profits of Transferor Ltd. based on 75% capacity are

Sales price per unit	Rs. 16
Profit per unit	Rs. 4
Profit per week = 4 x 7500 =	Rs. 30,000
Profit for 6 months (25 weeks)	Rs. 7,50,000

(a) Marginal Cost

No additional is earned.

Marginal cost per unit

	Rs.
Material	2.00
Labour	1.00
Overhead	1.00
Transfer price	4.00

Since no additional fixed costs are incurred then the cost of the additional output is the variable cost.

(b) Marginal cost + 25%

	Rs.
Marginal cost per unit	4
Profit @ 25%	1
Transfer price	5
Profit per week Rs. 1 x 2000 =	2000
Profit for six months	50,000

(c) Marginal Cost + 15% Return on capital

Capital employed	Rs. 20 lakhs
Return	15% per annum

$$\text{Profit} = \frac{15 \times 6 \times 20{,}00{,}000}{100 \times 12} = \text{Rs. } 1{,}50{,}000$$

(d) Existing cost

	Rs.
Marginal cost per unit	4
Profit	4
Transfer price.	8
Profit per week	8,000
Profit for six months (25 weeks)	2,00,000

(e) Existing cost + a portion of profits on the basis of

$$\frac{\text{Preparing cost}}{\text{Total cost}} \times \text{Profit}$$

Marginal cost per unit	Rs. 4
Transfer price Rs. 8 + (8/12 x 4)	10.66
Profit	Rs. 6.6
Profit per week	Rs. 13,300
Profit for six months	Rs. 3,30,000

(f) At an agreed Market Price of Rs. 8.50

Marginal cost per unit	Rs. 4
Transfer price	Rs. 8.50
Profit	Rs. 4.50
Profit per week	Rs. 9000.00
Profit for six months	Rs. 225000

In this problem the additional profit in the 6 months 25 weeks can vary from nil for the marginal cost transfer pricing policy to 3,30,000 for the existing standard cost - a portion of profit.

The choice of a transfer pricing systems should be fair and equitable to both the transferor & transferee divisions.

Administration of Transfer Prices

Most transfer price systems require formal administration procedures to operate successfully. They are described below.

Negotiation among Divisions

It most companies, divisions negotiate transfer prices with each other; that is, transfer prices are not set by a central staff group. Perhaps the most important reason for this is the belief that one of the primary functions of line management is to establish selling prices and to arrive at satisfactory purchase prices. If control of pricing is left to the headquarters staff, line management's ability to affect profitability is reduced. Also, many prices represent compromise positions by both buyer and seller. A headquarters group would have o rationalise the prices that it established. If the central staff group cannot defend the prices it sets, divisions managers can argue that their low profits are due to the arbitrariness of the prices. A third reason for having the divisions negotiate their prices is that they usually have the most information on markets and costs and, consequently, are best able to arrive at reasonable prices.

If the divisions are to negotiate prices, they must know the ground rules within which these negotiations are to be conducted. In a few companies, headquarters informs divisions that they are free to deal with each other or with outsiders as they see fit. Where this is done and there are outside sources and outside markets, no further administrative procedures are required, assuming that top management really means that the divisions are free to deal outside the company. As we described earlier, the market sets the price and, if divisions cannot agree on a price, they simply buy from or sell to outsiders. In most companies, however, some administrative procedures are established. If divisions are required to deal with one another, they do not have the threat of doing business with competitors as a bargaining point in the negotiation process.

Consequently, the headquarters staff must develop a set of rules that govern both pricing and sourcing of intracompany products.

Sourcing and Transfer Pricing Rules : The extent and formality of the sourcing and transfer pricing rules will depend to a great extent on the amount of intracompany transfers and the availability of markets and market prices. The greater the amount of intracompany transfers and the less the availability of market prices, the more formality and specificity of rules will be required. In some instances, all that is required is to tell the divisions that goods will be transferred at prevailing market prices. If such prices are readily available, there is little problem. Sourcing can be controlled by having headquarters review make-or-buy decisions that affect revenues in excess of a specified amount.

If there are significant amount of intracompany transfers and if competitive prices are not available for all products, guidelines similar to the following have been found to be useful.

1. Divide products into two main classes :

Class 1 includes all products for which top management wishes to control the sourcing. These would normally be the large volume products, products where no outside sources exist, and products where for quality or secrecy reasons the company wishes to maintain control over manufacturing. Class I products are further classified as follows : Class IA are products for which no outside, competitive prices are available. Class IB are products for which outside competitive prices are available.

Class II are all other products. In general, these are products that can be produced outside the company without any significant disruption to present operations. These are products of relatively small volume, produced with general purpose equipment.

2. The sourcing of Class I products can be changed only with permission of central management.
3. The sourcing of Class II products is determined by the divisions involved. Both the buying and selling divisions are free to deal either inside or outside the company.

Under this arrangement it is possible to concentrate on the sourcing and pricing of a relatively small number of high volume products. A list of products by classification should be provided as well as specific instruction as to how the prices of each product should be established. There should be rules for establishing market-based prices and rules for establishing cost-based prices. It is not unlikely that all of the different methods described in the preceding section would be used. If divisions are to negotiate, they must know how each product is to be priced, and this is the purpose of the set of rules.

It is important that line managers spend as little time as possible on transfer price negotiations and that the guidelines for these negotiations be specific enough so that skill in negotiations is not a significant factor in the determination of the transfer price. Without such rules, the most stubborn manager will negotiate the most favourable prices.

Arbitration

No matter how specific the pricing rules are, there may well be instances where divisions will not be able to agree on a price. For this reason, there should be some procedure for arbitrating transfer price disputes.

There can be widely different degrees of formality in transfer price arbitration. At one extreme the responsibility for arbitrating disputes is assigned to a single executive, for example, the financial vice president or the executive vice president, who talks to the division manager involved and then announces the price orally. The other extreme is to set up a committee. Usually such a committee will have three responsibilities: (i) to settle transfer price disputes, (ii) to review sourcing changes, and (iii) to change the transfer price rules where appropriate.

The degree of formality employed depends on the extent and type of transfer price disputes. In any case, transfer price arbitration should be the responsibility of a high level headquarters executive or group, since arbitration decisions can have an important effect on divisional profits. There are a number of ways in which arbitration can be conducted. With a formal system, both parties submit a written case to the arbitrator. The arbitrator, with assistance of the appropriate staff, reviews both positions and decides on the price. In doing so, he usually obtains the assistance of other staff officers. For example, he might have the purchasing department review the validity of a proposed competitive price quotation or the industrial engineering department review the appropriateness of a disputed standard labour cost. As indicated above, in less formal systems, the presentations may be largely oral.

It is important that relatively few disputes should be submitted for arbitration. If a large number of disputes are arbitrated, this indicated that the rules are not specific enough, the rules are difficult to apply, the divisional organisation is illogical, or divisionalisation should not have been adopted. In short, it is a symptom that something is wrong. Not only is arbitration time-consuming to both line managers and headquarters executives, but also arbitrated prices often satisfy neither the buyer nor the seller.

In some companies, there is such an onus involved in submitting a price dispute to arbitration that very few are ever submitted. If, as a consequence, legitimate grievances do not surface, the results are undesirable. Preventing disputes from being submitted to arbitration will tend to hide the fact that there are problems with the transfer price system.

Pricing Corporate Services

Some of the problems associated with charging divisions for services furnished by corporate staff units are discussed below. It is useful to classify central services in the following three types :

1. Those central services over which the division has no control.
2. Those central services that the division must accept, but for which the amount of the service is at least partially controllable by division.
3. Those central services over which the division has the discretion of using or not using.

No Control by the Division : Divisions ordinarily cannot control the services rendered by such staff offices as accounting, public relations, industrial relations and legal. The divisions must accept these services and have little, if anything, to say about the amount that is spent on them. The principal problem with these services is whether to allocate the costs to the operating divisions. The main reasons given for allocating them are :

1. If an operating manager pays for a service whether he uses it or not, he will be more likely to use it.
2. An operating manager will be more likely to exert pressure to keep down those costs (by complaining) if he must pay for them.
3. Divisional profits will be more realistic and comparable to outside firms because, presumably, the outside firm would have to pay for comparable services.

The main argument against allocation is that it is not controllable by the operating manager and, therefore, may only annoy him.

If top management does decide to allocate these costs, the usual cost accounting techniques for estimating the "fair share" applicable to each profit centre are satisfactory. However, when costs are allocated, the budgeted costs, not the actual costs, should be allocated. In this way, the allocation will not affect the comparison between budgeted and actual divisional profit performance, and variances will appear in the reports of the responsibility centre that incurred the costs. An exception to this generalisation might occur if personnel costs or prices for purchased services increase significantly during the budget period; it would seem appropriate to pass on these increased costs to the users.

Control over Amount of Service : In some cases, divisions must accept a central service, but the amount of the service that it accepts may be controllable. Data processing and research/development are two examples. There are three schools of thought about such services.

One schools holds that a division should pay the marginal costs of the discretionary services. If it pays less than this, it will be motivated to use more of the service than is economically justified. For example, if a divisional manager did not have to pay for his reports, he might request reports from the data processing department even though these were of little value to him. If, on the other hand, a divisional manager pays more for a service than the marginal cost to the company, he might not elect to use certain services because the value to him was not equal to the cost. If the value of the service was more than the marginal cost to the company, it might be a mistake for the operating manager to reject this service.

A second school advocates a price equal to the full cost, that is, marginal cost plus a fair share of the fixed costs. It is argued that if the divisions do not believe that the services are worth at least their full cost, then there is something wrong with either the quality or the efficiency of the service unit. Furthermore, as described, divisions may be permitted to obtain services from an outside source if they can do so at a price that is lower than the company's full cost. If services are in fact procured from an outside source, this is another signal that something may be wrong with the company's service unit. It is also argued that full costs represent the company's longrun costs and this is the amount that should be paid. If full costs are used, they should be budgeted costs, with the exception stated above.

A third school of thought advocates a price that is equivalent to the market price, or to full cost plus a profit margin. The market price would be used if one is available (e.g., the costs charged by a computer service bureau); if not, the price would be full cost plus a return on investment. The rationale for this position is that the capital employed by the service unit should earn a return just as much as the capital employed by manufacturing divisions.

TRANSFER PRICING PRACTICES

The earliest study on the subject appears to be the one published by the National Association of Accountants (NAA) in June 1956. National Industrial Conference Board's "Studies in Business Policy No. 122, based on investigation of practices in 190 companies in the United States was published in 1967. The notable and exhaustive study by David Solomons, published in 1965, contained a fairly detailed chapter (mostly a theoretical economic analysis) on inter-divisional relationship and transfer pricing. All these studies, though highly useful, are descriptive and do not give extensive numerical data on transfer pricing policies and practices employed in the United States.

Most recently, four surveys have been published :

1. BIM's management Survey Report No. 8 by A. Rook (1971)
2. Survey undertaken (on individual basis) by Cyril Tomkins (1973)

3. ICMA study by J. Finnie (1978)
4. FERF study (1979).

The major findings of three studies at Nos. 1, 3 and 4 (all these studies give numerical data regarding transfer pricing policies and practices) are presented below. Relevant comments are also offered.

BIM Study (1971)

In all 193 companies of all sizes belonging to various industries responded. Two thirds used only one method of transfer pricing for interunit transactions while majority of the remaining companies had two or three methods. Policies relating to the amount of control exercised by central management over company units varied widely and depended partly on the company size and structure. Most of the companies preferred administed prices. The largest number of the respondents (irrespective of the class they belonged to) had central management staff alone formulate policies for inter-unit prices and price changes. Other methods like committee of central management and staff from buying and selling units or committees from buying and selling units alone were in much less use. All this indicates that profit centre autonomy is regarded as secondary to main objective of goal congruence.

54% of the respondents used market price and the remaining 46% used cost of production as bases for determining transfer prices. Of the companies using market price as their basic approach, 40% used current market prices, which the remaining 60% modified it in one or the other manner to suit their particular circumstances. In companies using the adjusted market price, two methods commonly used were : (i) adjustment by negotiation, and (ii) adjustment by a fixed amount or percentage. The biggest drawback with negotiated prices felt was that it tended to become a test of mutual bargaining strength and skill amongst managers. The negotiated technique was found widely practised in large companies than in small companies. Overall, 62% of the companies that modified market price in some way stated that they were satisfied with the price.

Of the companies basing inter-unit prices on cost of production, 62% based them on standard costs and 38% on historical costs. Over 90% the companies included cost of direct materials, direct labour and elements of some factor overheads; 12% included all the elements of listed overheads. Of the companies using cost of production as basis for transfer pricing, 61% modified it in some way to give it is 'plus' effect. Nearly half of these companies modified it by negotiation and the others by a fixed percentage. Three-quarters of the companies revising the cost of production upwards to include the profit content stated that they were satisfied with their systems.

An interesting sidelight of the study is that none of the respondents used marginal costs, thus showing complete unpopularity of this approach of

Economic Analysis. The scope of the study did not include shadow prices or mathematical programming approaches.

ICMA Study (1978)

An open-ended study on transfer pricing of products and materials (rather than on allocation of charges of central service apartments to operating units) was done under the auspices of the Institute of Cost and Management Accountants (London) and was published in December 1978. Responses received covered 42 organisation. But 33 sent in complete questionnaires. The majority of respondents saw transfer prices as being about control (measuring management performance, identifying unit contribution to total profit) with motivation (encouraging profit consciousing) coming second, registering 30%, and other objectives sharing the remaining 10%. The main advantages were also seen in the same terms. Perception of disadvantages are more widely distributed, with most emphasis given to the tendency to prefer unit to corporate advantage and to time spent in arguing about prices. Central influence over the fixing of transfer prices (cost plus or some other centrally moderated arrangement) was shown in 70% of responses as opposed to 30% using inter-unit negotiation. The overall picture that emerged from the survey was of considerable diversity of practice but with the majority of instances stressing control and preservation of corporate interest above motivation and unit autonomy.

FERF Study (1979)

A research study prepared for the Financial Executive Research Foundation by Vancil showed that 85% of the sample (of 239) companies transferred goods among profit centres and the extent of transfers between profit centres varied from 0 to 65 percent. The study, not unsurprisingly, indicated that companies with lower level of diversification were more involved in transfer of goods than companies with higher levels of diversification.

68% (of 239) companies reporting the extent of their transfers of goods handled transfers as a purchases or sale transaction (this included transactions with profit). While 32% transferred goods at cost. In all, as many as eleven methods of transfer pricing were found to be used. Of the companies which treated transfers as purchases and sale, nearly a third used negotiations to arrive at transfer prices and about 40% of them made use of either list prices or competitor's prices. Full manufacturing costs (standard or actual) were used by over 70% of the companies which specified transfer prices on cost basis.

Of all the 239 companies (which specified transfer pricing practices) without first putting them into two broad categories as above, only 5% used variable cost for establishing transfer price. Full costs were used by nearly a quarter of the companies. Thus, about 70% of the companies specified transfer prices on the basis of cost plus, negotiation, and market price.

If variable cost, full cost, cost plus, negotiation, and market price (in that order) are to be taken as points on a continuum of transfer pricing methods ranging from the use of cost based transfer prices to the use of market based transfer prices; it has been observed (while examining the relationships) that in large companies transfer prices tended to be close to the market prices end of the spectum. It has been further observed that financially more successful companies were more inclined to use market based prices. From this the author infers that "companies which try to maintain the independence of the profit centres by using market based transfer prices tend to be more successful".

Study by Chakraborty (1974)

In a limited study of six companies in different industries, Chakraborty found that companies more concerned with assessing the profitability of products preferred to base transfer prices on cost of production even when market prices were available, while companies intending to judge profitability of units (rather than individual products) tended to prefer market price basis. In two companies cost plus basis was used, in three other companies market price was modified through limited negotiation. In view of the limited scope of the enquiry, it is difficult to make any generalisations on transfer pricing practices in India. The author himself recognised that one of the six companies did not constitute a typical transfer pricing case.

Concluding Comments

From the above discussion it would be discerned that there is possibly on basis of transfer pricing that satisfies all the criteria (or objectives) laid down in this behalf, except perhaps the market based transfer prices. But these are also frought with several practical difficulties, illstructured or imperfections of markets being one. Cost based transfer prices run counter to basic concept of decentralised profit responsibility. Transfer pricing based on marginal cost or shadow prices entails moving towards **centralised** management. The techniques of marginal costs and Management Science, by and large, call for elaborate processing of vast amount of data by the central planning group which may either impose a transfer price or output goals in order to induce goal congruity, and this distracts from a profit centre manager's perception that he is managing an independent business. The slow acceptance of the use of mathematical models set transfer prices is probably attributable to their lack of feasibility.

The alternative of dual pricing system which permits the use of two different prices for two different purposes (one for allocation and the other for performance evaluation) has been suggested. Under such a system, a profit is created for the supplying segment to afford a positive motivation to the manager while the buying segment is charged at the variable cost which is regarded appropriate to guide the manager's decisions. Though claimed to offer more flexibility and motivation, it results into subsidy for one and tax for another segment.

Moreover, the system is not completely consonant to the idea implied in profit centres. Since there is seldom a single transfer price that can meet all the criteria of a goods transfer pricing system, multiple transfer prices have also been suggested for different purposes. A single basis of transfer prices, it is contended, may not be soundly based. Real world situations are often too complex and varied to fit the straight-jacket of uniformity.

It is indeed difficult to achieve all the objectives of a sound transfer pricing system and, at the same time, keep all the parties involved happy. Management faces a real dilemma, Nevertheless, management has no option but to face the situation by developing an acceptable and practicable system of transfer pricing. While remaining reasonably stable, the transfer pricing policy has to be dynamic and flexible in view of the constant changes taking place in costs, prices and the marketing environment so that adjustments are made whenever warranted. Many of the pin-pricks can be avoided if the initial system of transfer pricing is designed and introduced after careful planning and analysis of all the relevant factors.

Often a decision on transfer pricing is a trade off between perceived benefits from goal congruence and administrative convenience on the one hand and perceived benefits from profit centre autonomy and profit awareness on the other. Profit centre managers generally do not appreciate complex control techniques or methods that burden them with providing profuse, detailed information. Such methods are viewed with suspicion. In the absence of availability of market prices, the management has to explore the most desirable or the least undesirable transfer pricing system, and in the process examine and assess the relative benefits and costs of each course open to it. This is particularly required when an elaborate transfer pricing model is intended to be installed. Rigid adherence to a particular approach or model may lead to needless complexities. Decentralisation, in fact, is a continuum and every management has to attempt some intermediate point between the two extreme points of least decentralisation and maximum decentralisation, depending, upon its objectives. The transfer pricing systems encountered in practice, therefore, represent compromises, with the nature of each compromise and its consequent strengths and weaknesses depending on the considerations which have weight most with its designors. To illustrate, a company with units operating in competitive markets and where internal trading is not much involved is likely to emphasise the autonomy of unit managers, leaving them free to settle such transfers as they choose to make on the basis of market prices, whereas another company with units of complementary character is likely to be more explicitly concerned with corporate interest, imposing limits on the autonomy of unit managers in the interest of ensuring fuller emplo[illegible]ent of its investments, etc.

In several situations, transfer prices may be viewed as constraints on complete profit centre autonomy since they link two or more segments. An appropriate and workable transfer pricing system may decrease some of the benefits of decentralisation but it may also decrease costs, particularly when interdependencies are overwhelming and mistakes costly.

The broad conclusion that emerges is that market based transfer pricing (including the negotiated prices) is ideal as it is likely to minimise dysfunctional decision making and maximise unit and overall company interests. It is straight forward in concept and provides credible basis for performance appraisal. In the absence of this, companies prefer to base transfer prices on simple and less complex ways by which they attempt to reach, as closely as possible, an approximation of market prices either by cost plus or by negotiation. The benefits and costs of a workable system of transfer pricing are hard to quantify. So, the corporate management must feel its way. The decision is bound to reflect their way of thinking, their overall philosophy, perhaps their value system.

REVIEW QUESTIONS

1. What do you understand by Transfer Pricing?
2. Why do transfer prices become necessary?.
3. What objectives should transfer prices attempt to meet?
4. Explain, briefly, the various issues involved in transfer pricing.
5. In what circumstances should central management intervene in selling transfer prices or transfer quantities?
6. Explain the different types of transfer prices. Also state the merits and drawbacks of each.
7 What is market based transfer pricing and why might there be difficulties in using this approach?
8. Describe full cost transfer pricing and its characteristics.
9. What is variable cost transfer pricing and how might possible disadvantages be overcome?
10. What is negotiated transfer pricing?
11. How will you formally administer transfer prices for evaluating divisional performance?
12. Summarise the findings of various studies/surveys on polices and practices of transfer pricing.

21
Proprietary Audit And Management Audit

Propriety Audit : Kholer, defines the term 'propriety' as "that which meets the tests of the public interest, commonly accepted customs and standards of conduct".* Propriety audit refers to an audit in which the various actions and decisions are examined to find out whether they are in public interest and whether they meet the standards of conduct. While undertaking a propriety audit, the auditor does not merely evaluate the evidence supporting a transaction. He attempts to examine the regularity, prudence and impact of the various actions and decisions of the authorities.

The conventional commercial audit is an examination of the transactions to ascertain the true and fair character of the financial statements. It is essentially a reporting function and does not concern itself with the propriety of transactions. However, propriety as an element of satisfaction exists in the audits conducted by the Comptroller and Auditor General of India. As Asok Chanda** points out, the purpose of the government audit is "to bring to the notice of the administration lacunae in the rules and regulations, and to suggest, wherever possible, ways and means for the execution of plans an projects with greater expedition, efficiency and economy". Actually, one of the specific objectives of government audit is to ensure that expenditure conforms to certain general principles which have, for long, been recognised as standards of financial propriety, namely, the following.

1. The expenditure should not be prima facie more than the occasion demands. Every public officer is expected to exercise the same vigilance in respect of expenditure incurred from public moneys as a person of ordinary prudence would exercise in respect of expenditure of his own money.

2. No authority should exercise its power of sanctioning expenditure to pass an order which will be directly or indirectly to its own advantage.

3. Public moneys are not utilised for the benefit of a particular person or section of the community unless (i) the amount of expenditure involved is insignificant; or (ii) a claim for the amount could be enforced in a court of law; or (iii) the expenditure is in pursuance of a recognised policy or custom.

---

* A Dictionary for Accountants, Eric L. Kohler, P.H.I. New Delhi, 1978, p. 384.

** Aspects of Audit Control, Asok Chanda, Asia Publishing House, 1960, p. 26

The audit as contemplated in section 227 of the Companies Act does not basically require the auditor to go into the financial propriety or prudence of transactions. However, some of the requirements of law introduced in the last two decades or so suggest that in certain specified areas, even the company auditor is required to go beyond his traditional function of reporting and express an opinion about the propriety or prudence of certain transactions. Thus, section 227(1A) of the Companies Act requires the company auditor to inquire whether the terms on which the loans and advances have been made by the company are prejudicial to the interests of the company or its members. Again, the auditor is required to inquire whether the transactions of the company which are represented merely by book entries are prejudicial to the interests of the company. Similarly, the auditor is to see whether personal expenses have been charged to revenue account. These provisions cast specific duty on the auditor to inquire into the propriety of certain transactions. Also, under section 227(4A), the central government has extended the duties of the company auditor to examining the financial propriety of transactions in certain areas. For example, the auditor of a manufacturing, mining or processing company has to state whether the rate of interest and other terms and conditions of certain loans are prima facie prejudicial to the interests of the company. Similarly, the auditor has to verify whether the transactions of purchase of goods and materials and sale of goods, materials and services with certain specified parties and aggregating to Rs. 50,000 or more in respect of each party have been made at reasonable prices. The cost audit report under section 233B of the Companies Act and the additional reporting requirements for government companies under section 619(3) of the Companies Act also include a number of issues regarding which an auditor has to conduct a propriety audit.

Audit of Financial Propriety under Government Audit

In conducting the audit to find out whether in incurring the expenditure, financial propriety has been observed or not, the auditor has to scrutinise the expenditure from the point of view of an administrative authority. He has to examine whether in making the expenditure, a reasonably high standards of public financial morality, sound financial administration and devotion to the financial interests of the government has been maintained. While no hard and fast rules can be laid down regarding the standards of financial propriety, the auditor should, while conducting this phase of audit, look into the following matters.

(a) The expenditure does not seem prima facie to be more than what the occasion demands.

(b) The authorities involved in the expenditure have made the expenditure with the same degree of caution as a person of ordinary prudence would exercise in respect of his own money.

(c) The authorities involved in the expenditure have not derived any direct or indirect advantage from the transaction.

(d) Public money is not utilised for the benefit of a particular person or section of community and the benefit accrues to the public in general.

Definition of Management Audit : The concept of management audit and operational audits is really not capable of statutory definition since it is a continuously by growing concept arising from the needs of management.

"Management audit is appraisal of managers as managers". Harold, Koontz, Cerill, O'Donell.

"The management audit may be defined as comprehensive and constructive examination of an organisational structure of a company, institution or branch or government or of any component thereof, such a division or department and its methods of controls, its use of human and physical facilities and its plans and objectives". Lenard, William P.

"Management audit is an appraisal of the enterprise in all its aspects, in the light of its present and probable future environment". McKinsey, J.O.

The above definitions elaborate the concept of management audit. Management audit cares for managerial decision and policies which determine the future of a business enterprise. The performance of managerial personnel is tested as to see to what extent the decisions and policies have been successful in achieving the objectives of a business. Because the entire edifice of a business is erected on the strength of the management's capabilities. So the functioning of management should also be subjected to check. The viability, correctness and effectiveness of decision making process should be tested comparing to the standards laid down for achieving the goals. Thus the management audit is total examination of an organisation or a part of it, it includes check on the effectiveness of managers, their compliance with company or professional standards, the reliability of management data, the quality of performance of duties, and recommendations for improvement.

Why Management Audit : Every science developed because our needs required so. Every invention is need based. Auditing or the need for auditing was felt to check whether the public funds are utilised according to the predetermined objectives? It poses some questions regarding the capabilities of persons (managers) at whose disposal the public funds are kept. Are they competent enough? Are they honest towards achieving objectives of enterprise? Are they aware of the fact that the money if employed in productive purpose yields rich dividends?

Anything which questions the capabilities of the persons who are at the helm of the affairs of a business enterprise comes under the review of management audit. That is, management audit has nothing to do with the profit and loss figures of a company; it concentrates upon the performance of management; whether the performance is according to the standards laid down by the top management. Because in the present situations, the ownership of companies is widely spread over many shareholders, a large proportions who comparatively hold small portion of equity capital. Such shareholders should be in position to see the immediate prospects of ownership. Published balance sheets and profit and loss accounts are grossly inadequate information on which to predict the probable future process of a company's management.

The management audit tries to check the following weakness which may creep in management or at any stage of functioning of business which may undermine all the good things done. The management audit can plug the loopholes if it is efficiently used and interpreted. The weaknesses are discussed hereunder.

Directorial Weakness : Directors of a company are brains of a company. Their decision and foresight goes to grassroot level of a company which helps in achieving the objectives. If at any stage of functioning of a directors' weakness or incapacity occurs, whether administrative or otherwise, it may jeopardise the entire business. Management audit evaluates the tasks performed by the directors minutely. It does interpretation of facts in analytical manner. If the interpretation shows deviations from standards then the management auditor presents corrective measures to accomplish the desired level of standards.

Managerial Weakness : The technology is changing very fast. The business is affected with this change and so the ways of doing things. If managers are unable to cope with this technological change, the business may face problems. Management may not be aware of developments in management science. May it be that the management facing hardships in delegating power and authority. Management may not be aware of latest changes in doing things in systematic and scientific manner. Management may be trained inadequately in some specialised field. All these things certainly affect business adversely, which management audit tries to remove. Though it is not business of management audit to teach the latest development in technology to managers but it can tell use where we can excel by adopting new methods.

Technological and Administrative Weakness : As above stated, technological changes have bearing on administrative behaviour of management. The management may be afraid of adopting the latest technological changes, which is essential for growth. The hesitation of adapting to the newer changes in technology is certainly weakness of administration. Management audit tries to remove this lacuna.

Who Should be Management Auditor

It is extremely difficult to prescribe any qualification for management auditor because management auditor has to deal with human behaviour, it has to establish whether the activities of management are according to pre-set targets or not; whether the management has been successful in leading the team of subordinates according to the directives of plans. That is, management auditor works as consultant within the business environment who suggest the alternatives to achieve business targets. As a consultant, management auditor's prime qualification is to possess a broad business experience in some business or profession such as engineering, accountancy, statistics, administration etc. That is management auditor should be a behaviourist and understand the psychology of doing things. For this he must have profound knowledge of developments in the fields of socio-economic, socio-politic, and socio-technological behaviour of the society as a work which affect the business environment directly and indirectly. To become competent management auditor, one should work a team to achieve useful results. Some of the team members should be specialists to solve the special types of problems. The team of management auditors work as in phased manner. The work starts from fact finding and collection of data from and completes when the problem are solved or alternatives are found. So the members of the team should be well experienced in their respective fields of activities.

As above stated that management auditor's task is as of a behaviorist-scientist. For examining the relevance of managerial actions for auditor's purpose, the management auditor must rely on trait theory. He must review his findings according to the traits possesed by management team. The following traits are necessary to examine for better results by management audit :

Intelligence : Intelligence can be appraised with reference to the faculty of comprehension and mental alertness in relation to activities performed.

Judgement : Managers are decision makers, the quality of their decision making can be asserted by comparing results yielded by their judgement.

Initiative : Business environment is full of uncertainties. Anyone who takes initiation, wins. Initiation involves intelligence and judgement power of the managers. The management auditor can appraise the initiative inclination of managers by the risk assumed by the managers while taking decision to start first.

Force : The forcefulness of managers in achieving targets can be measured by the actual results achieved.

Leadership : Managers, in other words, are leaders. The leadership quality of managers can be appraised with reference to directing, controlling, influencing other (subordinates) in a definite line of actions and maintaining discipline at every stage of functioning.

Moral Courage : This quality can be appraised by management auditor by examining the moral courage and character of managers. It is necessary that managers should be ready to do things fearlessly under all circumstances.

Cooperation : How a manager cooperates with his team-mates and subordinates? The team spirit of managers is examined by the management auditor by asking questions to subordinates and other team-mates under them.

Loyalty : Loyalty is the sum total of fidelity, faithfulness, allegiance and consistency and give respect to the higher order of management. This quality can be appraised by testing the inclination of managers as how prompt and obedient they are in performing duties.

Preservance : It can be appraised with reference to maintenance of purpose in spite of obstacles and discouragement by outer forces.

Reaction in Emergency : A manager may face emergency of taking decisions for betterment of result. This can be appraised whether the managers acted in logical manner depite emergency conditions.

Endurance : This can be appraised with reference to ability for carrying things under all circumstances.

Industry : This quality can be appraised with reference to performance of duties by managers in energetic manner for achieving results.

The above managerial qualities are appraised by management auditor for ascertaining the findings regarding the individual manager. A manager's performance is sequel to the qualities cherished by them. The task of management auditor is based on the managers performance. So these qualities must be paid profound attention as to what extent the managers stood by these qualities in crisis and in the normal course of functioning of business.

Management Audit Techniques

It is obvious that since management audit partly structured as mentioned above, the specific techniques for management audit would differ from organisation to organisation, depending upon the nature, activities, size, environment and goals of the organisation. Management Auditor has to design his own 'specific' techniques of audit, though the basic approach would remain the same, viz. to appraise the quality of management practice itself. Nevertheless, a broad outline as to the approach for selection of techniques of Management Audit can be laid down, based on the general techniques. These ar enumerated in Fig 21.1 in the next page.

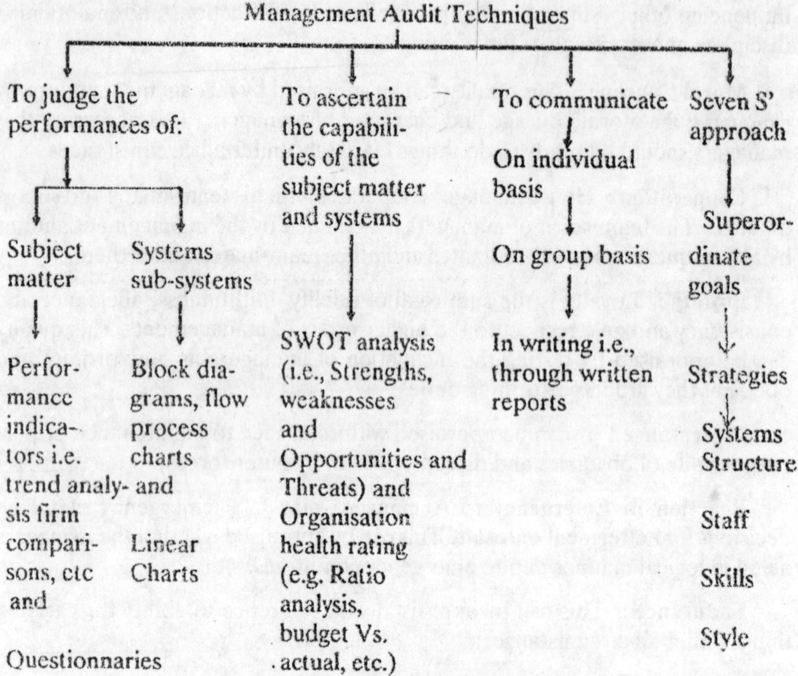

Fig. 21.1 Management Audit Techniques

Management Audit Methodology and Reports

As mentioned earlier, the very purpose of management audit is improvement for future. It is educative and consultative in nature and action-aid. Management audit methodology and reports, therefore, should be drafted with skill and competence. Let us now analyse these aspects in detail.

Management Audit Methodology : As the specific management audit techniques differ from organisation to organisation, the specific management audit methodology also differs depending upon the nature of organisation and management audit assignment. The general management audit methodology, however, can be described as follows :

1. Examining Organisational contexts and situations ; Whatever may be the management audit assignment, it is advisable to evaluate the environment to evaluate the environment and situations in which the organisation is working.

2. Obtaining Perceptions and views of managers : In order to understand the process of management, it is absolutely essential to obtain the perception and views of managers at various levels.

3. Obtaining and analysing data on organisation/assignment and performance results : The data and performance results relevant to the given management audit assignment and for organisation should be obtained and analysed thoroughly since it forms the very basis of the management audit assignment. This would also help management auditor to understand the relevant management aspects and emerging practices.

4. Evolving questionnaires and checklists : This is the most important aspect and the core of any management audit assignment. The approach for preparing questionnaires check-lists/involves the following steps :

(a) Obtaining overview of the organisation and its environment

(b) Preliminary findings should be outlined as follows :

- Goals and performance indicators should be listed and reviewed;
- Environmental opportunities and constraints should be studied with the help of SWOT analysis.
- Organisation resources should be evaluated.
- Organisation controls should be evaluated.

(c) The preliminary findings should be examined with 'Seven S' approach given below:

Seven 'S' Approach - Components of Management Inputs and Management Audit Approach Thereof

Main Classification	Components and Management Audit Approach
1. Super-ordinate Goals	(a) Are they defined? (b) Are performance indicators specified? (c) Are roles and responsibilities laid down? (d) Are they understood by Managers? (e) Are they translated into short-term objectives?
2. Strategy	(a) Is the management strategy specialised? (b) Are the criteria for choice laid down? (c) Are the strategies balanced?
3. Systems	(a) Are the information systems defined? (b) Are the standards laid down for control? (c) Are the systems intervened wher- ever necessary and corrective action taken?

4. Structure	(a) Are the functions and tasks defined? (b) Are the responsibilities defined? (c) Are the authorities delegated properly? (d) Is the Structure flexible enough to cope up with changes within and outside?
5. Staffing	(a) Are the selection criteria laid down? (b) Are the job descriptions specified? (c) Are the personnel appraisal systems, compensation policies, employee relation policies and procedures laid down?
6. Skills	(a) Are the techniques for skill development laid down? (b) Is the formal and informal development of individuals taken care of? (c) Are the training policies specified? (d) Are they problem-centered and development-oriented?
7. Style	(a) Are the degree of authorisation and participative practices laid down? (b) Are the motivating methods adequate? (c) Is the conflict management taken care of? (d) Are the decision making style and leadership style specified?

(d) Survey should be taken of emerging concepts and practices.

(e) Areas requiring in-depth examination should be identified and detailed check-lists should be evolved.

5. Obtaining answers to questionnaires and reaching agreement with managers on findings and issues : A constant interaction with management personnel and effective analysis of information being collected should be undertaken on continuous basis till all the points of the questionnaires or check-lists are answered or agreed upon.

6. Comparing Current Practices and agreed standards : The findings should be compared with the current practices and agreed standards so that they can form a basis for drafting recommendations for corrective action.

7. Drafting recommendations for corrective action : In the end, management auditor should draft his recommendations for corrective action. In short, a constant interaction with management personnel and effective analysis of information being collected are absolutely essential for a successful management audit.

8. Versatile approach : Management audit also requires a versatile approach to the assignment undertaken. To illustrate, in the case of management audit of marketing function, the following areas should be subjected to management audit : (a) marketing Environment, (b) marketing Strategy, (c) marketing Organisation, (d) marketing Systems, (e) marketing Productivity, (f) marketing Finance. Thus it can be seen that management auditor has to cover a lot of aspects while conducting management audit. It is possible that he may not be an expert or master of a particular trade or function which reflects on his management audit assignment. In such a case, he should take necessary assistance from his colleagues or experts in the field.

Management Audit Report : As a last step of management audit assignment, a management audit report should be prepared and submitted. In brief, therefore, it would be worthwhile to remember the following points while drafting a management audit report.

1. A management audit report should be exhaustive and must cover the assignment fully including its scope, approach, findings, and recommendations.

2. Management auditor has to be methodical while presenting his report. Following steps can be suggested for this purpose :

(a) Declaring the Purpose : The very purpose of undertaking the management audit assignment should be briefly outlined in the opening paragraphs of management audit report.

(b) Plan of Report : The plan of report, i.e., the methodology adopted for audit, the areas covered, the nature of assignment in brief, and the assumptions made, if any, should be elaborated in an orderly manner.

(c) Data and Facts : Data and facts are the very heart of a management audit report. It is, therefore, absolutely essential that the data and facts are sorted out properly and only relevant information is presented. All the data and facts should be cross-checked and should be specific as far as possible. Only main facts should be elaborated in a descriptive way, point by point, in the main body of the report and the data should be presented in annexures to the report. A mention of the annexures and relevant data (conclusive figures, etc.) must be made in the main body of the report.

(e) Agreement : The draft report should be discussed with all concerned and an agreement should be reached about the facts and data given in the draft report. The draft report may be suitably amended wherever necessary. In case an agreement cannot be reached on certain points, a mention to that effect should be made in the final report. In fact, it is better to prepare the minutes of discussions and the same may be circulated along with the final report.

(f) Final Report : Final Report, inter alia, should include the following ; (i) .Objective of assignment and terms of references, (ii) Process of examination, (iii) Finding, and (iv) Recommendations (including strategy for implementation) While items (i) to (iii) are already taken care of while correcting the draft report, item (iv) viz. Recommendations is to be freshly prepared which is the crux and crown of the management audit report. The recommendations, therefore, should be given step by step as per the findings. Above all, the implementation strategy must be specified along with the recommendations. For this purpose, management auditor must have absolutely clear knowledge of how to implement his own recommendations. It is very easy to recommend so many things but difficult to implement them all. Management auditor, therefore, should not recommend what he himself does not know how to implement.

3. Last, but not the least, management audit report should not only say what needs to be improved but should also state what needs to be preserved. It should conclude with acknowledgment of the information, help and support given by all concerned and should place on record the plus points of the management and organisation.

Management Audit - Indispensability

As already mentioned, management audit is 'voluntarily but compulsory' for every organisation. Nevertheless, it would be worth while to note some situations where management audit is just indispensable. In the following circumstances, management audit must be resorted to :

(a) Sick unit seeking for corporate turnaround : When a sick organisation is seeking for turnaround, i.e., revival to come out of sickness, it is absolutely necessary to perform management audit of the entire organisation.

(b) Declining market share/shrinking markets : Barring exceptional circumstances, when the market for the product is good but the market share of the organisation is declining, or alternatively, when the market for the product is itself shrinking, it would be essential to conduct management audit of marketing function of the organisation.

(c) High management/labour turnover : Sometimes an organisation is doing very well on overall basis, but despite this, there is high labour turnover at junior level or at managerial level. In such circumstances, management audit of human resources function is inevitable.

The total task of management may be divided into five elements : (i) Setting objectives (ii) Planning (iii) Organising (iv) Communicating and (v) Controlling. Each is vital to the success of management at all levels-from first line Supervisors to President. And these five elements are present in management of every kind of enterprise, small or large, manufacturing or selling, partnership or company. Hence, Management auditor has to critically examine these process and adopt certain checklist for their evaluation.

Setting Objectives

The definition and use of the term "Objective" may vary from organisation to organisation. An objective is result expected to be achieved within some time frame. An objective is also a mile post directed towards the achievement of some goal. Management wants to get maximum out of minimum. The resources- men, machines, money material etc., are to be so employed that there is minimum of wastage. The objectives are generally established on the basis of past experience and data available and the projection worked out considering new factors which are likely to affect the objectives whether in the current or the future situation. The changes expected are change in demand, machine and equipment, legal and environmental, etc. Further, the management prepares the objectives of the Organisation keeping in view the economic, competitive, technological, political and social aspects prevalent in the country which are likely to affect the objectives. The objectives once set should be reviewed from time to time keeping in view the new developments. The objectives can be achieved if the targets are set for each department, and responsibility is fixed and authority is given for execution of the responsibility. An **illustrative check-list on objectives** is given below :

Check-list

1. Does the Organisation have clearly defined the objectives in specific quantitative terms like (a) Maximisation of profit, (b) Cost reduction, (c) Public image, (d) Capturing Market, (e) Production improvement, (f) Return on investment, etc.
2. Are the broad objectives broken up into detailed targets? Are functional policies supportive of the master strategy.
3. Are the objectives revised periodically in the light of changes in internal and external environment?
4. Are the objectives/goals adequately supported by data?
5. Are the objectives attainable?

Planning : The management must have a plan-a strategy for achieving each objective. This strategy is best developed in consultation with managers. When the managers have agreed upon a set of measurable, and attainable objectives and a strategy to attain them, they should put everything in writing. This writing plan is the most important working tool for all managers. The entire management function revolves around accepted objectives and the strategy for reaching them.

Check-list

1. Is the planning related to objectives of the management?
2. Does the Organisation have a system of long-range and short- range planning?
3. What is the degree of involvement by various managers?
4. How are the budget estimates developed?
5. How are they reviewed in depth?
6. Are the budget conveyed to various operational managers in time?
7. Are they easily understandable?

Organising : When the management has completed planning sessions with its managers, it can assess fairly (a) its manpower requirements and (b) the manpower potential in the area of responsibility. At this point, the management can determine how many people are required to achieve the objectives. Organising helps the management to unite different people to achieve goals. Whether the number of people is only a few or thousand their effective cooperation requires organisation. Two elements are invariably present in organising dividing the work into jobs and simultaneously ensuring that these separate clusters of work are linked together into a team effort. The structure must be built around organisational needs and objectives. It should be simple with a minimum number of echelons. Top management must be able to see the entire operation.

Check-list

1. Whether the Organisation structure is in harmony with the objectives of the organisation?
2. What are the various levels in the organisation hierarchy?
3. Are the lines of authority and areas of responsibility clear.
4. Is there proper coordination and cross communication among different organisational levels?
5. Is the decision making centralised?
6. What is the usual span of supervision?
7. What is the nature of superior-subordinate relationship?
8. Is there any regular system of motivation?
9. Does the organisation structure provide for unity of command?

Communication : Without good communication there cannot be good management. At the top, the management must have a continuous flow of reliable and dependable information. In middle management, it is the responsibility of the manager to keep lines open so that good communication flows downward as well as upward. The middle managers must make sure that the policies and procedures, rules and regulations as developed by top management are getting through to lower echelons. At the same time, the communication upward must reflect such matters as what is happeing within the operating unit; employee attitude' acceptance or rejection of policies and procedure; quality and quantity of product being produced and sold, etc. The communication should be concise and to the point.

Check-list

1. Is the communication clear and understandable to the person to whom it is intended?
2. Does it indicate the procedure to be adopted to achieve the corporate plan?
3. Does the communication reach the desired person in time?
4. Are the methods of communication adopted by the Organisation are effective?

Controlling : Plans without corresponding controls are apt to be hollow hopes. So, to make the management really effective it should couple controlling with planning. The primary aim of controlling is to ensure that results of operations conform as closely as possible to established goals. A secondary aim is to provide timely information that may prompt the revision of goals. These aims are achieved by setting standards, comparing actual results against these standards and taking corrective action.

Check-list

1. Are the controls acceptable to various levels of management?
2. Is there a system of reward or punishment linked with control?
3. Have the standards been established for the completion of job?
4. Are the standards developed after giving due weightage to all the factors (quality, quantity, cost etc.)
5. Are the standards reasonable and achievable?
6. Does the system of control provide for good reporting system for evaluation of standards and then achievements.
7. Are the causes of variances and exceptions accepted as normal or efforts are made to eliminate, or reduce the variances?
8. How prompt is the determination of the action to correct deviation?

Management Functions

The functional areas of management may be broadly divided into five departments : Purchase, personnel, production, marketing and finance. Management auditor after analysing the process of management has to further look into the functional areas and adopt certain check-list for evaluation.

Purchase Department : Purchasing of goods is the starting point for any trading or manufacturing activity. The quality of the purchases will affect production efficiency and the quantity purchased will determine the efficiency of stock holding and return on capital employed. The basic role of the purchase department therefore is to purchase the right type of goods at the right price at the right time and at the right place.

Check-list

1. Is the purchase function centralised/decentralised?
2. Are the purchase requirements related to production schedules?
3. Are regular and dependable suppliers are ensured?
4. How are the suppliers selected and eliminated?
5. What is the system of purchase authorisation?
6. Is latest market information regularly collected regarding new products?
7. Are studies conducted regularly to analyse price trends?
8. Is comparison made between average price paid and average market price.
9. How effective is the system of follow-up orders?
10. What is the system of executing emergency purchases?

Production Department : The ingredients used in production are material, men, and machines. The task of production department is to produce the goods of specified quality within the desired time and at the cheapest costs. Management must first assess the existing capacity and if it is not adequate, consider how to increase the capacity and by purchasing additional facilities, getting the work done outside or working overtime, keeping in view the cost involved, quality of product and timing. The next step is scheduling to facilitate flow of production. The necessary manpower needed to run the machines and the procurement of raw- materials are other elements controlling the production. Effective handling of the various components of production (men, material and machine) will enable the organisation to produce the required goods.

Check-list

1. Is there an adequate system of production planning?

2. Are production schedules drawn-up to optimise various factors like plant capacity, raw-materials, skilled workers, availability of funds, machine hour, power, etc.?
3. Is there a close co-ordination with sales department to ensure acceptability of finished products by customers? How effective is the quality control in production?
4. Is the product design properly worked out? Is there a constant review of the product design to improve the cost benefit rates?
5. What is the system of reviewing delays in production?
7. How effective is the control over idle time?
8. Is each production process reviewed periodically to explore the possibility of having more efficient production method?

Personnel Department : The personnel department plays a leading role in any organisation. It is responsible to select, administer, develop and pay for the service of the people. The personnel department will have to ascertain the present as well as future needs of the manpower by the organisation and plan its activity accordingly.

Check-list

1. How is the manpower requirement assessed?
2. What is the recruitment policy? Is qualification for each job prescribed?
3. What is the promotion policy?
4. Are training programmes conducted periodically?
5. Are proper records maintained for all workers? Is time keeping effective?
6. How are the grievances of employees dealt with?
7. How is the discipline maintained? How are the erring workers dealt with?
8. Is the cost of labour turnover and absenteeism worked out?
9. Are demands of the workers legitimate?

Marketing Department : Basic function of Marketing department is the interpretation of the needs of the customer to plan the production of these goods needed by the market and to sell the same to the customer directly or through a network of distributors. The function of marketing department involves (a) Market Research (b) Production planning (c) Pricing (d) Sales promotion & advertising and distribution.

Check-list

1. How is the sales department organised? Is it adequately staffed? Are there any specific responsibilities fixed for development of products in various areas?
2. Are the market forecasts developed regularly?
3. What are the steps taken to improve the market share?
4. Is there any system of performance linked with rewards for sales men?
5. Are sales budget prepared? Is it realistic?
6. What control exists on the expenses incurred by the salesman?
7. How do marketing manager keeps in touch with the changing conditions in market? Are consumers survey conducted regularly?
8. Is there a constant review of order book?
9. Does a proper control over stock of finished goods exist? Are the slow-moving stock reviewed periodically?
10. Is there proper budget for advertising and sales promotion?
11. Are the advertising campaign well-planned? How is its effectiveness judged?

Finance Department : Financial management involves the evaluation of the company's needs for capital, both short-term and longterm. The objective is to satisfy both the needs at the lowest possible cost. The short term (working capital) is required for the day-to-day running of the business. It includes cash in hand, cash at bank, sundry debtors and stock in hand. This in turn depends upon cost of production and the total working cycle. The longterm capital requirements would arise for purchase of land, machinery, building, etc. The decision of financial strategy would depend upon many internal and external factors. The future borrowing and issue of further shares depends upon existing planning, products manufactured, cost estimates and returns expected on fresh investments.

Check-list

1. Is adequate fund available to carry on business?
2. Are the financial structure between debt and equity; fixed assets and current assets; current assets and current liabilities balanced?
3. Are the credit terms reasonable?
4. Are the funds invested judiciously?
5. Are there idle funds?
6. What is the return on capital?
7. Has the cost of capital been considered while borrowing and making investment

— —

8. Is the liquidity position sound?
9. Are too much funds locked in current assets?
10. How is future requirement of funds estimated?
11. How is working capital requirement assessed?

Management Performance

"What was achieved" is not more important than "how was it achieved". The former refers to output whereas the latter to performance which offers potential scope for purposeful evaluation. Performance being supposed as the product of management functions, it also depends upon management process as shown in Fig. 21.2.

	Purchase		Production		Personnel		Marketing		Finance	
Objectives	A_v	a_v	B_v	b_v	C_v	c_v	D_v	d_v	E_v	e_v
Planning	A_w	a_w	B_w	b_w	C_w	c_w	D_w	d_w	E_w	e_w
Organising	A_x	a_x	B_x	b_x	C_x	c_x	D_x	d_x	E_x	e_x
Communicating	A_y	a_y	B_y	b_y	C_y	c_y	D_y	d_y	E_y	e_y
Controlling	A_z	a_z	B_z	b_z	C_z	c_z	D_z	d_z	E_z	e_z

Fig. 21.2 Process-function Matrix

(In the matrix shown in the Fig.21.2, capital letters represent a set of parametres relating to relevant functions, small letters shown an accomplished set of parametres, and the subscript letters V W X Y Z refer to the process of management, i.e., objectives, planning, organising, communicating and control, respectively).

The process-function matrix is an attempt to show the possible areas where occurrence of deviations are common. Further, these deviations can be three dimensional as detailed below :-

(a) Process - Function deviation

1. (Av-av)
Proposed and actual purchase objectives deviations.
2. (Bv-bv)
Proposed and actual production objective deviations.
3. (Cv-cv)
Proposed and actual personnel objective deviations.

(b) Conceptual incongruities

1. (Av-Aw)
Purchase objective incongruent with purchase planning
2. (Bv-Bw)
Production objectives incongruent with production planning

3. (Cv-Cw)

Personnel objectives incongruent with personnel planning

(c) **Functional irrationalities**

1. (Av-Bv)

Purchase objectives incoherent with production objectives.

2. (Av-Cv)

Purchase objectives incoherent with personnel objectives.

3. (Av-Dv)

Purchase objectives incoherent with marketing objectives.

Such and many other deviations are quite inevitable. What is impôrtant is the reason(s) for deviations. No doubt, many such deviations are not measurable but their possible impact-whether gain or loss-can be assessed in terms of money. The total estimated loss or gain may be strictly viewed as an indicator of effectiveness of performance.

Identification of High Pay-off Areas (HPA)

From the process-function matrix high pay-off may be easily located. High pay-off areas are those in which we should invest our men, materials, machines, money etc., so that we realise the maximum return on our investment. The are those areas in which 20% of the results. Identification of these areas shall make significant economic different for any organisation by avoiding costly non-production work. In short, high pay-off areas relate to those areas in which the results are significant to the organisation.

SWOT Analysis

Once the management auditor identified the HPA, then SWOT analysis can be applied for each HPA to draw proper strategies.

Strength : Organisational culture plays a large role in development of strengths of organisation. But the environment (Govt. policies on various matters, the role of competitors, the behaviour, etc.) play equally important role in the evaluation of strengths. The strength of an organisation may be better planning, better coordination; effective communication; proper control; appropriate corrective actions; good industrial relations; sense of belonging among staff and workers; good will; monopoly condition, etc.

Weaknesses : Once again weaknesses may either emanate from the organisational structure or from environmental factors. Weaknesses may arise due to defective organisational set-up; lethargy on the part of the management; inter-union rivalries; frustration among staff and workers; improper fund management; indiscipline among staff and workers, etc.

Opportunities : Opportunities should be identified so that the organisation can plan for the future. Opportunities may exist to effectively utilise men, material, machine, money, etc., to increase the production and to reduce the cost; alternative products at a cheaper cost; diversification of products; expansion; capturing new market etc.

Threats : Equally important is the identification of threats. Unless threats are identified and actions are planned to face them, the very survival of the organisation is bound to suffer. Threats may be in the form of cutthroat competition, unwarranted union activities, continuous bad performance, high absenteeism, high labour turnover, improper maintenance of machine, obsolete machines, outdated methods and design of products, inferior quality, high cost of production, and distribution system, continuous losses, etc.

Further Process

SWOT analysis is a complex one. In certain cases excess strength may weaken the organisation. An organisation with goodwill and monopoly conditions may become weak due to lethargy and improper fund management in course of time. Likewise, excess opportunities may invite threats. If an organisation is in a position to produce goods at a cheaper cost due to favourable factors of production and make considerable margin of profit; it may attract competitors and invite unnecessary union activities. Hence, for success of any organisation appropriate action should be taken up to attain an optimum level.

Step 1 - Organise the Opportunities : All the opportunities available for better management, improving productivity, expansion etc., should be tapped. While tapping opportunities, care should be taken to attain the optimum level otherwise it may either lead to overflowing resulting into waste or bursting, resulting into complete crackdown. The existing and expected opportunities should be tapped in a systematic manner and analysed properly before implementation. Further, management should try out each opportunity on a small scale to start with so that little is lost if it does not work. While taking action, the management must foresee its impact on various goals. Its consequences are likely to be both desirable and undesirable, both immediate and long range, both tangible and intangible, both certain and uncertain, and the management should take all possibilities into account.

Step 2 - Thrash-out Threats : The opportunities available to improve the organisation in all its spheres should be formulated into action by stage by stage. Further, it should be analysed logically-which opportunity should be taken up first and its consequence. Again threats may exist within or outside the organisation which may impose problems and create hurdles. Attempts should be made to eliminate all threats at the beginning stage itself.

Step 3 - Stabilise Strength : Once the organisation has identified its strength while organising the opportunities, and effective steps have been taken to thrash-out threats, then it may further proceed towards stabilisation of its strength. While doing so, the management has to look into all technical, economical, political and social aspects very carefully. In this process excess flesh should be cut-off and all loose ends should be tied up. In other words, care should be taken to assess the exact requirement of factors of production-men, material, machine, money etc. Strength in management will not brook delay in operation that are unprofitable and inefficient should be discontinued. When a new opportunity has been tasted and proved, it should be fed into the stream of operation at once.

Step 4 - Weed-out Weaknesses : The inherent weaknesses in the management process and functional areas should be identified and eliminated to march towards better performance and progress. However, the cost of eliminating the weakness should not exceed its benefits. The management must catch incipient crisis long before they erupt. It should seek out problem areas and make sure they are resolved. Whenever a red light appears, the management should dig into reasons, find a solution, and not let the matter slide. The management should not rest until it is resolved.

Distinction Between Financial Audit, Cost Audit and Management Audit

Criteria	Financial Audit (statutory)	Cost Audit (statutory)	Management Audit
1. Time span	Immediate past	Immediate past and also a little bit of present and future	Present, future and past (in the order)
2. Field of audit	Financial accounting records and allied documents	Cost accounting records and allied documents	Records of all types, even things that are not documented depending on the scope of the audit
3. Principles, conventions, norms, practices and procedures	Available almost fully - detailed and well-structured	Available by and large and reasonably well-structured	Not available at all (barring only overlapping areas, if any)

4. Area and scope of audit	Statutorily defined/determined	Statutorily defined/determined	Determined with respect to the objectives/purposes of the audit and included in the terms of reference.
5. Rights, duties/ obligations and liabilities of the auditors	Statutorily determined (vide Section 224 to 233 of the Companies Act, 1956)	Statutorily determined (vide Section 224 to 233 of the Companies Act, 1956)	- do - (some legal obligations might arise under the common law, if not the Companies Act)
6. Reporting	To the share holders	To the Government (Company Law Board)	To the management (or the persons/entity at whose behest the audit is conducted)

Some Unresolved Issues in Management Audit

Some of the unresolved issues in management audit are as follows :

(i) There is no statutory status, protection or security of tenure for the management auditor, nor is there any uniformity in the range or depth of audit he has to undertake. His rights, duties and liabilities require clear determination;

(ii) Who are the persons qualified to conduct management audit? Chartered accountants, cost accountants, management experts (with formal management qualifications) or any other persons?

(iii) To whom will the management auditor send his report? The management, the shareholders or the government?

Any attempt to answer all such questions is deliberately avoided primarily because of the highly controversial nature of all the issues involved. But one observation in the area of qualification of management auditor may be made here. Considering the responsibility attached to and the challenge posed by the job, none of the professional groups mentioned above appears to be adequately equipped to do justice to the job themselves. The right approach would perhaps be to assign the management audit to a team (instead of one person) formed with both internal and external experts and represented by chartered accountants, cost accountants, management experts, etc. If the team be composed of say, three or four people, perhaps the best results could be obtained and at the same time, element of bias due to subjective value judgement could be reduced to the minimum.

Conclusion

A doer cannot be observer of his function, a writer cannot be a critic of his article, an actor cannot be director of his cast. Likewise, a performer cannot be an appriser of his function. Both have different vision and mission towards the same function with an end in view to improve the performance. The same principle applies to management and the management auditor. Management auditor can independently apprise the processes and functional areas of management. By doing so, he can identify the high pay-off areas and suggest further course of action to stabilise the strengths, weed out the weaknesses, organise the opportunities and and thrash out threats to the organisation.

REVIEW QUESTIONS

1. Explain the concept of Proprietary audit.
2. What is a management audit? How far is it different from Proprietary audit?
3. What are the steps involved in conducting a management audit?
4. Who should be management auditor?
5. State and explain the different aspects of management audit methodology.
6. List out the points to be considered while drafting a management audit report.
7. While conducting the management audit of a large enterprise which functional areas of management would you specifically review?
8. Differentiate management audit from financial audit and cost audit.

22
Production Control

Definition of Production Control : According to the British Standards Institute, production control is the mixture of the principles or factors namely planning, scheduling, despatching, stock control, routing and progress. In the light of these principles we can define the production control as, "it is a directive agency which regulates for an orderly flow of materials and coordination of the different production operations, following the scientific procedure of its principles viz., planning, routing, scheduling, despatching and inspecting, and taking the objective or producing the right quality in the right quantity at the right time at minimum cost". In the words of L.P. Alford and J.R. Bangs. "The highest efficiency in production is obtained by manufacturing the required quantity of product, of the required quality, at the required time, by the best and cheapest method".

Need for Production Control : Production control regulates systematic flow of materials, verifies the occurrence in conformity with the plan adopted and also corrects deviations from plans before they occur. Considering these functions, production control is a boon to an enterprise. Goods must be produced as much, and when it is required by the customers. Also it must be of right quality and produced with most economic cost. Production control take these responsibilities to perform in the current era where there is cut-throat competition and a constant tug of war between the customers and the products. Production control also maintains a balance in activities required for completing a job. Production control is the half mark of production efficiency, it is the pivot around which the success of production revolves and, it is necessity and not a luxury : a profitable investment and not an expense.

Objects of Production Control ; There are certain objects of production control which may be summarised as below :

(i) To arrange for the production of commodities according to the predetermined demand.

(ii) To arrange necessary raw-materials, machine, tools and workers for the production.

(iii) To utilise the available production facilities to its maximum so that the production cost is minimum and goods are available when required.

(iv) To arrange for product-development and design.

(v) To co-ordinate the activities of different departments relating to the production.

(vi) To arrange the activities of quality control and inspection so that the goods are produced according to the predetermined standards and specifications.

(vii) To determine economic lots and ascertain sequence of operations so that set-up cost is reduced.

(viii) To supply raw materials to the plant equipment at proper time, proper place and in proper quantity so that congestion and delays in production may be eliminated.

In short, the objective of an ideal production control is like a guide which should see that there is an orderly flow of materials and should boil down a long and complicated series of production operations into production orders so that product may be manufactured in the right quantity, of the right quality and at the minimum cost.

Difference between Production planning and Production control

Many people think of production control as a function embracing both planning and control. Since control amounts to compelling to conform to plans, it is evident that these two functions are intimately bound together. The planning function contributes to the smooth discharge of control through objectives, standing plans, programmes or budgets. On the other hand, the control function contributes to the adoption of new plans. Production control is a regulating or adjusting process and it follows operation just as operation follows production planning. Production planning is always tempered with production control information from current operations, and it undergoes to adopt or adjust according to the needs of the situation. Apart from their mutual contributions, production plans are required to be modified for successful controlling while, on the other hand the production control system is liable to be modified successful planning.

Advantages of Production Control

Production control is advantageous not only to the management but it also renders valuable services to the customers.

Production Control pays the management : Production control makes available the products to the customers of right quality, in right quantity and at most economic cost. It is necessary for every enterprise to allign productive activities with its sale programme. Such an allignment will initiate for the production of goods by the best and least cost methods, thereby the market can be captured and may captivate the customer's heart. The larger amount of sales will fetch greater amount of profit and prosperity and greater the chance to survive in the market.

Production control renders valuable services to customers : Customers are the soul of a manufacturing concern. They can be satisfied only by offering them products of right quality, right quantity at the right time and at the most economical cost. Thus production control tries to provide better products at lower prices for the consumers. An ideal production control balances while marching towards its predetermined goal and set of goals. One should not be sacrificed at the alter of the other.

Techniques or Mechanism of Production Control

Production control has to perform certain activities for which its principles and techniques must assemble these activities as given below :

1. Routing

Routing means determination of path or route on which manufacturing operations will travel, establishing the sequence of operations to be followed in manufacturing a particular product. In other words, routing is the selection of paths or route over which each piece is to travel in being transformed from raw material into finished product. Evidently, where one single product or part is manufactured by a fixed set of machines, the job of routing becomes mechanical. In the mass and process production systems with their fixed line layout, it needs no managerial effort for routing, though different sets of machines are used in manufacturing the products in such systems. But in job production and batch production, routing becomes a different task for manufacturing of a different product. It needs manufacturing process to be outlined on different route sheets for every item or lot of production.

Besides determining operation sequences, routing is concerned with the fixation of requisite facilities to be used in manufacturing. Routing designates the quantity of materials, tools, fixtures and jigs, number of skilled and unskilled operatives which are required for production. Broadly speaking, routing provides the basis for scheduling, dispatching and follow-up. Routing includes the planning of where and by whom work shall be done, the determination of the path that work shall follow and the necessary sequence of operation. It forms ground work for most of the scheduling and despatching functions of planning.

Routing Procedures

(i) To analyse the product and fabricate into constituent parts and then decide the number of items to be purchased and manufactured.

(ii) To analyse the product and component parts so that materials required may be determined. For this, a 'part list' containing if standard of quality, symbols for identification, specifications and drawing is prepared and then the routing section verify this test with available materials to see whether additional materials are needed to be purchased or not.

(iii) To determine manufacturing operations and their sequence for their performance. Such operations and their proper sequence are listed on route sheet.

(iv) To decide the required process time for each operation and the type and number of machines necessary to produce articles.

(v) To decide lot size of order quantity.

(vi) To determine scrap factors which leads to normal spoilage.

(vii) To design the forms which are necessary for plant departments. These forms are primarily influenced by the type of manufacture.

A careful study of the procedures in routing will reveal that there are certain factors which mainly influence the routing procedure. These are : the manufacturing type employed, availability of the plant equipment and its component parts, characteristics of the physical plant equipment and its component parts, and human elements.

2. Loading

After the route has been established, the work can be loaded against the concerned machines and equipment. Loading deals with the amount of work assigned to a machine or a worker. Persons concerned with loading keep all the records of the workload and capacity of different shops. The total time required to perform the workload is computed by multiplying the unit operation time given on the standard process sheet by the number of parts planned for the work station. This process results in a tabulated list or chart showing the planned utilisation of machines or work stations in the plant. The chart helps in assessing the spare capacity. If the loading charts indicate sufficient spare capacity, efforts should be directed through the sales department to obtain more orders for the utilisation of the spare capacity. Underload of certain departments may also arise from ineffective planning. In such a case, the remedy lies in proper planning. But if, on other hand, there is an overload in any work station, action on any one or more of the following lines may be taken.

(a) arrangement of overtime work;

(b) introduction of an additional shift;

(c) transfer of operations to another shop; and

(d) sub-contracting of the excess work-load.

3. Scheduling

Another important phase of mechanism of production control is scheduling. In production control scheduling means 'rating of the work at prescribed time in a prescribed sequence in the order of its priority'. In other words, Scheduling involves establishing the amount of work to be done, and the time when each element of the work will start or order of the work. Thus scheduling is a logical time-table of production which indicates when work will be released to the plant in a prescribed order in the proper sequence.

Objective

1. To eliminate idle capacity and thus to maximise production.
2. To eliminate or atleast to minimise the idel labour time.
3. To meet the established lead times.

Kinds : Usually three types of schedules are prepared for the production control :

1. **Master Schedule :** It tells the dates on which the various jobs are to be completed.
2. **Operation (Production) Schedule :** It indicates the total time needed to do a given piece of work with a given machine or process.
3. **Detail Operation Schedule :** It indicates the time required to do each detail operation of a given job with a given machine or process.

Production Control Charts

Following production control charts are very popular in production scheduling :

1. **Gantt Chart :** It points out plans for future, progress of present operations and a record of past achievements for future reference. Such charts are suitable for large scale production and are the most popular form of control devices.
2. **Load Chart :** It indicates the load on each machine and tells about the over-loading or under-loading of different machines at different of time.
3. **Man-Machine Chart :** It depicts through graphs the actual and potential performance of a worker in relation to his machine.
4. **Bar Chart :** It indicates the progress of work, that is, what has already taken place.

Factors Affecting Scheduling

Scheduling is affected by the following factors :

A. Internal Factors

1. **Position of finished good in stock :** Scheduling of production is done keeping in view the position of stock of finished goods with the firm.
2. **Availability of man power :** Scheduling should be made keeping in view the availability of manpower at different periods of time.
3. **Availability of machines and equipment :** Since production depends on the availability of machines and their capacity, scheduling is affected by this factor also.

4. **Availability of raw materials :** Even if adequate manpower and machines are available, production will depend on the availability of raw materials. Hence, scheduling is done keeping in view the avilability of raw materials.

5. **Process interval :** Since different processes have different process intervals, the early or late start of different processes also affect the scheduling of production.

B. External Factors

1. **Demand for the product in the market :** Scheduling has to be done keeping in veiw the demand for the product in the market so that it could be met easily.

2. **Delivery dates :** While scheduling, the delivery dates of the product(s) play an important role.

3. **Stock of finished goods with the dealers :** Scheduling is done keeping in view the stock position of finished goods with the dealers.

As compared to scheduling in continuous production, scheduling in intermittent production is a bit difficult because of variation in the order specifications, varying sequence of processes, need of different types of materials, changes in the machine set-up, etc.

Difference between Routing and Scheduling : Both routing and scheduling are important techniques of production control which are compensatory to each other. The object of routing is to determine the best production sequence which is most economical while on the other hand, the object of scheduling is to prepare a logical time-table which shows when production work will start and finish according to predetermined programme. Routing considers the 'Where' aspects as distinguished from the scheduling 'When'.

4. Despatching

Despatching is another important technique of production control. It is a doing function of production management and initiates actual manufacturing in accordance with the work of routing and scheduling. Despatching is the routing of setting production activities in motion through the release of order and instructions, in accordance with previously planned times and sequence, embodied in route sheets and scheduled charts. As a basic function in production activities, despatching is concerned with the issuance of orders, instructions and other communication to the workforce, demanding accountability of their performance, exercising leadership and supervision and maintaining discipline and morale of production personnel. In fact despatching translates into reality of physical work which has been planned by scheduling.

Functions of Despatching : The following functions may be included in despatching :

(i) To assign the work to definite machines or work places and men.

(ii) To issue the necessary materials, tools, Jigs, fixtures, dies and gauges for various jobs etc., to their correct points of use.

(iii) To release necessary orders and production forms so that the operations may be started by dispatcher.

(iv) To guide and control the materials and operations in processing on the basis of route sheets and schedules.

(v) To note the start and finish time of each and every job.

(vi) To make contact with routing and scheduling sections so that their plans and schedules may not overlap.

5. Follow-up

Follow-up or chasing is though last, but most important step of production control. It means to see whether it carries the progress of production operations according to the planning. In other words, follow-up is the means by which the execution of the production plan is efficiently coordinated so as to reveal, and as far as possible to eliminate any variations from the plan which has set the engine of productional control moving to a definite goal.

Follow-up function can be divided into three parts- follow-up of materials, follow-up of work in progress and follow-up of assembly and erection. The follow-up section should minutely discover the delays that have crept into industrial progress. The causes for delays may be scheduling of uneconomic lot sizes, scheduling of machinery beyond capacity, underestimation of materials, tools, equipment and man-power, errors in processing and inspection etc.

Manufacturing Systems

Methods, organisation and operation differs from company to company. They also differ with the types of production (normally two basic types) even when both the types are sued by a single enterprise. These types or systems are intermittent and continuous production. Intermittent system of production may further be divided in two types namely 'Job' and 'Bath' production, while continuous production may also be sub-divide in two types 'Mass' and 'Process' production. the usual scale of operation is small in the case of job production, medium in batch production, large in mass production and very large in process production.

Goods are produced either according to definite customer's orders or the are produced to stock. They are also produced by four general types of operations : job, batch, mass and process. Many combinations of goods are produced either to stock or to order by these types of operation. Both job order and stock production may be adopted by a single company and even under one building.

There are some companies which simplify job order and stock production mixtures by having code designations of their products :

A is used for products to be carried in stock.

B is used for products to be produced only on customer's orders, and for which raw materials are carried in stock.

C is used for products to be produced only on customer's orders, and for which no raw materials are carried in stock.

D is used for products to produce experimentally.

The above classification of products is helpful to production planners. For type A products planning methods based upon sales forecasts are used. For type B products job-order planning methods are used and raw materials are maintained within prescribed limits and reorder points. For type C products full job-order planning methods with raw materials ordered specifically for each customer order are used.

Some customers decide term contracts for commodities in the B and C types of products. These types of contracts help manufactures to plan production in advance and to avoid uneconomic lot sizes. The customer generally agrees that he will buy a specified quantity of certain product during a certain period. He generally specifies the estimated quantity he will require monthly, and the minimum quantity to order at one time. Under such a contract with customer the supplier may be able to produce the product specified in it on the basis of production to stock and can set upper and lower stock control limits. The commodities under such contract are designated as BA or CA on manufacturing orders to indicate that they are being carried in stock for the duration of the contract.

The system of production may be discussed here as follows :

i. Job Production : In this system goods are produced to definite customer orders. As in this type there is no assurance of a continued demand for specific items and the manufacturing is dependent on the receipt of orders from customers, job production is of intermittent character. Each product is a class by itself and constitutes a distinct and separate job for production purposes. In some instances there is no repetition of orders for exactly the same item, in such cases job production calls for an adjustment of tools and equipment in working out each individual job. An enterprise which produces capital goods such as heavy, special-purpose machinery generally use the job-order method of production.

ii. Batch Production : It involves the manufacture of a group, batch or lot of products on the basis of customer's orders or expected demand for products. Both batch and job production are similar in nature and have almost, the same features except in regard to the quantity of production. In job production, one single product is manufactured while a batch of group of products is turned out at a time under the system of batch production. Strictly speaking, batch production is only an extension of job production system. Peter. Drucker has grouped these two systems under a single title of "unique-product production". In the system of batch production, when the production of a batch is completed, the plant and machines become available to other batch of similar type of production. The best example of this type is chemical industry where different medicines are manufactured separately in batches. Machines tools, Printing press etc., may also be given examples of this type.

Thus is both job and batch systems of production goods are produced to definite customer orders. Regarding basic system of planning and scheduling employed in these systems, there is no clear-cut separation of functions in this field, nor are they clearly coordinated. By using diagrams for functions, rectangles for forms or documents, and solids for raw or processed matèrials much of the confusion is eliminated. Planning for these systems of production can not begin with a sales forecast giving the number of items that may be sold in a planning period. For example, a steel fabricator has no way of estimating how many roof trusses of certain dimensions will be sold during the first quarter of next year. He will have to estimate on the basis of general business conditions, past experience and having an idea of future sales efforts.

In the job or batch system, orders are placed on the load chart as they are received. Department schedules also are not made for total production period but are prepared after customer orders are received. Personnel schedules are also not prepared in advance. It should be noted here that when manufacturing to stock, load charts are prepared in advance of production for the period. There is also no procurement schedule for minimum balances of basic materials used in filling almost every order, as there is in manufacturing to stock.

iii. Mass Production : This system of production is used by companies where manufacturing is carried on continuously though not having always uniform demand. Standardisation is the keynote of mass production. Standardised materials and machines are used in a standard process of production for manufacturing standardised products or parts thereof. To maintain an even and continuous flow of production, machines and equipments are laid out in conformity with the sequence of operations required for manufacturing a particular product. In manufacturing two different products, two sets of machines are used to avoid interruptions and delays in setting tools or in adjusting equipments.

iv. Process Production : This system is an extended form of mass production in which manufacturing is carried on continuously through an uniform sequence of operations. Process production calls for the setting up of automatic machines and equipments as far as possible. Large industries like petroleum refining, plate-glass manufacturing, heavy chemical industries uses generally this system of production. Under this system, usually one principal raw material is transformed into several products at different stages of the operations, for example, crude petroleum is processed into kerosene, gasolene and other like products.

Manufacture to stock type of production is used by companies whose products are in continued, though not always uniform demand. Before planning of manufacture to stock, a sales forecast is made to understand the number of each item or product likely to be sole during a further period i.e., three months, six months, or a year. After, a master production schedule is prepared to adjust the sales forecast according to back orders and inventory. For example, if sales forecast calls for 4,00,000 of a certain items and 40,000 items are carried as a normal stock and 20,000 are on back order, the two latter numbers are added to the forecast, giving a master production schedule of 4,60,000. If, on the hand, there is no back order and 60,000 of this item are in stock the 20,000 in excess of normal inventory are substracted from the forecast, and the master production schedule then will become 3,80,000.

v. Production Control Mechanisms for Intermittent Manufacturing System : In this system of production, the goods are manufactured specially to fulfil orders made by customers rather than for stock. The following points of production control mechanism that applies to this system of production are worth noting :

1. As this type of manufacture covers specialities of every kind and sub-assemblies or parts which are required for manufacturing other products, it requires careful routing of the orders in the manufacturing schedule.

2. Due to large number of orders and separate lots, scheduling becomes rather elaborate and complex and requires wise and careful act for proper sequence of operations.

3. Proper regulation and close checking of work-in-process is required.

4. The job of stock control of raw materials should be given to the competent personnel who regulate the operations and eliminate such materials which do not move at all, or in case they move, the movement is slow hindering a steady flow of operations.

Production Control Mechanism for Continuous Manufacturing System : In continuous system of production, the production control mechanism is not as elaborate and complex as that for intermittent system of production as continuous system involves making of a large portion of standard products in large quantities. However, the following points of production control mechanism in regard to this system are worth noting :

1. As this system does not involve diverse work, routing is comparatively simple and follows either when plant-facilities are being organised in the operational sequence or when they are being revised for the manufacture of standard products.
2. In order to avoid confusion and to have proper scheduling specifications and route sheets are prepared.
3. In case for standard products meant for mass production master route sheets are also prepared to co-ordinate more effectively the various departments of the plant.
4. In continuous manufacturing system, scheduling is required to rate the output of various standard products in their order of priority, operations and correct sequence to meet sales requirements.
5. The work relating to despatching and follow-up is usually simple as despatchers in highly continuous manufacture usually release schedule to the different departments of the plant even before the start of the manufacturing period.

A comparative study of different Systems of Production : A comparative study explaining the distinct features of the different systems of production may be made in the following way :

1. Size and Capital Investment : As already pointed out, the usual scale of operation is small in case of job production, medium in batch production, large in mass production and very large in process production. Hence the need for capital investments differs from one system to another. In job production it requires the lowest amount of capital, batch production requires comparatively large capital investment than job production and so much so, the process production calls for highest amount of capital investment.

2. Cost of Manufacturing : The unit cost of manufacturing is the largest in the case of job production, while it is the lowest in process production. Mass production is inferior to process production but is better than job production in matters of production cost.

3. Required Technical Ability : Both job and batch production require high skilled technical foremen and other executives. But managerial ability is of greater importance in the case of mass and process production. It should also be noted that it requires higher ability for planning and co-ordinating several functions in mass production and process production than in the case of batch production and job production.

4. Industrial Application : The mechanism of job production applies in products of construction and manufacturing industries like buildings, bridges, special-purpose machines etc. Batch production is mostly used in mechanical-engineering and consumers goods industries like cotton, jute, machine-tools, shoe-making, etc. Mass production is found in automobiles, sugar-refining, electrical products, refrigerators etc. Process production is appropriate for petroleum-refining, milk- processing, chemical industries etc.

5. Organisational Structures : Functional organisation is mostly adopted in case of job production and batch production. On the other hand, mass production and process production is adopted mostly in divisional organisational pattern due to the greater emphasis for centralisation.

6. Flexibility in Production : Both job production and batch production are capable to adjust their production facilities shortly just after the change in demand for products and without incurring heavy expenses. But as both mass production and process production employ single-purpose machine in their manufacturing operations, these cannot adjust their production facilities so easily like job or batch production wherein general-purpose machines are utilised.

7. Job Security : As job and batch production possesses the intermittent characters of production, they cannot provide any job security. During bad times, workers particularly unskilled become out of job. On the contrary, in mass or process production workers enjoy a greater employment stability. Continuous production system applies only when there is a stable, expanding or dependable market. Moreover heavy overcost burden also prevents them from reducing their scale of operation.

Requirements of Efficient Production Control

In order to achieve an efficient system of production control, the following points must be given due consideration :

(i) Preliminary Appraisal : Preliminary appraisal is essential to understand the areas where there are possibilities of bottlenecks.

(ii) Continuous checking : Production control is a continuous process. In order to avoid higher wastage, it is essential to carry on checking of various processes when they are in the working order.

(iii) Freedback : Significant variations at different levels of production must be pointed out to the manager concerned. Limits should be laid down up to which the deviations from the standards are to be tolerated.

(iv) Flexibility : Sufficient flexibility should be ensured to meet emergencies which may arise because of power failure, breakdown of machinery etc.

(v) Up-to-date Information : The persons concerned with control of production should have up-to-date knowledge about the quantity of work-in-process, availability of various types of material, unused plant capacity etc.

(vi) Improvement : Production control should also concentrate on bringing about improvements in work methods. Alternative methods may be tried to handle peak load. The improved methods should be applied after giving sufficient instructions to the workers.

REVIEW QUESTIONS

1. Define 'Production Management' and discuss the various production systems used in modern industrial organisations.
2. Describe the process of Production Planning and Control in a manufacturing enterprise which undertakes production to order.
3. What is the purpose of production planning and control? Indicate the steps involved in production planning and control.
4. Discuss how far production planning and control can be introduced in various types of industries.
5. Discuss between routing and scheduling. Discuss the need of 'expediting' in production planning and control.
6. Discuss the application of production planning and control in (a) assembly industry, and (b) process industry.
7. What are the requirements of an efficient system of production control?
8. What are the objectives planning and control? Discuss the steps involved in production control.

23
Inventory Control

Proper control of materials or inventory can make a substantial contribution to the efficiency of a business. The success of a business concern largely depends upon efficient purchasing, storage, consumption and accounting. The uncontrolled inventories are dangerous and at times it is called as the grave yard of business. Hence, inventory control system should be designed to ensure the provision of the required quantity of material of the required quality at the required time to meet the needs of production and sales, while at the same time keeping the investment in them at a minimum.

Classification of Inventories

(i) Investment in Raw Materials : The investment in raw materials on a particular date represents the value of materials, components and parts required for use in the process of production. When purchases of raw materials increase, investment of funds in raw materials also increases and when they are issued to production, they decrease. The following are the important determinants as regard the level of raw materials to be maintained ; (a) the quantity representing safety stocks, (b) economy in the matter of purchases, (c) anticipated fluctuations in the prices of the materials in the future, (d) cost of carrying stocks, (e) funds available for investment in materials, (f) expected quantity of consumption, and (g) management's efficiency in the purchases and control of the materials.

(ii) Investment in Work-in-Progress : Investment in the cost of raw materials and the direct expenses connected with the production and allocation of proportionate overhead expenses. The cost of raw materials used, wages and other direct expenses included in work in progress are the factors that generally influence the investment in work in progress. The amount of funds tied up in work in progress will be directly influenced with the volume or production and the period of time taken in the manufacturing or production and the period of time taken in the manufacturing or production process. Thus if there is increase in production, the investment in work in progress also increase. If the volume of production is reduced, there is fall in investment. However, production should coincide with sales.

(iii) Investment in Finished Goods : Finished goods inventories are generally maintained to the minimum by providing only to orders. Some manufacturers maintain sufficient stock in anticipation of sales. In seasonal industries, retailers are forced to carry larger stock than the manufacturers.

(iv) Indirect Inventories : They include lubricants and other items (like spare parts) needed for proper operation, repair and maintenance during manufacturing cycle.

Motives in Holding Inventories : Generally three motives are involved in holding inventories (i) The *transaction motive* which emphasises the need to maintain inventories to facilitate smooth production and sales operations (called transaction inventory). (ii) The *precautionary motive* which necessitates holding of inventories to guard against the risks of unpredictable changes in demand and supply forces (called precautionary inventory). (iii) The *speculative motive* which influences the decision to increase or reduce inventory levels to take advantage of price fluctuations (called speculative inventory).

The main **reasons for holding inventories** can be summarised as follows :

(a) to ensure that sufficient goods are available to meet anticipated demand;

(b) to absorb variations in demand and production;

(c) to provide a buffer between production processes. This is applicable to work-in-progress stocks which effectively decouple operations;

(d) to take advantage of bulk purchasing discounts;

(e) to meet possible shortages in the future;

(f) to absorb seasonal fluctuations in usage or demand;

(g) to enable production processes to flow smoothly and efficiently;

(h) as a necessary part of the production process;

(i) as deliberate investment policy particularly in times of inflation or possible shortage.

Alternative Reasons for Inventories : The reasons given above are the logical ones based on deliberate decisions. However, stocks accumulate for other, less praise-worthy reasons, typical of which are of the following :

(a) Obsolete items are retained in stock.

(b) Poor or non existent inventory control resulting in over-large orders, replenishment orders being out of phase with production, etc.

(c) Inadequate or non-existent stock records.

(d) Poor liaison between the Production Control< Purchasing and Marketing departments.

(e) Sub-optimal decision-making, e.g, the Production Department might increase W.I.P stocks unduly so as to ensure long production runs.

Objectives of Effective Inventory Control

Inventory control is the process of deciding what and how much of various items are to be kept in stock. It also determines the time and quantity of various items to be procured. The basic objective of inventory control is to reduce investment in inventories and ensuring that production process does not suffer at the same time. An effective inventory management should (i) ensure a continuous supply of materials to facilitate uninterrupted production, (ii) maintain sufficient stocks of raw materials in periods of short supply and anticipate price changes, (iii) maintain sufficient finished goods inventory for smooth sales operation, and efficient customer service, (iv) minimise the carrying costs and time, and (v) control investment in inventories and keep it at an optimum level.

For attainment of higher production it is necessary to keep the plant and machinery in perfect order with minimum of repairs and maintenance cost possible and to produce goods in relation to market demand and future sales potentiality. To achieve these two-fold objectives requires multi-dimensional controls on various activities. In this context, inventories can be broadly classified into two, namely, *production inventories and repair/maintenance inventories.*

Broadly, the objectives of inventory control can be classified into operative objectives and financial objectives. *Operative objectives* aim at avoiding production bottle-necks by ensuring continuous supply of all types of materials, weeding out obsolete items, avoidance of wastages like theft, pilferage, leakage, spoilage etc., promotion of manufacturing efficiency and prompt execution of customers' orders. The *financial objectives* of inventory control include effecting economy in purchasing through 'economic order quantity' and taking advantages of favourable markets, maintaining optimum level of investment in inventories, etc.

This is achieved by, (a) Purchasing material at an economical price, at proper time and in sufficient quantities so as not to run short of them at any instant, (b) Providing a suitable and secure storage location, (c) Providing enough storage space, (d) A definite inventory identification system, (e) Adequate and responsible store room staff, (f) Suitable requisition procedure, (g) Up-to-date and accurate record keeping, (h) Periodic inventory check up, and (i) Division of inventory under A, B, and C items, exercising the control accordingly and removing obsolete inventory.

Functions of Inventory Control Department

In the case of a manufacturing organisation, the functions of inventory control department will be as follows :

1. Planning the inventories : It involves working out the periodic requirements of the inventories based on sales forecasting.

2. Procurement of inventories : Having planned the inventory requirements, the next function of the inventory control is to procure the required amount of inventories from the selected suppliers at competitive rates, of good quality, and in time.

3. Receiving and inspection : The inventory control department is then supposed to receive the purchased inventories inspect the quality and quantity by comparing it with the purchase order and packing slip etc.

4. Storing and issuing the inventories : Having received the inventories the same are to be properly stored and issued on proper requisition from the production department.

5. Keeping the required inventories in adequate quantity : So as to meet the requirements of the production department.

6. Maintaining the capital investments in inventories at the minimum desirable level : Without sacrificing the main interests of trading.

7. Safeguarding the inventories : From pilferage, damages, deterioration, losses, etc.

8. Coding, identifying all items : In a manner that the same can be located easily as and when required.

9. Maintaining proper records of inventories : All entries of receipt and issue of inventories should be properly recorded and balances worked out.

10. Physical verification : Inventory control department is also supposed to carry out periodic physical verification of inventories and prepare detailed report of losses, causes responsible for such losses and also suggest measures to overcome such causes.

11. Follow up : In case any fault in the functioning of inventory control department is identified, necessary steps are supposed to be taken by the inventory control department.

12. Material standardisation and substitution : Inventory control department is also expected to standardise the materials. It should also try to find out cheaper substitutes, if possible.

Inventory Costs

There are four cost factors involved in general inventory policies :

(i) The cost of materials itself i.e, material cost.

(ii) The cost associated with keeping the materials in stock i.e., inventory carrying charges, or storage costs. The following costs are incurred in keeping materials in stores, and the longer the period, the materials are stored, the greater these costs become : (a) Capital costs i.e., the loss of return that could be obtained if the capital tied up in stock was employed elsewhere, (b) Space costs such as rent, heating, lighting etc., (c) Equipment costs like bins, racks, etc., (d) Personal costs involved in storing, stock taking, security, etc., (e) Insurance costs i.e., protection against fire, theft, etc., (f) Property taxes, (g) Cost of handling the material, (h) Stationery and other consumables used by the stores, (i) Cost of wastage and material losses in the stores, (j) Obsolescence and deterioration costs. The higher the stock levels, the longer the time materials in stock, and so the greater the risk, and therefore ultimate cost of obsolescence, (k) Depreciation and repair cost for the stores facilities and handling equipment.

These costs come nearly 20 to 25%. These costs are arbitrary and vary from industry to industry and from time to time and also from item to item in the same industry.

(iii) The cost associated with the placement of a purchase order i.e., order costs. This consists of : (a) Salaries of the staff in administration and purchase department, (b) Rent for the space used by the purchase department, (c) Postage, telegram and telephone bills, (d) Stationary and other consumable, required by the purchasing department, (e) Entertainment charges on vendors, (f) Travelling expenses, (g) Lawyers and court fees due to legal matters arising out of purchase.

All these cost usually come to 15 to 20 percent, as ordering cost. The expenditure on ordering of material is directly proportional to the number of orders placed.

(iv) Carrying inventory which results where there is stock left on hand after the demand for the item has terminated. This cost is called the **overstock** cost or **under stock** cost.

INVENTORY CONTROL TECHNIQUES

In most manufacturing concerns inventories are controlled through the following techniques or tools :

(i) Economic Order Quantity.

(ii) Determination Stock Levels.

(iii) Inventory Turnover Ratio

(iv) Input-output Ratio Analysis.

(v) ABC Analysis.

(vi) Perpetual Inventory and Continuous Stock taking.

(vii) Value Analysis.

The scientific inventory management helps the purchase department to determine when to buy and how much to buy. The problem before the management is to be balance the following opposing costs.

S.No.	Cost to have inventory	Cost not to have inventory
(i)	Return on Investment	Stock out costs
(ii)	Storage cost	Lost sale. Loss of future sale (Demand x Future Profitability)
(iii)	Handling cost	Loss of customers/goodwill
(iv)	Handling equiptment	Down time cost
(v)	Obsolescence	Idle labour, Idle production
(vi)	Spoilage and shelf life	Capacity and other cost

Every businessman must have faced the problem of either being out of stock or a large amount of money tied up in the form of inventories. Some of the evils of excess inventory are given below.

(a) lock up of capital unnecessarily in inventories which could be invested in more profitable operations,

(b) excess inventory adds to the cost of carrying the inventory more store space, equipment and personnel, insurance, taxes, pilferage etc.,

(c) excess inventory invites risk of deterioration and obsolescence,

(d) changes in the prices of inventory materials sometime go unfavourable.

Economic Order Quantity (E.O.Q.)

The Economic Order Quantity (E.O.Q.) is the optimum or the most favourable quantity which should be ordered for purchase each time when the purchases are to be made. The Economic Order Quantity is one where the cost of carrying is equal to, or almost equal to the cost of not carrying. To sum up, E.O.Q. is that size of the order which gives maximum economy in purchasing any material and ultimately contributes towards maintaining the material at the optimum level and at the minimum cost.

The E.O.Q. is also known as Reorder Quantity or Standard Order Quantity and it depends upon two factors viz., cost of carrying and cost of ordering and receiving per order. The cost of carrying or holding costs can be estimated by the management on the basis of sales of past years but costs of not carrying enough are only estimated.

The widely used formula of E.O.Q. is $\sqrt{\dfrac{2.\,C.O}{I}}$

Where, C = Annual consumption of materials concerned in units,

O = Ordering and receiving cost per order,

I = Interest payment including variable cost of storage per unit per year. or

$$E.O.Q. = \sqrt{\frac{2AB}{C}}$$ Where, A = Annual consumption, B = Ordering cost per batch and C = Cost of carrying

or

$$E.O.Q. = \sqrt{\frac{2 R \times S}{I}}$$ Where, R = Annual consumption, S = storing cost, I = interest for carrying cost.

Illustration 1: A manufacturer buys certain equipment from supplier at Rs. 30 per unit. Total annual needs are 800 units. The following further data are available :

Annual return as investment 10%

Rent, insurance, taxes per unit per year Re. 1

Cost of placing an order Rs. 100

Determine the economic order quantity.

Answer. Cost of carrying inventory per unit = 30 x 10% + 1 = Rs. 4.

$$E.O.Q. = \sqrt{\frac{2 \times 100 \times 800}{30 \times 10\% + 1}} = 200 \text{ units}$$

Assumptions and Limitations of E.O.Q : The major weaknesses of the E.O.Q. model are associated with several of its assumptions, in spite of which the model tends to yield quite good results. Where its assumptions have been dramatically violated, the E.O.Q. model can generally be easily modified to accommodate the situation. The model's assumptions are as follows :

1. **Constant or uniform demand :** Although the E.O.Q. model assumes constant demand, demand may vary from day to day. If demand is stochastic - that is, not known in advance - the model must be modified through the inclusion of a safety stock.

2. **Constant unit price :** The inclusion of variable prices resulting from quantity discounts can be handled quite easily through a modification of the original E.O.Q. model redefining total costs and solving for the optimum order quantity.

3. **Constant carrying costs :** Unit carrying costs may vary substantially as the size of the inventory rises, perhaps decreasing because of economies of scale or storage efficiency or increasing as storage space runs out and new warehouses have to be rented. This situation can be handled

through a modification in the original model similar to the one used for variable unit price.

4. **Constant ordering costs :** While this assumption is generally valid, its violation can be accommodated by modifying the original E.O.Q. model in a manner similar to the one used for variable unit price.

5. **Instantaneous delivery :** If delivery is not instantaneous, which is generally the case, the original E.O.Q. model must be modified through the inclusion of a safety stock.

6. **Independent orders :** If multiple orders result in cost savings by reducing paper work and transportation cost, the original E.O.Q. model must be further modified. While this modification is somewhat complicated, special E.O.Q. models have been developed to deal with it.

These assumptions have been pointed out to illustrate the limitations of the basic E.O.Q. model and the ways in which it can easily be modified to compensate for them. Moreover, an understanding of the limitations and assumptions of the E.O.Q. model will provide the financial manager with a strong base for making inventory decisions.

Inflation affects the E.O.Q. model in two major ways. First, while the E.O.Q. model can be modified to assume constant price increases, many times major price increases occur only once or twice a year and are announced ahead of time. If this is the case, the E.O.Q. model may lose its applicability and may be replaced with anticipatory buying - that is, buying in anticipation of a price increase in order to secure the goods at a lower cost. Of course, as with most decisions, there are tradeoff's associated with anticipatory buying. The costs are the added carrying costs associated with the inventory that you would not normally be holding. The benefits, of course, come from buying the inventory at a lower price. The second way inflation affects the E.O.Q. model is through increased carrying costs. As inflation pushes interest rates up, the cost of carrying inventory increases.

E.O.Q. with Discounts : A particularly unrealistic assumption with the basic E.O.Q. calculation is that the price per item remains constant. Usually some form of discount can be obtained by ordering increased quantities. Such price discounts can be incorporated into the E.O.Q. formula, but it becomes much more complicated. A simpler approach is to consider the costs associated with the normal E.O.Q. and compare these costs with the costs at each succeeding discount point and so ascertain the best quantity to order.

Illustration 2 : A firm is able to obtain quantity discount on its orders of materials as follows :

Price per tonne	Tonnes
6.00	less than 250
5.90	250 and less than 800
5.80	800 and less than 2,000
5.70	2000 and less than 4,000
5.60	4,000 and over

The annual demand for the material is 4,000 tonnes. Stock holding costs are 20% of material cost per annum. The delivery cost per order is Rs. 600

Your are required to calculate the best quantity to order.

Ans. In next page.

Financial Effects of Discounts : Price discounts for quantity purchases have three financial effects, two of which are beneficial and one adverse.

Beneficial Effefts : Savings come from (a) Lower price per item, (b) The larger order quantity means that fewer orders need to be placed so that ordering costs are reduced.

Adverse Effects : (a) Increased costs arise from the extra stockholding costs caused by the average stock level being higher due to the larger order quantity.

Determination of Stock Levels

The demand and supply method of stock control technique determines different stock levels viz., maximum level, minimum level, re-order level, danger level, average level etc.

Maximum Stock Level represents the quantity above which inventory should not be allowed to be kept. This quantity is fixed keeping in view the disadvantages of over-stocking. The disadvantages of overstocking are : (i) working capital is blocked up unnecessarily in stores and interest may have to be paid thereon; (ii) more storage space is required, so more rent, insurance charges and other costs of carrying inventory have to be incurred; (iii) there is risk of deterioration in quality, depreciation in quantity due to evaporation, rusting, etc., and risks of obsolescence. There is risk of loss due to breakage, theft and excessive consumption also, and (iv) possibility of financial loss on account of subsequent fall in prices.

Answer

E O Q with Discounts

Ordering quantity Q Rs.	Price per ton C Rs.	Cost of purchases U X C Rs.	Cost of order $\frac{U}{Q} \times P$ Rs.	Cost of stock holding $\frac{Q}{2} \times I \times C$ Rs.	Total cost
200	6.00	4,000x6.00 = 24,000	$\frac{4,000}{200} \times 6 = 120$	$\frac{200 \times .2 \times 6}{2} = 120$	24,240.00
250	5.90	4,000X5.90 = 23,600	$\frac{4,000}{250} \times 6 = 96$	$\frac{250 \times .2 \times 5.9}{2} = 147.50$	23,843.50
800	5.80	4,000x5.80 = 23,200	$\frac{4,000}{800} \times 6 = 30$	$\frac{800 \times 2 \times 5.8}{2} = 464$	23,694.00
2,000	5.70	4,000x5.70 = 22,800	$\frac{4,000}{2,000} \times 6 = 12$	$\frac{2,000 \times .2 \times 5.7}{2} = 1,140$	23,952.00

Minimum cost = 23, 694
Economic Ordering Quantity = 800 Units

The following are the factors helpful in deciding the limits of inventory to be stored : (a) amount of capital available and required for purchases, (b) storage facilities and storage costs, (c) rate of consumption of the material, (d) possibilities of price fluctuations, (e) lead time i.e., the expected time lag between the date of issue of order and that of the receipt of materials (also known as cycle time), (f) seasonal nature of supply of materials, (g) possibility of loss due to fire, evaporation, moisture, deterioration in quality etc., (h) insurance costs, (i) possibility of change in fashion and habit which will outdate the products manufactured from that material, (j) restrictions imposed by government or local authority or Trade association in regard to materials in which there are inherent risks e.g., fire and explosion or restriction as to imports or procurement.

Minimum Stock Level represents the quantity below which stock should not be allowed to fall. This is known as **safety** or **buffer stock.** The main purpose of this level is to ensure that production is not held up due to shortage of any material. This level is fixed after considering (i) maximum consumption for day, (ii) average rate of consumption of materials, and (iii) lead time.

Reorder Level (or Order Level) is the point at which the store-keeper should initiate the purchase requisition for fresh supplies as and when materials in store approach that level. This level is fixed between maximum and minimum stock levels in such a way that the difference of quantity of the materials between the recorder level and the minimum level will be sufficient to meet the requirements of production up to the time the fresh supply of the material is received.

Reorder Quantity is the quantity of the replenishment order. In some types of inventory control systems this is the E.O.Q., but in some other systems a different value is used.

Danger Level means a point at which issues of the material are stopped and issues are made only under specific instructions. This level is generally fixed below the minimum stock level. When stock of materials reaches the danger level the purchase officer should take special arrangements to get the materials at any cost.

Optimum Stock Level is the level of stock that ensures that the requirements of production are met and that the amount of stock carried at any time is the minimum having regard to all relevant factors.

Physical stock. The number of items physically in stock at a given time.

Free stock. Physical stock plus outstanding replenishment orders minus unfulfilled requirements.

Marginal Stock Level is the stock level at which current orders cannot be met.

Revision of Levels. It has been experienced that persons concerned take the levels for granted once these are fixed. The various factors like lead time, consumption rate affecting the levels are dynamic and not static. The levels must be revised as and when changes occur in any one or all of the factors. It is a good practice to review levels periodically, say, at yearly intervals and revise these, if need be.

Formula for Determination of Stock Levels

(i) Maximum Level = Reorder level + Reorder quantity (Minimum consumption x Minimum Reorder period)

(ii) Reorder Level = Maximum consumption x Maximum Reorder period

or

Minimum stock + Average consumption during normal delivery time

(iii) Minimum Level = Reorder level - (Normal consumption x Normal reorder period)

or

(Maximum rate of consumption - Average Rate of consumption) x Lead time

(iv) Average stock level = Minimum level + 1/2 of Reorder quantity

or

1/2 (Minimum stock + Maximum stock)

(v) Danger level = Maximum delivery time x Maximum rate of consumption

or

Minimum rate of consumption x Emergency delivery time

Illustration : From the following information calculate the maximum stock level, minimum stock level, reordering level, average stock level and danger level.

(a) Normal consumption = 300 units per day
(b) Maximum consumption = 420 units per day
(c) Minimum consumption = 240 units per day
(d) Reorder quantity = 3,600 units
(c) Reorder period = 10 to 15 days

(f) Normal reorder period = 12 days

(g) Time required for emergency purchase = 4 days

Solution

Reordering level = Maximum consumption X Maximum reorder period
= 420 X 15 = 6,300 units

Minimum stock level = Reordering level - (Normal consumption X Normal reorder period)
= 6,300 - (300 x 12) = 2,700 units

Maximum stock level = Reordering level + Reorder quantity - (Minimum consumption X Minimum reorder period)
= 6,300 + 3,600 - (240 x 10)
= 9,900 - 2,400 = 7,500 units

Average stock level = 1/2 (Minimum stock level + Maximum stock level)
= 1/2 (2,700 + 7,500) = 5,100 units

Danger level = Minimum consumption per day X Time required for emergency purhcase
= 240 x 4 = 960 units

Lead Time or Procurement Time: From the time the requisition for an item is raised it may take several weeks or months before the supplies are received, inspected, and taken in stock. This time is called as "lead time" and involves the time for the completion of all or some of the following activities : 1. Raising of a purchase requisition, 2. Inquiries, tenders, quotations, 3. Receiving quotation, tenders, their scrutiny and approval, 4. Placement of order on a supplier/suppliers, 5. Suppliers time to make the goods ready (may have to be manufactured or supplied ex-stock), 6. Transportation and clearing, 7. Receipt of goods at the company, 8. Receiving inspection, and 9. Taking into stock.

This lead time required to procure any item can be divided into two parts namely internal lead time required for organisational formalities to be completed and external lead time as shown below :-

Total Lead Time			
Internal Lead Time (ILT)	External Lead Time (ELT)		Internal Lead Time (ILT)
Requisition order	Placement of order	Receipt of goods	Taking unit stock

It is a common belief that external lead time should be controlled and reduced but it has been found in actual practice that internal lead time constitutes a considerable part of total lead time and offers ample scope of reduction. The management must make a determined and deliberate effort to reduce lead time by selectively delegating powers, better paper work procedures, and fixing targets individually for all activities.

It is worth mentioning here that record should be kept of variations in lead time for at least A, B and other important items and it should be revised from time to time.

Obviously, in order to receive supplies before the stock reaches zero level, it is necessary to order the materials much in advance i.e., when the stock available in sufficient to last during the lead time.

Control Through Ratio Analysis

The following financial/business ratios, directly connected with inventory management, can be applied to appraise and review the effectiveness of inventory control.

(i) Inventory to working capital ratio,
(ii) Turnover (Net sales) to Total Assets,
(iii) Turnover (Net sales) to Fixed Assets,
(iv) Cost of goods sold to Average Stock holdings,
(v) Net sales to Inventory,
(vi) Net sales to Stocks and work in progress.

Inventory turnover ratio is also another method of exercising control. It is essential to compare the turnover of different kinds of materials to find out the items which are slow moving, thus helping management to avoid keeping capital locked up in such items. A low ratio is an indicator of slow moving stock, accumulation of obsolete stock, carrying of too much stock. A low turnover ratio will lead to the disadvantages arising out of over-stocking. On the other hand, a high turnover ratio is an indication of fast moving stock and less investment in stock. If the stock turnover ratio for a particular item (except for spare parts) is zero, it means that the item had not been used at all during the period and should be immediately disposed of otherwise the quality of the item may get deteriorated.

Input-Output Ratio Analysis

The input-output ratio is the ratio of the raw materials put into manufacturing and the standard raw material content of the actual output. A standard ratio of input of material and output of material should be determined and the actual ratio should be compared with the standard ratio, if the actual ratio is higher the standard ratio, the performance will be considered to be below the standard ratio, and vice versa. In process industries it is a valuable report to show the percentage of losses that have occurred at each stage. It measures the productivity of capital. This method is also useful to ascertain the raw material cost of finished output by multiplying the raw material cost per unit by this ratio.

Control Through ABC Analysis - Selective Control

Different types of analysis each having its own specific advantages and purposes, help in bringing a practical solution to the control of inventory. The most important of all such analysis is ABC analysis. This analysis is based on the principle of 'VITAL FEW-TRIVIAL MANY' and a higher degree of attention is focussed on VITAL FEW, which affect the result significantly. The others are :

F.S.N. - (Fast, Slow, Non-moving items) Analysis

H.M.L. - (High, Medium, Low cost) Analysis

S.D.E. - (Scarce, Difficult, Easily Available) Analysis

V.E.D. - (Vital, Essential, Desirable) Analysis

An effective inventory control system should classify inventories according to values so that the most valuable items may be paid greater and due attention regarding their safety and care, as compared to others. Hence, it is desirable to classify the production and supply items, both purchased and manufactured, depending upon their importance and subject each class and group of items to control commensurate with their importance. This is the principle of Control by Importance and Exception (C.I.E.) or selective control as applied to inventories and the technique of grouping is termed as ABC. analysis or classification which is said to be "Always, Better Control". As the items are classified on the basis of importance of their relative value, this approach is also known as Proportional (parts) Value Analysis (PVA).

The general procedure for implementing the ABC technique is as follows :

(i) Classify the items of inventories;

(ii) Determine the expected use in units over a given period of time;

(iii) Determine the total cost of each item by multiplying the expected units by its unit price;

(iv) Rank the items in accordance with total cost, giving first rank to the item with highest total cost **and so on;**

(v) Calculate percentage (ratio) of number of units of each item to total units of all items and the percentage of total cost of each item to total cost of all item;

(vi) Combine items on the basis of their relative value to form three categories - A, B and C.

Class	Percentage of item	Percentage of costs
A	8%	75%
B	25%	20%
C	67%	5%

The above mentioned example is clearly explained by the graph.

From the graphical analysis, it may be found that about 8% of items cost more than 75% of the cost on inventory. This is grouped as A items which form the most important items from the control point of view. B items forming 25% of total items constitute 20% of the total cost on inventory. These are of secondary importance and lie in between 'A' and 'C' items. Even though, they do not require as detailed and close control as 'A' items, they need more attention and control than 'C' items which are the numberous inexpensive items, i.e., about 75% of the items contributing to only 5% of the total cost of material.

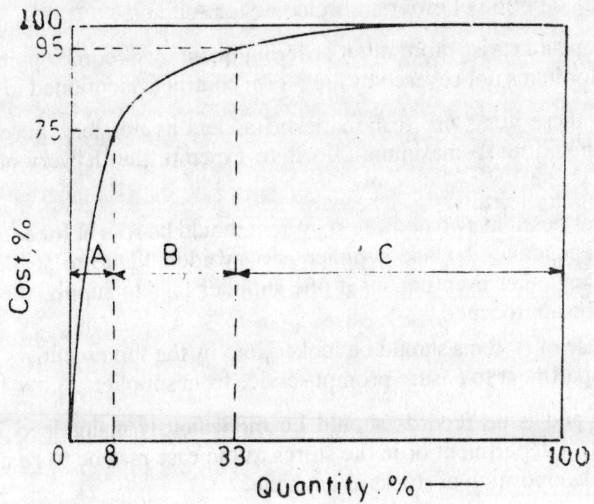

Controls for A, B & C Items

We are now ready to discuss the purchasing and stocking policies recommended for the different classes of items A, B & C. All these emanate from two basic requirements, viz., (i) to keep the capital tied-up in the inventories as low as is practicable, and (ii) to make sure that all the materials would be available when required for consumption.

Policies for A items : (About 8% items costing 75% in value).

1. Since these items account for over 75% percent of the value, they should be ordered more frequently to reduce the capital locked up at a time in inventories.

2. There would be many items for which the consumption varies considerably from time to time during a year. For such items the expected future consumption should be estimated in advance and they should then be procured on a planned basis, so that only the required quantities arrive a little before they are required for consumption. Of course, a small extra stock (buffer) would be carried throughout to meet any eventualities. It may be pointed out here that the advance estimation of future consumption can be made with the help of periodic production schedules and master schedules. In the absence of proper production schedules there is not reliable way of estimating what quantities would be required when and a planned procurement would be rather difficult. Thus, it may be emphasised that a proper inventory control basically calls for a good production planning system.

3. Annual or 6-monthly contracts with scheduled deliveries or deliveries within a specified period of order are welcome for A items.

4. Develop and revise more often ordering quantities, reorder points and safety stocks for items not covered by long term contracts mentioned in (3).

5. Since these items are to be stocked as less as possible, purchasing department should make maximum efforts to expedite the delivery of these items.

6. As far as possible, two or more suppliers should be sought for each item so that the dependency on one supplier is a avoided. Due to strike, fire, accidents, or any other eventualities if one supplier fails to supply, the other suppliers can be approached.

7. Purchase of A items should be looked into by the top executives in the purchasing department to ensure prompt service from suppliers.

8. Stock and issue records should be meticulously maintained in the inventory control department or in the stores as the case may be to be able to get the up-to-date position of stocks at any time.

9. The stock reports of A items should be sent more frequently to the top management. There can be no set rule, though once a month is good enough.

Policies for B Items (About 25% of items having 20% value)

1 The policies for B items in general are intermediate between those for A and C items.

2. Order quantities, reorder points and safety stocks should be fixed for B items and barring exceptions revisions once a year is adequate.

3. Annual or 6-monthly contracts with scheduled deliveries can be used to an advantage for B items.
4. Stock and issue records are necessarily to be maintained.
5. Should be ordered less frequently than A items about 3 to 6 order per year is the range of frequency.

Policies for C Items (About 67% items claiming 5% value)

Since the items are too many and the value is less the policies are to be aimed at reducing the ordering and stock keeping work to an extent possible and ensuring the availability at all times by stocking liberal quantities.

1. Liberal quantities (stock to last 6 months to over one year) can be kept in stock since in case of C items it does not involve much capital tie-up.

2. Annual or 6 monthly orders, should be pladed to reduce paper work in the purchasing department and also to take advantage of quantity discounts for bulk purchases.

3. Items should be grouped like all electricals, all hardwares, all paints, etc., and one group of items should be ordered all at once preferably from one or two vendors. This saves ordering work and also transportation costs. In additions, because of the inclusion of several items in one order, each order becomes sizable enough for the vendors to make concessions and give discounts.

4. Authority for the purchase of C items could be delegated to the Junior Executives in the purchasing department or even to the store-keeper so as not to bother the personnel at higher levels with work on these low-value sundry items.

5. Stock and issue records can be minimised to the extent the rules of the organisation allow. In some companies for most of the C items only records of receipts are kept. In others, one consolidated issue entry month for an item is recorded. However, in quite a few cases on records are maintained at all for C items barring some pilferable, and short-life items.

Variants of ABC Analysis

VED Analysis : This analysis is done to consider the vitality of an item and its effect on production and other services. It is specially used for classification of maintenance spares denoting the essentiality of stocking spares.

V - stands for vital items without which production would come to a halt.

E - is for essential items without which temporary losses of production or dislocation of production work occurs.

D - denotes desirable items-all other items which are necessary but do not cause any immediate loss in production.

SDE Analysis : This analysis is based upon the availability position of an item. Especially, in developing countries where certain items are scarce, this analysis is very useful.

S - refers to scarce items, especially imported items and those which are in short supply.

D - refers to difficult items, which are available in indegenous market but cannot be procured easily. For example, items which have to come from far off cities or for which reliable suppliers are difficult to find.

E - refers to items which are easily available; (mostly local items).

HML Analysis : The cost per item (per unit) is considered for this analysis and all items are classified as High Cost (H), Medium Cost (M), and Low Cost (L) items. This type of analysis is useful for keeping control over consumption at departmental level, and for deciding the frequency of physical verification.

FSN Analysis : Here the quantity and rates of consumption are analysed to classify the items as - Fast Moving (F), Slow Moving (S) and Non-moving (N) items. The Fast and Slow Moving classification help in arrangement of stocks in the stores and in deciding the distribution and handling methods. It is found that many companies maintain huge stocks of non-moving items and the number of such items run well over a thousand. The following steps are taken before disposal :

(a) circulate a list of non-moving to production, design and other departments and classify these into : (i) Items which can be used in future as such; (ii) Items which need modifications for use in future; (iii) Items which cannot be used.

(b) the list of items which cannot be used should be sent to all similar organisations and probable user for sale or exchange.

(c) these items, if cannot be disposed off to similar organisations, they should be put to open auction.

Advantages : The advantages of the ABC analysis are :

(a) Individual item analysis or Selective method ensures a closer, and more strict control over such items which represent a major portion of total stock value;

(b) It releases working capital, which would otherwise [illegible] up, for a more profitable channel of investment;

(c) it reduces inventory carrying costs;

(d) It enables the relaxation of control for the 'C' items thus makes it possible for a sufficient buffer stock to be created;

(e) It enables the maintenance of a high inventory turnover rate.

The techniques of ABC analysis is applicable to other area of business also e.g., quality control and inspection, customers services, maintenance of plants and equipments, and audit programmes of bills, vouchers etc.

Illustration : The following information is known about a group of items. Classify the material in A, B, C, classification.

Model Number	**Annual Consumption in pieces**	**Unit price in paise**
501	30,000	10
502	2,80,000	15
503	3,000	10
504	1,10,000	5
505	4,000	5
506	2,20,000	10
507	15,000	5
508	80,000	5
509	60,000	15
510	8,000	10

Answer

Model No.	Annual Consumption in pieces	Unit Price Rs.	Annual Consumption value	Rank (According to value)
501	30,000	0.10	3,000	6
502	2,80,000	0.15	42,000	1
503	3,000	0.10	300	9
504	1,10,000	0.05	5,500	4
505	4,000	0.05	200	10
506	2,20,000	0.10	22,000	2
507	15,000	0.05	750	8
508	80,000	0.05	4,000	5
509	60,000	0.15	9,000	3
510	8,000	0.10	800	7
Total	8,10,000		87,550	

	Model No.	Annual Consumption Value Rs.	% to total value	Rank
A category	502	42,000	48%	1
	506	22,000	25%	2
	Total	64,000	73%	
B Category	509	9,000	10%	3
	504	5,500	6%	4
	508	4,000	5%	5
	501	3,000	3½%	6
	Total	21,500	24½%	
C Category	510	800	1%	7
	507	750	1%	8
	503	300	¼%	9
	505	200	¼%	10
	Total	2,050	2½%	
Grand Total		87,550	100%	

Control Through Perpetual Inventory System

Perpetual inventory system is "a system of records maintained by the controlling department, which reflects the physical movements of stocks and their current balance". Thus, this is a method of ascertaining balance after every receipt and issue of materials through stock records, to facilitate regular checking and to avoid closing down for stock-taking. In order to ensure accuracy of perpetual inventory record, it is desirable to check the physical stocks by a programme of continuous stock- taking. Any discrepancy noted between physical stocks and the stock records can be investigated and rectified, then and there.

It is possible that the balance of stock shown by bin cards or stores ledger may differ from the actual balance of stock as ascertained by physical verification. It may be due to the following avoidable and unavoidable causes. Avoidable causes include (i) clerical mistakes i.e., wrong posting, non-posting of entries, wrong casting etc. Such errors can be corrected and actual balance can agree with book balance by making the required correction in bin cards or stores ledger; (ii) pilferage and thefts; (iii) carelessness in material handling; and (iv) short or over-issue of materials. Unavoidable causes include (i) actual balance may be less due to shrinkage and evaporation; (ii) actual balance may be more due to absorption of moisture; (iii) actual balance may be less due to breakdown of fire, riot etc., and (iv) materials may be lost due to breaking up bulk material into smaller parts for issue e.g., some iron is lost due to breaking up big iron rods in to smaller parts.

Advantages of the Perpetual Inventory Systems

1. **Planning of production** can be done according to availability of the materials in the stores because the management is constartly kept informed of the stores position.
2. A system of **internal check** remains in operation all the time because bin cards and the stores ledger act as a cross check on each other.
3. **Errors and shortage** of stock are readily discovered and efforts are made to avoid the shortage of stock in future.
4. It keeps the records of stocks **up-to-date.**
5. The **Capital investment** in stores can be kept under control because actual stock can be compared with the minimum and maximum levels.
6. The availability of correct figures of stocks helps in the **insurance of the stocks;** that is, it makes available correct stock figures for claim to be lodged with the insurance company for loss on account of stock destroyed by fire.
7. Continuous stock taking will make the store-keeper and the stores accountant more vigilant in their work and they will try to keep their records accurate and up-to date. The store-keeper will try to see that there is no leakage of the stores.
8. The materials getting stale or being wasted are detected and placed in right atmosphere. The slow moving inventories, obsolete or dormant stocks are brought to the notice of the Purchase Department so that such stocks may be purchased in future in lesser quantities are required.
9. It **obviates the necessity for the physical checking** of all items of stores at the end of the year and thereby avoids dislocation of production.
10. The prompt balancing of closing stocks enables quick preparation of financial accounts. It is also possible to **prepare Periodical Profit and Loss Account** and Balance Sheet without physical inventory being taken because figure for the closing stock can be taken from the bin cards or the stores ledger.

Value Analysis : The technique of 'Value Analysis' was first developed in General Electric Company in the U.S.A. by Lawrence D. Miles. 'Value analysis' or 'value engineering' is a technique which attempts to search for the cheaper substitute inventory items with a view to reducing the cost of the product. It attempts to reduce the cost of the product by studying the purpose it is to serve and constantly sees if there are less costly ways of manufacturing the product. According to the Handbook of Modern Manufacturing Management (edited by H.N. Maynard), "Value analysis is an arrangement of techniques which makes clear precisely the functions that the customer wants; establishes the appropriate cost for each function by comparison; and causes required knowledge, creativity, and initiative to be used to accomplish each function for that cost".

Another definition of value analysis is : "Value analysis is the organised systematic study of the function of a material, part, component or system, to identify area of unnecessary costs that can be eliminated without impairing the capacity of the item". Value analysis is also defined as a systematic application of recognised techniques which identify the function of a product or service; establish a monetary value for that function and provide the necessary function reliably at the lowest overall cost.

Objectives of value analysis : According to Lawrence D. Miles, "On an average one-fourth of manufacturing cost is unnecessary. The extra cost continues because of patterns and habits of thought, because of difficulties in promptly disseminating ideas, and because todays thinking is based on yesterday's knowledge". As a matter of fact, the objective of value analysis is to provide a means of total cost control anywhere within a product's life cycle. It stresses only the reduction or elimination of cost. This is done while maintaining required quality and reliability of the product to which value analysis is applied.

The basic objective of value analysis is to retain all the performance and aesthetic factors which now exist in the product, process or service, which the customer wants and is willing to pay for it, at the same time to put together practical alternatives which will accomplish them at still lower cost; e.g., instead of using the steel-made star or a brand name like Premier Padmini in a car, the chromium coated plastic items can serve the similar purpose at lower cost.* Another example can be quoted of an institute which used to mail lessons to students. Two pages were useless in very lesson i.e., the first page contained only lesson number while the last page contained a list of question only. Based on the suggestions given, these two pages were redesigned as the lesson number was mentioned on the lesson material itself and in the end the questions were

---

* Op. Cit., Awate, P.G., Chunawalla. S.A., Patel, D.R., and Bhandarkar, B.G., Industrial Organisation and Management.

given. This exercise saved Rs. 50,000 per year.* Though every product or service is bought by a customer because of its 'USE' function or the 'AESTHETIC' function or both, but the customer is basically interested in its 'USE' function and does not bother much for the 'AESTHETIC' function which is considered to be secondary. Therefore, more efforts should be made through value analysis to reduce the costs incurred on the secondary function. Thus, the purpose of value analysis is to provide each individual with a means of skillfully, deliberately, and systematically analysing and controlling the total cost of a product. This total cost control is accomplished by the systematic analysis and development of alternative means of achieving the function that are desired and required.

Since value analysis is a technique of inventory control which attempts to identify which of the several areas of the manufacturing system holds the solution to each specific component of unnecessary cost, it is necessary for the success of this technique that those who make use of this technique should possess thorough knowledge about the materials used in the product, uses of the product, motives of the product, motives of the buyers, and should also have initiative and innovative capacity required for making the product cheaper without hampering the cause that prompts the buyer to go for the product. The success of this technique also depends on the interest, cooperation, and motivation from the personnel of all functional departments in the organisation.

Process of Value Analysis : Following are the main steps involved in the process of value analysis :

(i) **Select :** First we have to select the item that we want to study.

(ii) **Gather information :** Then we collect all relevant information about the item.

(iii) **Analysis :** Then we analyse i.e., what does it do and what is its value for money.

(iv) **Speculate ;** Next we think of possible alternative ideas.

(v) **Assess :** Then we assess the worth of each of the ideas.

(vi) **Reach conclusions :** Next we decide what should be done.

(vii) **Implement :** Then we get the decision implemented.

(viii) **Evaluate :** Lastly, we evaluate to check if the expected result has been obtained or not.

The success of this process of value analysis depends largely upon the scientific attitude of the members, i.e., to keep an open mind to any suggestion that may be forthcoming from any corner.

---

* Op. Cit., Goel, S.L., Modernising Adminstrative Management.

INVENTORY VALUATION

Materials are issued to different jobs or work orders from the stores. These jobs or work orders are charged with the value of materials issued to them. Following are the important methods of valuing material issues :

A. Based on Cost Price

(i) The First in First Out (FIFO) Method
(ii) The Last in First Out (LIFO) Method
(iii) The Highest in First Out (HIFO) Method
(iv) The Next in First Out (NIFO) Method
(v) The Base Stock Method
(vi) The Specific (or Actual) Price Method
(vii) The Inflated Price Method
(viii) Average Cost Method -
- (a) Simple average price method
- (b) Periodic simple average price method
- (c) Weighted average price method
- (d) Periodic weighted average price method
- (e) Moving simple average price method
- (f) Moving weighted average price method

B. Based on Market Price Method

(ix) Realisable Value Method
(x) Replacement Value Method

C. Based on Standard Price Method

(xi) Current Standard Price
(xii) Basic Standard Price
(xiii) Re-use Price Methods

No single method can be appropriate in all circumstances. The selection of a proper method of pricing issues depends on the following factors :

(a) The nature of the business and type of production,(intermittent such as a job or continuous such as a process).

(b) The method of costing used (whether the cost accounts are maintained according to the standard costing system or if some method of issuing materials on standard cost is used).

(c) The nature of materials (if materials are to be kept for some time for maturing or seasoning, an inflated price will have to be charged).

(d) The frequency of purchases and issues.

(e) The extent of price fluctuations.

(f) The policy of the management (if the management wants that the cost accounts should represent the current position and correspond with estimates and besides that they should disclose efficiency in buying, pricing materials issues at market price may be suitable).

(g) Relative value of material issued and relative size of batch of material issued.

(h) Length of inventory turnover period and quantity of material to be handled; and

(i) The necessity for maintaining uniformity within an industry.

Methods Based on Actual Cost

(i) **First In First Out (FIFO) Price :** This method operates under the assumption that the materials which are received first are issued first and, therefore, the flow of cost of materials should also be in the same order. Issues are priced at the same basis until the first batch received is used up, after which the price of the next batch received becomes the issue price. Upon this batch being fully used, the price of the still next batch is used for pricing and so on. In other words, the materials issued are priced at the oldest cost price listed in the stores ledger account and consequently the materials in hand arè valued at the price of the latest purchases.

Example

Receipts	Issues	
2nd Jan. (First consignment)	7th Jan. 600 Kg.	
500 Kg.@ Rs. 8.00 per Kg.	500 Kgs. @ Rs. 8.00 per kg. =	Rs. 4,000
5th Jan. (Second consignment) 300 Kg. @ Rs. 8.20 per kg	100 Kgs. @ RS. 8.20 per kg. =	820
	Total issue value :	Rs. 4,820

Advantages

1. This method is realistic in so far as it assumes that materials are issued to production in the order of their receipts.
2. The valuation of closing stock tends to be nearer current market prices as well as at cost.
3. Being based on cost, no unrealised profits enter into the financial result.
4. The method is easy to operate if the prices do not fluctuate very frequently.

Disadvantages

1. The issues prices may not reflect current market prices and, therefore, in times of rising prices, the charge to production is unduly low.
2. The cost of consecutive similar jobs may differ simply because the prior job exhausted the supply of lower priced stock. This renders comparison between different jobs difficult.
3. The method may involve cumbersome calculations if the prices fluctuate quite frequently.

The FIFO method is most successfully used when (a) the size and the cost of raw material units are large, (b) materials are easily identified as belonging to a particular purchased lot, and (c) not more than two or three different receipts are on a materials card at one time.

(ii) Last In First Out (LIFO) : This method operates on the assumption that the latest receipts of materials are issued first for production and the earlier receipts are issued last, i.e., in the reverse order to FIFO. It uses the price of the last batch received for all the issues until all units from this batch have been issued after which the price of the previous batch received becomes the issue price. Usually, however, a new delivery is received before the first batch is fully used, in which case the new delivery price becomes the 'last-in' price and is used for pricing issues until either the batch is exhausted or a new delivery is received.

Example. Assuming the same figures which were taken in FIFO method, the issue of 600 Kgs, will be valued as shown below :

300 Kgs.	@ Rs. 8.20 per Kg.	=	Rs. 2,460
300 Kgs.	@ Rs. 8.00 per Kg.	=	Rs. 2,400
600 Kgs.	Total issue value	=	Rs. 4,850

Advantages

1. The method keeps the value of issues close to the current market prices.
2. No unrealised profit or loss is usually made by using this method.
3. In periods of rising prices, the high prices of the most recent purchases are charged to operations, thus reducing profit figure and resulting in a tax saving.

Disadvantages

1. The value of the closing stock may be quite different from the current market value and hence may not be acceptable for income tax purposes.
2. Comparison among similar jobs is very difficult because different jobs may bear different charges for materials consumed.

3. This method does not conform to the physical flow of materials.
4. The number of calculations complicates the stores accounts and increases the possibility of clerical errors when rates of receipt are highly fluctuating.

Under conditions of rising market prices, LIFO method is general considered better. This is so because under LIFO method reasonably correct effect of current prices is reflected in the cost and the cost is not understated. The quotation of prices for the products also becomes more safe than FIFO.

(iii) Highest In First Out (HIFO) Method : The method is based on the assumption that stock of materials should be always valued at the lowest possible price. Materials purchased at the highest price are treated as being first issued irrespective of the date of purchase. The method is very suitable when the market is constantly fluctuating because cost of heavily priced materials is recovered from the production at the earliest. But it involves too many calculations as in the case with the LIFO and FIFO methods. The method has not been adopted widely.

(iv) Next In First Out (NIFO) Method : The method attempts to value material issues at an actual price which is as near as possible to the market price. Under this method the issues are made at the next price i.e., the price of materials which has been ordered but not yet received. In other words, issues are at the latest price at which the company has been committed even though materials have not yet been physically received. This method is better than market price method under which every time when materials are issued, their market price will have to be ascertained. In case of this method materials will be issued at the price at which a new order has been placed and this price will hold good for all future issues till a next order is placed.

(v) Base Stock Method : The method is based on the contention that each enterprise maintains at all times a minimum quantity of materials in its stock. This quantity is termed as base stock. The base stock is deemed to have been created out of the first lot purchased and therefore, it is always valued at this price and is carried forward as a fixed asset. Any quantity over and above the base stock is valued in accordance with any other appropriate method. As this method aims at matching current costs to current sales the LIFO method will be most suitable for valuing stock of materials other than the base stock. The base stock method has the advantage of charging out materials at actual cost. Its other merits or demerits will depend on the method which is used for valuing materials other than the base stock.

(vi) Specific Price Method : Where materials are purchased for a particular job, they should be charged to that particular job at their actual cost. This method can always be used where materials are purchased and set aside for a particular job until required for production. This method is best suited for job order industries which carry out individual jobs or contracts against specific orders. From the point of view of costing, the method is desirable because it ensures that the cost of materials issued is actual and that neither profit nor loss arises out of pricing. This method however, is difficult to use if purchases and issues are numberous and the materials issued cannot be identified.

(vii) Inflated Price Method : In case of certain materials wastage is unavoidable on account of their inherent nature, e.g., if a log of timber is issued to various departments in pieces or if it is kept for seasoning, there will be some loss in its quantity. In such a case the production should be charged at an inflated price so as to recover the total cost of materials over the different issues.

(viii) Average Cost Method

(a) Simple Average Price : Simple average price is the average of the prices without any regard to quantities. The calculation of simple average price involves adding of different prices dividing by the number of different prices. The method operates under the principle that when materials are purchased in lots and are put in store, their identify is lost and, therefore, issues should be valued at the average price of all the lots in store. Though this method is very easy to operate, but it is crude and usually products unsatisfactory results. The value of closing stock may be quite absured. Moreover, materials are not charged but at actual cost and, therefore, a profit or loss will usually arise out of pricing.

(b) Weighted Average price.: Weighted average price is calculated by dividing the total cost of material in stock by the total quantity of material in stock. This method averages prices after weighting (i.e., multiplying) by their quantities. The average price at any time is simply the balance value figure divided by the balance units figure. Issue prices need only to be computed on the receipt of new deliveries and not at the time of each issue as in the case of FIFO and LIFO. Thus as soon as a fresh lot is received, a new issue price is calculated and all issues are then taken at this price until the receipt of the next lot of materials. This method operates under the assumption that the identity of the materials, when put in stores, is lost and therefore their cost should reflect the average of the total supply.

Advantages

1. Since the receipts are much less frequent than issues, the method is not so cumbersome because the calculation of the new issue price arises only when fresh lots are purchased. All subsequent issues are then charged at this price until the next lot is received.

2. The method evens out the effect of widely varying prices of different consignments comprising the stock.

3. A profit or loss may arise out of pricing.

4. Issue prices may run to a number of decimal points.

(c) Periodic Simple Average Price : This method is similar to the simple average price except that here the issue price is calculated at the end of each period (normally a month) covering the prices at which purchases were made during the period and not at the occasion of each issue of material.

(d) Periodic Weighted Average Price : The periodic weighted average price is the weighted average price of materials purchased during a period. It is calculated by dividing the total cost of materials purchased during a period by the total quantity of materials purchased during that period. A new average price is calculated at the end of each period (normally a month).

(e) Moving Simple Average Price :. This price is obtained by dividing the total of the periodic simple average prices of a given number of periods, by the number of periods, the last of the period being that for which material issues are valued. The calculation of moving simple average price requires to decide upon the number of periods (months), i.e., 3,5,7, etc. If, for example, a 5-monthly simple average is to be calculated, the periodic simple average prices of 5 periods have to be added and total of these prices divided by 5 would give simple moving average price.

(f) Moving Weighted Average Price : This is a derivation of the weighted average method. To obtain the weighted average price, the weighted average price of a given number of periods (including and preceding the period of accounting) have to be added and divided by the number of periods.

REVIEW QUESTIONS

1. What is inventory? Why do firms maintain inventory?
2. What are the objectives of inventory control?
3. What is the financial manager's role in respect of the management of inventory?
4. What purpose does safety stock serve? What are the benefits and costs associated with safety stock?
5. What are inventory carrying charges? How are they calculated?
6. What are ordering costs? How are they calculated?
7. What are the disadvantages of having excess inventories?
8. What are the costs of stock-outs? How should the costs of stock- out and the carrying costs be balanced to obtained the safety stock?
9. What is lead time? What are the various activities occuring during the lead time?

10. Explain the four cost factors involved in general inventory policies.
11. How would you determine economic ordering quantity?
12. What factors do you consider in fixing the maximum and the minimum stock levels?
13. State the points that should be considered in fixing reorder level and danger level limits for direct materials?
14. What do you understand by ABC analysis? What are its advantages? Discuss the inventory policies for A, B and C items.
15. Enumerate and explain briefly the advantages of perpetual inventory system and continuous stock taking.
16. Explain the techniques of control of inventories through turnover ratios with suitable illustration.
17. Explain the technique of Input-Output Analysis.
18. Distinguish between slow moving, dorment and obsolete stocks of stores items. What practical steps would you recommend with a view to minimising the losses and costs arising from existence of these stocks?
19. Explain the meaning, objectives and process of 'Value analysis' technique of inventory control.
20. Discuss and illustrate the following: "If purchase prices were to remain stable the LIFO. FIFO and Average Methods of determining inventories and cost flows would produce the same results".

24
Marketing Control

Marketing control is the tool for ensuring that the marketing programmes and activities of the firm always get directed towards the marketing objectives of the firm. In fact, many experts define 'Marketing Control' as the process that guides the marketing activity towards the marketing goals. Marketing control also provides the means of testing whether the desired goals and results are actually being achieved or not. Marketing control involves gathering information on marketing performance and comparing the achieved performance against the planned or budgeted performance, using predetermined standards and yardsticks. It provides feedback; it regulates; and it exercises a restraining influence or a redirecting influence. It ensures that the marketing activity does not derail or go off the track; it acts as a radar system for marketing, recording and signaling the ups and downs and deviations in the marketing performance; it also provides the required clues for the timely correction of the deviations. In a dynamic environment, the marketing programmes cannot be implemented effectively without continuous monitoring, controlling and corrective adjust ments. Marketing control takes care of this requirement. It paves the way for the maximisation of profitability and the maximisation of productivity of all the marketing activities. Marketing control is thus an integral part of management control.

Definition of Marketing Control : For the purpose of this text, however, control of marketing operations may be defined as the managerial function of monitoring and feeding back of actual marketing performance and its measurement and evaluation against the planned performance standards so as to identify deviations, correct them as they occur and provide inputs for plan reformulation. The monitoring and feedback of marketing performance entails surveillance of marketing operations and transmission of relevant information emanating from this surveillance. Measurement and evaluation entails assessment of marketing performance, whereas evaluation refers to the qualitative assessment of marketing control the qualitative assessment of marketing performance. In control the whole objective is to secure such information which may help detect and correct deviations from the planned effort and may serve as inputs for plan i.e., formulation.

Process of Marketing Control

From the above definition four important elements emerge which constitute the marketing control process. These are : formulation of performance standards, performance appraisal, correction of deviations and plan reformulation. Figure 24.1 illustrates this process which has been described in the next page.

1. Formulation of Performance Standards : The first stage in the control process is the formulation of standards of marketing performance. In fact, the moorings of this stage are located in the planning process and, therefore, it overflows therefrom. Performance standards refer to those criteria of expected marketing performance against which actual marketing performance is measured and evaluated. Standards indicate the managerial expectations of a certain level of sub-functional output over a plan period. The standards may be both quantitative and qualitative. Quantitative standards prescribe performance expectations in physical and monetary values in terms of sales- volume, profit, and expenses per product, region and customer; audience reach, calls per salesman, inventory levels etc., while qualitative standards prescribe performance expectations in non-tangible and behavioural values in terms of dealer's relations, consumer satisfaction, harmonious salesmen-supervisor relations, brand image, consumer attitude change, etc. Relative to quantitative standards, qualitative standards are easy to lay down but difficult to apply.

2. Performance Appraisal : The second stage in the marketing control process is to appraise the performance of the different sub-functions and people involved therein against the standards laid down. It involves collecting and collating information about performance, analysing it, and relating it to the standards so as to identify deviations and lapses, if any, and causes thereof. For this purpose, management has to develop an appropriate marketing information system so that it receives adequate and timely feedback from the market about the performance of the different components of the marketing-mix. The appraisal may be periodic or continuous. It is periodic when performance is measured and evaluated at the end of the plan period or after some interval(s). It is continuous when performance is continuously monitored from the market and corrections are triggered. In the subsequent pages are described some of the important methods and tools of performance analysis used for controlling marketing operations.

Performance appraisal in marketing is, however, relatively difficult. It is so because people involved in operations have to deal with many intangibles and qualitative aspects like consumer satisfaction, brand image, consumer attitudes, etc. Besides, the pay-off of marketing efforts is usually long term and, there fore, it is difficult to correlate current efforts with the current output. Also, the marketing performance may not always be the result of marketing efforts alone. Many environmental factors also impinge on it which is difficult to isolate in order to establish a cause and effect relationship between performance and operations. These and other problems make appraisal a difficult stage in the marketing control process.

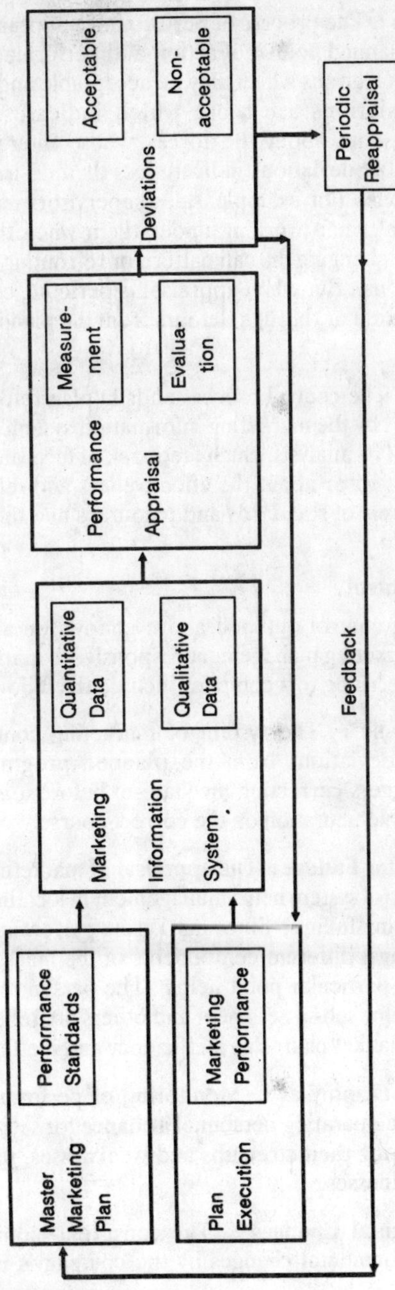

Fig. 24.1 Marketing Control Process

3. Correcting Deviations : The process of performance appraisal usually reveals deviations from the planned course of action and performance standards. These deviations are aberrations which may be acceptable and unacceptable. The acceptable deviations are those which indicate improved performance and impart wisdom about the forces whose interaction has brought it about. Unacceptable deviations indicate less than desired performance necessitating corrections. For example, sales supervisors may correct unacceptable deviations of salesmen working under them when they fail to achieve the sales target, say by changing the call pattern or re-routing salesmen. Such corrections are continuous. But when appraisal is periodic, corrections are made by tactics reformulation or through detours from the planned course of action.

4. Plan Reformulation : The control process ends in plan reformulation on the basis of inputs provided by the marketing information system in respect of marketing performance and its analysis. Such feedback of facts and analysis makes the marketing manager wiser about the effectiveness and relevance of certain policies, strategies, levels of standards and resources and the mode of their application.

Importance of Marketing Control

The system of marketing control outlined above endows on a company many benefits which make marketing management responsive to market needs. Some of the major benefits accruing to a company include the following :

1. Detection of Deviations : The system of marketing control helps management in identifying deviations from the planned programme. It monitors aberrations and triggers correcting mechanism before it is too late. Thus, it keeps programme implementation on the correct course.

2. Locate Responsibility for Failure : The appraisal of marketing performance as envisaged in the control system helps management in locating responsibility for any kind of marketing failure. Since marketing performance is the result of the interaction amongst different components of the marketing-mix, location of responsibility at a particular point helps. The person responsible for failure gets an opportunity for self- assessment and others are relieved of an unwarranted and misplaced blanket charge of inefficiency and ineffectiveness.

3. Self-Examination by Employees : Monitoring of performance and feedback of appraisal data give operating personnel a chance for self-examination. It helps them in identifying their strengths and weaknesses, reinforcing strengths and remedying weaknesses.

4. Matching Environmental Changes : The consistent monitoring of performance and other environmental changes by the company's marketing information system helps in continuously updating the company's marketing response so that it remains in equilibrium with its environment. It becomes all the more important in the context of rapid changes in technological, social and political fields, in consumers' preferences, and public policy postures.

5. **Organisational Complexity :** In modern business, organisations are growing in size. The vertical marketing system has more or less come to stay as a phenomenon of modern marketing. The organisational size and growth make control more complex and yet essential. Size has great potential to complicate the problem of control. The span of control enlarges with the size and creates problems of control. Therefore, a realistic, effective and yet simple marketing control system is a pre-requisite of effective marketing management.

6. **Assist Plan Reformulation :** The feedback provided by the marketing control system makes management wiser. It helps in re-appraising performance standards for their validity and applicability; policies and strategies for their relevance; and marketing programme for its effectiveness. The inputs provided by such a re-appraisal helps in the realistic re-formulation of the marketing plan.

Characteristics of an Effective Marketing Control System

The benefits of a marketing control system can accrue to a company when some of the following characteristics of an effective control system are present therein :

1. **Match Operational Needs :** Every control system in the marketing department should match the specific operational needs of its sub-functions. Performance of no two operations can be measured and evaluated by identical standards as, for example, the performance of marketing research men would require a set of standards different from that for salesmen or advertising men. Sales volume may be reasonable criterion for control of sales department but not for marketing research department. Also, the standards set should be within the reasonable reach of the persons who are suppose to meet them. Standards taller than the men would breed dissatisfaction and lower the morale.

2. **Ensure Prompt Detection of Deviations :** The control system should be such that deviations from the programme are promptly reported to the concerned manager(s) who can then trigger corrective mechanism. Delay in detection and reporting would make control irrelevant because manager then can do very little about it.

3. **It Should be Flexible :** The control system should not prove to be a straight-jacket. It must have the capacityto adopt to changes made in the plans or detours followed. The flexibility should be in terms of standards and appraisal techniques. Unforeseen circumstances should not impede the working of the control system.

4. It Should Match Organisation Pattern : It means that those incharge of marketing and its sub-functions should have the authority to control their respective operations. Although divergence from the organisational pattern may be developed by appointing separate controllers, experience shows that control works best when the man incharge of operations also control them. The manager should be the focal point in control.

5. It Should be Economical : The control system should be so economical as to be affordable by a company using it. A small company, for example, cannot afford an elaborate and sophisticated system of marketing control involving charts, detailed analyses, computor programs, etc., used by, say, Hindustan Steel Ltd. A reasonable test-stone of economy in control may be the trade-off in the cost of control and penalties of the absence of it.

6. It Should be Understandable : To be used, the control system should be understandable by managers. In India, one of the problems faced by managers is to comprehend the modern control methods based on break-even charts, statistical analysis and mathematical formula in spite of the advances made through management development programmes.

7. It Should Trigger Corrective Action : A good control system should activate corrective action no sooner deviations occur. It should reveal the points of deviations, pinpoint responsibility for failures, and indicate corrective measures.

TOOLS AND TECHNIQUES OF MARKETING CONTROL

There are several tools and techniques with which marketing control is exercised by a business firm. The important ones among them are : (a) Marketing audit, (b) Marketing cost analysis, (c) Credit control, (d) Market share analysis, (e) Budgetary control, (f) Ratio analysis, (g) Contribution margin analysis, (h) Marketing information inputs and warning signals, (i) Management By Objectives (M.B.O.)

Controls monitor the key result areas of marketing : All these control techniques have a common purpose, viz., monitoring the key result areas in marketing management. Some of the key result areas that are to be monitored by the various marketing controls are : (i) Sales volume, (ii) Market share, (iii) Market standing, (iv) Profits, (v) Productivity in each marketing activity.

A. Marketing Audit

Marketing audit is one of the most important tools of marketing control. Marketing audit is a continuous, systematic and objective and objective study of the total marketing efficiency of the firm. It exposes the business setting of the firm, critically evaluates the marketing policies and marketing activities of the firm, and measures the extent and direction of its growth. Marketing audit is concerned with the long term business interests and challenges of the firm rather than short term achievements.

No firm can ever take the stand that everything is fine with our marketing. It is essential to assess whether the marketing policies, programmes, systems and methods established in the distant past are valid and effective for the future. Marketing audit ensures such assessments.

Wide ranging scope of marketing audit : The strength of marketing audit lies in the fact that while other control techniques aim at a piecemeal evaluation of the various marketing functions, marketing audit aims at a total evaluation of the entire marketing system and process. It leads to specific plans for improving the marketing efficiency of the firm.

It also measures and evaluates the effectiveness of the other marketing control techniques employed by a firm. In this sense, marketing audit can be described as a control of controls. Several fundamental aspects of business are investigated through marketing audit. To tackle these aspects marketing audit raises some basic questions and seeks to answer them correctly. Some of these questions are :

1. What business are we in? Do we understand our business correctly?
2. What business are we heading for?
3. What is the business we should be doing tomorrow for our prosperity?
4. What change do we need in our current direction of growth?
5. What is our marketing strategy and plan?
6. Are they the right ones? Will they ensure the achievement of the objectives of our business?
7. What are the emerging trends in competition and the general business environment?
8. Do the marketing activities lend themselves for measurement?
9. Are they reviewed and measured periodically?

B. Marketing Cost Analysis

Marketing cost analysis is another important tool of marketing control. In recent years, business firms all over the world have experienced steep escalations in their marketing and distribution costs. They have found, to their dismay, that increased sales do not necessarily bring them increased profits. Containing marketing and distribution costs has become imperative for optimising profits.

The importance of marketing cost analysis : The marketing chief of any firm has to give the best of attention of marketing cost control. And if he has to effectively control the marketing costs, he has to, in the first place, comprehend the components of the marketing costs, their nature and the methods available for their control. He must have an effective system to track them down. He must also analyse them systematically. For, without systematic analysis of the marketing costs, it will not be possible to control these costs, and without such cost control, marketing control is meaningless. Today, in most firms, a marketing cost analysis has become a prominent marketing control technique.

Benefits flowing from marketing cost analysis : A variety of benefits is derived by the firm from a careful and systematic marketing cost analysis. The important ones among them as listed below :

(i) It helps to control and reduce the marketing costs, and thereby augments savings and surpluses.

(ii) It helps to identify costs of performing specific marketing functions/activities, throws up alternative ways of performing these functions/activities and provides an evaluation of relative cost benefits of various alternatives.

(iii) It helps to improve the competitive position of the products of the firm in the market. If costs are reduced, prices can be kept competitive.

(iv) It helps to drop unprofitable customers, products, channels and markets and enables the firm to identify and concentrate on relatively high profitable products, customers, channels and markets. The firm may even take a decision to carry on with the unprofitable customers, products and markets. But with marketing cost analysis, the decision is a conscious one, to support the long-term interests of the firm.

(v) It helps to appraise the true cost and true value of each marketing service provided by the firm - such as delivery, presale service, credit facilities, etc.

(vi) It helps to set responsibility and goals for individual executives in the marketing discipline, in the controlling of the costs and ensures cost-related performance.

Types of Marketing Costs : Marketing costs in modern large-sized firms pose a kaleidoscopic variety. There are may components to the marketing costs and they vary in their significance, size, measureability and controllability. Marketing costs can be broadly categorised as follows : (i) Physical distribution costs, (ii) Inventory costs or costs of holding stocks, (iii) Channel costs or costs of remunerating and administering the distribution channel, (iv) Selling sales administration costs, (v) Promotional costs, (vi) Cost of credit sales, (vii) Cost of marketing information and marketing research. As a rule, marketing costs are more difficult to measure and control compared with other costs, such as material costs and production costs. Within the various components of marketing costs, some are relatively more amenable for measurement and control than others.

Steps involved in marketing cost analysis : Marketing cost analysis and control involve the following steps :

(i) Assigning marketing costs to each of the major functions of marketing.

(ii) Analysing these costs by functions.

(iii) Assigning the functional expenses to the clearly identified marketing entities.

(iv) Each product.

(v) Each customer group.

(vi) Each territory.

(vii) Each channel type.

(viii) Analysing the costs by the marketing entitles.

(ix) Working out the cost benefit position for each function broken up for each entity.

(x) Determining what corrective action is needed.

Analysing the costs by the functions : The first step in marketing cost analysis is to gather the cost details by the various marketing functions and analyse the function-wise cost. For doing this, in the first instance, the various marketing activities have to be grouped into a few major and clearly identified functions. The marketing expenditure must be broken up into parts - each part clearly identified and related to the respective functions. The costs incurred by each of the major marketing function must be then measured against the budgeted figures and the standard costs for that function. Again, the cost incurred by the function should be compared with the results accomplished, for example, sales volume achieved, gross margins achieved and net realisations made.

Analysing the costs by the marketing entities : After identifying the major marketing functions of the firm and analysing the costs function-wise, the firm should analyse the cost by each marketing entity - each product, each territory, etc. For this purpose, there must be an accounting system which facilitates the assignment of functional expenses to the various products, markets and customers.

The analysis can be on the following lines :

I. By product

(a) By brand or by groups of related products.

(b) By 'order size' in each product.

(c) By stock turnover ratio of the respective product; expenditure for fast selling products and for slow selling products separately identified and analysed.

(d) By the share of promotion expenditure spent on each product.

(e) By the warehousing cost incurred by each product.

II. By customer group

(a) By customer type.

(b) By 'order size' of customers purchase.

(c) By the proportion of cash and credit sales in each customer group.

(d) By the mode or manner of delivery taken by customers.

III. By territory

(a) By the selling expenses incurred by each territory.

(b) By the promotion expenses incurred by each territory.

(c) By the cost of credit incurred by each territory.

(d) By the rate of turn round of stocks in each territory.

IV. By marketing method and channel type

(a) By method of sale; direct to customer, or through wholesaler or through retailer, or through commission agent.

(b) By order size and order handling cost to the firm.

(c) By salesmen; cost of sales calls, cost of orders booked, order to call ratio, etc.

(d) By price category and discount classification; cost incurred by each price category under which sales has taken place.

Cost-benefit analysis : The costs incurred by each of the above mentioned marketing entities should be measured against the results produced by the respective entities. Results for this exercise should mean sales volume generated, gross margins achieved and net realisation made by the entity. Furthermore, the productivity of each of these entities, i.e., how efficient or productive each product, each channel type, each customer (or customer class) and each salesman had been, should be analysed, by measuring their respective contributions to profits of the firm on the one hand and to the overheads of the firm on the other. The unprofitable product, channel or customer should be discontinued.

Comparison with Standard Costs : If marketing cost analysis be quite effective, it must be taken to its logical conclusion. It should include standard costing for the various marketing functions and entities. It may not be enough, if the marketing costs are compared with the budget. The firm should go one step further and develop standard costs for each function of marketing and measure the actual costs against the standards. The standard cost approach will reveal what ought to have happened or what could have happened under very efficient conditions. Cost can also be compared with industry averages, when they are available.

C. Credit Control

Business firms are often forced to extend credit to increase sales. In some businesses, the entire sales takes place on credit, cash sales being negligible. In certain other businesses, hire purchase and instalment payments are the normal practice. Even in those cases where the sales to consumers are on a cash basis, credit is extended to the distribution channels. It is essential for any business firm to evolve a proper policy on credit and exercise proper control on it.

Poor credit control drains away profit : As a part of credit control, it must be ensured that customers and the channel do not exploit the credit policy of the firm. Care should also be taken to see that credit transactions do not turn into bad debts. Credit has two cost dimensions : (i) the interest on the money involved in the credit transaction and (ii) the risk of bad debts. Bad debts must be seen and understood as an important part of the cost of credit. They erode the profits of the firm.

Obviously, every firm should have an efficient credit control system. Many marketing organisations are seen to be deficient in this aspect. They permit planned and unplanned, authorised and unauthorised credit to customers and the channel. They extend credit before a proper credit rating or appraisal of the credit worthiness of the client is made by the credit department. In other cases, they wait for the credit appraisal but do not adhere to the prescribed credit limits. In either case, the risk of bad debts is enhanced. Sometimes, it so happens that the cost of credit is not built into the price at all. These pitfalls must be avoided by instituting a proper credit control system and by ensuring that the system is strictly adhered to by all the marketing executives and salesmen. An analysis of outstandings and overdues will highlight the corrective action to be taken. It is also worthwhile to study the relative advantages of offering cash rebates to customers in lieu of credit. To the extent it is beneficial to the firm, such cash rebates can be used to reduce credit transactions and to accelerate recoveries.

Credit rating : Proper credit rating of the client or dealer is the fundamental step in credit control. Credit rating ensures that the credit-worthiness of the client or dealer as the case may be, is assessed objectively before the firm proceeds with the risk of extending credit facility to him. The firm can categorise the dealers into no-risk dealers, medium risk dealers and high-risk dealers. Such credit rating will help the firm to handle the dealers appropriately different dealers can be treated differently in fixing credit limits, interest rates, repayment periods, etc. For example, the no-risk dealer can be extended large credit limits; the high risk dealer will not get credit facility unless substantial bank guarantees or collateral security is made available. This way credit rating of dealers minimises the risk of the firm in extending credit. It introduces a vital role for managerial discretion in the matter of extension of credit facilities. And it provides analytical information to support the discretion. In the absence of such credit rating the firm has to either apply a blanket ban on credit or extend credit to every one without any regard to the safety factor. Neither of these alternatives would be appropriate for practice under competitive business conditions.

Control on price cuts : Just as credit control, control on price cuts is also very essential. Enthusiastic marketing men often try to push up sales by constantly reducing prices. Sometimes price wars among competitors become acute and salesmen start selling below costs. Even when there are no price wars, there is usually a strong temptation on the part of salesmen for striking special deals with customers, by offering price cuts, discounts and rebates of various kinds. Increasing sales volume by competitive pricing may be a good marketing strategy for a firm up to a point, but the firm must also realise the limits up to which it can go. Whenever sales are sought to be made below the normally fixed price, the marketing control system should be able to sense whether such price cuts will ensure compensating advantages to the firm.

D. Market Share Analysis

Market share analysis is another useful marketing control tool. However, if it is not handled properly and interpreted correctly, it can throw up highly misleading information. It becomes an effective control tool only when it meets the following pre- conditions - it is accurately measured; it is measured both at macro and micro levels; the comparisons of targeted and actual market shares are also made both at macro and micro levels; and the comparisons are made over reasonably long spells of time. Before a firm attempts a market share based evaluation and control, it must have clarity on whether it is consciously seeking a definite share of the market. It is implied in any market share evaluation that the marketing performance will be assessed based on the market share. It is also implied that a definite minimum share of the market is the real aim of the firm. Otherwise, the evaluation becomes a purely theoretical exercise and loses its control potential.

Market share analysis can be utilised for evaluating the market/business performance of a firm; for setting targets for the firm and for developing long term sales forecasts for the firm. Market share has to be measured on rational grounds. Comparisons may be made with the most efficient firms in the industry, or the industry leader, or a group of growing firms. Comparisons can also be made against industry average performance. Whatever be the criteria of comparison, the general economic conditions which have a bearing on the industry's performance have to be given due weightage. Quite often, the market share of a firm may go up substantially without any effort on the part of its marketing department. The increase may be due to environmental factors. Unless these dimensions are understood in the proper perspective, market share analysis will give the wrong interpretation. So it is essential to use market share analysis in an intelligent and objective manner. It is also essential to understand one's product/market boundaries correctly to make market share analysis purposeful. Shares can be worked out at product sub-category level, product category level, national level and regional level. Each measurement has its own use and implications.

E. Budgetary Control

Budgetary control is yet another marketing control device. It is applied to every function of the business including marketing. Budgeting in the area of marketing is usually quite an elaborate exercise, involving sales forecasting, sales budgeting, sales expense budgeting and profit planning. Budgetary control essentially involves preparation of control statements at specified intervals of time, showing the budgeted figures, the achieved figures and the variances. Review and remedial action is the other part of budgetary control. In marketing, sales volume, sales expenses and profits are the main aspects to be controlled through the budgetary control device. Budgetary control presupposes awareness of costs and profits associated with each product/territory/customer group. It involves the correct or near correct allocation of the total marketing effort in financial terms to each individual product, individual marketing function and individual marketing territory. The analysis should also be (a) by product, (b) by territory, and (c) by function.

F. Ratio Analysis

In addition to the budget-actual-variance analysis described above and the standard costing comparison described earlier, most firms use ratio analysis also as a control device in marketing as well as other areas. As far as marketing is concerned, ratio analysis seeks to measure the effectiveness and profitability of the various marketing functions and activities by the use of certain ratios. Whereas budgetary control reveals absolute figures, ratio analysis focuses attention on relative figures. Some of the important ratios used for marketing control are : 1. Return on Investment (ROI). It is the ratio of net profit to capital employed, 2. Return on new worth or (RONW). It is the ratio of net profit to net worth, 3. Net profit to sales ratio, 4. Sales to capital employed ratio, 5. Gross profit to sales ratio, 6. Turnover to bad debts ratio, 7. Turnover to working capital ratio, 8. Inventory to turnover ratio, 9. Turnover to distribution expenses ratio, and 10. Turnover to promotion expenses ratio.

G. Contribution Margin Analysis

We often come across instances where a particular product or customer does not bring in any net profit to the firm, but still makes a valuable contribution by carrying a significant part of the overheads. It is unwise to summarily drop such products or customers on the ground that they do not bring in any net profit. At the same time, they cannot be carried blindly. The firm should know whether these products and customers absorb at least a part of the firm's overheads and if so to what extent. The financial technique that comes to the rescue of the marketer in this respect, is called contribution margin analysis. It is partly a pricing technique and partly a marketing control technique.

To find out the contribution margin of a particular product, the costs incurred as a direct result of the particular product must be found first. In other words, those costs which could have been avoided if the particular product had been discontinued, must be found. Such costs are the escapable costs. The other costs are nonescapable costs or joint costs. Joint costs must be allocated to those products that are profitable and therefore, in a position to absorb these costs. It must then be examined whether the unprofitable product is in a position to absorb at least the escapable costs and produce a slight surplus. By this analysis, we can find out if a particular product is at least bringing in a little more revenue than the escapable costs, even though it may not be contributing to profits. As a part of marketing control, the firm should make such a contribution analysis and decide whether the 'not so profitable products and customers' should be dropped or continued.

Personal Observation

Personal observation as a method of marketing control refers to supervision, direction, deviation detection and its correction at the time and place of performance by those incharge of the job. It is one of the oldest and yet very potent method of controlling marketing operations. For examples, the job performance of a salesman or marketing research investigator may be personally supervised by the sales or research supervisor. In marketing, personal selling, research investigation, materials handling and office work easily lend to personal observation. It is a very effective method of control in that deviations are detected during the process of job performance and promptly corrected. There is not time lag between performance and control, which makes control effective. However, not all marketing operations lend themselves to control by personal observation like, for example, working of advertising message, transportation of goods, impact of price and discount structure. Also, it may not be applied to control persons' working at the middle or top management level, for example, the work of a sales manager cannot be controlled by personal observation of the marketing manager. Nevertheless, it is a very effective control method for those involved in marketing operations.

Evaluating the Sales Force

Evaluating performance of the sales force is difficult as is anything to do with the judgement of people. Even in advanced countries like U.K., a proper cost-benefit analysis into the productivity of the sales force is rarely carried out. This is because measuring merely the volume of sales will not determine the salesman's productivity. The simple yardsticks generally used for measuring the salesman's performance are 1. the number of calls per day; 2. the numb[illegible] of orders per day; and 3. the percentage of orders to calls.

However, these apply to comparatively simple sales situations. The more sophisticated approach would involve even grouping customers or users into size classes according to value or sub dividing the customers according to the volume of business they give. Thus in this sense, customers for examples may be divided into heavy users, medium users and light users in case of an industrial product. Whatever system of evaluation is introduced, it should help build morale and not harm it. However, evaluation is essential as it can help indicate areas where more training is needed and what further guidance can be given to the salesmen concerned. Establishment of standards however causes its problems. The establishment of sales quotas is an attempt to provide a standard. Once such a standard or quota is established properly, evaluation or measuring the performance becomes easy. For example, this can be done in terms of percentage above or below such quota. By establishing proper quotas, it is possible to project management's thinking to salesmen in terms of effort required from them with reference to products and customers by type and size. Another criterion used is expense standard; but here due weight must be given to territory differences. Other standards laid down generally are the number of calls made in a given period, average cost per call, new accounts secured in a certain period, and cost per unit of products sold. Despite such standards being prescribed, judgement cannot be avoided in evaluation. There are differences in personalities of both salesmen and customers, variations in territory potentials and differences in the impact of competition. Besides, salesmen who have provided poor sales at present may have contributed considerably in building good relations with dealers and distributors. Despite such difficulties, salesmen's performance must be evaluated. This is because, often (e.g., in case of industrial products) success of the entire marketing programme rests on the effectiveness of the sales force. Every effort must therefore be made to increase the salesmen's productivity. Constructive suggestions for improvement cannot be made unless an executive knows what his men are doing and can compare it with what results they should be producing. Performance evaluation can thus help management in determining factors responsible for success in selling and in-turn can show indicators as to how to help salesmen become more effective.

Evaluating Advertising Effectiveness

Daily, the average consumer is exposed to over 700 advertisements if we consider advertising in newspapers, magazines, hoardings, vehicles, films, radio, etc. It, therefore, becomes necessary to ascertain how far the company's advertising actually reached the consumer and what effect it had on him. As in case of all evaluation, effectiveness of advertising can be evaluated in terms of goals or objectives selected for a specific period. As advertising is a communication force, its goals or objectives must be communication goals such as orming people of new products and services and creating product preference. The advertising goals can be briefly summarised into the following three types, namely : 1. creating company awareness; 2. creating favourable company image; and 3. encouraging direct sales and service requests.

Thus the first goal involves creating of company awareness with the consumer or distributor by informing such person of the features, benefits and uses of the company's products and services. The second type of goal is concerned with creating a favourable company image to the same groups. Finally, the most important practical goal is to encourage direct sales and service requests which would result in consumer purchases requests for calls and demonstrations. The first type of goal is best measured by awareness and recalls surveys, the second type by attitude and psychological surveys and third type of goal is best measured by quantitative sales analysis and the use of coupons.

Awareness Surveys : Awareness tests are used to measure the public's knowledge of new product announcements and familiarity with name, trade mark, brand or product. The extent of knowledge gained from the advertising campaign, can be measured with the simple "Yes-No" type of questionnaires used before and after the campaign. The main advantages of awareness studies are low cost, speed, and ease of reporting and understanding. Mail and telephone surveys are typical examples of methods that give these qualities. The chief disadvantage of awareness techniques are their superficiality and difficulty in separating the results of the advertising campaign from other information sources. This is why recall or attitude studies are often used in addition.

Recall Tests : The objective of most advertising is to generate preference for the company's product which will later be used when the customer is ready for a purchase. The degree to which the messages are retained for such act is measured by the recall test. In both the awareness and recall measurement the question of the level of aid given becomes of importance.

Unaided recall may prove time-consuming but the suggestive recall may provide unrealistic indication of the respondent's knowledge. A common method of aided recall is more usually referred to as a "recognition test". The interviewee is asked if and where he has seen a series of advertisements from different sources. He may also be asked to interpret them. In another type of recognition test the main feature, identity, and message may be asked out. The interviewee is asked to name the company, message, and other factors. In either method, comparative data and preferences may be established by using company test advertisements or competitor's advertisements.

In general, the main factors that a recall study can quantify are the number of persons who "retained" one advertisement or the other; those who "retained" the general advertisement but missed the specific message; those who "retained" the specific message but did not know the brand; those who knew the message and the brand. These quantities, if properly interpreted, can be valuable for measuring the final results of the careful and time- consuming work done in formulating the goal, plans, and general campaign.

Attitude and Psychological Surveys : Attitude and psychological surveys are used to evaluate the favourable or unfavourable opinions about products, brands or advertisements. The objective of attitude surveys is to weigh personal opinions by getting answers to questions such as "Do You Like?" or "How would you describe the brand?". A positive or negative attitude formed about a product is a step beyond mere awareness or recall of a product. "Order-of-merit" is the common type of attitude test. The main risk here is that such aided tests may not be asking about the attributes that are most important to the respondent. The psychological surveys go a step beyond the attitude survey by further testing opinion at the mind's preconscious or unconscious level. These studies include depth interviews, group interviews and projective tests.

The depth interview is a typical psychological test which follows the vane of the interview used by psychiatry. In advertising research the main intent is to keep the respondent talking about the product until relaxed and frank opinion are revealed. Problems of expense and interpretation arise as one uses longer interviews and more expert interviewers. Usually depth interview tests are limited in number and the statistical significance may be questionable.

In the group interview method, some good attitude and frank opinion may be obtained. The counter argument is that known feeling may be more suppressed due to group pressure, status involvement or general lack of confidence. This method, of course, does not reveal the preconscious or unconscious.

The projective picture type of test is the second method beside depth interview which may reveal pre - or unconscious attitudes. Pictures of people and items, relating to the products or brand, are given to the respondent. He interprets the activity which has been carefully constructed. These tests, as with psychological tests in general, are highly effective but because of their non directive nature and complex interpretation are expensive and require great skill to use successfully. Another handicap is the difficulty in isolating and quantifying the effect of the advertising alone.

Sales Analysis : There are three approaches to sales analysis, namely, 1. Sales volume and mix changes; 2. Local market share change; and 3. Brand market share change. Sales volume and mix changes are measured by tabulating orders during the advertised period. It is effective to compare these sales with the previous year at the same time, if that period did not carry such advertising. Local market share change may generally be measured by a shift in a store's normal contribution, volume or mix. This is a gross store or brand measure and only relates to store or brand advertising rather than specific products. National brand market share is also only gross and reflects effect spread over a long period of time where many other factors dissolve a clear picture of advertising effectiveness. In general, sales analysis may not be as effectiveness as awareness type of studies.

Coupon Counting: Coupon counting and sorting are most commonly used to evaluate the results of different types of advertisements and media. This can be done by counting the response to coupon keyed advertisements in magazines and newspapers. If this methods is used regularly, it provides bench-marks over time and pinpoints sales trend, advertising effectiveness, and absolute performance. Another diversion is to measure the rupee value of request or response received. This is done by a follow-up sample of the responders to see what percentage have indeed purchased and are directly attributable to the advertisement or to direct sales call.

H. Using Marketing Information for Marketing Control

Timely and relevant marketing information facilitates the timely identification of variances between targets and achievements in respect of sales volume, market coverage and market share. It also throws light on market standing, advertising and personal selling effectiveness, and channel and physical distribution effectiveness. While using marketing information for marketing control, it is however essential that in the first place, control data, planning data and general purpose statistics are properly distinguished from one another out of the various marketing information outputs. Only then marketing information can be used as an effective control tool. The following are samples of marketing information, useful for control purpose.

- Information on marketing goals.
- Information on actual marketing performance.
- Information on emerging opportunities.
- Information on impending threats.

Secondly, the firm should properly tackle problems that arise commonly in the gathering of marketing information and in applying it for control. For example, at times, essential control information is left out and the available information is inadequate for control; at times, the information might lack clarity; there may be a mix up of vital information and trivial information; the information may not be related properly - it is disjointed; in some cases, the information may not be timely enough for effective control.

By instituting proper procedures for the information flow and by pinpointing the specific role of MIS in the matter of control the problems described above can be overcome. The firm must appreciate that the control system is essentially an information system or, more precisely, a cybernetics system, consisting of information flows and mechanisms for corrective action.

I. Marketing Control Through MBO

Today, management by objectives, or MBO is a popular and effective management technique. The technique consists of : (i) fixing of objective in each of the important areas of business; (ii) measuring performance against such pre-determined objectives; and (iii) carrying out the entire business operations keeping these objectives in focus. MBO can be used as a control technique in the area of marketing management. Marketing management is always oriented to results. And it is an area of business where measurable objectives can be set. The characteristics of the marketing function readily make marketing a fertile ground for the application of MBO. MBO is relevant to marketing controls in two ways. Firstly, through MBO, the top management of the firm can use control procedures to monitor the achievement of marketing objectives. Secondly, marketing executives at different levels can use it to ensure that their marketing programmes are the right one, that the programmes are being implemented in the right way and that the programmes take them to the objectives they have agreed upon.

The practice of MBO as a control technique in managing the marketing function actually starts with marketing planning and marketing goal setting. Once marketing objectives are set carefully, MBO in marketing is easy. As a matter of fact, more than objective setting, the important step in MBO is the identification of key results areas. The correct sequence is that Key Result Areas (KRAs) are specified first and the objectives are set in each of them. The KRAs may differ from industry to industry, company to company, department to department within a company, and manager to manager within a department. They may also differ somewhat from year to year depending on the state and nature of the business. The KRAs of marketing can be made the strategic points of control in marketing. If the KRAs are fixed carefully, MBO will serve as an effective marketing control device. It will eliminate other wasteful and dysfunctional controls. It will strengthen control in the strategic areas of marketing. KRAs must of course cover all those areas where results are important for marketing success, where success will be significant and where failures will be catastrophic. KRAs should include : market standing; innovation; sales volume; market coverage; market share; profitability; marketing productivity; productivity of advertising, personal selling and distribution.

Integrating Marketing Controls and Financial Controls : Marketing controls and financial controls are inseparable from one another in the sense that marketing and finance have the joint responsibility for ensuring the profitability of the enterprise. As such, proper integration of marketing and financial control tools is essential for meaningful and effective marketing control. The financial/accounting systems in some enterprises do not provide ready assistance to marketing control. This must be tackled in the first place. If the accounting system is at least capable of assembling the various marketing expenditures into suitable groups of clearly defined functions and allocating these functional costs over the relevant marketing activities, it can be used for marketing control. It is essential that finance and marketing travel hand in hand and assume joint responsibility for marketing control. Whether it is marketing audit, credit control or bad debts analysis, contribution margin analysis, or marketing cost analysis, successful application of control will need joint efforts of finance and marketing. Finance and marketing executives have to work as a team, understanding each other's role.

REVIEW QUESTIONS

1. "Planning and control are the 'siamese twins' of marketing management". Do you agree? Describe the meaning and scope of marketing planning and control.
2. Define marketing control and describe its process.
3. "The system of marketing control makes marketing management responsive to market needs". Discuss.
4. "The benefits of marketing control accrue when management follows some basic requisites of control". Discuss.
5. Describe the major methods and tools of controlling marketing operations.
6. "The rationale of performance analysis is rooted in the '80-20' principle". Is it true? Discuss the different types of analysis existing for measuring marketing performance.
7. "Personal observation is an inadequate while marketing audit is an impractical tool of marketing control". Discuss.
8. Explain the managerial significance or importance of marketing control.
9. Enumerate the characteristics of effective marketing control system.
10. Explain briefly : (a) Marketing Audit, (b) Market Share Analysis, (c) Marketing Cost Analysis, (d) Credit Rating of Dealers, (e) Coupon Counting and (f) Evaluation of Advertising Effectiveness.

25
Distribution Control

Changing Characters of Distribution Functions : A significant change has occurred in managements attitude towards the role and importance of the distribution function in business firms. The concept of integrated distribution management has progressed from the conceptual stage to a central part of forward-looking firm's strategic plans. Viewed in the historical perspective, prior to 1960, management did not view the distribution mission of the firm as an integrated task; instead, distribution was carried out in a series of fragmented uncoordinated movements of goods and information. For example, customer order processing was frequently the responsibility of the accounting function; traffic or transportation management the responsibility of the marketing function; while warehousing of raw materials and in-process goods was typically the responsibility of the manufacturing function. Similar fragmentation existed with respect to other activities which affected the flow of goods into, through, and out of a business to its customers.

It was virtually impossible to integrate the various activities involved in the distribution task, either conceptually or operationally, with the prevailing state of functional fragmentation. The sub optimisation that resulted from poor co-ordination not only led to poor distribution performance as viewed by the customers, but also frequently led to inefficiency, waste and morale problems within firms. The traffic manager, usually evaluated on the size of his freight bills, would try to ship in large quantities, frequently truck loads and by the most economical transport load.

The salesman, evaluated on the basis of his total sales, expected reliable and rapid customer order service, but was not concerned with the cost of providing that service. The manufacturing manager, evaluated on the basis of unit production cost, typically wanted to maximise the length of production runs of individual items to minimise his set-up and change-over costs. These type of conflicts within the organisation were frequently resolved on the basis of departmental power struggles which often resulted in adverse effects upon overall morale, efficiency and service of firms.

In view of these intricate problems, a number of progressive firms began in consider the potential of integrating the distribution function into a unified organisational whole for the purpose of planning operations and control during the 1960s. This trend gained momentum during the 1970s when the movement rapidly progressed from considering integration to actually implementing the integration of fragmented distribution activities into a systematic whole.

Integrated Distribution Management

Integrated distribution management is generally defined as :

The integration of two or more activities for the purpose of planning, implementing and controlling the efficient flow of raw materials, in process inventory and finished goods from the point of origin to point of consumption. These activities may include but are not limited to customer service, demand forecasting, distribution communication, inventory control, materials handling, order processing, parts and service support, plant and warehouse site selection, procurement, packaging, return goods handling, service and scrap disposal, traffic and transportation, warehousing and storage.

The following figure portrays the major component elements of an integrated distribution system :

Importance of integrated Distribution System : Empirical studies carried out, particularly, in the West, have shown that in most firms the cost of distribution alone represents a very significant proportion (18 to 45 percent) of total costs. These costs are, however, diffused throughout the company. Some of the costs are incurred in inventory, some in materials handling, some in transportation, others in warehousing and storage and so on. The principal method of securing cost reduction opportunity was to view distribution as an integrated rather than as the traditional fragmented task taking place in many parts of the firm.

A second major cause of the distribution revolution was the advent of new technology in data processing. As computer technology became increasingly powerful, less costly and more accessible, the possibility of automated inventory control procedures was increasingly realised. Distribution data are generally characterised as a high-input, low-calculation, and high-output form of processing. The new technology contributed to the technical capability of handling large amounts of distribution data in a rapid and efficient manner.

One side effect of the use of computer was its impact upon total integration of management within the firm. This has caused a break down in some of the traditional departmentalisation within the firm, and paved the way for integrated distribution management. Undoubtedly, increasing levels of computer technology will continue to contribute to expanding the data processing applications in distribution problem solving.

A third reason for the increased management attention to distribution management has been the management's recognition of its importance in providing customer satisfaction. Management began to realise that selling a product is really one one-half of the job. Getting the product to the customer at the right time in the right quantity and with the right logistical support (parts and service) is the other half, and, by far, the most important half.

There has been increasing recognition that marketing management cannot have a successful sales promotion programme unless the distribution system provides the logistic support for the promotion. This sector is of particular significance to those companies which sell relatively homogenous products. Such companies often compete on the basis of efficiency in distribution and their profits in large measure are determined by their success in effecting sound distribution.

The fourth major influence upon management thinking about distribution has been the emphasis on profit leverage available from reduced logistics cost Empirical exercises have generally shown that if a firm makes a 4 percent net profit from Rs. 1 sales, then, a saving of 4 paisa in legistics is equivalent to a Rs. 1 expansion in sales, assuming that all fixed costs remain constant. A Rs. 4 distribution cost saving is equivalent to Rs. 100 in sales expansion, a Rs. 400 savings in distribution cost is equivalent to Rs. 1,000 in additional sales. The profit leverage argument made a persuasive case for reviewing cost reduction opportunities available from integrated distribution management.

Finally, the rapid escalation of petroleum prices since 1974, coupled with the rising rate of inflation has brought transportation and distribution cots to a sharper focus and has forced managements' attention towards distribution system costs. Moreover, increasing interest costs have also forced firms to pay more attention to the rising inventory and distribution costs. Firms are increasingly paying more attention to the prunning of marginal product lines and marginal customers to assure that inventory investment is focussed on those products and customers which will yield the greatest return to the company.

Integrated Distribution Systems Objectives

(a) Cost Minimisation : The original objective of physical distribution practitioners has been cost minimisation. The minimisation of all distribution related costs remains one of contemporary physical distribution managements' primary objective.

(b) Service Maximisation : Some physical distribution managers, especially those in companies whose sales volume are very sensitive to the levels of service provided to customers, place maximisation of service even above cost minimisation. This may well be justifiable in situations where the market pays a premium service. It may also be warranted in situation where the market will not pay a premium price for superior service, but management recognises services as an integrated part of the marketing mix, and realigns marketing and sales budgets to be able to accommodate basic profitability.

(c) Profit Optimisation : As companies become more aware of the cost, service, and sales trade-offs, and more sophisticated in evaluating these trade-offs, they invariably move away from unilateral approaches to either cost minimisation or service maximisation towards profit optimisation. The profit equation is optimised when all relevant distribution costs are minimised within acceptable economical, and competitive service goals.

Energy Cost and Availability : The long term effects of the energy situation are significant :

(a) Products and processes must be redesigned to make them less energy intensive.

(b) Reduced location options due to limitations on energy availability will become a very important consideration in future site selection.

Components of Integrated Distribution Management : Specific functional areas that are encompassed by the integrated distribution systems or logistics could broadly be summarised as follows :

Inventory e.g. - Service level decisions -Materials requirement planning

Information e.g. - Order processing - Demand forecasting.

Warehousing and Handling e.g. - Depot location - Unitisation and packaging.

Transport e.g. - Mode decisions - Scheduling

Though each of the above elements enjoy their own importance and significance, they are not discussed in this short note in as much as each would in its own right deserve a comprehensive treatment. The primary purpose of this note is only to bring out an appreciation of the integrated distribution concept, as such. Only the significance of two elements e.g., customer service and channel strategy is mentioned below :

Customer Service : Customer service is the output of the logistics system within the 'logistics mix'. The provision of improved customer service will normally incur additional costs for the company. The higher the level of service ordered, the higher will be the costs. In fact, it can be shown that once the level of service increases beyond the 70-80 percent mark, the associated costs increase for more proportionately (the service level being defined as the percentage of orders that can be met from stock within a given period). The effect of offering a 97 percent level of service instead of 95 percent level may have only a slight effect on customer demand but will have a considerable effect on distribution costs. For normally distributed demand this 2 percent increase in the level of service would lead to a 14 percent increase in safety stocks.

One of the benefits of being able to identify the specific sources of total distribution costs is that it becomes easier to identify potential trade-offs. A trade-off occurs when an increased cost in one area is more than matched by a cost reduction in another area, thus, leading to an improved situation, overall.

Thus, a distribution system with ten regional depots has high warehouse and stockholding costs compared with a system of only five depots, but the savings in trunck haulage and the reduction of stock-outs may more than compensate for the extra costs involved in the ten depot system. In this case, an increase in warehouse and stock carrying costs can be traded against a reduction in total system costs.

Because of the multivariate nature of customer service and the delivering requirement of specific markets, it is essential for any business to have a defined policy towards customer service. In this context, the following points need to be recognised.

- the trade-off potential between the various components of the customer service mix must be evaluated.
- the unique customer service requirement of each product/channel/market segment must be identified.

A customer may be forced with alternative options of distribution service. He may choose between different levels of stock availability, order cycle time and delivery reliability. Hypothetically, a stock availability of 85 percent with 2 days delivery and reliability of % 1 day may be seen as being equally acceptable as a 95 percent availability with 2 days delivery and % days availability. Thus, suggesting that a tightening up on reliability might reduce stockholding, and still provide an acceptable level of customer service. The key question to be asked are :

- Do all our customers require the same level of service?
- Are all our customers equally sensitive to service?
- What are the different requirements of different market segments or trade sectors for customer service?

While designing customers packages, the following elements may be given their due recognition :

(a) Consider the impact on sales of a 'market presence', i.e., proximity of stocks to key markets.

(b) Provide quantity price brackets encouraging the buyer to 'stretch' for a lower price through purchasing greater quantities.

(c) Concentrate on improved ontime delivery consistency.

(d) Support promotion with superior distribution service.

Channels strategy : Channel length concerns the extent to which intermediates should be used or, customer sales should be made directly to the consumer. This decision is not just a question of economics but should be governed by the extent to which the firm is prepared to trade-off control of the marketing channel to intermediates.

The decision on channel breath is essentially one of market coverage. At the extreme are intensive distribution and 'selective' distribution. Evaluation of the channel strategy should focus on some important aspects like sales performance of channel members, marketing capability of channel members, motivation of channel members, competition faced by channel members and the growth prospects of channel members.

Distribution Cost Control

Distribution is one of the basic functions of marketing. The marketing job remains incompiete until the product reaches the consumer's door for ultimate use or consumption. This process of distribution involving different kinds of products and services is achieved at same cost. The nature and dimensions of these costs may vary with the product, manufacturer, channel and area. Concomitantly, these costs reflect in the price for the customer and the profit for the manufacturer. The force of demand determines the share of distribution costs to be borne by the manufacturer and his customer. It is evident, therefore, that marketing management should understand and if possible alter, to the company's advantage, these cost ratios for profitable selling and enlarged market penetration.

A significant and increasing part of many companies' expenditure is that incurred in keeping their products on the move through the channels of distribution to the final consumer. Physical distribution covers a broad range of activities concerned with this phase of corporate operations, such as transportation, warehousing, materials handling, packaging, inventory control, and administration.*

It is at those points in the distribution flow where goods stop moving that they accumulate costs. But it is also found that physical production developments have not kept pace with developments in physical distribution management. Physical distribution is an important aid to marketing, and must therefore be oriented towards meeting customers' requirements and securing the attainment of profit/market share objectives. This link adds great emphasis to the need for effective planning and control of distribution activities. However, distribution costs should be kept at a level that ensures an efficient system of operations. This follows from the inability of any distribution system to simultaneously maximise customer service and minimise distribution costs.

Analysis and Control of Distribution Costs

In essence, a manufacturer must be concerned with ensuring that his products are where the customer expects to buy them and when he wants them, at the lowest cost. The provision of a high level customer service (for example,

* These activities are directed towards order-filling, and this chapter complements chapter 24 which focussed on order-getting.

availability in a high proportion of possible sales outlets, or speedy delivery to the customer involving perhaps greater stocks, and more vehicles) may increase sales. However, the cost involved in despatching small quantities of the products to retailers, who are widely dispersed geographically, together with costs of ensuring quick delivery from the manufacturer's plant or distribution depots, may exceed any marginal benefit involved. The manufacturer has to balance the marginal costs of increasing customer service against the marginal gains he obtains.

Different Components

This brings one to the question of knowing the distribution cost in its various components as a first step in distribution cost analysis. The second step is to identify the characteristics of these costs in terms of whether they are fixed or variable in nature. The significance and impact of distribution cost would depend on a number of factors, some of which are :

single plant, single market;

single plant, multiple markets;

establishment of a regional manufacturing plant;

multiple plants, multiple markets;

inventory policies;

location decisions;

infrstructure facilities, like transport, etc.

All these factors individually or jointly influence the distribution cost in relation to the company objective of providing customer service (output of distribution system).

Based on the influencing factors, managements have to make decisions on the warehousing, freight, transport and inventory policies. The cost incurred in each of the distribution process has to be analysed and evaluated. If a company wants to evaluate the distribution cost in relation to its customer service, a norm for the incurrence of cost has to be established. This norm could take the shape of a standard or budget.

Method of fixing a budget for Distribution Expenses : The manager in charge of the distribution function must be provided with the cost data for a given level of distribution volume in respect of the past period. The cost data should clearly be classified into its basic characteristic as to whether they are fixed or variable. The actual cost incurred should be given before the distribution function starts its plan for the planning period in question. An illustration of presenting the actual cost incurred is given in next page.

Actual cost incurred in past 12 months related to level of activity

Item of Expenditure	Total
Despatch warehouse	
Fixed costs :	
- Salaries	
- Premises	
- Plant & equipment	
- Depreciation	
Variable costs :	
- Wages	
- Plant & equipment	
- Running cost/freight	
Motor lorries & vans	
- Drivers' wages	
- Manager's salary	
- Vehicle depreciation	
- Insurance	
- Licence fees etc.	
Variables :	
Fuel	
Oil	
Repairs etc.	
Total	

The level of performance for each month is to be expressed in some convenient units of measurement.

Based on these past data, the distribution manager would be in a position to calculate his budget of expenses giving due allowance for variable factors depending on the level of performance expected in the planning period. This budget, when approved by this marketing manager and the board, would form the criteria for judging the actual distribution cost incurred in two ways - first, to control the actual distribution cost in relation to the budget; second, to evaluate the cost incurred in relation to the physical performance of the distribution function. Any variation in the actual from the budget has to be further analysed to find answers to "What", "Why" and "Who" has been responsible for the variations and in terms of controllability aspects. The comparison of actual costs in relation to the budget should be prepared on a monthly basis and communicated to the distribution manager to enable him to control the distribution cost. The presentation could be as shown as given below :

Distribution Expenses

Month......... 1995

Budget Rs.
Actual Rs.

Despatch/Warehouses

Fixed :
Salaries
Premises (rent)
Depreciation (P & E)
Variables
Wages
Running cost (P & E)

Motor lorries & vans

Fixed :
Drivers' wages
Mgmt. salary
Depreciation
Insurance, licence fees etc.
Variables :
Fuel, oil
Repairs etc.

Total

This type of feedback information, when presented on a monthly basis with the least time lag, enables the functional managers to control the costs in relation to the budget. The other advantage of such periodical review is that it enables the management to evaluate functions and achieve the goal of the organisation.

Maximum customer service demands the existence of such facilities as high inventories, a large number of warehouses, and the fastest means of transportation. The *level of service* is usually defined in terms of either the number of days it takes to deliver an order, or the percentage of orders that can be filled from stock at any point in time. The desired level of service must be at least that of the firm's competitors, but it is extremely difficult to measure the value that consumers actually place on the level of service in selecting a supplier.

Figure 25.1 illustrates the relationship between the level of service (as the percentage of orders that can be filled from existing stocks) and the required inventory investment to provide this level of service. It is clear that no firm can realistically carry such large inventories to guarantee no stock outs (i.e., situations in which ordered goods are not available immediately from stock).

Minimising Distribution Costs : Minimising distribution costs would imply low stock levels, slow transport, few warehouses, and so forth. The aim should be to balance the costs inputs in an efficient manner to give the desired level of service as the output (i.e., efficiency replaces maximum and minimum concepts). This demands that costs be viewed as a whole, because a reduction in one area may produce a more than proportionate increase in another. For example, it may be cheaper in total terms, and more efficient in achieving the specified level of service (in terms of days required to deliver), to use an expensive means of transport (e.g., air freight) than to maintain a number of local warehouses, with related inventory and administrative expenses.

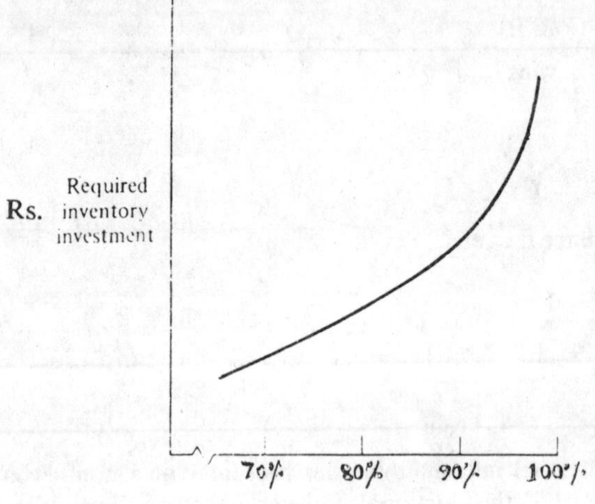

Fig. 25.1 Level of Service

Planning the Systems

Before financial control can be put into effect, the system of distribution itself must be specified. All the elements of a physical distribution system are interdependent, and should be planned, operated, and controlled as integrated part of the whole system. The nature of the distribution system will depend on the nature of the industry, the competition, the product, and so forth. Policy decisions must be made in relation to both the selection of channels and their management, as well as in relation to physical characteristics. For example, geographically scattered customers may favour public means of transport, whereas geographically, scattered warehouses may favour one's own means of transport. (A detailed analysis on tonnages to be delivered to different areas will aid decision- making on this point).

Whatever the system, it must facilitate the delivery of goods to the firm's customers in usable and saleable condition. This requires that they be undamaged, arrive at the specified time and place, and in the right quantities. These requirements are not as simple to meet as they may appear. Inadequate packaging, incorrect loading procedures, rough handling in transit, overloading, and similar matters all hinder their attainment. The packaging of the product may be influenced by the need to effect economy in shipping costs. Special packaging may be needed to secure protection from shock and weather, and special palletisation may be needed to facilitate handling. Improvements may be made in the product planning phase with respect to product design or packaging, in anticipation of distribution requirements. Such factors as shelf-life, attractive display, and final condition on delivery to the consumer may affect the design of the product. In addition, closer co-operation with carriers and other distributive agents may prove beneficial. (This is more likely to be the case if vehicles are engaged on a contract basis, rather than spot-hired, for instance).

The system that is eventually specified will consist of a unique physical distribution network based on decisions on transport, warehousing, inventory management, administration, and level of service to be provided. The total system's cost is given by the simple equation : $D = T + FW + VW + S$

Where D = total distribution cost
T = total transportation cost
FW = fixed warehousing costs
VW = variable warehousing costs (including inventory costs)
S = cost of lost sales due to average delivery delay.

Each alternative system should be costed using this equation before the best one can be selected. Two examples should clarify the approach that should be adopted.

1. XYZ Ltd has a national distribution system via six warehouses selling to wholesale customers. Ninety-five per cent of orders are delivered within 24 hours of receipt. Some figures from the last financial year are :

Sales	Rs. 5m.
Net profit (after tax)	Rs. 250 000
Finished goods inventory at factory*	Rs. 750 000
Finished goods inventory at warehouses*	Rs 1m.

(* average)

There is only one factory, and this works on a system of minimum- maximum levels of finished goods inventory to maintain the 95 per cent level of service. Each warehouse orders weekly from the factory, with special interim orders for urgent requirements. Warehouse inventory levels are based on lead times of 2-12 days from the factory. The firm's marketing director asks what the effect on costs would be if the warehouses were eliminated, and direct delivery was made to customers by outside carriers. The estimated effects for the next year are given in below:

		Shipments to warehouses Rs.	Shipments to customers Rs.
Transport	To Warehouses	150 000	
	Local	37 500	
	Direct		330 000
Warehousing	Rent	52 500	2 500
	Salaries	65 000	20 000
	Insurance	17 500	10 000
	Rates	7 500	5 000
	Other	15 000	5 000
	Communications	22 500	30 000
Total Distribution Costs		367 500	402 500

Fig. 25.2 Distribution Costs

On the basis of these figures, the present system appears to be least expensive. But all the relevant costs have not been considered.

It is assumed that both alternatives are based on a 95 percent level of service, so the cost of lost sales will be the same in each, and can thus be ignored for comparative evaluation purposes. However, to maintain this level of service under the present system involves an investment of Rs. 1m. in warehouse stocks. The cost of carrying this stock is given below..

Cost of capital	8%
Excess handling	2%
Obsolescence	7%
Deterioration	2%
Administration	1%
Total	20%

Fig. 25.3 Cost of Inventory

(The figure of 20 per cent excludes an allowance for the risks of price changes, variable markets, etc., which could make it even higher).

Thus 20 per cent of Rs. 1m. is Rs. 200 000, which is the amount saved by adopting the proposes alternative of direct delivery, and shows that this is, in fact, the better choice. Further savings could also be made in manufacturing costs as a result of producing for once central inventory rather than for a central inventory plus six warehouses. However, this example shows the need to consider the total situation, not merely segments of it.

2. A variation would have been to consider the financial alternatives of owning or leasing the warehouses. The leasing alternative provides greater flexibility and less risk unless volume is large and demand stable. This is so because the cost of storage should be related to the average number of square feet used per period, and leasing charges will be proportional to this area, whereas ownership costs remain the same regardless of usage.

Cost-volume analysis can be used to assist the decision-maker in choosing among : (a) leasing or buying premises; (b) leasing or owning vehicles; (c) using agents or branch offices, etc.

In the case of warehousing, the chart in Fig. 25.4 summarises the situation. showing the storage space at which ownership costs are identical with leasing charges (B). At greater volume requirements, ownership is cheaper; at lesser volumes, leasing is too be preferred.

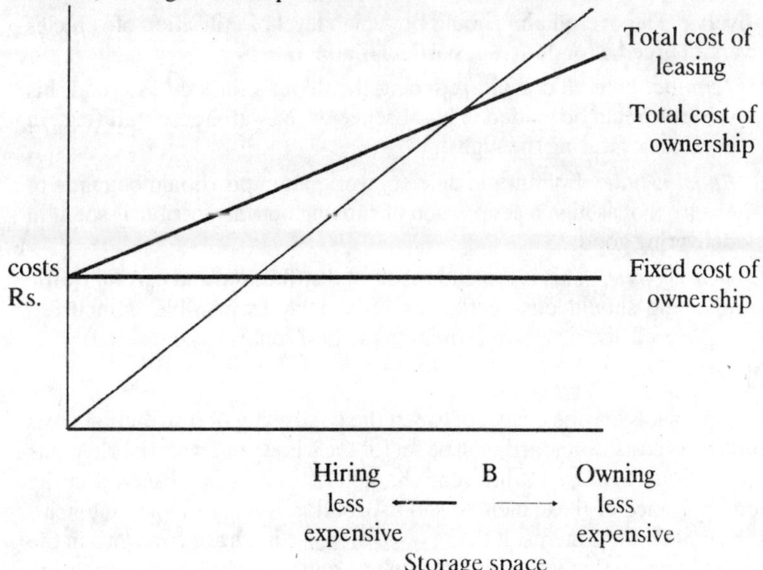

Fig. 25.4 **Break-even chart for Warehousing**

Resource Planning : Having determined the system, attempts must be made to achieve cost-effective results through the efficient utilisation of labour and equipment within the system. Work study standards of performance, where appropriate, should be established in the labour-intensive warehousing and delivery/driving spheres. Control action can be based on the subsequent application of these standards only if they are kept up-to-date. Variations in the traffic mix, the introduction of new products, and similar events render previously determined standards obsolete. As in the use of work study in setting manufacturing standards, its application in distribution must be carried out with the full knowledge of those whose performance is to be measured. It is also important that all management personnel are fully trained in the significance of this means of control

Warehousing ; Three areas of cost control are especially important within warehousing. They are :

1. *Space utilisation.* Since warehouse space, and the related costs (such as rates, lighting, heating) are expensive, a high rate of utilisation, hence low unit cost, should be sought.
2. *Labour utilisation.* Work study should be applied to goods receiving, stacking, materials handling, order assembly, outward loading, and stock control activities.
3. *Equipment utilisation.* The high costs of materials handling equipment should be justified by fairly intensive usage.

Delivery ; The overall aim should be a high level of utilisation of vehicles and drivers. Three factors warrant particular attention :

1. *Terminal time.* To avoid reducing the driver's time on the road, his vehicle should be loaded in his absence by the warehouse staff (e.g., in evenings or during the night).
2. *Running time.* In multiple delivery work, attempts should be made to ensure that as high a proportion of running time as possible is spent in delivering goods.
3. *Delivery time.* This is the end result of distribution, and careful traffic planning should ensure that as little delay as possible is incurred between deliveries by determining the best routes to be taken.

Cost Control

Close parallels may be drawn between the controlling of distribution costs and production costs. Standards can be set for the labour and material elements of both functional areas, but different characteristics will be observed in the relative importance of these elements. Distribution is more labour- intensive in most instances, with the result that a wage increase is harder to absorb in the distribution function that it is within manufacturing. Conversely, materials are a more significant aspect of manufacturing than they are of distribution.

In allocation costs to the two functions, wide variations are often found in practice as to what should be included in each. Some firms, for example, include all container costs as distribution costs, whereas others only show transit containers as distribution costs, with the unit pack being shown as a production expense. The decision frequently rests on such circumstances as whether the actual packing is a factory process or despatch process. The allocation of carriage costs is a similar problem, and the answer depends on the facts of each individual case.

Apart from these marginal problems of allocation, unit distribution costs show a marked tendency to increase disproportionately with volume. In contrast, unit production costs tend to decrease disproportionately with volume (Fig. 25.5). The optimal scale of operations is, prima facie, that shown by the lowest total unit cost, point V.

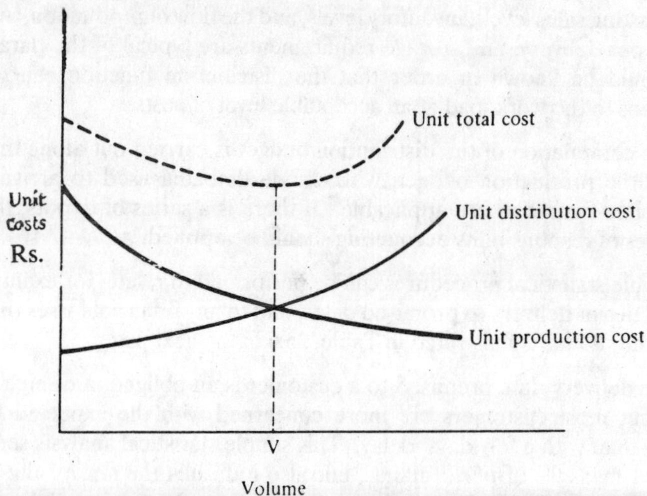

Fig. 25.5 Unit Cost Behaviour

In the light of the detailed planning steps and a knowledge of the behaviour of distribution costs, decision rules can be derived for the following areas :

(a) inventory rules to minimise the costs of ordering, stock-holding, and shipping for a given level of service;

(b) materials handling rules to minimise space, time, costs, and effort in warehousing;

(c) transportation rules to minimise the costs of scheduling and routing vehicles and deliveries; and

(d) communication rules to minimise the costs of information.

All these rules should be developed in such a way that more expensive activities can be traded off for less expensive ones in order to minimise the costs of providing the desired level of customer service.

A range of financial techniques can be used in conjunction with these decision rules. Distribution cost analysis offers a means of allocating costs to transport, warehousing, and inventory that help the budgeting process; marketing audits can be extended to distribution activities to reveal areas of inefficiency and highlight points that should be incorporated into Operation Research models or computer programmes; and a ratio hierarchy or pyramid can be specially drawn up for distribution expenses.

Flexible budgets can be compiled with any one of several volume bases-sales (in value terms), product units, cases, tons, or whatever measure best reflects cost performance. This requires that the marketing department and production department work closely with distribution management in relation to forecasting sales levels, inventory levels, and the flow of production. Average weights per delivery, and storage requirements are typical of the parameters that should be known in order that the distribution function can gear its operations to the work load at an acceptable level of costs.

The compilation of the distribution budget is carried out along the same lines as the production budget, with standards being used to arrive at the appropriate figures where applicable. If there is a series of depots, then the principles of responsibility accounting should be applied.

Simple statistical procedures can be performed to relate, for example, the actual dates of delivery to promised dates, and to any financial losses that arise from delays. This is illustrated in Table. 25.6 in the next page.

The delivery date promised to a customer is an obligation of high importance, but most customers are more concerned with the expected time of delivery than with a few days' delay. This simple statistical analysis serves not only as a measure of performance, but also indicates the size of the control problem- especially if related to lost orders and penalties due to delay.

Further statistical analyses can be carried out in the following areas :

1. Output, showing performance against standard for :
   (a) tons handled per man:
   (b) tons delivered per vehicle;
   (c) number of deliveries;
   (d) kilometers covered, etc.
2. Costs, showing monthly comparisons of budgeted figures with actual figures.

Shipping pattern	Number of orders	% of total
As promised	186	37.2
Late		
1 day	71	14.2
2 days	49	9.8
3days	35	7.0
4 days	38	7.6
5 days	28	5.6
6 days	14	2.8
7 days	13	2.6
8 days	10	2.0
9 days	8	1.6
10 days-2 weeks	17	3.4
2 weeks-3 weeks	15	3.0
3 weeks-4 weeks	10	2.0
4 weeks-5 weeks	6	1.2
Total	500	100.0

Fig. 25.6 Delivery control statistics

3. Miscellaneous, covering such matters as :
   (a) kilometers per litre;
   (b) life (in kilometers) of tyres;
   (c) accidents;
   (d) repairs, etc.

Control of the physical distribution aspects has been emphasised so far in this section, the essence of which is the planning and reporting of costs by responsibility centres. However, the control of sales through different channels should not be ignored. The aim should be to check on the profitability of each channel used in order that the optimum means of distribution may be determined.

The following example indicates how marginal analysis can be used to determine channel profitability. (The same technique can also be employed to calculate the minimum sales volume necessary to justify the use of a particular channel, and solutions to similar decision problems).

The marketing director of ABC Ltd suspected that one of his company's four channels of distribution was unprofitable, but had no concrete evidence of this.

Rs. 000		Total	Channel			
			A	B	C	D
Sales	Rs	1500	750	250	300	200
Variable Costs*	Rs	1050	400	100	300	250
Contribution	Rs	450	350	150	0	-50
Fixed Costs	Rs	300				
Net Income	Rs	150				

* (Including manufacturing costs)

Fig. 25.7 Channel Profitability

He asked the controller for an analysis showing the contribution margin of each channel, which was fairly straightforward because the same product was sold at the same price through each channel. The approach adopted was to separate fixed costs form the variable, and to compute a unit cost by dividing the variable costs by the number of units distributed. The variable channel cost can then be found for each of the channels by multiplying the unit cost by the number of units passing through each channel during the period (Fig. 25.7). It would appear that channel D is unprofitable since it does not even recoup its variable costs. The decision to drop this channel must be based on expected future costs and revenues not on past data alone.

Monitoring Results

The collecting and reporting of cost data only form the basis of control, and action must result if control is to be effective. A comparison may be made with the results of other comparable companies. In either case, however, it must be appreciated that all costs do not have the same relative importance. Consequently, the most significant cost factors should receive the greatest attention-the principle of management by exception.

REVIEW QUESTIONS

1. Explain the concept and components of integrated distribution management.
2. How is distribution control exercised in a manufacturing organisation?
3. Explain the different means and areas of minimising distribution costs.

26
Control in Personnel Area

Human behaviour is complicated and it is not easy to impose controls without leading to conflicts. Employees do not like controls because they give rise to pressures and strains. An operative attains greater psychological satisfaction if he is free in his functioning. The more controls on him the greater is his opposition to them. Following are some of the reasons for workers' resistance to controls :

1. **Failure to accept objectives :** If a worker fails to accept certain objectives he may find the control mechanism that pushes him towards those objectives a distinct annoyance. Thus a worker may not care to reduce waste because he thinks that the company is rich or a branch sales manager may not push a new product because he thinks it to be of poor quality.

2. **Feeling that the standard is unreasonable :** An operative may reject all standards and targets which have been fixed for him from above. He complains these standards are unreasonable because : (a) they are too high to be achieved, (b) the prescribed time within which they are to be achieved is too short, and (c) the company does not provide him with sufficient resources in terms of man, material, money and machines.

3. **Too many controls :** Too many controls act as irritants. If there are already many controls in operation any additional control may act as the last straw on the camel's back. There is not simple rule to alert the manager when this is going to take place. The point of redundancy depends on the nature of the job, the traditions of the company, the way the controls are administered and many other factors.

4. **Belief that measurements are inaccurate :** Sometimes people dislike controls because they believe that the measurement of results is inaccurate and consequently they do not get credit for what they do. Thus a man in the maintenance department may say "You cannot measure the breakdowns that did not take place".

5. **Fear of exposure or punishment :** Sometimes people dislike controls for fear of being exposed before others or punished for their weaknesses and failures.

6. **Social pressure running counter to controls :** Sometimes people are opposed to controls because the groups which they belong to do not like them.

People care more for the attitudes of their groups than for the dictates of their superiors.

7. Controls being exercised by wrong persons : Senior people resent receiving orders from their juniors in the management hierarchy.

Kinds of Control Devices

There are four kinds of control devices which are used by personnel managers viz., Reports and Budgets, Employee relation index, Personnel audit and Human resource accounting.

1. Reports and Budgets : These are perhaps the most obvious and frequent control devices. An established reporting system brings information on a daily, weekly or monthly basis. Such reports can be compared with earlier experience or with that of other organisations. A personnel budget is a personnel programme, expressed in monetary terms, that covers a specified period of time, usually one year. Broad categories of expenditure usually included in a personnel budget are :

(i) Expenses to be incurred by the personnel staff as such - that is, salaries, travel expenses, etc., of the personnel officer, welfare officer, training officer and their subordinates.

(ii) Expenses to be incurred for carrying out certain company-wide activities, such as, management training and development, employee services, medical, safety, and the like.

(iii) Expenses to be incurred on certain materials and services, such as printing of booklets, brochures, reporting services, etc.

(iv) Outside consulting fees.

(v) Miscellaneous, such as heat, light, space, etc.

Today's personnel administrator is interested not only in controlling his costs but also knowing whether his costs are reasonable and in line with general practice. Basically, this is a matter of establishing comparisons with other units. The personnel administrator can compare his expenditures under various heads with his own budgeted provisions and with those of other companies. This will enable him to know whether he is spending high or low, whether he is getting his money's worth and whether he is in danger of losing his better men. The expenditure and other data of different companies can be made comparable by converting them into ratios such as the training cost per employee per year or the average travelling expenditure per trip or the number of personnel, staff per 100 people in the total company population, and so on.

2. Employee Relations Index : This is a quantitative technique of measuring the overall effectiveness of the entire personnel programme. In this technique a composite index is prepared taking into account a number of strategic items such as absence, separations, visits to dispensary for occupational disease, suggestions made through suggestion systems, formal grievances, work stoppages, etc. These items are given weights according to their importance. An employee relations index of 100 indicates average industrial relations, of below 100 poor industrial relations and of above 100 good industrial relations.

3. Personnel Audit ; A personnel audit is a systematic and comprehensive analysis of all activities and results of a personnel programme. It assures a complete review, at regular intervals, of the effectiveness and utility of the various personnel functions and activities, policies and procedures. In the words of Dale Yoder, personnel audit is an investigative, analytical, comparative process. It not only listens but looks for and discovers answers. It undertakes a systematic search. It investigates formally and in depth, as contrasted with day-to-day informal impressions. It assumes that appropriate policies and programmes can produce positive results which can be identified and evaluated and that it is wrong to believe that achievements in the sphere of personnel management defy evaluation and measurement. Advantages of personnel audit are given below :

(i) It serves as a **check** on the activities of personnel management department.

(ii) It generates wide **understanding** of both policy and practice in manpower management.

(iii) It highlights the **need** for line staff co-operation.

(iv) It **focuses** attention on what is being done and what needs to be done.

(v) It **assists** staff in convincing higher management of the need for improved policy and practice.

(vi) It **brings** in fresh points of view and valuable suggestions based on the experience of auditors in other organisations.

A comprehensive personnel audit includes every phase of manpower management. One can group these phases as under :

1. Personnel policy, organisation and administration.
2. Procurement : Job analysis, Recruitment, Selection, Induction and Job change.
3. Utilisation : Productivity.
4. Training and Development : Training, Appraisal, Promotion, CareerPlanning and Counselling.
5. Compensation : Wage and salary administration.
6. Integration and Maintenance : Safety, health and employee service programmes, In plant communication, Job satisfaction and Morale.
7. Labour relations : Negotiation, administration.
8. Research.

Qualitative and Quantitative Indicators for Personnel Audit

Major functions	Qualitative Indicator	Quantitative Indicator
1. Procurement	Personnel inventory, Replacement tables, Organisation planning, Job descriptions and specification, Source evaluation, Exit interviews, Induction programme.	Turnover rates, Selection rates, Retrenchment, Dismissals and lay- offs, Recruitment time-lag and Recruitment ratios.
2 Utilisation	Identification of misfits.	Capacity utilisation, Idle time statistics, Extra-time statistics, Backlogs, Turnover per employee, Profits per rupee of personnel expenses, etc.
3. Training and Development	Training programmes, Supervisory and management development programmes, Systematic promotions, Career planning, Formal appraisals.	Time taken in training, Apprentice ratios, Scrap losses, Productivity increase.
4. Compensation	Job evaluation programme, Wage and salary surveys, Complaint from employees about wages and salaries.	Wage and salary differentials, Benefit range and costs, Number of employees earning bonus in excess of standard rate.
5. Integration and maintenance	House organ, Employee hand-book, Employee voluntary participation in-optional service programmes.	Measured morale, Measured communication, Absen teeism and turnover rates, Number of grievances, Suggestion ratios, Accident rates.
6. Labour relations	Labour-management committees, Contract interpretations, No strike clause.	Work stoppages, Grievances and their settlement, Arbitrations, Costs.

Audit may be carried out at various depth levels. It may be superficial or intensive and probing. Superficial audit generally limits its evaluations to such apparent results of management as labour turnover, absenteeism, selection ratios, promotions, transfers, and so on. It is, therefore, also known as the **'result audit'**. Here it is assumed that the results which are being probed represent the effects of managerial policies and practices. The following table outlines the most commonly used qualitative and quantitative indicators of effectiveness classified by major functions. It should be remembered that these indicators or symptoms provide only a superficial impression and may not be dependable in some cases.

Results audit is generally superficial because the meaning of indicators is taken for granted. Low turnover, for example, is supposed to reflect satisfied labour force and good management. But it may be that the real cause of low turnover is high unemployment and fewer opportunities to go elsewhere. In this way result may be satisfactory in spite of rather than because of existing programmes. To avoid this drawback the audit should, therefore, probe much deeper than mere results. Since all results depend on programmes, programmes on policies, policies on philosophies, and philosophies on the theory of management, probe can be continued deeper and deeper till the lowest level (theory) is reached. In practice, however, it is difficult to design and conduct an audit which may go beyond the third level and may expose the underlying philosophies and theory of management.

Levels of Audit

First level (superficial)	Results
Second level	Progammes (including practices and procedures)
Third level	Policies (both explicit and implicit)
Fourth level	Philosophy (values, goals and objectives)
Fifth level (deepest)	Theory (the assumed relationships and plausible explanations that explain and relate philosophies, policies, practices and continu-

There is no set procedure personnel audit. Like all other audits in personnel audit also the two basic sources of information are written records of facts and multiple opinions obtained from a sample of respondents from the groups interested in and concerned about the activity. A comprehensive personnel audit includes information analysis, Personnel department activity analysis, Survey of management opinion and survey of employee attitude.

(i) Information Analysis : Depending upon the amount and nature of audit available a personnel audit should analyse and interpret the following information both for the company and the industry as a whole :

- Number and type of grievances and the number which reach arbitration.
- Arbitration decisions.
- Turnover ratios for various classes of employees.
- Recruiting and employment costs.
- Staffing ratios as related to total employment and sales.
- Supervisory ratios.
- Accident frequency and security measures.
- Working men's compensation costs.
- Area wage and salary surveys.
- Wage and salary practices.
- Merit rating and performance appraisal systems.

(ii) Personnel Department Activity Analysis : The authority and responsibilities of the head of the personnel department should be carefully enquired into. Factual answers should be obtained to the question how he is spending his time in various functional areas, viz., department administration, planning, staffing, training, promotion and transfers, personnel rating, labour relations, employee service and benefits, health and safety, wage and salary administration, record and reports, audit and review, research and overhead and miscellaneous. If the answer is not readily available the head may be requested to keep a daily record of his activity, tabulated in half-hour units for 2 or 3 months. This data would reveal to the auditor whether the various functional areas are receiving the head's attention in terms of time as they deserve.

The activities of the personnel department should also be classified according to the level of professional competence needed for carrying them out and it should be seen how much of his time the head is spending in activities under each class. For this purpose activities may be divided into 3 levels.

Level 1 - Activities which can be handled by the head of the department only.

Level 2 - Activities which can be handled by their the head or his assistant.

Level 3 - Activities which can be handled by a secretary or a clerk, e.g., filing, completing routine reports, posting notices, etc.

As a matter of fact a head with his professional training and ability must spend most of his time in activities of the first level only. But if he spends much of his time in activities of lower levels which can be successfully handled by an assistant or clerk there is indication of serious understaffing which should be further probed.

(iii) Survey of Management Opinion : A sound personnel audit programme should also aim at making an assessment of the existing personnel organisation, policies and practices. This requires a detailed analysis of what is being done, by whom, when and how. A questionnaire should be developed for this purpose. It should raise questions about personnel policies, the personnel department's organisation and functions, employee recruitment, selection and placement, induction and follow-up of new employees, training and personnel development, transfer, promotion and separations, compensation, employee security and benefits, employee services, personnel records, labour relations, communication, community relations and other miscellaneous activities. Some sample questions are as follows :

- Who recommends establishment of or changes in personnel policy ?
- What controls are exercised to assure compliance with established policy?
- What are the responsibilities of the head of the personnel department? Are they defined and understood by line people?
- How does personnel department educate other departments regarding their statutory obligations?
- What records are kept of applicants interviewed, hired, rejected, held in reserve, source and method of recruitment?
- Are applicants measured against job specifications?
- What is the existing programme for supervisory and management development?
- Is there a job evaluation programme?
- How do the company's pay rates and other compensation practices (including fringe benefits) compare with other plants in the immediate geographical area with other companies in the same industry?
- What personnel records are maintained, what analyses are made and to whom they are reported?
- What important practices and understandings have developed that are not spelled out in the labour contract?
- What methods are used to communicate to (i) supervisors and (ii) employees information on matters of interest or importance to the company and/or its employees?
- Do company management members participate and co-operate in community programmes and activities?
- How are individual and union grievances attended to? Are decisions taken in respect of grievances fully implemented?
- Is there any personnel budget relating to expenses on staff welfare?

(iv) Survey of Employee Attitude : A survey should also be conducted of the attitudes of the employees toward those aspects of the company management and its services which relate to their well-being as individuals and their satisfaction with the organisation.

Personnel audit is generally criticised on two grounds. First, it is said that objective evaluations are not possible because the check list usually has not scaling or weighing procedure. Moreover, self-audit brings biases and blind spots to the audit. In some cases this defect may be present. But it is also possible that the personnel manager who is generally trained in self-analysis and criticism may be harder on himself than independent outsiders would be. Second, it is said that if the periodicity of audit is one or more than one year too much water would pass over the dam before corrective action is taken. Personnel audit is, in a sense, merely a rear-viewing mirror of management and is not forward looking.

One big advantage of personnel audit is that the personnel manager may use it for persuading top management that certain changes are desirable or for convincing line management that certain programmes are needed. Audit reports are more likely to catch the attention of busy top executives than several other types of reports.

4. Human Resources Accounting : The concept of human resources accounting is of recent origin. Working on the idea that human assets in an organisation are no less important than its material assets. human resources accounting refers to the method of reflecting the rupee value of the human asset in the company's balance sheet. A balance sheet that does not reveal the current value of company's human assets does not, to say the least, portray the true and fair picture of the company's affairs. This is because the present and future earnings of a company always depend upon the quality of its human organisation.

The following methods are generally used to compute the value of human resources of a concern :

(a) Valuation at Cost : Under this method the employees of an organisation are evaluated on the basis of the cost which the organisation has incurred in selecting and training them. It should be noted that under the traditional accounting system this cost is treated as a revenue expenditure and is charged to the profit and loss account. But in human resources accounting this cost is capitalised and is shown as an asset in the balance sheet.

(b) Valuation at Economic Cost : Under the first method the human asset is shown in the balance sheet at its historical cost which is not enough if the balance sheet is to serve as a health chart of the organisation. It is essential for this purpose to show all assets (including the human asset) in the balance sheet at their economic value. This is the capitalised value of future benefits expected of each asset. The present capitalised value of every employee in an organisation can be found out by estimating his remaining future earnings from employment (assuming the present promotion policy and pay scales to be constant). The aggregate of such present discounted values is then shown as the value of the human resources assets in the balance sheet. It is, however, questioned, how the capitalised value of future expenses can be asset? It is the value of the benefit expected to accrue that should be capitalised and not the amount to be spent for the use of the asset.

(c) Valuation of Replacement Cost : Employees can also be valued at their replacement cost, i.e., the amount which will be needed to replace them completely. It should be noted that it is always impossible to replace the present personnel by a new set of people and still have the same organisation.

REVIEW QUESTIONS

1. What are the reasons for workers' resistance to controls?
2. State the different kinds of control devices used by personnel managers
3. What is personnel audit? On what grounds is it criticised?

   What is the nature and purpose of a personal audit?
4. Which of the five operative functions of personnel management is most susceptible to close control? Why?
5. In what ways is controlling personnel activities different from controlling the output of a product?
6. What are the quantitative and qualitative indicators for personnel audit?
7. The personnel manager is in sharp controversy with the company's general manager. The latter suggested, in an executive committee meeting, that all departments, including staff, should prepare budgets and should be ready to justify their expenditures. He argued that all activities should be justifiable on a rupee-and- paisa basis.

   The personnel manager immediately expressed his disagreement on this point. He argued, **first**, that is was practically impossible to put a rupee value on many personnel programmes. **Second,** there is not good reason why every expenditure should be expected to "pay off" in rupee and paise. He cited the rug in the chairman's office as an example of the expenditure whose contribution could not be assessed and further suggested that no one had shown there was any economic contribution from the care of the front lawn. Prepare an answer to the personnel manager in which you outline the potential gains from a functional budget.
8. What is human resources accounting ?

27
Computer Systems : Decision Support Systems

Computers can be valuable tools for management control purposes for the same reasons as they are for all other applications, namely, speed, accuracy, filing and retrieval abilities, calculating and decision making capabilities, input and output facilities. These points are expanded below :

Speed : Relative to manual methods, all aspects of computer operations (except the initial manual input of data via the keyboard) take place at very high speeds. Whether the computer is calculating an overhead variance, making an entry on a job cost file, printing an actual/budget statement or carrying out some other task the computer does this in a minute fraction of the time it would take manually.

Accuracy : All computers incorporate inbuilt checking features which ensure for all practical purposes 100% accuracy in following a programme. If a programme has been thoroughly tested and produces the required output or performs the correct calculations, then this will be followed faithfully time after time after time. On occasions computer systems do produce errors but investigations invariably show that these errors arise from such factors as errors contained in the data input or programming errors or an unforeseen combination of circumstances not allowed for in the programme and not from computer malfunction.

Filing and Retrieval Abilities : Computer files, nowadays invariably maintained on some type of disk storage, and the associated software file handling systems, permit the rapid updating, amendment, cross-referencing and retrieval of huge volumes of data that would be virtually impossible using any manual system. Computer backing storage systems are becoming physically smaller, cheaper and permit faster access. These developments mean that accountants and managers can have more and more information readily available for instantaneous display on their terminal.

Calculating and Decision making Capability : Computer calculating speeds are measured in millionths of a second and are the heart of their power. In computer terms, the calculations required for management accounting purposes are very modest yet these same calculations done manually are tedious and time- consuming. Take for example the calculations required for apportioning various items of overhead expenditure over cost centres, which is a routine but necessary task. Each calculation is simple but the overall task, including cross and down totalling, can be lengthy when done manually, yet is ideally suited to the computer where it would be done virtually instantaneously.

Allied to the calculating power of the computer is its ability to test different values or conditions and depending on the results, take different actions. It is this ability which enables the computer to make decisions and makes it qualitatively different from other machines. The speed, calculating power and decision- making ability of the computer enables the accountant to extend the scope of his analysis beyond that which would be feasible manually, except for a special once-off exercise. As an example, manually-prepared variance statements typically highlight variances above a certain value (say, Rs. 1000) or those more than a given percentage (say $\pm$ 5) away from standard. The computer could be programmed to do this and also to analyse the variance and its significance by statistical methods - including the calculation of the standard deviation - and, where a significant variance is detected, to retrieve the history of this variance for comparison and to ascertain trends. In short, a more detailed analysis could routinely be undertaken, where required, without extra effort on the part of the accountant who would know that all truly significant variances would be highlighted so leaving more time for any personal investigations felt necessary. This, incidentally, is the key to effective use of computers for management accounting (or any other) purposes. They should be used, where feasible for all forms of routine ledger keeping, calculation, searching, periodic statement/report production and so on in order that there is more time for activities requiring the human touch; for example interpretation of results, special investigations, planning, interviewing and so on.

Input and Output Facilities : Computers can read and search files, print results or display information on VDU's at very high speeds. With modern software, report layouts can be altered at will, results can be displayed using a range of diagrammatic and graphical displays, often in full colour, and displays can be interrogated and manipulated by the user without leaving his desk. Taken together the various facilities provide a far more flexible and speedy service than would be possible using manual means.

Are Computers Essential for MIS?

The short answer to this question is, not essential but they can be very useful. The study of MIS is not about the use of computers, it is about the provision and use of information relevant to the user. Computers are one - albeit important - means of producing information and concentration on the means of producing information and concentration on the means of production rather than the needs of the user can lead to expensive mistakes. There is undoubtedly an important and growing role for computers in MIS but the technology must be used with discretion.

Table 27.1 Five Generations of Computer and Communications Technologies

Generation Years	**First** 1946-56	**Second** 1957-63	**Third** 1964-81	**Fourth** 1982-89	**Fifth** 1990-
Example computers	Eniac Edvac, Univac IBM 650	NCR 501 IBM 7094 CDC 6600,	IBM 360, 370,PDP 11, Spectra-70,Honeywell 200, Cray 1,Illiac IV, Cyber-205	Cray XMP,IBM 308 Amdahl 580	
Telecommunications technology	Telephone Teletype	Digital transmission Pulse code modulation	Satellitecommunications,Microwaves,Networking,Optical fibers, Packets witching,	Integrated systems digital network (ISDN)	Extensive development of distributed computing Merging of telecommunications and computer technologies, Extensive modularity
Computer hardware	Vaccum tubes Magnetic drum Cathode-ray tube	Transistors Magnetic-core memories	ICs, Semi-conductor memories,Magnetic disks,Minicomputers, Microprocessors	Distributed Computing systems VLSI Bubble memories Optical disks Microcomputers	Advanced packaging and interconnection techniques Ultra large-scale integration Parallel architectures 3-D integrated circuit design Gallium arsenide technology Josephson junction technology,Optical components
Computer software	Stored programs Machine code Autocode	High level languages Cobol Algol Fortran	Very high level languages Pascal operating Systems,Structured programming, Time sharing,LISP Computer graphics	Ada Widespread packaged programmes Expert systems Object-oriented languages	Concurrent languages Functional programming Symbolic processing (natural languages, vision, speech recognition, planning)
Computer performance	2-kilobyte memory 10 kiloinstructions per/second	32-kilobyte memory 200 KIPS	2-megabyte memory 5 megainstructions per second	8-megabyte memory 30 MIPS	1 gigainstruction per/sec to 1 tetrainstruction per/sec

Computers are good at rapid and accurate calculations, manipulation, storage and retrieval but less good at unexpected or qualitative work or where genuine judgement is required. It has been suggested that computers can be used to best advantage for processing information which has the following characteristics :

(a) a number of interacting variables
(b) speed is an important factor
(c) there are reasonably accurate values
(d) accuracy of output is important
(e) operations are repetitive
(f) large amount of data exist

These characteristics can be related to the needs of the various management levels as shown below :

Information Characteristics	Presence in Management Information		
	Operational Level	Tactical Level	Strategic Level
Interacting Variables	Frequent	——————→	Always
Speed Important	Usually	——————→	Rarely
Data Accuracy	High	——————→	Low
Output Accuracy	Always	——————→	Rarely
Repetition	Usually	——————→	Rarely
Data Volume	High	——————→	Low

Resulting Application of Computers

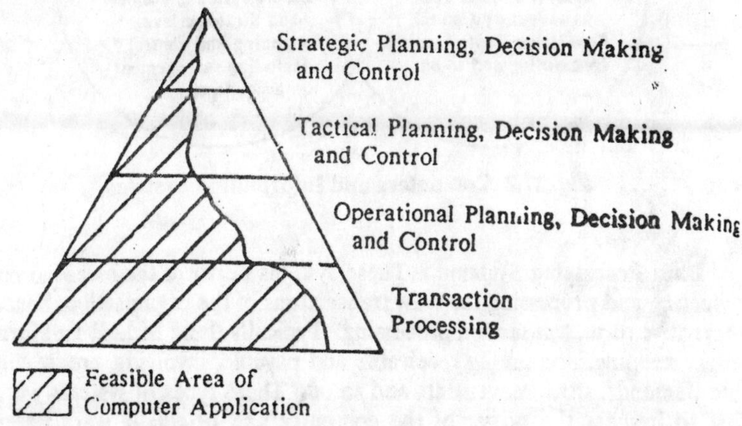

Fig. 27.1 Feasibility of Computer application by Management Level

The unshaded are of Figure 27.1 represents unstructured problems and decisions where human involvement is essential. The division between computer and human tasks is constantly changing. As software and hardware develops and organisations gain more skill in using computers, tasks previously requiring managerial expertise and judgement become worthwhile computer jobs.

An example is the now widespread use of 'credit scoring' in banks. An applicant for a loan fills in a detailed questionnaire and the answers are input into a computer. The programme carries out a series of checks and tests and decides whether or not the loan should be granted. Previously all loan applications required a managerial decision which is now needed only for unusual requests, large loans or industrial applications.

Computers and Information Systems : Although the boundaries between them are blurred and there is substantial overlap it is possible to distinguish two major areas of application of computers in information systems. These are (i) Data Processing (or Transaction Processing) and (ii) Decision Support Systems (or End User Computing). These categories are shown in Fig. 27.2 and developed in the Paragraphs which follow.

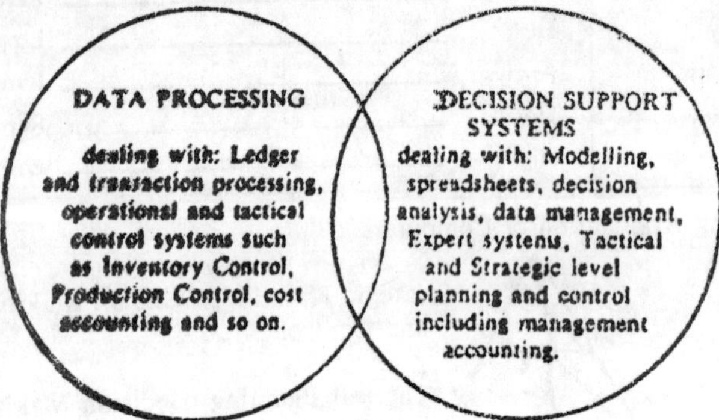

Fig. 27.2 Computers and Information Systems

Data Processing Systems : These systems perform the essential role of collecting and processing the daily transactions of the organisation, hence the alternative term, transaction processing. Typically these include : all forms of ledger keeping, accounting receivable and payable, invoicing, credit control, rate demands, stock movements and so on. These types of systems were the first to harness the power of the computer and originally were based on centralised mainframe computers. In many cases this still applies, especially for large volume repetitive jobs, but the availability of micro and mini computers has made distributed data processing feasible and popular. Distributed data processing has many variations but in essence means that data handling and processing are carried out at or near the point of use rather than in one centralised location.

Transaction processing is substantially more significant in terms of processing time, volume of input and output than say, information production for tactical and strategic planning. Transaction processing is essential to keep the operations of the organisation running smoothly and provides the base for all other internal informations support. This is shown in Figure 27.3

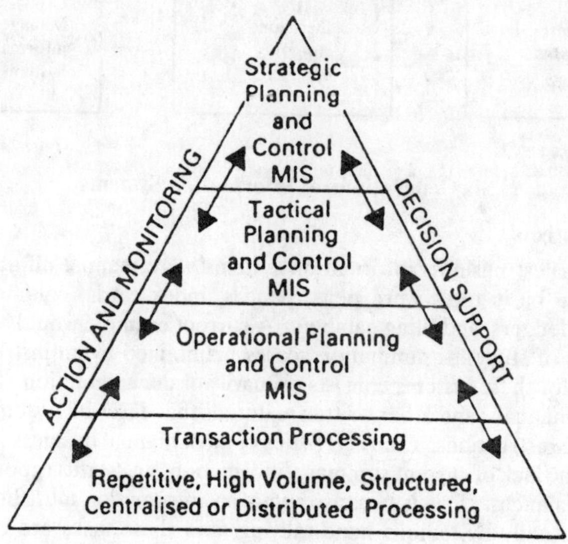

Fig. 27.3 Transaction processing as a base for MIS

GENERATIONS OF INFORMATION SYSTEMS

There are six distinct types, or generations, of information systems : (1) manual systems, (2) mechanical systems, (3) electronic data processing (EDP) systems, (4) management information systems, (5) decision support systems, and (6) expert systems. The word generation is used because these information systems evolved in a natural order, and each can be said to characterise a data processing era. However, these generations of information systems do not coincide with the generations of computer hardware, and, more importantly, each type of information system is still cost-effective today in the "right" application. Table 27.2 in page 502 summarises the characteristics of each type of information system.

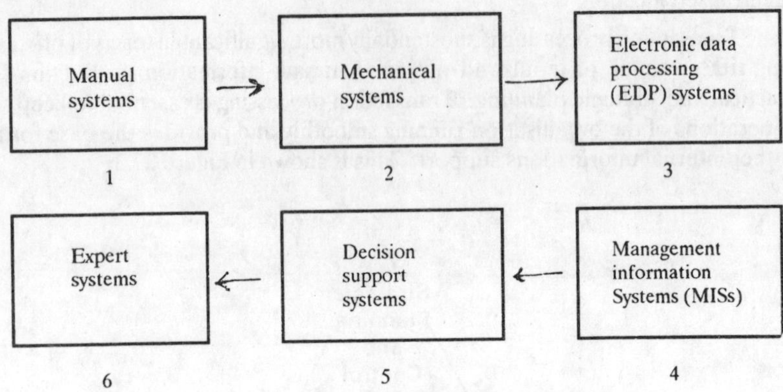

Six Generations of Information Systems

Manual Systems

The earliest business information systems were manual information systems, whose basic tools were pens, pencils, index cards, columnar tablets, accounting ledgers, and filing cabinets. A current example would be a manual grade book of student examination scores maintained by an instructor. The "software" for these systems consists primarily of documentation : handbooks, procedure manuals, and other written materials that describe systems functions and provide instructions. Characteristics of most manual business information systems is the lack of current summary information e.g., status reports showing inventory balances. This is because summary information must be generated manually, usually by tedious hand-tallying, and these tasks are often either impossible or too expensive to be cost-effective. Prior to computers, for example, few instructors teaching large classes compiled summary information on the number of students missing a given examination question or computed current averages.

Historically, manual systems in business settings also had a high potential for clerical and procedural errors. This created major obstacles for the preparation of such reports as financial statements and caused businesses to avoid preparing less-demand reports (e.g., marketing or production reports) altogether. Thus, manual systems, the data needed for managerial decision making was in the system, but there were not timely or cost- effective processes available to prepare it for managerial uses.

Mechanical Systems

Beginning in 1890 with the development of adding machines, sorting trays, and unit record equipment (i.e., card-processing equipment, businesses were able to substitute mechanical processes for manual procedures. These devices facilitated data processing, improved computational accuracy, and decreased the time required to prepare reports. Like manual systems, however, mechanical systems concentrated on the processing of data rather than the informational needs of managers i.e., they concentrated on data-processing efficiency rather than data processing effectiveness.

Electronic Data Processing (EDP) Systems

The first computerised applications (1953-1965) were basically automated manual or mechanical systems that simply computerised earlier processing methods. This approach was only logical since these systems were what businesses best understood and what employees best knew how to operate. These systems are known as *electronic data processing (EDP) systems or transaction processing systems.* The first EDP systems were exclusively batch-oriented. Early EDP system focused on volume-oriented applications (because this was where expensive computers were most cost-effective) and were first implemented in those applications that followed well- defined processing rules (because these applications were the easiest to programme). These twin considerations of high transaction volumes and well-defined rules made accounting applications among the most "natural" ones to computerise and help to explain why many of the first computer employees began their careers in accounting departments.

Management Information Systems (MISs)

As noted previously, one of the major deficiencies of early information systems was their inability to provide useful managerial reports. EDP systems were an improvement, but the fact that EDP systems were basically automated manual systems meant that they focused on operational detail, not managerially oriented overviews. Also, since most of the early EDP systems used batch processing, managers had to wait until needed reports were generated during their regular cycles. The development of management information systems or MISs in the late 1960s and early 1970s was in response to the need for managerial information as opposed to detailed, transactions information. To design useful MISs, therefore, it was important to understand the four most important informational needs of managers, mainly information that is : (i) timely, (ii) accurate, (iii) complete, and (iv) concise. A business information system accomplishes the first three of these by using a computer to process information quickly; by testing computer hardware, software, and procedures for computational accuracy; and by installing controls that assure the complete gathering, reading, and processing of data. Where an MIS excels over an EDP system is in its ability to generate management information in concise, useful formats. Examples of managerial reports that meet this objective include : Vide p.504

Table 2.1 Six Generations of Information Systems

	Manual systems	Mechanical systems	Electronic data processing (EDP) systems
Time span	Befor 1900	1900-1953	1953-1965
Primary functions	All uses before mechanical systems	All uses before computers	1. Automatic record keeping, 2. Volume data processing
File orientation	Manual files	Mechanical sequential files (e.g., card files)	Sequential files updated in batch
Type of data processing	Manual	Mechanical (e.g. with unit record equipment)	Batch
Primary users	All users before mechanical systems	All users before computers	Operational level employees
Types of decision making	All decisions	All decisions	Operational decisions
Types of reports	Minimal	Transaction, detailed listings	Transaction, detailed listings

Six Generations of Information Systems (contd)

Management information systems (MISs)	Decision support	Expert systems systems (DSSs)
1965-1975	1975 to present	1975 to present
Provide relevant information to management	Assist decision makers with unstructured problems	Assist users requiring and expert opinions on complex matters
Online, direct-access files, often in data bases	User-created files, often on microcomputers	Knowledge data bases and large programs containing detailed processing logic
Mixture of batch and real time	Almost exclusively interactive real time	Interactive, using programs employing artificial intelligence
Middle managers	Top management	Specialists requiring expert opinions
Tactical decisions	Strategic (policy) decisions	Expert decisions
Summary reports, exception reports	Customs-designed reports	Specific to the type of expert system

1. **Summary reports** that purposely omit detail in favour of activity summaries.
2. **Demand reports** that are prepared only when a manager requests them.
3. **Exception reports** that output data satisfying predetermined "exception" conditions e.g., a report showing only those accounts receivable more than 90 days past due.
4. **Custom reports** that are tailored to managerial specifications.

MISs also support online files that enable managers to access data of immediate interest and report generators that enable managers to design their own reports e.g., electronic spreadsheets or data base management systems.

Another problem with EDP systems was that managers often needed comparative information that EDP systems were not able to store conveniently in a single file. For example, an EDP system might store the information on employee health coverages in one file and the information on employee absenteeism in another file. The independence of these two files made it inconvenient to prepare a single report containing information from both. MISs improved this situation by integrating file information in the online data bases made possible by the development of hard disks and data base management systems. With these tools, MISs were better able to meet informational needs with more desirable printed reports and online access and retrieval.

To many, the concept of a management information system is more philosophy than technology. The overall objective is to provide the right information to the right manager at the right time-all in a cost-effective manner. This is a matter of determining informational needs and then developing business information systems that meet them. From a historical viewpoint, this was possible only after basic, transaction-processing requirements had been met and the information needs of managers were better understood.

Decision Support Systems (DSSs)

One of the characteristics of MISs is that designers must know in advance what managerial information is required before these systems can be developed. At higher organisational levels, however, managers often do not know in advance what data will be required or how this data must be processed to be useful. In such instances, the goal of providing meaningful managerial information is hindered by a lack of input, processing, or output specifications. These difficulties led to the development of a fifth generation of information systems-decision support systems or DSSs (Figure 27.4). DSS are alternatively termed end-user computing systems. Their objective is to support managers in their work, especially decision making. DSS tend to be used in planning, modelling, analysing alternatives and decision making. They generally operate through terminals operated by the user who interacts with the computer system. Using a variety of tools and procedures the manager (i.e., the user) can develop his own systems to help perform his functions more effectively. It is this active involvement and the focus on decision making which distinguishes a DSS from a data processing system. The emphasis is on *support for decision making not on automated decision making* which is a feature of transaction processing.

DSS are especially useful for semi-structured problems where problem solving is improved by interaction between the manager and the computer system. The emphasis is on small, simple models which can easily be understood and used by the manager rather than complex integrated systems which need information specialists to operate them.

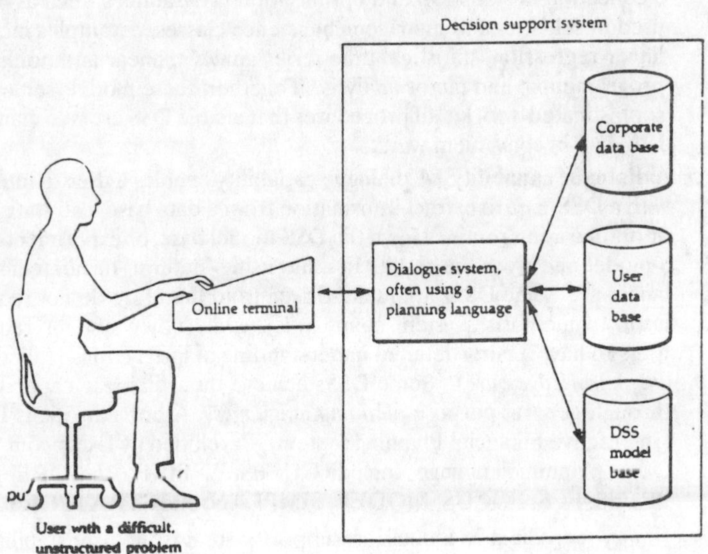

Characteristics of DSSs

1. **A user with unstructured or semistructured problems**. These are problems without known answers and also without clear procedures for answering them. An example of a structured problem would be to

solve the function 3x - 6 = 0 for x. An example of an unstructured problem would be : "What price should my company charge to maximise profits?"

2. **One or more corporate data bases.** Decision support systems often draw upon corporate data bases that store a company's financial and nonfinancial information. This data is then used by a DSS for some type of analysis e.g., to establish sales patterns or project future income.
3. **One or more user data bases.** User data bases are created by individuals rather than by the processing activities of a company. These files often store data about the external environment e.g., financial statistics concerning the activities of competitive firms or the results of previous attempts to solve specific problems.
4. **A set of quantitative models stored in a model base.** A model base is a collection of statistical and optimisation programmes, such as those used in statistics and management science classes. Examples include linear regression, statistical time series analysis, linear and nonlinear programming, and factor analysis. Together, these models serve as a sophisticated "tool kit" of procedures that enable DSS users to manipulate data in convenient ways.
5. **A dialogue capability.** A dialogue capability enables a user to interact with a DSS e.g., to extract information from a data base, call statistical or optimisation routines form the DSS model base, or experiment with a model and store the results in a file-using "natural" or nontechnical language. Some DSSs are menu-driven (and therefore do not require users to memorise system commands), while other systems require users to have a fairly detailed understanding of instructions (called the *user knowledge base*). Some DSSs achieve their dialogue capabilities through general-purpose *planning languages*. A popular one is IFPS (Interactive Financial Planning System), developed by Execucom, Inc. Other planning languages include CUFFS, EXPIRE, ENCORE, EXPRESS, FCS, FOCUS, MODEL, SIMPLAN, and STRATPORT.

A primary ingredient in a decision support system is the user's ability to simulate a business situation over and over using different parameters and solution values i.e., to perform "what- if" analysis. For this reason, decision support systems may also use special-purpose simulation languages, such as DYNAMO, GASP (General Activity Simulation Programme), GPSS (General Purpose Simulation Language), or SIMSCRIPT. Electronic spreadsheets, such as Context MBA, Framework, Javelin, Lotus 1-2- 3, Multiplan, or Symphony, are also sometimes called decision support tools because of their simulation capabilities.

It is unlikely that DSSs will replace MISs (as some MISs have replaced EDP systems) because the two fulfill different needs. An MIS is usually a large, complex computer information system, perhaps serving many managers and many different parts of the country. Often, it is also a standard part of corporate data processing so that managers can use corporate-wide information for their own needs. In contrast, a DSS is a personal tool that permits managers to generate their own models. Thus, DSS developers do not try to second-guess executive needs, but rather attempt to provide computing tools that permit managers to meet their own informational requirements.

Where to Apply DSS

DSS are man/machine systems and are suitable for semi-structured problems. The problem must be important to the manager and the decision required must be a key one. In addition if an interactive computer-based system is to be used then some of the following criteria should be met.

(a) There should be a large data base : A data base is an organised collection of structured data with a minimum duplication of data items. The data base is common to all users of the system but is independent of the programmes which use the data. If the data base is too large for manual searching then a computer-supported approach may be worthwhile.

(b) Large amount of computation or data manipulation : Where analysis of the problem requires considerable computation or data manipulation, computing power is likely to be beneficial.

(c) Complex inter-relationships : Where there is a large data base or where there are numerous factors involved it is frequently difficult to assess all the possible inter- relationships without computer assistance.

(d) Analysis by stages : Where the problem is an iterative one with stages for re-examination and re-assessment it becomes more difficult to deal with manually. The computer-based model can answer the question, 'what if?' quickly and effectively.

(e) Judgement required : In complex situations judgement is required both to determine the problem and the solution, unaided, no computer system can provide this.

(f) Communication : Where several people are involved in the problem solving process, each contributing some special expertise, then the co-ordinating power of the computer can be of assistance.

It follows from the above criteria that DSS are inappropriate for unstructured problems and unnecessary for completely structured problems because these can be dealt with wholly by the computer and man/machine interaction is unnecessary. In outline DSS require a database, the software to handle the database and decision support programmes including, for example, modelling, spread sheet and analysis packages, expert systems and so on.

Expert Systems

Expert systems are computer programmes that attempt to capture the experience, decision rules, and thought processes of experts in a given area. Such systems are often useful to managers in remote locations who do not have access to onsite experts, to businesses that cannot afford full-time consultants, to organisations that require the same expert to be several places at the same time, to businesses whose experts leave or retire, or to experts themselves who desire second opinions.

Expert systems are created by interviewing professionals and observing how they work to understand how they reason. As a result, expert systems often use *artificial intelligence* i.e., computer programmes that stimulate the thought processes of humans. When modeling these processes, some expert systems use "decision tree structures" i.e., networks of if-then statements that enable a system to reach conclusion through the process of elimination. This is called forward reasoning or forward chaining, and contrasts with those expert systems that start with evidence and work backward to determine causes i.e., that use back ward chaining.

Expert systems are like decision support systems in that both attempt to provide meaningful information for decision-making purposes and both usually employ interactive computer systems to facilitate user dialogues. Expert systems are unlike decision support systems in that expert systems emphasise structured problems, usually require specific information for input, and are often unable to explore "what-if" scenarios. Nonetheless, expert systems hold great promise for technical and managerial decision making because of their abilities to capture years of expert experience and to explore millions of unrelated possibilities.

The application areas of expert systems vary widely. As suggested already, medical diagnosis, geological exploration, and process control applications are particularly common. Currently, there are more than 1,000 large scale expert systems under development. Until recently, these were expensive to build partly because they are complex, custom creations. For large scale systems, average development costs typically exceed $ 500,000 and development time can span ten years. Many expert systems are also costly to maintain e.g., because they run on special computers, because new information must be entered to keep data bases current, and because they must be checked periodically to make sure they are solving problems correctly. These high maintenance costs cause some companies to abandon projects even after sinking thousands of dollars into them.

Recently, new software tools have been announced that should reduce development time and costs considerably. Examples of such tools include : Expert Systems Environment/VM (IBM), VM Programming in Logic (IBM), AI Vacstation (DEC), OPSS Expert System Development Language (DEC), Quintus Prolog (DEC), LISP/VE (CDC), and Knowledge Engineering System/VE (CDC). Expert system "Shells" or software packages have also been developed for micro computers, although there is some debate whether such packages are capable of developing "true" expert systems.

Table 27.3 Examples of Expert Systems

Name	Application Area	Uses
CADUCEUS	Medicine	Diagnosing medical problems from symptoms
Capital Investment	Investments	Making capital investment decisions
DELTA	Machine maintenance	Maintaining locomotives
DENDRAL	Chemistry	Outling the molecular structures of organic compounds
Dipmeter Advisor	Geological Exploration	Analysing geological data from oil dipmetres
MUDMAN	Geological exploration	Analysing "mud" extract from an oil shaft for content
MYCIN	Medicine	Diagnosing and treating bacterial infections
ONCOCIN	Medicne	Analysing medical symptoms for cancer
Prospector	Geological exploration	Locating mineral deposits
R-1	Computers	Designing computer systems for customers
STEAMER	Training in the navy	Training boiler room technicians
XCON	Computers	Evaluating a computer to make sure that it has correct parts
XSELL	Computers	Fitting computer hardware and soft ware to cutomer requirements

Matching Information Systems to Managerial Needs

An efficient business information system helps employees to perform their jobs, and this, in turn, leads to greater job satisfaction and worker productivity. Thus, it is important to consider what type of information system-manual, mechanical, EDP, MIS, DSS, or expert-should be developed to best meet the informational needs of the employees of a specific company. While it is tempting to assume that all employees will most profit from the newest, most advanced information system-perhaps implemented on a micro computer-this is rarely correct. It is more often a function of managerial level.

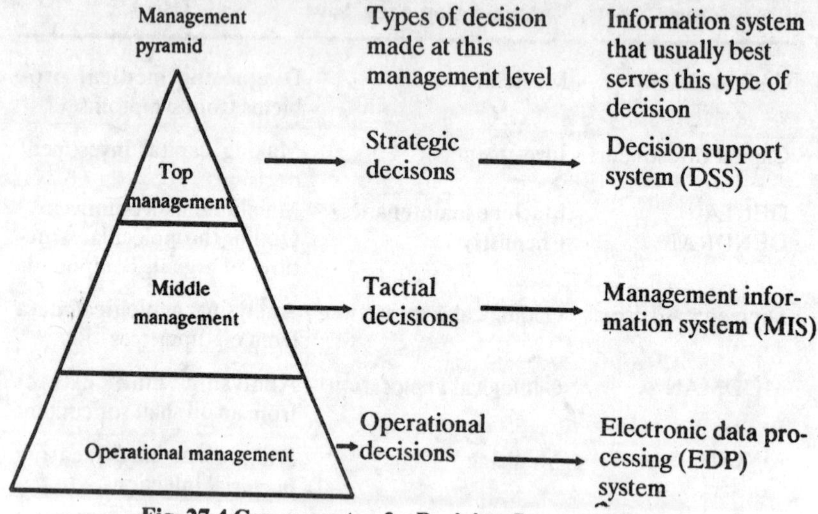

Fig. 27.4 Components of a Decision Support System

The information needs of management often differ according to the managerial level of the decision makers. Usually, different types of information systems best fulfill these different needs.

Three Levels of Management

Figure 27.4 suggests that a corporation can be divided into three corporate levels : (i) top managers, including executive officers and their immediate staffs; (ii) middle managers and their staffs; and (iii) operational managers and other lower-level employees. The decision-making roles of these three corporate levels also differ. Top managers, for example, are charged with decisions regarding overall corporate policy and therefore make *strategic decisions*. In contrast, middle managers translate broad policy objectives into specific methods for accomplishing them and therefore make *tactical decisions*. Finally, managers at the lowest level carry out the tasks determined by their superiors and therefore make *operational decisions*.

Information Needs and Management Levels

Providing the right information to the right manager at the right time in a cost-effective manner typically means choosing the right system to meet these informational needs. Since different managerial levels within an organisation tend to involve different types of decisions, informational requirements often differ as well. For many organisations, satisfying managerial needs for information means providing : (i) detailed, transaction-oriented information for operational managers; (ii) summary management for top managers .

These conclusions are perhaps oversimplified. There may be good cause for an operational employee to have access to a decision support system, just as there may be occasions when top management may best be served with an EDP system. Businesses must study the specific informational needs of their managers and how these needs can best be met.

REVIEW QUESTIONS

1. Briefly identify six types, or generations, of information systems. Which system was developed first? Which system or systems were developed last?
2. In what ways are manual information systems and mechanical information systems similar? In what ways are they different?
3. What are EDP information systems? Why are such systems also called transaction processing systems? How are EDP systems better than manual or mechanical information systems? How are they the same?
4. What are management information systems (MISs)? How are they better than EDP systems? In what ways are they the same as EDP systems?
5. Describe decision support systems (DSSs). What are their major components? How are they used? How are they similar to management information systems? How are they different?
6. What is an expert system? Why are there so few of them today? Why are more expected?
7. Define the following levels of management : (a) top management, (b) middle management, (c) operational management. What types of decisions does each managerial level most commonly make? What type of information system best provides the informational requirements of each management level?

28

Management Control in Service and Non Profit Organisations

In the preceding chapters our focus, at least implicitly, has been on organisations that produce and sell tangible goods. In this chapter, we discuss management control in organisations that provide intangible services, rather than tangible goods, with particular attention to organisations that provide professional services. Service organisations include hotels, restaurants, and other lodging and eating establishments; barbershops, beauty parlours and other personal services; repair services; motion picture, television and other amusement and recreation services; legal services; and accounting, engineering, research/development, architecture and other professional service organisations. Because of the similarity of their management control problems, we also include banks, insurance companies and other financial institutions. Government agencies, educational organisations and most other nonprofit organisations are service organisations, but in this chapter we focus on service/non profit-oriented organisations. In the 20th century the fraction of the work force employed in service organisations has been steadily increasing, and in India currently more people are employed in these organisations than in organisations that produce goods.

Characteristics of Service Organisations

The production and sale of services, as contrasted with tangible goods, has several important implications for the management control process.

(i) Absence of Inventory : Goods can be held in inventory, and this inventory is a buffer that dampens the impact on production activity of fluctuations in sales volume. *Services cannot be stored*. If the services available today are not sold today, the revenue from these services is lost forever. By contrast, in order to obtain in advantages of long production runs or for other sound reasons, manufactures often produce goods for which they have no current orders. Up to a point, they need not be concerned about the fact that these goods are not sold currently; the revenue should be earned in the near future. Thus, because of inventory the manufacturer can earn revenue in the future from production capacity that is not sold today, but the service company has no such option. To make this problem even worse, *the resources available for sale in many service organisations are essentially fixed.* In the short run, a hotel cannot increase the number of rooms that it offers for rent, and it does not reduce costs substantially by closing off some of its rooms. An accounting firm, law firm or other professional organisation could conceivably lay off some of its professional personnel in times of low volume, but for morale reasons it is most reluctant to do so.

(ii) Labour Intensive : Service organisations tend to be labour intensive, that is, they tend require relatively little-capital per unit of output. It is more difficult to control the work of a labour-intensive organisation than that of an operation whose work flow is paced or dominated by machinery. (Some service organisations are becoming capital intensive as computers replace clerks).

(iii) Quantity Measurement : It is easy to keep track of the quantity of tangible goods, both during the production process and when the goods are sold, but it is not so easy to measure the quantity of many services. We can measure the number of patients that a physician treats in a day, for example, and even classify these visits by type of complaint, but this is by no means equivalent to measuring the amount of service that the physician provides to each of these patients. For many services, the amount rendered can be measured only in the crudest terms, if at all.

(iv) Quality Measurement : The quality of tangible goods can be inspected, and in most cases the inspection can be performed before goods are released to the customer. If the goods are defective, there is physical evidence of the nature of the defect. The quality of a service cannot be inspected in advance; at best, it can be inspected during the time that the service is being rendered to the client. Judgments as to the adequacy of the quality of most services are subjective; measuring instruments and objective quality standards do not exist. A public accounting firm can measure the number of hours spent on an audit, but not the thoroughness of the work done during those hours. A consulting firm has no objective way of appraising the soundness of its recommendations. It a law firm may leave loopholes or ambiguities in documents it drafts that do not come to light until years later.

(v) Historical Development : Cost accounting started in manufacturing companies because of the necessity for valuing work-in-process and finished goods inventories for financial statement purposes. These amounts provided raw data that was easily adapted to use, first for setting selling prices and then for other management problems. Standard cost systems, the separation of fixed and variable costs, and the analysis of variances, buint and the foundation of actual cost systems, and the fact that managers in manufacturing companies were accustomed to using cost information facilitated the general adoption of these techniques. Until the last few decades, most books on cost accounting and related subjects dealt only with manufacturing companies.

(vi) Size : With some notable exceptions, service organisations are relatively small and operate in a single location. Top management in such organisations can personally observe what is going on and personally motivate employees. Thus, there is less need for a sophisticated management control system, with profit centres and heavy reliance on formal reports of performance. (Nevertheless, even a small organisation needs a budget, a regular comparison of actual performance against a budget, and the other essential ingredients of a management control system).

Implications for Management Control

There are some differences between management control systems in service organisations and those in manufacturing organisations. These are differences in degree, rather than in kind, however. The essential features are the same in both types of organisations. In both, planning is done in terms of programs and responsibility centres, including profit centres and investment centres for organisation units that meet the criteria. The management control process in both organisations involves the steps of programming, budgeting, the measurement of performance, and the appraisal of that performance.

Because of their relatively recent development, systems currently found in service organisations tend to be less advanced than those in manufacturing organisations. Because of the difficulty of measuring both the quantity and the quality of output, judgments about both the efficiency and the effectiveness of performance are more subjective than is the case when output consists of physical goods, which means that there is more room for legitimate differences of opinion about performance. Managers are coming to recognize that performance is not easy to measure; this suggests that a search for better tools for improving its measurement is likely to be eminently worthwhile.

FINANCIAL INSTITUTIONS

Commercial Banks

In the 1960s commercial banks began to create profit centres for their branches and for their corporate trust, personal trust, investment, and other revenue producing units. In doing so, they had to solve problems not faced by an industrial company. Perhaps the most serious problem is that of measuring the number that corresponds to gross profit in a manufacturing company, that is, the difference between the cost of obtaining money and the revenue earned on loaning or investing the money. Money is obtained by inducing customers to make deposits. (It is also obtained by borrowing from other financial institutions, but the cost of these funds can be readily measured). For savings deposits, the bank pays interest, and this interest, plus the cost of servicing accounts, is the cost of money obtained from savings accounts. For current accounts, however, cost is much more difficult to measure. Commercial banks are prohibited by government regulation from paying interest; therefore, in order to induce customers to make deposits in current accounts, banks provide a number of free services. The most obvious of these is the processing of cheques and deposits, but there are a number of others, ranging from informal advice to handling payroll records and accounts receivable records at no cost or at a price that is less than these services cost.

The problem is further complicated by the fact that some fraction of many corporate current accounts consists of compensating balances, that is, funds that the corporation is required to leave on deposit as a condition of a loan that the bank has made to it. Conceptually, a compensating balance reduces the net amount of funds made available to the borrower and thus increases his effective interest cost and the rate of return that the bank derives from the loan. As a practical matter, the problem of treating compensating balances separately from other current account balances is so difficult that banks do not attempt to make the separation in their formal control system, although they may do so in special analyses. These problems make it difficult to measure the profitability of individual branches and other profit centres.

Some branches typically generate more money in deposits than they loan out; they are "deposit-heavy", while other branches are "loan heavy". Some profit centres make only loans, using funds generated by deposits made in the branches. In order to measure the profitability of these profit centres, the cost of money must be correctly calculated. If it is set too low, too much profit will be reported for the loan-heavy units; Whereas if it is set too high, too much profit will be reported for the deposit-heavy units. The problem is further complicated by the fact that government regulations require that a certain proportion of deposits be held in reserves on which low interest rates, in some cases zero, are earned. Arriving at the cost of money is a difficult transfer price problem, and banks have devoted much attention in recent years to the best way of setting this price. Partly in order to arrive at a sound transfer price, and partly for other reasons, banks have also started to analyse carefully the real cost of services that they provide to customers and to measure the profitability of individual customer accounts.

Problems of joint costs and joint revenues are also prevalent in banks. Accounting and check processing are usually done centrally, and the costs of such work must be equitably assessed to the branches. A customer who maintains an account in one branch may use the services of another branch, or may be induced to use service provided by headquarters unit. The branches that "sell" such services should be given appropriate credit, but this is difficult to do in practice. With these important exceptions, the management control systems in commercial banks are similar to those described in earlier chapters.

Insurance Companies

Insurance Companies also deal with money. They collect money in the form of premiums, invest it, and subsequently pay out money in the form of claims, death benefits, or annuities. Many years may elapse between the time a policy is written and the time when benefit payments are completed. The profitability of the policy cannot be known with certainty until the last payment is made, but for management control purposes the company cannot, of course, wait; in needs information currently.

Traditionally, insurance companies measured the performance of their responsibility centres by rough rules of thumb, such as the amount of firstyear premiums or the face amount of insurance written. In recent years, they have begun to explore the possibility of measuring the approximate profitability of a policy at the time it is written. For example, the annual premium on an ordinary life policy is arrived at by taking into account life expectancy estimated investment income, selling costs, and recurring operating costs over the life of the policy, adjusted if necessary to meet rates charged by other companies. Each of these components is set conservatively; for example, the mortality table used in setting premiums understates the actual life expectancy. The ultimate profitability of the policy arises from the difference between these conservative estimates and the actual amounts experienced. The true expectations can be estimated, and from them the expected present value of the policy can be determined. Thus, a measure of profitability can be calculated at the time the policy is sold.*

With this measure of profitability as a starting point, insurance companies can organise their sales branches as profit centres, and they can also measure the performance of the investment, actuarial, and other parts of the company by comparing actual results with those used in the calculations of the present value of a policy's profitability.

PROFESSIONAL ORGANISATIONS

Research and development organisations, law firms, accounting firms, medical clinics, engineering firms, consulting firms, investment firms, and advertising agencies are examples of organisations whose product is professional services. These firms differ from manufacturing companies and from other service companies in ways that have a substantial impact on management control problems and practices.

Characteristics

(a) Organisational Goals : In a manufacturing company, and also in some service organisations such as hotels, the name of the game is return on assets employed. The organisation is successful if it earns a satisfactory return on assets employed, and capital investment decisions are made according to this return-on-investment criterion. The assets can be measured, and they are reported on the balance sheet. In a professional organisation, the amount of

* For a full description see James S. Hekimian. Management Control in Life Insurance Branches (Boston : Division of Research, Harvard Business School, 1965).

tangible assets employed is relatively insignificant. The principal resource of the organisation is the skill of its professional staff, and return on investment, as conventionally calculated, provides neither a basis for measuring success nor a criterion for decision making. The output of a professional organisation is intangible, is therefore not easy to measure in quantitative terms, and is difficult or impossible to measure in qualitative terms.

(b) Production Standards : The work done by professionals tends to be non-repetitive. No two consulting jobs or research and development projects are quite the same. Thus, it is difficult both to plan the time required for a task and also to set reasonable standards for task performance. This obviously makes it difficult to judge how satisfactory the performance was. Some tasks are essentially repetitive; the drafting of simple wills, deeds, sales contracts, and other documents, the taking of a physical inventory, and certain medical and surgical procedures, are examples. The development of standards for such tasks is worthwhile, although in using these standards, unusual circumstances affecting them must be taken into account.

(c) Marketing : In most professional organisations no clear dividing line exists between marketing efforts and production efforts. In some, such as law, medicine, and accounting, the reason is that the ethical codes of the profession prohibit overt marketing efforts. Since marketing is an essential activity in any organisation, if it cannot be conducted openly.

Because marketing is not an identifiable function and because new business is generated by the part-time activities of professional staff members who are primarily engaged in doing production work, it is difficult to assign appropriate credit to the person responsible for the generation of revenue. In a consulting firm, for example, a new engagement may result from a conversation between a member of the firm and an acquaintance in the client company, from the reputation of one of the firm's professionals.

(d) Professionals : Professionals often have motivations that are inconsistent with good resource **utilisation**, and their success, as perceived by their professional colleagues, reflects these motivations. Professionals are motivated by dual standards. (a) those of their organisations, and (b) those of their professional colleagues. The former standards are related to organisational objectives; the latter may be inconsistent with organisational objectives. The rewards for achieving organisational objectives may be less potent than those for achieving professional objectives.

Those professionals who are departmental managers tend to **work only part time** on management activities. They spend a substantial part of their time doing the same work that their subordinates do. The head of the surgical department in a hospital does surgery. The senior partner in the local office of an accounting firm participates actively in audit engagements. In organisations not dominated by professionals, management tends to be a fulltime job and managers do not do the same type of work that their subordinates do.

Many professionals, by nature, prefer to work **independently.** Examples are academicians, researchers, and physicians. Because the essence of management is getting things done through people, professionals with such a temperament are not naturally suited to the role either of managers or of subordinates.

In a professional organisation, the **professional quality** of the people is of primary importance, and other considerations are secondary. Therefore, managers in professional organisations spend much of their time recruiting good people and then seeing to it that they are kept happy. The manager has correspondingly less time available for those aspects of the job that relate to efficiency. In a professional organisation, the practice of recruiting many and then weeding out unsatisfactory workers is expensive, so management must concentrate on careful preselection. In some professions, promotion is geared to criteria established by the profession and tends to be a function of time (e.g., eight years for assistant professor; eight years for Army major). These criteria may not place much emphasis on efficiency and effectiveness.

Financial incentives tend to be less effective with professional people either because they consider their current compensation to be adequate or because their **primary satisfaction** comes from their work.

Although the leadership of an **organisation** may require more management skills than professional skills, tradition often requires that the manager be a professional. Traditionally, the head of a research and development organisation was a scientist; the president of a university, a professor; the head of a hospital, a physician. This tradition seems to be diminishing, however.

Professionals tend to give inadequate weight to the financial implication of their decisions. The physician feels that no limit should be placed on the amount spent to save a human life, although in a world of limited resources such an attitude is unrealistic.

(e) Differences Among Organisations : The characteristics described above are tendencies which are applicable to varying degrees in most professional organisations. There are also differences among professions and among the firms within a given profession that are relevant for management control. In some organisations, professionals work as a team on an engagement; in others they tend to work as individuals with perhaps some temporary assistance from colleagues. Organisations also, of course, vary in size and complexity. In small organisations with only one office, the management control system can be relatively simple and informal.

Implications of the Characteristics of Professional Organisations

Programming and Budgeting : In general, formal programming and budgeting systems are not as well developed in professional organisations as in industrial companies of comparable size. A good budgeting process helps to insure that departments are in balance with one another, and particularly that support departments are at an optimum size to service the professional staff; it determines the size and scope of the firm's operations for the coming year, particularly its capacity to take new business; it identifies the additional staff and other resources that must be acquired; it states permitted levels of spending, and it provides a basis for motivating desired spending performance and for judging actual performance.

Pricing : The criterion of return on assets employed provides both a conceptual basis for analysing and explaining the behavior of the prices of industrial products in general, and also a practical guide to pricing in individual companies. Since assets, in the conventional accounting sense, are relatively unimportant in professional organisations, the return-on-assets criterion does not provide a rationale for pricing in these organisations.

Lacking any conceptual basis for determining a profit margin, professional firms tend to price strictly according to tradition. In each profession, there is a traditional fee structure, usually related primarily to the time of the professionals, and firms use this structure in their pricing. The fee structure varies widely from one profession to another, and in ways that are unrelated to supply-demand relationships.

Control of Operations through Progress Reports : Because quality usually cannot be measured by physical instruments or by the other inspection procedures found in industrial companies, special control techniques are needed. Perhaps the most important is the creation of an atmosphere such that project leaders are willing to reveal actual or incipient problems to their superiors, rather than hiding them until it is too late to take remedial action. In such an atmosphere, progress reports are important control devices; whereas in an environment in which unpleasant reports invariably lead to destructive criticism, rather than helpful suggestions, the reports resemble works of fiction.

At best, formal reports are unlikely to provide the principal means of finding out about quality problems. Informal conversations, regularly scheduled meetings, and the manager's sensitivity to hints of trouble received from various sources are likely to be much more important. Expressions of satisfaction or dissatisfaction from clients are also an important basis for judging performance, although such expressions may not be forthcoming in many engagements. One firm that sells investment advice to institutional clients keeps a record of letters of commendation or criticism received from these clients, classifies these according to the analysts who made the relevant recommendations, and uses this information as part of its performance evaluation system.

Human Resource Accounting : The principal asset of a professional organisation is its professional staff. The value of this staff does not appear in its balance sheet, however. From 1967 on, accounting literature contains many references to the desirability of accounting for the asset value of human resources in a way that is analogous to the conventional accounting treatment of physical and financial resources.*

MANAGEMENT CONTROL IN NON PROFIT ORGANISATIONS

The management control process in nonprofit organisations is in many respects similar to that in profit-oriented organisations, but in other important respects it is different. The similarities and differences are discussed below:

Characteristics of Non profit Organisations

The dominant purpose, or at least one of the major purposes, of some organisations is earning profits. Decisions made by their managements are intended to increase (or at least maintain) profits, and success is measured, to a significant degree, by the amount of profits that these organisations earn.

By contrast, other organisations exist primarily to render a service. Decisions made by their managements are intended to provide the best possible service with the available resources, and the success of these organisations is measured primarily by how much service they render and by how well they render it. More basically (but unfortunately also more vaguely), their success should be measured by how much they contribute to the public welfare. This type of organisation is here labelled "nonprofit". Included in this category are government organisations, educational organisations, hospitals and other health care organisations, and religious and charitable organisations, clubs and similar membership organisations, and a variety of other types. They employ approximately five percent of the Indian work force.

Certain characteristics of nonprofit organisations affect the management control process in those organisations are given below:

1. Their tendency to be **service organisations.**
2. The dominance of **professionals.**
3. The absence of the **profit measure.**
4. The lesser role of the **market place.**
5. Differences in **ownership and power.**
6. Their tendency to be **political** organisations.
7. A **tradition** of inadequate management controls.

---

* **Detailed discussion was given in page 494.**

The first two characteristics were already explained in the previous part of this chapter. The other points are discussed below in the following pages.

The Profit Measure

All organisations use inputs to produce outputs. An organisation's effectiveness is measured by the extent to which outputs accomplish its objectives, and its efficiency is measured by the relationship between inputs and outputs. In a profit- oriented organisation the amount of profit provides an overall measure of both effectiveness and efficiency. In many nonprofit organisations, however, outputs cannot be measured in quantitative terms. Furthermore, even when outputs can be measured, many nonprofit organisations have multiple objectives, and there is no feasible way of combining the several outputs, each of which is intended to accomplish one of these objectives, into a single number that measures the overall effectiveness of the organisation.

The absence of a satisfactory, single, overall measure of performance that is comparable to the profit measure is the most serious management control problem in a nonprofit organisation. (It is incorrect to say that the absence of the profit **motive** is the central problem; rather, it is the absence of the profit **measure**). The profit measure has the following advantages : 1. It provides a single criterion that can be used in evaluating proposed courses of action; 2. It permits a quantitative analysis of those proposals in which benefits can be directly compared with costs; 3. It provides a single, broad measure of performance; and 4. It permits comparisons of performance to be made among responsibility centres that are performing dissimilar functions. The difficulties that arise when the profit measure is not present can be seen by discussing each of these points.

1. No Single Criterion : Since a nonprofit organisation has multiple goals and since these goals usually cannot be expressed in quantitative terms, there often is no clearcut objective function that can be used in analysing proposed alternative course of action. The management team of a profit-oriented com pany may debate vigorously the merits of a proposal, but the debate is carried on within the context of how the proposal will effect profits. The management team of a nonprofit organisation often will not agree on the relative importance of various goals; members will view a proposal in terms of the importance that they personally attach to the several goals of the organisation. Thus, in a municipality, all members of the management team may agree that the addition of new pumper will add to the effectiveness of the firm/department, but there will be disagreement on how important an expenditure to increase the effectiveness of the firm department is compared to a comparable expenditure on parks, or streets, or welfare. This greatly complicates the problem of decision making.

2. No Relation between Costs and Benefits : For most important decisions in a nonprofit organisation, there is no plausible way of estimating the relationship between inputs and outputs; that is, there is no way of judging what effect the expenditure of X rupees will have on achieving the goals of the organisation. Would the addition of another professor increase the value of the education that a college provides by an amount that exceeds the cost of that professor? How much should be spent on a programme to retrain unemployed persons? Issues of this type are difficult to analyse in quantitative terms because there is no good way of estimating the consequences of a given increment of spending.

3. Difficulty of Measuring Performance : When both revenues and costs can be measured, one goal of a nonprofit organisation should be to break even. But this is never the principal goal, not it is a very important goal except in times of financial crisis. The principal goal should be to render service, and the amount and quality of service rendered is not measured by the numbers in the financial statements. Performance with respect to the important goals is difficult to measure. The success of an educational institution depends more on the ability and diligence of its faculty than on such measurable characteristics as the number of courses offered, or the student/faculty ratio.

4. Comparison among Units : In nonprofit organisations, organisational units can be compared with one another only if they have similar functions. One fire department can be compared with other fire departments, and one general hospital with other general hospitals, but there is no way of comparing the effectiveness of a fire department with the effectiveness of a hospital. Dissimilar profit-oriented companies can be compared with one another in terms of the common measure of profitability.

Market Forces

Most nonprofit organisations are less subject to the forces of the marketplace than are profit-oriented organisations. The market dictates the limits within which the management of a profit-oriented company can operate. A company cannot (or, at least, should not) make a product that the market does not want, and it cannot dispose of its products unless selling prices are in line with what the market is willing to pay. A company cannot servive for long if it cannot equal the performance of its competitors. By contrast, many nonprofit organisations decide what services they should render on the basis of the judgement of their managements, rather than according to what the market wants. And, in many cases, a nonprofit organisation need not worry about competition. These differences have important implications for management control.

A profit-oriented company wants mor customers. More customers mean more profit. In many nonprofit organisations, however, there is no such relationship between the number of clients and the success of the organisation. If the amount of its available resources are fixed by appropriations (as in the case of government agencies) or by income from endowment or annual giving (as is the case with many educational, religious and charitable organisations), additional clients may place a strain on resources. In a profit-oriented organisation, therefore, the new client is an **opportunity** to be vigorously sought after; in many nonprofit organisations, the new client is only a burden, to be accepted with mis givings.

Ownership and Power

The statement that shareholders "run" a corporation is an oversimplification, but it is unquestionably true that shareholders have the ultimate authority. Although they may exercise this authority only in times of crisis, it is nevertheless there. The movement of stock prices is an immediate and influential indication of what shareholders think of their management. In profit-oriented organisations, policy and management responsibilities are vested in the board of directors, which derives its power from the shareholders. In turn, the board delegates power to the president, who serves at the board's pleasure, acts as the board's agent in the administration of the organisation, and who is replaced it there are serious differences of interest or opinion. In many nonprofit organisations the corresponding line of responsibility is often not clear. In nongovernment organisations, the presumably controlling body does not necessarily represent the source of the organisation's power. Instead of being selected formally by those ultimately responsible for the organisation, it may be self-perpetuating, selected by outside parties, or selected **de facto** by top management. Its members are seldom paid for their services. They feel little pressure from, or little responsibility to, outside groups.

Politics

Many nonprofit organisations are political; that is, they are responsible to the electorate or to a legislative body that presumably represents the electorate. Elected officials cannot function if they are not re-elected, and in order to be re-elected, they must-at least up to a point-advocate the perceived needs of their constituency, even though satisfying these needs may not be in the best interests of the larger body that they are supposed to govern.

Pricing

Although prices charged for services rendered are an important consideration in the management control structure, many nonprofit organisations have given inadequate attention to their pricing policies. To the extent that pricing of services is feasible, the following benefits can be achieved :

1. If services are sold at prices that approximate full cost, the revenue figure that is thereby generated is a measure of the quantity of services that the organisation supplies. In the absence of such an output measure, it is difficult to measure either efficiency of effectiveness.

2. Charging clients for services rendered makes them more aware of the value of the service and encourages them to consider whether the services are actually worth as much to them as their cost. If revenues generated by full-cost prices are not sufficient to cover total expenses, there is an indication that the service is not valuable enough to society to warrant the cost of providing for it. It may be that the organisation's costs are higher than necessary, or that a lower-cost service would satisfy the clients' needs.

3. If services are sold, the responsibility centre that sells them can become, in effect, a profit centre. The manager of a profit centre becomes responsible for operating the unit in such a way that revenue equals expenses. Such a manager is motivated to think of ways of rendering additional service that will increase revenue, to think of ways of cutting costs to the point where the corresponding price is one that clients are willing to pay, to become more vigilant in controlling overhead costs, and in general to behave like a manager in a profit-oriented company.

Notwithstanding these advantages of charging for services rendered, there are many situations in which prices should not be charged.

The most important class of these is public goods. Public goods are services which are for the benefit of the public in general, rather than for an individual client. Examples are police protection, as contrasted with a police officer who is hired by the manager of a sporting event; and foreign policy and its implementation, as contrasted with services rendered to an individual firm doing business overseas. In addition to the general class of public goods, prices should not normally be charged for services when it is public policy to provide the services (e.g., welfare investigations; legal aid services), when it is public policy not to ration the services on the basis of ability to pay, when the cost of collecting the revenue exceeds the benefits, or when a charge is politically untemable.

Full-Cost Pricing : As a general rule, prices should be equal to full cost. A nonprofit organisation often has a monopoly position. It should not set prices that exceed its cost, for to do so would be taking unjustifiable advantage of its monopoly status. Furthermore, the organisation does not need to charge prices that are higher than costs. If it does so, it generates a profit, and by definition no person can benefit from such a profit. Neither should a nonprofit organisation price below full cost because that would be providing services to clients at less than the services are presumably worth; this can lead to a misallocation of resources in the economy.

A full-cost pricing policy should normally apply to services that are directly related to the organisation's principal objectives, and to services that clients ordinarily take as a necessary concomitant to the organisation's principal objectives; but it does not necessarily apply to peripheral activities. Prices for these activities should ordinarily correspond to market prices for similar services. For example, in a hospital, prices for hospital care, surgical procedures, laboratory procedures, X- rays, and meals come within the general rule, but prices in the gift shop in the hospital should be market based.

Although the pricing strategy should normally be to recover full cost for the organisation as a whole, it may be desirable to price specific services above or below full cost. The relevant considerations are essentially the same as those that profit- oriented companies consider when they depart from full-cost pricing.

The Pricing Unit : In general, the smaller and more specific the unit of service that is priced, the better the basis for decisions about the allocation of resources and the more accurate the measure of output for management control purposes. An overall price is not a good measure of output because it masks the actual mix of services rendered. For example, a blanket daily charge does not provide as good a measure of output in a hospital as specific charges for room rental, use of the operating room, drugs, and so on. Separate charges for the day of admission (to cover "work up" costs), and for geriatric and infant patients as compared with other patients, are examples of opportunities to make the pricing unit even smaller.

This principle is subject to two qualifications. The first is the obvious one that beyond a certain point, the paperwork and other costs associated with pricing tiny units of serviced out weigh the benefits. The prices location of this point is of course uncertain. The second qualification is that the pricing policy should be consistent with the organisation's overall policy. It is a fact that undergraduate English instruction per student costs less than undergraduate physics instruction, and it would be feasible to reflect these differences in cost by charging different prices for each course that a student takes. Nevertheless, a separate price for each course may well lead students to select courses in a way that the university administration does not consider educationally sound.

Prospective Pricing : As a general rule, management control is facilitated when the price is set prior to the performance of the service, as contrasted with the alternative of reimbursing the service provide for the actual amount of costs incurred. When prices are set in advance, they provide an incentive for the organisation to keep costs with in the level of anticipated revenue, whereas no such incentive exists when the organisation knows that whatever the level of costs may be, they will be recouped. An organisation that knows that it is going to recover its costs, whatever they are, is not likely to do much worrying about cost control. When reliable methods of setting prices in advance can be worked out, the incentive is much stronger.

This principle can be applied, of course, only when it is possible to make a reasonable advance estimate of what the service should cost. For many research or development projects, for example, there is no good basis for estimating how much should be spent in order to achieve the desired result, and the reimbursement for such work is necessarily based on actual costs incurred.

Transfer Pricing : Most nonprofit organisations have not given much attention to developing a sound policy on transfer prices, even though goods and services are transferred from one responsibility centre to another to roughly the same degree as is the case in profit-oriented organisations. the basic purposes of a transfer price are the same in both types of organisations; that is, to measure the revenue of the responsibility centre that furnishes the product and the cost of the unit that receives the product in a way that aids management decisions and that motivates responsibility centre managers to work in the best interests or the organisation. The principles for transfer pricing in nonprofit organisations are essentially the same as those in profit-oriented organisations, as discussed in Chapter 20.

Non Monetary Output Measurement

Prices can be charged only by client-oriented organisations. In other organisations, and also in many circumstances in client- oriented organisation, output must be measured in Nonmonetary terms. Output measures can be classified in various ways. They can be subjective or objective; that is, they can be derived from a person's judgment or theymay be derived from numerical data. They can be quantitative or nonquantitative. They can be discrete or calar. They can measure either the quantity of output or the quality of output.

An important way of classifying output measures is according to what it is they purport to measure. Although many different terms are used in practice, they can be grouped into three categories : 1. result measures, 2. process measures, and 3. social indicators.

A **result measure** is a measure of output expressed in terms that are supposedly related to an organisation's objectives. In the ideal situation, the objective is stated in measurable terms, and the output measure is stated in these same terms. When this relationship is not feasible, as is often the case, the performance measure represents the closest feasible way of measuring the accomplishment of an objective that cannot itself be expressed quantitatively. Such a measure is called a surrogate or a proxy. A results measure relates to the impact that the organisation has on the outside world.

A **process measure** relates to an activity carried on by the organisation. Examples are the number of livestock inspected in a week, the number of lines typed in an hour, the number of requisitions filled in a month, or the number of purchase orders written. The essential difference between a results measure and a process measure is that the former is "ends oriented", while the latter is "means oriented". An ends-oriented indicator is a direct measure of success in achieving an objective. A means-oriented indicator is a measure of what a responsibility centre or an individual does. There is an implicit assumption that what the responsibility centre does helps achieve the organisation's objectives, but this is not always a valid assumption.

Process measures are most useful in the measurement of current, shortrun performance. They are the easiest type of output measure to interpret because there presumably is a close causal relationship between inputs and process measures. They measure efficency, but not effectiveness. Being only remotely related to goals, they are of little use in strategic planning. They are useful in constructing relavent parts of a budget, but only for those activities for which it is feasible to obtain process measures. They are useful in the control of lower-level responsibility centres. Process measures should not be used if results measures are available.

A **social indicator** is a broad measure of output which is significantly the result of the work of the organisation, but which is also affected by exogenous forces, and which therefore is at best only a rough indication of the accomplishment of the organisation itself. Social indicators are often stated in broad terms (e.g., "the expectation of healthy life free of serious disability and institutionalisation"). Such statements are generally not as useful as those expressed in more specific, preferably measurable, terms (e.g., infant mortality rates, life expectancy). Social indicators are useful principally for long- range analyses of strategic problems. They are so nebulous, so difficult to obtain on a current basis, so little affected by current programme effort, and so much affected by external influences, that they are of limited usefulness in day-to-day management.

Inputs as a Measure of Outputs

Although generally less desirable than a true output measure, inputs are often a better measure of output than no measure at all. For example, it may not be feasible to construct output measures for research projects. In the absence of such measures, the amount spent on a research project may provide a useful clue as to its output. In the extreme, if no money was spent, it is apparent that nothing was accomplished. (This assumes that the accounting records show what actually was spent, which sometimes is not the case). When inputs are used as proxy output measures, care must be exercised to avoid undue reliance on them, and the organisation should try to develop usable measures of output.

REVIEW QUESTIONS

1. Expalin the characteristics of service organisations.
2. What are the characteristics of professional organisations?

3. Suggest a suitable management control system to (a) Commercial Banks, (b) Insurance Companies, (c) Hospitals and (d) Advertising.
4. State the differences between management control systems in service organisations and those in manufacturing organisations.
5. Outline the characteristic features of non-profit organsiations.
6. Suggest a suitable management control system to non profit organisations.
7. Explain the merits and limitations of different approaches to the problem of pricing of services.
8. Explain briefly (a) Non-Monetary output Measurement (b) Human Resource Accounting (c) Profit Measure.

29
Management Control of Projects

A project is a set of activities intended to accomplish a specified end result, of sufficient importance to be of interest to management. In a shipyard, for example, the repair and overhaul work done on a single ship constitutes one project. The accomplishment of a project often involves more than one responsibility centre. In a shipyard, each of the production shops (electrical, sheet metal, plumbing, and so forth) is a responsibility centre, and several of these shops are usually involved in a single repair and overhaul project. An organisation in which employees have responsibilities both to a project and to a responsibility centre is called a matrix organisation.

Overall Nature of the Problem

Project management focuses on the accomplishment of a specific end result, that is, the successful completion of the project. Management control of projects therefore differs from that of responsibility centres in two respects :

1. In a project, the focus is on the work involved in producing the end item regardless of which responsibility centres participate in this work, whereas in a responsibility centre the focus is on all the work done by that responsibility centre.
2. In a project, the time period of interest is the time involved in the total project, whereas in a responsibility centre the time period of interest is a calendar period, such as a month.

As will be seen, these two differences lead to a quite different control process for projects than for responsibility centres.

Aspects of Control

Management control of projects has a planning phase and a control phase, as is the case with management control of responsibility centres. In each of these phases, attention must be directed to three aspects of the project : 1. time, 2. cost, and 3. quality. The time required for each activity involved in the project must be estimated in advance and set forth in a schedule. During the conduct of the project, actual time required is compared with the estimated time and significant variances are brought to light and acted upon. The cost estimate for a project is prepared in essentially the same way that a responsibility centre budget is prepared, except that the focus is on the whole project, rather than on a specified time period. In the control phase, actual costs are compared with budgeted costs and appropriate action taken. The third aspect, quality, refers to the specifications of the project, that is, the desired end product. The term "quality" although customarily used, does not indicate the full scope of this aspect. In the planning phase, the desired end product is stated as specifically as is feasible, and in the control phase, actual quality is compared with these specifications and appropriate action taken.

Each of these three aspects must be considered separately, and they also must be considered jointly, for they interact. A reduction in quality can lead to a corresponding reduction in cost, and time can be shortened by increasing overtime costs, to give two examples. These interactions will be considered in the discussion which follows. Also, as the project progresses, circumstances may suggest the desirability of revising any or all of the time, cost, or quality estimates. These revisions complicate the control process.

Work Packages : Most projects, except the smallest are broken down into pieces, in order to facilitate both planning and control. These pieces are here called *work packages, or activities*, although other terms are customary in various industries. A work package is a measurable increment of work which can be related to a physical product, milestone, or other indicator of progress. It should require a relatively short time (usually not more than a month, rarely more than a few months), it should have an identifiable starting point and completion point, and it should be performed in a single responsibility center.

Work packages always encompass the time and quality dimensions; they may or may not include cost information. Often it is not believed to be necessary to collect costs at the level of work packages, and in this case costs are collected in broader categories, which essentially are aggregates of individual work packages.

PROJECT PLANNING

The planning for a project may start with a rough, quite vague idea, which becomes increasingly definite on the basis of discussions, tests, various types of preliminary studies, and negotiations with clients. We start our description at the point where a decision to proceed with the project has been made, and its cost magnitude, the total time required, and the quality aspects have been pretty well agreed to. Such a point cannot be specified concretely, because at any time new information may lead to a change in any of these aspects, as will be discussed below. We shall describe how these general plans are translated into specific schedules and budgets that form the basis for project control. The preparation of these schedules and budgets is done as close to the inception of work on the project as is feasible. If they are prepared at an earlier stage last-minute changes in the nature of the project are likely to make them obsolve.

Planning the Time Dimension : Several tools are available for constructing the time schedule for the project. They go by such acronyms as PERT (Program Evaluation and Review Technique), CPM (Critical Path Method), LOB (Line of Balance method). Collectively, they are known as techniques for **network analysis.** Essentially, they involve the construction of a network which shows each subgoal, or **event**, that must be completed in order to accomplish the whole project, the time required for the **activity** that is necessary for the attainment of each event, and the chronological sequence in which events must be completed in order to complete the whole project.

Planning the Cost Dimension ; A technique called PERT/Cost attempts to incorporate a cost dimension into the network analysis. The objective is to develop a critical path that is optimum considering both the time aspects and the cost aspects jointly. For planning purposes. PERT/Cost is supposed to identify time/cost tradeoffs, that is, activities in which it would be desirable to increase costs in order to reduce time, and, conversely, activities in which it would be desirable to increase costs in order to reduce time, and, conversely, activities in which it would be desirable to lengthen the time in order to reduce costs. For control purposes, the PERT/Cost estimates are supposed to provide a basis for analysing actual times and actual costs jointly.

For practical reasons, therefore, cost estimates are often made at a level of aggregation that incorporates several work packages. For simple projects, the estimates may be for the whole project as one entity, but if this is done it is not feasible to establish cost checkpoints during the conduct of the project. Lacking such checkpoints, the assumption has to be made that planned spending will proceed at an even rate, for example, that when 25 percent of the project has been completed, 25 percent of the total estimated cost should have been spent. Such an assumption is likely to be, at best, only a rough approximation. If progress payments are to be made during the course of the project, the cost estimates will usually be in terms of full costs,because these provide a basic for such payments. In other cases, the costs may well include only the direct costs of the project. In project control, unlike responsibility centre control, it usually is unnecessary to separate variable costs from fixed costs since there usually is no need to analyse the behaviour of costs in relation to volume.

Planning the Quality Dimension : Presumably, the plan for the project specifies the end product that is desired, and in some cases it may contain considerable detail about the components that make up the end product. To the extent that such information exists, it provides that basis for constructing work packages and specifying their contents. In many cases, however, the nature of the work packages cannot be determined simply from the specifications for the end product, and engineers must develop a concrete plan, perhaps working backward from the end product, first to its components, and then to the activities that are required in order to obtain each component. In a complicated project it is often difficult to describe the work packages concretely enough so that the manager knows exactly when one has been completed, and this complicates the problem of control.

For some projects, there is no written description of the steps that are to be carried out in order to achieve the project's objective, that is, of the work packages. For short, simple projects, or for certain basic research projects where the nature of the work may not be forseeable, this may not be necessary. For other projects, the absence of a written plan greatly complicates the control problem. Furthermore, those who work on projects often find that their time is spent more effectively if they have done as much advance planning as is feasible.

PROJECT CONTROL

As a consequence of the planning process, there exists, for most projects, a schedule and a budget. The schedule shows the time required for each activity, or work package, and the budget shows estimated costs of each principal part of the project, but probably not at the level of individual work packages. In the control process, information on actual cost, time, and quality is compared with these estimates. The comparison may be made each time a designated milestone in the project is reached, or it may be made at specified time intervals, such as weekly or monthly. In the latter case, there is the problem of matching work packages to the work packages to the work actually done. It is likely that some work packages will be partially complete as of the reporting data, and this makes it necessary to estimate their percentage of completion as a basis for comparing the actual time. A similar procedure must be used for cost comparisons.

Basically, management is concerned with these questions : 1. Is the project going to be finished by the scheduled completion date? 2. Is the completed work going to meet the specifications that were contemplated when the project was approved? and 3. Is the work going to be done within the estimated cost? If at any time during the course of the project, the answer to any of these questions is "no", management needs to know the reasons and what can be done to correct the situation. These three questions cannot be considered separately from one another, for it is sometimes desirable to make tradeoffs among time, quality, and cost. For example, overtime might be authorised in order to assure ontime completion, but this would add to costs; or some of the specifications might be relaxed in order to reduce costs. In any event, a project control system is structured in terms of these three dimensions.

Reports on Cost and Time

Reports on actual cost compared to budget and actual time compared to the schedule are relatively straightforward. In interpreting the time reports, usual presumption is that if the project manager can complete a work package in less than the estimated time, he is to be congratulated, and if he takes more than the estimated time, questions are raised. The interpretation of the cost reports is somewhat different, for the possibility exists that if actual costs are less than budget, quality may have suffered. For this reason, unless there is some independent way of estimating the costs that should be required, good cost performance is often interpreted as meaning being on budget, neither higher nor lower.

In most companies, cost reports compare actual costs to date with budgeted costs for the work accomplished to date. In some companies, the reports show the current estimate for the entire project compared with the budgeted cost for the entire project. The current estimate is obtained by taking the actual costs to date and adding an estimate of the costs required to complete are properly calculated. In most circumstances, these estimates should be at least equal to the original estimates made for the remaining work; if project managers are permitted to use lower figures, they can hide overruns already incurred by making corresponding reduction in future estimates. Indeed, if overruns to date are caused by factors that are likely to persist into the future, such as unanticipated inflation, the current estimates of future costs may well be higher than the amounts estimated originally.

If only direct costs are matched with work done, reports on indirect costs must prepared separately. These reports measure costs in a different dimension than do reports on the direct costs of project work. In the case of direct costs, actual costs are compared with budgeted costs for the work actually accomplished. In the case of indirect costs, the actual costs for a period, such as a month, are compared with the budgeted costs for that same period.

Tradeoffs : The interpretation of time behaviour, taken by itself, or cost behaviour, taken by itself, is a relatively straight forward type of analysis. For a real understanding of accomplishment, however, one must also consider the interactions between cost and time, and between each of these and quality. Usually such interactions are not set forth in the reports themselves, but they are an important topic in meeting held to discuss progress.

Reports on Output

Reports on time and on cost consist of numbers that come out of a formal system, often from a computer. In part, information on what has been accomplished can also be stated in concrete terms : the completion of a specified component, or of a well defined task of the project, or the achievement of prescribed specifications. Usually, however, the full story of performance cannot be told in such objective terms. The most important information must be conveyed by words, and these reports on what has actually been accomplished usually must be prepared by a project manager personally. Managers usually dislike writing such reports, and even the best reports do not communicate precisely what is going on, because of the limitations inherent in words. There is much difference of opinion as to the appropriate content of such reports.

The question may be raised : If the project is proceeding satisfactorily, why is it necessary to have a report that says so? One possible answer is that even if the project *appears* to be satisfactory, difficulties may surface in the future, and a regular report of progress may help to identify why these difficulties arose and who was responsible for them. In particular, if a controversy arises about the project, a well documented description of "who did what" is a highly desirable starting point in analysing what went wrong. This reason does not justify lengthy reports on routine happenings, however.

One solution to the performance reporting problem is to classify projects as either high risk or low risk. For low risk projects, the performance reports would be simple, unless a problem was identified. For the high risk projects, the reports would be more detailed and more frequent. Such an approach is taken in research/development laboratories that have many projects underway at any one time and cannot devote an equal amount of management attention to all of them.

Written reports are, by themselves, an inadequate device for controlling progress on any except the most routine projects. An appraisal of performance is very much a matter of management judgment which is arrived at principally by actual observation of the work and by discussions with the persons involved in it. One of the purposes of these discussion is to uncover problems as early as possible, and if this purpose is to be achieved, there must be an atmosphere such that the project leader feels uninhibited about discussing incipient problems.

Revisions

If a project is complex, or if it is lengthy, there is good chance that the plan will not be adhered to in one or more of its three dimensions : time, cost, or quality. A common occurrence is the discovery that there is likely to be a cost overrun, that is, that actual costs will exceed budgeted costs. When indications of significant deviations of plan come to management's attention, there will naturally be a discussion of what should be done. In the case of a cost overrun, for example, management might decide to accept the overrun and proceed with the project as originally planned; it might decide to cut back on the specifications of the project with the aim of producing an end product that is within the original cost limitations; or it might decide to replace the project leader in the belief that the cost overrun was unwarranted. Whatever the decision, it usually leads to a revision of the original plans for the project, and a revised plan is therefore necessary.

The question then arises : Is it better to track future progress against the revised plan or against the original plan? The revised plan is presumably a better indication of the performance that now is expected, but the danger exists that a persuasive project leader can negotiate unwarranted increases in budgeted costs or that the revised plan will incorporate, and thus hide, inefficiencies that have accumulated to date. In either case, the revised plan is said to be a *rubber baseline*, that is, stretched so as to cover up inefficiencies. This danger can be minimised by taking a hardheaded attitude toward proposed revisions, but even if this is done, there is a tendency to overlook the fact that a revised plan, by definition, does not show what was expected when the project was initiated. On the other hand, if performance continues to be monitored by comparing it with the original plan, the fact that the original plan is obsolete is likely to cause the comparison not to be taken seriously.

A possible solution to this problem is to compare cost performance to both the original plan and the revised plan, along the lines indicated below. This summary report starts with the original budget, and in the first section sets forth the revisions that have been authorised to date and the reasons for making them. The lower section shows the current cost estimate and the factors that caused the variance between the revised budget and the current estimate of costs.

PROJECT COST SUMMARY
(000 Omitted)

Original budget		Rs. 1,000
Authorszed revisions to date :		
For inflation..		50
For specification changes		200
For time delays..		60
For cost savings		(30)
Revised budget		Rs. 1,280
Current estimate to complete		1,400
Variance		Rs. 120
Explanation of Variance :		
Material cost increases	Rs 20	
Overtime	60	
Spending variances	40	
	Rs. 120	

The Project Audit

A project audit is a formal and systematic examination of the performance of an ongoing project as compared to its requirements. Towards this end, the project auditor investigates the underlying records, the tangible results of work done, the project management, the project methodology and techniques, and the organisation and controls. This enables the project auditor to report a confirmed opinion regarding the five principal objectives of each project audit, as follows :

(a) The current status of the project at the time of the project audit as compared with the contractor's contractual obligations and management expectations;

(b) The forecast status of the audited project at various future times as compared with the contractor's contractual obligations and management expectations;

(c) The critical management issues that may have negative effect on the fulfilment of the contractor's contractual obligations and management expectations;

(d) The exposure to risks and potential for losses arising from the nature of the project and the contract for both the customer and the contractor;

(e) The lessons which can be usefully applied to other projects throughout the organisation.

A Formal and Systematic Examination : A project audit is an activity of measurement against predefined and relevant standards. Without such standards of measurement, a project audit is merely the expression of personal opinion which varies significantly depending on the examiner. At the same time, a project audit is necessrily an activity in which judgment on the part of the individual project auditor is required. The object of his examination, namely a project, is a complex entity. In order to achieve resulting opinion which is consistent, uniform and largely independent of the biases of the individual project auditor, the activity must be conducted according to formally established and applied methods and subject to formally established and applied guidelines and principles which are generally agreed upon and accepted by those who will commission project audits, and those whose work is to be subjected to them.

Reporting the Project Auditor's Opinion : A project audit is designed to be a practical, cost effective, independent and reliable source of information about a project. It is intended to serve as a support to, and a basis for, management decision making. It is not a substitute for management prerogative, nor does it relieve management of the responsibility of making management decisions. As a consequence, the information presented in the project auditor's report must be reliable and confirmed; formed as a result of an examination and analysis of appropriate data; performed in a way which is known by, and visible to, the responsible management; and presented in a form which is directly usable by management for decision making. The project auditor's report must aim to reduce uncertainty about the audited project so far as possible within the constraints and circumstances of any particular project audit. Where uncertainties remain, the auditor's report must clearly identify them and emphasise those which are significant and material. The decision as to what information is significant and material in any given case is one of the major judgments required of the project auditor.

The Project Auditor's Orientation : A project audit is concerned with the management's exposure to risk and potential losses arising out of the audited project. Therefore, it is by nature a critical activity which is primarily concerned with identifying actual and potential deficiencies related to the project's execution, and only secondarily with identifying and reporting exceptional strengths and accomplishments. In order for this orientation to be acceptable to the prefessional staff associated with the audited project, the project audit must be seen to be conducted as a formal and systematic examination which is impartial, objective and fair.

The Levels of Project Audit

A project audit must be a practical undertaking carried out withing the operational constraints of limited cost, availability of manpower, and the required timeliness of the resulting report. As a consequence, three different levels of project audits have been defined which differ according to the effort required, the time taken, and the results which can be expected from them.

The levels of audit vary by their scope of coverage and the level of detail involved. The *overview audit* can be considered as a 'quick and dirty' method of obtaining a well founded opinion as to whether or not a project is in trouble. An *administrative audit* is a thorough examination of a project covering all aspects except detailed examination of technical quality. *Technical quality audits* are concerned with specific technical issues and problems within a project. Normally, overview audits are performed first and then, when required, either an administrative and/or technical quality audit follows. An administrative audit may take place without a prior overview audit if the project is important enough to justify the effort and cost involved or the project is known to be in serious trouble. Technical audits should never be performed without being preceded or accompanied by an overview and/or an administrative audit.

When to Perform a Project Audit

As project audits have a direct cost in terms of the audit team and an indirect cost in terms of the efforts required by the project team to support the audit activity, it is important that the audit investment have an optimal return. Project auditing ought to be considered by an organisation as a normal part of its quality control activities and ought not to be considered to be unusual in nature.

Project audit is useful at every stage of the project as detailed below :

Project State/phase	Usefulness of a Project Audit
	Each of the phases below may be separately contracted. An audit is most useful when performed prior to signature of the final version of a contract/work statement.
Project Initiation	As each phase may be separately contracted each could have a separate start The project audit is also highly useful if it takes place after the project has started but before it has gone on for more than thirty percent of the estimated time.
(i) Definition Study	The project audit is useful.
(ii) Preliminary Design	The project audit is useful.
(iii) Detailed Design	The project audit's usefulness is slightly less.
(iv) Programme and Human Job Development	The further into this phase usually the less useful the project audit is because the design is frozen and the project has developed an almost unchangeable inertis. The main usefulness is related to the fact that the problems of managing this phase are usually greater than in the previous phases.
(v) Testing	The project audit is marginally useful.
(vi) Data Conversion and System Implementation	If this is done in parallel with iv, the project audit can be useful. This is mainly true because conversion is a major cause of project failures.
vii) System Operation and Maintenance.	This is a different type of audit, although the same principles apply.

Comparison of Financial and Project Auditing

The relationship between financial auditing and project auditing is not clear to many people. In order to clarify similarities and differences of these disciplines the following brief list of points is made*

1. Statement of status : The financial auditor is primarily concerned with confirming that the directors' statement of the status of the company is fair, true and correct. There are legal and other standards pertaining to the form and content of such statements of status. The project auditor in almost all cases has to create the statement of status. The project audit report is a standard form for presenting such a statement of status.

2. Predictions : The financial auditor normally makes only one main predictive statement, namely that the company will continue to stay in business. The project auditor is concerned with making predictions concerning the future status of the project.

3. Measurement : The financial auditor is concerned with measurement in almost purely financial terms. The project auditor attempts to measure in financial terms but he is also concerned with other means of measuring which are not purely financial, such as time, technical quality, etc.

4. Format and Content of record keeping systems : The financial audit has the advantage that the records of the company are kept in formats which are often governed by law and are otherwise governed by a limited number of standard alternatives accepted by the accounting profession. The project auditor will have to deal with record keeping systems which are not governed by generally accepted standards in regard to their form or content. Even within a company the record keeping systems may vary from project to project.

5. Existence of record keeping systems : There is a minimal set of record systems that must be kept by a company before the financial auditor can or will perform an audit. The existence of this minimal set is a precondition for an audit. The project auditor may encounter the situation that there is no such set of records for a given project. In such cases, the project auditor must create the minimal set of records and record keeping systems in order to carry out the auditing tasks.

6. Recommendations : The financial auditor does not normally make recommendations. In some cases, the financial auditor may make separate recommendations but will restrict these to the way the company handles its

---

* Turnet, W.S. Project Auditing Methodology, North-Holland publishing company, Amsterdam, 1980, pp 3-4

accounting systems and the accounting practices that it follows. The project auditor ideally does not make recommendations, but in practice, this is frequently required. Often he is required to make recommendations beyond those relevant to the record keeping and control systems of the project.

7. Qualifications : It is customary for financial auditors to make qualifying remarks concerning their of a company's statement of accounts. Financial auditors have been in more trouble for failing to make proper qualifications than for making such qualifications. Often they have to resist strong management pressure because the management does not like to have such qualifications as part of the auditor's report.

Project auditors should also make appropriate qualifications in their reports when it is necessary. It is often necessary for the project auditor to make qualifying remarks because the time provided for the audit was too short. Also he may have to make qualifications because he does not have certain specialised technical knowledge. Neither of the above cases normally occurs in financial auditing. The project auditor sometimes must make qualifying remarks in the same sense as a financial auditor. An example which would apply to both is when the liabilities involved in a contract are unclear.

REVIEW QUESTIONS

1. Define the term 'Project'. State the overall nature of the problem of project management.
2. How will you plan the time and cost dimensions in project management?
3. Explain in detail, the three dimensional structure of a project control system.
4. What is a project audit? State its principal objectives and advantages.
5. What are the different levels of project audit?
6. Compare and contrast financial auditing with project auditing.

30
Mathematical Models : O.R., & L.P.

In recent years quantitative techniques have been increasingly used to solve complex problems of business and industry. The quantitative techniques are now recognised as an effective tool for solving managerial problems. Business executives are expected to have a good knowledge of quantitative techniques. Quantitative techniques play a special role in the field of production for achieving cost minimisation and profit maximisation objectives. A production department has to solve many problems, e.g., what products to produce, in what quantities, by which processes, etc. Quantitative techniques are very helpful in solving these problems in the optimum manner. Quantitative techniques comprise those statistical and programming techniques which are helpful in managerial decision- making. These techniques involve the use of numbers, symbols and other mathematical expressions to express the problem in quantitative terms. These techniques serve as a useful supplement to human judgement and intuition. They provide a systematic means of analysis and choice for attaining predetermined objectives. Quantitative techniques involve the use of scientific method in management.

Concept of Mathematical Model

A model may be defined as a representation or abstraction of an actual object or real life situation. Any model can be looked upon as an attempt to simplify phenomenon belonging to the real world through a process of abstraction. The objective of model building is to learn more about the peration characteristics of the real world. Models are used in the place of the real system for many reasons. Economy and range of experimentation are considered to be the two important reasons. Models are of different types such as Iconic or physical models (sculpture, globe of the earth), Analogue models (graphs and maps), and Quantitative models (statistical and mathematical models). Symbolic models include quantitative models and logical models. Also in vogue is the broad classification of models as either descriptive or prescriptive. A descriptive model describes the way a system operates and all statistical models obviously fall under this category. A normative model may be aimed at finding "the best" alternative, the process being referred to as optimising. Almost all mathematical models and some logical models can be classified under this category.

Definition of Quantitative Model : A quantitative model may be defined as one which provides the user with a systematic and powerful means of analysis and help, based on quantitative data, in exploring policies for acheiving predetermined objectives or goals.

Classification of Quantative Models : Quantitative models may be classified either as **statistical models** *or* **mathematical models** *or* **logical models.** These models involve the use of numbers, symbols and other mathematical expressions and are essentially helpful supplement to judgement and intuition. Statistical models are used in conducting the statistical enquiry concerning a certain phenomenon and include all statistical methods, tools and statistical measures such as sampling theory, probability theory, statistical tables, charts, graphs, averages, variance, correlation, regression, etc. Statistical models, on the other hand, reflect uncertainty by incorporating random elements. Standard examples are the use of queuing models and regression analysis. Common applications are manpower planning, capacity planning for raw materials handling and design of appropriate distribution system to cater to varying demand.

A mathematical model is a representation of the real system in quantitative terms. It is also termed as operations research or programming model. Mathematical models include such techniques as linear programming, decision theory, network analysis, queuing theory, etc. A mathematical model explicitly states the mathematical structure that relates the inputs such as constraints, parameters, controllable and uncontrollable variables, etc., to the output i.e., values for the criterion as expressed through the objective function. It shows the relationship between all significant factors and their interactions and also specifies a measure of performance.

Mathematical models may be classified either as **deterministic models** and **stochastic models** or as static and dynamic models. If a model is based on probabilities and concerned with future uncertainties it may be termed as a stochastic or probabilistic model. If it does not include probabilistic considerations and is concerned with certainty conditions then it may be called as a deterministic or non-probability model. A third category is a hybrid or a combination of these two models. For example, linear programming models are deterministic models; queuing models are stochastic models; and network analysis and inventory models are hybrid models.

Mathematical models are, however, frequently criticised, for their resemblance to the real world system is not apparent. They need a stringent set of assumptions to be made to convert the real world system into an abstract model. But these assumptions do not fully describe the real world - if they did, there would be little purpose in making them at all. Hence, a model first be examined to see if it is consistent with the assumptions made. Quantitative models are the most abstract of all. Unlike physical or symbolic models, they initially appear to have no relationship to the real world. Yet, after careful scrutiny, they can be viewed as simply a more sophisticated abstraction than other models.

A **logical model** is the one which every one of us uses. A good administrator develops either explicitly or implicitly an appropriate logical model. For instance, the decision on the location of post offices for every one thousand population or for villages within a radius of 10 Km can be a good logical model. Again, to classify a firm as highly profitable if it made a profit in the last three years, finding out if the firm's ratio of net profit to net tangible assets is in the top 25 percent of the industry, and the firm's ratio of stocks to turnover is in the top 50 percent of the industry can be an appropriate logical model. These models are used when the situations are complex and when past experience in operations is considerable.

Relevance of Mathematical Models

The fast changing technologies and increasing complexities of business environment have made the process of managerial decision making more difficult and the decision maker cannot rely entirely upon his observation, experience, or evaluation to make a decision. Decisions have to be based upon data which show relationship, indicate trends and show rates of change in various relevant variables. Statistical and mathematical techniques have enabled the decision maker to collect such data and analyse the data more effectively. The developments in computer technology and advanced computer software have made the usage of these techniques very easy and the job decision making more scientific. Mathematical models are being used as power tools for solving a number of managerial problems such as profit maximisation, cost minimisation, optimal allocation of resources, etc.

In a corporate outfit there are functional areas or divisions with conflicting objectives. For example, there may be conflict between the production, finance, and marketing departments in the case of inventory problem. In such cases, the problem should be solved from the company's overall point of view and the mathematical model may be useful to find an optimum solution acceptable to all departments. In addition, the mathematical models provide the business executives such an understanding of the business operations which give them new insights and capability to determine better solutions for several decision making problems with great speed, competence, and confidence.

To conclude, the mathematical models and reasoning help managers incorporate estimated probabilities in their decisions so that their methods for monitoring production become more reliable and accurate. All manner of decisions can be reached by straightforward application of probability mathematics. In the real world of unknown phenomena, any information obtained through statistical analysis is too precious to be ignored.

Formulation of a Mathematical Model

A mathematical model is a representation of the system in quantitative terms. It shows the relationship between all significant factors and their interactions and also specifies a measure of performance. In order to construct a model, it is essential to formulate the problem clearly. The problem formulation should generate some very specific outputs, which will become basic building blocks for a quantitative representation of the problem. These products include the definition of variables, parameters, constrainsts, and the objective function.

Variables are measurable factors that bear on the problem of interest. They may be classified as controllable variables and uncontrollable variables. The controllable variables are purely internal which would be under the direct control of the decision maker. Conversely, the uncontrollable variables are exogenous and beyond the control of the decision-maker. Parameters are measurable conditions inherent in the structure of the problem, and in mathematical terms they are known as constants. Constraints represent restrictions placed on the controllable and uncontrollable variables. In actual practice very few problems can be considered unconstrained. For example, in an inventory problem the reorder level is a controllable variable while the demand for the inventory item might be an uncontrollable variable. The cost of carrying one unit of inventory over some period of time and the ordering cost or the start-up cost, etc., would be parameters. At the same time, the amount of capital invested in inventory or the amount of space allocated to inventory might be the major constraint.

The objective function is the representation of the criterion or criteria in the problem. The value of the criterion or the objective function is influenced by the controllable and uncontrollable variables, parameters and constraints. The relationships among variables and the conditions on their values are expressed in an appropriate set of mathematical equations. Once the objective function is defined and appropriate relationships and constraints are known, the problem might be solved by maximising or minimising the objective function subject to the given constraints.

Advantages of Quantitative Techniques

Quantitative techniques have proved useful in tackling the intricate problems of modern industry. These techniques facilitate managerial decision-making in the following ways :

(i) Simplify decision-making : Quantitative techniques simplify the decision-making process. Decision theory enables a manager to select the best course of action. Decision tree technique refines executive judgement in systematic analysis of the problem. These techniques permit scientific decision making under conditions of risk and uncertainty. Decision problems such as manpower forecasting, production capacities and capital requirements planning can be more effectively tackled.

(ii) Serve as a tool for scientific analysis : Quantitative techniques provide a basis for precise analysis of the cause and effect relationship. They make it possible to measure the risks inherent in business by providing an analytical and objective approach. These techniques reduce the need for intuition and subjective judgement in decision-making. In this way quantitative techniques enable managers to use logical thinking in the analysis of organisational problems.

(iii) Facilitate optimum allocation of resources : Quantitative techniques are very helpful in the optimum deployment of resources. For example, the Programme Evaluation and Review Technique (PERT) enables a manager to determine the earliest and the latest times for each of the events and activities involved in a project. The probability of completing the project by a specified date can be determined. Timely completion of the project helps to avoid time and cost overruns. Similarly linear programming technique is very useful in optimum allocation of scarce resources, production scheduling and in deciding optimal assignments.

(iv) Assist in profit maximisation : At any point of time, a firm can utilise its resources in alternative areas. Quantitative techniques are invaluable in assessing the relative profitability of alternative choices and identifying the most profitable course of action. What should be the relative mix of different products, which site to choose for location out of alternative sites, how to use the available men and machines so that none remains idle, which arrangement of orders in terms of time and quantity will give maximum profits. Such questions can be answered with the help of quantitative techniques. These techniques are, therefore, widely used in the field of production, procurement, marketing, materials management, finance, etc.

(v) Help in cost minimisation : Quantitative techniques are very helpful in tackling cost minimisation problems. For example, queuing theory or waiting line theory enables a manager to minimise waiting and servicing costs. This technique helps businessmen in taking a correct decision through analysis of the feasibility of adding facilities.

(vi) Facilitate forecasting : Quantitative techniques are useful in demand forecasting. They provide a scientific basis for coping with the uncertainties of future demand. Demand forecasts serve as the basis for capacity planning. Quantitative techniques enable a manager to adopt the minimum risk plan.

(vii) Improve competitive strength : Quantitative techniques like mathematical programming help to make a choice from conflicting objectives. They permit systematic evaluation of the alternative strategies technical and other innovations. These techniques help to decide the critical uncertainties so that necessary steps may be taken to face them. Game theory is particularly useful in selecting the optimum strategy in a competitive environment.

(viii) Improve inventory control : The inventory planning techniques help in deciding when to buy and how much to buy. It enables management to arrive at appropriate balance between the costs and benefits of holding stocks. The Integrated Production Models Techniques is very useful in minimising costs of inventory, production and workforce. Statistical quality control helps us to determine whether the production process is under control or not.

Thus, quantitative techniques render invaluable services to management. With the help of these techniques executives can gain better understanding of problems. These techniques provide a means for handling and processing information. The vision and perspective of executives is broadened. They get new insights and capability to design effective solutions to business problems with speed, accuracy and confidence. The utility and importance of quantitative techniques have increased tremendously since the advent of computers.

Limitations of Quantitative Techniques

Quantitative techniques are no doubt a valuable aid to management. But they cannot be a substitute for executive judgement and experience in decision-making. These techniques suffer from several limitations some of which are described below :

(i) Human factors : Quantitative techniques do not take into consideration important intangible factors. Human factors like skill, attitude and philosophy of management are non-measurable but they exercise paramount influence on managerial decision- making.

(ii) Mathematical limitations : Quantitative techniques involve the use of mathematical models, equations and other formulae. Derivation of a mathematical models or equation involves certain assumptions. When these assumptions do not hold good the quantitative techniques may yield misleading results. One must be very careful in the application of quantitative techniques.

(iii) Expensive : The application of quantitative techniques very often requires the services of specialists and computers. As such high costs are involved in the use of quantitative techniques. Small firms cannot always afford the costs. Moreover, in certain cases the application of quantitative techniques may not be worth the costs.

(iv) Analytical tool : Quantitative techniques are only a tool of analysis and they cannot by themselves make the final decision. These techniques are at best a supplement to managerial judgment and can never be a substitute for management.

Classification of Quantitative Techniques : Quantitative techniques may broadly be classified into two categories : 1. Statistical techniques, 2. Operations Research (OR) techniques.

Concept of Operations Research (O.R.)

Though a scientific approach has been used in decision making for centuries, Operations Research (O.R), as it is known today, first came to be used during World War II in Britain. The Americans used it for the development of new types of mine tactics for use in the war against Japan. After the war, the technique has been extensively applied in business and government with varying impact. The early Seventies saw increasing use of the technique in the United States and Europe so much so that the term "management science" was synonymously used for quantitative techniques. However, the trend did not last as the professional bodies were busy, complicating the operational science through use of trivial variants of mathematical models and thus divorcing the practitioners from the field. Also, the fact that the use of O.R models is a high risk-prone, alternative was not recognised by many corporate executives until they burnt their finger. Just as the expected pay-off can be significant so can be the expected loss if the model is not formulated properly. Only those with an inter-disciplinary strength in finance, operations, and organisational behaviour can make effective operations researchers (or an inter-disciplinary team if an appropriate person cannot be located). This fact was not recognised by many firms using these models and they came to grief because they associated operations researchers with skills in applied mathematics.

An attempt is made here to indicate first how O.R can be put to effective use for decision making and secondly to introduce the various techniques. O.R is often confused with statistics, accounting control systems, industrial engineering and market research. An operations researcher visualises the whole system unlike the other functional experts. Operations research, as the term implies, is the business of doing research on operations. An operation is a system consisting of men, machinery and money which can be isolated for study. Research obviously is to perform operations better. In the present study, operations will often be a model built in a convenient language like mathematics. A typical example of a model of communication in an organisation context is the organisation chart. An operating statement and balance sheet together form the model of operations of a firm. A physical model such as a see - saw at its equilibrium position can be described by the mathematical equation $W_1L_1 = W_2L_2$ where W_1 and W_2 are weights suspended at distances L_1 and L_2 from the fulcrum respectively.

Thus, O.R. is a comparatively new science devised from many disciplines such as mathematics, physics, engineering and economics. And, therefore, it rests on inter-disciplinary team approach. Wagner has defined O.R. as a scientific approach to solve problems for executive management. An application of O.R. include : (i) constructing mathematical, economic and statistical models to find solutions to problems under situations of complexity and uncertainty; (ii) analysing the relationships that determine the probable future consequences of decision choices, and devising appropriate measures of effectiveness in order to evaluate the relative merit of alternative actions.

In the most general sense, O.R. can be considered as the application of scientific methods, techniques and tools to problems involving the operations of systems so as to provide the executive management with optimum solutions. The five phases of an O.R. study are as follows :

1. Formulation of the problem,
2. Construction of a mathematical model,
3. Obtaining the solution from the model,
4. Testing the model and evaluating the solution, and
5. Implementing and maintaining the solution.

Although these phases of an O.R. study are normally taken up in the order shown above, they do not usually terminate in this order. Each phase normally continues until the study is completed and continuously interacts with the others.

Application of O.R. Techniques

O.R. has been applied in virtually every kind of business and industry. It has been applied to a variety of problems. Its application to tactical or short run problems is more common than to strategic or long run problems and this has facilitated to identify a small set of prototype problems. They are as follows:

1. Allocation Problems,
2. Inventory Problems,
3. Replacement Problems,
4. Queuing Problems,
5. Sequencing Problems,
6. Routing Problems.
7. Competitive Problems,
8. Search Problems

In real situations these problems frequently emerge from each other, not necessarily in the order listed. For example, many O.R.'s start with inventory problems. Inventories simply involve in holding or storing resources. The decisions required generally entail the determination of how much of a resource to procure and when to procure it. A large number of resources involved - for example, in determining how many of each of a large number of parts to purchase or produce, and when to do so. Once such a multi-item inventory problem is solved, it may become apparent that there are not enough facilities to produce all the items specified in the solution. It then becomes necessary to allocate the available production facilities to different jobs optimally.

The allocation problem always assumes uninterrupted availability of production facilities. In reality, interruptions may occur due to machine break-downs, power failures, repairs, shortage of raw materials or labour etc. Then the allocation problem may require solving queuing problem.

Queuing models assume a rule for selecting the next among the things (jobs) waiting for service (e.g., repairs). The servicing of jobs in a particular order may have significant effect on total time required for jobs and the distribution of such time. This may lead to sequencing problem. When this illustrative problem is considered over an extended period of time, it may require solving of replacement problem.

Upto this stage in the development of the problem, the concern was with the behaviour of the system under study and not with the behaviour outside parties who affect the performance of the organisation, such as suppliers, customers, or competitors. If their behaviour is considered in attempting to purchase materials at a lower price or to sell at a better price, a competitive problem is involved.

Finally the O.R. problems need more information and this results in study of information and communication support system. Problems that involves the determination how much and what information to acquire, how to acquire it and use it, etc., are search problems. From the above discussion it clear that management problems can seldom be isolated from one another. Hence, although O.R. can be organised on a problem or project basis, it may most effectively be used to incorporate simultaneously or sequentially a wide range of interacting problems also.

Models and Decision-making Process

Let us now have a close look at management models and the process of decision making. Decision-making involves three phases - the "Intelligence" stage of searching the environment calling for decision; "design" or finding and assessing the alternatives; and "choice" or selecting one from among the many available alternatives. The first phase calls for defining the problem. The second involves search for alternatives and their evaluation. The final phase selects the desired alternative.

McKhenna (1980) has illustrated the use of models in the decision process (see Figure 30.1)

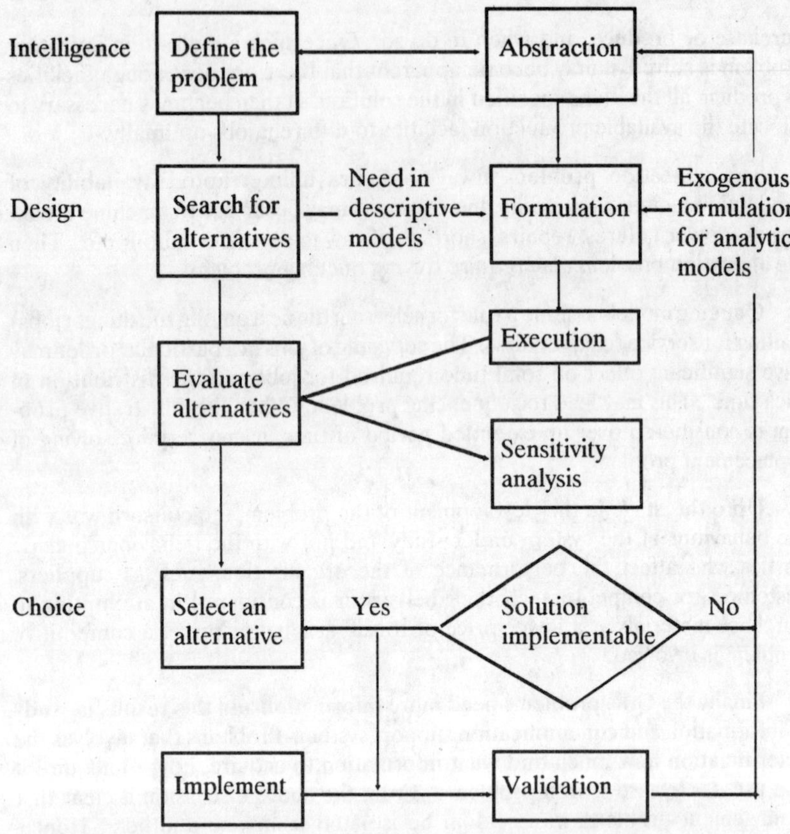

Fig. 30.1 Model showing three phases of a Decision Process

Validation, A Must

Most failures of O.R models can be traced to the skipping of the validation phase. Any model developed must be validated using past data. The results from the model must be compared with actual decisions taken to see whether the models can predict better alternatives than possible through the use of logical models.

If a multi-disciplinary approach is not used or if validation is not carried out, the use of O.R can affect a firm's financial viability. At the same time a well-versed operations researcher may be able to offer better alternative solutions to a problem. This can be illustrated through an example.

Let us take the accounting model of a firm. An operating statement and the balance sheet form an accounting model :

Accounting Model

	Rs. in lakhs
Sales (S)	100
Variable costs including raw materials, indirect materials utilities and direct labour	75
Fixed costs including general administration, selling expenses, depreciation and interest	15
Earnings before tax	10
Investment	
Permanent capital	30
Working capital	45

The accounting model indicates that the return on investment (ROI) is 13.33 percent. Assuming that the management sets a goal of increasing the ROI to 15 percent it may contemplate reducing overheads or have a tighter contrc' on inventory. If the general administration and selling expenses form two-thirds of fixed costs and if inventory forms half of the working capital then the alternatives before the top management are to reduce these two items of overheads by 13 percent or reduce inventory by 36 percent to achieve the 15 percent ROI. The management may decide on the former alternative as achievement of the latter is fraught with difficulties.

The operations researcher, on the other hand, constructs an extended model of the operation system. This is arrived at after discussion with the marketing manager about the nature of relationship of selling expenses with sales volume, with the materials manager about the relationship of inventory to sales volume, and with the finance manager about the relationship of permanent and working capital needs with sales volume. Supposing the O.R analyst finds that past data can be used to arrive at the relationship of sales volume to selling expenses in the following form

Log (sales volume) = a + b log (selling expenses) where a and b are constants then he can estimate possible sales volumes for varying selling expenses.

If the new sales is denoted by S and the old sales by S_0 then ROI (S) equals

$$\frac{[S - \text{Variable cost} \times S/S_0 - (\text{fixed cost} - \text{depreciation} - \text{interest} - \text{selling expenses}) \times 1 - (\text{depreciation} + \text{interest})\, S/S_0 - \text{new level of selling expenses}]}{[\text{Permanent capital} + \text{Working capital}]\, S/S_0}$$

His analysis may lead him to conclude that the best strategy to achieve a higher ROI will be to increase overheads (selling expenses) by 10 percent rather than decrease them by 13 percent. The apparent paradox is due to the fact that the conventional functional manager's decision was based on the assumption that selling expenses do not affect sales volume. Similarly, the operations researcher may suggest addition of balancing facilities even when the machines downstream and upstream are fully utilised in order to achieve a different mix of production with a higher proportion of more profitable items possible thanks to the use of a linear programming model.

These illustrations are meant to emphasis that the operations researcher may be able to point out better alternatives or bring into focus the assumptions made in conventional decision-making. Various applications of operations research models in functional areas in an organisational context are listed in the Table 1.1 The list is not exhaustive. Resourceful managers can add to it.

The O R tools are not for the exclusive use of organisations. Programming models can be effectively used by block development officers for planning the mix of crops to be grown; collectors may like to sue queuing, models to arrive at the optimum number of fire engines and hospital ambulances needed while the secretary attached to the legal department may examine various polices of controlled decentralisation to delegation of authority for clearing backlog of cases which have a waiting time of more than two or three years. The models can be of use to arrive at an appropriate metropolitan transport system or to determine the number of counters needed at railway stations or the number of houses to be allotted to lower middle income groups to reduce the waiting period. The scope for application of operations research in organisations, social services, transport systems, and other areas is indeed great and so are the pitfalls if the models are not fully representative or if the skills of the formulating team are under question !

Application of O.R. in Functional Areas

O.R. has been very successful in aiding executives in solving problems in their respective functional areas. To mention a few of such areas are as follows :

Production

Planning and Scheduling

Raw material and in-process inventory management

Make or Buy decisions

Allocation of fixed facilities and manpower

Maintenance and replacement of equipment and facilities

Waiting lines (bottlenecks)

Plant location

Tbale 1.1 Use of Operations Research Models in Functional Departments in an Organisational Context

O.R. Models Department	Queuing Model	Programming Models	Game Theory	Replacement	Networking	Inventory
Production	Production scheduling on critical machine centres	Modernisation\ expansion programmes for mulation	Assess competition process changes	Replacement policies groups Vs. Individual replacement interval determination	PERT/CPM, PERT/ Resource output for mega production runs SPAR for multi project	Setting up safety stock levels,re-order point determination, EOQ models, etc.
Marketing	Location and size of ware houses and sales offices scheduling	Resource allocation distribution channels; media mix selection	Plan competitive bidding; plan for price changes by customers	Rotation of sales person replacement for improved selling	Preparation of sales strategies	Warehousing needs analysis
Finance	Liquid assets level; projection for short-term borrowings	Capital budgeting portfolio management	Medium term long-term corporate strategies financial viability resulting from price process changes	Replacement sources of borrowing (short-term)	Public issues management long term source	Inver.tory of liquid and fixed assets
Personnel and Administration	Manpower requirement assessment office equipment capacity and number assessment	Assignment of men and office machinery	Key personnel technical/managerial recruitment	Projection of requirements of clerks, unskilled, skilled workers arising out cf retirement turnover etc.	Office recoras computerisation, setting up branches sales depots	Inventory or personnel records, office equipment, etc

Marketing and Distribution

Allocation of advertising budget

Product mix

Finished goods inventory management

Warehouse location

Transportation

Customer service

Investment and Finance

Selection of process and equipment

Replacement policy

Diversification and acquisition

Budgeting

Portfolio selection

Sampling in accounting

Organisation

Organisation structure

Centralisation vs. Decentralisation

Communication

Long range planning

Other Areas of Business

Research and development expenditure

Design of experiments

Credit analysis

Incentive plans

Decision-oriented MIS

Managerial Uses of O.R.

O.R. when applied to suitable problems by competent practitioners, leads to proper solution of problems - i.e., problems that could not be so clearly and decisively understood, stated, or handled by any other means. O.R. helps the decision maker in a number of ways. To mention a few are as follows :

1. It assists the decision maker in substantially improving the operations under his control and better achieving the organisation's goals.
2. It provides him with the increased knowledge and insight into the basic facts, characteristics and relationships of the business.
3. It enables him to have more effective, more responsive, and broader control.

4. It supplies better, more timely, and more quantitative information.
5. It facilitates to adopt management by exception by reducing the and effort required for routine decisions.
6. It helps him to have more time for planning and managing.

O.R. TECHNIQUES

The Linear Programming, Games Theory, Queuing Theory, etc., are some of the O.R. techniques often used in business and industry for operational and management control.

Linear Programming (LP)

The linear programming technique was formulated by a Russian mathematician L.V. Kantorovich. It was developed later by Georg B. Dantzig who evolved the simplex method in 1947. The word 'linear' means that the relationships handled are represented by straight lines or involve linear function. The word 'programming' implies use of mathematical procedure to find the best solution. Thus, linear programming may be defined as a mathematical techniques involving the maximisation or minimisation of a linear function (called objective function) of variables subject to a constraint of linear inequalities (called linear restraints). LP is a mathematical model for directing the most efficient use of limited resources such as raw materials, manpower, tools of production or capital etc., toward an objective, such as maximising profit or minimising the cost under certain constraints. Hence, it is primarily concerned with the optimal allocation of scarce resources for optimising the given objective function. The features of a LP problem are as follows :

(a) Existence of a set of constraints - where limitations or minimum requirements must be met.

(b) Choosing among the alternative courses of action.

(c) Linear relationship between different variables of the problem.

(d) A best solution - Optimisation of objective function.

Basically, the problem is how to assign the available scarce resources among the competing jobs to do each job best. LP problems may be used on many 'allocation' problems. Production/distribution problems, transportation problems, production mix and blending problems also fall into this category.

Requirements of Linear Programming : Linear programming can be applied to only those problems which satisfy the following conditions :

1. Objective Function : There must be a clearly defined objective which can be stated quantitatively. In business problems an objective is usually the maximisation of profits or the minimisation of costs.

2. Constraints : All restrictions relating to resources etc., should be fully spelt out. They must be capable of mathematical expression.

3. Linearity : The various relationships to be expressed in the form of equations or inequalities must be linear. Linear means proportional relationship between two or more variables. Under linear relationship, every increment in one variable results in proportionate change in another variable. Such a relationship is generally found between inputs and outputs.

4. Non-negativity : The values of variables must be positive and not negative. This suits the production decisions as negative values of physical quantities are never possible.

5. Finiteness : The number of inputs, outputs and activities need to be finite as otherwise an optimal solution is not possible to compute.

Thus, linear programming is applicable to problems of quantitative and linear nature where maximisation or minimisation objective is to be achieved under given constraints.

Methods of Linear Programming : A linear programming problem can be solved either by the graphical method or by the simplex method. The graphical method involves the use of graphs. It is relatively simpler but can be applied effectively, when only two decision variables are involved. The simplex method is useful in more complicated problems. But it requires comparatively advanced mathematics. The computation procedure is so wearisome that it is necessary to use computers to handle the volume of calculations involved in actual business problems. In simplex method, the computational routine is an iterative process, i.e., it is repeated again and again. Successive solutions are developed until the optimum solution is found. It always begins at the point of no production, technically known as the zero solution. The simplex method is based on the property that every successive solution is an improvement over the earlier solution.

Advantages of Linear Programming : Linear programming offers the following benefits :

1. **Analytical tool :** Linear programming facilitates logical organisation and study of data. It provides a better insight into the problem.

2. **Alternative solutions :** Linear programming enables a manager to consider all possible solutions to the problem.

3. **Optimal solution :** With the help of linear programming, a manager can evaluate the costs and benefits of different alternatives. He can select the best solution to optimise his objective.

4. **Re-evaluation :** Linear programming is helpful in making adjustments in the plan so as to meet changing conditions. When the plan is partly carried out, adjustments can be incorporated to achieve best results under changed conditions.

Linear programming is a flexible tool and it can be applied to a variety of multi-dimensional problems. It provides an information base for the optimum allocation of scarce resources. It leads to better use of productive resources by indicating the best use of existing facilities.

Limitations of Linear Programming : Linear programming is a powerful tool but it is not a panacea for all management problems. It suffers from the following drawbacks.

(i) Linear programming cannot be applied to all business problems. It is applicable to only to those situations where the objective function and the constraint set is linear in nature. Many problems do not satisfy the condition of linearity, i.e., returns to scale are not constant. In such cases non-linear programming is required.

(ii) Linear programming assumes that the values of the coefficients are known with certainty. Therefore, it cannot be applied to those problems where values of variables are uncertain and unknown.

(iii) Linear programming does not always give integer value solutions. In many cases, fractional value answers do not make much sense. For example, it may give a solution of 529 machines which has no sense in production planning.

(iv) In some business situations the number of variables and their relationships are so large that it becomes almost impossible to handle them with the help of linear programming. The reliability of linear programming also depends upon the reliability of values assigned to the variables.

(v) Linear programming cannot give a solution where management has multiple goals which are incompatible and cannot be satisfied simultaneously within the constraints of available resources. In such cases, goal programming has to be used.

Applications of Linear Programming

Linear programming is useful in wide range of production and procurement problems in industry. It is particularly applicable in product mix, resource allocation, production planning and scheduling, transportation, assignment, corporate planning, sales and advertising, financial planning, portfolio analysis, etc. Some industrial applications of linear programming are given below :

1. **Product-mix problem :** Very often a multipurpose plant has production capacity to produce a range of produces. The different products have different

unit costs and prices. The objectives in such a situation is to determine the product mix that will maximise the profits or minimise the cost of operations. Linear programming can solve this problem very well.

Illustration 1

A small-scale manufacturer has production facilities for producing two different products A and B. Each of the product requires three different operations - grinding, assembly and testing. Product A requires 15, 20 and 14 minutes to grind, assemble and test respectively, while product B requires 7.5, 40 and 45 minutes respectively. The production run calls for at least 7.5 hours of grinding time, at least 20 hours of assembly time and at least 15 hours of testing time. If the manufacturing cost of the two products are Rs. 60 and Rs. 90 respectively, how many units of each product should the firm produce in order to minimise the cost of operations.

Solution

Taking X_1 and X_2 as the number of units produced of products A and B respectively the above problem can be stated as follows :

Minimise Total cost (C) = $60X_1 + 90X_2$

Subject to

$$15X_1 + 7.5X_2 \geqslant 450$$
$$20X_1 + 40X_2 \geqslant 1200$$
$$14X_1 + 45X_2 \geqslant 900$$
$$X_1 \geqslant 0 \quad X_2 \geqslant 0$$

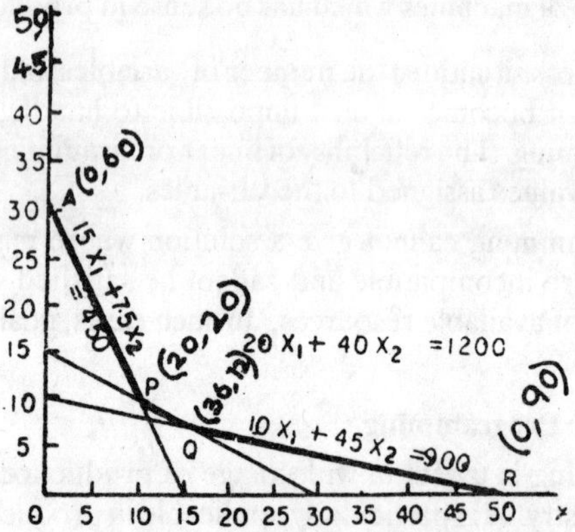

Fig. 30.2

Using the graphical procedure let us plot the linear constraints (Fig. 30.2). Since the inequalities in the constraint set are , the region of feasible solutions consists of all points falling on and above the line segments AP, PQ and OR.

The coordinates of the four vertices of unbounded convex region formed by the feasible region are given by

$A = (0, 60)$ $P = (20, 20)$ $Q = (36, 12)$ and $R = (90, 0)$

The values of the objective function for the different coordinates are :

$C(A) = 60(0) + 90(60) = 5400$; $C(P) = 60(20) + 90(20) = 3000$

$C(Q) = 60(36) + 90(12) = 3240$; $C(R) = 60(90) + 90(0) = 5400$

Since it is minimisation problem and the optimum solution is at the point P, i.e., 20 units each of products A and B with the cost of Rs. 3000.

2. Production Scheduling Problems : Linear programming is helpful in solving the problem of deciding a low cost production schedule for one or more products over future time periods. In such a problem the constraints of product demand, capacity, manpower and storage space have to be considered. A linear programming model can be developed for optimal scheduling.

Illustration 2

A firm makes two types of furniture - chairs and tables. The contribution for each product as calculated by the accounting department is Rs. 20 per chair and Rs. 30 per table. Both products are processed on three machines M_1, M_2 and M_3. The time required in hours by each product and the total time available in hours per week on each machine are as follows :

Machine	Chair	Table	Available Time
M_1	3	3	36
M_2	5	2	50
M_3	2	6	60

How Should the firm schedule its production in order to maximise the contribution ?

Solution

Step 1. The mathematical formulation of the problem is as under :

Maximise (Total profit) $Z = 30X1 + 20X2$ subject to constraints :

$$3X_1 + 3X_2 \leqslant 36; \; 5X_1 + 2X_2 \leqslant 50$$
$$2X_1 + 6X_2 \leqslant 60; \; X_1 \geqslant 0, X_2 \geqslant 0$$

where X_1 = number of chairs
X_2 = number of tables.

Step 2. Construct the graph by drawing a horizontal and a vertical axis which are represented by the X1 -axis and X2 - axis in the cartesian X_1OX_2 plane, since any point which satisfied the condition $X_1 > 0$ and $X_2 > 0$ lies in the first quadrant only and thus our search for the desired pair (X_1, X_2) is restricted to the points of the first quadrant only.

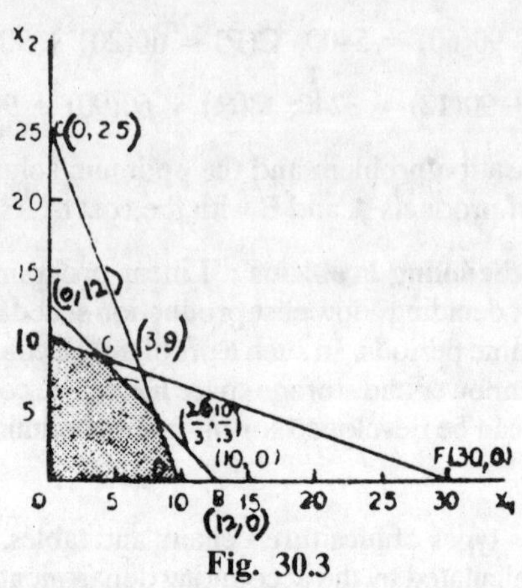

Fig. 30.3

Now the inequalities are plotted on a graph (Fig 30.3) taking them as equations.

Step 3. Identify the feasible resin or solution space which is the area containing all pairs of values that satisfy all the constraints. Here the possible region is bound by the two axes and the three lines :

$$3X_1 + 3X_2 = 36$$
$$5X_1 + 2X_2 = 50$$
$$2X_1 + 6X_2 = 60$$

It is the area which falls to the left of these constraint equations as all the three constraints are of the 'less than or equal to' type.

Step 4. Locate the solution points. The shaded area ODHGE represents the set of all feasible solutions. The five corners of the polygon are O = (0, 0), D = (10,0), H = (26/3, 10/3), G = (3, 9), and E = (0, 10).

Step 5. Evaluate the objective function. Dantzig's theorem guarantees that the optimal solution to an L.P.P. occurs at one or more of the corner points. Let us evaluate the objective function at each of these five corner points :

Corner point (X, X_2)	Objective function $Z = 20X_1 + 30X_2$	Value
O = (0, 0)	20x0 + 30x0	Z(O) = 0
D = (10,0)	20x10 + 30x0	Z(D) = 200
H = (26/3,10/3)	20x(26/3) + 20x(10/3)	Z(H) = 240
G = (3, 9)	20x3 + 30x9	Z(G) = 330
E = (0, 10)	20x0 + 30x10	Z(E) = 300

Optimal solution lies at the point G = (3, 9) i.e., $X_1 = 3$ and $X_1 = 9$ with the objective function value of Rs. 330 (largest value). Hence to maximise profits the company should manufacture 3 chairs and 9 tables.

3. Blending Problem : This problem arised when a product can be made form a variety of available raw materials of various compositions and prices. These materials have to be mixed up to make a product conform to given specifications. The objective function in a blending problem is to minimise the cost of the final product. The supply of raw materials and the specifications would state the number of units of each raw material which are to be blended to make one unit of the product. The blending problem frequently occurs in petroleum industry (e.g., blending crude oil to produce different octane gasoline), chemical industry (e.g., blending input ingredients to produce soft drinks), etc. In all such blending problems the technique of linear programming can be quite useful.

4. Production smoothing problem : An industrial enterprise faces the problem of scheduling its production or procurement over a number of future time periods with the total time span being considered the 'planning horizon'. Linear programming can be used to solve this problem.

5. Assignment problem : Allocation of employees or other facilities to different tasks is known as assignment problem. The objective function here is to minimise the cost of facilities and to meet the staff needs at all hours of the day. Availability of facilities serves as the constraint. Assignment problems arise in manufacturing concerns as well as in transport companies, hospitals, restaurants, etc.

6. Transportation problem. : This is also known as distribution problem. Transportation problem arises when there are a number of production centres from which goods are to be transported to various destinations. The objective function here is to minimise the cost of transportation. For example, a firm may have to determine the distribution system that will minimise total shipping cost from several warehouses to various market locations.

7. Inventory problem : A firm always faces the problem of minimising inventory costs to meet the demands over time. Linear programming is very helpful in determining inventory policy that will minimise the costs.

8. Trim loss problem : In several manufacturing situations products are produced in standard sizes while orders are received in different sizes or quantities. The problem is to determine the combination of requirements to be produced from standard materials that will minimise the trim loss.

In addition to the above, linear programming is also applied in balancing assembly lines, in structural design for maximum product, in scheduling of a military tanker fleet, in deciding which parts to make and which to buy, in selecting equipment, in designing optimum purchasing policies, in media selection, in portfolio selection, in profit planning, in farm planning, in routing aeroplanes, in deciding diet problems, etc. In fact S.J. Gars (An illustrated Guide to Linear Programming, McGraw Hill, New York, 1970) describes more than one hundred applications of linear programming.

Integer Programming (IP) : It is a special form of linear programming in which the decision variables have integer solutions (i.e., whole numbers) only. In LP the variables are allowed to take any non-negative value (even fractions) within the feasible region of the particular problem. The divisibility requirement in LP may not pose a serious problem in many practical situations. But in certain decision problems, the divisibility assumption is unrealistic and totally unacceptable. For example, in a product mix problem, a solution of 5.35 units of product X and 4.76 units of product Y or in a recruitment problem, selection of 3.4 persons would be meaningless. Such problems require integer values for the decision variables and integer programming technique is to solve problems of these types. The optimisation problems obtained from the linear programming model, when they are forced to take only integer values, are known as integer linear programming problems.

The essential features of IP problems are as follows :

1. a linear objective function,
2. a set of linear resource constraints,
3. integer value constraints for all or some variables, and
4. non-negativity constraints for the decision variables.

The IP is adaptable to problems that allow only integer values for final solutions. It can be applied to such areas as capital budgeting, research and development, location of warehouses, allocation and assignment of people to jobs, etc.

Similar to LP problem, the IP problem may also be formulated. IP model will be as follows :

To maximise $\sum C_j X_j$

Subject to $\sum a_{ij} X_j < B_{ij}$ *for i = 1, 2, 3, ..., m*

$X_j > 0$ for j = 1, 2, 3, ..., n

and X_j are integer values, for j = 1, 2, 3, ..., S

The integer programming problem may be pure or mixed integer programming problems. In mixed IP problems some of the variables are continuous while others have only integer values. Business situations of this type is more common and mixed IP is more applicable than the LP. One of the easiest ways of solving the IP problems is to transform the problem into a form that permits application of LP. However, the nature of transformation necessary to change it into an acceptable form for the simplex method varies with the type of problem under study.

Dynamic Programming (D.P.) : Dynamic programming is a mathematical model for solving problems involving a series of inter-related decisions. It is basically concerned with finding a combination of optimal decisions over a period of time which will optimise the overall effectiveness. For example, the production manager of a firm may wish to make a series of inter-related production scheduling decisions over a time which will minimise the production cost or minimise hiring and lay off personnel necessary to achieve some specified product goals. Thus, DP is used in situations where it is desirable to make a sequence of decisions that is needed to optimise some objective function. It can be applied to such areas as transportation problems, replacement problems, production scheduling problems, inventory control, financial planning, media planning, portfolio analysis, etc.

Goal Programming (G.P) : Goal programming is a mathematical technique used for optimising the multiple goals of the organisation. This technique uses the simplex method for finding optimum solution of a single dimensional or multi-dimensional objective function with a given set of constraints which are expressed in linear form. For example, in a production scheduling, employment smoothing problem, the management might consider the cost of shortages to be higher than costs of changing the employment level, and the latter costs to be higher than the inventory costs thus identifying three separate goals-the levels of production, employment, and inventory. In GP, management is made to set some estimated target for each of their goals and to rank them in order of their priorities. When the information is supplied, the GP tries to minimise the deviations from the targets that were set. It starts with the most important goal and continues until the achievement of a less important goal would cause the management to fail to achieve a more important one.

REVIEW QUESTIONS

1. What is meant by model building? State its objectives.
2. Define quantitative models and state its classification.
3. Explain the concept and relevance of mathematical models as applicable to management control.
4. Explain the concept of Quantitative Techniques. State its advantages and limitations.
5. What is meant by Operation Research? State the various areas of business and industry to which O.R. techniques may be applied effectively?
6. What do you understand by Linear Programming? Discuss its uses and limitations.
7. What is the general level of problems which may be tackled by linear programming?
8. Under what conditions can linear programming be utilised in the solution of allocation problem?
9. Write short notes on :

   (a) Integer programming (b) Dynamic programming (c) Goal programming.

31
Net Work Techniques : PERT & CPM

Network analysis involves the determination of an optimum sequence of performing certain operations concerning some jobs in order to minimise the overall time and/or cost. It is a generic name for a number of associated project planning and control procedures which are all based on the concept of network Network analysis involves the consideration of the time and resources profile of the project activities so as to identify the optimal course of action involving the amount of time, keeping in view the available resource constraints. It provides a clear picture of the work elements of the project and also their sequential relationship. A number of network techniques have been developed and a few of them are named below :

1. P.E.R.T : Programme Evaluation and Review Technique.
2. C.P.M. : Critical Path Method.
3. R.A.M.S. : Resource Allocation and Multiproject Scheduling.
4. P.E.P. : Programme Evaluation Procedure.
5. C.O.P.A.C. : Critical Operating Production Allocation Control.
6. M.A.P. : Manpower Allocation Procedure.
7. R.P.S.M. : Resource Planning and Scheduling Method.
8. L.C.S. : Least Cost Scheduling.
9. M.O.S.S. : Multi-Operations Scheduling System.
10. P.C.S. : Project Control System.
11. G.E.R.T. : Graphical Evaluation Review Technique.
12. L.O.B. : Line of Balance Technology.

Among the various network techniques, the Programme Evaluation and Review Technique (PERT) and the Critical Path Method (CPM) are the most widely used techniques.

Objectives of Network Analysis

Network analysis can be used to serve the following objectives :

1. Minimisation of total time : Network analysis is useful in completing a project in the minimum possible time. A good example of this objective is the maintenance of production line machinery in a factory. If the cost of downtime is very high, it is economically desirable to minimise the maintenance time despite high resource costs.

2. Minimisation of total cost : Where the cost of delay in the completion of a project exceeds cost of extra effort, it is desirable to complete the project of time so as to minimise total cost.

3. Minimisation of time for a given cost : When a fixed sum is available to cover costs, it may be preferable to arrange the existing resources so as to reduce the total time for the project instead of reducing total cost.

4. Minimisation of cost for a given total time : When no particular benefit will be gained from completing the project early, it may be desirable to arrange resources in such way as to give the minimum cost for the project in the set time.

5. Minimisation of idle resources : The schedule should be devised to minimise large fluctuations in the use of limited resources. The cost of having men/machines idle should be compared with the cost of hiring resources on a temporary basis.

6. Network analysis can also be employed to **minimise production delays, interruptions and conflicts.**

Managerial Applications of Network Analysis : Network analysis can be applied to a very wide range of situations involving the use of time, labour and physical resources. Some of the more common applications of network analysis in project scheduling are as follows :

1. Assembly line scheduling.
2. Installation of a complex new equipment, e.g., computers, large machinery.
3. Research and Development.
4. Maintenance and overhauling complicated equipment in chemical or power plants, steel and petroleum industries, etc.
5. Inventory planning and control.
6. Shifting of manufacturing plant from one site to another.
7. Development and testing of missile system.
8. Development and launching of new products and advertising campaigns.
9. Control of traffic flow in metropolitan cities.
10. Long range planning and developing staffing plans.

11. Budget and audit procedures.
12. Organisation of international conferences.
13. Launching space programmes, etc.

Advantages of Network Analysis

1. Network analysis is simple and easy to apply even by people without advanced knowledge of mathematics.

2. It is a powerful tool of planning, scheduling and control. In the planning stage, it helps to identify the tasks to be performed and the resources required. During scheduling, network analysis time and resources needed at each stage of activity can be calculated. In the monitoring phase, it is useful for measuring the actual against the planned performance.

3. Network analysis shows in a simple way the inter-relationship of the various activities constituting a project or a programme. This helps in bringing out clearly the technological interdependence of the various activities and so in integrating the project plan.

4. It helps the management to think through the project systematically ensuring that the sequence requirements are adequate and necessary. It also forces the management to prepare time estimates for individual portions of the total project. This in turn helps to identify possible improvements in these portions or in their relationship to the whole project.

5. Network analysis reveals the critical path or the series of activities that require longest time. When it is necessary to reduce the project completion time, the network technique can identify those activities for which extra effort would not be beneficial. Extra time can be taken for some of these without lengthening the total project time.

6. It develops a discipline and a systematic approach in planning and scheduling which is not accomplished to this extent by older and traditional methods.

7. Network analysis identifies the earliest possible starting date and latest allowable completion date for each activity.

8. It provides a comprehensive view of the project and brings about better communication and coordination between the concerned departments.

9. Network analysis facilitates control by exception whereby management need act only when the situation is out of control.

10. It focuses attention on the critical elements of the project and suggests areas for increasing efficiency and reducing costs.

11. Network analysis provides upto date information on the progress of the project through frequent reporting and accurate analysis.

12. It lends itself easily to computers. Several computer manufacturers provide standard packages of network analysis routines with their equipment.

Limitations of Network Techniques

Network techniques suffer from the following shortcomings.

1. It is very often difficult, if not impossible, to construct an accurate network for complex projects. In real world projects interrelationships between activities and events are not clear- cut and precise.

2. Network analysis is based on the assumption that all the resources required to perform any number of activities simultaneously are available. In reality, resources are very often limited and less than those needed for the network.

3. What may appear to be a non-critical path in the network of a project may actually be a semi-critical path. In such cases it is quite easy for delays to occur causing the path to became truly critical even though network does not show it critical.

4. Several complexities are involved in calculating the project duration in the form of alternative critical paths, compression and relaxation occurring simultaneously and critical activities changing to non-critical ones.

5. Project networks involve a large number of activities and it is very difficult to calculate valid time estimates for them. This problem applies especially to PERT analysis where three time estimates are required for each and every activity.

6. When the network has hundreds of activities use of computer becomes necessary. Network analysis becomes an expensive exercise.

Terminology of Network Analysis

The basic concepts, symbols and conventions commonly used in network techniques are described below :

1. **Activity :** An activity represents some action and as such it is a time consuming part of a project. It may be an operation, transportation or inspection. It consumes both time and resources. An activity is represented by an arrow. Each and every activity has a point of time where it begins and a point where it ends.

2. **Event :** An event represents the start (beginning) or completion (end) of some activity and as such it consumes no time. It has no time duration and does not consume any resources. It is also known as a node. An event is represented by a circle. An event is not complete until all the activities flowing into it are completed.

3. Network Diagram : It is a pictorial presentation of the various events and activities concerning a project. In a network diagram each arrow represents an activity and each circle an event. The event which is the ending point of two or more activities is called node.

4. Critical Path : Critical path is the longest path in a network. It is the sequence of activities that requires the maximum time for completion. It is critical because its length determines the minimum time in which the project may be completed. If there is any delay in the critical path activities the project is also delayed. The critical path is denoted by darker or double lines to distinguish it form the other non- critical paths.

5. Critical Activities : All the activities associated with the critical path are called critical or bottleneck activities. Such activities require special attention.

6. Slack : Slack is the time period for which an activity can be delayed without causing delay in completion of the project. Slack may be positive or negative. Positive slack represents idle time and resources whereas negative slack occurs when the project requires more resources than are normally available.

7. Float : While slack is used for events, float is applied for activities. There are various types of float, e.g., total float, free float, independent float.

8. Arrow Diagram : An arrow diagram is a network in which arrows are used to represent activities.

Construction of Network Diagram

In order to construct a network diagram, the project is split into activities, then the starting and finishing events of the project are decided. Thirdly, the precedence order is decided. The activities are then put in logical sequence by using the graphical notations. The following rules should be observed while constructing a network diagram :

(a) A complete network diagram should have only one start point and one finish point.

(b) Each activity must have one arrow only. No single activity should be represented twice in the network.

(c) The flow of the diagram should be from left to right.

(d) Arrows should not be cross unless it is absolutely essential.

(e) Arrows should be kept straight and not curved or bent.

(f) Arrows pointing in opposite direction must be avoided.

(g) There must be no loops in the network.

(h) Angle between arrows should be as large as possible.

(i) Dummy activities should be used only when completely unavoidable.

(j) Once the diagram is complete, the modes (events) should be numbered from left to right.

Critical Path Method (CPM)

Critical Path Method or CPM was developed in 1956 at the E.I. Dupont Nemours & Co., U.S.A., in connection with the periodic overhauling and maintenance of a Chemical Plant. It resulted in reducing the shut-down period form 130 hours to 90 hours and saving the company 1 million. CPM uses two time-cost estimates for each activity (one time-cost estimate for the normal situation and the other estimate for crash situation) but does not incorporate any statistical analysis in determining such time estimates. CPM operates on the assumption that there is a precise known time that each activity in the project will take.

The iterative procedure of determining the critical path involves the following steps :

(i) Break up the project into various activities systematically. Arrange all activities in logical sequence and label them. Construct the arrow diagram.

(ii) Number all the events and activities. Find the time for each activity considering it to be deterministic. Indicate the activity times on the arrow diagram.

(iii) Calculate the earliest start time, earlier finish time, latest start time and latest finish time. Construct a table showing earliest times, latest times and normal times.

(iv) Determine the total float for each activity on the basis of difference between the earliest time and latest time.

(v) Identify the critical activities and connect them with double line arrow. This gives the critical path.

(vi) Calculate the total duration of the project.

(vii) If it is intended to reduce the total duration, crash the critical activities.

(viii) Optimise the cost by shifting resources.

(ix) Update the network and smooth the network resources.

Illustration 1

Consider the following schedule of activities and related information for the construction of a new plant :

Activity	Expected time		Expected cost
	Months	Variance	Rs. '000
1-2	4	1	5
2-3	2	1	3
3-6	3	1	4
2-4	6	2	9
1-5	2	1	2
5-6	5	1	12
4-6	9	5	20
5-7	7	8	7
7-8	1	0	14
6-8	1	1	4

Construct a network diagram and calculate :

(a) the critical path

(b) expected cost of construction of the project

(c) expected time required to build the plant.

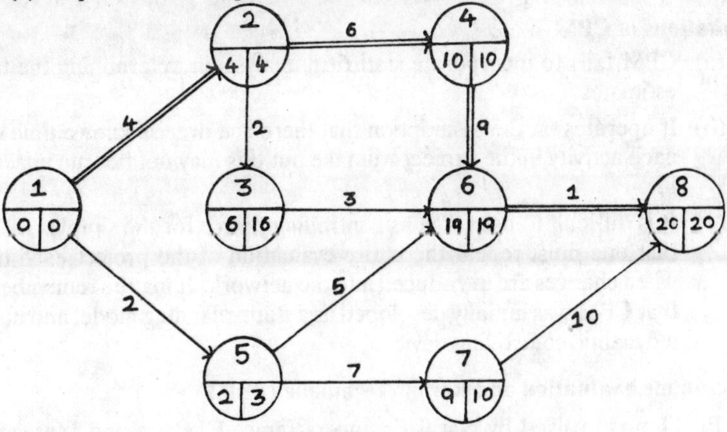

Fig. 31.1 Network Diagram

Solution

(a) From the above diagram, the critical path is : 1-2-4-6-8

(b) The expected cost is :
$5+3+4+9+2+12+20+7+14+4$ = Rs. 8,00,000

(c) The expected time of completion of the project will be the expected time of the critical path.

Activity	Expected time
1-2	4
2-4	6
4-6	9
6-8	1

Thus the expected time to build the plant is $4+6+9+1 = 20$ months.

Advantages of CPM

CPM technique is employed to schedule and control projects. It is applicable to both large and small projects. Some of the important advantages are listed below :

(a) It helps in ascertaining the time schedule.

(b) With its aid, control by the management is made easy.

(c) It makes better and detailed planning possible.

(d) It provides a standard method for communicating project plans, schedules, time and cost performance.

(e) It identifies most critical elements and thus more attention can be paid on these activities.

Limitations of CPM

(a) CPM fails to incorporate statistical analysis in determining the time estimates.

(b) It operates on the assumption that there is a precise known time that each activity in the project will take but this may not be true in actual life.

(c) It is difficult to use CPM as controlling device for the simple reasons that one must repeat the entire evaluation of the project each time when changes are introduced into the network. It may be remembered that CPM was initially developed as a static planning model and not as a dynamic controlling device.

Programme Evaluation and Review Technique (PERT)

PERT was evolved by Naval Engineers James E. Casie and Margan E. Walter in charge of special projects office of the United States navy. It was formally applied to planning and control of Polaris Missile Programme (Fleet Ballistic Missiles Programme) in October 1958 and worked well successfully expediting the completion of that programme i.e., the estimated duration of the project was reduced from 7 years to 5 years. Since that time PERT has spread rapidly throughout the U.S.Defence and Space Industry. Currently almost every major Government and military agency concerned with Space Age Programmes is utilising the technique as well as large industrial contractors in this field. Its various forms include PERT. time for reducing the duration of project, PERT cost for controlling cost of Project, and PERT Resources for optimum allocation of resources.

PERT deals with the problem of uncertain activity times by the application of statistical analysis to the determination of estimated time for each activity concerning the project. This technique, as a manager's tool, defines and co-ordinates what must be done to successfully accomplish the objectives of a project on time. It aids the decision maker but does not make decisions for him.

In order to arrive at a most reliable estimate of time three time estimates are usually employed under this technique as given below :

(i) *The optimistic time :* It is the shortest time possible if everything goes perfectly with no complications, the chance of this optimum actually occurring might be one in hundred.

(ii) *The pessimistic time :* It is the longest tome conceivable; it includes time for unusual delays and thus the chance of its happening might be only one in a hundred;

(iii) *The most likely time :* It would be the best estimate of what normally would occur.

The differences in these three times give a measure of the relative uncertainty involved in the activity.

Methodology of PERT

The steps involved in PERT are :

1. Preparation of the Network : First of all a list of activities that constitute the project is prepared. The predecessor and successor activities are determined. A network diagram is prepared on the basis of dependence between different activities and events. This is project planning phase of PERT. Events are numbered in ascending order from left to right.

2. Network Analysis : Estimates of the time required to perform each activity are made. These estimates are based upon manpower and equipment availability. At this stage the probability of completing the project or a part of it by a specified time can be computed.

3. Scheduling : Expected time for each activity is computed from the three time estimates. Earliest and latest start time and finish time for each activity are determined. Then the critical path through the network is determined. The slack time associated with the non-critical activities is also computed.

4. Time cost trade-offs : If management wants to reduce the project completion time, crashing or compressing of the project is done. The cost of reducing the project completion time is computed. Time cost trade-offs for the critical path are considered.

5. Resources Allocation : The feasibility of each schedule is checked with respect to manpower and equipment requirements. Replanning and rescheduling may be necessary if the resources are limited.

6. Project control : Once the network plan and schedule are developed to satisfactory level, they are finalised. The project is controlled by checking progress against the schedule, assigning and scheduling manpower and equipment and analysing the effects of delay. Whenever major changes are made in the schedule, the network is revised accordingly and a new schedule is prepared. Thus, monitoring of progress may require periodic updating of the project and rescheduling to ensure completion of the project in time.

Illustration 2

Present the following activities in the form of a PERT network and determine :

(a) critical path,

(b) earliest and latest expected time, and

(c) probability of completing the project within scheduled completion of 48 days.

Activity	Completion time		
	Optimistic (t_o)	Pessimistic (t_p)	Most expected (t_m)
1-2	4	12	8
2-3	1	7	4
2-4	8	16	12
3-5	3	7	5
4-5	0	0	0
4-6	3	9	6
5-7	3	9	6
5-8	4	8	6
7-9	4	12	8
8-9	2	8	5
9-10	4	16	10
6-10	4	8	6

Solution

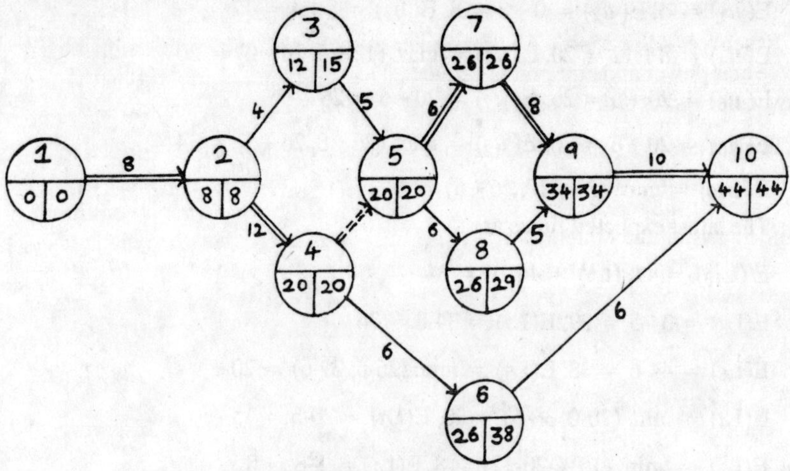

Fig. 31.2 PERT Network

The expected time (tm) and the variance for the various activities are given in the following table :

Activity	Optimistic (t_o)	Most expected (t_m)	Pessimistic time (t_p)	Expected $t = [t_o + 4t_m + t_p)/6]$	Variance $= [(t_p - t_o)/6]^2$
1-2	4	8	12	8	$(8/6)^2 = 1.78$
2-3	1	4	7	4	$(6/6)^2 = 1.00$
2-4	8	12	16	12	$(8/6)^2 = 1.78$
3-5	3	5	7	5	$(4/6)^2 = 0.44$
4-5	0	0	0	0	$0 = 0.00$
4-6	3	6	9	6	$(6/6)^3 = 1.00$
5-7	3	6	9	6	$(6/6)^2 = 1.00$
5-8	4	6	8	6	$(4/6)^2 = 0.44$
7-9	4	8	12	8	$(8/6)^2 = 1.78$
8-9	2	5	8	5	$(6/6)^2 = 1.00$
9-10	4	10	16	10	$(12/6)^2 = 4.00$
6-10	4	6	8	6	$(4/6)^2 = 0.44$

The earliest expected times are :

$E(u_1) = o, E(u_2) = 0+8 = 8, E(u_3) = 8+4 = 12$

$E(u_4) = 8+12 = 20, E(u_5) = \text{max.}\ (12+5, 20+0) = 20$

$E(u_6) = 20+6 = 26, E(u_7) = 20+6 = 26$

$E(u_8) = 20+6 = 26, E(u_9) = \text{max.}\ (26+8, 26+5) = 34$

$E(u_{10}) = \text{max.}\ (34+10, 26+6) = 44$

The latest expected times are :

$E\ (L_{10}) = 44, (L_9) = 44\text{-}10 = 34$

$E(L_8) = 34\text{-}5 = 29, E(L_7) = 34\text{-}8 = 26$

$E(L_6) = 44\text{-}6 = 38, E(L_5) = \text{min.}\ (26\text{-}6, 29\text{-}6) = 20$

$E(L_4) = \text{min.}\ (20\text{-}0, 36\text{-}6) = 20, E(L_3) = 20\text{-}5 = 15$

$E(L_2) \text{-}= \text{min.}\ (15\text{-}4, 20\text{-}12) = 8, E(L_1) = 8\text{-}8 = 0$

The critical path as shown in the above network is

1 - 2 - 4 - 5 - 7 - 9 - 10

Expected project completion time is $= 8+12+0+6+8+10 = 44$ days.

Project variance is :

$(\sigma T)^2 = 1.78+1.78+0+1+1.78+4 = 10.34$

$\sigma T \ = \sqrt{10.34} = 3.216$

If due date of completion of the project is 48 days then :

$$Z = \frac{48 - 44}{3.126} = 1.24$$

From the standard normal table, the probability of meeting the due date is 0.3925.

Advantages of PERT

(a) This technique gives the management the ability to plan the best possible use of resources to achieve a given goal within overall time and cost limitations.

(b) It helps management to handle the uncertainties involved in programmes where no standard time data of the Taylor-Grantt variety are available.

(c) It presses for right action, at right point, and at right time in the organisation.

Limitations of PERT

(a) The basic difficulty comes in the way of time estimates for the completion of activities because activities are of non-repetitive type.

(b) This technique does not consider the resources required at various stages of the project.

(c) Use of this technique for active control of a project requires frequent updating and revising the PERT calculations and this proves quite a costly affair.

Differences Between PERT and CPM

The fundamental network PERT and CPM are though identical, yet there are certain differences in details as listed below :

PERT	CPM
1. The origin is military (naval)	The origin is industrial
2. It is an event-oriented approach.	It is an activity-oriented system
3. There is allowance for uncertainty	No such allowance
4. It has three time-estimates	There is only single estimate of time and the emphasis is on cost.
5. It is a probabilistic model with uncertainty in activity duration	It is a deterministic model with well-known activity (single) time based upon past experience
6. It does not demarcate between critical and non-critical activities	It marks critical activities
7. It is especially suitable when high precision is required in time estimates e.g., defence projects.	It is suitable when reasonable precision is required e.g., civil construction projects, industrial expansion schemes, etc.
8. Time is averaged	No averaging of time is involved
9. The concept of 'crashing' is not applied	The concept of crashing is applied.
10. It lays emphasis on reduction of the execution time of the project without too much concern for cost implication. Hence, it is time-based.	It lays emphasis on greatest reduction in completion time for the least increase in project cost. Thus it is cost-based

REVIEW QUESTIONS

1. What do you mean by Net Work? What are Net Work techniques?
2. Discuss the importance and role of Network Techniques in planning and control of project and programmes.
3. What are the advantages of Net Work planning and where can Net Work techniques be applied effectively?
4. Explain the concept of PERT. State its uses.
5. What is meant by Critical Path Method?
6. State the differences between PERT and CPM?

32
Queuing Theory, Game Theory And Simulation

Queuing (or Waiting Line) Theory

Queuing theory deals with mathematical study of queues. The queuing problem arises whenever the current demand for service exceeds the current capacity to provide that service. The queuing theory concerns itself with the random arrival of customers at a service station where the facility is limited. In queuing problem, two types of costs are involved namely the cost of providing the service and the cost of waiting for the service. The object of queuing theory is to achieve a good economic balance between these two types of costs. This technique is used in handling arrivals requiring some kind of service e.g., arrival of vehicles in a petrol pump for filling petrol or arrival of machine for repair in a workshop. The application of the queuing theory includes the scheduling computer facilities, health care system facilities, transportation services, etc. It is probabilistic model.

Thus, a queuing problem arises when the current service rate of a facility falls short of the current rate of customers' demand. The word queue refers to customers. Waiting for service is a line. It may be a physical line of customers or a waiting list for berth on a train, etc.

Terms Commonly Used in Queuing Theory

(i) *Customer:* Persons or units arriving at a station for service. Customers may be either persons or machines or other items.

(ii) *Service station :* Point where service is provided.

(iii) *Waiting time :* Time a customer spends in the queue before being serviced.

(iv) *Time spent by a customer in the system* : Waiting time plus service time.

(v) *Number of customers in the system :* Number of customers in the queue plus the number of customers being served.

(vi) *Queue length :* Number of customers waiting in the queue.

(vii) *Bulking :* Customer decided not to join the queue.

(viii) *Reneging :* Customer joins the queue but leaves it afterwards.

(ix) *Jockeying :* Customer leaves the first queue and joins another one.

(x) *Queuing system :* The system consisting arrival of customers, waiting in queue picked up for service according to a certain discipline, being serviced and the departure of customers.

Some common examples of waiting lines are given in the following table :

Waiting Line or Queuing Situations

Example	Unit arriving	Service or facility required	Process performed
Manually paced assembly line	Parts to be assembled	Assembly line or assembly operations	Assembling
Inventory of items in a warehouse	Order for withdrawal	Warehouse	Replenishment of inventory
Tools in the tool room	Tools for service	Tool room	Servicing the tools
Ships entering a port	Ships	Docks	Loading and unloading
Maintenance and repair of machines	Machine breakdown	Repair crew	Repair work
Customers at checking counters at airports	Customers	Checking counters	Customs clearance
Buses at Bus terminal	Buses	Bus terminal	Parking
Purchase of groceries in super bazaar	Customers loaded with grocery	Check out counter	Billing and payment

Purpose of Queuing Theory : When adequate number of customers is not there service facilities might stay idle and there are service costs. On the other hand, where there are queues customers have to wait for service. The time lost in waiting is expensive and there are waiting time costs. The purpose of the queuing theory is to create a proper balance between the two types of costs. When the total waiting and service costs are minimum, the optimum solution is found.

Elements of Queuing System : The basic elements of characteristics of the queuing theory are given below :

1. The Input Process : This element is concerned with the pattern in which the customers arrive and join the system. An input source is characterised by :

(a) its size,
(b) arrival time distribution of customers,
(c) mean arrival rate,
(d) mean time between intervals,
(e) attitude of the customers.

In terms of size, an input source (population) is finite or infinite. If the rate at which the source generates the customers is affected by the number of customers in the service system (customers in queue and those in service) population is considered finite, otherwise it is infinite.

The periods between the arrival of individual customers may be constant or scattered in some fashion. For example, in a restaurant the arrival times of customers are distributed randomly. But in a clinic appointments can be so given that patients arrive at specified intervals of time.

Mean arrival rate refers to the average number of customers arriving per unit of time. It is often represented by Greek letter λ known as 'Lambda'. Mean time between intervals is represented by $1/\lambda$.

Attitude or behaviour of customers joining the service system may be of several types. If customers stay in the system until served they are called 'patient' customers otherwise they are known as 'impatient' customers. Impatient customers may wait for some time and leave the system if not served or they move from one waiting line to another.

2. Service mechanism : The service mechanism is concerned with service time and service facilities. Service time is the time interval from the commencement of service to the completion of service. It may either be fixed or distributed in accordance with some probability distribution. Service facilities or service channels may be in a sequence or parallel. In the former case a customer must go through one facility after another in a particular sequence. In the latter case customers are serviced in no particular sequence, e.g., parking of vehicles. Service facilities can be of the following types :

(a) Single channel facility, i.e., one queue-one service station facility wherein the customer waits till the service point is ready to take him for servicing.

(b) One queue-several service station facilities wherein the customers wait in a single queue until one of the service stations is ready to take them for servicing.

(c) Several queues-one service station wherein there are several queues and the customer can join any one of these but there is only one service station.

(d) Multi-channel facility where there are many service station facilities and many queues.

(e) Multi-stage channel facilities wherein several service stations are there each providing a specialised service. Customers pass through each of the service stations before leaving the system.

With respect to service mechanism the following information is considered relevant :

(i) Average number of customers being served in one unit of time at a service station. This is often represented by Greek letter μ, known as "mue"

(ii) Average time taken to service a customer (represented by $1/\mu$).

3. Queue discipline : Queue discipline refers to the order in which the service station selects the customers from the waiting line. Customers may be taken into service in order of their arrival. This is called the 'first come first served' service discipline. Sometimes customers may be given a priority basis for service or may be selected at random. Another aspect of queue discipline is whether a customer in a queue can move to a shorter queue in the multi-channel system. Queue discipline also refers to the manner in which the customers form into queue and the manner in which they behave while being in the queue.

4. Output of the Queue : Generally this factor is not important but in some cases it may influence the service/arrival rate. For example, if there is only one door to service point through which people enter and leave after being served, it is possible that people leaving could affect the rate of arrival. In a single channel facility the output of the queue does not pose any problem because the customer departs after receiving the service. But the output of the queue becomes important when the system is of multistage channel facilities due to the possibility of a service station breaking down can have repercussions on the queues. The line before the breakdown will lengthen and the line following the breakdown will diminish.

Thus, a queuing model can be described as composed of customers arriving for service, waiting for service and then leaving the system after being served. It essentially involves the study of behaviour of waiting lines with the help of mathematical techniques utilising the concept of stochastic process.

Assumptions in Queuing Theory

The following assumptions are usually made in queuing theory :

1. There is only one type of queue discipline, i.e., first come first served.
2. There are steady state (stable) conditions, i.e., the probability that *n* item are in queue at any time remains the same with the passage of time.
3. Mean service rate exceeds the mean arrival rate.

4. **Arrival rates follow Poisson distribution and service rates follow exponential distribution.**
5. Both the number of items in queue at any time and the waiting line experienced by a particular item are random variables.

Symbols and Notations

The following symbols and notations are generally used in queuing models :

n = total number of customers in the system, both waiting and in service

λ = average number of customers arriving per unit of time

μ = average number of customers being served per unit of time

$\lambda/\mu = \rho$ = traffic intensity or utilisation factor

C = number of parallel service channels

E(n) = average number of customers in the system, both waiting in service

E(m) = average number of customers waiting in the queue

E(v) = average waiting time of a customer in the system both waiting and in service

E(w) = average waiting time of a customer in the queue.

Pn(t) = Probability that there are n customers in the system at any time t, both waiting and in service.

Operating Characteristics of Queuing System

The operating characteristics of a queuing system refer to the numerical values of the probability distributions of various decision variables like arrival rate, number of facilities, service time, line length, priority system, etc. Some common characteristics are given below :

1. Queue length : Probability distribution of queue length can be obtained with the help of the given probability distribution of the arrival and service process. A large queue indicates poor service facility or a need for more space. On the other hand, small queue indicates excess of service facilities.

2. Waiting time in queue : It refers to the time spent by a customer in the queue before the commencement of his service. Long waiting time may increase the customer's dissatisfaction and potential loss of future revenues.

3. Waiting time in system : This is the total time spent by a customer in the queue plus service time. Long waiting time may indicate need for a change in priority rules.

A queuing system is said to be in transient state when its operating characteristics are dependent upon time. If the operating characteristics become independent of time, the queuing system is said to be in steady state.

Types of Queuing Models : There are several types of queuing models. Some of them are :

1. Single queue - single service point
2. Multiple queues - multiple service points
3. Single queues - multiple service points
4. Multiple queues - single service point.

The most common case of queuing models is the single channel waiting line.

Illustration 1

A repair shop attended by a single mechanic has an average of four customers an hour who bring small appliances for repair. The mechanic inspects them for defects and quite often can fix them right away or otherwise render a diagnosis. This takes him six minutes on the average. Arrivals are Poisson and service time has the exponential distribution. Find :

(a) the proportion of time during which the shop is empty
(b) the probability of finding at least one customer in the shop
(c) the average number of customers in the system
(d) the average time spent including service.

Solution

Mean arrival rate (λ) = 4 customers per hour

Mean service rate (μ) $= \frac{60}{6} =$ 10 customers per hour

Traffic intensity (ρ) $= \frac{\lambda}{\mu} = \frac{4}{10} = 0.4$

(a) Probability of no body in the system $= 1\text{-}p = 0.6$

(b) Probability of at least one customer $= 1\text{-}(1\text{-}p) = 0.4$

(c) Average number of customers in the systems

$$= Ls = \frac{\lambda}{\mu-\lambda} = \frac{4}{10-4} = \frac{2}{3}$$

(d) Average time spent in the system

$$Ws = \frac{1}{u-\lambda} = \frac{1}{10-4} = \frac{1}{6} \text{ hours or 10 minutes}$$

Illustration 2

A firm has several machines and wants to install its own service facility for the repair of its machines. The average breakdown rate of the machines is 3 per day. The repair time has exponential distribution. The loss incurred due to the lost time of an inoperative machine is Rs. 40 per day. There are two repair facilities available. Facility X has an installation cost of Rs. 20,000 and facility Y costs Rs. 40,000. The total labour cost per year for the two facility are Rs. 5,000 and Rs. 8,000 respectively. Facility X can repair 4 machines daily while facility Y can repair 5 machines daily. The life span of both the facilities is 4 years. Which facility should be installed ?

Solution

Total annual cost of a facility = 1/4 (total investment) + (annual labour cost) + (annual cost of revenue lost due to down machines).

Facility X :

Annual capital cost = 1/4(20000) = Rs. 5000
Annual labour cost = Rs. 5000
Annual cost of lost machine time = Daily cost of lost time x 365

Daily cost of lost time = expected number of customers in the system x Loss incurred per day =

$$= \frac{3}{4-3} \times \text{Rs. } 40 = \text{Rs. } 120 \text{ per day}$$

Annual cost of revenue lost due to break down = Rs. 120 x 365 = Rs. 43,800

Total annual cost = 1/4(20,000) + 5000 + 43800 = Rs. 53800

Facility Y

Annual capital cost = 1/4(40000) = Rs. 10000
Annual labour cost = Rs. 8000
Annual cost of lost machine time

$$= \frac{3}{5-3} (40) \times (365) = \text{Rs. } 21900$$

Total annual cost = Rs. 10000 + 8000 + 21900 = RS. 39900

Since Annual cost of facility Y is less than facility X, facility Y should be preferred.

Advantages of Queuing Theory

Queuing theory is a valuable tool for business decision-making. It can be applied to a wide variety of situations for scheduling.

(a) mechanical transport fleets
(b) scarce defence equipment
(c) issue and return of tools from tool cribs in plants
(d) aircrafts at landing and take-off from busy airports
(e) jobs in production control
(f) parts and components in assembly lines
(g) routing sales persons
(h) inventory analysis and control
(i) replacement of capital assets
(j) minimisation of congestion due to traffic delays at booths.

Queuing theory has been applied in factories, transport companies, telephone exchanges, computer centres, retail stores, cinema houses, restaurants, banks, insurance companies, traffic control, hospitals, etc. It offers the following benefits :

(i) Queuing theory provides models that are capable of determining arrival pattern of customers or most appropriate number of service stations.
(ii) Queuing models are helpful in creating balance between the two opportunity costs for optimisation of waiting costs and service costs.
(iii) Queuing theory provides better understanding of waiting lines so as to develop adequate service with tolerable waiting.

Limitations of Queuing Theory

Most of the queuing models are very complex and cannot be easily understood. The element of uncertainty is there in almost all queuing situations. Uncertainty arises due to :

(i) We may not know the form of theoretical probability distribution which applies.
(ii) We might not know the parameters of the process even when the particular distribution is known.
(iii) We would simply be knowing only the probability distribution of outcomes and not the distribution of actual outcomes even when (i) and (ii) are known.

In addition to these complications, queue discipline may also impose certain limitations. If the assumptions of 'First come first served' is not a true one (and this happens in many cases) queuing analysis becomes more complex.

In many cases the observed distributions of service times and time between arrivals cannot be fitted in the mathematical distributions usually assumed in queuing models. For example, the Poisson distribution which is generally supposed to apply may not fit many business situations. In multi-channel queuing, the departure from one queue often forms the arrival of another. This makes the analysis more difficult. Thus, queuing models variable arrival and/or service times are much more complex and in many such situations Monte Carlo Method of simulation is considered more useful than queuing analysis.

Decision Theory : The decision theory is concerned with choosing among several alternative courses of action, the best one under conditions of uncertainty. The decision situations may be classified as deterministic situation or state of certainty, stochastic or risk situation, and situation of uncertainty. The decision theory explains how to select a suitable decision strategy to achieve some objective under each of the three situations. It is a very useful analytical tool for managers when managerial decisions are taken under conditions of risk and uncertainty. It uses the probability theory for selecting the best course of action. It is used in competitive type problems such as bidding, pricing and some other marketing problems. The decision theory approach can be used in a wide range of managerial problems such as make or buy, inventory decisions, capital budgeting and portfolio decisions. The decisions theory provides a framework to analyse the decision situations in which the decision-maker has many alternatives with different possible consequences i.e., pay offs in terms of potential profit or loss for each alternative. The essence of decision theory rests on quantifying the unknown outcomes.

Game Theory : The term 'game' relates to conditions of business conflict over a period of time. Game theory is really the 'science of conflict'. The theory of games applies to competitive situations or situations where there are conflicts between parties. In such situations the game theory is used to arrive at an optimal strategy. Simplest possible competitive situation is that of two persons playing zero-sum game which is a situation where one person wins exactly what the other loses. It may also be used to determine the optimal strategy for more complex competitive situations. It can be applied in business and industry to develop pricing policies, advertising strategies, bidding strategies, and timing of new product introduction, etc. The theory provides the basis for rational decisions and thus improves the decision-making process.

Underlying Assumptions or Rules of Game : Games theory is applicable to situations that satisfy the following conditions :

1. The number of competitors is finite
2. The players act rationally and intelligently
3. Each player has available to him a finite set of possible courses of action

4. There is a conflict of interests between the participants
5. The players make individual decisions without direct communication
6. The rules governing the choice are specified and known to the players.
7. The players simultaneously select their respective course of action
8. The payoff (outcome) is fixed and determined in advance.

Basic Terminology : The basic elements of game theory are as follows :

1. Payoff : It is the outcome of playing the game or the net gain the strategy brings to the firm for any given counter- strategy of the competitor. The payoff is measured in terms of the objective of the firm like increase in profits, expansion in actual market share, etc.

2. Payoff Matrix : This is a table showing the outcomes or payoffs of different strategies of the game. The following table illustrates a payoff matrix of a 2 person zero sum game

Player A	Player B		
	B_1	B_2	B_3
A_1	24	36	8
A_2	32	20	16

In this payoff matrix, a positive payoff denotes gain to the maximising player (shown as row) and loss to the minimising player (shown as a column). For example, if player A chooses strategy A_2 and player B the strategy B_1, this results in the gain of 32 to A and loss of 32 to B.

3. Optimal strategy : It is the course of action or plan which puts the player in the most preferred position. Any deviation from this strategy results in a decreased payoff for the player.

4. Value of the game : It is the expected payoff of play when all the players of the game follow their optimal strategies. The game is called fair if the value of the game is zero, and unfair if it is non-zero.

5. Rules of the play : These rules constitute the framework within which players choose their strategies. They determine whether the game is played entirely in one move or is played sequentially in a series of moves. The rules also specify whether or not the players are permitted to communicate and collude with one another.

6. Saddle point : It is the point where **maximin** value equals the minimax value. The saddle point is the solution or value of the game. Once saddle point exists for a game, the optimal strategy for two players can be identified. Solution of games with no saddle point is possible only through the use of mixed strategies.

7. Rules of dominance : A strategy is called dominant if each payoff in the strategy is superior to each corresponding payoff in an alternative strategy. The alternative strategy can be ignored because it will not affect the solution in any way. For example, in the above table, for player B (who is a minimiser) strategy B_3 dominates both strategies B_1 and B_2. While solving this game, columns 1 and 2 of the table can, therefore be removed from the payoff matrix. Thus, the principle of dominance is used to reduce the size of payoff matrix and thereby simplify the computation.

The Two Person Zero Sum Games

In a zero sum game what one player gains the other player loses. For example, when two firms compete with each other for market share, the gain of one will match the market loss of the other. There are two types of 2 person zero sum games. 1. Pure strategy games, and 2. Mixed strategy games.

Pure Strategy Games : In a pure strategy game, the maximising player arrives at his optimal strategy on the basis of maximin criterion, while the minimising player's strategy is based on the minimax criterion. The game is solved when the maximum value equals minimax value.

Let us take an example to illustrate the 2 person zero sum pure strategy game. Suppose firm A has two strategies and firm B has three strategies. These strategies and their corresponding payoffs are given in the following table :

	Firm B			Row minimum
	B_1	B_2	B_3	
Firm A				
A_1	2	18	4	2
A_2	16	10	8	8 → maximin
Column maximum	16	18	8	
			Minimax	

In this table firm A is the maximising player. Now if firm a chooses strategy A1 firm B will choose B_1 as a counter-strategy resulting in payoff equal to 2 to firm A. On the other hand, if firm A chooses A_2 then firm B will choose B_2 as a counter strategy thus giving firm A a payoff equal to 8. So the most preferred position for firm A would be the latter strategy where it gets a high payoff.

From the point view of firm B, strategy B2 dominates the strategy B_2. Thus, effectively firm B has only two strategies B_1 and B_2. Now, if firm B choose strategy B_1 firm A will chooses counter- strategy A_2 and firm B will lose 16 units. On the other hand, if it chooses B_2 firm A will again choose A_2 but the loss to firm B will be 8. Thus, the most preferred position for firm B is strategy B.

The extensive calculations of moves and countermoves of the competitors as described above can be simplified with the help of maximim and minimax criteria.

(i) Finding maximin value (for the maximising player)

(a) Find the minimum value in each row (shown as row minimum in above table) denoting minimum possible gain from each strategy of A

(b) The maximin value is the maximum of these minimum values (values 8 in the row column of above table)

(ii) Finding minimax value (for the minimising player)

(a) Find the maximum value in each column (shown as column maximum in above table) denoting minimum possible loss from each strategy of B

(b) The minimax value is the minimum of these maximum values (value 8 is the column maximum in the above table)

Mixed Strategy Games : In the following table firm A has two strategies and firm B has three strategies to make moves and countermoves. The payoffs are given in the table.

		Firm B		Row minimum
	B_1	B_2	B_3	
Firm A				
A_1	1	5	9	1
A_2	4	2	7	2 ← maximin
Column Maximum	4	5	9	
	↑ Minimax			

In this table maximin value is not equal to the minimax value. Therefore, there is no saddle point. There are two methods of solving such a problem -

graphical method and linear programming technique. Graphical method does not provide much insight and its scope is limited to 2 x 2 games. Therefore, linear programming is a popular method of solving mixed strategy games. Games theory bears a strong relationship to linear programming because every finite two person zero sum game can be expressed as a linear programme and conversely every linear programme can be represented as a game.

Using linear programming technique we can write the problem as follows:

Firm A	Firm B
Minimise	Maximise
$A_1 + A_2$	$B_1 + B_2 + B_3$
Subject to	Subject to
$1A_1 + 4A_2 \geqslant 1$	$B_1 + 5B_2 + 9B_3 \leqslant 1$
$5A_1 + 2A_2 \geqslant 1$	$4B_1 + 2B_2 + 7B_3 \leqslant 1$
$9A_1 + 7A_2 \geqslant 1$	
$A_1 \geqslant 0,\ A_2 \geqslant 0$	$B_1 \geqslant 0,\ B_2 \geqslant 0,\ B_3 \geqslant 0$

These two linear programming formulations are simply the dual of each other. If first formulation is considered the primal, then the second is the dual, and vice-versa. In order to get the solution of the game problem we can take any one of them and solve it with the help of standard linear programming techniques : the graphical method or the simplex method.

Advantages of Games Theory

1. Game theory helps in determining the best course of action for a firm in view of the expected countermoves from the competitors.

2. It provides a scientific quantitative technique for arriving at an optimal strategy to realise given objectives.

3. Game theory gives insight into several less known aspects of situations involving conflicting interests. For example, it describes and explains the phenomena of bargaining and coalition formation.

4. Businessmen have very often to make decisions under conditions of conflict. Game theory is helpful in handling the situation of interdependence of firms. It provides a framework for decision-making when the competitor's reactions to the firm's action are uncertain and unknown.

Limitations of Game Theory

1. Businessman do not have all the knowledge required by the theory of games. They do not know alternative strategies available to themselves and to their rivals. They can only make a guess of these strategies and their payoffs.

2. There is a great deal of uncertainty which cannot be considered in game theory models. The outcome of a game may not be known with certainty.

3. The minimax strategy implies that the players are risk averters or conservative. In actual practice dynamic businessmen constantly take risks in quest of profits.

4. As the number of players increase in the game, the analysis of game theory becomes increasingly complex and difficult.

5. Game theory does not offer an optimum or winning strategy for a particular conflict and it only provides general rules concerning the logic that underlies strategic behaviour.

Despite its limitations, game theory provides the basis for rational decisions and improves the decision-making process. It helps to learn how to approach and understand a conflict situation. Game theory has been used in business and industry to develop pricing policies, advertising strategies, timing of the introduction of new models in the market, bidding tactics, etc.

Simulation Analysis

Simulation may be defined as "a quantitative technique that uses a computerised symbolic model in order to represent actual decision-making under uncertainty for evaluating alternative courses of action based upon facts and assumptions". Simulation is a technique of testing a model which resembles a real life situation. It is used for evaluating alternative courses of action based upon facts and assumptions with a computerised mathematical model in order to represent actual decision-making under conditions of uncertainty. Monte carlo method and system simulation method is used where mathematical formulation is not possible. It uses random numbers and is used to solve problem under conditions of uncertainty. System simulation is very complicated and costly. It allows for analysing the operating environment for taking alternative management actions. Simulation can be applied to a wide variety of problems ranging from queuing problem, inventory, capital budgeting, marketing and many other problems.

Elements of Simulation : A simulation process consists of the following phases :

1. **Define the problem :** First of all the decision-making problem is clearly defined. Its elements and inter-relationships among them are identified.

2. **Construct an appropriate model :** A model is a replica of basic data and inter-relationships. It represents a real life problem and describes the system's operation. For example, an aeroplanes manufacturer will always test

a scale model of a new type of aircraft in an air tunnel before building a full sized aeroplanes.

3. **Experimenting with the model :** Sample experiments are performed on the model. The experiments are carried out on the model because experiments on real system may disrupt the system, may be too expensive or may not at all be possible. Therefore, simulation is a technique of testing a model which represents a real life situation. It is mathematical experimentation.

4. **Evaluate the results :** The results of experiments are evaluated and an appropriate solution is found to the problem.

A simulation model may be considered to be consisting of two basic elements, namely, data generation and book-keeping. Data generation involves the sample observations of variables and can be carried out with the help of the following methods.

(a) using the random number tables

(b) resorting to mechanical devices

(c) using electronic computers

The book-keeping phase of a simulation model deals with updating the system when new events occur, monitoring and recording the system states as they change and keeping track of quantities of interest, such as idle time and waiting time to compute the measures of effectiveness.

Advantages of Simulation

Simulation is probably the most important technique used in analysing several complex problems where analytical methods become inadequate. Many real life systems are so complicated that it is impossible to transcribe them in mathematical equations or to solve them even if they could be so formulated. It is possible to simulate in such cases. The main advantages of simulation technique are as follows :

1. Simulation is a flexible and straightforward technique. It is easier to apply than pure analytical method.

2. It can be used to analyse large and complex real work systems that cannot be solved by conventional quantitative techniques.

3. It is useful in solving problems where all values of the variables are not known or partly known in advance and there is no easy way to find these values.

4. Simulation may be the only method available when it is difficult to observe the actual reality.

5. It does not interfere with the real work system as experiments are done on the model and not on the system itself. The effect of using model can be observed without actually using it in the real system.

6. Once a model has been constructed it may be used over and over again to analyse different situations.

7. Simulation can be used to foresee unknown bottlenecks in problems where it is difficult to predict or identify bottlenecks.

8. It can be used to study the interactive effect of individual components or variables in order to determine which ones are important.

9. Simulation is a valuable method of breaking down a complicated system into sub-systems and then study each of these sub-systems individually or jointly with others.

10. Usually data for further analysis can be generated from a simulation model.

Limitations of Simulation

Despite its advantages simulation is considered a method of last resort and is used when all other techniques fail. The analytical methods are considered more accurate and reliable where a problem can be reduced to a mathematical problem. Simulation suffers from the following drawbacks :

1. Simulation does not generate optimal solutions to problems as do other quantitative techniques. It is a trial and error approach that may produce different solutions in repeated runs.

2. Simulation model does not produce answers by itself. It is 'run' other than solved.

3. In very large and complex problems the large number of variables and the inter-relationships between them makes the problem very unwieldy and hard to programme.

4. It is often a long and complicated process to develop a model. It is a time consuming and expensive process because a number of simulation runs are required to solve a problem.

5. Each simulation model is unique and its solutions and inferences are not usually transferable to other problems.

In spite of its limitations simulation is a useful technique because it provides management with an opportunity to observe and analyse the dynamic behaviour of a changing business environment. It permits management to analyse and evaluate problems for which there are no other practical analytic methods and for which experimentation with the real world system would be too expensive or inconvenient.

Practical Applications of Simulation

Some of the applications of simulation in real world are given below :

1. Aircraft scheduling
2. Assembly line scheduling
3. Bank teller scheduling
4. Bus scheduling
5. Telephone traffic routing
6. Brand selection
7. Advertising allocation
8. Locating warehouses
9. Job shop scheduling
10. Library operations design
11. Maintenance Scheduling.
12. Parking facility design
13. Railroad operations
14. Traffic light timing
15. Water resource development
16. Ambulance and fire fighting
17. Testing inventory order policies
18. Manpower hiring decisions
19. Development and evaluation of military systems
20. Design and operation of hospital facilities

Generation of Random Numbers

The essence of simulation activity is the recreation of a real world situation including its most important feature i.e., the random number of the real world situation. Random numbers are the numbers which have equal probability of being generated. For example, when we are interested in one digit numbers 0, 1, 2,.......9. there are in all ten numbers and each of the numbers should have 1/10 probability of being generated.

There are several manual methods of generating numbers, e.g., the rolling of dice, the tossing of coins, the spinning of roulette wheels, etc. But these days there are published tables of random number (digits). These tables are very economical and convenient to use.

Monte Carlo Technique

The Monte Carlo technique is the most popular method of simulation. It uses random numbers and is employed to solve problems requiring decision-making under uncertainty and where mathematical solution is not possible. The general procedure of Monte Carlo simulation comprises the following steps :

1. *Define the problem.* This involves defining clearly the objectives of the system and identifying the variables (constraints) which have maximum effect on the problem objectives.

2. *Construct an appropriate model.* The model should represent the real situation.

3. *Specify values of variables to be tested.* Supply values for input parameters and measure the output values.

4. *Collect the information required* and determine the functional relationships and the types of probability distribution which one to apply.

5. *Define a coding system* that will correlate the factors identified in step 1 with the random numbers that will be generated for the simulation.

6. *Select a random number generator* and create the random numbers to be used in the simulation.

7. *Correlate the generated random* numbers with the factors identified in steps 1 and 5.

8. *Summarise and examine* the results in an appropriate table.

9. Evaluate the results of the simulation and select best course of action.

10. Formulate proposals for advice to management on the course of action to be adopted and modify the model, if necessary.

Illustration 3

A production line turns out about 50 cars per day with the following probability distribution :

Production/day	Probability	Production/day	Probability
45	0.03	51	0.15
46	0.05	52	0.10
47	0.07	53	0.07
48	0.01	54	0.05
49	0.15	55	0.03
50	0.20		

Finished cars are transported by train at the end of the day. If the train capacity is only 51 what will be the average number of cars waiting to be shipped and what will be the average numbers of empty spaces on the train ?

Devise a simulation model to solve this problem.

Solution. If the numbers 00-99 are allocated in proportion to the probabilities associated with each production level as shown below then the daily production levels can be sampled, using random number tables.

Production per day	Probabilty	Cumulative probability	Random number
45	0.30	0.03	00-02
46	0.05	0.08	03-07
47	0.07	0.15	08-14
48	0.10	0.25	15-24
49	0.15	0.40	25-39
50	0.20	0.60	40-59
51	0.25	0.75	60-74
52	0.20	0.85	75-84
53	0.07	0.92	85-91
54	0.05	0.97	92-96
55	0.03	1.00	97-99

Assuming random number to be taken from tables, a work sheet can be completed as follows :

Random number	Daily production	Cars left overnight	Total cars waiting	Cars shipped	Empty places
37	49	0	49	49	2
35	49	0	49	49	2
63	51	0	51	51	0
25	49	0	49	49	2
50	50	0	50	50	1
71	51	0	51	51	0
95	54	0	54	51	0
16	48	3	51	51	0

The following rules were used in preparing the above table :

(i) Cars waiting = cars left overnight + day's production.

(ii) If cars waiting $\geqslant 51$, then empty spaces = 0, and cars left overnight = cars waiting - 51

(iii) If cars waiting < 51 then empty spaces > 0 cars waiting and cars left overnight = 0

Illustration 4

An engineering concern wants to manufacture shafts and rings of definite sizes and specifications. Quality control data reveal that shaft diameters are normally distributed with a mean average of 0.980 inches and a standard deviation of 0.010 inches. Similarly rings have a mean average of 1.000 inches and a standard deviation of 0.020 inches. You are required to locate the number of misfits, i.e., shaft diameter exceeding the ring diameter, through the Monte Carlo technique of simulation.

Solution

In order to locate the number of misfits, it is necessary to simulate the sizes of shafts and rings through random numbers and to find the corresponding random deviates (z) from the table giving area under the normal curve with mean equal to zero and standard deviation equal to one. The calculations are given in the following table in the next page.

Explanatory Notes

1. In finding random normal deviate from the table showing area under the normal curve, four digit random numbers are generally used.

2. The following procedure is used for finding 'z' corresponding to a random number :

(a) If the random number varies between 0 and 5000, z can be found out from the table by looking against the respective row and column. Suppose the random number is 2952 the 'Z' (against area 0.2952) is 0.82.

(b) If the random number exceeds 5000, then 5000 is subtracted from the random number and 'z' corresponding to the remaining figures is found. But negative (-) sign is given to the z so found. Suppose the random number is 6641 then z for 1641 (6641- 5000) is 0.42 but this will be read as -0.42 as the original random number was more than 5000.

3. Since $z = \frac{X - \mu}{\sigma}$, therefore $X = \mu + z(\sigma)$ and the same can be used to find the simulating size concerning the variable.

Table I Simulating Sizes to Locate the Number of Misfits

	Shats			Rings		
Assembly No.	Random numbers	Random normal deviate (z)	Simulating size $X = \mu + z(\sigma)$	Random numbers	Random normal deviate (z)	Simulating size (z)$X = u + 2(\sigma)$
1	2952	0.82	.980 + .82(.01) = .9882	3992	1.28	1.0 + 1.28(0.2) = 1.0256
2	3170	0.91	.980 + .91(.01) = .9891	4167	1.38	1.0 + 1.38(.02) = 1.0276
3	7203	- 0.59	.9808 -.59(.01) = .9741	1300	0.33	1.0 + 0.33(.02) = 1.0066
4	3408	1.00	.980 + 1.0(.01) = .9900	3563	1.06	1.0 + 1.06(.02) = 1.0212
5	0560	0.14	.980 + .14(.01) = 9814	1112	0.28	1.0 + .28(.02) = 1.0056
6	6641	- 0.42	.980-.42(.01)- = .9758	9792	-2.04	1.0-2.04(0.2) = 0.9592
7	5624	- 0.16	.980-.16(.01) = .9784	9525	- 1.67	1.0-1.67(.02) = 0.9666
8	5356	- 0.09	.980-.09(.01) = .9791	2693	0.74	1.0 + .74(.02) = 1.0148
9	2769	0.76	.980 + .76(.01) = 9876	6107	- 0.28	1.0-.28(.02) = 0.9944
10	5246	- 0.06	.980-.06(.01) = .9794	9025	- 1.29	1.0-1.29(.02) = 0.9742

The above table shows that in assembly No. 6, 7, 10 the shaft size turns out to be longer in diameter than that of the ring and, therefore, these are the cases of misfit out of the ten assemblies simulated here.

Optimal Control Theory

The framework of the optimal theory aims at finding the most optimal way to control a dynamic system. It requires the system to exist in various 'states'. The state of the system is defined by the state variables, and it is controllable through 'control variables'. Thus, inventory level x(t) can be defined as state variable at time. The control variable u(t) could be the production rate. Having defined the state variable and control variable a 'state equation' is formulated, which determines the instantaneous rate of change in the state variable. An objective function is maximised for given state constraints, control constraints and terminal constraints and the 'exogenous function'. In case of the inventory model, the 'exogenous function' include demand rate, inventory holding cost and product cost. The 'parameters' such as terminal time, minimum ending inventory, lower value of production rate, upper value of production rate and initial inventory level are also specified. The setting up of a model for the optimal control theory involves the identification and specification for the state variable, control variable, state equation, objective function, state constraints, control constraints, terminal constraints, exegenous functions and its parameters.

As indicated earlier, the optimal control theory delas with the problem of the optimisation of dynamic systems. Before attempting a solution to such problems, a mathematical model of the system to be optimised is formulated, the constraints on the system are identified and the objective function to be maximised or minimised is defined. The solution for the optimal values of the control variables, is obtained using the mathematical technique of 'calculus of variations'. The optimal control theory has been applied to problems in finanace, production, inventory, marketing, transfer pricing and resoruce allocation. As a resource allocation technique, it has a definite place in the field of management control.

Catastrophe Theory

The routine existing activities of an organisation might be affected or dislocated owing to certain abrupt changes or criticalities in the organisational system created by certain environmental factors (internal or external). For example, a drastic change in the industrial policy of the government or the sudden demise of the chief executive may have a catastrophic effect on the organisation. An analysis of the past working of the organisation might help to identify the critical events that created the catastrophic effects and led to reconfigurations and a new emergent behaviour. The catastrophe theory provides a framework to analyse these reconfigurations and emergent behavior. This theory attempts to deal with the properties of abstract spaces and explain how discontinuities arise from continuously changing causal factors. A catastrophe is a sudden changing effect created by such factors which can be shown on a graph or diagram.

When catastrophes occur, the existing control systems break and new controls emerge in consonance with new reconfigurations and new emergent organisational behaviour. This theory can be applied to motivational dynamics, cooperation and conflict, economic stability and instability, organisational dynamics, anxiety and frustration, stock market crashing, perpetual shifts and value changes, etc. The theory is based on topology - a branch of mathematics. It has been applied in other fields such as economics, anthropology, computer and behavioural sciences.

Behavioural Field Equations

In an organisational situation power and actions are the important aspects. Power has its own influence on the actions in an organisation. When an action say, a decision, is taken depending upon the power behind it, the repercussions may be felt across the organisation. Hence, power and action constitute the key elements in an organisation's behaviour. Attempts have been made to formulate mathematical equations to explain the dynamics of power and influence similar to Lewin's force field. If P stands for Power field and A for the Action field one can formulate mathematical equations using two vector calculus concepts namely, divergence (DIV.) and curl. The divergence indicates the spread of the field and curl denotes curling around or encircling. Since the power lies with the boss, the equation for this would be :

$$\text{Div. } P = O$$

It means that the divergence or spread of power is nil. When an action is taken, its impact would be felt by the affected managers. That is, the action waves will pass through the various units of the organisation.

The equation that represents the impact or repercussions would be : $\text{Curl } A = f(P)$

Where f is a function that indicates the intensity of relationship between power and action. Though these two equations have little practical relevance for managers they, however, provide a theoretical framework for conceptualising the behaviour in an organisation.

Inventory Control Models

Each business firm, as regards their inventory planning and control is confronted with the problem of meeting two conflicting objectives : (i) To maintain a large size of inventory for efficient and smooth production and sale operations. (ii) To maintain minimum investment in inventories to maximise the profitability. Both excessive and inadequate inventories are not desirable. Hence, the object of inventory control is to determine and maintain the optimum level of inventory investment. Inventory control models enable the management to achieve this objective more effectively.

The two basic decisions concerning inventory levels are :

1. How much should be ordered?
2. When should it be ordered?

The first question relates to the problem of determining economic ordering quantity (EOQ) and is answered with an analysis of the cost of maintaining certain inventory level. The second question arises because of uncertainty and it is a problem of determining the reorder point. Mathematical models are used to determine the EOQ, various inventory levels, and reorder point. Perpetual inventory control system and the Selective inventory control system (ABC Analysis) are also used as inventory control techniques.

REVIEW QUESTIONS

1. Outline and compare four alternative structures of Waiting Line situations. Give a physical example of each situation.
2. Discuss the advantages and limitations of Waiting Line Theory.
3. Describe the nature, importance and limitations of Games Theory.
4. What is meant by Simulation Analysis. State the practical applications of Simulation Technique.
5. Explain the different phases of a Simulation process.
6. What are the advantages and limitations of Simulation Technique.
7. Explain (a) Monte Carlo Technique (b) Catastrophe Theory (c) Behaviour Field Equations (d) Inventory Control Models.

33

Hierarchical Systems and Expert Systems

MATHEMATICAL MODEL OF CONTROLS IN HIERARCHICAL SYSTEMS*

According to Mesarovic, there are two basic approaches for specifying behaviour of systems whose variables are calssified as inputs and outputs, namely, the input-output approach and the goal-seeking approach. The former is referred to as causal stimulus-response while the later is teleological decision-making problem solving. In goal seeking the system responds to any given stimulus so that a given goal is pursued

Let the set X and Y define the inputs (stimuli) and outputs (responses) respectively. Then, the system S is a relation on inputs and outputs and using the abstract algebra concepts we can express it as S X x Y, in case of input-output approach of system specification. In case of goal seeking approach, in addition to X and Y, we have a 'decision object' M and 'value set' V. Further, we have an 'outcome (process) function'and a 'performance function'. Using abstract algebra concepts, these functions can be expressed as :

(i) Outcome (process) function $P : X \times M \longrightarrow Y$
(ii) Performance function $G : M \times Y \longrightarrow V$

The outcome function specifies the constraints. The goal of the system is to optimise G. In goal seeking approach, for any input x X, the system's response (output), y Y is such that G is optimised while constraints as specified by outcome function are observed.

In Hierarchical systems, there are multiple levels of decision making, and there are multi-level controls. There are local control processes and first level decision units. Using the concepts discussed earlier, each local process has a performance function and outcome function. Further, there are interactions at the first level, which are expressed as 'inter-action functions'. The task of the second level sub-systems, termed as coordinator is to select 'corordination terms' so that the first level units satisfy the control objective of the toal system, and at the same time they take care of the local control problems. Figure 33.1

---

* Based on : " A Mathematical Theory of General Systems", by Mihaljo D. Mesarovic, in Trends in General Systems, ed, George J. Klir, John Wiley and Sons, New York, 1972 (pp. 250-269).

indicates the block diagram of a hierarchical system. This is typical of a multi-division organisation with a corporate head-quarters which plays the coordination role.

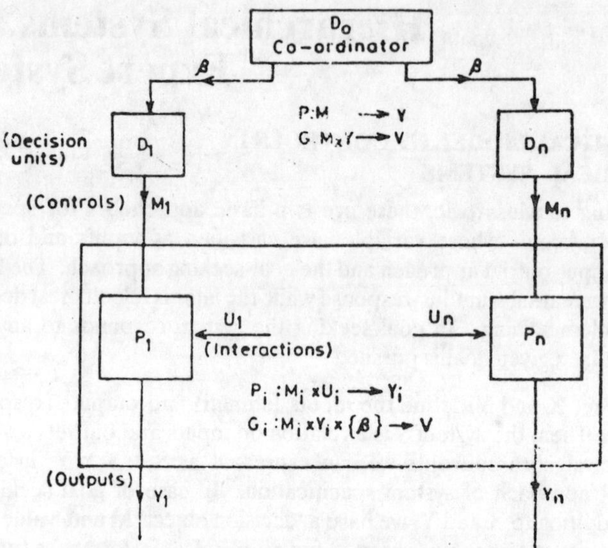

Fig. 33.1 Block diagram of Hierarchical Systems

Figure the $D_1, D_2..., D_n$ represent the first level decision units, e.g., divisions of an organsiation. D_o is the Coordinator, e.g., corporate head-quarter. $P_1, P_2,...P_n$ denote the local sub-processes, i.e., the local outcome functions. The objective of the entire system is to achieve overall goal G, given overall outcome function. $P : M \rightarrow Y$ and an overall performance function $G : M \times Y \rightarrow V$. The overall outcome function $P : M \rightarrow Y$ can be decompassed into n interacting sub-process, $P_i : M_i \times U_i \rightarrow Y_i$, where $M = M_1 \times M_2 \times....M_n$ are controls, $Y\ Y_1 \times Y_2.....Y_n$ are outputs and $U = U_1 \times U_2.....U_n$, are interactions. The interactions are expressed in terms of controls by 'interactions functions' $K_i : M \rightarrow U_i$. A local control process can now be expressed as,

$$P_i : M_i \times U_i \rightarrow Y_i$$

A local performance function is

$$G_i : M_i \times Y_i \times \{B\} \rightarrow V,$$

Where $\{B\}$ is the coordination term and V is the value set

Now, the key issues involved in the controls in hierarchical systems are, (i) The second level unit should decide a 'coordination strategy' and therefore select the coordination term $\{\beta\}$. (ii) The local control objective is to optimise G_i for given coordination term β. (iii) The overall objective is to optimise G.

Mathematical theorems have been formulated in respect of the above key issues. These theorems specify the conditions under which the system is coordinable, i.e., there exists optimal coordination term β.

EXPERT SYSTEMS FOR MANAGEMENT CONTROL

The gathering, assimilating and disseminating information is basic and essential for decision making and exercising control. An individual's response to information is guided through a cognitive process, which is depicted in Fig. 33.2

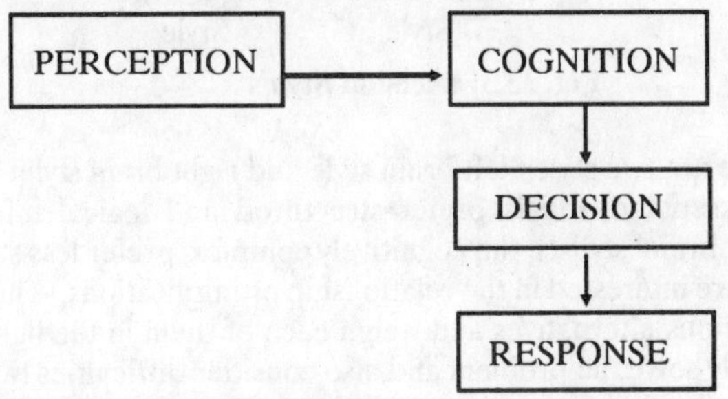

Fig. 33.2 The Cognitive Process

In the context of an organisation, the information is dove-tailed as in the cognitive process to stimulate a response appropriate to the problem suggested by a given set of information. It may be noted that during the cognitive process, the processing of information is done differently by each person, thus, effecting different responses.

One might wonder how a person could be called an expert? Even though experts have different personal characteristics, they come up with a solution which is effective in the light of the nature of the decisive problem; and only this criterion allows us to call them experts are: the cognitive process, decision styles and the experiences of the person in the light of the problem. The human element starts exerting its influence from the first step in the cognitive process, i.e., perception. All information is not perceived as stimulus. The selection of information depends on the individual's mental make-up and the threshold that the individual maintains for stimulus detection. The perceived quality of information depends on the decision maker's cognitive complexity, response to uncertainty, risk taking propensity, prior experience with the problem at hand, structure of the organisation and the ability to tolerate variety.

Variation among individuals in the second stage, i.e., cognition, is greater. Cognition is the way in which the human mind builds a picture of reality. These pictures are processed differently in line with the individual's decision style and the nature of decisions in terms of structured and unstructured decisions. Fig 33.3 relates the decision styles and the nature of decisions.

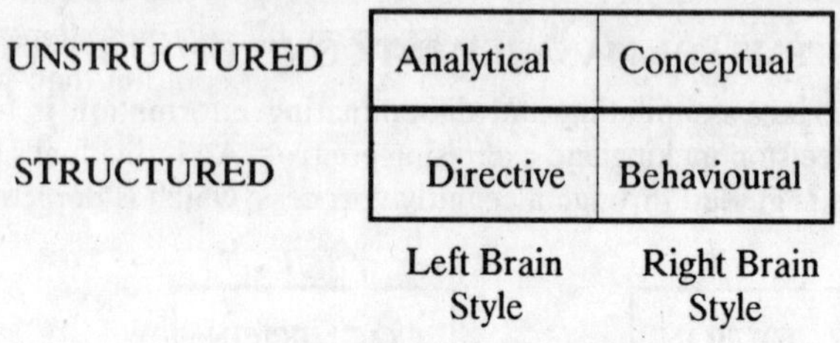

Fig. 33.3 Decision Styles

Broadly there are two styles-left brain style and right brain style. The 'left brained' or focussed individuals prefer structured and logical information whereas the 'right brain' stylists, the cognitively complex, prefer less structured information and are interested in the relationship or implications. They, therefore, generate various alternatives and weigh each of them in the light of how they will effectively solve the problem and also consider difficulties that will be encountered while implementing the solution. The focussed individuals, however, dove-tail all the parameters of the cognitive process towards a simple and direct action. Thus, decision styles of 'left brained' managers are directive and analytical, while decision styles of 'right brained' managers are conceptual and behaviour-oriented.

The problems that managers usually confront in their day-to-day functioning, can be categorised as follows :

(a) Deterministic-structured and operational in nature
(b) Stochastic-involving uncertainty and unknowns
(c) Complex-involving interacting variables which change structure too often for control
(d) Organisational-dealing with the behaviour of highly creative and divergent thinkers called human beings.

It may be observed that these categories represent the increasing order of complexity of the problems confronted by the managers. Given that such complexity and unstructuredness is sometimes involved in managerial decision making, how can computer systems, a collection of ligic gates, help in making managerial decisions? Alternatively, can human thinking be reduced to if-then or test- operate-test-exit rules so that it can be incorporated in a computer?

Artificial Intelligence : There is not denying that today Artificial Intelligence (AI) is a by-word in technological and management circles due to which many areas developed in the past are now in the domain of AI. The rapidly expanding boundary of AI calls for general definitions like "imitating human thinking" (Turing) or "ideas which enable computers to do the things that make people appear intelligent" (Winston). A slightly more precise definition is provided by Rowe and Somers*, who refer to it as "computer based systems that enhance the decision maker's ability to arrive at a better solution than what could be done without such systems".

The generality of the above definitions gives us a clue as to how AI developed from electronic data processing state to state-of-the-art expert systems. Fig.3 indicates the domain of AI. We will now discuss the important aspects of each quadrant in Fig.33.4.

UNSTRUCTURED	Q2 Expert Support Systems	Q4 Expert Systems of Future
STRUCTURED	Q1 Programmed Approach	Q3 Programmed Decsions of Management Science
	Data Processing Systems	Expert Systems

Fig. 33.4 Domain of Artificial Intelligence (Adapted from Rowe & Somers)

Quadrant 1 depicts the data processing systems which are used for structured and deterministic operations like invoicing, scheduling and material requirement planning.

Quadrant 2 addresses those systems that have incorporated in them mathematical models like linear programming, travelling, salesman, forecasting methods, etc. They can help extrapolate and therefore can answer what-if and should-I questions. Systems of Quadrant 2 fall in rule-based behaviour category, in that they operate on a set of rules that have been built into the system (Rasmussen, 1976). A robot, then, will fall in the category of skill-based behaviour.

---

* Rowe A.J. and Somers I, A, "Management Use of Artificial Intelligence", working paper, University of Southern California, March 1987.

The joint human-machine cognitive system is implicit in a hypothetical computer consultant (Woods,* 1986). Here design focusses primarily on building a machine expert that outputs usually correct solutions. The human user's role is to gather data and to filter any poor machine solutions. Systems of Quadrant 2 will be very nearly described by Wood's model in which the human being plays a very important role, both as a data gatherer and a solution filter. Fig.33.5 indicates the mechanism of expert systems.

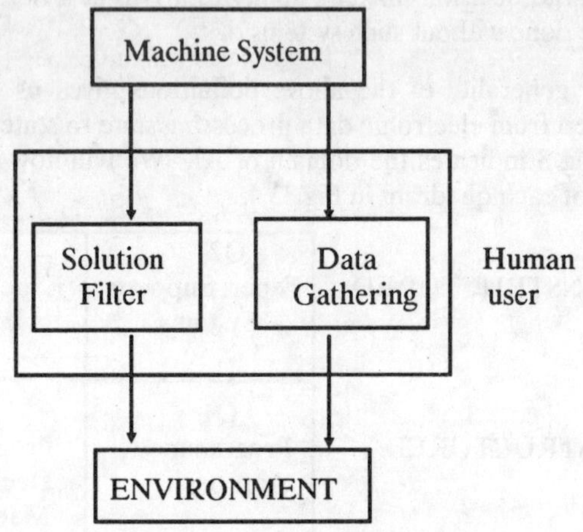

Fig. 33.5 Mechanism of Expert Systems (Adapted from AI magazine)

Recently, Quadrant 3 and 4 are attracting a lot of attention. The systems of Quadrant 3 relate to those that have available data bases built with knowledge and tools provided by the science of knowledge acquisition-heuristic and repertory grids being two of them. Heuristic is a technique that improves the efficiency of a search process, possibly by sacrificing claims of completeness. Employing heuristic grids helps in better knowledge representation and formulation of solutions for decision problems because of the better understanding of the cognitive process. Repertory grids are representations of the expert's view of a particular problem. It is useful to the knowledge engineer for two reasons (Anna Hart, 1986) :

(a) The elicitation of a grid makes the expert think twice about a problem and helps clarify issues in his mind.

---

* Woods, David, D. "Cognitive Technologies, The Acting of Joint Human-Machine, Cognitive Systems", The AI Magazine, Vol. 6, No.4, winter 1986, pp 86-91.

(b) Grids can be analysed to find patterns of associations for further investigation.

Figure 33.6 represents the design of an expert system. The information is drawn from the available data bases through an inference engine to the computer which then interacts with the decisions systems to effectively solve the decision problem in conjunction with the human user. The knowledge engineer builds expert systems for managerial decision making by matching cognitive complexity with machine intelligence by augmenting machine intelligence with machine reasoning. With this, the power and structure of the computers will be combined with the intuition, creativity and heuristic capability of the human mind to give a highly powerful managerial decision making tool. Such a tool will belong to the highest category of knowledge-based behaviour.

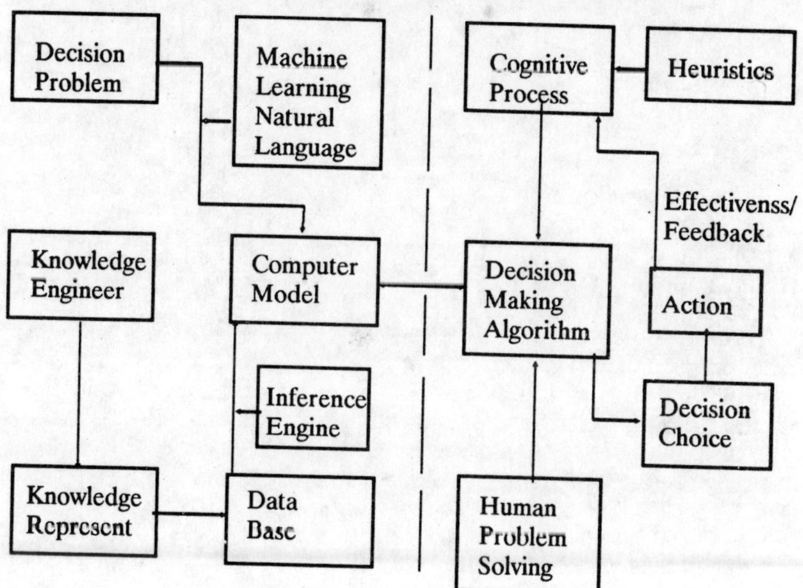

Fig. 33.6 Expert System (Quadrant 4)

Quadrant 4 is the expert system of the future. It will incorporate a natural language interface, adaptive machine learning that has complete and correct knowledge representation and that builds on the natural relationship between the decision maker and the computer so as to facilitate dealing with complex, unstructured and novel problems (Rowe and Somers, 1987).

The above discussion is aimed at providing the managers an exposure to the conceptual basis of the expert systems. With the increasing use of computers for decision making and control, the management use of expert system will increase in future.

REVIEW QUESTIONS

1. Explain the mathematical model of controls in Hierarchical Systems.
2. Explain the Expert Systems for management control.

TABLE II : CASH FLOW STATEMENT FOR THE MONTH OF --------- 1993 All Figures in Rupees Lakhs

	Week number 1		Week number 2		Week number 3		Week number 4		Total for month	
	Expected	Actual	Expected	Actual	Expected	Actual	Expected	Actual	Expected	Actual
1. CASH INFLOW										
1.1 Sale Proceeds										
1.2 Others										
1.3 Total										
1.4 CUMULATIVE TOTAL										
2. CASH OUTFLOW										
2.1 Bills										
2.2 Factory Expenses										
2.3 Head Office Exp.										
2.3 Interests										
2.5 Others										
2.6 Total										
2.7 CULULATIVE TOTAL										
3. EXCESS CASH INFLOW OVER CASH OUTFLOW FOR THE WEEK (1.3-2.6)										
4. EXCESS CASH INFLOW OVER CASH OUTFLOW CUMULATIVE (14.-2.7)										
5. OPENING CASH BALANCE										
6. CLOSING CASH BALANCES (3+5)										

TABLE III A : CAPITAL EQUIPMENT BUDGET MONITOR SUMMARISED POSITION AS ON -------

	Amount Budgeted for 1993		Amount Budgeted for Commitment/Disbursement till date		Actual Performance till date		Balance to be spent in the rest of the year		
	Commitment	Cash Flow	Commitment	Cash Flow	Commitment	Cash Flow	Commitment	Cash Flow	Remarks
A Plant & Machinery									
B Civil works									
C Officeequiptment									
D Miscellaneious									
Total									

TABLE III B : CAPITAL EQUIPMENT PROCUREMENT & COMMISSIONING MONITOR

		Procurement Follow-up								Installation		
	Qtns.Recd.	Purchase	Order	Advance	Sent	Dely.	Date	Date Insptd	Date	Date	Date	
A Plant & marchy	1 2 3 4	No.	Date	Yes	No	Promised	Delivered	Accepted	Started	Compltd	Commd.	Remarks

NOTE : Similar Procurement & Commission Monitors are made for Civil Works & Office Equiptment and Miscellaneious items.

TABLE IV A : PRODUCTION (QTY) FOR THE MONTH OF ---------- 1993

Last Month	Product	Budget	This month actual	Variance	Budget	Cumulative Actual	Variance	Cum. same period last year	Incr/Decr over the last year	Closing Stock-End of Month at factory
	A									
	C									
	D									
	E									

SALES (QTY) FOR THE MONTH OF ---------- 1993

Last Month	Product	Budget	This month Actual	Variance	Budget	Cumulative Actual	Variance	Cum. same period last year	Incr/Decr over the last year	Closing Stock-End of Month at Sales Depot
	A									
	B									
	C									
	D									
	E									

TABLE IV B : SALES (QTY) BREAK-UP GEGIONWISE FOR THE MONTH OF ---------- 1993

Last Month	Sales (region I)	Budget	This Month Actual	Variance	Budget	Cumulative Actual	Variance	Cum. sales period last year	incr/Decr over the last year	Closing Stock-End of Month at Sales Dept
	A									
	B									
	C									
	D									
	E									
	Sales (Region 2)									
	A									
	B									
	C									
	D									
	E									
	Sales (Region 3)									
	A									
	B									
	C									
	D									
	E									

SUGGESTED READINGS

Anthony R. N. and John Dearden	:	Management Control Systems
Arnold S. Tannebaum	:	Control in Organisation
Bhadada B. M.	:	Management Control Systems
Bhattacharya S. K.	:	Managerial Planning & Control System
Billy E. Goetz	:	Management Planning and Control
Buffa Elwood	:	Modern Production Management
Chadda H. L.	:	Industrial Purchasing & Materials Management
Charles T. Hongren	:	Accounting for Management Control
Harold Koontz and Cyril O'Donnell	:	Management
Kamal Gupta	:	Contemporary Auditing
Kothari C. R.	:	Quantitative Techniques
Kothari C. R.	:	Operation Research
Lucey, T.	:	Management Accounting
Mammoria C. B.	:	Personnel Management
Manohar L. Batia	:	Profit Centre
Mark G. Simkin	:	Computer Information Systems for Business
Peter A. Pyhrr	:	Zero - Base Budgeting
Peter F. Drucker	:	Management of Non-Profit Organisation
Philip Kotler	:	Marketing Management - Analysis, Planning & Control
Richard M. Lynch and Robert M. William	:	Accounting for Management Planning and Control
Robert J. Mockler	:	Readings in Management Control
Robert J. Thicrau	:	Decision Support System for Effective Planning & Control
Rose T. G. and E. D. Farr	:	Higher Management Control
Saravanavel P.	:	Financial Management
Subash Sharma	:	Management Control Systems
William L. Ferrare	:	Roadings in Cost Accounting, Budgeting, and Control
Willsmore A. W.	:	Accounting for Management Control
Willson R. M. S.	:	Financial Control

INDEX